CASES IN STRATEGIC MANAGEMENT

Jeffrey S. Bracker
George Mason University

John R. Montanari
California State University-San Marcos

Cyril P. Morgan
Washington State University

The Dryden Press
*Chicago   Fort Worth   San Francisco   Philadelphia
Montreal   Toronto   London   Sydney   Tokyo*

Acquisitions Editor: Butch Gemin
Project Editor: Susan Jansen
Design Manager: Alan Wendt
Production Manager: Bob Lange
Permissions Editor: Cindy Lombardo
Director of Editing, Design, and Production: Jane Perkins

Text Designer: C.J. Petlick, Hunter Graphics
Copy Editor: Sarah Russell
Compositor: Impressions
Text Type: 10/12 Times Roman

Library of Congress Cataloging-in-Publication Data

Bracker, Jeffrey S.
    Cases in strategic management / Jeffrey S. Bracker, John R.
Montanari, Cyril P. Morgan.
        p.   cm.
    ISBN 0-03-055858-1
    1. Strategic planning—Case studies.   I. Montanari, John R.
II. Morgan, Cyril P., 1936–   .   III. Title.
HD30.28.B694   1991
658.4′012—dc20   90-46427
                                                  CIP

Printed in the United States of America
123-017-987654321
Copyright © 1991, 1990 by The Dryden Press, a
division of Holt, Rinehart and Winston, Inc.

Requests for permission to make copies of any part of the work
should be mailed to: Permissions Department, Holt, Rinehart
and Winston, Inc., 8th Floor, Orlando, FL 32887.

Address orders:
The Dryden Press
Orlando, FL 32887

Address editorial correspondence:
The Dryden Press
908 N. Elm Street
Hinsdale, IL 60521

The Dryden Press
Holt, Rinehart and Winston
Saunders College Publishing

The Dryden Press Series in Management

Bartlett
Cases in Strategic Management for Business

Bedeian
Management, *Second Edition*

Bedeian and Zammuto
Organizations: Theory and Design

Boone and Kurtz
Contemporary Business, *Sixth Edition*

Bowman and Branchaw
Business Report Writing, *Second Edition*

Bracker, Montanari, and Morgan
Cases in Strategic Management

Cullinan
Business English for Industry and the Professions

Czinkota, Rivoli, and Ronkainen
International Business

Daft
Management, *Second Edition*

Efendioglu and Montanari
**The Advantage Ski Company:
A Strategic Simulation**

Foegen
**Business Plan Guidebook with Financial
Spreadsheets**

Forgionne
Quantitative Management

Gaither
**Production and Operations Management: A
Problem-Solving and Decision-Making Approach**
Fourth Edition

Gatewood and Feild
Human Resource Selection, *Second Edition*

Greenhaus
Career Management

Higgins
**Strategy: Formulation, Implementation,
and Control**

Higgins and Vincze
Strategic Management: Text and Cases
Fourth Edition

Hills
Compensation Decision Making

Hodgetts
Modern Human Relations at Work, *Fourth Edition*

Holley and Jennings
The Labor Relations Process, *Fourth Edition*

Huseman, Lahiff, and Penrose
Business Communication: Strategies and Skills
Fourth Edition

Jauch, Coltrin, and Bedeian
**The Managerial Experience: Cases, Exercises,
and Readings,** *Fifth Edition*

Kemper
Experiencing Strategic Management

Kuehl and Lambing
Small Business: Planning and Management
Second Edition

Kuratko and Hodgetts
Entrepreneurship: A Contemporary Approach

Lee
Introduction to Management Science
Second Edition

Luthans and Hodgetts
Business

Montanari, Morgan, and Bracker
Strategic Management: A Choice Approach

Northcraft and Neale
**Organizational Behavior:
A Management Challenge**

Tombari
**Business and Society: Strategies for the
Environment and Public Policy**

Varner
Contemporary Business Report Writing
Second Edition

Vecchio
Organizational Behavior, *Second Edition*

Wolters and Holley
**Labor Relations: An Experiential
and Case Approach**

Zikmund
Business Research Methods, *Third Edition*

Preface

When we conceived the idea for *Cases in Strategic Management* we conducted a survey to determine what potential users would like to see in a strategic management casebook. The survey results indicated that a need exists for a book that provides current cases representing a mix of small and large firms, entrepreneurial and established firms, and service and manufacturing organizations. Survey respondents also desired cases covering a range of industries and strategic issues. We believe that our casebook answers these needs.

Features of the Book

Four features of the casebook reflect our personal philosophies toward education in strategic management and, we believe, contribute to meeting the needs of future strategic managers.

1. *Cases.* The cases selected for this text focus on the strategic management issues faced by managers of today and of the future. The cases feature a diverse set of companies and industries from which students will develop a strong appreciation for the strategic management concept; from small entrepreneurial companies to large corporations, from the high-tech industry to home video.

Many cases feature nationally known organizations, such as Wal-Mart, Inc., Xerox, and Boeing, while others focus on firms of all sizes. For courses that stress entrepreneurship, both large and small entrepreneurial organizations are presented here. Follow the growth of such firms as Sam Walton's Wal-Mart, Inc. and compare the entrepreneurial spirit of America West Airlines to the tradition of USAir and the airline industry. Recent entrepreneurial successes such as The Home Depot, Inc. and Blockbuster Video are profiled along with the relative failure of Yugo automobiles. The problems and issues of an LBO led by Genicom Corporation's new managers and the management of growing high-tech businesses such as Brooktrout Technology, Inc. and Applied CAD Knowledge, Inc., are profiled. Xerox's venture into the high-end printer industry is featured as well. Award-winning cases on Ramsey Paint and Walsh Petroleum are written from an insider's point of view. Outstanding cases about Environcare and CrossLand Savings Bank are featured and an industry note on entrepreneurship is presented.

Current issues involving technology and innovation, global strategy, entrepreneurship, quality assurance, and turnaround and restructuring are highlighted in the cases. Many of the cases are developed and drawn on insider information, giving the cases an added dimension regarding the issues faced by the company's management.

2. *A choice perspective.* We agree with many other strategic management writers that the primary function of a strategic manager is to make choices or decide among alternatives. The correct solution is seldom obvious to senior executives of an organization, whether the organization is private, public, or not for profit. Often information is incomplete, the problem poorly defined, and the results uncertain, which creates an ambiguous decision-making situation. Under these conditions, the manager must conduct the appropriate analyses, evaluate the alternatives, and choose the best direction for his or her organization. The brief text portion of this book focuses on the content and process of the choices that managers make in the strategic management of their organizations. It thus provides a realistic look at the complexity of managing strategically and suggests tools to help tomorrow's managers make better choices.

3. *An applications orientation.* We have attempted to make the text portion of the book easy to understand. By combining descriptions of what managers do with advice given by scholars about what managers should do, we provide a brief description of how to perform the strategic management process.

4. *Case analysis and financial analysis appendixes.* Both were written specifically for this book. The case analysis format described in Appendix A shows how to analyze a case. Financial analyses (Appendix B) are presented in a manner that highlights the practical uses of the results obtained from such analyses.

Supplements

A comprehensive teaching package has been assembled to support the casebook.

- An extensive *Instructor's Manual* prepared by the authors includes a chapter outline, and a chapter summary for the overview chapter. Complete casenotes for the 28 cases are presented in a consistent format to make case analysis more convenient.

- A *Videotape* is available to supplement several of the cases in the text, featuring America West, the NASA Space Shuttle Challenger, and others.

- A *Computer Disk* of templates provides financial data from selected cases and guides the student through several important strategic analyses.

A computer simulation entitled *The Advantage Ski Company: A Strategic Simulation* is available for the IBM PC and compatibles. The software and accompanying manual allow students to strategically manage their own firm in a competitive arena consisting of other companies (teams) in the class. The simulation is written by Alev M. Efendioglu and John R. Montanari.

Acknowledgments

Many competent professionals and policy-making groups have contributed to the material contained in this book. To the pioneers who first conceived of strategic planning and strategic management as a discipline worthy of study and research, we owe a special debt of gratitude. To the AACSB, who recognized strategy as an important component of a business education, we applaud their foresight. To the Academy of Management and the Strategic Management Society, which provide forums to present and discuss strategic issues, many of them having become the foundations for the field of strategic management, we express our thanks. Finally, to the universities that have encouraged our pursuit of strategy knowledge and experience, we are extremely grateful.

Special gratitude must be expressed to the people who were responsible for the creation, assimilation, and preparation of the content of this book. For the many strategic management scholars who conducted the research to write the cases for this text, no expression of gratitude is sufficient. We must also recognize the strategy practitioners who contributed many of the insights contained in this book through their writings in the popular business press and their willingness to let case writers document their experiences as strategic managers.

More directly involved in the creation of *Cases in Strategic Management* were those who contributed illustrations, figures, and quotations for inclusion in the book. We wish to acknowledge and thank the colleagues who contributed many of the cases for this text. They are Sexton Adams, *University of North Texas*; Michael D. Atchison, *University of Virginia*; Mark Aucutt, *Washington State University*; Douglas D. Baker, *Washington State University*; Charles Boyd, *Southwest Missouri State University*; Dorothy Brawley, *Kennesaw State College*; James W. Clinton, *University of Northern Colorado*; David B. Croll, *University of Virginia*; Robert F. Elliott, *Texas A & M University*; Howard D. Feldman, *University of Colorado-Boulder*; Adelaide Griffin, *Texas Women's University*; M. Ray Grubbs, *Millsaps College*; John M. Gwin, *University of Virginia*; Tommy Hackney, *Kennesaw State College*; Jeffrey S. Harrison, *Clemson University*; Carl Honacker, *Kennesaw State College*; Richard Hubbard, Jr., *George Mason University*; Jean-Pierre Jeannet, *IMEDE*; Per V. Jenster, *University of Virginia*; Gareth R. Jones, *Texas A & M University*; Karen Jones, *George Mason University*; Jon G. Kalinowski, *Mankato State University*; Raymond M. Kinnunen, *Northeastern University*; Charles R. Klasson, *University of Iowa*; Joseph Lampel, *New York University*; Michael W. Lawless, *University of Colorado-Boulder*; Robert Lewis, *George Mason University*; Mike Mahoney, *Kennesaw State College*; Stewart C. Malone, *University of Virginia*; Patricia P. McDougall, *Georgia State University*; Douglas D. Moesel, *Texas A & M University*; Bernard A. Morin, *University of Virginia*; Susan Nye, *IMEDE*; George A. Overstreet, Jr., *University of Virginia*; Dan S. Prickett, *University of Dayton*; Glynn Rawson, *Millsaps College*; Richard Reed, *Washington State University*; Joseph A. Schenk, *University of Dayton*; Sandra L. Schmidt, *University of Virginia*; William D. Schulte, Jr., *George Mason University*; John A. Seeger, *Bentley College*; Jamal Shamsie, *McGill University*; Carolyn Silliman, *Clemson University*; Denise West-Smith, *Kennesaw State College*; Stanley J. Stough, *University of Dayton*;

Linda F. Tegarden, *University of Colorado-Boulder*; Julian W. Vincze, *Rollins College*; Wendy Vittori, *Northeastern University*; William D. Wilstead, *University of Colorado-Boulder*; James A. Wolff, *Washington State University*; and Shaker A. Zahra, *George Mason University.*

The organization and development of the vast amounts of material necessary to complete this project was no small task. We would like to acknowledge the help, patience, and professionalism of the staff at The Dryden Press. To Bill Schoof, Butch Gemin, Susan Jansen, and others with whom we have worked, we express our gratitude for their guidance, encouragement, and commitment to our project.

We would also like to thank the people who contributed to the preparation of the manuscript. A thank you is owed to the many students who contributed their ideas, experiences, and stimulation. Of special note are research assistants Paul Walker, Greg Dunn, and Alan Belton and our secretary, Caryl Jones, who were extremely helpful in the preparation of drafts of the manuscript.

Finally, thank you to our families, who encouraged and motivated us through the preparation of the manuscript. Ellen was a constant source of encouragement for Dick at times when the work on the project seemed most difficult. Sharon, Pat. Sean, and Matt, having suffered through several books, knew when to stay out of the way and when to get Cy to go fishing, as well as when he needed "strokes." Peggie and Rachel were there when Jeff needed them most. To all of our families we owe more than gratitude. They shared our joys and frustrations and continued to provide selfless support throughout the entire project.

John R. Montanari
Cyril P. Morgan
Jeffrey S. Bracker

February 1990

About the Authors

Jeffrey S. Bracker (Ph.D., Georgia State University) is an Associate Professor of Strategic Management at George Mason University. He was one of the founders and former chief executive officer of Biosurge Inc., a New York–based medical products firm. He has more than 75 articles, proceedings, and scholarly presentations to his credit. Some of his work appears in the *Academy of Management Review, Strategic Management Journal, Journal of Applied Psychology*, and *Planning Review.*

John R. (Dick) Montanari received his Doctorate in Business Administration from the University of Colorado in Management and Administrative Policy. He has served on the faculties of the University of Houston, Arizona State University, and California State University-San Marcos since receiving his degree in 1976. He is currently Professor of Management at California State University-San Marcos. He has published several articles on management and business strategy in journals such as the *Academy of Management Review, Strategic Management Journal, Human Relations, Journal of Management*, and *Journal of Management Studies.* He is on the Editorial Review Board of the *Journal of Management* and *Executives Academy of Management.* His awards include several grants for research in the area of strategic management. Dr. Montanari was selected as a Distinguished Visiting Professor by the United States Air Force Academy. He has been actively involved in consulting and training for a number of firms in the private and public sectors. His consulting and training experiences include strategic management, long-range planning, and leadership. He has helped a number of public and private organizations develop strategic plans and strategic management systems.

Cyril P. Morgan is a Professor and Chairman of the Department of Management and Systems at Washington State University. His research interests include organization structure as well as its interface with business policy and organizational behavior, collaborative group processes, risk taking, and R&D project management. He has taught courses in business strategy and policy, organizational theory, organizational behavior, and introduction to management. His work has been published in such journals as *Administrative Science Quarterly, Journal of Experimental Psychology, Management Science, Academy of Management Journal, Journal of Management Studies, Human Relations*, and *Management Informational Review.* He is also the author of case studies and articles for practitioners. He is the coauthor of *Organizational Theory* (three editions) and *Administering Real Property.* Dr. Morgan has engaged in extensive consulting and training with public and private organizations. He received his Ph.D. from Case Institute of Technology, his M.B.A. from Xavier University, and his B.S. from Miami University. He has also received three teaching awards from M.B.A. and doctoral students.

Contents

Part One   **Introduction to the Strategic Management Process** *1*

Appendix A Strategic Case Analysis *29*

Appendix B Financial Statement Analysis *39*

Part Two   **Cases** *67*

Case 1   Industry Note on the Commercial
Aircraft Manufacturing Industry *69*
by Jeffrey S. Bracker

Case 2   Boeing's Commercial Jet Aircraft Business *83*
by Jeffrey S. Bracker

Case 3   The Kellogg Company and the Ready-to-Eat Cereal Industry *91*
by Joseph A. Schenk, Dan S. Prickett, and Stanley J. Stough
Case 3 Update *114*

Case 4   The American Express Company *121*
by William D. Wilsted
Case 4 Update *141*

Case 5   The John Hancock Mutual Life Insurance Company *153*
by Raymond M. Kinnunen
Case 5 Update *174*

Case 6   CrossLand Savings, FSB *181*
by Karen Jones and Shaker A. Zahra

Case 7   Cineplex Odeon *195*
by Joseph Lampel and Jamal Shamsie

Case 8   Blockbuster Video   *213*
              by Dorothy E. Brawley, Brian Cone, Linda Kobel, Jody Prentice, and Jeffrey Sowell

Case 9   The Restructuring of Ramada Inc.   *235*
              by Jeffrey S. Bracker

Case 10   Merck: Strategy Making in
              "America's Most Admired Corporation"   *249*
              by Shaker A. Zahra, Robert Lewis, Richard Hubbard, Jr., and William D. Schulte, Jr.

Case 11   The Airline Industry   *271*
              by Patricia P. McDougall
              Case 11 Update *281*

Case 12   USAir's Competitive Response to Deregulation:
              Key Policy and Tactical Choices of the CEO   *285*
              by Jon G. Kalinowski and Charles R. Klasson
              Case 12 Update *299*

Case 13   America West Airlines   *309*
              by Jeffrey S. Bracker

Case 14   Hanson—1989   *325*
              by Richard Reed

Case 15   Xerox's Competitive Dilemma in the High-End,
              Nonimpact Printer Industry   *343*
              by Michael W. Lawless, Linda Finch Tegarden, and Howard D. Feldman

Case 16   Robert F. Ramsey, Inc. and Ramsey Paint Manufacturers, Inc.
              353
              by Michael D. Atchison, Stewart C. Malone, and Sandra L. Schmidt

Case 17   Genicom Corporation   *381*
              by Per V. Jenster, John M. Gwin, and David B. Croll

Case 18   Applied CAD Knowledge, Inc.:
              The "Boom/Splat" Syndrome   *411*
              by John A. Seeger and Raymond M. Kinnunen

Case 19   Applied CAD Knowledge, Inc. (B)   *429*
              by Raymond M. Kinnunen and John A. Seeger

Case 20   The Lincoln Electric Company   *435*
              by Arthur Sharplin

Case 21   Wal-Mart Stores, Inc.   *455*
           by Sexton Adams and Adelaide Griffin
           Case 21 Update *468*

Case 22   The Home Depot, Inc.   *477*
           by Dorothy E. Brawley, Tommy Hackney, Carl Honaker,
           Mike Mahoney, and Denise West-Smith

Case 23   The Rise and Fall of Yugo America, Inc.   *501*
           by Carolyn Silliman and Jeffrey S. Harrison

Case 24   Harley-Davidson: How Long Can the Eagle Stay Aloft?   *511*
           by James A. Wolff and Douglas D. Baker

Case 25   A Note on Starting an Entrepreneurial Business through
           Venture Capital   *531*
           by Jeffrey S. Bracker

Case 26   Walsh Petroleum   *543*
           by George A. Overstreet, Jr., Stewart C. Malone, and Bernard A. Morin

Case 27   Brooktrout Technology, Inc.   *583*
           by Raymond M. Kinnunen, Wendy Vittori, and John A. Seeger

Case 28   Environcare   *599*
           by James W. Clinton

Alphabetical Listing of Cases

The Airline Industry *271*

The American Express Company *121*

America West Airlines *309*

Applied CAD Knowledge, Inc.: The "Boom/Splat" Syndrome *411*

Applied CAD Knowledge, Inc. (B) *429*

Blockbuster Video *213*

Boeing's Commercial Jet Aircraft Business *83*

Brooktrout Technology, Inc. *583*

Cineplex Odeon *195*

CrossLand Savings, FSB *181*

Environcare *599*

Genicom Corporation *381*

Hanson—1989 *325*

Harley-Davidson: How Long Can the Eagle Stay Aloft? *511*

The Home Depot, Inc. *477*

Industry Note on the Commercial Aircraft Manufacturing Industry *69*

The John Hancock Mutual Life Insurance Company *153*

The Kellogg Company and the Ready-to-Eat Cereal Industry *91*

The Lincoln Electric Company *435*

Merck: Strategy Making in "America's Most Admired Corportion" *249*

A Note on Starting an Entrepreneurial Business through Venture Capital *531*

The Restructuring of Ramada Inc. *235*

The Rise and Fall of Yugo America, Inc. *501*

Robert F. Ramsey, Inc. and Ramsey Paint Manufacturers, Inc. *353*

USAir's Competitive Response to Deregulation: Key Policy and Tactical Choices of the CEO *285*

Wal-Mart Stores, Inc. *455*

Walsh Petroleum *543*

Xerox's Competitive Dilemma in the High-End Nonimpact Printer Industry *343*

Part 1

Introduction to the Strategic Management Process

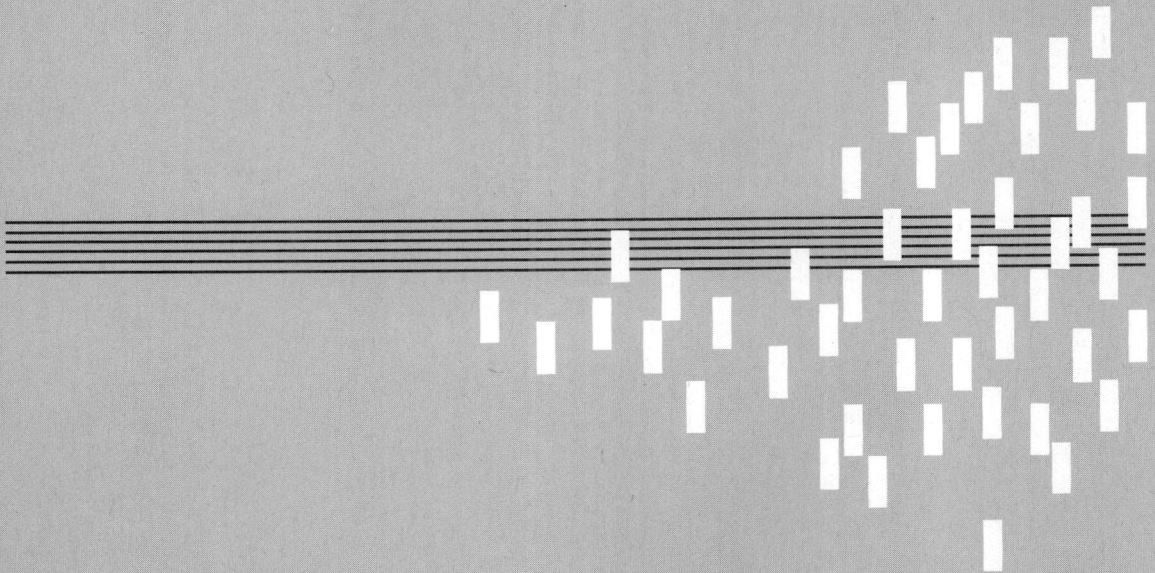

Part 1

Introduction to the
Strategic Management Process

We've come to praise strategic planning, not to bury it.
                    —Daniel Gray, President and CEO of Gray-Judson, Inc.[1]

Learning Objectives

- To discover the difference between strategic management and strategic planning.
- To learn how strategic management thought developed and why it is important today.
- To understand the levels of strategy development and the stages of the strategic management process.
- To be introduced to the choice model of strategic management.
- To appreciate the flow and direction of the strategic management process.
- To learn the situational, organizational, group, and personal factors that influence managers' strategic choices.
- To understand how to recognize effective organizations.

The Strategic Management Perspective

When Lee Iacocca came to Chrysler Corporation, the company was on the verge of closing its doors. The K-car was on the drawing boards, but Chrysler's management could not generate financing to bring it to market. Sweeping changes under Iacocca's administration have since turned the company around dramatically.

Why do some firms succeed while others fail? Why do similar firms in the same industry pursue different courses of action? The answers to these questions lie in the strategic direction that top-level decision makers such as Iacocca set for the organization.

The strategic direction is based on answers to questions such as "What business should we be in?" and "Which approach to that business should we take?" These answers determine the other individuals and organizations with which the firm must transact its business. Asking and answering such questions is the basis of the **strategic**

management of the organization—that is, the choices of the analyses, plans, decisions, and actions that determine the strategic direction of the organization and lead to accomplishment of its strategic goals and objectives in a dynamic environment. Whether a firm is large or small, is not-for-profit or profit-making, or is privately held or a publicly traded corporation, successful strategic managers engage in similar activities. The senior executives who make the top-level, long-term decisions of strategic management are referred to as **strategic managers**. These managers spend most of their time analyzing, planning, and deciding on issues that give the firm a competitive advantage in an increasingly turbulent business environment. To accomplish this, managers must perform in different capacities in the organization.

Mintzberg refers to these as the roles that top managers occupy in the organization.[2] According to Mintzberg, the primary roles involve making decisions, handling information, and managing people. Strategic managers handle external and internal information by matching external environmental opportunities with internal organizational capabilities. Once the managers believe they have a match, they make strategic choices as to how to use the firm's capabilities to take advantage of the opportunity. Last, they organize, motivate, and direct people to utilize their capabilities to contribute to the success of the organization. Performing all of these roles well is the key to being an effective strategic manager.

At the very top levels of the organization, management is more complex than it is at lower levels. Strategic managers make novel choices that involve the success and survival of the organization. Because strategic problems are unique, managers draw upon their judgment and experience to commit vast amounts of the organization's resources to projects that may or may not be appropriate for tomorrow's marketplace. The amount of resources and degree of uncertainty involved make the strategic manager a key figure in the firm's success. The central challenge of tomorrow's strategic manager is to match the opportunities in the environment to the firm's capabilities and then manage those capabilities toward accomplishment of organizational goals.

Strategic managers are the captains of their organization. They set the long-term course of the firm and ensure that resources are available to steer the organization along that course. Therefore, it is not surprising that the average chief executive officer (CEO) of a major corporation receives total compensation of over $1.1 million.[3] These managers are highly valued because they deal with strategic issues that are critical to the firm's survival. Iacocca, for example, was a creative and charismatic CEO who was able to convince suppliers, unions, bankers, and the government to fund Chrysler until he could turn it around. He was the right strategic manager for the environment that Chrysler faced and the right person to manage Chrysler's turnaround.

Why Learn about Strategic Management?

Learning about strategic management is more important today than it has been at any time in the past. The growth of a world economy, rapid technological advances, and the shortage of critical resources (for example, crude oil and water) are just a few of the factors that make today's business conditions more dynamic and complex than those of even a decade ago. Effective strategic management is typically associated with improved organizational performance. Those who learn to view the organization from a strategic perspective will benefit personally and professionally.

Changing Business Conditions

In the early 1960s, the big three U.S. automobile manufacturers were in the driver's seat in the huge U.S. auto market. These companies were increasing the size of cars to improve their profit margins, and demand was strong. Foreign automobile manufacturers had only five to seven percent of the market, and brand loyalty for GM, Ford, and Chrysler was high. But during the next two decades, the United States experienced two fuel crises, which created a demand for smaller, fuel-efficient foreign cars. Impressed by the high quality of these autos, many U.S. consumers switched loyalties to the foreign manufacturers. Today foreign autos enjoy a 30 to 35 percent share of the market.

This cycle of rapid and dramatic change is not limited to the automobile industry. Many other industries as diverse as semiconductors and home appliances are experiencing turbulent change. Not only has the environment in which managers conduct business changed, but so have the nature of organizations and the view that managers hold in setting the strategic direction for their firms.

Before the mid-1950s, most organizations were thought of as **closed systems**. That is, strategic managers assumed that knowledge would expand at a steady rate that would allow ample time to plan for obsolescence. They also assumed that resources were abundant and available, both in terms of the materials and knowledge needed to provide a good or service and in terms of the customers for that good or service. Thus, the success and survival of the organization depended upon the efficiency of its internal operations. Planning concentrated on internal processes associated with operations. Managers did not need to look outside the organization, because the environment would favor the firm with the most efficient operations.

Strategic managers of some organizations, such as General Electric and Du Pont, recognized early that there was a need for a more external or open view of the firm. However, several events that occurred after 1960 convinced other strategic managers to change the way they viewed their organizations.

One such event was the energy crisis of 1973, which dramatically illustrated to managers the degree to which U.S. business had become internationally dependent. Another event was the widespread acceptance of the computer in scientific and business applications. The processing speed of computers dramatically shortened the time required to analyze data, greatly increasing the rate at which new knowledge is created and transferred. The effect of the resulting knowledge explosion has been more rapid technological development, which causes more rapid obsolescence of existing products and services. Today's strategic managers must expend more energy looking outside of the firm for new competing technologies and market entrants.

These events and many others highlighted the importance of the firm's external environment, forcing strategic managers to view the organization as an **open system**. This perspective entails viewing the organization as being open to changes in the environment and in a state of continuous interaction with it. Managers depend upon the environment for opportunities, resources, and customers. They are also the key individuals responsible for adapting the firm to its dynamic environment. Today's successful managers have adopted a more open perspective in order to strategically manage both the organization and its interactions with the environment.

Improved Organizational Performance

Mounting evidence indicates that firms using formal strategic planning and management outperform firms without it.[4] In one review of prior research, 12 of 20 studies conclude that strategic planning improved organizational performance. According to many studies, as strategic plans become more sophisticated, performance improves. Other research reports that the mere practice of strategic planning results in improved performance. Based on these studies and the experience of practicing managers, strategic planning is generally acknowledged as a way to improve organizational performance.

Personal and Professional Benefits

On a more personal note, if you, as a possible future strategic manager, learn to view the firm from a strategic perspective, you will be better prepared to understand your organizational surroundings. In addition, this book will give you a better understanding of the decisions that top managers make in the firms in which you are employed. The insights that you gain will help you prepare to chart your course up the career ladder through the organization. In many cases, advancement in a firm depends on being in the right place at the right time. Understanding which factors affect top management improves your chances of being where you need to be when you need to be there.

The Evolution of Strategic Management

Strategic planning and management have interested senior executives for the past two decades. **Strategic planning** is the analysis of environmental conditions and organizational capabilities, and the formulation of plans to match the firm's capabilities with those conditions. Most managers consider strategic planning absolutely necessary to allow their organization to cope with a more dynamic environment. Others believe that the planning process has been overformalized to the point of little use.[5] As one senior executive put it: "What we had [our plan] was a kind of strategic rain dance—war cries, smoke signals, sacrificial offerings."[6] However, a recent survey of senior-level executives reported that most companies remain firmly committed to strategic planning.

Why this confusion about strategic planning? As the business environment became more turbulent,[7] managers discovered that strategic *planning*, with its emphasis on environmental assessment, analysis of internal capabilities, and plan formulation, was insufficient. They realized that the strategic planning process did not specify how plans should be translated into action. A gap existed between the strategic direction set by senior executives and the results obtained by the firm.

As Alex R. Oliver, vice president at Booz, Allen and Hamilton, Inc., suggests, one of the most common strategic planning mistakes is inadequate involvement of line management in strategic planning.[8] In addition, discussions with 216 strategic managers indicated that the greatest source of frustration and disappointment in their strategic planning systems was difficulties in implementation.[9] As one executive stated, "We actually used to tell ourselves our planning system was OK, even though we admitted it fell apart at implementation. That was our way of telling ourselves that the trouble was not at the top."

These problems with the implementation of the strategic plan led to the evolution of **strategic management**. Strategic management includes not only the elements of strategic planning, environmental analysis, and strategy formulation, but also strategy implementation and control. This current view of strategically managing the enterprise extends the responsibilities of strategic managers beyond planning to the design of implementation and control systems. Therefore, strategic management is not merely a new name for strategic planning. It is a comprehensive process for strategically managing the organization, a process that evolved in response to the demands of changing business conditions.

The Strategic Management Process

In a survey of CEOs, 91 percent stated that their firms engaged in some type of formal long-range planning.[10] However, planning does not always result in effective organizational performance. If plans are to succeed, they must be developed and implemented with equal care. Once implementation begins, managers must evaluate actual performance to verify progress toward accomplishing the plans and trigger corrective action when needed. Depending on the organization, this process can operate at any of four levels.

Levels of Strategy Development

In most larger firms, strategies are developed at various levels within the firm. It makes sense that department heads will develop strategies that are different from those developed by top-level managers. Managers at each level have a different perspective of the organization, and managers at higher levels are responsible for choices that have a greater impact on the organization. The choices at all levels are important, but some have consequences that are farther reaching for the firm than others.

A useful way to view these levels of strategy development is to use the four levels first specified by Schendel and Hofer,[11] drawing from the work of Ansoff.[12] They are the functional, business, corporate, and enterprise levels. Figure 1.1 illustrates each of these levels and the areas of the firm's environment addressed by managers at each level.

Figure 1.1   Levels of Strategy Development

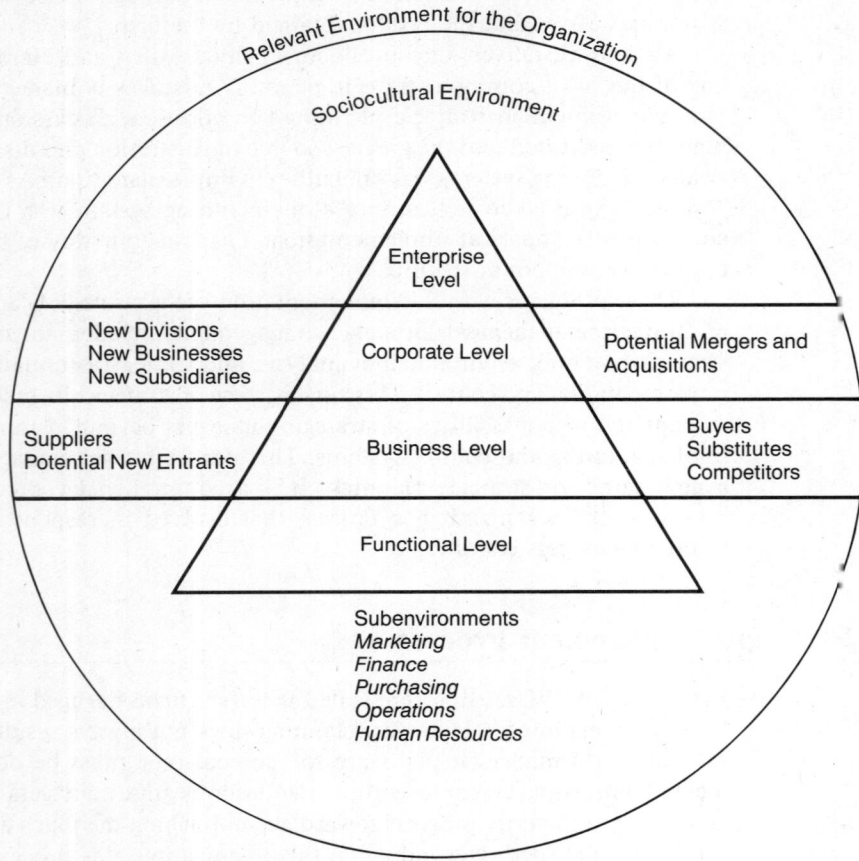

Relevant Environment for the Organization

Sociocultural Environment

Enterprise
Level

| New Divisions
New Businesses
New Subsidiaries | Corporate Level | Potential Mergers and
Acquisitions |

| Suppliers
Potential New Entrants | Business Level | Buyers
Substitutes
Competitors |

Functional Level

Subenvironments
Marketing
Finance
Purchasing
Operations
Human Resources

The levels at which strategies must be developed depend on the type of organization. Smaller, single-purpose businesses in a large community may not need to be as concerned with strategies for the enterprise and corporate levels, whereas large, visible, multibusiness firms may need to devote management attention to all levels.

According to Schendel and Hofer, the strategic management process can be applied to each level at which strategies are developed. In other words, regardless of level, strategies must be effectively managed to ensure that they move the organization toward its goals.

Enterprise Level   The highest level of strategy development, the enterprise level, involves strategies that encompass the organization's interactions with its publics. In a broad sense, the publics include the firm's sociocultural environment, which consists of the general publics that provide the culture, populations, communities, and economic system in which the firm conducts its business. The organization not only is influenced by the sociocultural environment in which it conducts business, but also influences that environment through its products and the choices that it makes. Society can accept the firm's choices or act through special interest groups or legislators to object to the firm's actions. The organization therefore must be prepared to analyze its sociocultural environment and develop enterprise-level strategies appropriate to this environment.

The society in which the firm is located gives it both legal and practical permission to operate. This permission from society is referred to as a **charter**. The **legal charter** is the granting of the licenses, registrations, and permissions that the organization needs in order to conduct business. The **practical charter** is society's willingness to purchase the firm's products or services at a price that allows the firm to make a profit. In many situations, these charters are influenced as much by the way the organization interacts with its relevant publics as by the products or services it provides.

The enterprise level of strategy development also includes strategies for social responsibility and ethics. The awarding of the legal and practical charters depends in part upon the public's belief that the company conducts its business responsibly and ethically. **Social responsibility** is the posture a firm takes in its attitudes, policies, and actions with respect to the duties, obligations, and expectations for which society believes the business should be held accountable in the conduct of its affairs or pursuit of its purpose. Fundamentally, it is the expectations that society holds for the manner in which the firm conducts its business. **Ethics** is a set of moral principles or values that forms the basis for accepted professional standards of conduct.

Society demands ethical and responsible behavior as a precondition for giving an organization a charter to operate. At the enterprise level, managers must therefore develop strategies for this behavior. Failure to do so may result in scenarios such as the alleged one in the Strategic Application "The Saga of Paul Bilzerian."

Corporate Level Firms engaged in multiple businesses or single-business firms pursuing growth through diversification into other businesses need to develop corporate-level strategies. The corporate level of strategy development requires the manager to analyze the environment for opportunities to acquire, develop, or divest businesses that will strengthen the organization's portfolio and to develop strategies to capitalize on those opportunities. The central issue is how best to manage the firm's portfolio of businesses to achieve the organization's strategic goals and to protect it from unexpected changes in the environment. This is one of the most important strategic choices for the top executives of a multibusiness firm.

Managing the firm's business portfolio involves integrating businesses with different market and operating characteristics. For example, many businesses are affected differently by general economic cycles, so that some are strong during periods of economic decline, whereas others closely follow the economic cycle. Another reason for corporate-level strategies is to manage the product life cycles of the various businesses.

Business Level Most discussions of strategic planning and management focus on the business level of strategy development. This level involves the choices relating to the strategies the firm will use to compete in a single business area. At this level, strategic managers are responsible for analyzing the environment for opportunities and threats in the firm's chosen business. They must then match the organization's internal capabilities to these opportunities and threats, and develop the strategies that will direct organizational members toward accomplishment of the organization's goals. Next, they must design structures, processes, and systems to guide all of the functional areas of the firm toward implementation of those strategies. If the organization consists of many businesses, then each business develops strategies for its product-markets. For example, the Strategic Application "Audi Aims for the U.S. Market" describes strategy development at the international business level at the Audi Car Company.

Functional Level Functional units of the firm handle business functions such as marketing, production, and finance. Each functional unit must develop strategies that contribute to the success of the overall business strategy.

Variations in functional strategies reflect that each functional unit of the organization interacts with unique segments of the environment. Purchasing deals with suppliers. Personnel recruits and trains employees. Marketing is responsible for distribution and sales. Operations must maintain the systems to produce the product or service.

The manager of the functional unit not only monitors the actions of organizations outside the firm but also integrates the unit's activities with those of other units in the firm. For example, the personnel department must be aware of the local labor market and also coordinate with the other departments within the firm to ensure that the right employees are hired for each department.

Phases of Strategic Management

Regardless of the level at which the manager develops strategy, the same basic process is used to manage the strategy. This process consists of three phases: strategy formulation, strategy implementation, and strategic control and evaluation.

Strategy Formulation In the first phase of strategic management, the manager assesses current business conditions, analyzes internal capabilities, and develops plans. Like strategic planning, strategic management considers the environment a source of opportunities and threats for the organization. A strategically well-managed firm scans the environment for opportunities and threats as an initial stage in the planning process. In addition, it continually monitors the environment for changes that will present new opportunities or interfere with the achievement of the organization's goals.

At the same time, managers analyze the organization's internal capabilities. These include the managerial, technical, informational, organizational, and financial resources necessary for the business to continue to serve existing customers and clients plus what is needed to pursue new opportunities or respond to new threats. The capabilities analysis provides information upon which the manager can base a decision whether to adapt to environmental changes by using internal capabilities or by acquiring needed capabilities from outside the organization.

Combining the environmental assessment and the analysis of internal capabilities allows the manager to progress to formulating a strategy. Here, the manager chooses the firm's principal business relationships and develops a mission and strategy to take advantage of opportunities. This phase also includes strategic goals and objectives to guide the activities of members of the organization.

Strategy Implementation The action phase of strategic management is strategy implementation. This is the phase at which lower level managers must convert the strategic plans received from the strategic managers into the functional plans and strategies that guide the activities of organization members in a way that should lead the firm to achieve its strategic goals. Senior executives design organization structures and develop annual objectives to guide this process. These objectives are converted into functional-level plans, including objectives and strategies, that specify each unit's contribution to meeting the organization's overall strategic goals.

Good implementation requires that each department fulfill its purpose in the best way possible to contribute to the firm's strategic goals. It is hard to recommend specific implementation principles for department managers, because what they need to do varies with the organization and the strategic plan. In addition, these managers are seldom rewarded for their contributions to the strategic plan because of the difficulty in tying one unit's efforts to overall organization performance. The combination of few guidelines and little recognition makes the implementation phase extremely challenging for functional-level managers.

Strategic Control and Evaluation A plan must be developed in the present to prepare for the future. But conditions inside and outside the firm change rapidly, making some aspects of the plan obsolete. Therefore, businesses need processes for evaluating these changes to determine their source (inside or outside) and importance. In addition, systems and techniques must be in place to trigger action to adjust to the changes and return the firm to the planned course, or to modify the plan to reflect the real world that the firm now faces. By using these processes and systems, the business completes the final phase of strategic management: control and evaluation.

A Choice Model of the Strategic Management Process

Most issues that senior managers address are either strategic or operational. **Strategic issues** concern the future decisions and actions that set the long-term direction of the firm.[13] Examples of strategic issues are: Which business(es) should the firm be engaged in over the next three, five, or ten years? Which major market segments, consumer or commercial, should the firm concentrate on over the next decade?

Operational issues are shorter-term decisions made in order to keep the firm competitive. These issues typically concern the functional areas of the firm rather than the entire organization. Examples of major operational issues are: Which manufacturing processes should be used? How can we best market our product or service?

Which inventory costing method is most appropriate for our firm? Although operational issues have a narrower scope and focus on shorter time periods, they are as important as strategic issues. Both categories of issues influence the overall success of the organization.

Strategic issues are the focus of the strategic management process. The outputs of this process are the choices that managers make to direct the firm toward the pursuit of its mission. Unlike the daily operating choices of the lower level managers, these choices are strategic in nature.

Strategic choices usually depend on the prior experience of senior executives. They involve unique problems with major long-term consequences for the organization. Very little precedent exists to guide the manager, and an incorrect choice can seriously impair the success and survival of the firm. Therefore, these choices reflect the manager's best judgments among alternatives generated from previous analyses. The specific alternative that the executive chooses reflects environmental conditions, situational and organizational factors, and the individual and collective personalities of senior executives involved in the strategic management of the firm.

To make these choices successfully, managers should follow a logical process of analyzing information, formulating strategies, implementing the strategies, and evaluating and controlling them. Figure 1.2 illustrates the way many executives perform these tasks. Notice that strategic management is a series of choices. These choices determine the success and survival of the organization. Besides the strategic choices, Figure 1.2 indicates some of the important functional-level choices that are necessary to effectively implement top management's strategies.

Environmental Assessment Why have foreign automobile manufacturers captured one-third of the U.S. car market? Why did so many savings and loan associations go under in the late 1980s while other financial institutions thrived? The answers to such questions are complex, but the single most important reason for the success or failure of an organization is its ability to assess current business conditions, accurately predict future trends, and use this information to make good strategic choices.

Strategic management therefore begins with acquiring an understanding of the business environment in which the organization operates. The firm's environment consists of other organizations, government agencies, special interest groups, and individuals with which the firm must transact business. From this arena, the firm draws its life's blood in the form of capital, raw materials, labor, and operating revenue (whether from sales or appropriations). This information does not come cheaply. Indeed, deciding how much to spend for the acquisition of environmental data is one of top management's most important strategic choices.

Determination of Internal Strategic Capabilities Strategic management must also look inward to the organization and determine the capabilities of its technical and human systems. This analysis reveals the demands that current operations place upon the firm's resources, material and human. It also provides information about the slack that the firm has available to absorb new demands that may emerge from the environment. A thorough analysis of internal strategic capabilities allows the manager to

Figure 1.2 Choice Model of the Strategic Management Process

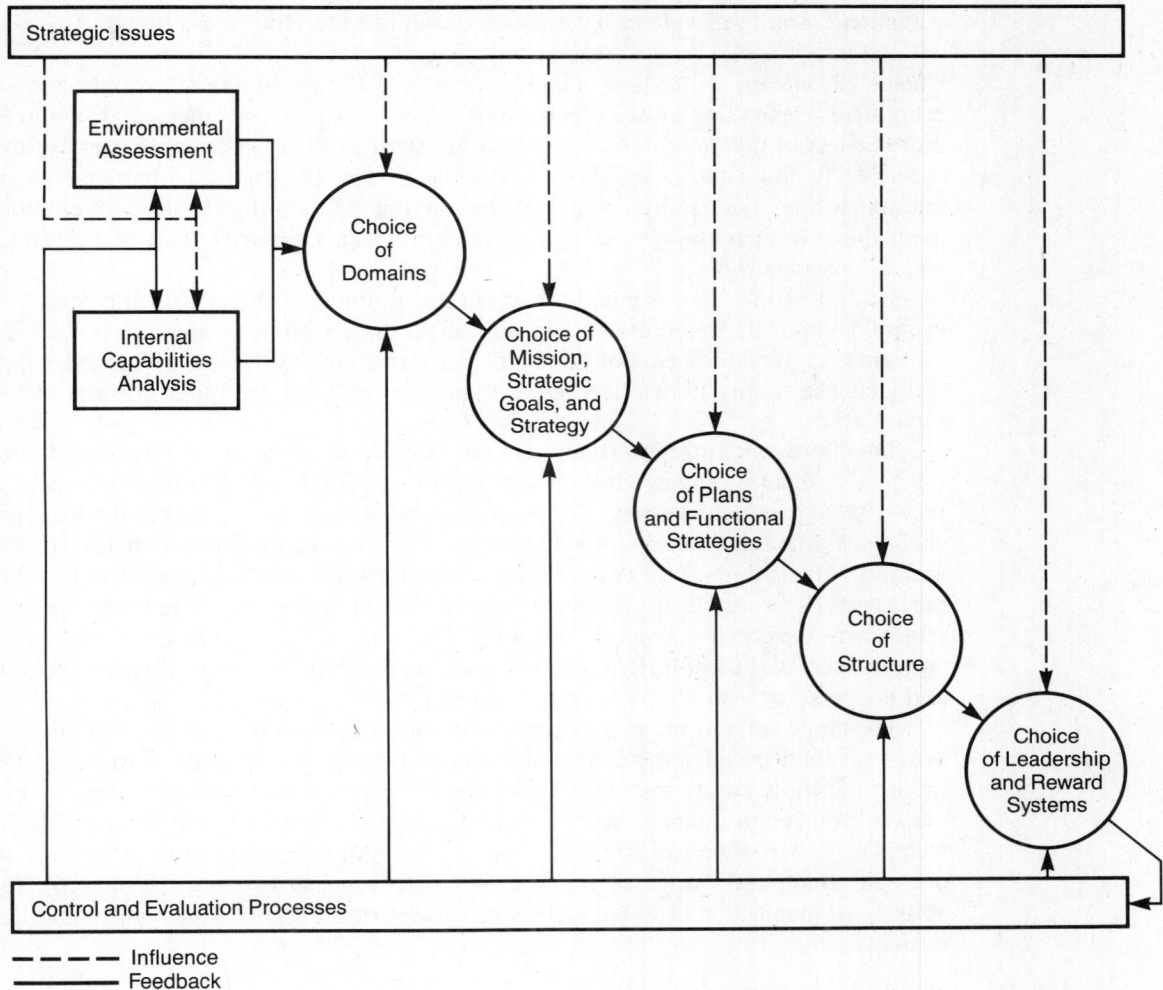

match current capabilities to environmental conditions and to assess the feasibility of possible strategies. If additional resources are necessary, then the acquisition of those resources can be incorporated into the strategic plan.

This stage of the strategic management process is extremely important. The strengths and weaknesses of the firm's managerial, technical, financial, and human resource capabilities determine to a large extent which environmental opportunities the firm can pursue in the short run. For example, Sony used its strength of an innovative culture to shift its dependence from the highly competitive consumer electronics market to new opportunities in commercial telecommunications, office automation, and health care. With its relatively high commitment to research and development, Sony was able to use existing capabilities to enter these markets.[14]

Choice of Domain Not all of the components of the environment are relevant for every firm. Depending on the organization's size, industry, customers, and products, more or less of the environment will be important to the organization's success and survival. To use a term chosen by Dill,[15] the part of the total environment that is relevant to the organization for goal setting and goal attainment is the task environment. Most business task environments are limited geographically to a single nation, region, city, or town.

Not all of the components of a firm's environment transact with the firm. For example, suppliers of inputs and buyers of the firm's products may be potentially relevant and, therefore, part of the firm's task environment. However, managers typically choose to buy from a few reliable suppliers and sell to only a segment of the total market.

Therefore, once strategic managers are familiar with the environment and with the firm's capabilities, they must choose the portion of the task environment in which they wish to conduct business. The portion of the task environment that the manager chooses is called the **domain**. It is defined as all of the organizations, agencies, groups, and individuals in the task environment with which the manager chooses to transact business.[16] For example, the decision to make Dillards' a national rather than regional retailer was the specific choice of William T. Dillard.[17] He chose this expanded domain with its increased complexity on the basis of his assumptions about the environment and his personal aspirations for the organization.

The choice of a domain is extremely important. The correct choice will give the firm a competitive advantage, while an incorrect choice will force the firm to operate in an unfriendly environment, as Quadram Corporation unfortunately learned. Explosive growth and financial success caused J. Leland Strage, CEO of this small high-tech firm, to rapidly make a series of acquisitions. An 80 percent drop in earnings in one year convinced him that the company's domain had expanded faster than his ability to manage it. He later decided to restrict expansion to more familiar businesses.[18]

Choice of Mission, Strategic Goals, and Strategy Within the selected domain, the manager must choose which environmental opportunities to pursue. This choice results in a clear statement of the firm's primary business or **mission**. A mission states the firm's primary purpose or business, indicating to its employees and publics the firm's products, markets, method of conducting business, and approach to dealing with constituents. The mission specifies whether the firm intends to be proactive or reactive and whether it will emphasize R&D, finance, operations, or marketing. Finally, the mission gives the firm's employees and publics a clear picture of where it is positioned in its competitive arena and who are its primary stakeholders.[19] The Strategic Application "Mission Statement" provides examples of mission statements for several types of firms.

Strategic management is designed to enable the firm to accomplish its mission over an extended period. To plan how the firm can do this, managers set **strategic goals**, sometimes called long-term objectives. These goals state the general targets that the firm intends to achieve in strategic areas such as market share, profitability, productivity, growth, and return. To serve their purpose, strategic goals must be consistent with the mission of the firm. For example, to fulfill a mission of being a proactive, high-growth firm, managers might set a strategic goal of 15 percent annual growth rate in an industry in which growth of seven to eight percent is average. These are strategic-level goals that reflect the combined performance of all of the organizational units (strategic business units, divisions, or departments).

The specifics of how the firm will exploit the opportunities that top management has chosen from among those available are laid out in the **strategy**. This functions as the organization's compass to point to the general methods that the organization will use to achieve its strategic goals. The strategy guides and directs the activities of organization members toward accomplishment of the mission.

Strategies fall into three general types: generic strategies, master strategies, and ancillary strategies. Table 1.1 shows these types along with brief definitions of strategy categories under each type. Many of the master strategies in these categories are most appropriate for the business level of strategy development. Others apply more directly to the corporate level.

Strategies describe broad ranges of actions available to the organization to accomplish its strategic goals. For example, a cost-leadership generic strategy helps the firm be a more effective competitor within its industry by incurring the lowest costs to provide its product or service. Internal-growth master strategies promote the firm's growth through developing new products or services in-house, whereas external-growth master strategies use acquisition or merger as the method for growth. In some cases,

Table 1.1 Types of Strategies

Strategy Type	Definition	Examples of Strategies
Generic	Generic approaches to outperform industry competitors.	Cost Leadership Differentiation Niche (Focus)
Master	Strategic actions that a single business or SBU takes to achieve its strategic goals.	Vertical Integration Concentration Product Diversification Concentric Diversification Conglomerate Diversification Rejuvenation through Retrenchment Stabilization through Maintenance Termination through Divestment
Ancillary	Strategies that work in conjunction with other strategies and facilitate achievement of strategic goals.	Rationalization through Consolidation Cooperation through Joint Venture

a firm may need to shrink to control costs and improve management control before launching into a growth mode. This would require rejuvenation master strategies. At other times, it is financially more appropriate to concentrate on maintaining the current level of business performance than to attempt to grow. This frequently happens in times of economic decline and results in the adoption of a stabilization master strategy. On occasion, it may be best to harvest or divest all or part of the business, which calls for a termination master strategy. Last, a manager may choose to focus on establishing cooperative ventures with other organizations as a means to improve organization performance. These strategies are referred to as ancillary strategies. The factors that determine the choice of a strategy are discussed later in this introduction.

Choice of Plans, Objectives, and Functional Strategies Strategies and strategic goals are implemented through plans that include objectives and functional-level strategies. Objectives provide specific targets that indicate expected levels and time frames and serve as guides to organization action. Functional-level strategies are the means or activities that the organization will use to achieve its objectives. Managers are responsible for selecting the best strategy for each objective.

To merely develop a new strategy is not enough. Organizational performance depends on effectively implementing strategies through plans and functional-level strategies. For example, after Black & Decker, the medium-sized power tool manufacturer, experienced a $158 million loss in 1985 due primarily to foreign competition, the board hired a new CEO, Noland D. Archibald, with a background in consumer marketing. Archibald immediately devised a retrenchment–turnaround strategy designed to position the company to face foreign competition head-on and diversify its product mix. He purchased GE's small-appliance division and devised an implementation plan that included closing seven plants, eliminating 2,000 jobs, and reorganizing operations around product-markets.[20]

A formulated strategy is lifeless until members of the organization implement it. All of an organization's activities either help or hinder the successful implementation of the strategy.

Choice of Organization Structure Implementation plans usually include changes to the structure, processes, and systems of the organization. Choosing the appropriate organization structure involves selecting the structural design that leads to accomplishment of strategic goals. General Electric appeared to pursue a master strategy of external growth when it acquired Kidder, Peabody & Company, one of the larger Wall Street brokerage houses. To implement this growth strategy and integrate Kidder, Peabody into its organization, GE had to modify its structure by creating a new division for financial services.[21] Not only acquisition but most changes in strategy are accompanied by alterations in the firm's structure. Motorola Inc. has an implementation procedure that automatically elevates a unit from division to group status when it reaches a certain level of sales. Staff functions are then added to the group's organization chart, and group managers receive more decision authority.

The organization structure is originally designed during the initial stages of strategy implementation. Senior executives handle this formal organization design, which is represented by the organization chart. So that it will help managers and employees implement the strategy, the organization design must be consistent with the mission and strategy stated in the strategic plan. However, organizations also have an informal structure that is based on past working relations and friendships among employees, developed over a period of time. This informal structure can either help or hinder the successful accomplishment of the firm's goals and objectives.

While senior management must design an appropriate overall organization structure, unit managers must modify the department's structure. All levels of management need to closely monitor the informal structure to determine whether changes are necessary. For example, Gillette formally committed $7 million to the introduction of its electric shaver produced by its West German subsidiary. However, Gillette's top management remained apathetic about the project. As one executive put it, "Those electric razors are getting better, but they're still not as good as a blade."[22] The informal structure did not truly support the product development strategy, and as a result the product was not successful.

Choices of Leadership, Culture, and Human Resource Processes and Reward Systems
To implement new or changing mission, strategic goals, and strategy, the organization needs new processes and systems for leading and rewarding employees. A **process** is a series of actions or operations directed toward a particular result. A process or several processes focused on a particular aspect or activity of the organization form a **system**. Leadership processes play an important role in the implementation of plans and strategies. The system of rewards with which the organization acknowledges the contributions of its members also encourages employees to perform the actions necessary to achieve strategic goals and objectives.

The implementation of strategic and functional plans depends on the choices of the most effective leadership processes and reward systems. For example, Intel Inc., a large semiconductor manufacturer, has a master strategy of internal growth through innovation. To implement this strategy, the company decided to make leadership more participative and to reward creative thinking. In contrast, Texas Air has chosen external growth through acquisition and low-cost leadership. Texas Air reward systems place less emphasis on people and rewards using traditional means such as money and movement up the hierarchy. In both cases, the implementation processes and systems must be consistent with the mission and strategy.

The culture operating at all levels of the organization can be a key to the efficient and effective implementation of a strategy. Organization culture is the structures, behaviors, processes, rites, rituals, myths, symbols, and traditions that distinguish the organization from other organizations. In many respects, culture is the link between plans and action. Well-developed plans clearly specify what actions are necessary. However, unless the organization has a culture that supports taking the specified actions, the plan cannot be successfully implemented. Managers should be sensitive to the organization's culture and to how employees operate within that culture, so that they can design a process that maximizes each employee's contribution to achieving functional objectives and strategic goals.

Senior management also must choose the most appropriate reward system for the organization's mission and strategy. The reward system gives managers a powerful tool to use in influencing the actions of organization members toward accomplishment of strategic goals and functional objectives. The expectation of receiving a desired reward usually motivates employees to higher performance. Managers can modify organizational rewards to reflect what employees value. Managers can use the promise of rewards as an incentive and the awarding of rewards as a reinforcement.

A company that designed a reward system to direct and reward action toward the firm's goals and objectives is Mesa Petroleum. When T. Boone Pickens, the celebrated corporate raider, was chairman of Mesa Petroleum, the strategy was external growth through acquisition. A unit of the company was devoted to searching for potential acquisitions. In this unit, the speed with which information was obtained and decisions were made was critical for taking advantage of the very narrow windows of opportunity that appeared for corporate takeovers. The unit's performance appraisal system was designed to reward analysts for their thorough and timely research and willingness to make risky decisions. In that regard, the system was designed to facilitate movement in the strategic directions set forth for the organization.

Choice of Processes and Techniques for Control and Evaluation Throughout each phase of the strategic management process, management must control and evaluate the activities of the organization. Control processes and techniques provide the means to monitor the firm's progress toward its goals and objectives. Evaluation criteria are the triggers that tell when the limits of the objectives have been reached.

Senior management designs and activates the control processes, techniques, and evaluation criteria used to keep the organization's progress on track. A variety of control techniques are available, including statistical testing, employee surveys, and financial reports. These techniques use several different evaluation criteria such as cost, stress levels, profitability, and satisfaction levels. The manager must design the most effective process and appropriate techniques with relevant criteria to ensure that the firm is on track toward meeting its strategic goals and objectives.

Control mechanisms should include recommendations for corrective action. A report that simply observes that an objective was missed is of little use to a manager. By the time the manager receives the report, it may be too late to take any timely corrective action. Therefore, the control mechanism itself should initiate intermediate corrective action until the manager can analyze the condition in more detail.

One clear example is Pan American World Airways. Pan Am's management was aware that its Panamac reservation system was obsolete and costing sales. Yet the control mechanisms that alerted management to the problem failed to indicate a way to respond. Because other matters were more pressing for the airline, nothing was done. Finally, the problem became a crisis, and Pan Am was forced to negotiate the use of the reservation system owned by American Airlines.[23] Pan Am could have avoided this threat if the company's control mechanism had been designed to initiate action to develop a new reservation system as soon as Pan Am learned the old system was hurting sales.

Choices of control processes, techniques, and evaluation criteria are, perhaps, some of the most important choices that managers must make as part of the strategic management process. Top-level executives specify overall strategic goals and approve budgets that serve as standards by which to judge the firm's performance. Unit managers then must design control processes and techniques that monitor the day-to-day activities of their unit and that prompt corrective action when the managers detect a deviation from objectives. This arrangement allows unit managers to identify and quickly correct small internal deviations, freeing senior management to focus on attempting to adapt to external factors such as changes in the actions of competitors or general business conditions.

Feedforward and Feedback Any dynamic process such as strategic management must include a feedback loop to the preceding stages. Control mechanisms compare actual performance to desired levels specified in strategic goals and objectives. If an unacceptable gap exists between desired and actual performance, corrective action must be taken. Short-term corrective action should be specified as part of the control mechanism. However, long-term remedies require the manager to review the preceding stages of the process to determine the source of the gap and take more permanent corrective action. The feedback indicated in Figure 1.2 directs the manager back to preceding stages. If strategic plans are carefully developed, the gap is more likely caused by an implementation or control issue than by a faulty strategic plan.

Recent writings in strategic management suggest that control and evaluation include more than merely reacting to gaps between the desired and actual levels of performance.[24-27] After all, even if the organization has quick-reacting control mechanisms, the gap already exists and part of the damage is done. These strategic management experts argue that management should continually look forward to try to anticipate future gaps rather than waiting until they happen. This idea, referred to as **feedforward** control, is the active anticipation of strategic and operational gaps, and the timely and effective closing of those gaps. By using a combination of feedforward and feedback control, managers at all levels can provide better direction toward the accomplishment of the organization's strategic goals and objectives.

Flow and Direction of the Strategic Management Process

One frequent misconception regarding the process of strategic management is that it always flows from the top-level decision makers down to lower level managers. Although the determining of the strategic direction for the firm is the responsibility of top management, much information about the internal and external environment comes from department managers, sales staff, and other employees. Once the strategic direction is decided, it is communicated downward, where it starts a series of cycles for objective setting, strategy formulation, implementation, and monitoring, as shown in Figure 1.3. Note that the levels in Figure 1.3 refer to level of responsibility rather than level of strategy development.

The first two cycles involve formulating enterprise-, corporate-, and business-level strategic goals, and forwarding them upward or downward for review and approval. Next, divisions and departments develop budgets based on the approved objectives and again forward them to higher level management for review and approval. In the fourth cycle, department managers report their performance to top management, where performance is compared to objectives to determine if strategy adjustments

Figure 1.3 Strategy Development Cycles

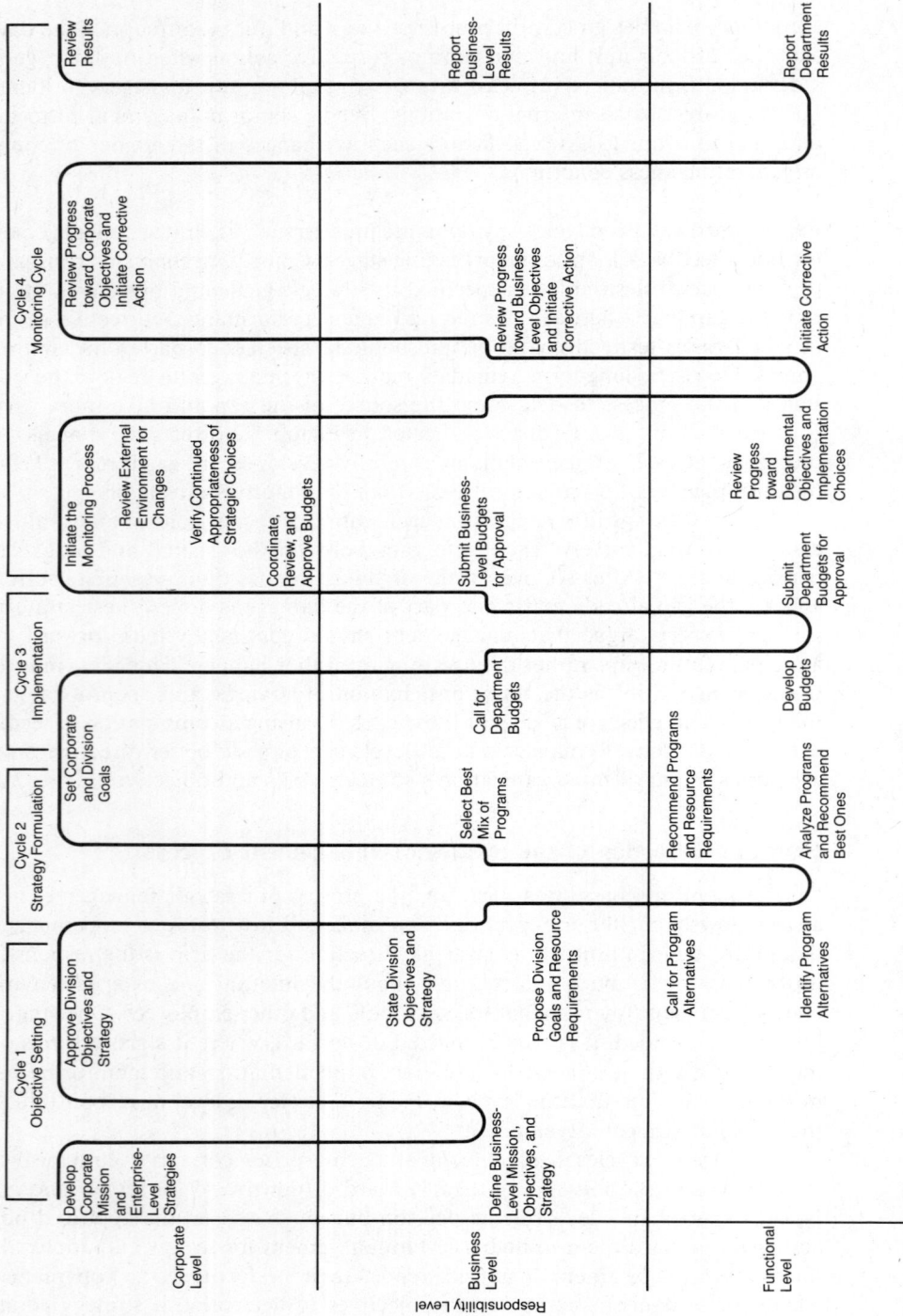

	Cycle 1 Objective Setting	Cycle 2 Strategy Formulation	Cycle 3 Implementation	Cycle 4 Monitoring Cycle
Corporate Level	Develop Corporate Mission and Enterprise-Level Strategies	Approve Division Objectives and Strategy	Set Corporate and Division Goals	Initiate the Monitoring Process / Review External Environment for Changes / Verify Continued Appropriateness of Strategic Choices / Coordinate, Review, and Approve Budgets	Review Progress toward Corporate Objectives and Initiate Corrective Action	Review Results
Business Level	Define Business-Level Mission, Objectives, and Strategy	State Division Objectives and Strategy / Propose Division Goals and Resource Requirements	Select Best Mix of Programs	Call for Department Budgets	Submit Business-Level Budgets for Approval	Review Progress toward Business-Level Objectives and Initiate Corrective Action	Report Business-Level Results
Functional Level		Call for Program Alternatives / Identify Program Alternatives	Recommend Programs and Resource Requirements / Analyze Programs and Recommend Best Ones	Develop Budgets	Submit Department Budgets for Approval	Review Progress toward Departmental Objectives and Implementation Choices	Initiate Corrective Action	Report Department Results

Responsibility Level

Source: Modified and reprinted by permission of *Harvard Business Review*. An exhibit from "Strategic Planning in Diversified Companies" by Richard F. Vancil and Peter Lorange, January–February 1975, pp. 84–85. Copyright © 1975 by the President and Fellows of Harvard College; all rights reserved.

are necessary. This process is consistent with the ideas of many experts, who say that strategy development is highly interactive among top management and operational units (divisions or departments). It also suggests a sequence that will result in more effective strategic management for the organization.

The cycles in Figure 1.3 correspond to the stages in the choice model (Figure 1.2). The development of a mission, enterprise-level strategy, or charter is assumed to be based on an environmental assessment and analysis of internal capabilities. This mission or charter is a formal statement of the domain that the firm's management has selected. Division objectives and strategies are the choices of strategic goals and master strategies. The third cycle involves the flow of plans, objectives, and functional-level strategies required to effectively implement the firm's strategic goals. The last cycle describes the possible flow of review activities undertaken in the control and evaluation stage of the strategic management process.

Influences on Managers' Choices

Because the essence of strategic management is making choices, it is important to understand what influences these choices. Many firms that are in the same industry and are apparently facing identical environmental conditions elect to pursue different strategies. One explanation for these differences is that factors within the organization and unique to the manager may influence the manager's choice of one strategy over others.

The influences on the choices that managers make in the course of strategically managing their organizations fall into five basic categories: environmental, situational, organizational, group, and personal. Environmental factors are the forces in the firm's business arena that cause the manager to select a course of action. These factors are the focus of most discussions of strategy formulation and provide the opportunities and threats that act on the organization. Situational, organizational, group, and individual factors also exert substantial influence on managerial choices but have received much less attention from management writers.

Situational Factors   Situational factors include organization size, shape, and technology. Size usually refers to the level of the firm's sales, value of assets, or number of employees. Managers of larger organizations have the option to choose strategies that require large amounts of extra resources typically unavailable in smaller, leaner organizations. However, smaller firms are usually less constrained by rigid bureaucratic structures or inflexible cultures and can be more responsive to opportunities by pursuing rapid-growth strategies than their larger counterparts. Thus, size can expand or limit the number of strategies available to the organization.

Organization shape is the configuration of the firm's structure at the corporate, business, and functional levels. This is typically represented by the organization chart. The shape of the organization limits the choices of the strategic manager.[28] If the organization has a history of a tall, rigid structure, the strategic manager will likely choose a strategy that fits within that structure. The manager who is accustomed to operating in a very flexible, organic structure is less limited in selecting strategies because he or she knows that the organizational configuration can adjust to the design requirements of the new strategy.

The level of sophistication of the organization's technology influences the strategic manager's choices in two ways. First, the type of technology directly limits the number of alternatives available to the manager. Traditional smokestack industries—for example, steel producers or auto makers—require large capital investments. Strategic managers are frequently reluctant to abandon such a large asset base to pursue a completely different strategy. This limits strategic options to those that fit within the constraints of the current industry. Second, the type of technology inevitably influences the manager's point of reference. That is, a manager trained in a particular industry, with its associated traditions and accepted practices, would probably continue to evaluate choices based on this initial point of reference. The Strategic Application "Sun National Bank" provides a case in point.

Organizational Factors: Culture and Politics Organizational factors that influence managers' choices include the organization's culture and politics. Remember from page 17 that an organization's culture is the structures, behaviors, processes, rites, rituals, myths, symbols, and traditions that distinguish the organization from other organizations. Interest in organization culture grew with the publication of Peters and Waterman's book *In Search of Excellence*.[29]

Peters and Waterman studied several successful firms and determined that they had certain aspects of culture in common. Some readers assumed that all organizations that have or acquire these characteristics will be successful. However, just three years after publication of their book, a report in *Business Week* indicated that 13 of the 25 firms listed as excellent by Peters and Waterman were no longer excellent according to their same criteria.[30] This suggests that no one culture is best.

On one hand, the manager's experience in the firm's existing culture will bias him or her toward choosing a strategy that is compatible with the firm's current culture. On the other hand, it is most important that the culture match the demands of existing business conditions. Furthermore, changing an entire organization's culture is slow and difficult. These opposing forces push the manager to choose the best strategy that is acceptable to the firm's current culture, even though this may not be the best strategy for prevailing business conditions.

Organizational politics are especially likely to affect strategy development if strategic choices are made by a group of top-level senior executives rather than a single CEO. In many organizations, such a group is called the executive committee, strategic planning committee, or planning committee. Its purpose is to draw from the collective experience and knowledge of several senior executives to arrive at a consensus regarding the strategic direction of the firm. When strategy development involves the high stakes of corporate leadership, organizational politics are highly likely to become important.

Robert E. Jones[31] warns of several political games that are played in organizations. These games diminish the advantages of using a group for strategy development because little exchange of ideas takes place. Furthermore, these games can be harmful if they result in political infighting among the members of the senior executive group.

Group Factors Strategic managers seldom act in isolation. More often, their choices and actions result from input and discussions with trusted individuals or their peer group. Members of this group may come from various levels of the organization and have varying degrees of influence on the choices of the manager. James D. Thompson refers to this group as the dominant coalition of organization decision makers.[32] They are the "relevant others" who apply direct and indirect pressure on the executive to conform to the choices that are acceptable to the entire group.

The manager may reject feasible strategies because he or she knows that they are inconsistent with the wishes of the management group. In some instances, the manager's choice may not be his or her preferred strategy but a consensus of the members of the executive group. Other choices may merely be influenced by information from members of the group. Regardless of the degree of influence, the opinions and suggestions of the executive's peer group affect the executive's choices.

Personal Factors Strategic managers are not robots, but thinking and feeling human beings. When senior executives make choices, they typically use a combination of intuition and analysis based on aspects of their personalities. In addition, their diagnosis of a strategic situation is frequently biased by their preferred choices.[33] It is important to understand the personality factors that contribute to intuition and, therefore, influence strategic choices. Three of the most important personality factors that influence managers' choices are their functional perspective, individual characteristics, and previous professional experience. Definitions and examples of these factors are provided in Table 1.2.

Performance and Organization Effectiveness

The central theme of this introduction is that strategic managers make complex choices that influence the success and survival of the firm. Effective strategic management results in improved short- and long-term performance. To relate the strategic manager's choices and actions to the firm's performance, managers need to understand the complex nature of organizational performance and effectiveness. Furthermore, managers need to understand how to measure effectiveness in a way that will provide accurate feedback on how effectively they are strategically managing their firm.

Effectiveness is a measure of the long-term viability of the organization. This definition, which pertains to organizations in all sectors of the economy, is too broad to be used by individual organizations to determine their long-term performance. Therefore, managers have developed more direct ways to measure effectiveness. Table 1.3 provides a list of 15 effectiveness measures, their time perspectives, and the organizational setting in which they would be most appropriate. When selecting the most appropriate measure, managers should consider the time perspective and the type of measure that are appropriate.

Three broad time periods are usually considered: short range (one to three years), intermediate (two to five years), and long range (three to 15 years). Some measures are more suited to assess performance over the long term. For example, the organi-

Table 1.2 Personality Factors Influencing Choices

Factor	Definition	Examples
Functional perspective	The functional background of the managers, such as accounting, engineering, or production/operations	Functional area of the firm in which the manager received his or her formal education (e.g., engineering, accounting)
		Functional area of the firm in which the manager received his or her on-the-job training
Individual characteristics	The personality attributes that managers bring to strategic choice situations	Values: Managers tend to choose the strategies that promote what they personally value (e.g., creativity).
		Geographical perspective: Managers think in either global or local terms.[a]
		Demographics: Sex and ethnic background may influence values and biases.[b]
		Judgment biases: Managers can display biases in their judgment when making choices based on partial data.[c]
		Problem simplification: Because managers have varying abilities to mentally process complex strategic data, they use simplification processes.[d]
		Use of power and authority: All managers have authority but vary in their power to implement strategic choices.[e]
		Degree of assertiveness: Managers vary in the degree to which they are assertive or aggressive.[f]
		Decision-making profile: Managers differ in how they gather and evaluate information for decision making.[g]
		Cognitive beliefs: Managers have varying beliefs about which factors cause which outcomes.[h]
		Motivational orientation: Managers are motivated by different factors.[i]
Professional experience	The experiences of the manager during his or her professional career that have influenced the way he or she evaluates strategic choices and makes decisions.	Initial professional exposure: The first professional job or activity performed by a manager in an organizational setting. This is the period when the new professional is most impressionable and results in lasting opinions of what constitutes good management practice.[j]
		Role models: Superiors or peers of the manager whom he or she admired for their management accomplishments. Attempts to emulate the role model result in lasting management preferences and opinions.

[a]Frank Feather, "Geo-Strategic Thinking . . . and Its Courageous Application to Planning," *Managerial Planning* 33 (November–December 1984): 4–8, 60.

[b]Andre Von der Merwe, "Strategic Leadership and the Chief Executive," *Long Range Planning* 18 (February 1985): 100–111.

[c]James H. Barnes, Jr., "Cognitive Biases and Their Impact on Strategic Planning," *Strategic Management Journal* 5 (April–June 1984): 129–137.

[d]Charles R. Schwenk, "Cognitive Simplification Processes in Strategic Decision Making," *Strategic Management Journal* 5 (April–June 1984): 111–128.

[e]David C. Calabria, "CEO's and the Paradox of Power," *Business Horizons* 25 (January–February 1982): 29–31.

[f]James A. Walters, "Managerial Assertiveness," *Business Horizons* 25 (September–October 1982): 24–29.

[g]John W. Slocum, Jr., and D. Hellriegel, "A Look at How Managers' Minds Work," *Business Horizons* 26 (July–August 1983): 58–68.

[h]Jeffrey D. Ford and W. H. Hegarty, "Decision Makers' Beliefs about the Causes and Effects of Structure: An Exploratory Study," *Academy of Management Journal* 27 (June 1984): 271–291.

[i]H. R. Bobbit, Jr., and J. D. Ford, "Decision-Maker Choice as a Determinant of Organizational Structure," *Academy of Management Review* 5 (January 1980): 13–23.

[j]John R. Montanari, "Managerial Discretion: An Expanded Model of Organization Choice," *Academy of Management Review* 3 (April 1978): 231–241.

Table 1.3 Effectiveness Measures

Criteria	Time Perspective[a]	Type[b]
Adaptability	I	Beh
Productivity	SR	Ops
Satisfaction	SR	Beh
Profitability	SR-I-LR	Fin
Resource Acquisition	SR-I	Ops
Absence of Strain	SR-I	Beh
Control over Environment	I-LR	Fin-Ops
Development	I-LR	Beh
Efficiency	SR-LR	Ops
Employee Reaction	SR-I	Ops
Growth	LR	Fin
Integration	I-LR	Ops-Beh
Open Communication	SR-I	Beh
Survival	LR	Fin-Ops
Financial Operations (e.g., return on investment, gross profit margin, inventory turnover, cash flow)	SR-I-LR	Fin

[a] SR = Short-Range (1–3 years), I = Intermediate (2–5 years), LR = Long-Range (3–15 years)
[b] Fin = Financial Effectiveness Criteria, Ops = Operational Effectiveness Criteria, Beh = Behaviorial Effectiveness Criteria

zation's ability to adapt to a rapidly changing environment is critical to the long-term success of the enterprise, but this criterion is impossible to assess in the short run.

The effectiveness measure may be financial, operational, or behavioral. Financial measures assess the financial performance of the organization or unit. Operational measures assess the effectiveness of work flow and work support. Behavioral effectiveness measures determine individual performance. The type of measure used depends on which aspect of performance the manager wishes to evaluate.

Managers can select effectiveness measures using this straightforward method:

1. Determine the type and time perspective that is most appropriate to determine the organization's and/or unit's performance.

2. Review the list of criteria available (see Table 1.3), and select the most appropriate criteria.

In today's dynamic business environment, firms must be effective to survive. Thus strategic managers must be able to assess the effectiveness of their organization over the correct time period, using the proper measure. Strategic managers cannot hope to correctly determine the effectiveness of a selected strategy unless they use an accurate measure of the performance attributed to that strategy. Therefore, the selection of the appropriate measure of effectiveness is an important managerial choice in the strategic management process.

Summary

Unlike strategic planning, strategic management recognizes the need for extensive strategy implementation and control to effectively manage organizations under dynamic business conditions. The strategic management perspective, like strategic planning, is based on the open-systems view of the organization. It has evolved in response to the changing needs of the organization in a more uncertain environment.

Strategy development takes place on four levels. First, enterprise-level strategies focus on the firm's transactions with its sociocultural environment. Corporate-level strategies are concerned with the mix of the firm's various businesses to create a portfolio to achieve corporate strategic goals. Business-level strategies integrate the efforts of several components of a single business to take advantage of the opportunities present in the business environment. Finally, functional-level strategies assure that each functional unit manages its environment in a manner that will contribute to the accomplishment of strategic goals and objectives. The strategies that are appropriate for each level vary depending on the type of organization.

The strategic management process involves a series of choices. First, the manager assesses current business conditions to determine opportunities and threats and analyzes the firm's internal strategic capabilities. Then senior managers determine the gaps between opportunities and capabilities and select the domain that offers the most opportunities with the fewest threats. Then these managers choose the firm's mission, strategic goals, and strategy. At this stage, the managers are in a position to develop a mission and specific strategic goals. These goals guide the choice of a strategy to specify how the firm intends to accomplish its goals and objectives.

The strategic management process continues with the choices necessary to implement the strategies developed. Managers choose plans and functional-level strategies necessary to transform the strategic plan into action. Depending on the nature of the strategic and implementation plans, a new or modified organization structure may be necessary. Leadership and culture processes and reward systems also must contribute to the successful implementation of plans. Last, control processes, techniques, and evaluation criteria must be set in place to anticipate and track the progress of actual organization performance toward the goals and objectives. If the actual results fail to meet the levels specified in the strategic goals and objectives, feedback from this last stage triggers corrective action at preceding stages. If changes in conditions could hinder the accomplishment of strategic goals and objectives, feedforward triggers the required changes in plans, implementation strategies, or evaluation criteria.

The fundamental goal of the strategic management process is improved performance. The choice model presented in this chapter shows the type and location of critical choices that the manager must make to ensure effective organizational performance.

Notes

1. Daniel Gray, "Uses and Misuses of Strategic Planning," *Harvard Business Review* 64 (January–February 1986): 89–97.

2. H. Mintzberg, *The Nature of Managerial Work* (New York: Harper and Row, 1973): 92–93.

3. John A. Byrne, Ronald Grover, and Todd Vogel, "Is the Boss Getting Paid Too Much," *Business Week*, May 1, 1989, 46–93.

4. John A. Pearce II, D. K. Robbins, and R. B. Robinson, Jr., "The Impact of Grand Strategy and Planning Formality on Financial Performance," *Strategic Management Journal* 8 (March–April 1987): 125–134.

5. "Business Fads: What's In—and Out," *Business Week*, January 20, 1986, 52–61.

6. Gray, "Uses and Misuses of Strategic Planning," 88–89.

7. F. E. Emery and E. I. Trist, "The Causal Texture of Organizational Environments," *Human Relations* 18 (Feb. 1965): 21–32.

8. Alex R. Oliver and J. R. Garber, "Implementing Strategic Planning: Ten Sure-Fire Ways to Do It Wrong," *Business Horizons* (March–April 1983): 49–51.

9. Christopher Oyeen, "Long Range Planning in Large Corporations: A Cross-National Survey," *Managerial Planning* 33 (November–December 1984) 18–23.

10. Ibid.

11. D. E. Schendel and C. Hofer, eds., *Strategic Management: A New View of Business Policy and Planning* (Boston: Little Brown and Co., 1979): 11–13.

12. H. Igor Ansoff, *Corporate Strategy: An Analytic Approach to Business Policy* (New York: McGraw-Hill, 1965), 37–38.

13. Jane E. Dutton and R. B. Duncan, "The Influence of the Strategic Planning Process on Strategic Change," *Strategic Management Journal* 8 (March–April 1978): 103–116.

14. "Sony's Challenge," *Business Week*, June 1, 1987, 64–69.

15. W. R. Dill, "Environment as an Influence on Managerial Autonomy," *Administrative Science Quarterly* 2 (March, 1958): 409–442.

16. James D. Thompson, *Organization in Action* (New York: McGraw-Hill, 1967), 25–27.

17. Jim Hurlock, "Why William Dillard Loves a Lost Cause," *Business Week*, May 5, 1986, 100.

18. Pete Engardio, "How Last Year's No. 11 Tumbled Off the List," *Business Week*, May 26, 1986, 102.

19. R. Edward Freeman, *Strategic Management: A Stockholders Approach* (Boston: Pitman, 1984).

20. Christopher S. Eklund, "How Black & Decker Got Back in the Black," *Business Week*, July 13, 1987, 86–90.

21. Anthony Blanko, "Generous Electric: We Bring Good Things to Kidder Peabody," *Business Week*, May 12, 1986, 27–28.

22. Alex Beam, "Gillette: Not Quite So Sharp," *Business Week*, May 12, 1986, 92 and 94.

23. Chuck Hawkins, "Does Pan Am Have a Ticket Out of the Industry Slide?" *Business Week*, May 5, 1986, 32.

24. Georg Schreyogg and H. Steinmann, "Strategic Control: A New Perspective," *Academy of Management Review* 12 (January 1987): 91–103.

25. J. Camillus and R. Velizath, "Organization Control: A Conceptual Typology." Paper presented at the Academy of Management annual meeting, Boston, August 1984.

26. J. K. Gardner, "A Systems Approach to Bank Prudential Management and Supervision: The Utilization of Feedforward Control," *Journal of Management Studies* 22 (January 1985): 1–24.

27. P. Lorange, "Strategic Control: Some Issues in Making It Operationally More Useful," in *Competitive Strategic Management*, ed. R. B. Lamb (Englewood Cliffs, N.J.: Prentice-Hall, 1984), 247–271.

28. D. J. Hall and M. A. Saias, "Strategy Follows Structure!" *Strategic Management Journal* 1, (April/June 1980): 149–163.

29. Thomas J. Peters and R. H. Waterman, *In Search of Excellence: Lessons from America's Best-Run Companies* (New York: Harper & Row, 1982), x.

30. "Who's Excellent," *Business Week*, November 5, 1984, 76–79.

31. Robert E. Jones, "Internal Politics and the Strategic Business Plan," *Journal of Small Business Management* 23 (January 1985): 31–37.

32. Thompson, *Organization in Action*, 125–127.

33. Daniel J. Isenberg, "How Senior Managers Think," *Harvard Business Review*, 62 (November–December 1984): 81–90.

Appendix A

Strategic Case Analysis

Both the format and the focus of the case analysis presented here stress strategic-level analysis. The approach is applicable to historical cases such as those in this text as well as real-world strategic situations. The format is not the only one acceptable for student case analyses; in fact, most instructors have a preferred case analysis format.

For this presentation, we have selected the short case on Holiday Inns Inc. reproduced at the end of the appendix. Any case provides only limited information, and some interpretation and interpolation are required. However, here we have attempted to limit our analyses to the facts of the case. This limits, to some degree, the richness of the analysis. Before proceeding with the analysis, please turn to page 33 and read the Holiday Inns case.

Introduction

Set the stage by describing relevant characteristics of the case; for example, industry, main thrust of the case, products(s), your assumptions, and so on.

- Describe the firm's position on the product or firm life cycle.
- Describe the strategy level the case is focused on.
- Discuss the firm's competitive portfolio (business or product-markets).

Case Analysis Holiday Inns Inc. (HI) is the world's largest hospitality company. Its primary thrust is lodging with interests in hotels, casino gaming, and restaurants. The case is written on HI as it existed in 1984. It focuses on HI's attempts to segment the lodging market into upscale business traveler hotels, budget hotels, standard Holiday Inn hotels, and gaming hotels.

The lodging industry appears to be in the mature stage of its life cycle. HI's attempts to segment the market are aimed at increasing the company's market share. Because the case concentrates on the lodging part of HI's business and mentions little of the gaming operation, the case is focused on the business level of strategy development.

Although it is difficult to determine from the case, Crowne Plaza, Embassy Suite, and Hampton Inn hotels appear to be question marks using the BCG portfolio analysis. Gaming seems to be the star of HI's current businesses. Exhibit A.1 on p. 34 shows that gaming is the only business to realize an increase in revenues in 1982. The traditional Holiday Inn hotels are probably cash cows.

Environmental Assessment and Capabilities Analysis

Conduct a SWOT (strengths, weaknesses, opportunities, threats) analysis. Strengths are the positive internal capabilities of the organization that give it a strategic advantage in achieving its objectives. Weaknesses are the internal liabilities or limitations that the organization currently possesses that prevent it from effectively achieving its objectives. Opportunities are usually external factors that an organization can exploit to give it a strategic competitive advantage. Threats are external factors that have the potential of adversely affecting the organization's effectiveness and/or survival. The SWOT analysis helps locate problems associated with exploiting opportunities, protecting against threats, building on strengths, and correcting weaknesses.

Case Analysis A SWOT analysis for Holiday Inns might consist of the following:

Internal Strengths: market leadership, broad product line, industry's largest reservation system, strong financial position, excellent reputation and name recognition, and properties in the prime gaming locations.

Internal Weaknesses: low operating margins due to competitive pricing strategy, expensive remodeling and construction campaign underway, decreasing operating income in all business segments except gaming, and concentration in hospitality industry.

External Opportunities: Greater segmentation in the lodging industry, increase in business travel, growth in gaming market, and foreign markets.

External Threats: clouded economic picture, mature product-market, increased competition in all market segments, massive federal budget deficits, and possibility of a collapse of hospitality market due to world recession caused by business downturn.

Strategic Problem Definition

Clearly state your view of what the primary strategic problem is and label it as such. Next, briefly discuss the causes and effects of the strategic problem as stated in the case.

Case Analysis An interpretation of the strategic problem might be: "How can HI reduce its vulnerability to a decline in the hospitality market?" This vulnerability was caused by the reversal of HI's previous diversification strategy, which culminated with the divestment of Delta Steamships. Strategic management's strategic choice to concentrate in the hospitality business created a situation in which the effect of an economic downturn that curtails business travel will be a rapid decline in HI's profits.

Generation of Strategic Alternatives

List at least three alternative solutions to the problem you have stated. We assume that you have reviewed many alternatives and the three that you present are the three best.

Case Analysis Three possible alternatives that would reduce HI's vulnerability to a downturn in the hospitality business are the following:

▪ Return to a diversification master strategy involving acquisition of new but related product lines for new and existing customers that would be countercyclical to the hospitality business.

▪ Develop a cost leadership strategy that reduces HI costs to the point that a decline in occupancy to recession levels will continue to generate profits.

▪ Develop a conglomerate diversification master strategy that provides a mix of businesses that will generate a profit even in the event of a hospitality market collapse.

Evaluation of Alternatives

Include the following three subsections in this section:

▪ Evaluation criteria: You should use the same criteria to evaluate each alternative (you want to compare apples to apples).

▪ Evaluation method: You may use a quantitative technique (e.g., payoff matrix) if you wish. However, a well-developed pros versus cons analysis can also be used. Remember to use the same criteria to determine whether each alternative is a pro or a con.

▪ Presentation and discussion of results: Here you should present a table that summarizes the results of your alternative analysis. For example, you might use a pros versus cons analysis for which the table would consist of the alternatives on the horizontal axis and the criteria on the vertical axis. The cells would contain the word *pro* or *con*. Next, develop a method to compile these data and discuss the rationale for the results.

Case Analysis The criteria that one would use to evaluate the alternatives depend, to a large extent, on the information in the case. For our illustration here, we will use these criteria:

▪ Efficacy: Does the alternative solve the strategic problem over the long term?

▪ Cost: Does HI have the financial resources to implement this alternative?

▪ Acceptability: Is this alternative acceptable to HI management or will it be resisted if chosen?

▪ Efficiency: How should HI's stated criteria be weighted?

▪ Consequences: What are the chances that negative consequences will evolve from the choice and implementation of this alternative?

Analyses Method One way to evaluate alternatives is to use a payoff matrix. This would be set up as shown in Matrix A.1. The numerical evaluation indicates that the second alternative is the strategy that will be most appropriate to recommend to HI for the situation described in the case. The presentation of the table with a complete explanation of the scale used and how the scores were determined will give a clear illustration of the evaluation procedure used.

Recommendations

Present your recommendations to solve the strategic problem and discuss how they will address/alleviate the effects of the strategic problem. The discussion should include the impact of your recommendations on the firm's actions, structure, process, and performance.

Case Analysis Here we would recommend that HI management adopt a cost leadership strategy that reduces costs to a point that will maintain profitability during a downturn in the hospitality market. This strategy has only a moderate ability to solve the problem (3 on a scale of 5) because it depends on an accurate prediction of the bottom of the market slide. If the hospitality business falls below projections, HI has no contingency to draw upon. However, this alternative is well within HI's financial capabilities and will be readily embraced by management. Finally, it is associated

Matrix A.1   Payoff Matrix

| | Criteria | | | |
Alternative	Efficacy (3)	Cost (1)	Acceptability (2)	Calculation
Horizontal or Concentric Diversification Master Strategy (0.6)	5	4	3	$(3 \times 5) + (1 \times 4) + (2 \times 3) = 25$ $(25 \times 0.6) = 15$
Cost Leadership Strategy (0.8)	3	5	5	$(3 \times 3) + (1 \times 5) + (2 \times 5) = 24$ $(24 \times 0.8) = 19.2$
Conglomerate Diversification Master Strategy (0.3)	5	4	2	$(3 \times 5) + (1 \times 4) + (2 \times 2) = 23$ $(23 \times 0.3) = 6.9$

Efficacy, cost, and acceptability are evaluated on a numerical scale: 1 = "no" answer to the question asked in the criterion; 2 = "probable no" answer to the question asked in the criterion; 3 = neither "no" nor "yes" to the question asked in the criterion; 4 = "probable yes" to the question asked in the criterion; 5 = "yes" answer to the question asked in the criterion.
Efficiency is indicated by the numerical weight in parentheses (3–1) under the criterion. These weights were determined by subjective analysis of the case.
Consequences are indicated by the probabilities shown in parentheses under each alternative. They are determined by calculating $(1 - p)$, where p is the subjective probability that negative consequences will be associated with the alternative.

with only a slight probability of negative consequences from employees or the marketplace.

The discussion of the impact of the recommendations on the firm's actions, structure, process, and performance is an opportunity for the case analyst to integrate material from previous business courses and apply that knowledge to this aspect of the analysis. It should be thoughtful speculation regarding the impact of a recommendation on the critical dimensions of the organization's operations and performance.

Suggestions for Implementation

Present ways in which the recommendations can be implemented in the organization. For example, what should key managers do now, six months from now, and so on? How can the chief executive know the plan is working?

This is a general outline of how the organization might go about implementing the recommendations. This section encourages the case analyst to deal with the practical realities of introducing change into an organization. For example, cost leadership strategy, if implemented by HI, might precipitate some employee layoffs and changes in cost reporting procedures. These changes can be difficult for managers to implement.

Holiday Inns Inc. (1984)*

Holiday Inns Inc. (HI), headquartered in Memphis, Tennessee, is the world's largest hospitality company, with interests in hotels, casino gaming, and restaurants, having sold its Delta Steamships subsidiary in 1982. For the first half of 1983, 64.6 percent of operating income came from hotels, 32.9 percent from gaming, and 1 percent from restaurants. First-half net income and sales were at respective annual rates of $123 million and $1.5 billion. More detailed financial information is provided in Exhibits A.1 and A.2.

The Holiday Inn hotel system includes 1,744 hotels with 312,302 rooms in 53 countries on five continents and produces an estimated $4 billion in annual revenues. Licensed, or franchised, hotels account for 86 percent of total Holiday Inn hotels, 81 percent of total rooms, and 6 percent of HI sales. Franchisees pay $300 a room initially plus a royalty of 4 percent of gross room revenues and a fee for marketing and reservation services of 2 percent of gross room revenues. The company's reservation system is the largest in the hotel industry.

In 1982, less than 3 percent of Holiday Inn customers dropped in without room reservations, down from 95 percent in the 1950s. In 1981, the company started to deemphasize highway locations. Virtually all new Holiday Inn hotels are placed near airports, industrial parks, and similar sites.

*(This case was prepared by Arthur Sharplin, McNeese State University, Lake Charles, LA. Connie Shum provided research assistance. Reprinted with permission. The case protrays neither the effective nor the ineffective handling of an administrative situation. Rather, it is to be used as the basis for classroom discussion.)

Exhibit A.1 Holiday Inns Inc. and Consolidated Subsidiaries Statements of Income
(in thousands, except per share)

	Three Quarters Ended		Fiscal Year Ended	
	September 30, 1983	October 1, 1982	December 31, 1982	January 1, 1982 (Restated)
Revenues				
Hotel	$ 667,644	$ 651,740	$ 840,698	$ 853,645
Gaming	449,239	360,608	472,792	388,148
Restaurant	71,016	70,865	100,584	96,366
Other	4,183	7,624	11,224	13,616
Total revenues	1,192,082	1,090,837	1,425,298	1,351,775
Operating income				
Hotel	143,552	132,280	150,205	170,944
Gaming	98,576	63,647	74,595	56,291
Restaurant	3,486	2,714	5,029	6,547
Other	2,741	3,424	4,999	10,826
Total operating income	248,355	202,065	234,828	244,608
Corporate expense	(22,058)	(17,860)	(24,487)	(25,736)
Interest, net of interest capitalized	(31,725)	(38,738)	(50,965)	(65,540)
Foreign currency translation gain (loss)	—	—	—	1,889
Income from continuing operations before income taxes	194,572	145,467	159,376	155,221
Provision for income taxes	85,612	58,187	62,157	56,515
Income from continuing operations	108,960	87,280	97,219	98,706
Discontinued operations				
Income from operations, net of income taxes	—	(22,100)	4,671	38,652
Loss on disposition, plus income taxes Payable of $5,505	—	—	(25,910)	—
Net income	$ 108,960	$ 65,180	$ 75,980	$ 137,358
Income (loss) per common and common equivalent share				
Continuing operations	$ 2.86	$ 2.23	$ 2.50	$ 2.68
Discontinued operations	—	(.58)	(.56)	.98
Total income (loss)	$ 2.86	$ 1.65	$ 1.94	$ 3.66
Average common and common equivalent shares outstanding	38,055	38,305	38,216	39,449

Exhibit A.2 Holiday Inns Inc. and Consolidated Subsidiaries Balance Sheets
(in thousands, except share amounts)

	December 31, 1982	January 1, 1982 (Restated)
Assets		
Current assets		
Cash	$ 49,945	$ 39,655
Temporary cash investments, at cost	32,544	20,181
Receivables, including notes receivable of $12,618 and $31,927, less allowance for doubtful accounts of $18,925 and $15,080	73,008	91,782
Supplies, at lower of average cost or market	21,871	23,424
Deferred income tax benefits	13,510	11,190
Prepayments and other current assets	18,101	9,775
Total current assets	208,979	196,007
Investments in unconsolidated affiliates, at equity	108,480	46,535
Notes receivable due after one year and other investments	44,186	49,214
Property and equipment, at cost		
Land, buildings, improvements, and equipment	1,635,310	1,496,491
Accumulated depreciation and amortization	(367,434)	(313,947)
Subtotal	1,267,876	1,182,544
Excess of cost over net assets of business acquired, amortized evenly over 40 years	54,314	55,787
Deferred charges and other assets	24,172	31,275
Net assets of discontinued operations	—	111,297
Total assets	1,708,007	1,672,659
Liabilities and shareholders' equity		
Current liabilities		
Accounts payable	77,867	66,375
Long-term debt due within one year	31,267	30,478
Accrued expenses	123,283	133,256
Total current liabilities	232,417	230,109
Long-term debt due after one year	436,356	581,465
Deferred credits and other long-term liabilities	33,938	34,851
Deferred income taxes	62,334	53,857
Shareholders' equity		
Capital stock		
Special stock, authorized—5,000,000 shares; series A—$1.125 par value; issued—491,541 and 576,410 shares; convertible into 1.5 shares of common stock	553	648
Common stock, $1.50 par value; authorized—60,000,000 shares; issued—40,218,350 and 32,909,606 shares	60,327	49,364
Capital surplus	294,517	161,188
Retained earnings	671,609	626,310
Cumulative foreign currency transaction adjustments	(3,804)	—
Capital stock in treasury, at cost; 3,036,081 and 2,439,500 common shares and 72,192 series A shares	(78,660)	(63,170)
Restricted stock	(1,580)	(1,963)
Total shareholders' equity	942,962	772,377
Total liabilities and shareholders' equity	$1,708,007	$1,672,659

Business travelers account for about 60 percent of Holiday Inn room nights occupied. The company is launching two new hotel chains aimed at the upscale business traveler. The first, Crowne Plaza hotels, offers fine dining, complimentary morning newspapers, continental breakfasts, 24-hour maid service, bellmen, and free HBO movies. Rates are $15 to $20 higher than the average rate of $44 at existing company-owned Holiday Inns. Crowne Plaza hotels are now located in Rockville (Maryland), San Francisco, Miami, and Dallas. Four more will open in Stanford (Connecticut), Houston, and New Orleans by year-end. The second new chain, Embassy Suite hotels, is targeted primarily at the business traveler near the upper end of the lodging market who stays three or four days instead of the usual two, and will pay for specialized service. Each suite will offer a separate living room with a wet bar and the option of one or two bedrooms. The company plans to have six all-suite hotels in varying stages of development in 1984.

In December 1983, the company announced plans to develop a new budget hotel chain, called Hampton Inn hotels, to include 300 company-owned and franchised units within five years. The first will open in Memphis, Tennessee, in 1984. Room rates at these hotels will average about $30. They will feature rooms for smokers and nonsmokers, free television and movies, local telephone calls, continental breakfasts, and arrangements for children under 18 to stay free with their parents.

The Holiday Inn hotel group spent $60.1 million in 1982 to upgrade and renovate company-owned hotels. Old franchises were eliminated at the rate of about one a week, as minimum operating standards were raised. So drastic was the pruning that, even with 569 new hotels in the past eight years, there has been a net gain of only 45 in the number of Holiday Inns. At the end of 1982, there were 48 Holiday Inn hotels under construction worldwide. The Holiday Inn sign is being replaced with a new rectangular one bearing the chain's name topped with an orange and yellow starburst on a green background.

In March 1983, Roy E. Winegardner, chairman, and Michael D. Rose, president and chief executive officer, briefed stockholders on Holiday Inn's preparations for the future. Some excerpts from their comments follow:

"With the disposition of our steamship subsidiary, Holiday Inns Inc. is now strategically focused on the hospitality industry. We also introduced a new sign and logo for our Holiday Inn hotel system, better reflecting the range of property types and level of product quality that will characterize the Holiday Inn hotel system in the decades ahead. Recognizing the increasing segmentation of the lodging market, we also began construction on two new hotel products. We also embarked on an aggressive expansion plan for our core Holiday Inn hotel brand. This represents the most aggressive company hotel development effort in recent years, and reflects our continuing belief in the long-term strength of the lodging market and of our Holiday Inn brand within the large moderate-priced segment of that market.

"Our company has prospered with the growth of Atlantic City, as our Harrah's Marina facility there has proven to be the most profitable hotel/casino in that market on a pretax, preinterest basis. We entered into a joint venture to build a new 600-room hotel and 60,000-square-foot casino on the Boardwalk. We believe this should contribute to Harrah's ability to achieve the same brand leadership position in Atlantic City that it now enjoys in Northern Nevada.

"As a result of [a competitive] pricing strategy, operating margins suffered in our hotel business. However, this approach enabled us to maintain occupancy levels despite the fact that occupancies declined throughout the rest of the hotel industry. At Perkins Restaurants Inc., our restaurant subsidiary, this pricing strategy paid off, contributing to substantially higher customer count and improved unit profitability. We also made the decision to dispose of a number of restaurants and hotels which were not performing to our financial standards.

"In addition to strengthening our market position, we also strengthened our balance sheet. The company's 9⅝-percent convertible subordinated debentures were called for redemption on March 2, 1982. The result was conversion to $143 million of additional equity, which provides the basis for significant new debt capacity to fund our future expansion. Consistent with our stated intention to reduce floating rate debt, we issued $75 million in fixed-rate, 10-year notes in August. In 1982 we commissioned an update of an independent study of the appreciated value of the company's tangible assets and certain contract rights. This study indicated that the net market value of these assets approximated $2.5 billion. [This] appraisal reflects the value of the company's franchise and management contract income streams as well as the appreciation of our real estate assets. [We have] also made substantial progress in improving the productivity of our most important resource, our people. We undertook a thorough review of staffing levels and programs to assure that we were bringing sufficient resources to bear on those things that matter the most, and not expending time or money on those efforts that yield more limited returns. As a result, we have eliminated significant overhead costs and focused our attention more clearly on those things that are most critical to our success in the future. We deliberately increased our expenditures on training and development. We believe that in our businesses, people represent the greatest opportunity for competitive advantage.

"As we look ahead, the economic picture remains clouded. We cannot accurately predict the impact of the unprecedented massive federal budget deficits on our economy. We remain confident in our ability to manage our businesses effectively under both good and difficult economic conditions."

Appendix B

Financial Statement Analysis

The Purpose of Financial Analysis

The primary purpose of financial analysis is to help in evaluating management performance by appraising financial condition, efficiency, profitability, and risk. Each analyst may have a different point of view in conducting the appraisal. For example, possible creditors may be concerned with the company's liquidity or ability to cover interest payments as they try to decide whether to extend credit to the firm. Investors want to know whether the firm represents a good investment. The executive wants to know how the firm looks to outsiders like banks, investors, and bondholders, but also needs to know how well it is doing compared to competitors and to past performance. Most of these analysts are concerned with projecting how well the firm will perform in the future, and for this purpose they use financial statement analysis.

The financial statements most frequently used to provide information for analysis are the balance sheet, the income statement, and the sources and uses of funds statement. They indicate the state of the firm at a particular time, such as the end of the year or quarter (balance sheet), or for a particular period of time, such as one quarter or one year (income statement and uses and sources of funds statement). The balance sheet indicates the assets controlled by the company and how the company financed their acquisition. A balance sheet for the Cascade Corporation is shown in Exhibit B.1. The income statement indicates sales generated, the expenses incurred in generating the sales, and the earnings obtained from the sales over a period of time. Exhibit B.2 is an income statement for Cascade Corporation. These two statements will be the primary sources of information used in the analysis performed later in the appendix. The sources and uses of funds statement employs information from both the balance sheet and the income statement to provide a summary of where funds were obtained and where the company used its funds. Exhibit B.3 is the source and use of funds statement for Cascade Corporation.

The data on which financial statement analysis is performed is historical. The basic assumption is that past performance is a reliable predictor of how management will perform in the future. The assumption may be reasonably sound for well-entrenched firms with good management teams in fairly stable environments. In other cases, the assumption could easily mislead an analyst. In a rapidly changing industry past performance may not be a good predictor of the future. For example, Microsoft, a software company, produces MS-DOS, the operating system used in many personal computers. This operating system accounts for over 50 percent of Microsoft's revenues. The company has been highly dependent on its relationship with IBM and is now developing an OS/2 operating system for IBM's new personal computers. If Microsoft

Exhibit B.1   Balance Sheet for Cascade Corporation, 1983–1987 (in $000)

	1987	1986	1985	1984	1983
Assets					
Cash	$ 776	$ 205	$ 8,394	$ 7,733	$ 2,438
Marketable Securities	10,100	8,600	NA	NA	NA
Receivables	16,945	13,784	12,411	11,096	893
Inventories	20,246	19,452	16,890	17,110	19,497
Raw Materials	3,421	3,512	3,122	2,045	3,742
Work in Progress	3,578	3,968	3,452	3,497	3,255
Finished Goods	13,247	11,972	10,316	10,568	12,500
Notes Receivable	NA	NA	NA	NA	NA
Other Current Assets	726	522	571	464	356
Total Current Assets	48,793	42,563	38,266	36,403	32,984
Property, Plant, and Equipment	29,465	49,897	42,439	22,211	24,829
Accumulated Depreciation	NA	23,250	20,426	NA	NA
Net Property and Equipment	29,465	26,647	22,013	22,211	24,829
Investment and Advances to Subsidiaries	NA	NA	NA	NA	NA
Other Non-Current Assets	NA	NA	NA	NA	NA
Deferred Charges	NA	NA	NA	NA	NA
Intangibles	NA	NA	NA	NA	NA
Deposits and Other Assets	350	614	400	565	404
Total Assets	$78,608	$69,824	$60,679	$59,179	$58,217
Liabilities					
Notes Payable	$ 5,249	$ 3,123	$ 2,269	$ 2,931	$ 4,101
Accounts Payable	6,305	6,645	5,050	4,773	2,685
Current Long-Term Debt	1,154	2,602	1,891	3,298	1,331
Current Portion Capital Leases	NA	NA	NA	NA	NA
Accrued Expenses	5,725	5,205	5,184	4,977	2,736
Income Taxes	1,183	946	1,262	908	769
Other Current Liabilities	NA	NA	NA	NA	NA
Total Current Liabilities	19,616	18,521	15,656	16,887	13,016
Mortgages	NA	NA	NA	NA	NA
Deferred Charges/Income	4,169	3,599	2,613	2,553	2,273
Convertible Debt	NA	NA	NA	NA	NA
Long-Term Debt	7,501	6,587	7,333	7,138	10,388
Non-Current Capital Leases	NA	NA	NA	NA	NA
Other Long-Term Liabilities	NA	NA	NA	NA	NA
Total Liabilities	31,286	28,707	25,602	26,578	25,677
Minority Interest (Liabilities)	NA	NA	NA	NA	NA
Preferred Stock	NA	NA	NA	NA	NA
Common Stock Net	1,549	387	387	387	387
Capital Surplus	2,045	2,045	2,045	2,045	2,045
Retained Earnings	46,454	43,772	39,575	35,734	34,506
Treasury Stock	686	686	686	1,220	1,220
Other Liabilities	−2,040	−4,401	−6,244	−4,345	−3,178
Shareholder Equity	47,322	41,117	35,077	32,601	32,540
Total Liabilities and Net Worth	$78,608	$69,824	$60,679	$59,179	$58,217

Source: Cascade Corporation 10K reports, 1983–1987.

Exhibit B.2 Income Statement for Cascade Corporation, 1983–1987 (in $000)

	1987	1986	1985	1984	1983
Net Sales	$98,682	$86,664	$84,090	$67,708	$63,045
Cost of Goods	63,840	56,222	55,003	45,391	44,330
Gross Profit	34,842	30,442	29,087	22,317	18,715
R&D Expenditures	NA	NA	NA	NA	NA
Selling, General, and Administrative Expense	19,748	16,738	15,609	13,980	14,914
Income before Depreciation and Amortization	15,094	13,704	13,478	8,337	3,801
Depreciation and Amortization	4,619	3,854	3,701	4,006	4,037
Nonoperating Income	−253	−164	−347	−160	−396
Interest Expense	482	353	263	812	1,168
Income before Taxes	9,740	9,323	9,167	3,359	−1,800
Provision for Income Tax	4,095	3,700	3,900	1,455	−1,620
Minority Interest (Income)	NA	NA	NA	NA	NA
Investment Gains/Losses	NA	NA	NA	NA	NA
Other Income	NA	NA	NA	NA	NA
Net Income before Expense Items	5,645	5,623	5,267	1,904	−180
Expense Items and Discount Operations	NA	NA	NA	NA	NA
Net Income	$ 5,645	$ 5,623	$ 5,267	$ 1,904	$ −180
Outstanding Shares[a] (000)	3,002	751	751	774	713
Earnings per Share	1.88	7.49	7.01	2.46	−.25

[a]Three-share dividend declared May 1986.
Source: Cascade Corporation 10K reports, 1983–1987.

failed to land the contract for the new OS/2 operating system or if the system did not perform well, the company's future performance would decline rapidly.

The projection of future performance from historical financial statements can be a valuable tool in evaluating a firm's situation. It can point out potential problems for the firm and suggest additional analysis to be performed. The analyst with good judgment who corroborates the data with additional information can learn much about the firm, gaining clues as to how it is managed and how performance can be improved. A mechanical analysis will not provide this insight. Data must be analyzed in the context of the company's situation, the nature of the industry, and the economic conditions the company faces. Several ratios may be needed to understand the results of one. For example, return on investment can be arrived at as follows:

$$ROI = Turnover \times Operating\ Profit\ as\ a\ Percent\ of\ Sales$$

By probing deeper we can see:

$$Turnover = \frac{Sales}{Total\ Investment}$$

Exhibit B.3 Sources and Uses of Funds for Cascade
Corporation, 1985–1987 (in $000)

	1987	1986	1985
Annual Sources			
Income/Loss before Expense Items	$ 5,645	$ 5,623	$ 5,267
Depreciation and Depletion	4,619	3,864	3,701
Deferred Income Taxes	506	848	199
Minority Interest—Subsidiaries	NA	NA	NA
Other Funds from Operations	NA	NA	NA
Total Funds—Operations	10,770	10,335	9,167
Funds Used for Extraordinary Item	NA	NA	NA
Sale of Property, Plant, and Equipment	NA	NA	NA
Issue Long-Term Debt	107	NA	1,049
Sale of Stock	NA	NA	NA
Other Sources of Funds	922	900	165
Total Sources of Funds	$11,969	$11,235	$10,381
Annual Uses			
Dividends	$ 1,801	$ 1,426	$ 1,426
Capital Expenditures	5,197	6,521	4,435
Increase in Investment	NA	NA	NA
Decrease Long-Term Debt	NA	1,642	622
Purchase of Stock	NA	214	NA
Acquisitions	NA	NA	NA
Other Uses of Funds	264	NA	804
Total Uses of Funds	$ 6,734	$ 9,803	$ 7,287
Increase/Decrease in Working Capital	$ 5,135	$ 1,432	$ 3,094

Source: Cascade Corporation 10K reports, 1985–1987.

and

$$\text{Operating Profit as a Percent of Sales} = \frac{\text{Operating Profit}}{\text{Sales}}$$

Breaking out the components of ROI allows us to understand which components contributed to the ratio and trace the causes of good or poor performance. Each of these components can also be broken down until we can see which component is responsible for changes in the ratio.

As another example, return on equity is an important measure of the rate of return on common stockholders' investment. Normally it can be arrived at, provided there is no preferred stock, using this formula:

$$\text{ROE} = \frac{\text{Net Income}}{\text{Equity}}$$

It can also be seen as deriving from three other ratios:

$$\text{Total Asset Turnover} = \frac{\text{Sales}}{\text{Total Assets}}$$

$$\text{Financial Leverage} = \frac{\text{Total Assets}}{\text{Equity}}$$

$$\text{Net Profit Margin} = \frac{\text{Income}}{\text{Sales}}$$

Now the same ROE can be found as follows:

$$\text{ROE} = \frac{\text{Sales}}{\text{Total Assets}} \times \frac{\text{Total Assets}}{\text{Equity}} \times \frac{\text{Income}}{\text{Sales}}$$

The first formula suggests that, to increase ROE, management must increase net income and/or decrease equity. The second formula suggests that management could improve ROE through increasing asset turnover, by using its assets more efficiently, by increasing financial leverage, by changing the capital structure, or by improving the profit margin.

Using Ratios

Ratios are used in most financial analysis for strategic decision making. They allow the analyst to put the results in context and make comparisons. For example, knowing a company earned $50,000 in net income last year means very little in itself. The net income figure could reflect a good or bad performance depending on such considerations as the amount of sales required to produce it, the total equity invested, the amount of debt employed, the industry, performance of the company's major competitors, and the state of the economy. The use of a ratio also allows comparison of numbers of quite different sizes. A $50,000 net income of one company, for example, may represent a much better performance than $100,000 net income of another company because the second company has three times the asset base of the first. The use of ratios helps the analyst make meaningful interpretations of how management has obtained and used the resources of the company.

The ratios obtained must be put into perspective if they are to be meaningful. The results will vary with time, industry, and economic conditions. A firm with a profit margin that does not change during an economic expansion may be showing signs of weakness while the same profit margin may indicate strength if obtained during an economic contraction. Most firms are affected by business cycles, although some are more severely affected than others. Learning how a firm performs through a business cycle can lead to better predictions of future performance.

Perhaps the most common comparisons sought by an analyst are the company's figures relative to its industry. Firms in the same industry are most frequently the company's competitors and face similar conditions, especially when there is a rela-

Exhibit B.4 Sample Trend Analysis of Financial Ratios

Quick Ratio

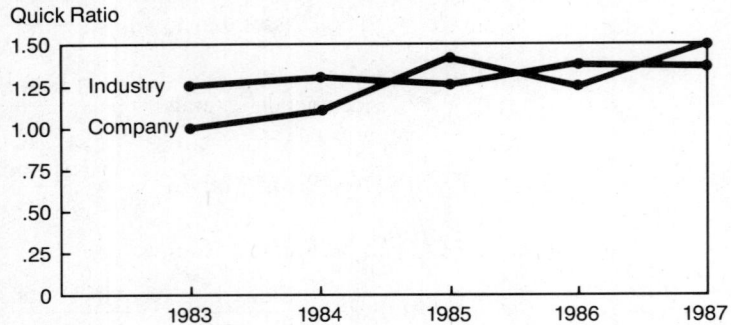

Average Collection Period

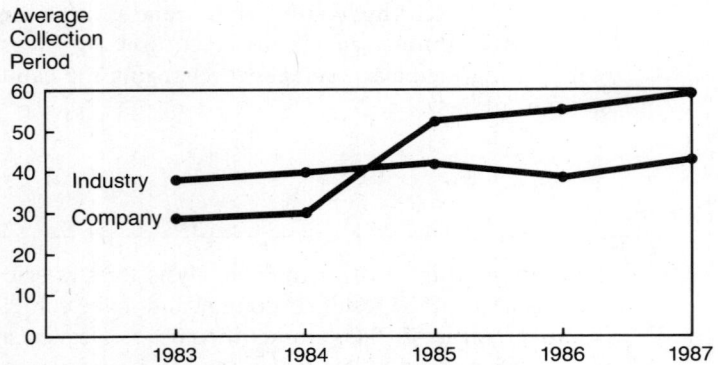

tively homogenous or standardized product, for example, lumber. The technology and production processes may be similar. The "economics of the industry" may implore rather common uses of capital and lead to such characteristics as labor or capital intensity. The firms may also be subject to similar demand characteristics. When firms are subject to similar conditions a more meaningful comparison of management performance can be made. Nevertheless industry comparisons are subject to a couple of caveats. The less homogenous the industry, the less meaningful will be the comparisons. If firms produce different products for different clientele, their demand curves may be significantly different. Firms of quite different size may use different production processes and compete on a different scale. In addition a particular firm may not be typical of the industry norm. In cases in which comparison to an industry average would be misleading, a better comparison would be to selected firms in the industry that are similar in product, service, size, or clientele.

Often a more meaningful comparison is to be found in the trend of a firm's performance. Is it improving or becoming worse? Has the firm recognized its problems or is it heading toward trouble? Here the analyst needs to track the ratios over time. Comparisons can be made with past performance. Here again the most meaningful information may be obtained when the analyst can relate the trend of the firm to economic conditions of the time period considered and to the trends of the industry and firm's competitors. Simple graphs plotting the performance of key ratios for the firm along with the industry norm and key competitors can vividly show the comparisons. Exhibit B.4 is an example of how such a comparison might look.

A sampling of relevant sources of information needed for these comparisons can be seen in Exhibit B.5. From such sources an analyst can obtain or construct ratios for the industry and key competitors as well as the company being analyzed. Com-

Exhibit B.5 A Sampling of Sources of Information Used in Financial Ratio Analysis

Economic

Business Conditions Digest	Contains leading, coincident, and lagging indicators based on time series that allow analysts to predict trends and identify business cycles. Published by the Department of Commerce.

Industry

Standard & Poor's Industry Survey and S&P Analysts Handbook	Cover the major domestic industries with the industry's prospects and trends. Latest developments and statistics for industries. Handbook has income and balance sheet items and ratios.
Trade associations	Often provide extensive statistics. Each trade association is established by members of the industry.
Dun & Bradstreet's Industry Norms and Key Business Ratios	Provides industry averages for 14 different ratios for 800 types of business. Data are grouped by Standard Industrial Classification number and broken down by size.
Robert Morris Associates, Annual Statement Studies	Provide industry averages for 16 different ratios. Data are grouped by SIC number and by size.

Individual Company

Annual reports	Published by publicly held companies. Often available in university libraries.
Security and Exchange Commission 10K Reports	Required annually by publicly held companies. Available from the companies.
Moody's Manuals	Provide financial information for numerous companies.
Standard & Poor's Value Line	Provides financial information for numerous companies.
Compustat	A data bank on computerized tape from Standard & Poor's data. The tapes contain 20 years' data for about 120 banks, 1,000 OTC companies, 2,200 industrials, 175 utilities, and 500 Canadian companies. Complete balance sheet and income statements. An analyst can use the data to construct industry ratios. Frequently available at universities.
Compact Disclosure	A data bank for microcomputers that contains balance sheet, sources and uses of funds statement, income statement, calculated ratios, and a president's report to the stockholders. Typically carries data for five years or more. Available in many libraries.

prehensive reviews of the many sources of information available on the economy, industries, and individual firms include Jugoslav S. Milutinovich, "Business Facts for Decision Makers: Where to Find Them," *Business Horizons,* March–April 1985, 63–80; David M. Brownstone and Gorton Carruth, *Where to Find Business Information: A Worldwide Guide for Everyone Who Needs the Answers to Business Questions* (New York: Wiley, 1979); Oscar Figueroa and Charles Winkler, *A Business Information Guidebook* (New York: AMACOM, 1980); and Paul Wasserman, C. C. Georgi, and J. Woy, *Encyclopedia of Business Information Sources,* 4th ed. (Detroit: Gale Research, 1980).

Calculating Financial Ratios

The balance of this appendix is devoted to the most common financial ratios used in financial analysis. The calculation of each ratio is demonstrated using data from the Cascade Corporation in 1987. The primary business of the firm is indicated by its Standard Industrial Classification (SIC) code: 3537, Industrial Trucks and Tractors. Exhibit B.6 provides a summary list of the ratios and gives the formulas employed. It also provides a format for a worksheet that could be used to record ratios for both the company and the industry for a period of five years.

Liquidity Ratios

Liquidity ratios indicate the firm's ability to meet its future short-term obligations. The focus here is on whether the company's most liquid assets are adequate for paying its potential short-term obligations.

Current Ratio. The current ratio is the most well-known measure of liquidity. Current assets such as cash, inventories, and accounts receivables are matched against current liabilities such as accounts payable. The current ratio is calculated as follows:

$$\frac{\text{Current Assets}}{\text{Current Liabilities}}$$

For the Cascade Corporation the current ratio for 1987 was:

$$\frac{48,793}{19,616} = 2.49$$

A popular guideline for the ratio is 2 or 3 to 1; however, the ratio will vary by industry. An industry with a stable cash flow such as a public utility may not need as high a ratio as a retailer who has a high investment in inventory and accounts receivable, which are subject to rapid change in value. The composition of the assets should also be considered because they may affect the firm's ability to turn the assets into cash as needed. Inventories or accounts receivables that are slow to turn over may impair the firm's ability to meet short-term obligations. Conversely, a firm with a high current ratio may have the ability to meet obligations to short-term creditors, but may not be wisely using its current assets to generate business.

Acid Test or Quick Ratio. This ratio represents the ability of the firm to meet its short-term obligations without sale of its inventories. Inventories may not turn over quickly or they may be obsolete. Other current assets that are of questionable or unknown liquidity should also be deducted for this test. It is a more severe test than the current ratio because it concentrates on the most liquid of assets. It is calculated as follows:

$$\frac{\text{Liquid Current Assets}}{\text{Current Liabilities}}$$

When inventories are the only nonliquid asset, the formula can be written in this way:

$$\frac{\text{Current Assets} - \text{Inventories}}{\text{Current Liabilities}}$$

For the Cascade Corporation the quick ratio for 1987 was:

$$\frac{48,793 - (20,246 + 726)}{19,616} = 1.42$$

The typical guideline is 1 to 1. Again, volatile industries require higher figures. Assets such as cash, marketable securities, and receivables are considered to be current and liquid. If the asset is of suspect liquidity a conservative approach would be to exclude it.

Because receivables and inventories can be a major portion of current assets, the liquidity of the receivables and inventories can be a concern. Three ratios to be considered under efficiency ratios can be used to shed light on the liquidity: accounts receivables turnover, average collection period, and inventory turnover.

Efficiency Ratios

Efficiency ratios indicate how management is performing in using the assets and capital of the firm.

Total Asset Turnover. This ratio is a measure of the volume of business generated by the asset base. It indicates how efficiently company management is using all the assets of the firm to generate sales. It is calculated with the formula:

$$\text{Total Asset Turnover} = \frac{\text{Net Sales}}{\text{Average Total Net Assets}}$$

Net assets are found by subtracting depreciation on fixed assets from gross assets. (The average is calculated by adding together the amounts for the beginning and the end of the year and dividing by 2.) Total net assets are listed as simply total assets on the Cascade balance sheet. For the Cascade Corporation the 1987 total asset turnover was:

$$\frac{98,682}{(78,608 + 69,824)/2} = 1.33$$

Exhibit B.6 Financial Analysis Worksheet

		Company Year					Industry				
Ratio	Formula	1	2	3	4	5	1	2	3	4	5

Liquidity Ratios

Current Ratio: $\dfrac{\text{Current Assets}}{\text{Current Liabilities}}$

Quick Ratio: $\dfrac{\text{Current Assets} - \text{Inventories}}{\text{Current Liabilities}}$

Efficiency Ratios

Total Asset Turnover $\quad = \dfrac{\text{Net Sales}}{\text{Average Total Net Assets}}$

Fixed Asset Turnover $\quad = \dfrac{\text{Net Sales}}{\text{Average Net Fixed Assets}}$

Equity Turnover $\quad = \dfrac{\text{Net Sales}}{\text{Average Equity}}$

Inventory Turnover $\quad = \dfrac{\text{Net Sales}}{\text{Average Inventory}}$

Accounts Receivable Turnover $\quad = \dfrac{\text{Net Annual Sales}}{\text{Average Accounts Receivables}}$

Average Collection Period $\quad = \dfrac{365}{\text{Annual Turnover}}$

Profitability Ratios

Gross Profit Margin $= \dfrac{\text{Gross Profit}}{\text{Net Sales}}$

or

$= \dfrac{\text{Net Sales} - \text{Cost of Goods Sold}}{\text{Net Sales}}$

Operating
Profit Margin $= \dfrac{\text{Earnings before Interest and Taxes}}{\text{Net Sales}}$

or

$= \dfrac{\text{Operating Profit}}{\text{Net Sales}}$

Net Profit Margin $= \dfrac{\text{Net Income}}{\text{Net Sales}}$

Expense Analysis
(Percentage of Sales) $= \dfrac{\text{Expense Item}}{\text{Net Sales}}$

Expense Analysis
(Percentage of Costs) $= \dfrac{\text{Expense Item}}{\text{Total Costs}}$

Common Size
Income Statement $= \dfrac{\text{All Income Statement Items—Individually}}{\text{Net Sales}}$

Exhibit B.6 *(continued)*

Ratio	Formula	Company Year					Industry				
		1	2	3	4	5	1	2	3	4	5
Return on Total Assets	$= \dfrac{\text{Net Income}}{\text{Average Total Assets}}$										
Return on Total Capital	$= \dfrac{\text{Net Income + Interest}}{\text{Average Total Assets}}$										
Return on Total Equity	$= \dfrac{\text{Net Income}}{\text{Average Total Equity}}$										
Return on Common Equity	$= \dfrac{\text{Net Income} - \text{Preferred Dividend}}{\text{Average Common Equity}}$										
Return on Equity	$= \text{Equity Turnover} \times \text{Net Profit Margin}$ or $= \text{Total Asset Turnover} \times \text{Financial Leverage} \times \text{Net Profit Margin}$										
Equity Turnover	$= \dfrac{\text{Sales}}{\text{Equity}} = \dfrac{\text{Sales}}{\text{Total Assets}} \times \dfrac{\text{Total Assets}}{\text{Equity}}$										
Financial Leverage	$= \dfrac{\text{Average Total Assets}}{\text{Average Equity}}$										
Growth	$= \text{Earnings Retention} \times \text{Return on Equity}$ $(1 - \% \text{ of payout})$										
Earnings per Share	$= \dfrac{\text{Net Income} - \text{Preferred Stock Dividends}}{\text{Number of Common Shares Outstanding}}$										

Business Risk $= \dfrac{\text{Standard Deviation of Operating Earnings (OE)}}{\text{Mean Operating Earnings}}$

$$= \dfrac{\sqrt{\sum_{i-1}^{n} (OE - \overline{OE})^2/N}}{\sum_{i-1}^{n} OE/N}$$

Sales Variability $= \dfrac{\text{Standard Deviation of Sales (S)}}{\text{Mean Sales}}$

$$= \dfrac{\sqrt{\sum_{i-1}^{n} (S_t - \overline{S})^2/N}}{\sum_{i-1}^{n} S_t/N}$$

Operating Leverage $= \sum_{i-1}^{n} \left| \dfrac{\%\,\Delta OE}{\%\,\Delta S} \right| / N$

Exhibit B.6 *(continued)*

Ratio	Formula	Company Year					Industry				
		1	2	3	4	5	1	2	3	4	5

Financial Risk

Proportion of Debt:

Total Debt to Total Capital $= \dfrac{\text{Total Debt}}{\text{Total Capital}}$

Debt to Capital $= \dfrac{\text{Total Long-Term Debt}}{\text{Total Long-Term Capital}}$

Debt to Equity $= \dfrac{\text{Total Long-Term Debt}}{\text{Total Equity}}$

Debt Coverage:

Interest Covered $= \dfrac{\text{Income before Interest and Taxes}}{\text{Debt Interest Charges}}$

Earnings Decline Coverage $= 1 - \text{Coverage Ratio} \times 100\%$
Reciprocal

Fixed Asset Turnover. This ratio indicates how efficient the company is in using its plant and equipment in generating sales. The ratio is found by the formula:

$$\text{Fixed Asset Turnover} = \frac{\text{Net Sales}}{\text{Average Net Fixed Assets}}$$

For the Cascade Corporation the 1987 fixed asset turnover was:

$$\frac{98,682}{(29,815 + 27,261)/2} = \frac{98,682}{28,538} = 3.46$$

Both the fixed asset and the total asset turnover ratios should be compared to industry ratios because there is considerable variation among industries. Capital intensive industries may yield low ratios (1 to 1) whereas those that are low capital intensive may yield much higher figures (between 7 and 10 to 1). Old depreciated plants would also contribute to a high ratio as would the use of leased equipment and plants. Thus it is possible for a firm to have a high ratio and look efficient when in fact it has neglected the fixed asset base.

Equity Turnover. Another measure of efficiency is to see how well management is using the firm's capital to generate sales. Different components of capital can be used to determine the dollar amount of sales generated for each dollar of the respective capital component. Of these ratios perhaps the most interesting is equity turnover. The interest is in how many dollars of sales are generated for each dollar of owner (shareholder) equity. Owner equity excludes long-term debt, current liabilities, and preferred stock in this ratio calculation. It can be found with the formula:

$$\text{Equity Turnover} = \frac{\text{Net Sales}}{\text{Average Equity}}$$

For the Cascade Corporation the 1987 equity turnover was:

$$\frac{98,682}{(47,322 + 41,117)/2} = \frac{98,682}{44,220} = 2.23$$

Changes and trends in this figure need to be interpreted along with other capital figures such as the proportion of debt. For example, a firm may rely on increasing debt to finance increased sales, which would make it look efficient in its use of owner equity, but would also increase the financial risk.

Inventory Turnover. This ratio indicates whether a firm has excessive inventory, how liquid the inventory is, and how efficient the firm is in moving inventories into sales. It is computed using the following formula:

$$\text{Inventory Turnover} = \frac{\text{Net Sales}}{\text{Average Inventory}}$$

The 1987 inventory turnover for Cascade Corporation was:

$$\frac{98,682}{(20,246 + 19,452)/2} = \frac{98,682}{19,849} = 4.97$$

Because inventories are carried at cost, the use of cost of goods sold is preferable to net sales although the services reporting ratios use net sales.

Again, good judgment must be used when interpreting the figures. The results vary by industry, although 9 is about "typical." Supermarkets have a low profit margin, but depend on high turnover of inventories. On the other hand, some furniture stores have a low inventory turnover, but have a high profit margin because of a 200 percent to 300 percent markup. Other furniture stores use the supermarket approach. The nature of the strategy, the industry, and the products can make a major difference in this ratio. When the ratio is out of line with the industry average, the analyst should look for the reasons. The ratio may be either too high or too low. A ratio that is high for the industry might indicate inadequate stocks to support sales, shortages, and a loss of customers. A low ratio might indicate the firm is carrying too much inventory, is not planning production and sales wisely, or is incurring excessive carrying costs.

Accounts Receivable Turnover. The turnover of accounts receivable can indicate the quality of the asset for liquidity, but it can also be an indicator of management's performance. It tells the analyst the average collection period on sales. It is calculated as follows:

$$\text{Accounts Receivable Turnover} = \frac{\text{Net Annual Sales}}{\text{Average Accounts Receivables}}$$

For the Cascade Corporation the 1987 accounts receivable turnover was:

$$\frac{98,682}{(16,945 + 13,784)/2} = \frac{98,682}{15,365} = 6.42$$

A ratio that is too low may indicate a tight credit policy that means a loss of sales. If the ratio is too high, management may have established a credit policy that is too loose. Management may be failing to collect debts, may be extending credit too easily, or may be tying up too much capital in accounts receivables.

Average Collection Period. The average collection period can be found as follows:

$$\text{Average Collection Period} = \frac{365}{\text{Annual Turnover}}$$

In 1987 the average collection period was:

$$\frac{365}{6.42} = 56.8 \text{ days}$$

This figure gives the average length of time in days that it takes to collect on sales. Again, the figure must be related to the industry, the current trend, and the firm's credit policy. Comparisons can be distorted by differences in credit policy among firms and whether the firm sells for cash as well as on account. For example, cash sales will make the ratio appear stronger because receivables will be smaller in relationship to sales.

Profitability Ratios

Profitability ratios are measures of the firm's ability to generate profits from its sales and its capital. The ratios will vary widely across industries. Within industries comparisons can give some indication of how well the firm has been managed overall. However, a high return on sales may not mean a high return on investment if sales volume is relatively low or investment relatively high. Thus, returns on both sales and capital should be examined.

Gross Profit Margin. Gross profit margin is the total margin available to cover operating expenses and provide a profit. It gives some indication of the firm's basic cost structure. When compared over time with industry margins it can give a good indication of the firm's relative cost and price position. It is found with the formula:

$$\text{Gross Profit Margin} = \frac{\text{Gross Profit}}{\text{Net Sales}}$$

or

$$\text{Gross Profit Margin} = \frac{\text{Net Sales} - \text{Cost of Goods Sold}}{\text{Net Sales}}$$

The Cascade Corporation's gross profit margin in 1987 was:

$$\frac{34,842}{98,682} = 35.3\%$$

Operating Profit Margin. Operating profit margin indicates the firm's profitability without the effect of interest or taxes. It can be found as follows:

$$\text{Operating Profit Margin} = \frac{\text{Earnings before Interest and Taxes}}{\text{Net Sales}}$$

The operating profit margin for the Cascade Corporation in 1987 can be found by picking up the figure for income before taxes and adding back in the interest expense:

$$\frac{9,740 + 482}{98.682} = 10.36\%$$

Some analysts use the variability of the operating profit margin over time to indicate business risk.

Net Profit Margin. The net profit margin is the after-tax profit per dollar of sales. Net income is earnings after taxes but before preferred and common stock dividends are subtracted. Net profit margin is found with the following formula:

$$\text{Net Profit Margin} = \frac{\text{Net Income}}{\text{Net Sales}}$$

In 1987 the net profit margin for the Cascade Corporation was:

$$\frac{5,645}{98,682} = 5.72\%$$

The net profit margin will vary considerably across industries, but the average for U.S. companies is about 5 percent. Below-normal profit margins may indicate relatively low prices, relatively high costs, or a combination of the two.

Income and Expense Analysis. The profitability ratios already discussed can give an indication of the overall cost–price structure and the ability to generate profits. However, a more detailed analysis of the firm's sources of expense and income is often useful. Are certain expenses increasing over time relative to other firms in the industry? If there is an increase or decline in gross profit margin, what is the source of the change? In addition to helping answer questions such as these, a more detailed analysis that looks at all expenses and income items as a percentage of sales allows a comparison of the firm's efficiency of operations with the efficiency of other firms. Such ratios can be used to compare performance from one period to another and in management control activities. The particular ratio used depends on the needs of the analyst. For example, one analyst may be interested in R&D costs as a percentage of sales, particularly in such high-technology industries as pharmaceuticals. If the percentage of R&D expenses is too low, it may be cause for concern that the firm is not investing in its future. However, if other pharmaceutical firms are selling for relatively low prices, the firm may be showing good management by acquiring another firm. Rather than developing products through its own R&D, the company acquires a firm—and thus its products. Often this can be done more cheaply than developing a new product through R&D. Another example might be to examine administrative costs by determining the percentage of total costs or the percentage of sales. If administrative costs are creeping up when compared to past periods and to industry averages, the firm should be examined more closely for inefficiency or increased bureaucracy. For the Cascade Corporation an analysis of selling, general, and administration expenses as a percentage of sales gives the following:

$$\frac{19,748}{98,682} = 20.01\%$$

Another measure related to sales is the firm's sales growth relative to the industry's sales growth. This measure will indicate the change in market share. If it is calculated for each competitor in the industry, relative market share can be seen. Market share is important in many strategic decisions and can be an important indicator of management's performance.

The discussion of income and expense analysis has focused thus far on the selective use of percentages for a particular purpose. Another approach is to prepare common size income statements such as the one for the Cascade Corporation in Exhibit B.7. Each item on the income statement is shown as a percentage of sales. The selling, general, and administrative expenses as a percentage of sales, which was calculated earlier to be 20.01% for Cascade, can be read directly from the common

Exhibit B.7 Common Size Income Statement for Cascade Corporation, 1983–1987 ($000)

	1987		1986		1985		1984		1983	
Net Sales	$98,682	100.00%	$86,664	100.00%	$84,090	100.00%	$67,708	100.00%	$63,045	100.00%
Cost of Goods	63,840	64.69	56,222	64.87	55,003	65.40	45,391	67.03	44,330	70.31
Gross Profit	34,842	35.30	30,442	35.12	29,087	34.59	22,317	32.96	18,715	29.68
R&D Expenditures	NA	0	NA	0	NA	0	NA	0	NA	0
Selling, General, and Administrative Expense	19,748	20.01	16,738	19.31	15,609	18.56	13,980	20.64	14,914	23.65
Income before Depreciation and Amortization	15,094	15.29	13,704	15.81	13,478	16.02	8,337	12.31	3,801	6.029
Depreciation and Amortization	4,619	4.680	3,854	4.447	3,701	4.401	4,006	5.916	4,037	6.403
Nonoperating Income	−253	−0.25	−164	−0.18	−347	−0.41	−160	−0.23	−396	−0.62
Interest Expense	482	0.488	353	0.407	263	0.312	812	1.199	1,168	1.852
Income before Taxes	9,740	9.870	9,323	10.75	9,167	10.90	3,359	4.961	−1,800	−2.85
Provision for Income Tax	4,095	4.149	3,700	4.269	3,900	4.637	1,455	2.148	−1,620	−2.56
Minority Interest (Income)	NA	0	NA	0	NA	0	NA	0	NA	0
Investment Gains/Losses	NA	0	NA	0	NA	0	NA	0	NA	0
Other Income	NA	0	NA	0	NA	0	NA	0	NA	0
Net Income before Expense Items	5,645	5.720	5,623	6.488	5,267	6.263	1,904	2.812	−180	−0.28
Expense Items and Discount Operations	NA	0	NA	0	NA	0	NA	0	NA	0
Net Income	5,645	5.720	5,623	6.488	5,267	6.263	1,904	2.812	−180	−0.28
Outstanding Shares[a] (000)	3,002		751		751		774		713	
Earnings per Share	1.88		1.87		1.75		0.65		−0.06	

[a]Three-share dividend declared May 1986.
Source: Cascade Corporation 10K reports, 1983–1987.

size income statement. When this is done for several years, trends can be spotted. When they are compared to trends of other firms or the industry as a whole, management can better understand the firm's performance.

Return on Total Assets. Ratios related to the rate of return generated by the firm's assets are generally considered a better indication of management's success and the firm's efficiency and profitability than are the profitability ratios related to sales and expense. Return on total assets, sometimes called return on investment, is an indicator of the after-tax returns per dollar of assets. Because the firm may buy and sell assets and the capital employed may change, an average figure for total assets should be used. Thus the formula is:

$$\text{Return on Total Assets} = \frac{\text{Net Income}}{\text{Average Total Assets}}$$

The return on total assets for the Cascade Corporation in 1987 was:

$$\frac{5,645}{(78,608 + 69,824)/2} = \frac{5,645}{74,216} = 7.61\%$$

Total assets are financed by creditors as well as stockholders. To reflect the earnings available to all investors, interest paid on debt can be added to net income to find out how productive total assets are, as indicated by the following modification:

$$\text{Return on Total Capital} = \frac{\text{Net Income} + \text{Interest}}{\text{Average Total Assets}}$$

The 1987 return on total capital for the Cascade Corporation was:

$$\frac{5,645 + 482}{(78,608 + 69,824)/2} = \frac{6,127}{74,216} = 8.26\%$$

Return on Equity. Return on equity (ROE) is a measure of how well management has earned profits using the owners' investment. It is the rate of return earned on the capital provided by the stockholders after paying all other suppliers of capital. It is calculated as follows:

$$\text{Return on Total Equity} = \frac{\text{Net Income}}{\text{Average Total Equity}}$$

The return on total equity for the Cascade Corporation in 1987 was:

$$\frac{5,645}{(47,322 + 41,117)/2} = \frac{5,645}{44,220} = 12.8\%$$

Total equity is all shareholder equity including preferred stock. If the analyst is interested in common equity only, it would be calculated as follows:

$$\text{Return on Common Equity} = \frac{\text{Net Income} - \text{Preferred Dividend}}{\text{Average Common Equity}}$$

For the Cascade Corporation in 1987 the return on common equity was:

$$\frac{5,645 - 0}{(47,322 + 41,117)/2} = \frac{5,645}{44,220} = 12.8\%$$

Common equity is found by subtracting the par value of preferred stock from total equity. Because the Cascade Corporation has no preferred stock, common equity and total equity are the same.

ROE can be broken down into several subcomponent ratios.

$$\text{ROE} = \text{Equity Turnover} \times \text{Net Profit Margin}$$

or

$$\text{ROE} = \frac{\text{Net Income}}{\text{Equity}} = \frac{\text{Sales}}{\text{Equity}} \times \frac{\text{Net Income}}{\text{Sales}}$$

These two components indicate two ways to improve ROE. Management can increase the company's equity turnover by using equity more efficiently. Equity turnover can also be broken down into additional components for examination:

$$\text{Equity Turnover} = \frac{\text{Sales}}{\text{Equity}} = \frac{\text{Sales}}{\text{Total Assets}} \times \frac{\text{Total Assets}}{\text{Equity}}$$

Management can also increase the company's net profit margin because

$$\text{Net Profit Margin} = \frac{\text{Net Income}}{\text{Sales}}$$

Because total assets divided by equity is a measure of financial leverage, management can manipulate three components in improving ROE. The formula is rewritten as follows:

$$\text{ROE} = \text{Total Asset Turnover} \times \text{Financial Leverage} \times \text{Net Profit Margin}$$

$$\text{ROE} = \frac{\text{Sales}}{\text{Total Assets}} \times \frac{\text{Total Assets}}{\text{Equity}} \times \frac{\text{Income}}{\text{Sales}}$$

The only component of this formula not previously calculated is financial leverage:

$$\text{Financial Leverage} = \frac{\text{Average Total Assets}}{\text{Average Equity}}$$

Financial leverage for the Cascade Corporation in 1987 was:

$$\frac{(78,608 + 69,824)/2}{(47,322 + 41,117)/2} = \frac{74,216}{44,220} = 1.68$$

Thus, using figures already calculated for total asset turnover (1.33) and net profit margin (5.72), the ROE for the Cascade Corporation in 1987 was:

$$\text{ROE} = 1.33 \times 1.68 \times 5.72 = 12.8\%$$

By breaking down ROE the analyst can sometimes determine the actions management has taken as well as actions that can be taken to improve ROE. For example, management can increase equity turnover by using more debt capital. However, this would also increase financial risk and likely increase the required rate of return on equity.

Growth The growth of a company is usually important to its strategic goals. Expected growth affects the price buyers are willing to pay for the company's stock. It also affects lender decisions because earnings growth provides protection to debt holders. Earnings growth also affects a firm's ability to finance the investments required to carry out its strategy. It is generally assumed that the more a company reinvests in itself, the more it will grow. We can look at growth by focusing on (1) the percentage of earnings retained for reinvestment and (2) the rate of return earned on equity retained. The indicator is as follows:

$$\text{Growth} = \text{Earnings Retention} \times \text{Return on Equity}$$

Earnings retention is found by subtracting the percentage of payout from 1. Again, trends are important in estimating future growth. If the growth rate is declining, expected return on equity should decline, whereas an increasing rate would predict an increase in return on equity. Based on figures in the sources and uses of funds statement, the earnings retention for the Cascade Corporation in 1987 was:

$$1 - (1,801/5,645) = 1 - .319 = .681$$

The growth rate for Cascade Corporation in 1987 was:

$$.681 \times 12.8 = 8.72\%$$

Earnings per Share Earnings per share shows the earnings available to owners of common stock and is found as follows:

$$\text{Earnings per Share} = \frac{\text{Net Income} - \text{Preferred Stock Dividends}}{\text{Number of Common Shares Outstanding}}$$

Earnings per share for the Cascade Corporation in 1987 was:

$$\frac{5,645 - 0}{3,002} = 1.88$$

Risk

The uncertainty of returns and income is important to strategic analysis of a firm. The volatility of sales, operating earnings, and earnings available to stockholders can be important to assessing risk. If another firm is an acquisition or merger candidate, the risk connected with the volatility of its sales and earnings may be an important consideration. Business and financial risk can also affect the alternatives available to a firm in financing the company; that is, its capital structure.

Business Risk Business risk is concerned with the uncertainty of future earnings. A firm's earnings vary because its sales and production costs vary. The products and customers in some industries lead to more variability in sales and costs over time. For example, capital goods like machines and tools have a more volatile history than retail soft goods or grocery products.

Business risk can be gauged by looking at the variability of the company's operating earnings over time. The more variable the operating earnings over time, the more uncertain are the future earnings and the greater is the business risk. The coefficient of variation of operating earnings is used here because it allows comparison of companies of different sizes. Data for at least five to ten years should be used for a meaningful measure.

$$\text{Business Risk} = \frac{\text{Standard Deviation of Operating Earnings (OE)}}{\text{Mean Operating Earnings}}$$

$$= \frac{\sqrt{\sum_{i=1}^{n} (OE_t - OE)^2/N}}{\sum_{i=1}^{n} OE_t/N}$$

The business risk for the Cascade Corporation is based on minimum data points, but for illustration is:

$$\frac{4,220.46}{10,882.80} = .388$$

Business risk can be broken into its two components: (1) sales variability and (2) operating leverage.

Sales Variability. The most powerful component of earnings availability is greatly affected by the general economic environment and the company's industry. Machine tools or steel, for example, are more affected by the economic cycle and are a more cyclical industry than groceries. The former will have a greater sales variability. The sales variability can be found using the coefficient of variation of sales. Sales are substituted for operating earnings in the previous formula. The basic formula is as follows:

$$\text{Sales Variability} = \frac{\text{Standard Deviation of Sales (S)}}{\text{Mean Sales}}$$

$$= \frac{\sqrt{\sum_{i=1}^{n} (S_t - \overline{S})^2/N}}{\sum_{i=1}^{n} S/N}$$

The sales variability for the Cascade Corporation was:

$$\frac{13,028.52}{80,037.80} = .163$$

Operating Leverage. The mix of costs from producing goods or services affects the variability of a company's operating earnings. Production costs may be viewed as variable and fixed cost. If all production costs were variable, the total production costs would vary directly with sales, and operating earnings would be a constant proportion of sales. But because of fixed or relatively fixed production costs (such as plant, machinery, and management), earnings will not remain a constant proportion and will vary more than sales. In periods of decline, earnings will decline more than sales, whereas during expansion periods earnings will increase more than sales. Thus the greater the fixed production costs, the more variable will be the operating earnings relative to the sales variability. Operating leverage is determined by comparing the percentage of change in operating earnings to the percentage of change in sales for several years:

$$\text{Operating Leverage} = \sum_{i-1}^{n} \left| \frac{\% \, \Delta \, \text{OE}}{\% \, \Delta \, \text{S}} \right| / \text{N}$$

The operating leverage for the Cascade Corporation was:

$$\frac{19.94}{4} = 4.99$$

Financial Risk. In addition to business risk there is the risk to the owner derived from the use of debt obligations because the payment on debt capital comes prior to earnings available to common stock. If there were no debt, the only risk would be to that of business risk. The use of fixed debt obligations produces an effect similar to that of fixed production costs on operating earnings variability. That is, during favorable business conditions earnings on equity will be relatively larger than for operating earnings, whereas during unfavorable times the earnings available will be relatively less. Financial risk is measured by looking at the proportion of debt and the coverage of interest and fixed charges.

Proportion of Debt. The greater the proportion of long-term debt in a company's capital, the more volatile will be earnings available to common stock and the greater the chance of defaulting on the bonds. In other words, the higher the proportion of debt, the greater the financial risk will be. As financial risk increases, the interest rate demanded becomes higher and equity capital becomes more difficult to obtain. The level of acceptable financial risk is affected by the company's business risk. Companies with stable earnings have lower business risk and can tolerate higher debt ratios; an example is public utilities. Several ratios may be used to examine proportion of debt.

$$\text{Total Debt to Total Capital} = \frac{\text{Total Debt}}{\text{Total Capital}}$$

Total debt includes both current liabilities and long-term liabilities. It is most useful when the company utilizes considerable short-term borrowing. The total debt to total capital for the Cascade Corporation in 1987 was:

$$\frac{31,286}{78,608} = 39.8\%$$

A second ratio for examining proportion of debt is the following:

$$\text{Debt to Capital} = \frac{\text{Total Long-Term Debt}}{\text{Total Long-Term Capital}}$$

Long-term debt includes all long-term fixed obligations. Long-term capital includes all long-term debt, total owner equity, and preferred stock. The Cascade Corporation long debt to long capital for 1987 was:

$$\frac{31,286 - 19,616}{78,608 - 19,616} = 19.78\%$$

A third ratio is:

$$\text{Debt to Equity} = \frac{\text{Total Long-Term Debt}}{\text{Total Equity}}$$

Total equity includes preferred stock, common stock, and retained earnings and is essentially the book value of equity. The Cascade Corporation long-term debt to equity in 1987 was:

$$\frac{31,286 - 19,616}{47,322} = 24.66\%$$

Coverage Ratios. Coverage ratios indicate the adequacy of earnings to pay the interest on debt obligations. The greater the coverage, the smaller the financial risk will be.

$$\text{Interest Covered} = \frac{\text{Income before Interest and Taxes}}{\text{Debt Interest Charges}}$$

The interest coverage for the Cascade Corporation in 1987 was:

$$\frac{9,740}{482} = 20.21$$

This ratio indicates how many times fixed interest charges could be covered by earnings available to pay the charges. It can also be used in another ratio to determine the extent to which earnings can decline before the company can no longer meet its interest charges. This can be found as follows:

$$\text{Earnings Decline Coverage} = 1 - \text{Coverage Ratio Reciprocal} \times 100\%$$

$$\left[1 - \frac{1}{N}\right] \times 100$$

For example, if the ratio yields a 3, then 1 minus 1/3 equals .67; this means earnings could decline 67 percent and the company could still pay its charges. The earnings decline coverage for the Cascade Corporation in 1987 was:

$$\left[1 - \frac{1}{20.21}\right] \times 100 = 95.05\%$$

Exhibit B.8 provides the calculated financial ratios for the Cascade Corporation for the years 1983 through 1987.

Exhibit B.8 Calculation of Financial Ratios for Cascade Corporation, 1983–1987

	1987	1986	1985	1984	1983
Current Ratio	2.4874	2.2980	2.4441	2.1556	2.5341
Quick Ratio	1.4182	1.2196	1.3288	1.1149	1.0088
Total Asset Turnover	1.3296	1.3281	1.4031	1.1534	
Average Net Assets (000)	74,216	65,251	59.929	58,698	
Fixed Asset Turnover	3.4579	3.4893	3.7217	2.8206	
Average Net Fixed Assets (000)	28,538	24,837	22,594	24,004	
Equity Turnover	2.2316	2.2748	2.4850	2.0788	
Average Equity (000)	44,220	38,097	33,839	32,570	
Inventory Turnover	4.9716	4.7693	4.9464	3.6991	
Average Inventory (000)	19,849	18,171	17,000	18,303	
Accounts Receivable Turnover	6.4227	6.6168	7.1544	11.295	
Average Receivables (000)	15,365	13,097	11,753	5,994.5	
Average Collection Period	56.830	55.162	51.017	32.315	
Gross Profit Margin	0.3531	0.3512	0.3459	0.3296	0.2968
Operating Profit Margin	0.0987	0.1075	0.1090	0.0496	−0.028
Net Profit Margin	0.0572	0.0648	0.0626	0.0281	−0.002
Percent of Sales Example: Selling, General, and Administrative Expense	0.2001	0.1931	0.1856	0.2064	0.2365
Return on Total Assets	0.0761	0.0861	0.0878	0.0324	
Return on Total Capital	0.0826	0.0915	0.0922	0.0462	
Return on Total Equity	0.1276	0.1475	0.1556	0.0584	
Average Total Equity	44,220	38,097	33,839	32,570	
Return on Common Equity	0.1277	0.1475	0.1556	0.0584	
Return on Equity	0.1277	0.1475	0.1556	0.0584	0
Financial Leverage	1.6783	1.7127	1.7710	1.8021	
Growth	0.0870	0.1101	0.1135		
Earnings Retention	0.6810	0.7463	0.7292		
Dividends (000)	1,801	1,426	1,426	NA	
Earnings Per Share	1.8804	7.487	7.013	2.459	−0.252
Debt to Capital	0.3980	0.4111	0.4219	0.4491	0.4410
Long-Term Debt to Long-Term Capital	0.1978	0.1985	0.2209	0.2291	0.2801
Long-Term Debt to Total Equity	0.2466	0.2477	0.2835	0.2972	0.3890
Interest Covered	20.207	26.410	34.855	4.1366	−1.541
Earnings Decline Coverage	95.051	96.213	97.131	75.826	164.88

Source: Cascade Corporation 10K reports, 1983–1987.

Part 2

Cases

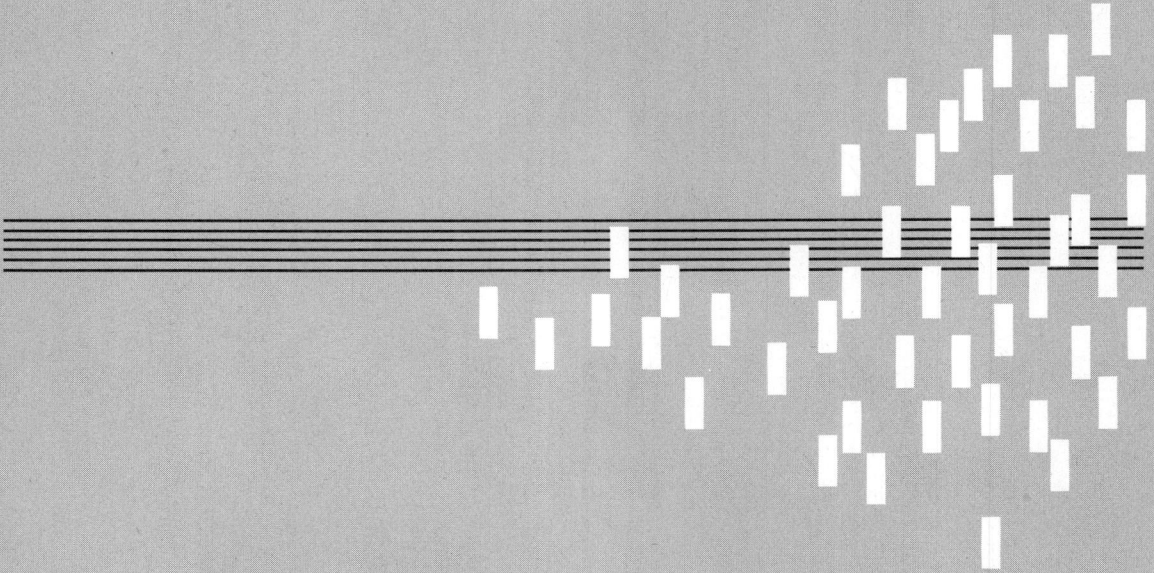

Case 1

Industry Note on the Commercial Aircraft Manufacturing Industry

Three of the four giants of the commercial aircraft industry have their roots in the World War I era. In 1916 William Edward Boeing began building seaplanes in Seattle. The same year, the Loughead brothers founded Lockheed in Santa Barbara, California. In 1924, the Douglas Corporation became a late entry into the fledgling aircraft manufacturing industry. Until 1953, Douglas Corporation was the industry giant, having produced the most successful family of propeller planes ever built, the DC-3 through the DC-7. In 1954, however, the industry environment changed abruptly when Boeing Corporation convinced the United States government that the proposed long range strategic bomber, the B52, should be jet powered.

The Beginning of the Commercial Jet Age

The U.S. government's acceptance of Boeing's proposal to equip the B52 with jet engines ushered in the commercial jet age. Boeing used the knowledge gained from producing the B52 and the KC135 (jet tanker) to launch the Boeing 707 in the early 1960s. The rapid success of these aircraft gave Boeing immediate industry dominance, relegating Douglas and Lockheed to second and third positions in the growing commercial aircraft industry. Also contributing to Boeing's position was the fact that Douglas Corporation and Lockheed had gambled unwisely. Both companies concluded that the time saved flying coast to coast on a jet aircraft was not worth the additional costs to the airlines. This

miscalculation put Douglas, formerly number one, in a catch-up position. Douglas did not introduce its first jet liner for several years after Boeing; the DC-8 was delayed with production problems and suffered cost overruns. By the late 1960s Douglas was on the verge of collapse. Fortunately, the McDonnell Corporation, primarily a military aviation firm, became interested in a merger, and the two companies formed McDonnell Douglas Corporation.

Lockheed experienced major problems with its turboprop Electra, which was plagued by crashes in its first years of operation. Further, the plane reportedly experienced vibrations, causing it to become structurally unstable. After this fiasco, Lockheed management decided to sit out the first round of the jet powered commercial aviation battle.

The Market for Commercial Aircraft in the 1960s

Commercial airlines began to realize that the corporation that offered a family of planes, including short-to-long range aircraft, was the most viable producer. During the 1960s, Boeing became the only such producer.

Manufacturers of commercial airplanes face an enormous expense in developing a new aircraft. Like many industries, the aircraft industry relies on a highly skilled work force to ensure success. However, few other industries are as capital intensive or as involved with such a high volume of new technologies. Thus two factors set the airplane industry apart from others: the major costs incurred in developing a new plane and the monumental amount of moneys risked.

The aircraft industry is often compared to the automobile industry; however, Ford Motor Corporation was reported to have lost over $300 million on the Edsel and yet it remains a viable healthy organization today. On the other hand, Glenn Martin Company, General Dynamics, and Lockheed are no longer in commercial aircraft because each manufactured one unsuccessful plane. Through 1988 a total of 26 commercial jet-powered aircraft have been introduced in the marketplace, but few have been profitable.

In the late 1960s the enormous growth in profitability of commercial airlines began to decay. Even though forecasts indicated a slowing in growth of passenger miles, airlines were purchasing new jet aircraft. Major carriers bought aircraft they could not operate successfully. For example, Pan Am, the inaugural flyer of the 747, applied competitive pressure to force TWA, its major U.S. competitor for international flights, to purchase 747s—even though TWA could not justify the size of the plane.

The market in the 1960s saw an environment that demanded a twin-aisle, wide-body, two-engine, fuel-efficient aircraft that could carry between 200 and 280 passengers. Both Lockheed and McDonnell Douglas worked feverishly to produce such a plane. Their entrants, the L-1011 and DC-10, respectively, were among the most technologically complete planes ever built. They were also major failures. Lockheed is reported to have lost over $1.5 billion on the development of the L-1011, while McDonnell Douglas lost hundreds of millions as well as the confidence of the flying public because of the tragic DC-10 crashes in Turkey and Chicago. At a time when commercial producers could ill afford further competition, a consortium of European countries founded Airbus Industrie.

A major contributor to the loss of profitability of commercial airlines was fuel costs. Fuel rose from about 11 cents a gallon in the 1960s to over a dollar a gallon in 1981. The spiraling costs of operating an airline, the deregulation in 1978, and the recession of the early 1980s combined to send the airlines into a tailspin. This sharp downturn in the fortunes of commercial carriers ushered in one of the most difficult periods in the history of commercial aircraft manufacturers.

The Differences between Defense and Commercial Markets

Though military and commercial planes may appear to be similar, the commercial aircraft industry has a longer road to profitability. It takes many years and often the sale of hundreds of planes before initial R&D costs are recovered. For example, Lockheed had to sell 400 L-1011s before realizing any profit. In the military aircraft industry, however, R&D costs are often recovered immediately because the federal government assumes these costs. The defense industry provides an immediate customer that orders large quantities and pays on time. Conversely, commercial aircraft customers stagger orders over the plane's projected life. Because the manufacturer has no guarantee on the reliability of future orders, it is less inclined to use the learning curve economies of scale. On the other hand, dependence on the military does have drawbacks. The most notable is the often irrational method for selecting contractors. Some observers suggest that the best design among competing entries often loses out because of political considerations. Other differences include the military priority of performance over reliability, whereas most commercial airlines stress reliability for safety. Thus these two criteria involve different design parameters for the two markets.

The Bonanza Market: 1985 to 1995

In early 1985 both U.S. and foreign commercial air carriers prepared to purchase new aircraft needed to replace their aging, loud, fuel-inefficient jets. Boeing estimated that over 8,000 new jet airliners would be sold by Western manufacturers from 1989 through 2004 (Exhibit 1). This estimate is 1,500 more aircraft than Boeing's 1987 estimate. Of this $100 billion increase in business, more than $90 billion was on order by 1988.

The gloom of earlier years turned into a manufacturer's bonanza. In the first four months of 1989 Boeing received orders in excess of $17 billion. Its sales for all of 1988 were $30 billion. In a single week Airbus received orders and options for more than $7 billion. McDonnell Douglas also benefited from large orders by Delta and American. Aircraft sales for 1988 are presented in Exhibit 2.

This wild growth according to industry analysts is attributable primarily to three factors. First, growth in air travel is fueling the sales boom. RPMs, the number of passengers carried on a flight times the distance, will grow at a rate of 5.4 percent a year. This will double the current market by the year 2005. Seventy percent of all new aircraft purchased will accommodate this growth. The second factor is the replacement of old aircraft. Renewed concerns about geriatric jets falling from the sky and noise regulations are forcing replacements. Airlines want to use new, more efficient jets to serve new marketplaces also. Finally, the stretched-out delivery dates for new aircraft are forcing airlines to make their purchases quickly or be shut out of the market.

Exhibit 1   Actual and Estimated Commercial Aircraft Sales, 1970–2004

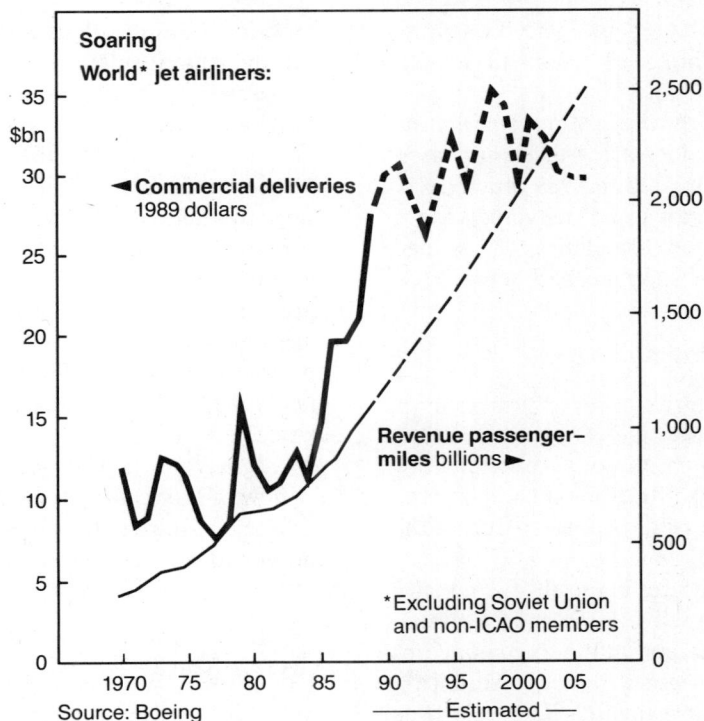

Exhibit 2   1988 Commercial Jetliner Firm Orders (through September)

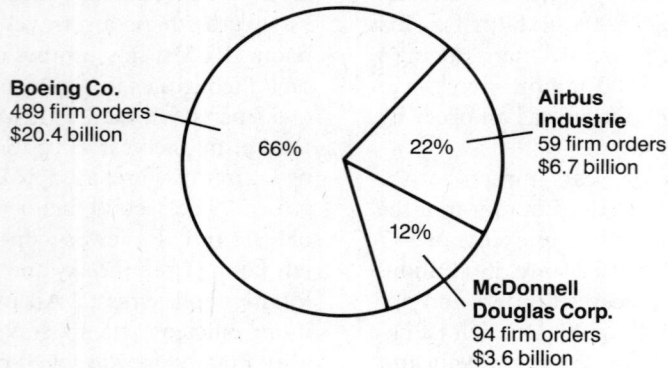

Boeing Co.
489 firm orders
$20.4 billion

66%

22%

Airbus
Industrie
59 firm orders
$6.7 billion

12%

McDonnell
Douglas Corp.
94 firm orders
$3.6 billion

Total: 642 orders; $30.7 billion value.

Source: Prudential-Bache Securities

As an example, Cathay Pacific placed an order for Airbus 330s on April 3, 1989 but will not take delivery until early 1995.

Because many airlines are strapped for cash, leasing firms are also increasing their purchases. GPA Group Ltd. of Ireland in 1989 ordered $17 billion worth of aircraft to be delivered over a ten-year period. Of the 308 planes, 182 valued at $9.4 billion will be supplied by Boeing.

Competitive Pressure among Manufacturers

Even with the strong demand, some doubt exists about whether the three major commercial aircraft builders—Boeing, McDonnell Douglas, and Airbus—can all successfully compete during the 1990s.

Competitive pressures in the airline industry have drastically thinned the ranks of airframe and engine manufacturers. Of the six major companies that remain viable, four are American. Airframe manufacturers include Boeing, Airbus Industrie, and McDonnell Douglas. Engine manufacturers are Pratt & Whitney, General Electric, and Rolls Royce. The two American engine man-

ufacturers (GE and Pratt & Whitney) are larger than the American airframe manufacturers; this increases the pressures on aircraft producers because of vulnerability to these suppliers.

The engine totals one-third of the cost of a jetliner. To develop a completely new jet engine may cost hundreds of millions of dollars and take as long as five years in research time. Nonetheless, airframe manufacturers still sell their planes with a choice of two or three types of engines. These engine options increase engineering and development costs for the airframe manufacturers and affect the profitability of the aircraft. For example, Airbus Industrie offers Pratt & Whitney engines on its A300–600 series. This limits the flow of profits to Europe from an aircraft sale because one-third of the revenue is engine related and would revert to Pratt & Whitney.

The 150-Seat, Narrow-Body Aircraft Market

Delta Air Lines initiated the idea of the 150-seat aircraft in the mid-1970s. This plane would fly more frequently to more places, which would create a need for more, not necessarily larger, aircraft. Most carriers prefer long-haul, wide-body aircraft, but the shorter high-frequency flights—less than two hours in duration and about 800 miles in distance—constitute 75 percent of all scheduled flights. Certainly, the market for the 150-seater appears to exist. However, the cost of developing such an airplane is staggering. One calculation shows that it would cost Boeing, the world's most efficient aircraft manufacturer, almost $2 billion to get this plane off the ground.

Despite staggering start-up costs, Airbus Industrie began development of a 150-seat market with reengineered existing aircraft. Nor have American companies abandoned the concept of a 150-seat aircraft. Their strategy is to update existing designs. Even though their entries to the marketplace lack the fuel efficiency of the A320, they are $1 million to $5 million less expensive and immediately available. In the early 1980s Boeing announced its intent to produce a new 150-seat aircraft by the year 1992. According to industry sources, this plane will be more cost effective than the A320. Boeing's message was clear; the A320 would be an inferior design by the year 1992. McDonnell Douglas also chose to build a new derivative of its successful MD-80 series that flew on Propfan-powered engines. However, changing factors in the marketplace caused Boeing to shelve its all-new 7J7. McDonnell Douglas also put its new Propfan-powered plane on hold.

The Trend Toward Larger Aircraft

A major factor in the current buying spree of commercial airlines is a move toward larger aircraft. Boeing estimates that almost 90 percent of all aircraft delivered after 1995 will have more than 170 seats, compared to 120 to 170 seats for the preceding few years. All three major airframe manufacturers are studying ways to meet this demand.

The cramped space at many airports has caused airlines to rethink plane size for their hub and spoke system. Both Delta and American have lost business travelers to other airlines when flights on 727s and 737s were sold out. Thus Airbus and McDonnell Douglas consider the junior jumbo, with a range of up to 8,000 miles and seating of 270 to 330 passengers, to represent a major market niche for the future. Both manufacturers are developing and taking orders for such planes. Airbus expects its long-haul 330 will compete with Boeing's 767ER and its A340 mini-jumbo will not only compete with the 747 series but will establish itself as the market leader in the mini-jumbo niche.

In a move that surprised some in the industry, American Airlines in early 1989 ordered 75 Fokker 100s and took option on another 75. This deal has a value of close to $3 billion. The aircraft seats 95 to 97 and is part of a strategy at American to fill the low end of its capacity range.

American Airlines had identified 100 markets for the 100-seat airplane. According to chairman Robert Crandall, "With the Fokker 100, we can bring larger numbers of passengers into our hubs, where they in turn will fill connecting flights, allowing those flights to operate at higher load factors."[1] He cited three reasons for selecting the Fokker 100 over the MD-87 or Boeing 737–500: The aircraft is available in 1991, the agreement limits the airline's vulnerability to a recession, and the aircraft will pay for itself once it enters service.

Product Line Decisions

Product line decisions take place in a dynamic environment, even for products with such long lead times as commercial aircraft. For example, within a short while after the idea of the 150-seat airplane was conceived in the early 1980s, a great deal of new information became available and the environment changed considerably.

Some of the issues driving the fleet-planning decisions for airlines are engine-noise restric-

---

[1]James T. Mckenna, "American Fokker 100 Order Caps Carrier's Growth Plan," *Aviation Week and Space Technology*, March 27, 1989, 88–89.

tions at domestic airports, new engine and avionics technology, and aging fleets. The engine-noise issue has been controversial for at least a decade. The very popular 727 series and the 737–100 and 737–200 aircraft have Pratt & Whitney JT8D engines in almost all their configurations, and they exceed noise limits at most domestic airports. The FAA has authorized installation of "hush kits" on these engines to allow the airlines to continue operating during the staged restrictions on engine noise. However, by 1992, when Stage III is implemented, even the hushed engines will not meet noise standards. These airplanes will have to be replaced. No replacement engine is currently available or planned.

New engine and avionics technology will be also necessary for the airlines to remain competitive in their operations beyond the year 2000. General Electric and Pratt & Whitney are both developing new engines that are more fuel efficient as well as much quieter than the engines on the Boeing 767 and the Airbus 320.

Airbus

The Airbus consortium is presently comprised of Aero Spatiale (France), 37.9 percent, and CASA (Spain), 4.2 percent. Fokker (Netherlands) and Belairbus (Belgium) are associates participating only in the larger A310 (220 seats).

Interestingly, until 1978 the Airbus was a typical European airplane; it was well produced but a commercial failure. However, when Eastern Airlines purchased 24 A300s, Airbus's fortune began to change. Soaring fuel costs and stiff competition among airlines had created a demand for a large, fuel-efficient airplane. Only Airbus had such a plane. Up to 1978, only 38 had been sold, but by the end of 1979 sales totaled over 300 planes. This was the highest figure for any European commercial aircraft. Airbus has since followed Boeing's strategy by introducing a family of aircraft (Table 1). Conventional wisdom in the industry argues that an aircraft manufacturer must offer a family of aircraft in order to sell any single model.

Table 1 Airbus Current Family of Planes

| | | General Data | | | Dimensions and Weights | | |
Name	Primary Mission	Crew	Passengers	Wingspan, ft.	Wing Area, sq. ft.	Max. Length, ft.
A300B4/C4	Medium-haul/convertible	3	220-345	147.1	2,800	175.9
A300-600	Medium-haul	2	230-375	147.1	2,800	177.4
A300-600C	Convertible	2	230-375	147.1	2,800	177.4
A300-600R	Medium-long haul	2	230-345	147.1	2,800	177.4
A310-200 Standard	Medium haul	2	210-280	144.0	2,357	153.1
A310-200 Option	Medium-haul	2	210-280	144.0	2,357	153.1
A310-300	Medium-long haul	2	210-280	144.0	2,357	153.1
A310-200C	Convertible pax/cargo	2	210-280	144.0	2,357	153.1
A320-200	Short-medium haul	2	140-179	111.3	1,318	123.3

[a]A330 and A340 are scheduled for introduction in the early 1990s, will be part of the Airbus family.
Source: "Leading International Aircraft, Spacecraft, Weapons," *Aviation Week & Space Technology,* March 20, 1989, 153.

Airbus is government supported and, by French law, not required to publish financial statements. However, many industry experts believe the company's orientation toward economic efficiency differs dramatically from its American counterparts. The underlying objective of Airbus may be employment of its own 180,000 direct and indirect employees. Industry experts suspect that Airbus Industrie is selling planes below cost; in that case, the government would be fostering employment through subsidies. If Airbus's financial statements were in the public domain, the demands for efficiency could cause significant layoffs and production slowdowns. Thus the very fact that Airbus does not openly report financial figures may be the method by which the company is able to preserve its existence. Boeing estimates that Airbus will not break-even in sales until 2001.

Airbus has been very successful in marketing its family of jets to both European and Asian carriers. It has capitalized on the theme "buy European." In addition, sales to air carriers in the Middle East (particularly Kuwait and Lebanon) have been brisk.

Airbus has developed a strategy of negotiating with government leaders instead of airline executives. For the many countries in which air carriers are state owned, the ultimate decision to purchase a plane becomes an upper level governmental policy decision. Thailand's purchase of A310s is an example. Airbus presently holds a 75 percent share of the market in new sales in South America; almost 80 percent in Europe, the Middle East, and Africa; and 70 percent in Asia.

Airbus's recent success is a result of shrewd planning. The consortium targeted market niches not occupied by Boeing, the first being junior jumbo jets with ranges approaching 8,000 miles (similar to the Boeing 747) but with a capacity of only 300 seats. The second is the 150-seat passenger jet replacement market. Airbus has 134 orders for junior jumbo jets and a remarkable 450-plus orders for the 150-seat A320.

Table 1 *(continued)*

Dimensions and Weights				
Max. Height, ft.	Empty Weight, lbs.	Gross Weight, lbs.	Powerplant: Number, Make, and Model	Max. Speed, mph.
54.2	195,100	363,760	2 GE CF-6-50C2 tf. or 2 P&W JT9D-59A tf.	M.86
54.2	195,500	363,760	2 GE CF6-80C2, or 2 P&W 4000	M.82
54.2	196,300	375,400	Same as A300-600	M.82
54.2	194,600	375,300	2 GE CF6-80C2 tf. or 2 P&W PW 4000	M.82
51.9	174,800	305,560	2 CF6-80C2 or 2 P&W 4000	M.84
51.9	174,800	313,100	Same as A310-200 std.	M.84
51.9	175,600	330,690	Same as A310-200 std.	M.84
51.9	176,800	305,560	Same as AP310-200 std.	M.84
38.6	87,100	162,000	2 CFM56-5 or IAE V2500	M.82

Airbus Industrie members in March 1989 approved a significant reorganization plan, designed to move the airframe manufacturer toward profitability and to increase its competitiveness. The changes involved the structure and size of the supervisory board, the structure of senior management, and the creation of an executive board. The supervisory board, which has responsibility for strategic decisions concerning current and future programs, shrank from 17 to 5 members. A new position of financial director was created to ensure full open accounting.

The newly created executive board has responsibility for Airbus's operations. Jean Pierson, managing director, will coordinate the firm's commercial needs with the industrial and financial capabilities of its four partner companies.

McDonnell Douglas

Historically, McDonnell Douglas has generated most of its revenue outside the sales of commercial aircraft. Defense contracts have been the company's lifeblood. However, February 1989 brought an order from American Airlines for 150 planes valued at $7 billion. The company had taken orders for 203 MD-80 jets and 43 MD-11 long-range trijets in 1988. This compared with 138 orders for commercial aircraft in 1987.

McDonnell Douglas held 23 percent of the commercial aircraft market with revenues of $4.9 billion and earnings of just $127 million in 1988. This low return (2.6 percent), according to McDonnell Douglas sources, is a function of high production costs, inability to meet some deliveries, or missed performance schedules.

The company restructured the Douglas aircraft division in 1989. A management team dedicated to bringing about fundamental changes and improvements in the production process was put in place. Newly elected president of McDonnell Douglas, Robert H. Hood, said, "Growth is always hard to deal with if you don't have the proper systems in place. You can't just throw people at a problem." The company planned to

deliver 135 commercial aircraft in 1989. Although it had no plans to boost production, an unplanned increase could result from a new quality management structure.

McDonnell Douglas, in its MD-80, a derivative of the DC-9, has developed a counterpart to the Boeing 737–300 and Airbus A320 in the 150-seat market. McDonnell Douglas's strategy assumes that new, high-technology aircraft cannot compete successfully with derivative re-engined aircraft that match the efficiency levels of newly developed equipment. The reengined aircraft has a lower purchase price, less technical risk, and is available currently.

McDonnell Douglas designed its MD-11 series for the 270- to 400-seat market. By early 1989 the firm had orders and options totaling 250 for the mini-jumbo jets. In September 1988 Delta picked the MD-11 over Boeing and Airbus planes for its expansion of its Pacific routes. American placed a large order in early 1989 for MD-11s and, like Delta, will use them to expand its Asian network.

The MD-11 may be stretched to add 70 seats. Another possible configuration would include a lower lobe "panorama deck" and seat close to 600. A new wing has been discussed to regain the range that would be lost because of the proposed changes.

McDonnell Douglas has made a commitment to its role in the commercial aircraft industry with the MD-80 series. The MD-83 (Super 83), a derivative of the original design, has a 2,500-mile range and features high-technology engines and a seating capacity of 169 in an all-economy configuration. McDonnell Douglas has boasted that this plane has a lower cost per seat than either Boeing or Airbus planes. This family of aircraft, according to McDonnell Douglas, comes within 10 percent of the operating costs of the newly developed aircraft.

The MD-80 series spearheaded a long-awaited McDonnell Douglas turnaround. MD-80 sales have been made to foreign carriers such as Scandinavian Airlines and China Air, and orders and options from various sources totalled 885 by early 1989; 568 MD-80 series planes had been delivered.

The strength of the commitment McDonnell Douglas has made to the MD-80 series has been expressed in the creative financing packages offered to commercial airline carriers. For example, the company leased 20 MD-80s to American Airlines and picks up the major maintenance and training costs associated with the sales. Similar arrangements were made with TWA and Texas Air.

McDonnell Douglas's family of planes is presented in Table 2.

Boeing

Boeing is the world's largest aircraft producer, operating primarily in two industries: transportation equipment and related services and missiles and space. Through 1988 the company had manufactured almost 58 percent of all jet airliners ever made outside the Soviet Union. Its market share is projected at 58 percent of the commercial market. America's largest exporter, Boeing holds close to 75 percent of the North American medium- to long-range market. However, its overall market share declined from a high of 63 percent to as low as 51 percent in 1987.

Orders in 1987 were for 461 aircraft valued at $20 billion. In its best year ever, Boeing booked orders for 636 commercial aircraft valued at $30 billion in 1988. Its market share also jumped from a low of 51 percent to 56 percent. The firm was at a record production rate of 32 planes a month. Its backlog of jets exceeded 1,000.

Technology is a major factor for continued success of Boeing's derivative models and for newly developed aircraft. At one time some industry watchers believed that Europe lagged behind the United States in technological innovation. This gap, if it ever existed, has been closed by Airbus.

In addition, the $2 to $3 billion estimated by Boeing for introducing a new aircraft only scratches the surface of total costs. Nonrecurring cost of investment and an expansion of existing plant capacity, needed to implement programs, machinery, labor, and so on, could inflate costs far beyond initial investment projections. Therefore, Boeing feels it must be sure about the size and duration of the market before it embarks on a new aircraft development program. Potential major carriers have given conflicting signals about the characteristics of this new market or the potential size of the market.

Before 1967, Boeing had identified a market for a 200-seat airplane that had the capacity of flying 800 miles or more and for longer than two hours. The project team assigned to this potential aircraft was initially dubbed "the 747 project." Then the 150-seat market was identified and Boeing assigned project team 7N7 to design the aircraft. Now the 100-seat market is hot and so is the over-170 market.

Boeing worked closely with the major airlines in "feeling out" a product it could produce to satisfy a majority of the demand requirements such as number of aisles and body size. However, Boeing was unable to obtain a consistent description of the demand characteristics for this new dynamic market. This is one possible reason that Boeing has used its derivative models rather than developing entirely new planes.

Boeing is committed to satisfying the variety of tastes and needs of commercial aircraft buyers. Table 3 lists the models that the commercial airplane division is actively developing. It does not include all the models that the company is contemplating.

The 737–400 is Boeing's major competitive entry in the Airbus A320 150-seat market. The plane contains such features as longer fuselage, improved stability, increased tail and wing spans, new fuel efficient engines, reinforced wings, advanced tires and brakes, improved aerodynamics and avionics. Its 737–500 will compete in the 100-seat market, while its 757 competes in the 170–220 market and 767 and 747 variations compete in the wide-body marketplace.

Table 2 McDonnell Douglas Family of Planes

Model designation	Popular Name or Subtype Designation	Flight Crew	Passengers	Cargo Capacity, lb.	Wingspan, ft.	Wing Area, sq. ft.	Maximum Length, ft.
DC-8	Series 30[a]	3	116-176	20,850	142.3	2,758	150.5
DC-8	Series 40[a]	3	117	20,850	142.3	2,758	150.5
DC-8	Series 50[a]	3	116-189	20,850	142.3	2,884	150.5
DC-8	Super 61[a]	3	259	66,665	142.3	2,884	187.4
DC-8	Super 62[a]	3	189	42,580	148.4	2,927	157.4
DC-8	Super 63[a]	3	259	66,665	148.4	2,927	187.4
DC-9	Series 10[a]	2	85	9,000	89.4	934	104.4
DC-9	Series 20[a]	2	85	9,000	93.3	1,001	104.4
DC-9	Series 30[a]	2	110	13,425	93.3	1,001	119.3
DC-9	Series 40[a]	2	120	15,285	93.3	1,001	125.6
DC-9	Series 50[a]	2	135	15,510	93.3	1,001	133.5
MD-81	—	2	155	18,795	107.8	1,209	147.9
MD-82	—	2	155	18,795	107.8	1,209	147.9
MD-83	—	2	155	15,195	107.8	1,209	147.9
MD-87	—	2	130	14,195	107.8	1,209	130.4
MD-88	—	2	155	—	107.8	1,270	147.9
DC-10	Series 10	3	250-380	4,618[b]	155.5	3,550	182.3
DC-10	Series 15	3	250-380	4,618[b]	155.3	3,550	180.6
DC-10	Series 30	3	250-380	4,618[b]	165.3	3,647	181.6
DC-10	Series 40	3	250-380	4,618[b]	165.3	3,647	180.6
MD-11	—	2	321-405	5,630[b]	169.3	3,618	200.8
MD-11ER	—	2	277	4,670[b]	169.5	3,648	182.3

[a]Production terminated.
[b]Cubic feet of cargo space.
[c]P&W = Pratt & Whitney; R-R = Rolls Royce; GE = General Electric.
Source: "Leading International Aircraft, Spacecraft, Weapons," *Aviation Week & Space Technology,* March 20, 1989, 150.

In facing the competition from Airbus, Boeing has also been creative in new areas of financing, that is, leasing, trade-ins, price cutting, discounts, offering free training and support services, and taking competitors' planes as trade-ins. The tax incentives created by leveraged leases now help Boeing finance foreign aircraft sales at rates several points below those offered by commercial banks. When loan levels for the Export-Import Bank were cut in 1983, these deals became even more popular. In 1983 Boeing delivered twelve 747s to foreign airlines through leveraged lease financing. The total value of this deal was about $1 billion.

Congress has proposed cutting the 10 percent investment tax credit and five-year accel-

Table 2 *(continued)*

Maximum Height, ft.	Empty Weight, lb.	Typical Gross Weight, lb.	Max. Landing Weight, lb.	Powerplant: Number Make, and Model^c	Maximum Speed, mph.	Best Cruise Speed, Mach or mph.
43.3	26,525	315,000	207,000	4 P&W JT4A-9, -11	600	544
43.3	24,369	315,000	207,000	4 R-R R, Co. 12	600	544
43.3	34,854	325,000	207,000	4 P&W JR3D-3B	600	544
43.0	48,897	328,000	240,000	4 P&W JT3D-3B	600	580
43.3	41,903	350,000	240,000	4 P&W JT3D-7	600	586
42.3	53,749	355,000	258,000	4 P&W JT3D-7	600	583
27.5	51,000	90,700	81,700	2 P&W JT8D-1 or 7	576	.76-.80
27.5	56,000	98,000	95,300	2 P&W JT8D-9 or 11	576	.76-.80
27.5	59,000	108,000	98,100	2 P&W JT8D-9	586	.76-.80
27.5	62,500	114,000	102,000	2 P&W JT8D-11 or 15	586	.76-.80
27.5	65,150	121,000	110,000	2 P&W JT8D-15 or 17	586	.76-.80
29.6	78,421	140,000	128,000	2 P&W JT8D-209 or 217A	576	.76-.80
29.6	78,549	149,500	130,000	2 P&W JT8D-217A	576	.76-.80
29.6	80,503	160,000	139,500	2 P&W JT8D-219	576	.76-.80
30.5	73,157	140,000	128,000	2 P&W JT8D-217C	576	.76-.80
29.6	78,000	149,500	130,000	2 P&W JT8D-217C	576	.76-.80
58.1	243,000	440,000	363,500	3 GE CF6-6D	593	0.82
58.1	248,500	455,000	363,500	3 GE CF6-50C2F	593	0.82
58.1	267,200	572,000	403,000	3 GE CF6-50C2	593	0.82
58.1	271,000	572,000	403,000	3 P&W JT9D-59A	593	0.82
57.8	277,300	602,500	430,000	3 P&W PW4360 or 3GE CF6-80C2-DF1	588	0.82
57.8	264,500	602,500	410,000	3 P&W PW4360 or 3 GE CF6-80C2-DF1	588	0.82

erated depreciation on equipment leased to foreign users. This, Boeing fears, will present a threat to sales of its commercial aircraft and initiate large decreases in cash flows.

Financing arrangements for aircraft purchasers are a key part of the competition for the non-U.S. market. If the Export-Import Bank budget is reduced sharply, Boeing fears it will have to fund more financing incentives to attract foreign buyers. This represents a major portion of company sales.

Finally, through creative efforts to sell additional aircraft, Boeing has become an industry giant in the free world. Boeing frequently takes trade-ins of used aircraft toward the purchase of new ones.

Outlook for the Future

No one can tell what sort of aircraft most passengers will choose over the next few decades: quieter aircraft, slower aircraft with sleeping

Table 3 Boeing Family of Planes

Model Designation	Popular Name or Subtype Designation	Flight Crew	Passengers	Cargo Capacity, lb.	Wingspan, ft.	Wing Area, sq. ft.	Maximum Length, ft.
707-320B[a]	Intercontinental	3	165	1,700[2]	145.8	2,892	152.9
707-320C[a]	Intercontinental	3	165	1,700[2]	145.8	2,892	152.9
727-100[a]	—	3	94	900[2]	108.0	1,560	133.2
727-200[a]	Advanced	3	145	1,525[2]	108.0	1,560	153.2
737-100	—	2	103	650[2]	93.0	980	94.0
737-200	Advanced	2	120	875[2]	93.0	980	100.2
737-200	Advanced[b]	2	120	640[2]	93.0	980	100.2
737-300	—	2	141	1,068[2]	94.8	980	109.6
737-300	—	2	141	1,068[2]	94.8	980	109.6
737-300	—	2	141	853[2]	94.8	980	109.6
737-400	—	2	159	1,375	94.8	980	119.6
737-400	—	2	159	1,160	94.8	980	119.6
747-100B	Superjet	3	452	6,190[2]	195.7	5,500	231.9
747SR	Superjet	3	550	6,190[2]	195.7	5,500	231.9
747-200B	Superjet	3	366-452	6,190[2]	195.7	5,500	231.9
747-300B	Stretched upper deck	3	400-490	6,190[2]	195.7	5,500	231.9
747-200C	Convertible	3	366-452	5,990[2]	195.7	5,500	231.9
747SP	Superjet	3	276-343	3,860[2]	195.7	5,500	184.7
747-400	Advanced Superjet	2	412-509	6,030[2]	211.0	5,650	231.9
757-200	—	2	186-220	1,790[2]	124.8	1,951	155.3
767-200	—	2	174-290	3,070[2]	156.1	3,050	159.2
767-200ER	—	2	174-290	3,070[2]	156.1	3,050	159.2
767-300	—	2	204-290	4,030[2]	156.1	3,050	180.3
767-300ER	—	2	204-290	4,030	156.1	3,050	180.3

[a]Production terminated.
[b]High gross weight structure.
[c]P&W = Pratt & Whitney; R-R = Rolls Royce; GE = General Electric; CFM = CFM International S.A.
[d]GE, R-R engines optional.
Source: "Leading International Aircraft, Spacecraft, Weapons," *Aviation Week & Space Technology,* March 20, 1989, 150.

berths, aircraft with greater operational flexibility, or "economy" aircraft. This uncertainty adds to that already facing commercial airframe manufacturers in today's volatile aircraft market.

A major question in the manufacturers' battle to fill the marketplace remains: Can the market support three competitors? All three aircraft manufacturers are utilizing their fullest resources and talent to gain that elusive edge needed to win customers and market share. However, one

Table 3 *(continued)*

Maximum Height, ft.	Empty Weight, lb.	Typical Gross Weight, lb.	Max. Landing Weight, lb.	Powerplant: Number, Make, and Model[c]	Maximum Speed, mph.	Best Cruise Speed, Mach or mph.
42.4	138,518	336,000	247,000	4 P&W JT3D-7	600	.8-.83
42.4	146,400	336,000	247,000	4 P&W JT3D-7	600	.8-.83
34.0	87,600	170,000	142,500	3 P&W JT8D-1, 7 or 9	600+	.8-.84
34.0	98,300	191,500	154,500	3 P&W JT8D-15A	600+	.8-.84
37.0	62,000	111,000	101,000	2 P&W JT8D-7 or 9	586	.73-.78
37.0	60,660	116,000	103,000	2 P&W JT8D-15A	586	.73-.78
37.0	62,445	128,600	107,000	2 P&W JT8D-17A	586	.73-.78
36.5	69,730	125,000	114,000	2 CFM 56-3-B1	566	.745
36.5	69,730	135,500	114,000	2 CFM 56-3-B1	566	.745
36.5	70,780	139,000	114,000	2 CFM 56-3-B2	566	.745
36.5	73,170	139,000	121,000	2 CFM 56-3-B2	566	.745
36.5	74,170	150,500	124,000	2 CFM 56-3C	566	.745
63.2	373,300	750,000	564,000	4 GE CF6-45A2[d]	640	M.84
63.2	356,400	600,000	525,000	4 GE CF6-45A2[d]	640	M.84
63.5	374,100	833,000	564,000	4 P&W JT9D-7R4G2[d]	640	M.84
63.5	380,000	833,000	574,000	4 P&W JT9D-7R4G2[d]	640	M.85
63.5	386,500	833,000	630,000	4 P&W JT9D	640	M.84
65.4	333,300	700,000	475,000	4 RR RB.211-524D4	640	M.85
63.5	390,200	870,000	630,000	4 GE CF6-80C2[d]	630	M.85
44.5	125,940	240,000	198,000	2 RR RB 211-535E or 2 P&W PW2037	593	M.8
52	176,100	315,000	272,000	2 P&W JT9D-7R4 or GE CF6-80A	594	M.8
52	179,900	351,000	278,000	2 P&W JT9D-7R4 or GE CF6-80A	594	M.8
52	190,200	351,000	300,000	2 P&W JT9D-7R4 or GE CF6-80A	594	M.8
52	196,100	400,000	320,000	2 P&W 4000 or GE CF6-80C2	594	M.8

factor may be overlooked. Ultimately, the winners of this race will be the commercial airlines and the consuming public. The advent of U.S. deregulation of this industry has allowed free market principles to work. The results are evident in lower fares and better service.

The same can be said of the fierce competition between the airframe manufacturers. For some time, Boeing has been the principal supplier and leader in producing commercial aircraft. This fact alone worried many commercial carriers, especially foreign airlines, who were apprehensive of being dependent on American-made aircraft. This fact, not entirely by itself but with a host of other factors, presents a distinct advantage to Airbus.

Any commercial airline CEO would agree that the most important factors needed for the business are high load factors and at least two competing aircraft suppliers. As in all free market competition, concessions relating to cost, financing, and special incentives are more readily obtained from the suppliers where there is competition. For example, since the 747 has no real competition, Boeing is less likely to offer creative pricing or special financing arrangements. Conversely, the 767 and A310, two relatively similar aircraft, are more vigorously marketed. Often manufacturers make concessions that may not be economically sound. Boeing's sale of 767s to TWA or Airbus's lease of A300s to Pan Am are two good examples. In both cases, these aircraft giants probably incurred losses to make the deal. Boeing provided TWA a guarantee that its 767 would meet specific fuel-burn requirements, probably with the knowledge that its quoted figures were beyond the capability of the aircraft. Airbus, at least in the assessment of industry analysts, leased A300s to Pan Am below cost.

The question of what the Boeing corporation will do remains. The age distribution of the commercial carriers' short- and medium-haul fleets supports Airbus Industrie's belief that the A320 is the right plane for the right time. According to Interavia, by 1988 110 Boeing 727s would be 20 or more years old, 200 will be between 15 to 19 years old, while over 420 will be 10 to 14 years old. The youngest 727 will be at least 16 years old by the year 2000. Airbus's strategy is not just to fill the replacement market for the 727 but to offer A320 to replace more than 1,500 DC-9 and 737–200 aircraft that will also be obsolete by the 21st century.

The battle for this market and the others not only exists in the manufacturing end of the industry but is related to the commercial airlines, engine manufacturers, and all the industry's support services. A loser or winner in one area will cause ripple effects in related areas, resulting in other winners and losers. The race is more costly than it seems at first glance, because American and European jobs, as well as the survival of many companies, are at risk. Many companies are betting their future on commercial aviation.

Case 2

Boeing's Commercial Jet Aircraft Business

The Current Marketplace

Maker of half the airliners produced since the jet age began, Boeing is flying high. The year 1988 was the best ever for its commercial airplane division. The company sold close to $30 billion worth of jetliners. This amounted to a staggering 636 jets, up from the 1978 record of 461 planes and the 1987 record of orders valued at $19.9 billion. A breakdown of company performance for five years is given in Table 1.

Much of Boeing's recent success is attributable to chairman Frank Shrontz (profiled in Exhibit 1). Serving under him, Dean Thornton is president of the commercial airplane division. Nine other key executives in the division and the positions they hold are shown in Exhibit 2, the organization chart for commercial airplanes.

To stay on top in an industry that exists at the boundary of technology, massive amounts of money are needed to develop aircraft. Dean Thornton has pointed out, "Hell, if we wanted to maximize earnings, we'd just cancel research."[1] No research would mean no new products or refinements to existing ones. This formula for short-term gain would lead to sure demise over time.

The Family of Planes

Boeing's dominance in the commercial aircraft industry was achieved through the strategy of

This case represents neither effective nor ineffective handling of an administrative situation. Rather, it is to be used as a basis for classroom discussion.

[1]"The Higher the Flight, the Farther the Fall," *The Economist,* May 3, 1986, 23.

offering a family of planes. Boeing airliners range from the narrow-body 737 and 757 series to the wide-body 767 and 747. Within each of these plane types, numerous configurations are available.

In 1987, the 737 surpassed the 727 as the most successful jet plane of all time with more than 1,800 units sold. Within the 737 series there are five configurations, four of which were being produced in 1988, when the 737–200 was phased out. Its replacement is the 737–500. This plane, which seats 100, has advanced avionics and all the sophistication of the larger 737–300 and 737–400. The 737 series enables operators to meet market requirements ranging from 100 passengers to nearly 170 on planes with a high degree of commonality. Flight crews can be cross-qualified on all versions. Airlines benefit from increased flexibility, reduction of inventory, and better usage of manpower.

Boeing's 757, its most fuel-efficient airplane, seats 180 to 220 passengers. This large, highly efficient plane fits well into the hub-and-spoke systems of numerous airlines. It gained renewed interest in 1988. In its first ten years, only 239 planes were sold. In 1988 Boeing took orders for 161 of the 757s. The plane is most effective on highly traveled congested routes that don't warrant a wide-body version but need 170-plus seating. A new all-cargo version is suitable for air delivery service because it can operate at night from the most noise-sensitive airports.

After what British Airways described as "a most careful study," the airline picked the wide-body 767–300 over the Airbus 300. The extended-range 767ER has been ordered by

Table 1 Five Year Summary (Dollars in millions except per share data)
(Per share data restated for 1985 three-for-two stock split)

	1988	1987	1986	1985	1984
Operations					
Sales (including other operating revenues)*					
Commercial	$ 12,170	$ 10,623	$ 11,060	$ 9,002	$ 6,114
U.S. Government	4,792	4,882	5,384	4,743	4,328
Total	16,962	15,505	16,444	13,745	10,442
Net earnings	614	480	665	566	390**
Per primary share	4.02	3.10	4.28	3.75	2.67**
Percent of sales*	3.6%	3.1%	4.0%	4.1%	3.7%
Cash dividends paid	$ 237	$ 217	$ 186	$ 157	$ 136
Per share	1.55	1.40	1.20	1.04	.93
Other income, principally interest*	378	308	304	184	153
Research and development expensed	751	824	757	409	506
General and administrative expensed	880	793	606	477	420
Additions to plant and equipment	690	738	795	551	337
Depreciation of plant and equipment	541	486	433	356	337
Salaries and wages	5,404	5,028	4,374	3,442	3,011
Average employment	147,300	136,100	118,500	98,700	86,600
Financial position at December 31					
Total assets	$ 12,608	$ 12,566	$ 10,910	$ 9,153	$ 8,423
Working capital	1,856	2,246*	2,819	2,349	2,130
Long-term customer financing	1,039	392	195	514	541
Cash and short-term investments	3,963	3,435	4,172	3,209	1,595
Total borrowings	258	270	277	34	299
Long-term debt	251	256	263	16	284
Long-term deferred taxes	205	189*	219	326	322
Stockholders' equity	5,404	4,987	4,826	4,364	3,695
Per share	35.27	32.75	31.12	28.12	25.34
Common shares outstanding (000's)	153,233	152,273	155,095	155,189	145,837
Firm backlog					
Commercial	$ 46,676	$ 26,963	$ 20,084	$ 18,637	$ 15,949
U.S. Government	6,925	6,241	6,304	6,087	5,562
Total	$ 53,601	$ 33,204	$ 26,388	$ 24,724	$ 21,511

*Restated to conform to 1988 presentation.
**Exclusive of cumulative DISC adjustment to federal income tax provision. Net earnings after cumulative DISC adjustment were $787 or $5.39 per share.
Cash dividends have been paid on common stock every year since 1942.

Table 1   *(continued)*

Year ended December 31,	1988	1987	1986
Revenues			
Commercial transportation products and services	$11,369	$ 9,827	$ 9,820
Military transportation products and related systems	3,668	3,979	4,882
Missiles and space	1,457	1,063	1,126
Other industries	468	636	616
Operating revenues	16,962	15,505	16,444
Corporate income	378	308	304
Total revenues	$17,340	$15,813	$16,748
*Operating Profit**			
Commercial transportation products and services	$ 585	$ 352	$ 411
Military transportation products and related systems	(95)	60	367
Missiles and space	124	119	55
Other industries	(28)	(34)	(9)
Operating profit	586	497	824
Corporate income	378	308	304
Corporate expense	(144)	(147)	(100)
Earnings before taxes	$ 820	$ 658	$ 1,028
Identifiable assets at December 31			
Commercial transportation products and services	$ 4,558	$ 5,170	$ 3,533
Military transportation products and related systems	2,923	2,846	2,285
Missiles and space	684	548	434
Other industries	319	362	364
	8,484	8,926	6,616
Corporate	4,124	3,640	4,294
Consolidated assets	$12,608	$12,566	$10,910
Depreciation			
Commercial transportation products and services	$ 243	$ 218	$ 200
Military transportation products and related systems	188	170	136
Missiles and space	52	42	34
Capital expenditures, net			
Commercial transportation products and services	$ 326	$ 286	$ 332
Military transportation products and related systems	241	316	356
Missiles and space	62	72	82

*The implementation of SFAS No. 87 (see Notes 1 and 9) increased 1987 operating profit by $33 for commercial transportation products and services, $24 for military transportation products and related systems, $4 for missiles and space and $4 for other industries.

Exhibit 1   Profile of Frank Shrontz

You'd think Boeing chairman Frank A. Shrontz would be on easy street. A $54 billion order backlog will keep Boeing plants humming into the mid-1990s and send its earnings up. Yet the giant planemaker suffers from an embarrassment of riches. Customers are fuming over production delays on the new 747–400 jets they've ordered. And in the clamor over air safety, Boeing Company has come under intense scrutiny from regulators and the traveling public. Shrontz' biggest challenge is ensuring that the No. 1 planemaker keeps its reputation for quality and safety.

The pressures on the composed and urbane Shrontz, 57, come just as earnings are taking off. Thanks to a five-year buying binge by airlines, the Seattle company's profits are expected to jump 50 percent this year [1989] to $918 million, on a 29 percent gain in revenue, to $22 billion. Profits next year should rise 25 percent, and revenues 7 percent. "We have plenty of business," says Shrontz, a 30-year Boeing veteran. "Our big job is to execute."

Shrontz will have his hands full getting 747 production back on schedule. Because the company is overcommitted, it's running several months behind in delivering the jumbo jets—Boeing's first missed deliveries in 20 years. The company's top brass is busy negotiating concessions with irate airlines.

Employees are none too happy, either. Boeing has increased its work force 83 percent in the past five years, to 155,000, but it's still so short of manpower that it took the unusual step in early March of "borrowing" 760 Lockheed Corporation workers for its 747 production line. When labor negotiations start this fall, Boeing's unions will grouse most about excessive overtime.

As production pressures increase, Shrontz will have to be more vigilant about safety and quality. Boeing's image has slipped because of miswirings and plumbing problems on 59 of its jets and several crashes involving its planes. Although investigators may exonerate Boeing, the Federal Aviation Administration has stepped up its oversight of production and quality control.

Shrontz' problems on the military side are more commonplace: Business is just too slow. And while the former Assistant Defense Secretary would love to restore profitability to Boeing's military transport business, which last year [1988] lost an estimated $60 million, shrinking defense budgets may block his way. Defense and space will probably drop to 22 percent of Boeing's sales by 1991, from 29 percent last year. In the face of numbers like that, Boeing's backlog doesn't look so bad after all.

Source: Maria Shao, "Frank Shrontz," 129. Reprinted from April 14, 1989 Top 1000 Special Bonus Issue of *Business Week* by special permission, copyright © 1989 by McGraw-Hill, Inc.

American, Canadian Airlines, SAS, and LTU. The 767ER has a range of almost 6,000 miles and can carry up to 290 passengers.

The 747 is the mainstay of the free world's international airlines and Boeing's cash cow at over $110 million per plane. It enjoyed outstanding years in 1987 and 1988. Sales of this plane alone accounted for over $17 billion. In 1988 Boeing rolled out its new 747–400, with a range of 8,000 miles and passenger capacity of 400 to 600. However, production problems slowed the delivery of this advanced jetliner. Boeing officials conceded that earlier delivery positions played a role in the American Airlines $7.4 billion order for MD-11s and MD-80s.

Many people still remember the expense involved in developing this successful plane. In the years 1969 through 1971, development of this plane and the cancellation of the SST supersonic

transport almost bankrupted Boeing. "It's like living on the damn San Andreas fault all the time. The fact that it hasn't moved for ten years doesn't mean a thing," observed Boeing's economist Tom Craig. In a drastic retrenchment the airline cut its work force by over 60,000 workers.

Marketing Strategy

Boeing works closely with its customers in planning new or derivative product offerings. As with any product line, but especially for one that requires the tremendous resources required to produce an airliner, it is imperative that new products meet the needs of customers. Domestically, Delta and American have been the primary sources of market information. United more recently has also been a prime source of information. Among European airlines, SAS, British

Exhibit 2 Organization Chart for Boeing Commercial Airplane Division

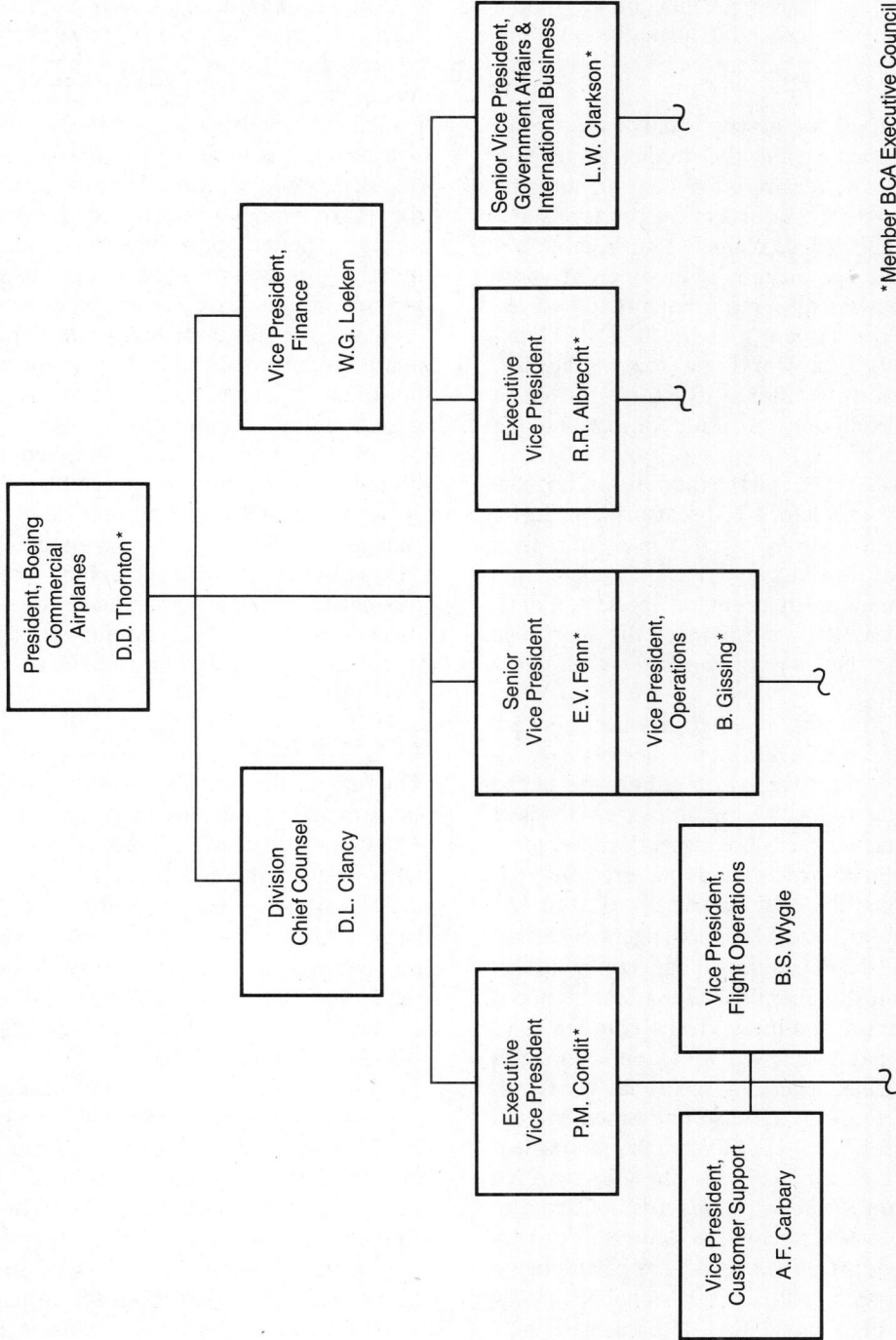

President, Boeing Commercial Airplanes

D.D. Thornton*

Division Chief Counsel

D.L. Clancy

Vice President, Finance

W.G. Loeken

Executive Vice President

P.M. Condit*

Vice President, Flight Operations

B.S. Wygle

Vice President, Customer Support

A.F. Carbary

Senior Vice President

E.V. Fenn*

Vice President, Operations

B. Gissing*

Executive Vice President

R.R. Albrecht*

Senior Vice President, Government Affairs & International Business

L.W. Clarkson*

---

*Member BCA Executive Council

Source: The Boeing Company

Airways, and Lufthansa provide input. In the Orient, Japan Airlines and to a small extent Singapore Airlines are the sources of primary market information.

Boeing gives the market what it wants, not what its engineers think the market wants. European state-owned aircraft makers in the past have tailored their products to the needs of state-owned airlines. These planes often became unsuitable for other airlines with different route networks or passenger requirements. Good examples are the Trident and the BAC 1–11 designed to fulfill the workhorse role of the 727. These planes were tailored to British European Airlines and sold only 351 units compared to the 727's 1,832.

Almost a decade ago the input from the market indicated a need for a 150-seat airplane. Delta had expressed a strong interest in a short-haul airplane that would carry 150 passengers between its many destinations on the East Coast. Delta also was the champion of the twin-aisle configuration that is now standard on all wide-body aircraft.

Market information emerged that indicated that two or more niches could be served with new products that resided on either side of the 150-passenger mark. For example, in its fleet planning meetings with Boeing, SAS presented a plan for a fleet of airplanes having three different configurations: 75 to 95 passengers, 120 to 140 passengers, and 160 to 180 passengers. SAS also indicated a desire to fill those configuration needs with only two airplane types. Similar needs have been expressed by domestic companies as well. Delta has purchased McDonnell Douglas MD-88 (142-passenger) aircraft to fill their 150-seat need. American has also purchased MD-80 series planes, Fokker 100s for the 95- to 100-seat market, and Boeing 757s for the 170- to 220-passenger configuration. It appears the demand for a new 150-seat plane, widely believed by some at the start of the decade to be the plane of choice to replace the 727, has changed. Boeing does have the 146-passenger 737–

400 to compete head to head with the Airbus A320. It has the same engines as the A320 and has technically equivalent avionics. A foreshortened version of the 737, the 737–500, became available in the summer of 1989. This 737-lite will compete in the 100-seat market.

Boeing is positioned to compete in all segments of today's marketplace. In the "Boeing first and better" days, Boeing airplanes commanded a premium price because there was no genuine competition for its products. Also, in exchange for substantial input to the final configuration of the airplane, airlines would prepay up to 25 percent of their committed purchases, which helped finance development of new planes. However, Airbus has taken a market-driven position in the marketplace. Through government subsidizing of interest rates and exchange rate fluctuations, it competes on price. The selling of aircraft now revolves around lease buy-backs, recession insurance, trading in of used planes, and other deal making or breaking issues that fall squarely on financial concerns.

The Future

The market for aircraft is difficult to define, because conflicting signals are given by the airlines. The threat is that the characteristics and the potential size of the new market are not very well defined. What is known is that 8,000 jets may be purchased between 1989 and 2004. Of these the majority, or close to 70 percent, will handle the explosive growth experience worldwide in air travel. The rest will replace the aging fleet of the world.

Boeing is facing a volatile aircraft market requiring huge investments. Even when a product is established, airlines tend to order little by little, so Boeing is unable to make any long-term plans for a large number of planes. The company cannot take advantage of either learning curves or economies of scale. Large orders are more frequent with the military, but the military sector is a function of the Administration in power.

Moreover, military budgets are the first targets for cuts and searches for abuse.

A possible threat is the flying public's loss of confidence in a Boeing product. A series of incidents that have involved older planes could incite the consumer to avoid airlines using Boeing planes, similar to the experience of the airlines flying the DC-10.

The greatest potential competition in the next century could come from Japan. The Japanese would like to erase a multibillion-dollar deficit in aerospace trade and become a front runner in this technology. One way for the Japanese to achieve this goal is to acquire technology and thus enter the airline market through cooperation with foreign firms.

Cooperation is a fashionable management technique in the aerospace industry. International cooperation, however, is difficult and nearly always more expensive. Political motives also play an important role, because partners may look for different benefits. Some examples of cooperation are the tactical fighter produced by Brazil and Italy; a commuter plane produced by the United States and Sweden; Concorde, produced by France and Great Britain; and a commuter series produced by Indonesia and Spain. Numerous joint productions between France and Germany also helped the German aerospace industry to develop after World War II. McDonnell Douglas had been planning to license its MD-80 to China for production, but the negotiations took place prior to the 1989 violence.

The Japanese are willing to push the cooperation between Japan and Boeing. Boeing was willing to share in the costs and the risk of developing a new 150-seat aircraft called the 7J7 with Japan Aircraft Development Corporation. This company is composed of Mitsubishi Heavy Industries (manufacturer of the Zero during World War II), Kawasaki Heavy Industries, and Fuji Heavy Industries. All of these companies are presently engaged in home designs or in license production. They have facilities and money, but each needs technology and expertise.

For the 150-seat aircraft, the Japanese company was willing to provide 25 percent of the development costs in exchange for more management, technical, and marketing responsibilities. The Japanese wanted the plane to be ready by 1989 to compete with the A320, which was introduced in 1988.

In February 1985, however, Boeing postponed the development of the 150-seat aircraft. Boeing's position was that the agreement made in March 1984 was not a joint venture but simply an agreement to study the possibilities of a new plane. The studies would have considered the 150-seat aircraft and a 100-seat aircraft.

Boeing's 747–400 program, as mentioned earlier, is behind schedule with only one of three engine combinations certified and only one aircraft delivered. The company will be at a record 34 planes per month by 1992. According to executive vice president Philip Condit, "Whatever we do, we do it carefully and logically—we won't try to do it all at the same time. At these high rates, we must stay in control, or we won't be able to meet our commitment."[2] Industry experts have indicated that investments in technology that have been unbalanced toward engineering will be applied more to manufacturing. The industry is in a phase in which there are no radical new technology breakthroughs. Condit believes that the primary attributes airlines are seeking are operating economies across the board and reasonable first cost.

The commercial airplane division's president has summed up his feelings about Boeing: "This is a hell of a company and it's got a hell of a group of people. We fight and we make love and it's fun to work here. You look at a company making toothpaste, or a new kind of bread. . . . We've got something to be proud of."[3]

---

[2]Richard G. O'Lone, "Commercial Airframe Makers Take Conservative Approach," *Aviation Week and Space Technology,* March 20, 1989, 198.

[3]"The Higher the Flight, the Farther the Fall," *The Economist,* May 3, 1986, 26.

Case 3

The Kellogg Company and the Ready-to-Eat Cereal Industry

You take care of the outside.
We'll help take care of the inside.
    1985 ad for Kellogg's All Bran

Advertising campaigns for Kellogg products in the 1980s stress the healthy, nutritious quality of cereal flakes—corn, bran, wheat, oats—a Kellogg theme that began almost a century ago. Dr. John H. Kellogg and W. K. Kellogg sought to develop a cereal that could replace meat in the diets of the patients at the Battle Creek sanitarium that the Kelloggs managed. The product of their efforts, Corn Flakes, became popular enough with the patients that the Kelloggs formed two companies that became the Kellogg Company in 1899.

Eighty-six years later Kellogg is one of the largest food companies in the world, with annual sales exceeding $2.5 billion and earnings greater than $250 million. Kellogg has established a position in the ready-to-eat (RTE) cereal market almost twice as large as either of the two nearest competitors, General Mills and General Foods. "Kellogg knows the cereal business better than anyone else" said William Wason of Brown Brothers Harriman & Co., "and the management has had the wisdom to stick with what they know." In December 1985, Kellogg was named one of the five best managed companies in the

United States by *Dun's Business Month* (Dec. 1985). Kellogg won this acclaim because of its performance throughout the 1970s and early 1980s, the darkest time in the industry's history, and the progress Kellogg made in recovering during 1984 and 1985.

The Ready-to-Eat Cereal Industry

The RTE cereal industry is composed of firms that are engaged in the manufacture and sale of prepackaged, processed foodstuffs made primarily of grain products. The user does not have to prepare the product prior to use, and it can be eaten in dry form or with the addition of other substances, such as milk and sugar. Advantages of the product from a consumer perspective include convenience of use and easy satisfaction of nutritional requirements. Consumption of the products takes place primarily at breakfast, but they are also used as between-meal snacks. The first products in the market were introduced by W. K. Kellogg, Wheat Flakes in 1894 and Corn Flakes in 1898.

The $4 billion RTE cereal industry is composed of several large companies that dominate the market. Led by Kellogg, the industry includes General Mills, General Foods, Quaker Oats, Ralston Purina, and Nabisco. Table 1 lists the market share performance of the major competitors as of 1984.

The significance of cereals within the product lines of the competitors changes as a result of competition and developments within the companies themselves. Although cereals represent more than 75% of Kellogg sales, cereals are

This case was prepared by Joseph A. Schenk, Dan S. Prickett, and Stanley J. Stough. © Joseph A. Schenk, 1986. Reprinted with permission. Address reprint requests to: Joseph A. Schenk, Management Department, University of Dayton, 300 College Park, Dayton, OH 45469–0001.

Table 1. The Ready-to-Eat Cereal Industry: Market Share Data[a]

Company	1976	1977	1978	1979	1980	1981	1982	1983	1984
Kellogg	42.6	42.5	42.0	41.5	40.9	39.3	38.5	38.5	40.3
General Mills	20.8	20.5	20.4	22.2	22.4	23.0	23.1	23.2	23.1
General Foods	15.7	16.8	16.0	15.4	15.0	15.0	16.0	16.1	13.3
Quaker Oats	8.9	8.9	8.7	8.6	8.6	8.6	8.9	8.9	8.6
Ralston Purina	4.9	3.4	5.7	5.6	6.2	6.1	5.6	6.1	6.3
Nabisco	4.0	4.2	4.2	4.1	3.8	3.9	3.8	3.8	4.2
All others	3.1	3.7	3.0	2.6	3.1	4.1	4.1	3.4	4.2

Source: Advertising Age: Aug. 5, 1985, p. 42; Jun. 14, 1982, p. 62; May 25, 1981, p. 62; Aug. 28, 1978, p. 217.
[a]All figures are percentages.

estimated to constitute no more than 13% of General Foods sales and 7% of General Mills sales. Kellogg sales and estimated operating profits by division are listed in Table 2.

Vigorous competition in the RTE cereal industry requires intensive and decisive actions to expand investments in research, in the development of new products, and in marketing. Marketing plans generally center on facing the competition squarely and forcefully. Budgets for advertising and promotions have increased substantially in recent years, both to give additional support to established products and to success-

fully support new product introductions. Market shares for the top ten products in the industry are listed in Table 3. Selected information regarding each major competitor is presented below.

General Mills
General Mills managed to increase its market share significantly during the 1976–1981 period. Since then market share has stabilized, and General Mills has been able to maintain a share position in the industry at about 23%. Recent new product activity included the national roll-out of

Table 2. Kellogg Company: Operating Profit at Year End December Estimated by Division ($ millions)

	1982	1983	1984	1985	1986 (estimated)
Net sales	$2,367	$2,381	$2,602	$2,930	$3,250
Operating profits					
Domestic RTE Cereals	238.0	255.0	311.0	395.0	450.0
Mrs. Smith's	29.0	28.5	31.5	36.9	43.0
Salada	9.0	10.0	11.0	12.5	14.0
Fearn	13.8	15.5	17.0	19.0	21.0
International	107.9	105.4	96.7	95.0	110.0
Total operating income	397.7	414.4	467.2	558.4	638.0
Net income	227.8	242.7	250.5	281.3	320.5

Source: Prudential-Bache Securities, Inc., Apr. 2, 1986.

Table 3. Cold Cereal's Top Ten in Market Share[a]

Brand (company)	1983		1984	
	Pounds	Dollars	Pounds	Dollars
Corn Flakes (K)	6.8	4.7	6.8	4.7
Frosted Flakes (K)	5.2	4.8	5.6	5.2
Cheerios (GM)	5.5	5.8	5.2	5.5
Raisin Bran (K)	4.6	4.1	4.5	4.0
Chex (RP)	4.3	4.4	4.3	4.6
Shredded Wheat (N)	4.0	3.1	4.0	3.3
Rice Krispies (K)	3.6	3.9	3.5	3.8
Raisin Bran (GF)	3.0	2.5	2.7	2.1
Cap'n Crunch (Q)	2.9	3.5	2.7	3.2
Honey-Nut Cheerios (GM)	2.3	2.6	2.6	2.9
Total	42.2	39.4	41.9	39.3

Source: *Advertising Age,* Aug. 5, 1985, p. 42.
Abbreviations: K = Kellogg; GM = General Mills; GF = General Foods; Q = Quaker Oats; N = Nabisco; RP = Ralston Purina.
[a]All figures are percentages.

E.T.'s, which failed to produce significant sales, reflecting a decline of consumer interest in licensed properties. Cinnamon Toast Crunch, Fiber One, Bran Muffin Crunch, and S'More's Crunch are all expected to perform well after national roll-out in early 1986. General Mills' brands and the market share performance of each brand for the period 1982–1984 are shown in Table 4.

General Mills has concentrated its efforts on its snack food, yogurt, and restaurant businesses. It has divested some toy operations and repurchased 7 million shares of its own stock (44 million shares outstanding). General Mills net sales and operating profit by segment are listed in Table 5.

General Foods
Throughout the 1970s, General Foods relied on coffee—Maxwell House, Sanka, Yuban, and Brim—for approximately 40% of its total revenue (*New York Times,* Sep. 15, 1985). Since then, it has made major acquisitions. Currently, the company gets 40% of its revenues from packaged groceries, 28% from coffee products, and 18%

from processed meats (*Economist,* 1985). Coffee is still General Foods' largest single product, and it holds a 38% share of the coffee market (Philip Morris, 1986). In fiscal year 1985, General Foods achieved total revenues of $9 billion and the RTE cereal sales accounted for $512 million of total sales (Drexel, Burnham, & Lambert, May 20, 1985).

Sales of Post Toasties and Grape Nuts are eroding. Raisin Bran and Honey Nut Crunch Raisin Bran are reported to be performing well in the health-conscious market segment (*New York Times,* Sep. 15, 1985). Table 6 lists General Foods' RTE cereal products and market share performance for the 1982–1984 period.

Most of General Foods' development in the 1980s has consisted of creating or acquiring product lines to enter new markets, particularly convenience, low-calorie foods. Acquisitions include Oscar Meyer, Entenmann's bakery, Ronzoni, and Orowheat. New products developments include Crystal Light, Pudding Pops, Sun Apple, Lean Strips, and Crispy Cookin' French Fries, of which only Crystal Light and Pudding Pops had met with success as of the end of 1985.

Table 4.   General Mills' Ready-to-Eat Cereals: Market Share Data[a]

	1982		1983		1984	
Brand	**Pounds**	**Dollars**	**Pounds**	**Dollars**	**Pounds**	**Dollars**
Cheerios	5.6	5.9	5.5	5.8	5.2	5.5
Honey Nut Cheerios	2.1	2.4	2.3	2.6	2.6	2.9
Total	1.7	2.4	1.9	2.6	2.1	2.8
Lucky Charms	1.7	2.2	1.6	2.1	1.7	2.1
Trix	1.5	1.9	1.5	1.9	1.5	1.9
Wheaties	2.5	1.9	2.3	1.7	2.0	1.4
Golden Grahams	1.3	1.3	1.3	1.3	1.3	1.3
Crispy Wheats 'n Raisins	1.1	1.3	1.1	1.3	1.0	1.1
Licensed Products	0.4	0.5	1.1	1.3	0.7	1.0
Monsters, etc.	0.7	1.0	0.6	0.9	0.5	0.8
Cinnamon Toast Crunch	—	—	—	—	0.6	0.7
Cocoa Puffs	0.7	1.8	0.7	0.8	0.6	0.7
Buc Wheats	0.5	0.6	0.4	0.5	0.3	0.4
Others	0.3	0.2	0.5	0.4	0.6	0.5
Total	20.7	23.1	20.8	23.2	20.7	23.1

Source: Advertising Age, Aug. 5, 1985, p. 42.
[a]All figures are percentages.

Table 5.   General Mills: Operating Profit at Year End May, by Segment ($ millions)

	1983	1984	1985	1986 (estimated)
Net sales	$4,082	$4,118	$4,285	$4,550
Operating profits				
Consumer foods	269.4	275.3	265.6	300.0
Restaurants	80.0	70.0	91.5	97.0
Specialty retailing and other (loss)	10.4	19.8	(1.7)	23.0
Total operating profit	359.8	365.1	355.4	420.0
Net income (loss)	245.1	233.4	(72.9)	182.9

Source: Prudential-Bache Securities, Inc., Apr. 2, 1986.

Simultaneously, General Foods has divested its pet foods division and the Burger Chef restaurant chain and repurchased 11% of its stock. In 1985, Philip Morris acquired General Foods to integrate its food operations into the tobacco products company. General Foods sales and operating profits by segment are listed in Table 7.

Quaker Oats
In the 1960s, Quaker Oats acquired many diverse businesses. By the 1980s, Quaker Oats had divested its restaurants and chemical products units and was concentrating on acquiring packaged foods and specialty companies including Brookstone (tools), Jos. A. Bank (clothiers), Eye-

Table 6. General Foods' Ready-to-Eat Cereals: Market Share Data[a]

Brand	1982		1983		1984	
	Pounds	Dollars	Pounds	Dollars	Pounds	Dollars
Post Raisin Bran	3.1	2.8	3.0	2.5	2.7	2.1
Grape-Nuts	2.9	2.4	2.5	1.9	2.2	1.5
Super Sugar Crisp	1.4	1.6	1.5	1.6	1.4	1.4
Honeycombs	1.1	1.5	1.2	1.5	1.1	1.3
Post Fruit & Fibre	1.5	1.7	1.3	1.4	1.3	1.4
Pebbles	1.2	1.4	1.2	1.4	1.1	1.3
Smurf Berry Crunch	—	—	1.0	1.1	0.5	0.6
Post Toasties	1.3	0.9	1.2	0.9	1.0	0.8
Alpha-Bits	0.8	0.9	0.8	0.9	0.7	0.8
Bran Flakes	0.8	0.8	0.8	0.8	0.8	0.8
Honey-Nut Crunch Raisin Bran	0.3	0.3	0.7	0.7	0.2	0.2
Raisin Grape-Nuts	0.8	0.8	0.6	0.6	0.4	0.4
Fortified Oat Flakes	0.6	0.5	0.6	0.5	0.5	0.4
C.W. Post Hearty Granola	0.2	0.2	—	0.1	0.1	0.1
Others	0.4	0.2	0.1	0.2	0.3	0.2
Total	16.4	16.0	16.6	16.1	14.3	13.3

Source: *Advertising Age,* Aug. 5, 1985, p. 42.
[a]All figures are percentages.

Table 7. General Foods: Operating Profit at Year End March, by Segment ($ millions)

	1983	1984	1985	1986 (estimated)
Net sales	$8,256	$8,599	$9,022	$9,500
Operating profits				
Packaged groceries	427.8	470.5	419.3	451.0
Coffee	131.1	107.9	127.2	135.0
Processed meats	90.1	96.9	104.2	115.1
Food services and other	38.4	39.9	51.2	55.0
Total operating income	686.6	715.2	701.9	756.1
Net income	288.5	317.1	302.8	316.4

Source: Prudential-Bache Securities, Inc., Oct. 1, 1985.

lab (eyeware retailing), and Stokely Van Camp (pork and beans, Gatorade). In addition, Quaker Oats repurchased 5% of its own shares in March 1985. The 1980s witnessed an aggressive Quaker Oats expanding its operations throughout its product lines.

Quaker Oats has bundled its product devel-opment (20 new products and line extensions since 1983) under the Quaker umbrella and has pushed those lines in which it has a leadership position: hot cereals, granola bars, and Gatorade. Spending $200 million in 1985 for advertising, Quaker Oats has shown a 16% growth in adver-tising expenditures and a 31% growth in merchandising expenditures since 1984.

As a result of this strategy and increasing new product development at Kellogg, General Mills, and Ralston Purina, Quaker Oats has allowed its share of the RTE cereal market to erode from 8.9% in 1983 to 8.6% in 1984. Halfsies and Cap'n Crunch have lost market share, whereas Life and 100% Natural have maintained their sales levels. Quaker Oats RTE cereal brands and market share performance are listed in Table 8, and Quaker Oats net sales and operating profits by segment are shown in Table 9.

Ralston Purina

Ralston Purina led the RTE cereal industry in restructuring through the use of share repurchase. Ralston Purina has acquired almost 40 million shares of its own stock, and, through divestiture of its Foodmaker division, can acquire more. Ralston Purina acquired Continental Baking in 1984, which added the Hostess brands to the Ralston Purina product lines.

Ralston Purina is expected to focus on its pet food operations and the Hostess lines for the foreseeable future. New product activity in 1985,

Table 8. Quaker Oats' Ready-to-Eat Cereals: Market Share Data[a]

	1982		1983		1984	
Brand	Pounds	Dollars	Pounds	Dollars	Pounds	Dollars
Cap'n Crunch	3.2	3.8	2.9	3.5	2.7	3.2
Life	2.5	2.3	2.4	2.2	2.4	2.2
100% Natural	1.6	1.5	1.6	1.5	1.5	1.4
Halfsies	—	—	0.7	0.7	0.2	0.3
Corn Bran	0.7	0.6	0.7	0.6	0.6	0.6
Others	0.9	0.7	0.6	0.4	0.9	0.9
Total	8.9	8.9	8.9	8.9	8.3	8.6

Source: Advertising Age, Aug. 5, 1985, p. 42.
[a]All figures are percentages.

Table 9. Quaker Oats: Operating Profit at Year End June, by Segment ($ millions)

	1983	1984	1985	1986 (estimated)
Net sales	$2,611	$3,344	$3,520	$3,650
Operating profits				
U.S. and Canadian grocery	193.8	219.5	250.0	272.0
International grocery	49.1	32.9	49.7	60.0
Fisher-Price	29.6	43.6	47.1	50.0
Specialty retailing	15.8	12.7	15.2	18.0
Total	288.3	308.7	362.0	400.0
Net income	119.3	138.7	156.6	174.2

Source: Prudential-Bache Securities, Inc., Apr. 2, 1986.

greatest in company history, brought extension of the Chuck Wagon line with three new dog food products, expansion of the dog treats line with Waggles and T-Bonz, and new cat foods. New products in cereals include Sun Flakes, Rainbow Brite, and Cabbage Patch. Ralston Purina's RTE cereal products and market share performance for the 1982–1984 period are presented in Table 10. Ralston Purina's net sales and operating profits by segment are listed in Table 11.

Nabisco

Since 1983, Nabisco has introduced 140 new products and line extensions globally. This aggressive posture indicated a recognition by Nabisco of the importance of the international market, which accounts for 40% of its normalized operating income.

In 1985, Nabisco was acquired by R. J. Reynolds, a tobacco products company. The com-

Table 10. Ralston Purina's Ready-to-Eat Cereals: Market Share Data[a]

	1982		1983		1984	
Brand	Pounds	Dollars	Pounds	Dollars	Pounds	Dollars
Chex	4.2	4.0	4.3	4.4	4.3	4.6
Donkey Kong	—	—	0.7	0.7	0.6	0.6
Cookie Crisp	0.6	0.6	0.5	0.7	0.4	0.7
Others	0.3	0.2	0.3	0.2	0.6	0.4
Total	5.9	5.6	5.9	6.1	5.9	6.3

Source: Advertising Age, Aug. 5, 1985, p. 42.
[a]All figures are percentages.

Table 11. Ralston Purina: Operating Profit at Year End September, by Segment ($ millions)

	1982	1983	1984	1985	1986 (estimated)
Net sales	$4,803	$4,872	$4,980	$5,864	$5,350
Operating profits					
Pet food	227.0	263.5	303.0	350.0	399.0
Seafood (loss)	(11.0)	14.5	9.5	10.0	11.5
Cereals	38.5	43.5	41.5	45.5	50.0
Continental baking	—	—	—	84.0	94.0
Other consumer goods	3.7	5.5	1.6	6.6	8.0
Agriculture	96.6	105.6	92.5	74.9	82.0
Restaurant	46.7	58.5	61.4	47.2	0.0
Diversified operations	27.1	33.6	35.9	24.2	30.0
Total operating income	428.6	524.7	545.4	642.4	674.5
Net income	69.1	256.0	242.7	256.4	371.0

Source: Prudential-Bache Securities, Inc., Apr. 2, 1986.

bined R. J. Reynolds and Nabisco advertising budget weighs in at $1 billion. This financial strength is to be applied, among other things, to joint product marketing. For example, Del Monte coupons may come with Shredded Wheat. It is hoped that this mixed marketing approach will boost sales of product lines throughout the combined companies.

Nabisco's major product in the RTE cereals market is Shredded Wheat. Shredded Wheat held a 3.3% dollar market share in 1984 (4.0% in pounds). All Nabisco RTE cereal products held a total market share of 4.2% on a dollar basis (4.9% on a poundage basis) (*Advertising Age,* Aug. 5, 1985).

Industry Challenges

The RTE cereal industry emerged from the 1970s facing continuing challenges from the Federal Trade Commission (FTC). Founded in 1914 to combat monopolies, the FTC is charged with preventing unfair methods of competition and unfair or deceptive acts or practices that affect commerce. For almost a decade, the FTC had pursued the RTE industry leaders on two issues: children's television programming and advertising, and the operation of an oligopolistic "shared monopoly."

Children's Television and Advertising
As early as 1970, consumer groups pressed for greater regulation of children's television and advertising (*Federal Register,* vol. 49). A group called Action for Children's Television (ACT) prodded the FTC to establish minimum requirements for age-specific programming for children. In 1971, ACT petitioned the FTC to ban all vitamin advertising on programs intended for children. (One third of advertising on TV programs for children had been for vitamin products.) To avoid further pressure, the manufacturers voluntarily complied with the petition (Ward, 1978).

From 1971 through 1974, the Children's Tele-vision Task Force studied the state of children's television and recommended that licensees increase the amount of television programming created for children, particularly programs of educational and informational content. The task force recommended that selling, promotion, or endorsement of a product by the host of the program be prohibited, and that program content be clearly distinguished from commercial messages.

The ACT and other watchdog groups increased their efforts to influence the FTC in the late 1970s, with the result that the FTC introduced proposals for regulations to limit advertising on programs whose primary audience was children. Despite efforts toward self-regulation by industry groups such as the Children's Advertising Review unit of the National Council of Broadcasters and the Codes of the National Association of Broadcasters (Ward, 1978), the FTC banned all commercials on shows aimed at children of a very young age and commercials for highly sugared foods on programs directed at older children. The regulation also required advertisers to devote money to public service announcements to promote good dental and nutritional habits.

In 1980, Congress limited the scope of the FTC's attempts to regulate children's advertising to matters of deception and "unfair" or misleading advertising (Dewar, 1980). By October 1981, the FTC dropped its pursuit of the broadcasters and advertisers with respect to "Kid Vid" issues (*Federal Register,* vol. 46). The ACT continues to monitor television and file complaints to the FTC on those companies that ACT believes exploit the innocence of youth. The ACT has filed against Quaker Oats (1982), General Mills (1983), and General Foods (1983), charging unfair or deceptive advertising by each company (*Associated Press,* Jul. 18, 1983).

In 1983, Kellogg was brought to court in Canada to force the company to cease advertising to children. Kellogg claimed that such a ban would limit the company's ability to release new products and thus freeze competitors' present market shares. The availability of U.S. television in Canada obscures any verification of Kellogg's claim. However, Kellogg and other companies marketing products aimed at children, including games, toys, and foods, were restricted from advertising to children on Canadian television. The Canadian court stated that ads are presumed to be intended for children if they include "themes related to fantasy, magic, mystery, suspense or adventure," if they depict authority figures, role models, heroes, animals, or "imaginary or fanciful creatures," or if they rely on cartoons, children's music, or attention-getting technical devices (Lippman, 1983). Products of interest to children can be presented on Canadian television only if addressed to adults in a mature fashion.

Shared Monopoly
In the ten years that followed the FTC's initial complaint against Kellogg, General Mills, General Foods, and Quaker Oats, 243 days of testimony produced more than 36,000 pages of transcript and 60,000 pages of documents. The FTC charged the industry leaders with operating a "shared monopoly" that resulted not from conspiracy or collusion but from the collective power of the few firms (Kiechel, 1978).

The concept of shared monopoly arose from a study by a Massachusetts Institute of Technology economist, Richard L. Schmalensee. He argued that the cereal companies crowded the supermarket shelves with a large number of brands that left little space for new entrants. The flood of products into the market invited competition among those brands with similar characteristics—crunchiness, flavor, sweetness—but not competition between all brands on the market. The profusion of brands ensured that only existing firms could afford to compete; a new entrant would be required to invest $150 million in development with little assurance that it could gain the 3–5% share necessary to gain scale economy in production (Sebastian, 1979).

Specifically, the FTC charged the companies with the following practices (FTC vs Lonning & Kellogg).

Brand Proliferation. "The four companies introduce a profusion of ready-to-eat cereal brands into the market," that fill the "perceptual space" of the consumer with over 200 brands on the supermarket shelves.

Aggressive Marketing. "The brands are promoted by intensive advertising aimed primarily at children, which . . . conceals the true nature of these cereals." For example, Honey and Nut Corn Flakes implies significant sweetening by honey; in fact the flakes contain more brown sugar, white refined sugar, vegetable oil, salt, and malt flavoring than honey (Sebastian, 1979).

Product Differentiation. The four companies produce "basically similar" ready-to-eat cereals that are artificially differentiated through trivial differences.

In addition to creating barriers to entry into the RTE cereal market, the companies were also accused of other unfair methods of competition in advertising and product promotion. The charges included:

1. Cereal advertising is false and misleading. This issue, also raised by ACT, pits the claims of nutrition and health against the high sugar content of many cereals. The sugar content has been blamed for health and dental problems.

2. Kellogg's program of shelf-space allocation, a program emulated by other cereal manufacturers, controls the exposure of breakfast food products. Kellogg records the sales of cereals in the supermarket and recommends brand selection and shelf-space allocation to the supermarket manager.

3. The companies made numerous acquisitions to eliminate competition in the RTE cereal mar-

ket. These acquisitions have enhanced the shared monopoly structure of the industry.

4. The companies have exercised monopoly power by refusing to engage in price competition or other consumer-directed promotions.

The FTC claimed that the results of these acts were artificially inflated prices, excessive profits, and an absence of price competition. Government economists used the concept of shared monopoly to explain the reluctance of large consumer-products companies, such as Procter and Gamble, to enter the lucrative, albeit competitive, cereal market.

The FTC hoped to apply shared monopoly or oligopolistic behavior restrictions to other industries after establishing the validity of the concept in a landmark decision with references to the RTE cereals industry case. Any industry in which relatively few companies hold 90% market share (examples include telecommunications, oil, automobiles, and computers) would then be vulnerable to FTC action (Cowan, 1981; *Time*, Oct. 5, 1981).

Demographic Changes

Another basic challenge facing the industry has been a slowdown in the rate of growth of cereal consumption, brought about, in part, by the aging of the U.S. population. The U.S. median age is now 30 and is forecasted to reach 35 by the year 2000. The total population is expected to grow by less than 1% per year during the 1980s, primarily because of a slowdown in the U.S. birthrate.

Age-group populations do show different growth rates. Several changes expected in the 1980–1990 decade are listed below.

- The 15–24 year age group will decrease by 17% or 7.1 million.

- The 25–34 year age group will undergo a strong 14% increase.

- The 35–54 year age group will undergo the largest increase of all age groups, 25%.

- The 55–64 year age group will shrink by 2%.

- The over-65 age group will show the second largest increase, up by 20% (*Newsweek,* Jan. 17, 1983).

These demographic trends pose a threat to companies that sell a significant portion of their production to the youth market. The greatest consumers of RTE cereals are children under the age of 13. In the 1970s, the industry had experienced a decline in the population of this group. Tables 12–15 provide additional data on demographic changes facing the industry and on consumption of RTE cereal products.

Despite the challenges faced by the industry, the 1980s held some promise for the RTE cereal makers. Grain prices were weakening, with strong gains in production continuing through mid-decade. Moreover, cereal companies were able to levy 5% and 6% price increases while maintaining cereal at the lowest cost-per-serving of any breakfast food.

Kellogg's Business Situation

For Kellogg, the end of the 1970s and the beginning of the 1980s was an era of severe problems. The company retained its market leadership po-

Table 12. Age Distribution Changes and Composite Percentage Change

Age (yr)	1970–1980	1980–1985	1985–1990 (estimated)
<5	−8.7	32.1	7.6
5–13	−16.3	1.2	25.6
14–17	2.3	−11.6	−11.3
18–21	16.6	−9.9	−6.1
22–24	21.6	2.3	−14.3
25–34	38.5	13.8	3.1
35–44	8.6	24.8	16.6
45–54	−1.5	−2.2	12.7
55–64	12.3	3.7	−4.4
65+	22.8	10.7	9.2
Total	8.1	7.4	6.6

Source: U.S. Bureau of Census.

Table 13. Ready-to-Eat Cereal Consumption: Percent of Total Consumption by Age Group

Age (yr)	1984	1983	1982	1981	1980	1979	1976	1972
<13	31.0	31.5	31.5	31.6	31.8	31.9	32.2	36.1
13–18	13.9	13.9	13.8	13.8	13.8	13.9	14.0	12.9
19–49	28.9	28.1	28.0	28.2	28.1	28.0	27.9	25.7
50+	26.2	26.5	26.7	26.4	26.3	26.2	25.9	25.3
Total	100	100	100	100	100	100	100	100

Source: Drexel, Burnham, & Lambert Brokerage House Report, "Kellogg Co.," Apr. 8, 1985.

Table 14. Pounds Per Capita Ready-to-Eat Cereal Consumption by Age Group

Age (yr)	Pounds
<6	11.5
6–11	14.3
12–17	13.4
18–24	7.0
25–34	5.6
35–49	5.8
50–64	7.7
65+	11.3

Source: Kellogg Company publication.

Table 15. Ready-to-Eat Cereals: Consumption and Tonnage Shipped

Year	Pounds consumed per capita	Percent change in year-to-year tonnage
1971	6.76	3.00
1972	7.75	9.30
1973	8.30	15.20
1974	8.62	7.20
1975	9.03	5.40
1976	9.06	5.80
1977	8.89	1.00
1978	9.07	0.20
1979	9.07	1.30
1980	9.13	2.80
1981	9.26	2.40
1982	9.30	2.10
1983	9.41	2.30
1984	9.74	4.20

Source: Drexel, Burnham, & Lambert Brokerage House Report "Kellogg Co.," Apr. 8, 1985.

sition, but their erosion of market share in the United States was a growing concern.

Domestic Sales

The introduction of generic and private-label brands contributed to a loss of Kellogg market share. Kellogg's position in the industry weakened as its market share dropped from a high of 43% in 1972 to a low of 38.5% in 1983. Consumers appeared to switch to the less-expensive generic brands as the rate of inflation grew to double digits in the 1970s. The cost of this share erosion was substantial: each percent of the RTE cereal market is valued at approximately $40 million.

Kellogg executive Arnold Langbo stated that Kellogg was particularly vulnerable to the generic and private-label inroads in the RTE cereal market. He observed, "The whole philosophy or principle of the private label is to copy the leading products in the market" (Johnson, 1983).

Kellogg fought the invasion of generic and private-label cereals with aggressive price decreases, recovering 1.8% of market share in 1984 as generic goods dropped 10% in tonnage shipped. Kellogg's two primary competitors held 36.4% of the market, considerably less than Kellogg's 40.3% share. In 1984, General Foods market share dropped 2.8% to 13.3%; General Mills held constant at a 23% share. Sales trends for several of Kellogg's products are presented in Table 16. Market share performance of the Kellogg brands for the years 1982–1984 is presented in Table 17.

Research and Development
In addition to price decreases, Kellogg increased its efforts in research and development (R & D) advertising, and new product introduction. With an R & D budget of $6.5 million in 1978, Kellogg began to develop cereals to appeal to different segments of the cereal market. By 1981, Kellogg was investing $20 million a year in research. Kellogg built two advanced research centers and acquired Agrigentics, a research company exploring improvements in grain development. Kellogg's efforts in research produced the first flaked cereal with no sugar or preservatives, Nutri Grain in 1981, the first cereal to combine two grains with identity separation, Crispix in 1983, and the first cereals to fully enrobe fruit, Raisin Squares and OJ's in 1984 (Patent numbers: 4,178,392, 4,103,035, and 3,952,112).

Advertising
In 1984, Kellogg increased its advertising budget by 49% to $160 million, an aggressive move when compared to the 16% increase (to $52 million) of General Foods, and the 1% decrease in advertising by Post. As General Foods limited its primary advertising on its top five (of 14) leading brands, Kellogg was able to devote considerable push to its new products (*Forbes,* Oct. 7, 1985). Kellogg advertising themes for selected products are presented in Table 18.

Kellogg was able to take advantage of reports connecting a high-fiber diet with a reduced risk of colon cancer and they positioned their new All Bran cereal as a cancer-preventative tool. Kellogg advertised, "At last, some news about cancer you can live with." By the end of 1984, $250 million of Kellogg's sales came from bran cereals: All Bran, Bran Buds, Cracklin' Oat Bran,

Table 16. Kellogg's Principal Products' Sales Trends ($ millions)

Product	1983	1984	Change (%)
Corn Flakes	$141.3	$162.5	15.0
Rice Krispies	144.1	141	−2.2
Raisin Bran	134.3	151.9	13.1
Special K	70.3	82.9	17.8
Fruit Loops	88.9	103.6	16.5
Frosted Flakes	188.8	217.9	15.4
Total	767.5	859.7	12.0

Source: Drexel, Burnham, & Lambert, Inc.

Fruitful Bran, Kellogg's Bran Flakes, Kellogg's Raisin Bran, and, in 1985, All Bran with Extra Fiber (Tracy, 1985).

The advertising campaign sparked controversy among industry, medical, and government groups. Officials at the FTC hailed the campaign as "the type of advertisement that we believe should be encouraged" (Kronhelm, 1985; Wollenberg, 1985). The Food and Drug Administration, however, protested that Kellogg was making medical claims for its product and considered seizing all boxes of All Bran from the shelves (Marwick, 1985). The National Food Processors Association petitioned the FDA to allow its member manufacturers to tout the health benefits of their products as long as the labeling was truthful and could be substantiated.

"Everyone has his opinions of advertising, but we didn't think anyone would misinterpret our commercials," explained Kellogg Vice President of Public Affairs, Peggy Wollerman. "Our goal is to communicate recommendations of the National Cancer Institute's findings that maintaining a high-fiber diet is a direct means of reducing the risk of cancer" (Rotenberk, 1984). The Kellogg advertisement had been cleared by Kellogg and National Cancer Institute scientists and lawyers for accuracy, and it had been passed by lawyers for the three television networks.

Table 17. Kellogg's Ready-to-Eat Cereals: Market Share Data[a]

Brand	1982		1983		1984	
	Pounds	Dollars	Pounds	Dollars	Pounds	Dollars
Frosted Flakes	5.2	4.8	5.2	4.8	5.6	5.2
Corn Flakes	6.8	4.7	6.8	4.7	6.8	4.7
Raisin Bran	4.7	4.2	4.6	4.1	4.5	4.0
Rice Krispies	3.9	4.2	3.6	3.9	3.5	3.8
Fruit Loops	2.2	2.8	2.2	2.8	2.3	2.9
Special K	1.5	2.1	1.7	2.3	1.9	2.5
Bran Products	2.7	2.0	2.8	2.1	3.1	2.3
Frosted Mini-Wheats	1.8	1.8	1.8	1.8	1.9	1.9
Apple Jacks	1.0	1.5	1.0	1.5	1.0	1.5
Sugar Smacks	1.3	1.3	1.3	1.3	1.2	1.3
Sugar Pops	1.1	1.3	1.0	1.2	1.1	1.2
Product 19	0.8	1.1	0.8	1.1	0.9	1.1
Nutri-Grain	1.0	1.0	1.0	1.0	1.2	1.1
Crispex	—	—	0.7	0.7	0.5	0.5
Honey & Nut Corn Flakes	0.6	0.7	0.6	0.7	0.5	0.6
Marshmallow Krispies	0.5	0.7	0.5	0.7	0.4	0.6
Cocoa Krispies	0.5	0.7	0.5	0.7	0.6	0.8
Frosted Rice	0.6	0.8	0.5	0.6	0.4	0.4
Fruitful Bran	—	—	—	—	0.7	0.6
C-3PO	—	—	—	—	0.5	0.6
Apple Raisin Crisp	—	—	—	—	0.5	0.6
Raisin Squares	—	—	—	—	0.3	0.3
Most	0.3	0.4	0.3	0.4	0.2	0.3
Raisins Rice & Rye	0.5	0.6	0.3	0.4	0.1	0.1
Others	1.2	1.4	1.0	1.3	0.8	1.4
Total	38.5	38.5	38.5	38.5	40.5	40.3

Source: Advertising Age, Aug. 5, 1985, p. 42.
[a]All figures are percentages.

Until 1970, the FDA prohibited manufacturers from making any health claims on behalf of food products. In the following years, the FDA relaxed its standard for claims of "low calorie" and "low cholesterol." If a product is claimed to be useful in the treatment of a disease, it is considered a drug and the manufacturer must prove the efficacy of its claims (Cowart, 1985).

New Marketing Developments
Kellogg's move into the adult market in the late 1970s and early 1980s signaled a new direction for the cereal industry. Kellogg's strategy included promoting vitamin-enriched, whole grain, and sugarless cereals to the 25–49 year age group, high fiber to the 65+ age group, and C-3POs and OJs to the under 17 market (*Business Week,* Jan. 8, 1977).

Recognizing sociological changes in the United States, Kellogg introduced all-family cereals to enhance the convenience of shopping. Kellogg also introduced Smart Start, a cereal aimed at the working woman (*Business Week,* Nov. 26, 1979). Key to Kellogg's development

Table 18. Kellogg's Cereal: Products and Advertising Themes

Product	Themes
Special K	Thanks to the K, Staying in Shape Never Tasted so Good—Can't Pinch an Inch
Product 19	Flaky, Bumpy, Crispy, Crunchy *Vitamins*—100% of Your Daily Allowance of 10 Vitamins
Fruitful Bran	Bushels of Taste!—Fiber Rich
Nutri-Grain	Whole Grain Goodness . . . No Sugar Added—Dedicated to the Ones We Love
Apple Raisin Crisp	New Great Taste—New, Big, Juicy Chunks of Real Apple
Frosted Flakes	Gr-r-reat Taste—Tony the Tiger—The Taste Adults Have Grown to Love
Raisin Bran	Two Scoops of Raisins—Fiber Rich—Here is the Goodness of Fiber
All Bran	High Fiber—The Highest Fiber Cereal Ever
Rice Krispies	More Vitamin Nutrition than Old Fashioned Oatmeal—Snap! Crackle! and Pop!—The Talking Cereal Talks about Nutrition
Corn Flakes	The Original and Best—Provides 8 Essential Vitamins and Iron—How 'bout these Kellogg's Corn Flakes Now?—The Surprise is the People Who Eat Them
Just Right	High Nutrition . . . Uncompromising Taste—Kellogg's Just Right Cereal
Bran Flakes	Fiber-rich *Bran Flakes*—We'll Help Take Care of the Inside, You take Care of the Outside
Fruit Loops	Natural Fruit Flavors with 100% U.S. RDA of Vitamin C—All Natural Flavors: Orange, Lemon, Cherry—Delicious Natural Fruit Flavors with a Full Day's Supply of Vitamin C

Source: Kellogg advertisements.

and marketing were the themes of health, diet, convenience, and taste (Brody, 1985). Numerous surveys and surveying organizations, including the Bureau of Labor Statistics, have recorded significant social demographic changes in the last 15 years. A few of the changes that Kellogg and the other cereal companies had to address are listed below.

▪ In 1985, the numbers of families with school-age or preschool-age children increased by 460,000; the number of employed mothers increased by 765,000 to 18.2 million.

▪ In 1985, the median family wage and salary earnings increased 4.6%. Since 1982, the median family earnings increased 16% compared to a consumer price increase of 11% over the same period (*New York Times,* Feb. 19, 1986).

In the 1980s, breakfast has become a more significant part of the American diet, with 89% of the populace eating breakfast each day. Frozen

breakfast foods were also becoming an important part of the breakfast food industry. In 1985, sales of all frozen foods totalled $849.3 million, 15% more than in 1984. In part, this increase was caused by the fact that more than 44% of American homes now had a microwave oven, making cooking at home easier. Sales of frozen breakfast entrees tripled from 1979 to 1985: sales of frozen pancakes increased 390%; frozen toaster items increased 1000%. Moreover, between 1978 and 1984, the number of Americans eating breakfast at a restaurant increased 45.7% compared to the overall restaurant increase of only 6.3% (Callahan, 1986).

Despite the decline in the population of children under 13 years of age, competition in breakfast food market segment continued without any slackening of intensity. As consumers of the greatest per capita amounts of cereal, children have long been the focus of cereal company advertising. Although Tony the Tiger has represented Kellogg's Sugar Frosted Flakes for many years, General Mills broke new ground in products for children with the first licensed character, Strawberry Shortcake. This was a move to link the cereal with other commercial media. Other RTE cereal companies followed quickly. The RTE cereal companies' licensed character products now include General Mills' ET, General Foods' Smurf Berry Crunch, Ralston Purina's Donkey Kong, Rainbow Brite, and Gremlins, and Kellogg's C-3PO's.

The benefit of tying a cereal to an established figure from television, movies, comics, or toys (character licensing) is a quick gain in market share through exposure in a good trial period. Although traditional cereal products have existed for more than 30 years, the licensed-character cereals may have a life cycle of only 6–18 months. "The first licensed characters did well for about a year. Now their life span is about six months," said Nomi Ghez of Goldman Sachs & Co. (Spillman, 1985). The editor of *New Products News,* Martin Friedman, stated, "the characters that have been created by cereal companies go on forever, and the others don't" (Hollie, 1985). To seek a license for a character, Kellogg depended on assurances that the character would continue, that the character had personality and integrity, and that the character would not alienate adults.

By 1986, the cereal companies had less interest in developing licensed-character products because of a general decrease in the popularity of the characters with consumers (Friedman, 1986).

International Operations
By 1980, Kellogg measured sales in 130 countries from 19 manufacturing locations (Kellogg Annual Report, 1982). Kellogg International was divided into four divisions: Canada; United Kingdom and Europe; Latin America; and Africa, Australia, and Asia. International sales accounted for 30% of Kellogg's total sales. In France, Kellogg planned to target all segments of the population in hopes of replacing the croissant with cereal. In Japan, Kellogg has targeted children to establish the habit of eating cereal (*Dun's Business Month,* Dec., 1985). Financial results for several geographic operating segments are detailed in Table 19.

Federal Trade Commission Case Revisited
In addition to the problems created by the introduction of generic and private-label brands, Kellogg management also attributed the previously mentioned loss of market share to the inability of top management to concentrate on operating the business. The Chairman of the Board, William E. Lamothe, estimated in 1982 that 40% of top management time had been spent on the FTC litigation (*Business Week,* Dec. 6, 1982).

For Kellogg, losing the FTC case would have been significant. If the FTC had won the case, it would have divided Kellogg into five separate operating companies organized around its major product lines. Additionally, the FTC would have required Kellogg to license its brands to smaller, regional manufacturers. Kellogg argued that such actions would place Kellogg at a competitive disadvantage in the RTE market and would produce inconsistent quality within Kellogg's brands.

As the trial entered the 1980s, Kellogg changed its passive strategy of litigation, becoming an aggressive champion of the industry's positions. Kellogg sponsored intense letter-writing campaigns to congressional representatives from districts in which Kellogg maintained facilities. As a result, the FTC received numerous inquiries from congressional representatives regarding the efficacy of continuing the case further (*Business Week,* Nov. 26, 1979).

In 1981, Kellogg created Project Nutrition, a teaching unit for secondary grade school children, as well as nutrition inserts for children's television. Kellogg also provided cereals in 33,000 school breakfast programs. In 1982, Kellogg introduced Fitness Focus, a physical education program for high schools. Kellogg be-

Table 19. Kellogg Company: Geographic Operating Segments ($ millions)

	1985	1984	1983	1982	1981
Sales					
United States	$2,074.9	$1,789.6	$1,560.0	$1,514.3	$1.454.0
Canada	177.6	178.9	176.0	169.0	170.2
Europe	474.9	425.9	437.8	453.0	435.9
Other	202.7	208.0	207.3	230.8	261.2
Total	2,930.1	2,602.4	2,381.1	2,367.1	2,321.3
Net Earnings					
United States	222.7	194.7	170.5	163.0	150.7
Canada	11.7	11.6	27.6	15.2	13.1
Europe	38.8	35.0	38.6	36.9	34.0
Other	7.9	9.2	6.0	12.7	7.6
Total	281.1	250.5	242.7	227.8	205.4
Assets					
United States	833.6	731.6	677.1	639.0	606.9
Canada	262.7	247.5	192.3	143.4	130.2
Europe	337.9	223.3	195.4	199.0	197.5
Other	158.9	148.6	139.8	153.7	178.0
Corporate	133.0	316.1	262.6	162.3	166.5
Total	1,726.1	1,667.1	1,467.2	1,297.4	1,279.11

Source: Kellogg Annual Reports.

lieved that the program would enhance its image as a producer of health-related foods, an image that could benefit Kellogg in its case against the FTC as well as in its position in the market.

Procedural errors in the handling of the case by the administrative judge and the FTC raised challenges from Kellogg and the other cereal companies. Judge Harry R. Hinkes decided in 1978 to retire from the judiciary in order to gain full pension benefits, some of which he would lose if he postponed his retirement. The FTC, fearing a considerable delay and possible dismissal of the case, offered the judge a salary to stay on the case. The impropriety of such an arrangement, alleging a possible conflict of interest, was raised by Kellogg as grounds for dismissal. A new judge was appointed to continue the suit in 1981. Later, in 1982, the FTC dropped its suit (*Federal Register,* vol. 47).

Following the collapse of the FTC lawsuit against its four largest companies, the RTE industry witnessed increased competitive rivalry. This increased rivalry manifested itself in new product releases and advertising, and in corporate-development activities including acquisitions, divestitures, and share repurchases.

Diversification. The slowing growth rate in the cereal industry compelled Kellogg to look toward diversification for continued growth and comparable rates of returns for reinvestment of its retained earnings. In 1970, Kellogg entered the frozen food industry with the acquisition of Fearn International. In 1976, Kellogg acquired Mrs. Smith's Pie Co. and in 1977, it acquired Pure Packed Foods. Products such as Eggo waffles, salad dressings, LeGout soups, Salada Tea, Whitney Yogurt, Mrs. Smith's Pies, and pickles entered Kellogg's lines. Kellogg consolidated its frozen food operations under the Mrs. Smith's label in 1980 to gain greater efficiencies in manufacturing, warehousing, transportation, and marketing as well as a stronger product identity in the marketplace (Prokesch, 1985). By 1984, 25% of Kellogg's sales were noncereal (Blyskal, 1984). Table 20 presents net income contributions of several elements of Kellogg, and Table 21 presents sales and operating income for several segments of the company.

Despite LaMothe's declaration that Kellogg was "gung ho" on diversification, Kellogg lost in three attempts to acquire Tropicana and in attempts to acquire Binney and Smith, manufacturers of Crayola crayons, and Seven-Up. Kellogg believed in each case that the price was too high for the company. "Today we are kind of

Table 20. Kellogg Company: Net Income Contributions

Product/division	1981	1982	1983	1984	1985 (estimated)	1986 (estimated)
Domestic cereals	$121.0	$135.7	$138.0	$169.9	$206.0	$231.0
Canadian operations	11.0	13.0	13.8	9.4	10.0	12.0
Salada	12.1	13.0	14.0	15.0	16.0	18.0
Fearn International	9.0	9.5	10.5	11.6	12.0	14.0
Mrs. Smith's Pie Co.	8.7	7.0	8.0	8.9	10.0	11.0
Kellogg International	41.6	49.6	44.6	39.2	42.0	50.0
Total	203.4	227.8	228.9	254.0	296.0	336.0

Source: Drexel, Burnham, & Lambert, Inc., Oct. 7, 1985.

Table 21. Kellogg Company: Estimated Sales and Operating Income ($ millions)

	1979	1980	1981	1982	1983	1984	1985
Sales							
RTE cereals	$1,426	$1,687	$1,802	$1,792	$1,755	$2,000	$2,260
Salada	128	140	154	165	182	180	190
Fearn International	118	132	145	165	177	165	180
Mrs. Smith's Pie Co.	157	172	200	218	239	222	235
Other	18	19	20	27	50	35	35
Total	1,847	2,150	2,321	2,367	2,381	2,602	2,900
Operating Income							
RTE Cereals	240	297	331	343.7	370	408.2	510
Salada	12	12	13	14	16	14	15
Fearn International	8	9	10	11	12.5	11.5	13
Mrs. Smith's Pie Co.	19	20	22	24	27.5	25	28
Other	2	2	2	3	4	4.5	5
Total	281	340	378	395.7	430	463.2	571

Source: Merrill, Lynch, Pearce, Fenner, & Smith brokerage house report: "Kellogg Co.," Oct. 31, 1985.

glad we did [lose]," said LaMothe, "There is no embarrassment in losing. The big embarrassment is to win by paying too much and then never being able to make a return to your shareholders" (*Dun's Business Month,* Dec. 1985).

Capital Projects. Productivity improvements were made at many Kellogg manufacturing facilities in the late 1970s and 1980s, culminating in a $100 million expansion and improvement in the Battle Creek plant in 1985, the largest single capital expenditure in the company's history. Kellogg's ability to improve productivity is dem-

onstrated by the 50% increase in revenues per employee that the company enjoyed between 1979 and 1985 (Drexel, Burnham, & Lambert, Oct. 7, 1985). Early in 1986, Kellogg ended a long practice of public tours of the Battle Creek facility because of a desire to protect proprietary information. Several Kellogg capital projects for the years 1980–1983 are listed in Table 22.

Preventing Takeover. Matching Kellogg's rates of return in an acquisition candidate is difficult. Moreover, the consumer-products companies such as Kellogg are attractive takeover targets

Table 22. Kellogg Company: Capital Projects

Year	Location	Project
1980	Rexdale, Ontario	Frozen food manufacturing facility
	Wrexham, England	Expanded capacity for Super Noodles
	Valls, Spain	New cereal plant
	Rooty Hill, Australia	Expansion of frozen food plant
	Queretro, Mexico	New corn milling operation
	Sao Paolo, Brazil	Expansion of cereal plant
	Maracay, Venezuela	New office building, processing, and packing
	Guatemala	Expansion of grain storage
	Arlington, TN	Pure Packed dry materials warehouse
	McMinnville, OR	Expansion of Mrs. Smith's plants
	San Jose, CA	Expansion of plant
	Blue Anchor, NJ	Mrs. Smith's facility
	Milpitas, CA	Eggo salad dressing plant
1981	Battle Creek, MI	Expanded for Nutri-Grain cereal
	Lancaster, PA	Increase capacity for cereal
	Battle Creek, MI	Advanced technology facility for research and development
	South Korea	New processing plants
	London, Ontario	Advanced technology center
	Manchester, England	Expansion of packing facility
	Bremen, West Germany	Purchased land
1982	London, Ontario	Expansion of plant
	Seoul, South Korea	Plant completed
	Manchester, England	Conversion of packing line
	Sao Paolo, Brazil	Expansion of facilities
1983	Pottstown, PA	Expansion of office space, storage Warehouse

Source: Kellogg Annual Reports.

themselves because of their high returns. To reduce the risk of a takeover, Kellogg purchased 20% of its own stock in 1984, an "investment in our own business," said LaMothe. The effect of the stock repurchase added $500 million of debt to the Kellogg balance sheet. Before the transaction, Kellogg enjoyed only $19 million of debt against $1 billion in equity. The 20% block of stock had been held by the Kellogg Foundation. Any potential sale of the stock, said LaMothe, was a "cloud we didn't think was good to leave hanging out there in today's time" (Willoughby, 1985).

Kellogg's competitors employed a range of strategies in response to the same takeover challenge. Ralston Purina also acquired blocks of its own stock, continuing this strategy through mid-decade. In 1985, R. J. Reynolds acquired Nabisco Brands, itself a result of a merger between Nabisco and Standard Brands. Phillip Morris acquired General Foods. Table 23 lists several recent acquisitions of established brands.

Some of the largest companies in the food industry have been built through a series of acquisitions: Beatrice and Sara Lee Corporation are both the products of acquisitions. Traditionally, regional brands were acquired to take advantage of a larger, national sales force, as well as the financial strength of the parent company. When product lines of the two companies overlapped, the strength of the broader product line commanded greater influence in attracting shelf space in the supermarket, and greater discounts in advertising rates (Brown, 1985).

For Reynolds and Phillip Morris, acquisition of food products carried other benefits. Slower sales of cigarettes and pending lawsuits and legislation about smoking are expected to eventually erode profitability in the cigarette industry. The higher than average returns of the cereal and food companies, with a strong brand image of health and nutrition, is an attractive inducement for investment.

According to Marc C. Patricelli of Booz Allen & Hamilton Inc., 19 of 24 RTE cereal brands retained their leadership position from 1923 to 1983. "So if a company buys a leader, and if they run it correctly, they are buying an annuity, because brand leadership is sustainable" (Brown, 1985). Kellogg's financial performance and dominance in the cereal industry makes it an appealing target for merger or acquisition. Tables 24–26 give financial information on Kellogg.

Table 23. Recent Acquisitions of Established Brands

Buyer	Acquisition	Brands
Procter and Gamble	Richardson-Vicks	NyQuil, Vidal Sassoon, Clearasil
Phillip Morris	General Foods	Jell-O, Maxwell House
Monsanto	G.D. Searle	Nutrasweet, Metamusil
Brown-Forman	California Cooler	California Cooler
Greyhound	Purex' Cleaning	Purex Bleach, Brillo
Sara Lee	Nicholas Kiwi	Kiwi shoe polish
Nestlé	Carnation	Carnation Milk, Friskies pet food
Ralston Purina	Continental Baking	Hostess Twinkies, Wonder Bread
R.J. Reynolds	Nabisco Foods	Oreo cookies, Life Savers, Ritz Crackers, Shredded Wheat
Beatrice Foods	Esmark	Wesson Oil, Playtex
R.J. Reynolds	Canada Dry	Canada Dry soft drinks
Quaker Oats	Stokely-Van Camp	Gatorade, canned goods

Source: Brown (1985).

Table 24. Kellogg Company: Consolidated Balance Sheet ($ millions)

	1985	1984	1983	1982	1981
Current Assets					
Cash and temporary investments	$ 127.8	$ 308.9	$ 248.8	$ 159.8	$ 163.7
Accounts Receivable	203.9	182.5	157.1	140.7	158.9
Inventory					
Raw materials	135.6	119.7	115.7	128.8	129.4
Finished goods and work in progress	110.3	101.4	101.1	98.9	101.8
Prepaid expenses	40.5	39.0	40.4	35.9	28.4
Total current assets	618.1	751.5	663.1	564.1	582.2
Property					
Land	25.6	25.6	26.3	25.1	24.0
Buildings	321.2	277.7	274.1	263.4	263.8
Machinery and equipment	903.2	762.4	692.7	677.6	620.6
Construction in progress	280.4	215.7	143.7	83.5	90.0
Total property	1503.4	1281.4	1136.8	1049.6	998.4
Less accumulated depreciation	494.5	425.4	393.6	367.4	340.0
Net property	1035.9	856.0	743.2	682.2	658.4
Intangible assets	28.3	30.5	29.0	33.6	32.2
Other assets	43.8	29.1	31.9	17.5	6.3
Total assets	1726.1	1667.1	1467.2	1297.4	1279.1
Current Liabilities					
Current maturities of debt	34.8	340.6	20.0	6.5	16.5
Accounts payable	189.7	127.4	116.8	99.1	104.5
Accrued liabilities					
Income tax	29.4	51.4	85.0	81.9	77.4
Salaries and wages	41.8	38.7	36.2	31.4	29.9
Promotion	71.3	60.2	66.4	45.0	30.9
Other	46.4	45.8	36.3	43.7	41.7
Total Current Liabilities	444.3	664.1	360.7	307.6	300.9
Long-term debt	392.6	364.1	18.6	11.8	88.2
Other liabilities	12.3	9.5	9.2	11.0	9.8
Deferred income tax	193.9	142.2	100.8	82.3	69.9
Shareholder's Equity					
Common stock	38.4	38.4	38.2	38.2	38.2
Capital in excess of par value	44.5	40.8	34.4	32.9	32.5
Retained earnings	1288.5	1118.4	991.5	872.8	761.6
Treasury stock	−576.8	−577.8			
Currency translation adjustment	−111.6	−132.6	−86.2	−59.2	−22.0
Total equity	683.0	487.2	977.9	884.7	810.3
Total liabilities and equity	1726.1	1667.1	1467.2	1297.4	1279.1

Source: Kellogg Annual Reports.

Table 25. Kellogg Company: Consolidated Earnings and Retained Earnings ($ millions)

	1985	1984	1983	1982	1981	1980
Net sales	2930.1	2602.4	2381.1	2367.1	2331.3	2150.9
Interest revenue	7.2	27.7	18.6	21.3	18.2	18.7
Other, net	−2.8	3.9	18.1	2.1	0.0	0.0
Total revenue	2934.5	2634.0	2417.8	2390.5	2339.5	2169.6
C.O.G.S.	1605.0	1488.4	1412.3	1442.2	1447.8	1385.2
S, G, & A Exp.	766.7	650.8	554.4	529.2	501.1	435.7
Interest Exp.	35.4	18.7	7.1	8.2	12.0	10.4
Total	2407.1	2157.9	1973.8	1979.6	1960.9	1831.3
EBT	527.4	476.1	444.0	410.9	378.6	338.3
Income taxes	246.3	225.6	201.3	183.1	173.2	154.3
Net earnings	281.1	250.5	242.7	227.8	205.4	184.0
Retained earnings, Jan. 1	1118.4	991.5	872.8	761.6	665.1	583.5
Dividends	−111.0	−123.6	−124.0	−116.6	−108.9	−102.4
Retained earnings, Dec. 31	1288.5	1184.4	991.5	872.5	761.6	665.1

Source: Kellogg Annual Reports.

Conclusion

"The question is not whether this is a mature market," said LaMothe, "it's whether we can be inventive enough. . . . [Americans now have] the highest level of per capita [cereal] consumption in U.S. history. A lot of areas are close to 13 pounds. Why not make the whole country average 13?" (Willoughby, 1985). Kellogg's challenge is to increase the market for cereals, both domestic and foreign, by increasing consumption. In the United States, middle-aged and older Americans are the target segments. According to LaMothe (*Dun's Business Month,* Dec. 1985):

Dr. Kellogg and Mr. Kellogg were going on either intuition or their basic beliefs coming out of a Seventh Day Adventist background, where they believed that meats were not healthful for the diet . . . We think that it (cereal) has a tremendous future . . . The whole grains . . . healthy lifestyle . . . avoidance of major disease in the Western World . . . more grains, fruit and vegetables. Where else can you get such nutrition for 20 cents a serving? There will be 6 billion people on the face of the earth by the year 2000 and grains will continue to be the most efficient way for most people to get their calories and nutrition. We are going to help feed them, that's what Kellogg is all about.

Table 26. Kellogg Company: Changes in Consolidated Financial Position ($ millions)

	1985	1984	1983	1982	1981	1980
Source of funds						
Net earnings	281.1	250.5	242.7	227.7	205.4	184.0
Depreciation	75.4	63.9	62.8	55.9	49.1	44.7
Deferred tax/other	54.9	62.6	12.0	27.1	10.4	12.0
Total funds provided by operations	411.4	377.0	317.5	310.7	264.9	240.7
Changes in working capital components						
Accounts receivable	−21.4	−25.4	−16.4	18.2	−9.2	−17.0
Inventory	−24.8	−4.3	10.9	3.5	26.1	−19.2
Prepaid expenses	−1.5	1.4	−4.5	−7.5	−3.7	−7.1
Current debt maturity	−305.8	320.6	13.5	−10.0	−10.0	5.7
Accounts payable	62.3	10.6	17.7	−5.4	−1.5	−9.8
Accrued liability	23.7	−27.9	21.9	22.1	25.2	46.2
Net change	−267.5	275.1	43.1	20.9	26.9	−1.2
Funds provided by operations and changes in working capital	143.9	652.1	360.6	331.6	291.8	239.5
Long-term debt	31.5	348.1	1.5	0.0	7.9	0.4
Common stock	3.7	6.7	1.1	0.4	0.0	0.0
Property disposal	4.3	12.0	38.0	5.3	2.9	5.0
Tax-lease benefits	1.2	3.1	6.2	12.0	0.0	0.0
Other	7.9	0.9	0.5	3.1	0.5	1.4
Total source of funds	192.1	1022.9	407.9	352.4	303.1	246.3
Use of funds						
Property	245.6	228.9	156.7	121.1	146.4	122.9
Cash dividends	111.0	123.6	124.0	116.6	108.9	102.4
Treasury stock purchases	0.0	577.9	0.0	0.0	0.0	0.0
Investment in tax leases	0.0	0.0	11.6	14.2	0.0	
Long-term debt reduction	2.8	2.7	3.6	75.7	0.4	2.8
Other	23.8	14.7	10.5	13.9	6.4	1.1
Total use of funds	383.2	947.7	306.4	341.5	262.1	229.2
Exchange rate effect on working capital	10.0	−15.1	−12.5	−14.9	−9.1	0.0
Increase in cash and temporary investments	−181.1	60.1	89.0	−4.0	31.9	17.1

Source: Kellogg Annual Reports.

References

Advertising Age, Aug. 5, 1985, p. 42.

Associated Press, "FTC Accused of Sanctioning Bad Advertising Practice," Jul. 18, 1983.

Blyskal, Jeff (1984) "Branded Foods," *Forbes,* Jan. 2, p. 208.

Brody, Jane E. (1985) "America Leans to a Healthier Diet," *New York Times,* Oct. 13, p. 32, section 6.

Brown, Paul B., et al. (1985) "NEW? IMPROVED? The Brand Name Mergers," *Business Week,* Oct. 21, p. 108.

Business Week, Industrial Edition, Jan. 8, 1977, p. 46.

Business Week, Industrial Edition, Nov. 26, 1977, p. 80.

Business Week, "Too Many Cereals for the FTC," Mar. 20, 1978, p. 166+.

Business Week, "Still the Cereal People," Nov. 26, 1979, p. 80+.

Business Week, "Kellogg Looks Beyond Breakfast," Dec. 6, 1982, p. 66+.

Callahan, Tom (1986) "What's New With Breakfast; Morning Meals, Fresh from the Freezer," *New York Times,* Feb. 16, p. 17, section 3.

Cowan, Edward (1981) "F.T.C. Staff is Rebuffed on Cereals," *New York Times,* Sep. 11, p.D1.

Cowart, V. (1985). "Keeping Foods Safe and Labels Honest; Food Safety and Applied Nutrition," *Journal of the American Medical Association,* 254, 2228–2229.

Dewar, Helen (1980) "FTC Curbs are Adopted by Senate," *Washington Post,* Feb. 8, p.A1.

Drexel, Burnham, & Lambert, Brokerage House Report, "Kellogg Co.," Apr. 8, 1985.

Drexel, Burnham, & Lambert, Brokerage House Report, "General Foods," May 20, 1985.

Drexel, Burnham, & Lambert, Kellogg Company, Research Abstracts; Food Processors, Oct. 7, 1985.

Dun's Business Month, "Kellogg: Snap, Crackle, Profits," Dec. 1985, p.32+.

The Economist, "Philip Morris/General Foods: Chow Time for the Marlboro Cowboy", Oct. 5, 1985.

Federal Register, Federal Trade Commission, "Children's Advertising", 46 FR 48710.

Federal Register, "Childrens Television Programming and Advertising Practices," 49 FR 1704.

Federal Register, Federal Trade Commission, "Kellogg Company, et al; Prohibitive Trade Practices, and Affirmative Correction Actions," 47 FR 6817.

Federal Trade Commission v. J. E. Lonning, President, and Kellogg Company, a Corporation, Appellants, 539 F2nd 202.

Forbes, Oct. 7, 1985, p.126.

Friedman, Martin (1986) "Cereal Bowls Spill Over with Nuttiness," *ADWEEK,* Feb. 10.

Hollie, Pamela G. (1985) "New Cereal Pitch at Children," *New York Times,* Mar. 27, p.D1.

Johnson, Greg (1983) "Who's Afraid of Generic Cereals?" *Industry Week,* May 16, p.33.

Kellogg Company Annual Reports, 1981, 1982, 1983, 1984, 1985.

Kiechel, Walter III (1978) "The Soggy Case Against the Cereal Industry," *Fortune,* Apr. 10, p. 49.

Kronhelm, William (1985) "Should Food Labels Carry Health Claims, FDA's Policy Challenged," *Associated Press,* May 15.

Lippman, Thomas W. (1983) "Quebec's Ad Ban No Child's Game; Advertisers, TV Try to Adjust," *Washington Post,* Apr. 17, p.G1.

Marwick, C. (1985). "FDA prepares to meet regulatory challenges of 21st century," *Journal of the American Medical Association,* 254, 2189–2201.

Meadows, Edward (1981) "Bold Departures in Antitrust," *Fortune,* Oct. 5, p.180.

Newsweek, "A Portrait of America," Jan. 17, 1983, pp. 20–33.

New York Times, Sep. 15, 1985, section 3, p.1.

New York Times, "More Mothers are Working," Feb. 19, 1986, p. C4+.

Patent Number 3,952,112, "Method for treating dried fruits to improve softness retention characteristics," Fulger et al., April 20, 1976.

Patent Number 4,103,035, "Method for retaining softness in Raisins," Fulger et al., July 25, 1978.

Patent Number 4,178,392, "Method of Making a ready-to-eat breakfast cereal," Gobble et al., December 11, 1979.

Philip Morris Co., Press Release, Apr. 24, 1986.

Prokesch, Steven (1985) "Food Industry's Big Mergers," *New York Times,* Oct. 14, p.D1.

Prudential-Bache Securities, Inc., Oct. 1, 1985.

Prudential-Bache Securities, Inc., Apr. 2, 1986.

Rotenberk, Lori (1984) "Ad Exec Blasts JWT's All-Bran Ad," *ADWEEK* (Eastern edition), Oct. 29.

Sebastian, John V. (1979) "A Slight Taste of Honey," *Business Week,* Reader's Report, Dec. 17, p. 10.

Spillman, Susan (1985) "It's a Kid's Market," *USA Today,* Oct. 7.

Tracy, Eleanor Johnson (1985) "Madison Avenue's Cancer Sell Spreads," *Fortune,* Aug. 19, p.77.

Ward, S., "Compromise in Commercials for Children," *Harvard Business Review,* Nov. 1978, p. 128+.

Willoughby, Jack (1985) "The Snap, Crackle, Pop Defense," *Forbes,* Mar. 25, p. 82.

Wollenberg, Skip (1985) "Reagan's Cancer Diagnosis Sparks Prevention Ads," *Associated Press,* Jul. 29.

Case 3 Update*

To Our Stockholders:

A broad increase in consumption of ready-to-eat cereal products helped make 1987 another record year and one of substantial growth for Kellogg Company. Sales increased for the 43rd consecutive year, earnings improved for the 36th consecutive year, and dividends were raised for the 31st consecutive year, with a per-share increase from $1.02 to $1.29. A further increase of the quarterly dividend, to $0.38 per share, was announced in January 1988.

Consumer recognition of the importance of diet to good health and longevity continues to grow worldwide. This trend strongly favors nutritious, grain-based, ready-to-eat cereal products.

Traditionally, cereal consumption has been highest among children under 17 and adults over 50. In recent years, however, consumption increases in the 18–49 age group have represented not only a commitment by young adults to better health and fitness, but also an additional opportunity for long-term growth of our business.

Cereal consumption growth in more recently developed international markets has been very encouraging, with growth rates in several major countries currently exceeding 20 percent.

Marketplace competition in 1987 was more intense than ever before, challenging Kellogg Company to be even more innovative and aggressive in responding to the needs of consumers.

To strengthen our leadership position and our prospects for long-term growth, we continue to invest heavily in new technologies, product research and development, and effective marketing support programs.

Particularly noteworthy in 1987 was our substantial investment in modernizing and expanding our production facilities. Among major

*Excerpts from Kellogg Company 1987 annual report, pp. 3, 16–17, 20–22.

projects, we made significant progress in updating our Sydney, Australia facility; we began a further expansion of our Manchester, England plant; and we continued the work on our major addition to the Battle Creek, Michigan cereal plant. This new Battle Creek facility began producing cereal ahead of schedule in February 1988.

In January 1988, we announced the start of an additional expansion project in Battle Creek and plans to construct a new cereal production plant in Memphis, Tennessee.

Kellogg Company's strong financial condition provides great flexibility as we continue to invest in our business and seek new growth opportunities. In recognition of this strength, three major rating agencies—Moody's, Standard & Poor's, and Duff & Phelps—currently assign their highest debt rating to Kellogg Company.

Management Reorganization and Changes

In December 1987, Kellogg Company consolidated its U.S. subsidiary operations into Kellogg North America. This expanded division also includes our U.S. Food Products Division and our Canadian operations, Kellogg Salada Canada Inc. Concurrently, Horst W. Schroeder, president of Kellogg North America, was named group executive vice president, Kellogg Company.

We believe that bringing together all of our U.S. and Canadian operations provides greater synergisms within our organization and positions us to take better advantage of growth opportunities in all lines of our business.

In October 1987, Dr. Theodore Cooper, chairman of the board and chief executive officer of The Upjohn Company, was elected to the Kellogg Company Board of Directors.

Earlier in 1987, Walter T. Redmond, former vice chairman and chief administrative officer of Kellogg Company; Paul J. Kehoe, former vice chairman; and Gerald D. Robinson, former president and chief operating officer, retired from the Board of Directors. Also during 1987, W. Lawrence Romans was named corporate vice president-internal auditing.

In January 1988, Louis R. Somers, senior vice president-finance, retired from Kellogg Company and, in February 1988, Robert L. Burrows, vice president-materials planning, announced his plans to retire in March 1988. Concurrent with Mr. Somers' retirement, John R. Hinton was named vice president-finance and Jay W. Shreiner was named corporate treasurer.

No investment is more important than our continuing commitment to the growth and well-being of our most valuable asset, Kellogg employees. Their skills and dedicated performance have made us the leader in our business and provide strong encouragement as we face the challenges of the future.

William E. LaMothe
Chairman of the Board
Chief Executive Officer

Robert L. Nichols
Vice Chairman

Eleven-Year Summary (dollar amounts in millions, except share data)

Summary of Operations

	Net Sales	% Increase	Pretax Earnings	% Increase	Net Earnings	% Increase	Per Common Share Data			Average Shares (000's) Out-standing	Share-holder's Equity
							Net Earnings	Cash Divi-dends	Book Value		
10-year Compound Growth Rate	9%		10%		11%		14%	9%			
1987	**$3,793.0**	**14%**	**$665.7**	**13%**	**$395.9**	**24%**	**$3.20**	**$1.29**	**$9.82**	**123,668**	**$1,221.4**
1986	3,340.7	14%	586.6	11%	318.9	13%	2.58	1.02	7.27	123,481	898.4
1985	2,930.1	13%	527.4	11%	281.1	12%	2.28	.90	5.54	123,275	683.0
1984	2,602.4	9%	476.1	7%	250.5	3%	1.68	.85	3.96	149,380	487.2
1983	2,381.1	1%	444.0	8%	242.7	7%	1.59	.81	6.39	152,934	977.9
1982	2,367.1	2%	410.9	9%	227.8	11%	1.49	.76	5.79	152,878	884.7
1981	2,321.3	8%	378.6	12%	205.4	12%	1.34	.71	5.30	152,864	810.3
1980	2,150.9	16%	338.3	20%	184.0	14%	1.20	.67	4.81	152,860	735.8
1979	1,846.6	9%	281.6	4%	161.5	12%	1.06	.65	4.28	152,846	654.2
1978	1,690.6	10%	271.7	4%	144.4	5%	.94	.60	3.87	152,808	590.9
1977	1,533.4	11%	261.4	4%	137.6	6%	.90	.56	3.52	152,622	537.0

Other Information and Financial Ratios

	Property, Net	Capital Expend-itures	Depre-ciation	Total Assets	% Increase	Number of Em-ployees	Financial Ratios				Working Capital	Long-term Debt
							Current Ratio	Pretax Interest Coverage (times)	Return on Average Equity	Debt to Total Capital		
1987	**$1,738.8**	**$478.4**	**$113.1**	**$2,680.9**	**13%**	**17,762**	**.9**	**14**	**38%**	**27%**	**$(51.5)**	**$290.4**
1986	1,281.1	329.2	92.7	2,084.2	11%	17,383	1.1	13	40%	31%	43.2	264.1
1985	1,035.9	245.6	75.4	1,726.1	11%	17,082	1.4	11	48%	38%	173.8	392.6
1984	856.0	228.9	63.9	1,667.1	7%	17,239	1.1	26	27%	59%	87.4	364.1
1983	743.2	156.7	62.8	1,467.2	8%	18,293	1.8	64	26%	4%	302.4	18.6
1982	682.2	121.1	55.9	1,297.4	9%	19,290	1.8	51	27%	2%	256.5	11.8
1981	658.4	146.4	49.1	1,279.1	12%	20,260	1.9	33	27%	11%	281.3	88.2
1980	582.2	122.9	44.7	1,181.9	20%	21,285	2.0	34	26%	12%	276.3	82.7
1979	509.0	80.9	40.5	1,049.8	4%	20,818	2.1	28	26%	15%	258.0	84.6
1978	474.0	86.7	36.3	941.9	4%	20,905	2.1	29	26%	16%	222.3	84.0
1977	422.1	75.9	31.9	839.0	4%	20,405	2.2	29	27%	17%	206.7	80.3

Kellogg Company and Subsidiaries Consolidated Earnings and Retained Earnings
  Year Ended December 31

(millions)	1987	1986	1985
Net sales	$3,793.0	$3,340.7	$2,930.1
Interest revenue	14.1	11.7	7.2
Other revenue (deductions), net	(8.4)	(31.0)	(2.8)
	3,798.7	3,321.4	2,934.5
Cost of goods sold	1,939.3	1,744.6	1,605.0
Selling and administrative expense	1,162.5	948.7	766.7
Interest expense	31.2	41.5	35.4
	3,133.0	2.734.8	2,407.1
Earnings before income taxes	665.7	586.6	527.4
Income taxes	269.8	267.7	246.3
Net earnings—$3.20, $2.58, and $2.28 a share	395.9	318.9	281.1
Retained earnings, beginning of year	1,481.5	1,288.5	1,118.4
Dividends paid—$1.29, $1.02, and $.90 a share	(159.5)	(125.9)	(111.0)
Retained earnings, end of year	$1,717.9	$1,481.5	$1,288.5

See notes to financial statements.

Kellogg Company and Subsidiaries Changes in Consolidated
  Financial Position Year Ended December 31

(millions)	1987	1986	1985
Source of funds			
Net earnings	$395.9	$318.9	$ 281.1
Depreciation	113.1	92.7	75.4
Deferred income taxes and other	40.5	31.2	54.9
Funds provided by operations	549.5	442.8	411.4
Changes in components of working capital:			
Accounts receivable	(57.6)	(13.6)	(21.4)
Inventories	(45.5)	(19.5)	(24.8)
Prepaid expenses	(41.1)	(8.1)	(1.5)
Current maturities of debt	15.8	100.8	(305.8)
Accounts payable	49.1	73.1	62.3
Accrued liabilities	102.1	68.2	23.7
Net change	22.8	200.9	(267.5)
Funds provided by operations and changes in working capital	572.3	643.7	143.9
Issuance of long-term debt	52.4	22.6	31.5
Issuance of common stock	8.8	4.8	3.7
Property disposals	10.2	4.1	4.3
Other	9.5	13.5	8.7
Total source of funds	653.2	688.7	192.1
Use of funds			
Additions to properties	478.4	329.2	245.6
Cash dividends	159.5	125.9	111.0
Purchase of treasury stock	22.6		
Reduction in long-term debt	29.1	151.3	2.8
Other	30.6	15.4	23.8
Total use of funds	720.2	621.8	383.2
Effect of exchange rate changes on working capital	(4.9)	3.4	10.0
Increase (decrease) in cash and temporary investments	$(71.9)	$ 70.3	$(181.1)

See notes to financial statements.

Kellogg Company and Subsidiaries Consolidated Balance Sheet at December 31

(millions)	1987	1986
Current assets		
Cash and temporary investments	$ 126.2	$ 198.1
Accounts receivable, less allowances of $2.6 and $2.3	275.1	217.5
Inventories:		
Raw materials and supplies	161.9	147.7
Finished goods and materials in process	149.0	117.7
Prepaid expenses	89.7	48.6
Total current assets	801.9	729.6
Property		
Land	34.7	29.7
Buildings	568.3	439.0
Machinery and equipment	1,427.2	1,172.6
Construction in progress	387.8	213.1
Accumulated depreciation	(679.2)	(573.3)
Property, net	1,738.8	1,281.1
Intangible assets	77.4	28.0
Other assets	62.8	45.5
Total assets	$2,680.9	$2,084.2
Current liabilities		
Current maturities of debt	$ 151.4	$ 135.6
Accounts payable	311.9	262.8
Accrued liabilities:		
Income taxes	113.5	72.2
Salaries and wages	56.3	51.0
Promotion	151.9	101.2
Interest	30.0	25.6
Other	38.4	38.0
Total current liabilities	853.4	686.4
Long-term debt	290.4	264.1
Other liabilities	69.3	16.4
Deferred income taxes	256.4	218.9
Shareholders' equity		
Common stock, $.25 par value—shares authorized 165,000,000; issued 154,015,283 and 153,744,802	38.5	38.4
Capital in excess of par value	58.1	49.3
Retained earnings	1,717.9	1,481.5
Treasury stock, at cost—30,607,683 and 30,182,783 shares	(598.2)	(575.6)
Currency translation adjustment	(4.9)	(95.2)
Total shareholders' equity	1,211.4	898.4
Total liabilities and shareholders' equity	$2,680.9	$2,084.2

See notes to financial statements.

The American Express Company

American Express company executives, meeting in their new fifty-one-story headquarters in the financial district of lower Manhattan, look to the future with a certain optimism. As the chairman and CEO, James D. Robinson, III, put it, "We are extremely active in two of the world's greatest growth industries: financial services and tourism."[1] A trusted name since 1850, AMEXCO looks to the second half of the eighties and into the nineties with a corporate philosophy and values anchored in entrepreneurship, quality, integrity, and service. A brief history of the company appears in Appendix A.

Flushed with the apparent success of its major acquisitions, AMEXCO's total assets had tripled from 1982 to nearly $62 billion by the end of 1984. This international financial supermarket (Exhibit 1) employs 77,000 people in more than 2,000 offices spread throughout 131 countries. Much of its incredible growth has occurred in only 3 years, "faster than expected because of profound changes in insurance, banking and securities wrought by the interplay of higher interest rates, technology and deregulation."[2]

During this period of expansion, AMEXCO revenues doubled to almost $13 billion with net income increasing from $466 million to $610 million (Exhibit 2). Through 1982 AMEXCO enjoyed its thirty-fifth consecutive year of increased earnings. This ended in 1983 with an 11 percent decrease in net income primarily attributed to problems at Fireman's Fund. By the end of 1984, AMEXCO showed respectable growth in net income of 18 percent.

The competition has a very healthy respect for the strength of AMEXCO. Dee Hock, former managing director and CEO of VISA International, commenting on combat with AMEXCO, said:

> They [AMEX] are rough, tough, smart competitors with tons of money. There is very little they will not do to achieve their objectives. The advantage of American Express is that James Robinson can say, "To the left, march" and they do. I couldn't think of doing that. Each of our institutions [members] is totally independent.[3]

George Ball, president and CEO of Prudential-Bache Securities Inc., was quoted in April 1984 as saying, "Four years ago [AMEX] was a plastic card company, but with the addition of Lehman, AMEX is a fully fleshed-out financial services confederation of the type that will be dominant in tomorrow's marketplace."[4] Herbert E. Goodfriend, an analyst with Prudential-Bache, calls American Express "unquestionably the premier company in the financial services industry."[5]

---

[1]"American Express: Financial Powerhouse," *Dun's Business Month*, December 1983, p. 39.

[2]Arlene Hershman, "The Supercompanies Emerge," *Dun's Business Month*, April 1983, p. 44.

© William D. Wilsted. Financial and organizational data are taken from *American Express Company 1984 Annual Report* unless otherwise noted. Used by permission of the author.

[3]Leonard A. Schlesinger, Robert G. Eccles, John J. Gararro, *Managing Behavior in Organizations* (New York: McGraw-Hill, 1983), p. 479.

[4]"The Golden Plan of American Express," *Business Week*, April 30, 1984, p. 118.

[5]"American Express: Financial Powerhouse," p. 38.

Exhibit 1   The American Express Company (December 1984)

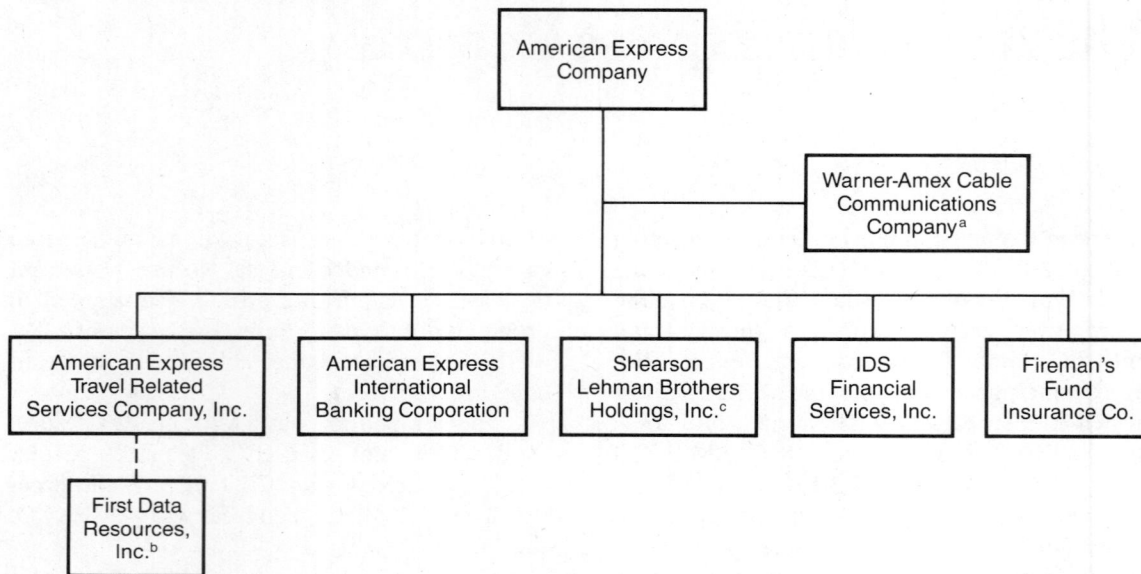

Source: Constructed from information contained in American Express Company 1984 Annual Report.
[a]AMEXCO owns 50 percent.
[b]TRS owns 75 percent of capital stock of the largest third-party processor of debit and credit cards in the United States.
[c]Includes fourteen major subsidiaries of which Shearson Lehman Brothers, Inc. is the principal.

The financial services supermarket is considered to operate in one or more of five major businesses. They include banking, credit cards, insurance, real estate, and securities. AMEXCO is looking for ways to enter the domestic U.S. banking business; Citicorp wants to enter the securities business. Sears, Roebuck, and Co. and Bank America are both involved in all five major businesses. Prudential-Bache and Merrill Lynch, the other two principal financial supermarkets, like AMEXCO, lack domestic banking operations.[6] AMEXCO currently outstrips all the others in the travel-related services industry. Exhibit 3 shows six companies that have major positions in a number of critical financial-services businesses (at end of 1982).

According to a 1984 survey conducted by the *American Banker,* people rate American Express products and services higher than those of any other top financial services firm in the United States. The same survey indicates that the American Express name is best known among consumers.[7]

AMEXCO's Major Companies

Assembled under the American Express corporate roof are five major companies. They include American Express Travel Related Services Company, Inc. (TRS), American Express International Banking Corporation (AEIBC), Shearson Lehman Brothers, Inc. (SLAX), IDS Financial

---

[6]"The Supercompanies Emerge," p. 45.

[7]*American Express Company 1985 Annual Report,* p. 4.

Exhibit 2   Consolidated Summary of Selected Financial Data

	1984	1983	1982	1981	1980
Operating results					
Revenues	$12,895	$ 9,770	$ 8,093	$ 7,291	$ 6,426
Percent increase in revenues	*32%*	*21%*	*11%*	*13%*	*26%*
Expenses	12,159	9,253	7,339	6,586	5,830
Income taxes	126	2	173	181	130
Net income	610	515	581	524	466
Percent increase (decrease) in net income	*18%*	*(11)%*	*11%*	*12%*	*23%*
Assets and liabilities					
Time deposits	$ 5,470	$ 4,071	$ 2,127	$ 1,784	$ 1,120
Investment securities					
Carried at cost	13,449	12,766	7,163	6,446	6,026
Carried at lower of aggregate cost or market	315	211	81	148	166
Carried at market	8,566	1,709	948	917	1,235
Accounts receivable and accrued interest, net	14,802	11,497	9,204	8,191	6,825
Loans and discounts, net	7,089	6,642	4,379	3,929	3,811
Total assets	61,848	43,981	28,311	25,252	22,731
Customers' deposits and credit balances	13,262	12,511	6,810	6,218	5,818
Travelers checks outstanding	2,454	2,362	2,177	2,468	2,542
Insurance and annuity reserves	8,831	7,667	4,323	4,110	3,856
Long-term debt	3,839	2,643	1,798	1,293	1,293
Shareholders' equity	4,607	4,043	3,039	2,661	2,430
Common share statistics					
Net income per share	$ 2.79	$ 2.53	$ 3.02	$ 2.79	$ 2.59
Cash dividends declared per share	$ 1.28	$ 1.26	$ 1.125	$ 1.025	$ 1.00
Average number of shares outstanding	217	203	192	188	180
Shares outstanding at year-end	217	213	191	188	185
Number of shareholders of record	*51,211*	*45,753*	*36,580*	*36,611*	*34,735*
Other statistics					
Number of employees at year-end					
United States	*59,420*	*53,740*	*48,533*	*43,315*	*39,475*
Outside United States	*17,027*	*16,716*	*15,472*	*14,994*	*15,556*
Total	*76,447*	*70,456*	*64,005*	*58,309*	*55,031*
Number of offices at year-end					
American Express offices worldwide	*1,472*	*1,356*	*1,160*	*1,066*	*1,046*
Representative offices	*810*	*797*	*760*	*782*	*782*
Total	*2,282*	*2,153*	*1,920*	*1,848*	*1,828*

Note: Data in millions, except per share amounts and where italicized.
Note: Operating results for the year ended December 31, 1983 do not include the effect of the acquisition of Investors Diversified Services, Inc., accounted for as a purchase as of December 31, 1983. Where applicable, amounts and percentages for 1984 include the effect of the acquisition of Lehman Brothers Kuhn Loeb Holding Co., Inc., accounted for as a purchase as of May 11, 1984.
Source: American Express Co. 1984 Annual Report.

Exhibit 3   The Six Financial-Services Leaders

	Banking	Credit cards	Insurance	Real estate	Securities
American Express Co. Assets: $30 billion Revenue: $8.1 billion Net income: $581 million	—	(1)	(2)	(3)	(1)
BankAmerica Corp. Assets: $122.5 billion Revenue: $4 billion Net income: $451 million	(1)	(1)	(3)	(1)	(2)
Citicorp Assets: $130 billion Revenue: $5.2 billion Net income: $723 million	(1)	(1)	(3)	(1)	—
Merrill Lynch & Co. Assets: $20.7 billion Revenue: $5 billion Net income: $309 million	—	(3)	(2)	(2)	(1)
Prudential Insurance Co. of America Assets: $76.5 billion Revenue: $18.5 billion Net income: $2.13 billion	—	(3)	(1)	(2)	(1)
Sears, Roebuck & Co. Assets: $36 billion Revenue: $30 billion Net income: $861 million	(2)	(1)	(2)	(2)	(1)

(1) = Major factor in this industry.
(2) = Medium-sized factor in this industry.
(3) = Small factor in this industry.
Source: "The Supercompanies Emerge," *Dun's Business Month*, April 1983, p. 44.

Services Inc. (IDS), and Fireman's Fund Insurance Companies (FF). Additionally, AMEXCO owns 50 percent of Warner AMEX Cable Communications. Appendix B presents 1982–1984 financial data by service category. Appendix C presents 1983–1984 financial data by subsidiary. Following is a discussion of each of these companies.

American Express Travel Related Services Company

Perhaps the oldest name in travel is TRS, the flagship organization of AMEXCO. The company was founded in 1850 and became a separate company under the AMEXCO banner in 1983. Annual growth in revenues exceeded 18 percent from 1982 to 1984. TRS is in the process of modernizing and is emerging as the most customer-responsive travel and credit card service company in the world with great profit potential.

TRS has grown and developed a great deal since its early days as a small package and funds freight company. Currently, TRS is best known for its worldwide network of travel offices, charge card, and traveler's cheques (without which you do not leave home). In addition, TRS offers direct mail merchandise services, publishing (*Travel and Leisure* and *Food and Wine*), and data processing services. TRS is also moving into communications, providing AMEX card members access to MCI. This is primarily a billing service providing MCI long-distance dialing through what AMEXCO calls "Expressphone."

In 1985, TRS launched "Project Hometown America" which raises money for local communities by contributions from American Express Card purchases, AMEX traveler's cheques, purchases of travel packages, and new card applications. TRS continues to utilize extensive advertising which, among other things, features tie-ins with major hotels, resorts, car-rental companies, and Eastern and United Airlines.

TRS operates 1,200 offices in more than 131 countries. Overseas travel has been popular due to the strength of the American dollar and TRS has capitalized on this opportunity. In 1984 and early 1985, TRS acquired new travel companies in Pittsburgh, Denver, and thirty-eight locations in the United Kingdom.

While the proliferation of plastic money and automatic teller machines (ATM) have eaten into the traveler's cheque market, AMEXCO still sold $15.1 billion in 1984, an increase of 9.1 percent over 1983. The average outstanding traveler's cheque's volume in 1983 was $2.6 billion, up 8.3 percent. It is on these outstanding cheques, or "float," that TRS makes its profit, which in 1982 was $76 million before taxes. In 1962 the traveler's cheque float accounted for 80 percent of AMEXCO's total income. Twenty years later, it was responsible for only 11 percent of the total income. (Credit cards accounted for 24 percent of income; Fireman's Fund, 36 percent; and Shearson, 18 percent in 1982.) It is the lessons learned from managing the traveler's cheque float that make AMEXCO's management of cash balances anywhere within the corporation masterful.[8]

By the end of 1984 there were more than 20 million American Express Cards in force

throughout the world, an increase of 17 percent over 1983. Credit card charge volume grew 24 percent to $47.6 billion during the same time. One out of every four cardholders lives overseas and the card is issued in twenty-eight currencies. In 1984, 125 mainland Chinese establishments accepted the card compared to 14 in 1983.

In August 1984, the platinum card ($250 fee, by invitation only) was offered in addition to the green card (offered since 1958) and the gold card (first offered in 1981). In 1984, AMEXCO added major retailers such as the May Company and the J. C. Penney Company as establishments that accept the American Express Card. TRS also acquired Health Carecard, Inc., a company whose product combines medical record keeping with payment capabilities.

The American Express Card differs from other plastic cards in distinct ways. It must be paid in full monthly (unless special arrangements have been made in advance) and the annual fee is more than other cards. (In 1985 the green card fee increased by 30 percent to $45.) These facts, coupled with economies of scale in billing and extensive experience in managing moving cash balances, make the American Express Card unique and highly profitable.

Another segment of TRS is direct marketing. When American Express began in 1974 to include product inserts in its 5 million monthly bills, it did not envision a merchandise services division of $185 million in sales just 10 years later. The growth of TRS's direct mail business is largely the result of its sophisticated use of customer segmentation based on the exact purpose for which each cardholder uses the card. Particular product mailings are targeted with precision to those customer groups with the greatest potential buying interest in that product. The merchandise services division has six target customer segments:

The frequent traveler, to whom it sells products and services to make business and travel more enjoyable

The upscale male consumer, to whom it sells

---

[8]Priscilla S. Meyer, "Cheques and Balances," *Forbes,* March 14, 1983, p. 50.

state-of-the-art electronics for home entertainment and personal productivity

The upscale female consumer, to whom it sells products related to home design and household invention

Business executives of small- to medium-sized companies, to whom it sells products for the office that will increase chances for success

Portions of each of the above, to whom it offers new products on a test basis

Portions of each of the first four groups, to whom it offers various services, including magazine subscriptions at discounted prices[9]

A key to the merchandise services division's success is its strategy of offering exclusive merchandise. Whenever possible, TRS strives to be the sole source of the merchandise it offers. More than 90 percent of the noncatalog merchandise offered is exclusive. TRS seeks manufacturers who will modify certain aspects of a product just for AMEXCO. As a result, TRS sold 18,000 IBM electric typewriters in 1983 and 42,000 Gucci watches in 1982 and 1983.[10]

The strengths that TRS has identified as its basis for its marketing approach are:

The prestige attached to owning an American Express card

The excellent customer service provided by AMEXCO

A vast, affluent cardmember customer base (over 11 million in the United States)

AMEXCO's orientation toward business

AMEXCO's adeptness at packaging goods and services

A very strong overall quality image

Strong information processing skills[11]

The goals of the merchandise services division are: to continue to use the strong name recognition of American Express to generate sales to new customers; to provide the best service available in direct merchandising, with new, quality products tailored to the customers' needs; and to go outside the AMEXCO cardmember base to allow customers to pay for merchandise by Visa, MasterCard, or other credit cards.[12]

In publishing, TRS saw new highs in both ad pages and revenues in 1984. With almost a million paid subscribers, *Travel and Leisure* saw an increase of 23 percent in advertising revenues over 1983. *Food and Wine,* with 600,000 paid subscribers, saw an 18 percent increase in advertising revenues over 1983.

Since 1984, TRS has owned 75 percent of the capital stock of First Data Resources, Inc. This data processing company is the largest third-party processor of debit and credit cards in the United States. It is this acquisition that gives AMEXCO its economies of scale in processing transactions.

Historically TRS has exhibited a great deal of support for the arts. From 1979 through 1984 TRS sponsored fifty projects, in one hundred cities, over five continents, to bring the arts closer to the people (at a cost of $20 million in 1984).[13] In AMEXCO's opinion, it has been worth the investment. AMEXCO has gained recognition within these communities and increased opportunities to attract potential customers and financial institutions. The "Project Hometown America" mentioned earlier is an extension of AMEXCO's charitable, goodwill efforts, while it offers potential tax advantages.

American Express International Banking Corporation

Growing out of a need to provide the travel-hungry American tourist financial services

[9]Larry Jaffee, "AMEX Targets Mailings Precisely to List Segments," *Direct Marketing,* May 1984, p. 78.

[10]Ibid., p. 79.

[11]Ibid., p. 78.

[12]Ibid., p. 86.

[13]Susan Bloom, "Beauty and the Bottom Line," *Business Quarterly,* Fall 1984, p. 86.

abroad after World War I, AEIBC was founded in 1919 as the American Express Company, Incorporated. In 1968, the name was changed to American Express International Banking Corporation.

By 1980 AMEXCO was itching to get rid of its overseas bank, AEIBC. The bank, under the direction of Richard Bliss, had been attempting to establish itself as a big investment banking concern in London. In 1981 Robert F. Smith, formerly AMEXCO's treasurer, took over as vice-chairman of the bank. Smith quickly changed the direction of the bank by slashing its operating costs and paring down its attempt to offer every service imaginable. The bank began to focus on trade finance and private banking for wealthy individual clients. AEIBC evolved into a deal-making organization with trade-related transactions involving export credit guarantees from Western governments.

The big improvement in AEIBC performance through 1983 was clearly a result of sheer cost-cutting. Total operating expenses fell from 63 percent of net financial revenue in 1981 to 52 percent in 1983. Also figuring prominently in the improvement was the acquisition of the Trade Development Bank (TDB) in Switzerland in March 1983. At $800 million in shareholders' equity, the combined bank has more than twice the equity of the old AEIBC. That, in turn, reduced AEIBC's Latin American debt from four times equity to a more manageable, yet still concerning, two times equity.[14]

To acquire the TDB, AMEXCO paid more than 50 percent over the book value of TDB stock. Many believe that AMEXCO paid the premium price to obtain the services of Edmond J. Safra, Lebanese-born banking genius and owner of TDB.[15] Safra needed U.S. government approval to become CEO of AEIBC (a condition of sale). Although the sale was made in January 1983, Safra did not set foot in AMEXCO's corporate offices in New York throughout the year. While waiting for U.S. approval, AMEXCO top executives visited and called Safra frequently (he has controlling interest in other U.S. banks) at his TDB office in Geneva to get the benefit of his advice and banking instincts.[16] Safra continued running TDB and in 1984 was elected to AMEXCO's board of directors.

As a result of these moves, the AEIBC was a welcome member of the AMEXCO family in early 1984. The former wallflower is a highly profitable bank with $13 billion in assets.[17] The AMEXCO hierarchy sees a great potential for marketing Shearson/American Express Inc. services through the AEIBC. 1984 was a year of record profits for AEIBC, even though it was a year that will be remembered as one of the most difficult in international banking. Net income in 1984 increased 15 percent to a record $156 million after a 126 percent increase to $136 million from 1982 to 1983.

Today, with 82 offices in 39 countries, AEIBC includes international private banking, trade financing operations, correspondent banking (more than 2,000 active correspondent bank relationships worldwide), treasury and foreign exchange services, equipment financing (American Express Leasing Corporation), and military banking for the U.S. Armed Forces overseas.

Citicorp has been a pioneer among the major financial supermarkets in pushing for changes in the law that would permit it, a leader in domestic banking, into the insurance field.[18] Citicorp has made inroads in this regard in South Dakota. If Citicorp is successful on a national basis, the door would be open for AMEXCO, if they so choose, to move into the domestic banking in-

[14]"AMEX's Bank: A Wallflower Suddenly Blossoms," *Business Week,* January 9, 1984, p. 101.

[15]Gwen Kinkead, "The Mystery Man American Express Is Banking On," *Fortune,* December 12, 1983, p. 142.

[16]Ibid.

[17]"AMEX's Bank: A Wallflower Suddenly Blossoms," p. 101.

[18]Carol J. Loomis, "Fire in the Belly at American Express," *Fortune,* November 28, 1983, p. 87.

dustry either as a separate AMEXCO company or as a division of AEIBC.

Fireman's Fund Insurance Company

Since 1863, when it was founded in San Francisco, Fireman's Fund Insurance Company has grown to be a leading provider of insurance protection for individuals, groups, businesses, and institutions, offering a broad range of property, liability, life, accident, and health insurance. Acquired by AMEXCO in 1968, FF products are offered through more than 10,000 independent agents and brokers throughout the United States.

In 1979 and 1980 the property and casualty industry experienced serious trouble due to price-cutting on many types of policies. In 1981, under the leadership of Fireman's Fund CEO Myron Dubain, FF cut a deal with the Insurance Company of North America to swap certain casualty policies. The swap allowed both companies to discount the loss reserves required on their newly acquired policies, without disclosing a change in accounting practices on their financial statements or to their respective boards of directors. This accounting sleight-of-hand increased FF's reported pretax profits by $66 million in 1981–1982, but resulted in a negative cash flow due to an additional $30 million tax bill[19] (Exhibit 4).

In 1982, Edwin F. Cutler became FF's CEO with guidance from AMEXCO to further increase profits. From January to September 1983, FF dropped its premium prices and generated a 13 percent increase in written premiums while the insurance industry average was only about 4 percent.[20]

In the third quarter of 1983, a sharp rise in claims forced FF to add $10 million to its loss reserves, which resulted in a fourth-quarter after-tax net loss of $10 million.[21]

A *Fortune* article in November 1983 ex-

---

[19]Carol J. Loomis, "How Fireman's Fund Stoked Its Profits," *Fortune,* November 28, 1983, pp. 99–104.

[20]Carol J. Loomis, "How Fireman's Fund Singed American Express," *Fortune,* January 9, 1984, p. 80.

[21]Ibid.

Exhibit 4 Fireman's Fund Net Income

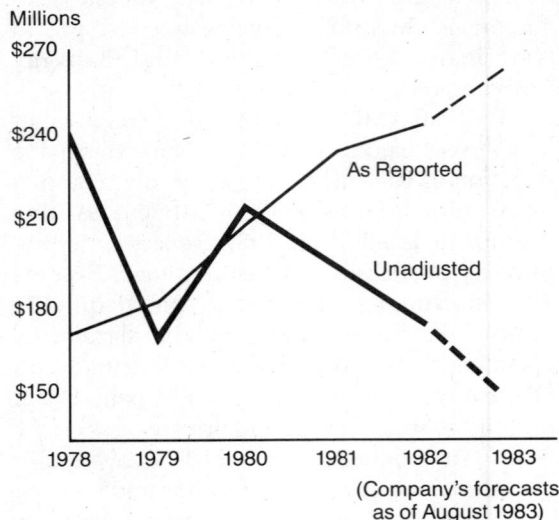

(Company's forecasts as of August 1983)

The dollar gap between "reported net income" and "unadjusted net income" at Fireman's Fund in the 1978–83 period was recapped in an August 1983 memo from Edwin F. Cutler, then chairman of the American Express subsidiary, to his boss, James D. Robinson III, chairman of the parent. Unadjusted profits were those earned on the subsidiary's basic insurance business, which as time went on felt increasing cyclical pressure. But "special items" added to or subtracted from those profits allowed Fireman's Fund to report figures that showed the smooth uptrend American Express loves to see. Cutler's memo forecast a further gain for reported profits in 1983. But a subsequent spike in claim costs and a $230-million addition to reserves blitzed 1983 profits. Reported net income for 1983 was $30 million; unadjusted net income was not announced.

Source: "The Earnings Magic at American Express," *Fortune,* June 25, 1984, p. 58.

posed the paper profits of 1981–1982 and seriously undermined the credibility of FF's and AMEXCO's financial statements.[22]

In December 1983 Cutler was removed as CEO and replaced by acquisition and financial

---

[22]Loomis, "How Fireman's Fund Stoked Its Profits," pp. 99–104.

wizard Sanford Weill, an executive with no prior insurance experience. FF simultaneously announced a reduction in its work force of 14,000 by more than 10 percent through retirement and attrition in an effort to reduce costs.

In December 1983, AMEXCO's board of directors added $230 million to FF's loss reserves which contributed to a drop in AMEXCO earnings from $700 million to $520 million for 1983. A public announcement by AMEXCO on December 12, 1983 regarding FF's financial problems caused a single-day drop in AMEXCO stock from $32 to $29 per share.[23] FF's performance, or lack thereof, was the principal reason why AMEXCO had its first downturn in earnings in 36 years.

In the first quarter of 1984, Sandy Weill cut 1,200 employees from the payroll, estimating a $40–50 million annual saving. Weill announced a three-step strategy to become the low-cost producer in the industry: lay-offs and cost cutting, combined with increased efficiencies in decision making due to more autonomy at lower levels; top management compensation tied to performance; and a revamping of FF's data processing system.[24]

The first quarter of 1984 saw a modest $10 million profit, but in the second quarter 1985 FF reported a quarterly loss of $71.7 million on revenues of $1 billion. Once again AMEXCO felt compelled to add $187 million to FF's loss reserves.[25]

By July 1985, Sandy Weill was replaced as CEO of Fireman's Fund by John J. Byrne, former CEO at Government Employees Insurance Company.[26] In December 1985, FF changed executive vice-presidents, with James Ridling, formerly of Crum and Foster, replacing Donald McComber.

As the year closed, AMEXCO owned 41 percent of FF.[27]

Shearson Lehman/American Express

Synergy—the art of making one plus one equal three—was the underlying impetus behind the broad concept of creating financial supermarkets, which, in turn, led to the stampede of acquisitions of large brokerage firms by giant outsiders in 1981. As part of the stampede, AMEXCO acquired the prestigious Wall Street brokerage firm Shearson at a price of approximately $1 billion. The merger was, to some degree, a response to the Prudential-Bache merger. Sandy Weill, Shearson's CEO at the time, did not want to risk being left behind by the entry of the largest U.S. insurer into the securities business. The merger between AMEXCO and Shearson was brought about by the two firms' belief that the barriers of tradition and regulation separating banking, brokerage, and insurance would eventually evaporate.[28]

In 1984 Shearson, under the leadership of their new CEO, Peter Cohen, purchased the 134-year-old investment bank of Lehman Brothers Kuhn-Loeb. This acquisition provided AMEXCO with additional strength in investment banking and fixed-income trading. As a result, SLAX wields this investment banking strength with a broadbased, soundly capitalized trading capacity and a global distribution network with over 5,000 professional financial consultants in 354 offices located in forty-four states and fifteen countries. Through these consultants, SLAX offers stocks, bonds, options, futures, commercial paper, certificates of deposit, insurance, and tax-advantaged investments as well as investment banking, pension and investment management, real estate, and mortgage banking services.

Mergers such as this have had the effect of moving retail brokers closer to becoming finan-

[23]Loomis, "How Fireman's Fund Singed American Express," p. 80.

[24]Mary Row, "Can Sandy Weill Turn Fireman's Fund Around," *Institutional Investor,* May 1984, pp. 110–112.

[25]Carol J. Loomis, "The Earnings Magic at American Express," *Fortune,* June 25, 1984, p. 60.

[26]"A New Chief for Fireman's Fund," *Business Week,* August 5, 1985, p. 38.

[27]"Who's News," *Wall Street Journal,* December 19, 1985, p. 14.

[28]Anthony Bianco, "How A Financial Supermarket Was Born," *Business Week,* December 23, 1985, p. 10.

cial consultants, although the SLAX brokers can now refer their clients with specific problems to the specialists who may reside in one of their sister companies and who also fall under the AMEXCO umbrella. This is due in large part to AMEXCO's purchase of such firms as Balcor (the nation's largest real estate syndicator) and Investors Diversified Services and Ayco (both well-known financial planning firms).[29]

Among the mergers' by-products, none seems to have benefited the brokers more than the reputation of AMEXCO. SLAX staff members acknowledge an overnight surge in client confidence. "Once Shearson teamed up with American Express, we got the credibility we needed."[30] Other beneficial side effects include the infusion of capital by AMEXCO (which has enabled many of the brokers to obtain desktop computers, which improves their service to the client); the ability to attend workshops on specific products and selling skills; and stepped-up advertising campaigns to enhance their visibility.

The effect of these advantages can be seen in the year-end summary of activities for SLAX for 1984. The company managed over 300 underwritings in U.S. and international markets. The corporate finance division represented clients in more than 70 completed mergers, acquisitions, and divestitures with an aggregate transaction value of over $12 billion. The public finance division managed tax-exempt financings of $28 billion for state and local governments in 1984. Shearson also recognized a 135 percent rise in revenues in the fixed-income sector and an 8.4 percent increase in revenues from the sale of tax-advantaged investments.

However, there have been certain drawbacks to the merger. The presence of AMEXCO has diminished the informal atmosphere that previously existed at Shearson. "A certain impersonality has emerged, it is no longer the closely

knit firm it once was."[31] The bureaucratic system of the conglomerate is also frustrating to the Shearson staffers: "It takes six weeks to get some requests through."[32] Along with the abundance of products has come an abundance of paperwork. Equally as frustrating is the fact that the parent company, as of March 1984, had not yet released the names of its 9 million green-card holders to the brokerage firm. This single source of potential clients could easily double or triple Shearson's client base.[33]

Despite these drawbacks, it is the consensus of the brokerage community that the full effects of the mergers will not be felt for some time. They are convinced that these mergers will give rise to a new breed of broker, one able to deal with a larger client base by supplying a wider range of financial services.

IDS Financial Services, Inc.
IDS Financial Services, Inc. (IDS) was established in 1894 to help people and businesses manage money and achieve their financial goals. Through its sales force of more than 4,400 representatives, IDS offers sound financial plans and the products and services to fulfill those plans. Among its offerings are investment certificates, mutual funds, life insurance, annuities, unit investment trusts, IRAs, limited partnerships, and management and fiduciary services for pension and employee benefit plans. IDS has traditionally concentrated on the lower end of the investing public (incomes in the $25,000–$75,000 range).

IDS was acquired by AMEXCO in January 1984 as part of its multibrand approach to providing financial services.[34] In addition to adding the American Express name to the IDS banner, this merger has also resulted in more training opportunities for the IDS sales force and a con-

[29]Andrew Marton, "What Have the Megamergers Meant for Brokers," *Institutional Investor,* March 1984, pp. 147–150.

[30]Ibid., p. 148.

[31]Ibid.

[32]Ibid.

[33]Ibid.

[34]"The Golden Plan of American Express," p. 119.

tinual flow of new and upgraded products. With AMEXCO's support, IDS has launched its most aggressive advertising campaign ever in an attempt to provide the company with further exposure.

Investors were apparently not impressed by AMEXCO's purchase of IDS. In fact, AMEXCO's stock plummeted from $45 to $28 in the year after the announcement of the merger. This was a much greater drop than that of the stock market averages during the same period. However, at the end of 1985, AMEXCO's stock was up to approximately $52.

Warner Amex (W-A)

In the late seventies, "gripped with doubts about its competitive position in checks and cards,"[35] AMEXCO sought acquisitions in the communications arena. After trying to buy the McGraw-Hill publishing company and looking at others in the field, AMEXCO settled on 50 percent of Warner-AMEX, a cable TV company that has grown to be the sixth largest cable operator in the United States.

W-A owns 104 cable television systems in twenty-one states serving 1.2 million subscribers, but has done poorly with big-city franchises. In its first 5 years of co-ownership, AMEXCO has contributed more than $300 million to W-A's operations.[36] In 1983, AMEXCO's share of operating losses was close to $40 million. In 1984, Drew Lewis, W-A CEO, reduced pretax losses to $94 million with net losses falling from $99 million to $25 million. Looking to 1985 and beyond, W-A owns almost two-thirds of MTV Network which also includes the VH-1 and the Nickelodeon Children's channels. W-A also owns 19 percent of the Showtime Movie channel.

The Cable Company Policy Act of 1984 provided for rate deregulation after 2 years, which will allow cable operators to function in a more competitive market, which may contribute to greater economic stability in the industry. In 1984 W-A sold cable systems in Pittsburgh, Chicago, St. Louis, and twenty smaller locales as well as its regional sports programming service and its security division. Contract modifications in its urban franchises in Milwaukee, New York City, and Dallas were also a part of the cost-containment strategy launched in 1984.

According to Drew Lewis:

> This year [1984] marked a turning point for Warner-Amex. The foundation for the future is now in place and Warner-Amex is moving forward toward its goal of profitability. The cable industry is entering an era of realism and its future is bright. Warner-Amex is well positioned for a key role in that future.[37]

The Financial Supermarkets

Deregulation has given rise to many investment alternatives. Americans spent $200 billion in 1982 for financial services with an estimated margin of 25 percent.[38] These facts, coupled with tax breaks for IRAs and capital gains, stimulate demand and encourage supplies of financial services to enter the market. A major barrier to expansion into the financial supermarket category has been the legal restrictions on combining banking operations with insurance or investment banking, or interstate branching by security brokers with investment banking.

As the supermarkets emerge, there is competition to become the low-cost financial service provider. ATMs and 800 telephone numbers make personal banking more efficient and easier for most types of financial transactions. Technology with its inherent efficiencies makes pursuit of a low-cost strategy more feasible. Other ways to pursue a low-cost strategy include the use of service representatives (rather than more expensive account executives) to handle walk-in low-margin investment clients, selling to indi-

[35]Loomis, "Fire In the Belly At American Express," p. 88.
[36]Ibid.

[37]*American Express Company 1984 Annual Report*, p. 47.
[38]Hershman, "The Supercompanies Emerge," p. 44.

viduals at the workplace (corporate benefit programs), and vertical integration.[39]

The supercompanies plan to go after the middle-income families earning $20,000 to $50,000 a year. The company that can profitably serve the middle-income investor is going to make a potload of money, as this market group contains the most people. Further strategies will be to have a broad and diversified base of revenues to overcome the large cycles of financial services. Furthermore, geographic diversification will be necessary to cover costs and enjoy the economies of scale of mass marketing. One method of mass marketing is the national ad campaigns that have just begun. These mass marketing strategies will be aimed at reaching as many people as possible and trying to gain national recognition for each company as a full-service financial provider. Banks have the inside track here as cash and checks are the centerpiece of financial transactions.[40]

AMEXCO considers itself to be in the financial and travel-related service industries. While each of its corporate companies is a separate profit center, AMEXCO attempts to capitalize on its corporate synergy by using multiple distribution channels that target select market segments with strong brand-name products and services. Cross marketing, another synergy of the financial supermarket, allows an AEIBC customer in West Germany, for example, to buy securities or real estate in the United States through SLAX.

In terms of vertical-integration economies, AMEXCO owns Balcor, a firm that puts together and manages real estate syndications which can then be sold through SLAX account executives to potential investors. Another economy of scale is its low-cost, high-speed data processing capability (First Data Resources, Inc.) on which AMEXCO spends $300–400 million annually for hardware and software improvements. A clear goal is for AMEXCO to be the low-cost processor of financial transactions.[41]

As a financial supermarket, AMEXCO competes on many levels within international, national, and regional markets. In the industry, AMEXCO competes with the other financial supermarkets on a corporate basis. This competition includes Sears Roebuck, Prudential-Bache, Bank America Corporation, Citicorp, and Merrill Lynch. To a lesser degree, AMEXCO competes with potential financial supermarkets such as Travelers, Transamerica, Aetna, and Security Pacific Bank. On a regional basis, AMEXCO competes with growing financial empires such as First Interstate Bancorp.

Looking at the leaders (AMEXCO, Sears, Prudential, and Merrill Lynch), it is clear that all are spending money as never before in efforts to revamp their business identities. The strategy for these firms is twofold: first, to make consumers comfortable with once unheard-of combinations of merchandise the supermarkets now offer (e.g., risky tax shelters and riskless life insurance or, in Sears' case, stocks and socks) and, second, to distinguish each firm from its competitors.[42]

Achieving the first goal (one-stop shopping) will take time. A recent sampling survey revealed that most respondents did not see many benefits in one-stop financial shopping. The survey results indicated that younger adults are more receptive to the idea than older ones.[43]

In terms of differentiation, Merrill Lynch ("to be all things to some people") has said frankly that it is after affluent households with incomes over $50,000.[44] This involves courting young professionals, who may not have big incomes now, but seem likely to at some point in the future. Sears is capitalizing on its image of trustworthiness and is using a celebrity spokes-

[39]Ibid., p. 49.

[40]Ibid., pp. 44–50.

[41]Ibid., p. 50.

[42]Geoffry Colvin, "Would You Buy Stocks Where You Buy Stocks?" *Fortune,* July 9, 1984, p. 50.

[43]Ibid., p. 130.

[44]Ibid.

man, Hal Holbrook, to convey that image in TV advertising ($3.1 million in first-quarter 1984).[45]

American Express is trying to cover all the bases. The company offers its credit card in three versions—green, gold, and the ultraexclusive platinum card—with the intent to intercept investors at three levels of wealth.

IDS Brokerage firm has always concentrated on the lower end of the investing public (incomes in the $25,000–$35,000 range). For the middle and upper range, there is Shearson. And then for the corporate client, Shearson has the investment banking firm of Lehman Brothers.[46]

American Express ads reflect its multibrand approach. There is intentionally no similarity between IDS ads and those for Shearson Lehman. It is too early to judge the effectiveness of the IDS ("IDS doesn't cater to get-rich-quick schemes") or the Shearson ads ("for the serious investor").[47]

Prudential's advertising is aimed at households with annual incomes of at least $50,000.[48]

The Outlook

Synergy was touted as the motivation behind the rash of acquisitions and mergers among the financial giants in the early 1980s, but, halfway through the decade, analysts claim that "when it comes to the financial supermarkets' synergy, one plus one well might end up equaling one."[49]

The torrid pace of AMEX's diversification drive is, however, straining its ability to control its far-flung operations. "Their management team has been assembled mostly by purchase," says Walter B. Wriston, CEO of Citicorp. "I don't think there's any question that if a team has played together for 10 years, you have a bet-

ter chance on Saturday afternoon than the all-star team that was assembled that morning."[50]

Sanford Weill, who brought Shearson into the AMEXCO family in 1981 and started to turn FF around in 1984, left AMEXCO in 1985. The leadership position at FF has been anything but stable with five CEOs in 6 years. Lewis Gerstner, Jr., CEO of the TRS, is rumored to be unhappy with decisions being made at New York corporate headquarters.[51] Weill's protégé, Peter Cohen, CEO at Shearson Lehman at thirty-six, may not sit well with some of AMEXCO's older executives. If AMEXCO has a major weakness, it may be in senior management, which is often accused of buying its talent rather than grooming it, notwithstanding the fact that such notables as Henry Kissinger and Edward Safra have recently been added to the AMEXCO board of directors. Could the problems at Fireman's Fund mean the beginning of the end of AMEXCO's involvement in insurance? Down to only 41 percent ownership, AMEXCO could be looking to cut bait altogether if and when the price is right.

Warner-Amex has yet to see black ink. How long will AMEXCO dabble in the communications/entertainment industries without a winner?

Visa, MasterCard, and others (including possibly Sears' new entry, Discover) pose a challenge to the AMEX card's dominance. They have erased all vestiges of complacency at TRS.[52]

IDS margins have been considered thin and visibly low. An announcement in December 1985 indicated that AMEXCO was pumping $65 million to expand IDS's business lines, giving IDS capital of more than $900 million.[53] In the same announcement, AMEXCO added $175 million to AEICB, which apparently is now a successful member of the AMEXCO family.

[45]Ibid., p. 133.

[46]Ibid., p. 131.

[47]Ibid., p. 133.

[48]Ibid., p. 131.

[49]Bianco, "How a Financial Supermarket Was Born," p. 10.

[50]"The Golden Plan at American Express," p. 118.

[51]Ibid., p. 120.

[52]"The Golden Plan of American Express," p. 119.

[53]"Business Briefs," *Wall Street Journal,* December 20, 1985, p. 8.

Will AMEXCO, regulations permitting, expand into domestic banking? Will AMEXCO's success in direct marketing take it into retail sales to compete with Sears through acquisition of a retailer such as J. C. Penney or Montgomery Ward? Can AMEXCO make greater use of First Data Resources to further cut internal costs or sell data processing services at a profit?

Are there economies to be gained, as well as synergistic effects, by placing IDS under SLAX management? Would such a move reduce internal competition for investors in AMEXCO's three-tiered investment strategy (Lehman—wealthy corporate, Shearson—middle income, IDS—small investor)? Or, conversely, is this too broad a front on which to attack?

Appendix A: History of Growth of AMEXCO

1850: American Express evolves from the merging of three small freight companies for delivery of small packages and funds by rail and horseback. American Express agents are expected to foil the efforts of masked bandits.

1891: The first traveler's checks are introduced by American Express.

1900: American Express opens the first overseas travel office in Paris.

1919: The American Express Company, Incorporated (known as the "Inc Company") is formed to provide financial services for post–World War I American travelers.

1958: The famous green travel and entertainment charge card is introduced.

1968: The international banking operation known as the Inc Company changes its name to the American Express International Banking Corporation (AEIBC).

American Express acquires the Fireman's Fund Insurance Company.

1981: Shearson investment firm is added to the growing AMEXCO financial empire.

1983: AMEXCO buys the Geneva-based Trade Development Bank and joins it to AEIBC.

AMEXCO formally establishes the American Express Travel Related Services Company, Inc., as one of the five major entities of AMEXCO.

IDS Financial Services, Inc. (a leader in financial planning) joins the AMEXCO corporate family.

1984: Shearson/American Express acquires Lehman Brothers, Kuhn, Loeb Holding Co. Inc. to join the AMEXCO financial conglomerate as Shearson Lehman Brothers, Inc.

Appendix B: Financial Performance by Service Category

The company is principally in the business of providing travel related services, international banking services, investment services, investors diversified financial services and insurance services throughout the world. Travel Related Services principally consists of the American Express Card and Travelers Cheque operations. The results of the company's 50 percent interest in Warner Amex are included in "Other and Corporate." Tables 1, 2, and 3 present certain information regarding these industry segments at December 31, 1984, 1983 and 1982 and for the years then ended (millions).

Appendix C: American Express At-A-Glance

This appendix contains excerpts from the American Express 1984 Annual Report, wherein American Express explains its different activities, with accompanying data.

1. American Express: Top Rated by Independent Study. American Express products and services hold the confidence of millions of people. They look to American Express brand names for better ways to make, use and protect their money. In a survey in 1984, the *American Banker* found that people rate American Express products and services higher than those of any other top financial services firm in the United States *(continues page 138).*

Table 1 1984 Data

	Travel Related Services	International Banking Services	Investment Services	IDS Financial Services	Insurance Services	Other and corporate	Adjustments and eliminations	Consolidated
Revenues	$ 3,620	$ 1,548	$ 2,280	$1,576	$4,025	$ 82	$ (236)	$12,895
Pretax income (loss) before general corporate expenses	$ 625	$ 193	$ 168	$ 95	$ (114)	$ 16	$ (18)	$ 965
General corporate expenses	–	–	–	–	–	(229)	–	(229)
Pretax income (loss)	$ 625	$ 193	$ 168	$ 95	$ (114)	$ (213)	$ (18)	$ 736
Net income	$ 387	$ 156	$ 103	$ 62	$ 43	$ (125)	$ (16)	$ 610
Assets	$12,542	$13,768	$22,735	$6,411	$7,735	$1,239	$2,582	$61,848

Insurance services comprises the following:

	Property-Liability				Life and other	Total insurance services
	Commercial Lines	Personal lines	Investment income	Total		
Revenues	$ 2,017	$ 817	$ 429	$3,263	$ 762	$ 4,025
Pretax income (loss)	$ (558)	$ (40)	$ 404	$ (194)	$ 80	$ (114)

Table 2 1983 Data

	Travel Related Services	International Banking Services	Investment Services	IDS Financial Services	Insurance Services	Other and corporate	Adjustments and eliminations	Consolidated
Revenues	$ 2,889	$ 1,437	$1,826	–	$3,784	$ (6)	$ (160)	$ 9,770
Pretax income (loss) before general corporate expenses	$ 445	$ 183	$ 326	–	$ (242)	$ (17)	$ (10)	$ 685
General corporate expenses	–	–	–	–	–	(168)	–	(168)
Pretax income (loss)	$ 445	$ 183	$ 326	–	$ (242)	$ (185)	$ (10)	$ 517
Net income	$ 301	$ 136	$ 175	–	$ 30	$ (117)	$ (10)	$ 515
Assets	$10,226	$13,287	$9,060	$5,410	$7,057	$1,095	$(2154)	$43,981

Insurance services comprises the following:

	Property-Liability				Life and other	Total insurance services
	Commercial Lines	Personal lines	Investment income	Total		
Revenues	$1,925	$ 783	$ 437	$3,145	$ 639	$3,784
Pretax income (loss)	$ (609)	$ (95)	$ 452	$ (252)	$ 10	$ (242)

Table 3 1982 Data

	Travel Related Services	International Banking Services	Investment Services	Insurance Services	Other and corporate	Adjustments and eliminations	Consolidated
Revenues	$2,516	$1,025	$1,318	$3,356	$ 14	$ (136)	$ 8,093
Pretax income before general corporate expenses	$ 363	$ 101	$ 228	$ 220	$ (5)	–	$ 907
General corporate expenses	–	–	–	–	(153)	–	(153)
Pretax income	$ 363	$ 101	$ 228	$ 220	$(158)	–	$ 754
Net income	$ 247	$ 60	$ 124	$ 244	$ (94)	–	$ 581
Assets	$8,445	$7,681	$6,351	$6,513	$ 784	$ (1,463)	$28,311

Insurance services comprises the following:

	Property-Liability				Life and other	Total insurance services
	Commercial Lines	Personal lines	Investment income	Total		
Revenues	$1,947	$ 640	$ 348	$2,935	$ 421	$3,356
Pretax income (loss)	$ (95)	$ (22)	$ 328	$ 211	$ 9	$ 220

	Who consumers know (%)[1]
American Express	75
Prudential Insurance	72
Bank of America	70
Merrill Lynch	66
Beneficial Finance	55
Sears Roebuck	54
Citicorp	53
Chas. Schwab	21

2. Travel Related Services. Travel Related Services began the American Express tradition of reliable service in 1850 by moving freight. Today, it moves people and their buying power around the world. People know the quality of the American Express Card, Travelers Cheque and Travel Services. *(See Table A)*

3. International Banking Services. At American Express International Banking Corporation, the accent is on "international." The Bank helped American Express expand internationally following World War I. Today, 82 offices in 39 countries offer export financing, private banking and other select services. *(See Table B)*

4. Investment Services. Shearson Lehman Brothers Inc. evolved from strategic acquisi-

tions—most recently, Lehman Brothers. Today, Shearson Lehman melds this investment banking franchise with strong trading and distribution capabilities.[2] *(See Table C)*

5. IDS Financial Services. IDS Financial Services Inc. and its subsidiaries have earned people's trust, through outstanding financial advice and services, since 1984. The 4,400 representatives of IDS provide financial plans and products that stand the test of time.[3] *(See Table D)*

6. Insurance Services. Fireman's Fund Insurance Companies was born in San Francisco in 1863 to provide protection against the frequent fires that ravaged the city. Today, Fireman's Fund is an industry leader in developing new products and new approaches to marketing. *(See Table E)*

---

[1]Multiple responses permitted. Adapted from the *American Banker.*

---

[2]Note: Investment Services 1984 amounts include the effect of the acquisition of Lehman Brothers Kuhn Loeb Holding Co., Inc., accounted for as a purchase as of May 11, 1984.

[3]Note: The acquisition of IDS Financial Services was accounted for as a purchase effective December 31, 1983. Therefore, revenues, pretax income and net income for 1983 are not presented.

(Table A)

(Millions, except percentages)	1984	1983	Percent increase
Revenues	$ 3,620	$ 2,889	25%
Net income	$ 387	$ 301	29
Card charge volume	$47,638	$38,356	24
Travelers Cheque sales	$15,116	$13,862	9
Total assets	$12,542	$10,226	23
Average Travelers Cheques outstanding	$ 2,634	$ 2,437	8
Cards in force	20.2	17.3	17
Return on average shareholder's equity	25.3%	24.1%	

[1]Multiple responses permitted. Adapted from the *American Banker.*

(Table B)

(Millions, except percentages)	1984	1983	Percent increase (decrease)
Net income from International Banking Services	$ 156	$ 136	15%
Loans and discounts	$ 6,272	$ 6,290	—
Reserve for loan losses	$ 165	$ 162	2
Total assets of American Express International Banking Corporation	$13,875	$13,309	4
Customers' deposits and credit balances	$10,517	$10,328	2
Shareholder's equity of American Express International Banking Corporation	$ 897	$ 819	10
Primary capital to average assets	7.64%	7.05%	
Return on average assets	1.15%	1.04%	
Return on average shareholder's equity	17.81%	17.67%	

(Table C)

(Millions)	1984	1983	Percent increase (decrease)
Revenues	$ 2,280	$ 1,826	25%
Pretax income	$ 168	$ 326	(49)
Net income	$ 103	$ 175	(41)
Total assets	$22,735	$ 9,060	151
Total capital, including subordinated debt, of Shearson Lehman Brothers Inc.	$ 1,896	$ 1,057	79
Assets managed and/or administered	$64,939	$47,144	38

(Table D)

(Millions)	1984	1983	Percent increase (decrease)
Revenues	$ 1,576	—	—
Pretax income	$ 95	—	—
Net income	$ 62	—	—
Individual life insurance in force	$13,818	$11,424	21%
Assets owned and/or managed:			
Assets managed for institutions	$ 3,080	$ 3,650	(16)
Assets owned and managed for individuals:			
Owned assets	$ 6,411	$ 5,410	19
Managed assets	$ 9,812	$ 9,162	7

(Table E)

(Millions, except percentages)	1984	1983	Percent increase
Fireman's Fund Insurance Companies			
Revenues	$ 4,025	$ 3,784	6%
Net income	$ 43	$ 30	42
Total assets	$ 7,735	$ 7,057	10
Shareholder's equity	$ 1,485	$ 1,304	14
Return on average shareholder's equity	3.1%	2.2%	
Property-Liability Companies			
Premiums written	$ 2,834	2,781	2
Underwriting ratio	121.1%	126.0%	
Loss and loss expense ratio	86.4%	86.5%	
Expense ratio	32.2%	36.6%	
Policyholder dividend ratio	2.5%	2.9%	
Life Companies			
Premiums written	$ 655	$ 539	21
Life insurance in force	$23,133	$15,493	49

Case 4 Update*

This report is dedicated to the men and women of American Express whose initiative, creativity and commitment to service and excellence enable us to be—and stay—ahead of the curve.

Ahead of the pack. State of the art. Cutting edge. There are a lot of ways to put it. At American Express, we say "ahead of the curve." Which, quite simply, means being proactive, innovative and entrepreneurial—a leader in everything we do. It means anticipating customer demands for greater choice in credit cards and devising creative approaches to dealing with the debt burdens of developing nations; providing flawless service face-to-face and unrivaled efficiency in our operating centers; building globe-spanning data networks and creating eye-catching advertising. being ahead of the curve is the basis for American Express' 137-year history of success and our growing preeminence worldwide in financial and travel services.

Who We Are

American Express Company

American Express Company, founded in 1850, is a diversified financial and travel services company. Through its four principal operating units—American Express Travel Related Services, IDS Financial Services, Shearson Lehman Hutton and American Express Bank—the Company is a leader in the payment systems, travel, data based services, personal financial planning, asset management, brokerage, investment banking and international banking industries.

American Express' goal is to be the best financial and travel related services company in the world by applying shared values to anticipate and fulfill the requirements of its customers.

*Source: Excerpts from American Express Company 1987 annual report, pp. 1–3, 5–9, 51–55.

These values encompass a never-ending search for excellence through:

- Outstanding people who embrace entrepreneurship and flexibility in managing change;

- Premium products with strong brand names provided through carefully targeted marketing channels;

- Individual and corporate commitment to community involvement and citizenship; and

- Above all, consistent and uncompromising *quality* in all that we do.

Travel Related Services

American Express Travel Related Services (TRS)—the foundation of the modern American Express Company—markets some of the world's most distinguished brand names: the American Express Card, Gold Card, Platinum Card, Optima Card, Corporate Card, American Express Travelers Cheques and American Express Money Orders.

Its direct marketing arm offers premium merchandise, life insurance, credit lines from American Express Centurion Bank and publications, including *Travel & Leisure, Food & Wine* and *New York Woman* magazines.

The company's network of over 1,400 travel offices serves millions of people around the world each year. In addition, TRS' Travel Management Services helps businesses schedule travel and control travel and entertainment expenses.

The First Data Resources Inc. (FDR) subsidiary provides data processing for a wide variety of industries. It is one of the largest third-party processors of debit and credit card transactions in the United States, and offers billing services for securities systems and cable television companies. FDR also supplies billing and management services to hospitals and doctors.

IDS Financial Services

IDS Financial Services is the industry leader in personal financial planning. Its nearly 6,200 financial planners meet face-to-face with more than 1.2 million clients throughout the United States, providing detailed programs designed to help those clients attain their personal financial goals, and products and services needed to make those programs work.

IDS products include investment certificates, mutual funds, life insurance, annuities, tax-exempt investments, limited partnerships and unit investment trusts. IDS also provides management and fiduciary services for employee benefit and pension plans, consumer banking and tax preparation services, and financial planning for the employees of client companies.

IDS maintains rigorous qualification standards for its representatives and acts as an industry leader in promoting uniform regulation of financial planning throughout the United States.

IDS measures itself by its success in helping clients manage their income and balance sheets. It has achieved broad-based recognition not only for its investment performance but also for its integrity and creativity.

Shearson Lehman Hutton

Shearson Lehman Brothers enhanced its industry position in the first quarter of 1988 when it acquired The E. F. Hutton Group. The combined firm—Shearson Lehman Hutton—will have approximately $4.2 billion in capital, over $95 billion in assets under management for others and will serve nearly three million households in the United States through a network of almost 12,000 Financial Consultants in over 600 offices.

Throughout the world, Shearson Lehman Hutton applies proven creativity and expertise to meet a broad diversity of financial needs for corporations, institutions, governments and individuals. The firm delivers one of the most comprehensive arrays of investment banking, merchant banking, investment advisory, asset management, securities trading and real estate services available from a single source. Its state-of-the-art data processing technology contributes to Shearson Lehman Hutton's leadership in productivity and service.

Through its worldwide facilities in investment banking and brokerage, Shearson Lehman Hutton provides quality service that sustains long-term client relationships.

American Express Bank

American Express Bank, incorporated in 1919, maintains a network of 103 locations in 42 countries. Through two subsidiaries—the Trade Development Bank, Geneva, and American Express Bank (Switzerland) A.G., Zurich—the Bank offers private banking services for high net worth individuals, including asset management, discretionary accounts, trust and estate planning, and investment services for securities and precious metals. The Bank's global office network offers corporate, governmental and institutional clients, including central banks, a broad range of treasury, foreign exchange, investment and correspondent banking services.

American Express Bank is committed to provide exceptional service to all clients at all times. To meet that pledge, the Bank selectively adds new services to meet growing client needs in constantly changing global financial markets. The Bank continues to build on its unique competitive advantages: a strong balance sheet, an extensive branch network and the singular ability of its bankers to provide clients a broad range of quality personalized services.

Letter to Shareholders

On a consolidated basis, 1987 was a disappointing year. Earnings from continuing operations of $533 million were down from $1.1 billion in 1986, and per share net dipped to $1.20 from $2.48.

But 1987 was a year unlike any other in recent history. It was a year the stock market experienced a one-day 508-point plunge, banks added billions to reserve for troubled loans, and changes in ways of doing virtually everything in financial services came fast and furious.

Managing change, particularly in periods of high volatility, is what leadership is all about, of course. We've said that before, but 1987 was the test. Happily, we passed.

Travel Related Services, the core of our Company, continued to demonstrate its remarkable talent for adding value and utility to the American Express Card, Travelers Cheques and its other businesses. TRS' net income rose 16 percent to a record $655 million.

IDS Financial Services, our newest major operating unit, turned in its best year ever, too, lifting earnings 21 percent to $124 million.

Shearson Lehman was buffeted by adverse market forces, the strains of rapid growth and consolidation within the industry. The sale of 18 million shares of Shearson Lehman common stock to the public and two other major strategic alliances—one with Nippon Life Insurance Company, which purchased a 13 percent voting interest in Shearson Lehman, the other with E. E. Hutton, which became part of Shearson Lehman early in 1988—turned Shearson Lehman Hutton into what many see as the prototype investment firm of the future.

Additions of $950 million to credit reserves caused American Express Bank to report a loss in 1987. However, as a result of the reserve additions and a capital infusion from American Express, the Bank now has one of the strongest balance sheets in its industry and is more clearly focused on private banking and other fee-generating businesses.

The bottom line reads like this: despite being hit with everything but the proverbial kitchen sink, American Express earned more than half a billion dollars in 1987. The Company also ended the year in a strong position, well prepared for the challenges and opportunities we'll face in 1988 and the years beyond.

Much of that strength comes from TRS, which has shown earnings increases every year for the past two decades. Earnings during the last 10 years have grown at a compound annual rate of better than 17 percent. Cynics—and we have our share—might scoff, saying that American Express has always had charge cards and Travelers Cheques locked up and that the rising economic tide of the past decade carried all boats higher.

The facts are somewhat different. The past 10 years have seen recession and growth, sky-high interest rates, periods of galloping inflation, a strong dollar, a weak dollar, the emergence of tenacious overseas competitors, the decline of others, and a stock market that experienced its most violent swings in history.

It also was a period in which all members of the financial services business encroached on each other's turf: dozens of banks began issuing travelers checks during the decade, and one of the largest acquired Diners Club and Carte Blanche, two big names in the card business.

So much for locks and rising tides.

How'd we do it? Well, we don't want to give away trade secrets, but it boils down to a set of basics that are followed by all our business units:

- Assembling the smartest, most entrepreneurial people we can find, giving them the resources and freedom to do their thing and holding them accountable for results.

- Remembering we are market driven, which means listening and responding to customers.

- Constantly reminding ourselves that our goal is to deliver high-quality, prestigious products and services to carefully targeted market segments that want and appreciate them.

Not very original, but with the right commitment, it's a formula that works. It worked last year when American Express Company's revenues rose to a record $17.8 billion, up from $16.7 billion in 1986.

Earnings were considerably less robust, as the gains at TRS and IDS were overtaken by shortfalls elsewhere. American Express Bank incurred a loss of $625 million, the result of the $950 million addition to reserves that was made to reflect the status of developing nation debt and provide the Bank flexibility in managing its balance sheet. Shearson Lehman's 1987 earnings of $101 million were less than one-third the $341 million of 1986, reflecting the turmoil in world financial markets. Our share of Shearson Lehman's 1987 earnings was $89 million.

Earnings also reflected a $200 million after-tax net gain from rule changes required by the Financial Accounting Standards Board and a $142 million after-tax gain from the sale of the Shearson Lehman stock. (Earnings in 1986 included an after-tax gain of $88 million from the sale of common stock of Fireman's Fund Corporation.) Absent these nonrecurring items and the Bank's addition to credit reserves, American Express' consolidated income from continuing operations would have totaled $1.1 billion in 1987 and $1.0 billion in 1986.

Other statistical benchmarks also were mixed—some very impressive, others so-so. We ended 1987 with $71 billion of assets owned and managed, up 20 percent from 1986. Assets managed and/or administered for others soared 47 percent to $211 billion.

Return on equity from continuing operations was 11 percent in 1987, compared with 23 percent in 1986.

A record 27.1 million American Express Cards were in force at year-end, up 14 percent from a year ago. Travelers Cheque sales rose 16 percent in 1987, reaching a new high of $19.9 billion.

We split our stock 2-for-1. The quarterly dividend was increased from 18 cents to 19 cents a share. And shareholders' value was further augmented by the continuation of stock repurchase programs begun in 1985; since then, some 50 million shares of American Express common stock have been repurchased.

The operating highlights of 1987—TRS' successful introduction of the Optima Card, the American Express Gift Cheque and the "Membership Has Its Privileges" advertising campaign, IDS' dramatic progress as the country's leading financial planner, Shearson Lehman's acquisition of E. F. Hutton, and the swaps and debt sales that significantly reduced American Express Bank's cross-border term loans—are described in detail on the following pages.

They add up to an impressive list of accomplishments, one that was capped, fittingly enough, early in 1988 when American Express was cited in a *Fortune* magazine poll as the most admired firm in the diversified financial services industry. The citation speaks volumes about the American Express employees worldwide whose dedication, skills and plain old hard work made us No. 1 and—in keeping with the theme of this report—have kept us out front and constantly ahead of the curve.

But this is hardly the time to rest on laurels. Everywhere we turn we see intensifying challenges from well-heeled companies. Domestically, they are the familiar institutions that have branches on most downtown corners, plus others in shopping malls and elsewhere. It's no secret, meanwhile, that the world is fast becoming an integrated global market, nor that many of the banks, insurance companies and financial services firms in Japan and Europe outrank us in terms of assets.

We never set out to be the biggest, of course, only the best. We have no doubt of our determination and ability to remain a leader, extend that leadership and further distance ourselves from the competition.

Our goal remains simple—to be the world's top provider of travel and financial services. We have the financial wherewithal to make it happen. And we have a road map to get us there. It consists, among other things, of:

▪ A decentralized, entrepreneurial approach to business;

- The application of state-of-the-art technology to enhance productivity, develop new products and deliver superior service;

- Recognizing the diverse corporate cultures within American Express and how this diversity fosters innovation; and

- Contributing to the well-being of the communities in which our employees and customers live through a broad sweep of philanthropic and volunteer service activities.

The glue that binds all this together is a commitment to quality in everything we do. It's what's gotten American Express where it is today and it's the "patent protection" that will keep us ahead of the curve of the future.

James D. Robinson III
Chairman and
Chief Executive Officer

Louis V. Gerstner Jr.
President

March 1, 1988

Staying Ahead of the Curve

The United States of the mid-19th century had a broad frontier and a need for capital to fuel commercial growth. Funds transport was risky. Banks charged up to 10 percent to cover the cost of special couriers and insurance. These conditions gave rise to a new business, the express industry, whose economies of scale vastly reduced the cost of moving money safely. The industry's leading entrepreneurs included Henry Wells, William G. Fargo and John Butterfield—the founders of American Express Company.

The early 1880s ushered in the greatest immigration in American history and new needs for secure, transportable and easy-to-use financial instruments. Money orders sold by the U.S. Post Office required completion of complicated forms. "Persons who cannot read or write have to blunder about until some outsider takes pity and writes out their application for them," noted American Express executive Marcellus Fleming Berry. To solve the problem, Berry devised and patented a money order that was easy to use, easy to purchase and resistant to forgery.

In 1890, Berry's inventive mind put American Express well ahead of the curve of another historic trend: the growing eagerness of Americans to travel abroad. His innovation, the Travelers Cheque, had first-year sales of just over $9,000. By 1900, however, volume topped $6 million.

"The greatest rendezvous for Americans which has ever existed in Europe"—that was the goal of William Swift Dalliba, American Express Company's first representative in Europe, as he scouted for office space in Paris at the turn of the century. The site selected, 11 Rue Scribe, was the forerunner of today's global network of American Express Travel Service Offices. This facility quickly fulfilled Dalliba's vision as the spot for tourists to meet, conduct financial transactions and pick up their mail.

In August 1914, American Express was one of the few financial institutions in Europe prepared for the coming of war. The month before, European Director General Dalliba had ordered American Express offices to build up cash reserves. When World War I broke out, American Express was able to redeem not only its own Travelers Cheques but also the financial paper of other institutions. The Paris office proved so effective in meeting the financial, communications and travel needs of Americans that the U.S. embassy directed tourists seeking emergency help to 11 Rue Scribe, not vice versa.

Two decades later, American Express was ahead of the curve at another calamity, the Great Depression. When depositories across the United States closed their doors during the Bank Holiday of 1933, the Company's offices remained open and continued to cash American

Express Travelers Cheques—demonstrating the unequaled dependability of the Cheque.

The end of World War II, coupled with advances in air transport and telecommunications, prompted a global boom in tourism and business travel. American Express responded with a greatly expanded travel office network and, on October 1, 1958, a brand-new product—the American Express Card—that enabled users to charge travel and entertainment outlays. The American Express Card has since earned the loyalty of millions of Cardmembers and gone on to become one of the world's great venture capital success stories.

In more recent years, as technological advances have increased global economic interdependence and financial volatility, American Express has remained in the vanguard of change by selectively expanding its quality services to meet customer needs. Whether building its capabilities as an asset manager (through the landmark 1981 acquisition of Shearson Loeb Rhoades) or attaining preeminence in financial planning (via the 1984 acquisition of Investors Diversified Services), American Express has stayed well ahead of the curve.

The past year was no exception.

Transnational Alliance. American Express initiated the first strategic partnership between U.S. and Japanese financial services providers, when Nippon Life Insurance Company purchased a 13 percent voting interest in Shearson Lehman Brothers and established a series of cooperative ventures with the Company.

The Optima Card. American Express introduced its first revolving credit product, the Optima Card, with an interest rate far below that charged by most credit cards.

Developing Nation Debt. The debt problems of developing nations demand creative solutions.

In Mexico, American Express converted a portion of its loans into investments in major tourist development projects.

Asset Management Leadership. Few companies equal American Express in its control of every phase of mutual fund operation, from investment to distribution to service. Based on 1987 industry rankings of top investment managers, the Company stands second in the United States in assets under management.

Technological Expertise. American Express has earned wide recognition for the Authorizer's Assistant, an "artificial intelligence" computer system that automates routine card charge authorizations to provide significant gains in productivity.

American Express is one of the world's largest users of computers and telecommunications, operating 19 major information processing centers and 15 worldwide data and voice networks, and over 120 mainframe central processing units, 170 minicomputer systems and 46,000 individual work stations. The First Data Resources Inc. subsidiary helps clients maximize the value of their data bases and perform transactional services.

At times, customer needs demand the resources of two or more subsidiaries. American Express makes such partnerships a success. In the past five years, over 260 joint operations by subsidiaries have been tested, and a significant majority has worked.

American Express will continue to evolve to meet the changing needs of a dynamic world. Whether safeguarding funds across the wilds of 19th-century America or, today, helping people and assets move swiftly around the world, American Express has stayed in front for 137 years. In the years to come, it will continue to do business in the same place . . . ahead of the curve.

Consolidated Statement of Income—American Express Company

Year Ended December 31, (millions, except per share amounts)	1987	1986	1985
Revenues			
Commissions and fees	$ 8,455	$ 7,477	$ 6,020
Interest and dividends	6,084	5,915	4,431
Life insurance premiums	786	1,149	1,059
Annuity premiums	1,382	967	860
Other	1,061	1,230	530
Total	17,768	16,738	12,900
Expenses			
Compensation and employee benefits	3,721	3,438	2,573
Interest	4,899	4,776	3,415
Provisions for losses and benefits:			
Annuities	1,810	1,371	1,238
Life insurance	666	941	860
Investment certificates	99	109	107
Banking, credit and other	1,818	951	693
Occupancy and equipment	957	789	636
Advertising and promotion	877	696	528
Communications	515	472	415
Taxes other than income taxes	270	242	197
Printing and supplies	223	199	154
Other	1,226	1,212	930
Total	17,081	15,196	11,746
Pretax income from continuing operations	687	1,542	1,154
Income tax provision	154	426	458
Income from continuing operations	533	1,116	696
Discontinued operations (net of income taxes):			
Loss from operations	—	—	(2)
Gain on disposal	—	140	—
Net income	$ 533	$ 1,256	$ 694
Income (loss) per common share:			
Continuing operations	$ 1.20	$ 2.48	$ 1.52
Discontinued operations	—	0.31	(0.01)
Net income per common share	$ 1.20	$ 2.79	$ 1.51

Consolidated Balance Sheet—American Express Company

December 31, (millions of dollars)	1987	1986
Assets		
Cash	$ 3,130	$ 2,650
Time deposits	5,395	4,989
Investment securities—at cost:		
U.S. Government and agencies obligations	1,994	2,817
State and municipal obligations	5,428	4,862
Corporate bonds and obligations	13,566	9,137
Foreign government obligations	910	900
Investment mortgage loans and other	1,269	768
Total (market: 1987, $23,166; 1986, $19,421)	23,167	18,484
Investment securities—at lower of aggregate cost or market (cost: 1987, $2,402; market: 1986, $1,406)	2,265	1,396
Investment securities—at market:		
Preferred stocks	267	525
Common stocks	668	962
Bonds and obligations	9,039	10,729
Commercial paper, bankers' acceptances and time deposits	4,530	3,058
Other	1,435	1,287
Total	15,939	16,561
Securities purchased under agreements to resell	19,160	12,626
Accounts receivable and accrued interest, less reserves: 1987, $941; 1986, $829	26,529	22,685
Loans and discounts, less reserves: 1987, $800; 1986, $223	11,394	11,634
Land, buildings and equipment—at cost, less accumulated depreciation: 1987, $875; 1986, $617	2,571	2,172
Assets held in segregated asset accounts	1,811	1,304
Other assets	5,073	4,801
	$116,434	$99,302

Consolidated Balance Sheet—American Express Company *(continued)*

December 31, (millions of dollars)	1987	1986
Liabilities and Shareholders' Equity		
Customers' deposits and credit balances	$ 26,308	$22,446
Travelers Cheques outstanding	3,602	2,990
Accounts payable	9,792	8,414
Securities sold under agreements to repurchase	21,485	18,573
Securities and commodities sold but not yet purchased—at market	5,950	4,835
Insurance and annuity reserves:		
Fixed annuities	5,900	4,849
Life and disability policies	1,969	1,554
Investment certificate reserves	1,753	1,507
Short-term debt	16,902	14,620
Long-term debt	10,639	8,400
Liabilities related to segregated asset accounts	1,786	1,280
Other liabilities	5,794	4,959
Total liabilities	111,880	94,427
Shareholders' equity:		
Money Market Preferred shares—authorized 600 shares of $1.66⅔ par value; issued and outstanding 600 shares in 1987 and in 1986, stated at liquidation value	300	300
Common shares—authorized 600,000,000 shares of $.60 par value; issued and outstanding 420,802,173 shares in 1987 and 430,555,204 shares in 1986	252	258
Capital surplus	1,516	1,474
Net unrealized security gains (losses)	(41)	11
Foreign currency translation adjustment	35	46
Deferred compensation—Stock Ownership Plan	(80)	—
Retained earnings	2,572	2,786
Total shareholders' equity	4,554	4,875
	$116,434	$99,302

Consolidated Statement of Shareholders' Equity—American Express Company

Three Years Ended December 31, 1987 (millions)	Total	Money Market Preferred Shares	Common Shares	Capital Surplus	Other	Retained Earnings
Balances at December 31, 1984						
As previously reported	$4,607	$225	$130	$1,224	$(56)	$3,084
Adjustment for 2-for-1 stock split			130	(130)		
Cumulative impact of changes in accounting policies	(740)					(740)
As restated	3,867	225	260	1,094	(56)	2,344
Net income	694					694
Change in net unrealized securities gains	14				14	
Foreign currency translation adjustments	21				21	
Repurchase of common shares	(136)		(4)	(18)		(114)
Dividend Reinvestment Plan	54		2	52		
Acquisition of minority interest of First Data Resources Inc.	85		2	83		
Issuance of Money Market Preferred shares	75	75				
Issuance of common stock in exchange for warrants	47		2	45		
Other changes	100		4	94		2
Cash dividends:						
Money Market Preferred	(17)					(17)
Common	(291)					(291)
Balances at December 31, 1985	4,513	300	266	1,350	(21)	2,618
Net income	1,256					1,256
Change in net unrealized securities gains	20				20	
Foreign currency translation adjustments	58				58	
Repurchase of common shares	(871)		(18)	(84)		(769)
Issuance of common stock in exchange for warrants	145		6	139		
Other changes	72		4	69		(1)
Cash dividends:						
Money Market Preferred	(14)					(14)
Common	(304)					(304)
Balances at December 31, 1986	4,875	300	258	1,474	57	2,786
Net income	533					533
Change in net unrealized securities gains (losses)	(52)				(52)	
Foreign currency translation adjustments	(12)				(12)	
Repurchase of common shares	(478)		(9)	(57)		(412)
Deferred compensation	(80)				(80)	
Other changes	106		3	99	1	3
Cash dividends:						
Money Market Preferred	(14)					(14)
Common	(324)					(324)
Balances at December 31, 1987	$4,554	$300	$252	$1,516	$(86)	$2,572

Consolidated Statement of Changes in Financial Position—American Express Company

Year Ended December 31, (millions)	1987	1986	1985
Financial Resources Provided By			
Income from continuing operations	$ 533	$ 1,116	$ 696
Add items not requiring funds:			
Provision for losses and benefits	3,495	2,153	2,201
Depreciation, amortization, deferred taxes and other	64	267	322
Minority interest in subsidiary	12	—	—
Deduct net gain from:			
Sale of Shearson common stock	(142)	—	—
Sale of Fireman's Fund Corporation units, warrants and common stock	—	(88)	(52)
Funds provided by continuing operations before dividends	3,962	3,448	3,167
American Express cash dividends declared	(338)	(318)	(308)
Funds provided by continuing operations after dividends	3,624	3,130	2,859
Increase in:			
Short-term debt	2,282	4,219	2,460
Long-term debt	2,239	3,001	1,543
Travelers Cheques outstanding	612	311	225
Accounts payable	1,378	36	3,707
Securities sold under agreements to repurchase	2,912	8,613	2,163
Securities and commodities sold but not yet purchased—at market	1,115	306	1,531
Customers' deposits and credit balances	3,862	6,243	2,941
Other liabilities and other items	723	562	1,218
Common shares	111	223	288
Money Market Preferred shares	—	—	75
Proceeds from sale of Shearson common stock	574	—	—
Proceeds from sale of Shearson preferred stock to Nippon Life	508	—	—
Proceeds from sale of 50% interest in Warner Amex Cable Communications Inc.	—	450	—
Proceeds from sale of Fireman's Fund Corporation units, warrants and common stock	—	386	910
	$19,940	$27,480	$19,920
Financial Resources Used For			
Increase (decrease) in:			
Cash and time deposits	$ 886	$ (329)	$ 750
Accounts receivable and accrued interest	4,758	5,452	5,593
Securities purchased under agreements to resell	6,534	4,881	2,830
Investment securities	4,930	12,041	6,111
Loans and discounts	776	2,621	2,295
Other assets	899	1,245	544
Purchases of land, buildings and equipment	679	698	1,081
Purchases of Life Operations from Fireman's Fund Corporation	—	—	330
Repurchase of common shares	478	871	136
Acquisition of minority interest, including goodwill, of First Data Resources Inc.	—	—	250
	$19,940	$27,480	$19,920

Case 5

The John Hancock Mutual Life Insurance Company

John G. McElwee, Chairman of the Board and Chief Executive Officer of the John Hancock Mutual Life Insurance Company,[1] asked himself three questions in the spring of 1984 as he prepared the company for the 1990s and beyond: "What is it you want the institution to be? What do you think the world will be like? How do we prepare for that in terms of what business the company will be in and what it will need in terms of talent?" A move to financial services came out of that analysis and, more specifically, an analysis of what McElwee saw as his six criteria: economy, demographics, attitudes and lifestyles,

competition, technology, and government action. In McElwee's view, however:

> Nobody *really* knows what the financial services industry (FSI) will be. We all admit to that. We are all trying to be flexible. We know we all are not doing everything right, and the jury is still out as to which companies will have the right combination and the wisdom and courage to remedy the situation as it evolves. When will this happen? When will the paradigm of the new FSI be in place? In my view it won't be before 1990.[2]

The John Hancock Mutual Life Insurance Company began its move into financial services in 1968. This case offers some background on the financial services industry, the insurance industry, and the nature of the issues and problems facing the company in 1984.

Trends in the Industry

The late 1970s and early 1980s saw a significant trend toward the provision of fuller financial services being offered by numerous financial-based institutions:

The FSI is a huge amalgam of firms ranging in size from the CitiCorp with well over $130 billion in assets to many small credit unions with a few hundred thousand dollars of assets. In

---

[1]See Appendix A for biographical sketches.

This case has accompanying video-tapes featuring John G. McElwee, Chairman of the Board and CEO of the John Hancock Mutual Life Insurance Company in a question and answer session with the Executive MBA class that can be purchased from Northeastern University, College of Business Administration, Boston, Massachusetts 02115.

This case was prepared by Raymond M. Kinnunen, Associate Professor of Business Administration, and L. Jake Katz, Research Assistant, with the cooperation of the John Hancock Mutual Life Insurance Company and its Chairman, John G. McElwee and the support of the Instructional Development Fund at Northeastern University. It is intended to be used as the basis for class discussion rather than to illustrate either effective or ineffective handling of an administrative situation. The research and written case information were presented at a North American Case Research Symposium and were evaluated by the North American Case Research Association's Editorial Board.

Distributed by the North American Case Research Association. All rights reserved to the author(s) and the North American Case Research Association. Permission to use the case should be obtained from the North American Case Research Association. Copyright © Raymond M. Kinnunen. Reprinted with permission.

[2]From Gregory L. Parsons, *The Evolving Financial Services Industry: Competition and Technology for the '80s,* 9–183–077, pp. 1–3. Copyright © 1982 by the President and Fellows of Harvard College. Reprinted by permission of the Harvard Business School.

1980, there were over 40,000 individual firms competing in the FSI with a mix of products including savings accounts, life insurance policies, pension management services, and stock brokering. The size of the FSI as measured by financial assets under control was nearly $4 trillion in 1980, and was experiencing nearly 11% growth [See Exhibit 1].

Historically, the various segments of the FSI have been primarily defined by government regulation. In fact, this is the reason many firms in the FSI are considered institutions rather than firms in the economic sense. The institutional segments of the FSI have been controlled and defined by their relationships to regulatory agencies. For example, banks are regulated at the federal, state, and local levels by various agencies. Securities firms are regulated only at the federal level by the Securities and Exchange Commission (SEC). Insurance companies, since 1946, have been regulated by state agencies. The result is an industry where products have been defined by regulation and customer markets have been given access to those products only through specific institutions. Until fairly recently, a customer went to a bank for a loan, to an insurance company for an insurance policy, and to a securities firm to trade stock. In this regulated environment, which defined the channels between customers and the financial products, the FSI was, on average, very profitable. Between 1975 and 1980, the banking industry reported annual profit growth of 18%, the life insurance industry reported 30% annual profit growth, and the securities industry reported 7% profit growth (for a scale of measurement, all U.S. industry reported 12% profit growth during that time).

Competition in the FSI has not been very intense compared to other industries; in fact, the common view of many financial institutions has been that the main objective is not to compete, but to provide public services. This view has been allowed and reinforced by: a) the regulatory environment, b) the web of relationships among

Exhibit 1 Assets

Company	Dollar Amount of Total Assets*
Prudential	$66,707,209
Metropolitan Life	55,731,371
Equitable Life of New York	40,285,559
Aetna Life	28,551,098
New York Life	22,549,386
John Hancock	21,710,494
Travelers	17,440,305
Connecticut General	15,660,054
Teachers Insurance and Annuity	13,519,897
Northwestern Mutual	13,252,835

*Figures do not include assets of subsidiaries.
Source: *Best's Insurance Management Reports,* October 1983.

financial institutions which required a large degree of coordination and cooperation and c) the historical values and culture which preside in most financial institutions. (The "lean and mean" operation has not been the role model for most financial organizations.) Regulations, severely limiting the dimensions of competition, have sought to create a sort of economic DMZ (demilitarized zone) between the customers and financial markets, reasoning that unlimited competition, by nature, causes behavior and results which are not in the best interest of the customer. The regulatory thinking assumed that unbridled competition would certainly mean more failures of weak and poorly run institutions. This would, over time, create a more efficient marketplace, but the result on the customer of a failing institution could be devastating. Also, it was expected that competition would drive institutions to more predatory and less benign behavior towards their customers and competitors as the scramble for profits intensified.

Traditionally, different types of institutions offered different types of products and services. Banks have concentrated on offering transaction products, and many kinds of loan products to individuals and corporations. Savings and loans (thrifts) have provided savings products and specialized mortgage lending to individuals. Securities firms have tended to specialize to a degree, with different firms offering "wholesale" products to corporations such as underwriting and other investment banking activities (e.g., Goldman Sachs and Salomon Brothers) and other firms specializing in "retail" brokerage and trading for consumers (e.g., Merrill Lynch, Shearson and E. F. Hutton). Insurance companies have generally specialized in either life insurance products (e.g., Prudential, Metropolitan and New York Life), or property and casualty insurance (e.g., State Farm, AllState, INA). To a degree they have also been involved in mortgage and commercial lending. Traditionally, most insurance companies have served both individual and corporate customers. Finance companies have concentrated on consumer lending and mortgage lending primarily to individuals. As noted above, a dominant reason in the traditional product/institution relationship has been regulation, but institutional thinking has also greatly influenced how the industry has defined itself.[3]

Consolidations Hindered by Sales Force Organization

While the level of merger and acquisition activity within the financial services industry over the last decade seemed to suggest an inevitable fusion of services under one roof, companies found that sales personnel trained to move one service were not necessarily well suited at uncovering client needs for another. For example, Merrill Lynch, the largest marketer of securities, found it inefficient to have their stockbrokers selling insurance policies. "Meanwhile, Merrill has begun experimenting with a more specialized approach to selling. Convinced that the average broker is unable to sell insurance, Merrill last June [1983] began installing life insurance specialists in 32 branches. It plans to hire 100 more this year."[4]

David Koehler, President of Financial Learning Systems, a firm training both securities and insurance personnel to sell new products and to prepare for licensing exams, cites five major barriers insurance agents face when selling non-insurance products. These barriers include: (1) licensing (state licensing exams are relatively easy for the insurance industry but fairly rigorous exams exist for securities); (2) product knowledge (the level necessary for agents to be comfortable selling securities may be underestimated); (3) skills to sell the product (different skills are required to sell a life insurance policy than a mutual fund); (4) commissions (to get a similar dollar-for-dollar commission, an agent has to sell a fund possibly 50 times the "value" of a life policy); and (5) attitude (life agents are accustomed to selling "guaranteed" products).[5]

Others in the industry acknowledge these barriers but conclude that the lines between agents and brokers are becoming blurred. Because of competition, the agent has diversified his product line while the broker has added more service through financial planning.[6]

To make matters more complex, some feel that both agents and brokers will be competing with other brokers selling products based more on price than on service.[7] The vast majority of consumers' liquid assets are held in depository institutions which gives the banking industry an advantage. One way for insurance companies to

---

[3]Ibid.

[4]"Merrill Lynch's Big Dilemma," *Business Week,* January 16, 1984, p. 62.

[5]Stephen Piontek, "Securities Products Face Agents with Problems," *National Underwriter, Life and Health Insurance Edition,* July 17, 1982, pp. 28–36.

[6]Ibid., p.3

[7]Ibid., p. 43.

compete with banks is to offer transaction accounts. To do this, however, they must acquire a bank image.[8]

Total Lines of Services

Standard and Poor's Industry Surveys note the following in regard to the trend toward full service:

> The emergence of alternative products, along with general deregulation of the financial industry, has intensified competition in the life insurance industry. The successful life insurance company will be one that adapts quickly to the changing environment. The competitiveness of life insurance will increasingly depend not only on innovations in products and services, but also importantly on the quality of marketing and distribution systems.
>
> Insurers are aware of the need for more effective marketing strategies and some already are making changes. One approach that is taking hold is the combination of insurers and other major financial institutions to form broad-based financial services conglomerates. The goal here is to bring together a variety of financial products and services, provide one-stop access to the consumer, and allow cross-marketing of product and service combinations as financial services packages. This approach to market expansion is evidenced by such recent acquisitions as Bache Group Inc. by Prudential Insurance Co. of America and Shearson Loeb Rhoades by American Express (which owns Fireman's Funds Insurance Co.) among others.[9]

Theodore Gordon, president of the Futures Group, summed it up this way:

> The whole marketplace for insurance is becoming very dynamic. It will be increasingly difficult in the future to tell the difference between a brokerage house, an insurance company, a bank, and a

large-scale credit card company. To some degree, the functions of these institutions already overlap.[10]

Are Synergistic Benefits Possible?

A May 1982 article in *Institutional Investor* questions the effects of mergers that result in extended financial services:

> While it is too early for a verdict on that, however, there's another critical question at stake here. These firms have also been trumpeting the *synergistic* benefits that are supposed to flow from these mergers. American Express, for example, hopes to sell a wide variety of financial services through its credit cards, opening up vast new vistas for Shearson. Sears can envision its millions of customers buying Dean Witter products at its stores. And the Pru can look forward to its agents selling Bache products nationwide. Bache chairman Harry Jacobs Jr. perhaps best sums it up when he says, "We expect the merger to extend the range of services both firms provide."
>
> Yet, amid all the euphoric talk, no one has really stopped to ask whether these future synergistic wonders will actually come to pass, whether synergy on such a grand scale can really work in the financial services business. Will the vaunted synergy ever materialize to any *significant* extent? Will the diverse parts of these financial services conglomerates truly mesh and spur each other on to new heights—boosting sales, cutting costs and, adding up to more than the sum of the parts?
>
> Actually, there's plenty of evidence to suggest these companies may be in for a tougher time of it than most people suspect. For one thing, there's the nagging fact that dozens of previous attempts to create synergy in the financial services industry have, at best, been somewhat disappointing. It was fashionable in the early 1970s, for example, to suppose that retail brokers could sell life insurance as a sideline, thereby increasing their earnings and those of their firms. As it turned out, however, these brokers either lacked the skills to

[8]Barbara E. Casey, "Customer is Key to Insurance-Banking Rivalry," *National Underwriter, Life and Health Edition,* July 17, 1982, pp. 8–9, 36.

[9]*Standard & Poor's Industry Surveys,* July 7, 1983 (Vol. 151, no. 27, sec. 1), *Insurance & Investments Basic Analysis,* p. 155.

[10]Theodore J. Gordon, "Life Insurance Companies in the 80's: A Quiet Revolution," *Resources,* July/August 1981, p. 3.

sell insurance or were too busy with stocks to bother with it. No precise figures are available, but Securities Industry Association statistics indicate that Wall Street firms gathered revenues of less than $500 million from insurance in 1980, compared with their total revenues of $16 billion.[11]

The article goes on to detail the experience of Continental Insurance.

Continental Insurance made little progress toward the synergy that was supposed to accrue from its consumer finance subsidiary and its Diners Club credit card operations—both of which have since been sold. Other than the relatively minor business of travel life insurance, Continental found it difficult to sell policies via the credit card. It was hard, says one Continental official, to design a home insurance application form to mail out with bills because it entailed asking so many detailed questions. Nor was it really feasible to sell insurance through consumer finance outlets—local Continental agents would have been annoyed by the competition. Reports Continental chairman John Ricker sadly: "One-stop financial shopping is a buzzword returning to our vocabulary. I am skeptical, not by nature, but by experience. Continental has tried the full financial services approach, and it didn't work."[12]

Robert Beck of Prudential is quoted later in the same article with this view:

"I don't think previous attempts have *all* been failures," is the way Prudential chairman Beck shrugs it off. Or perhaps a better way of putting it is that they're persuaded that times have changed dramatically since their previous efforts to achieve financial services synergy were made. Notes American Express chairman Robinson, "The environment today is 100 percent different than it was when those (previous) relationships were formed." For one thing, he notes, "there's a trend toward constructing hybrid financial products," begun by Merrill Lynch's CMA account—

a trend Robinson thinks multifaceted houses may be able to exploit.[13]

Consumer Base

The customer base is also an important factor when it comes to offering financial services.

Sears Roebuck and Company, American Express Company and Prudential Life Insurance Company currently sell their services to some 50 million Americans. The three companies intend to bombard these clients with new financial services products. But according to conventional wisdom in the financial services business, it's not really the quantity of customers that counts, but the quality—how rich the customers are. . . . It's generally assumed that servicing well-heeled folk will be more profitable in years to come than pushing financial products at people of moderate means.[14]

"Well-heeled" is typically defined as meaning an annual family income of $50,000 or more; there are an estimated 3.2 million households in this group. Some experts fear that, with a large number of big as well as small institutions competing, few will make a profit. Given those estimates "the supercompanies plan to concentrate on the vast middle market of families earning $20,000 to $50,000 a year."[15]

Current Actions

The supercompanies (Sears Roebuck and Company, Prudential-Bache Securities, Bank America Corp., American Express, CitiCorp, and Merrill Lynch and Co.) continue to expand into new businesses as fast as the law and technology permit (Exhibit 2 compares some financial and product data on the supercompanies with those of the John Hancock). Some large insurers are acquiring small securities firms, money man-

[11]Neil Osborn, "What Synergy," *Institution Investor,* May 1982, p. 50.

[12]Ibid., p. 52.

[13]Ibid., p. 52.

[14]Ibid., p. 54.

[15]Arlene Hershman, "The Supercompanies Emerge," *Dunn's Business Month,* April 1983, p. 46.

Exhibit 2   Financial Industry Major Competitors Comparative Data

Financial Data (all figures in millions of dollars)	American Express	BankAmerica	Citicorp	Merrill Lynch	Prudential	Sears	John Hancock*
Revenues	7,800	13,112	18,258	4,590	13,200	29,180	4,422
Net Income	559	425	774	220	Not Comparable	735	NC
Assets	27,700	120,498	128,430	20,940	62,500	34,200	**23,714
Customers' deposits	5,700	93,208	77,359	3,930	—	2,300	—
Customers' credit balances	1,200***	—	—	2,700	740	200	—
Money market funds	17,200	—	—	48,900	5,000	9,000	1,125
Commercial loans	4,200	48,800	60,411	400	1,560	—	2,000
Consumer loans	1,000	25,100	22,029	5,000	3,900	4,250	1,900

What They Do	American Express	BankAmerica	Citicorp	Merrill Lynch	Prudential	Sears	John Hancock
Securities brokerage	•			•	•	•	•
Securities trading	•	•	•	•	•	•	•
Cash management services	•					•	•
Investment management	•	•	•	•	•	•	•
Commodities brokerage	•			•	•	•	
U.S. corporate underwriting	•			•	•	•	
International corporate underwriting	•	•	•	•	•	•	
U.S. commercial banking		•	•				
International commercial banking	•	•	•	•			
Savings and loan operations			•			•	
Small loan offices		•	•			•	
Credit card, charge cards	•	•	•			•	
Traveler's checks	•	•	•				
Foreign exchange trading	•	•	•	•	•	•	
Leasing	•	•	•	•	•		•
Data processing services	•	•	•	•			•
Property-casualty insurance	•			•	•	•	•
Life, health insurance	•			•	•	•	•
Mortgage insurance						•	•
Mortage banking	•	•	•	•		•	•
Real estate development	•				•	•	•
Commercial real estate brokerage				•		•	
Residential real estate brokerage				•		•	
Executive relocation services				•		•	

Source: *The New Financial Services*, Alliance of American Insurers, Shaumburg, Ill., 1983 (reprinted with permission of Prudential-Bache Securities).
*Source: John Hancock Internal documents.
**Not including subsidiary assets.
***Total assets under management $37 million.

Exhibit 3   Financial Services Announcements The First Half of 1983

Travelers owns Securities Development Corporation (securities clearing subsidiary).

President of American Express joins Travelers (hiring said to be influenced by his financial services background).

Equitable Life and First National Bank of Chicago to market cash management services.

Prudential to buy Capital City Bank of Hopeville, Georgia.

Sears to have Dean Witter offices in 100 stores by the end of 1983, 150 by the end of 1984, and eventually 400.

CIGNA buys automatic Business Centers, commercial payroll processing centers.

Kemper's regional brokerage houses earned $8.3 million in 1982.

Nationwide to offer insurance in offices of Banc One.

John Hancock's Independent Investment Associates to offer financial services for corporations and institutions.

Prudential to have 30 joint offices with Bache by the end of 1983.

Travelers to offer insured cash management services through its trust company.

Hartford to buy 24 percent of Minneapolis brokerage firm.

Aetna Life & Casualty buys majority interest in Federal Investors.

Mutual of Omaha plans to acquire investment banking and brokerage firm of Kilpatrick, Pettis, Smith, Polian, Inc.

J.C. Penney to buy First National Bank of Harrington, Delaware.

Merrill Lynch to buy Raritan Valley Financial Corporation, a New Jersey savings and loan.

Kemper announces intention to buy a savings and loan.

Chairman of Manufacturers Hanover says much of the euphoria about financial supermarkets may be exaggerated.

Source: Bull, Robert A. "Insurance and the Financial Services Industry," *United States Banker*, August 1983, p. 118.

agers, and mortgage bankers. Alexander Clash, President at New York's John Alden Insurance Company, expressed one view that acquisitions are a cheap form of R&D and added, "Buying a foothold in every conceivable financial service is a way of participating in every business because no one is sure what the hot areas will be in 1990."[16]

Obviously, there are considerable mixed feelings in the financial services community concerning recent changes. Movement continues to take place even in light of the questionable results companies may achieve when they offer one-stop financial services, in effect becoming financial supermarkets (see Exhibit 3). Part of the reason for this trend may be the estimated $200 billion that Americans spent on financial services in 1982, reportedly earning suppliers of those services $42 billion.[17]

The decade of the 1980s promises to be an exciting one for the huge American financial services industry, which has, until now, been fragmented. Some uncontrollable factors, such as interest rates, the economic climate, the regulatory climate, and the role of technology, will also affect the industry. Many experts believe that technology (especially computers and telephones), with its costs and unpredictable product breakthroughs, will play such a large part in product cost and delivery that the big competition to worry about may not be other companies in the financial services industry but AT&T and IBM.[18]

[16]Ibid., p. 47.

[17]Ibid., p. 44.

[18]Ibid., p. 50.

The John Hancock Mutual Life Insurance Company[19]

The John Hancock Company began in 1862 when John Hancock started selling life insurance. By 1864 the company had over $500,000 of insurance in force. In less than ten years, the company's insurance in force grew to nearly $20 million. In the early part of the twentieth century, the company pioneered a number of products, including group life insurance. The John Hancock Company prospered during the boom years following World War I and continued to grow through the Depression. As late as the mid-1960s, the company was still primarily a seller of insurance. A hundred years after its founding, the company's pool of capital had been invested in nearly every imaginable sector of the economy, both private and public.

In December 1983, in an internal bulletin to all home office employees, the John Hancock Mutual Life Insurance Company announced a definitive merger agreement with the Buckeye Financial Corporation of Columbus, Ohio. The merger agreement provided for the acquisition of Buckeye by the John Hancock subsidiary for approximately $28 million in cash, equal to $13.50 per share of Buckeye common shares on a fully diluted basis. Buckeye, a savings and loan holding company in Columbus, Ohio, is the parent of Buckeye Federal Savings and Loan Association. Buckeye Federal, a federally chartered savings and loan association, conducts its business through 19 offices located throughout central Ohio. With assets of approximately $1.2 billion as of September 30, 1983, Buckeye Federal is one of the largest savings and loan associations in Ohio and is the largest mortgage lender in central Ohio. In April 1982, less than two years prior to this merger agreement, the Hancock had acquired Tucker Anthony Holding Corporation,

the parent of Tucker Anthony and R. L. Day Inc., a regional brokerage house with 30 offices in the Northeast.[20] These two announcements were the latest of a number of financial services subsidiaries (most developed internally) that had been added since 1968. In a letter dated December 23, 1968, and addressed to home office associates, then-President Robert E. Slater discussed the concept of subsidiaries:

> We think of them (the subsidiaries) as a device through which we can develop markets and new products and, as a corollary, other new avenues toward increased compensation for our sales forces. They also provide investment vehicles to enhance the return on total investable funds. Life insurance is still our main business—by a very wide margin—but in the larger view we can use these subsidiaries to augment or supplement our life insurance sales with the marketing of a wide array of financial services.

Background on the Insurance Industry

Today in the United States the insurance industry is divided into three major categories: life, health, and property and casualty. The life and health areas are further divided into group and individual categories. In 1981 new purchases of life insurance in the United States amounted to $812.3 billion.[21]

Commercial life insurance companies are divided into two categories: stock and mutual companies.[22] A company that has stockholders is a stock company, whereas a mutual company is owned by its policyholders. Just over 2,000 life insurance companies were doing business in the

---

[19]Historical facts on the company were taken from *A Bridge to the Future; One Hundredth Anniversary 1862–1962,* copyright 1962, John Hancock Mutual Life Insurance Company, Boston, Mass.

[20]"Hancock to Acquire Tucker Anthony at up to $47 Million," *Wall Street Journal,* April 15, 1982, p. 16.

[21]Sources of factual data on the insurance industry were: *1983 Life Insurance Factbook* (Washington, D.C.: American Council of Life Insurance, 1983), and S. S. Hubner and Kenneth Black, Jr., *Life Insurance,* 9th ed. Englewood Cliffs. N.J.: (Prentice Hall, Inc., 1976).

[22]For data on the top ten insurance companies, see Exhibit 29.1.

United States and accounted for 43 percent of the life insurance in force in 1982.

Stock companies seek to earn the highest possible profits for their shareholders. Policy owners do not benefit from any gains the stock company enjoys nor are they hurt by any losses the company suffers. Because they are not directly affected by the company's financial experience, their policies are called nonparticipating. Because no dividend is expected, the premium paid by a stock company must meet capital and surplus requirements as well as other requirements established by its home state. Having met these requirements and having had its stock subscribed, a stock company may begin doing business. Because a stock company is owned by its shareholders, the first responsibility of the directors is to those shareholders. Because shareholders can vote on major issues and elect the board of directors, control of the company rests with the owners of a majority of the stock. Shareholders may sell their stock or buy more shares at prevailing market prices.

Mutual insurance companies are owned by policyholders. Management's first obligation is to create profit for policyholders, who have the right to vote for directors. When funds available exceed solvency requirements, the directors may pay policyholders a dividend, although such payment is not mandatory. The cost of a policyholder's premium less the dividend paid determines the final cost of the insurance coverage. Because the policyholder may benefit from the favorable financial experience of a mutual company, that policy is called participating. Owners of mutual companies are numerous and scattered and have proportionately small ownership positions. For these reasons, control of a mutual company remains largely with management.

By the end of the 1960s, the rising inflation rate caused a number of people to seek new investment vehicles that offered higher returns than life insurance. The public's attention turned to the stock market. Many viewed life insurance as a high-opportunity cost versus returns they imagined were available through stock market investments. A number of investment firms answered that market's desire by offering mutual fund shares. The public sank dollars into a new breed of mutual fund called money market funds. Securities firms (such as Merrill Lynch) and fund operators (such as Fidelity) invested billions of dollars in low-risk securities offering record levels of income. Banks began offering certificates of deposit (CDs) with very high returns. The insurance industry found itself fighting not only for new business but to retain the reserves that they already held.

To grow and, indeed, to survive, traditional insurance institutions like John Hancock found themselves forced to compete with higher-yielding instruments offered by the federal government, municipal governments, and brokerage houses.

John Hancock Subsidiaries Inc. (JHSI)

In 1980, the structure of the John Hancock Company was changed to incorporate the existence of ten subsidiaries in the form of a downstream holding company (see Exhibits 4 and 5). Exhibit 6 describes the products and services offered by the subsidiaries. Selective financial data on the parent company and the subsidiaries can be found in Exhibits 7 and 8.

Stephen Brown, Executive Vice-President of Financial Operations of the John Hancock Mutual Life Insurance Company and President and Chief Executive Officer of John Hancock Subsidiaries Inc., had worked for the Hancock for 22 years when he became president of the holding company in 1981. Brown offered the following explanation on the origins of the holding company and its operations. Initially when the individual companies were started (the first in 1968), they became part of an existing department of the company. For example, Hanseco, which offered a line of casualty insurance, operated as a part of the Marketing Department and was expected to attract more revenue to the

Exhibit 4   John Hancock Mutual Life Insurance Company, Boston, Massachusetts, Organization Chart, Effective April 1, 1983

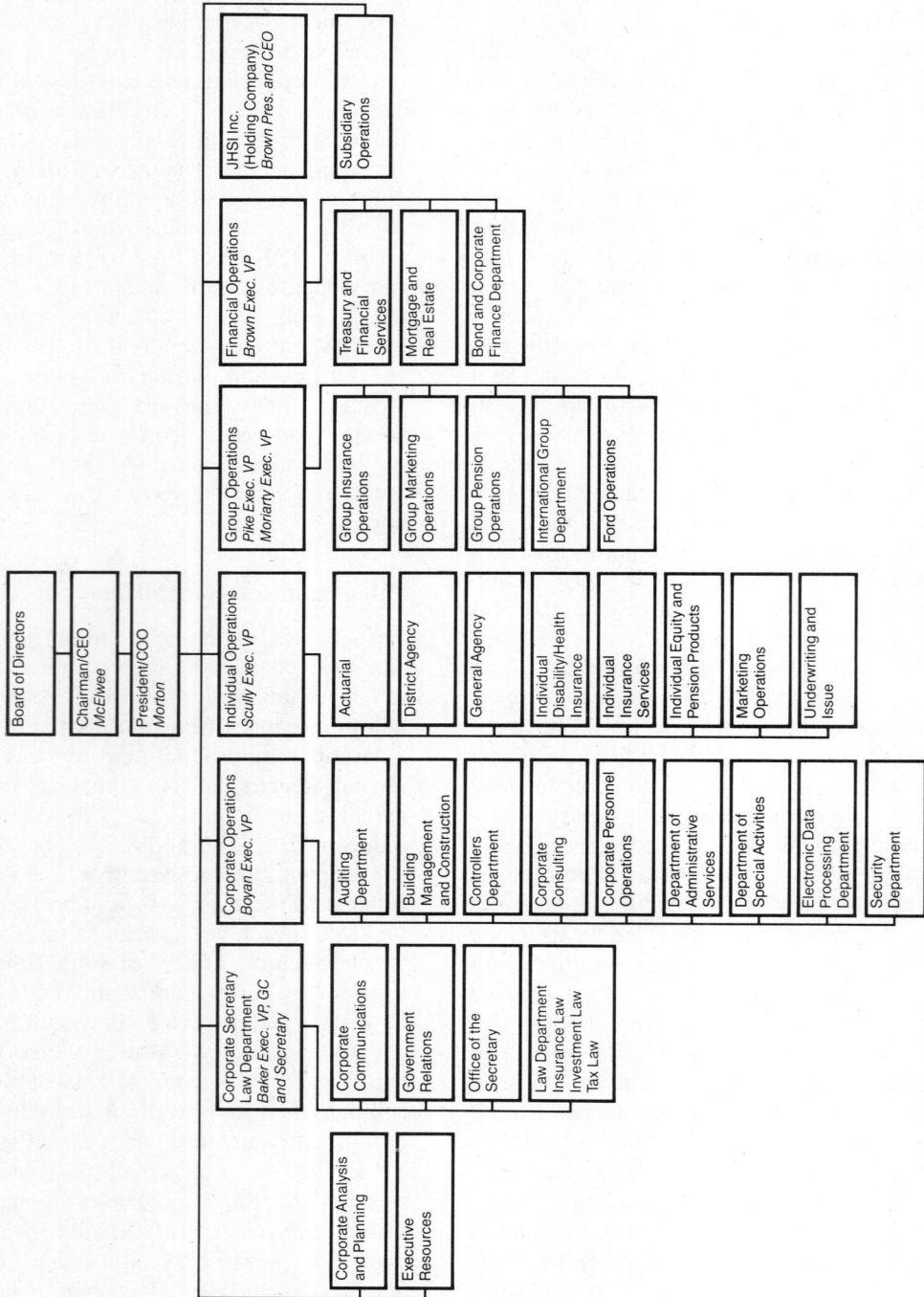

Exhibit 5 Subsidiary Organization Chart

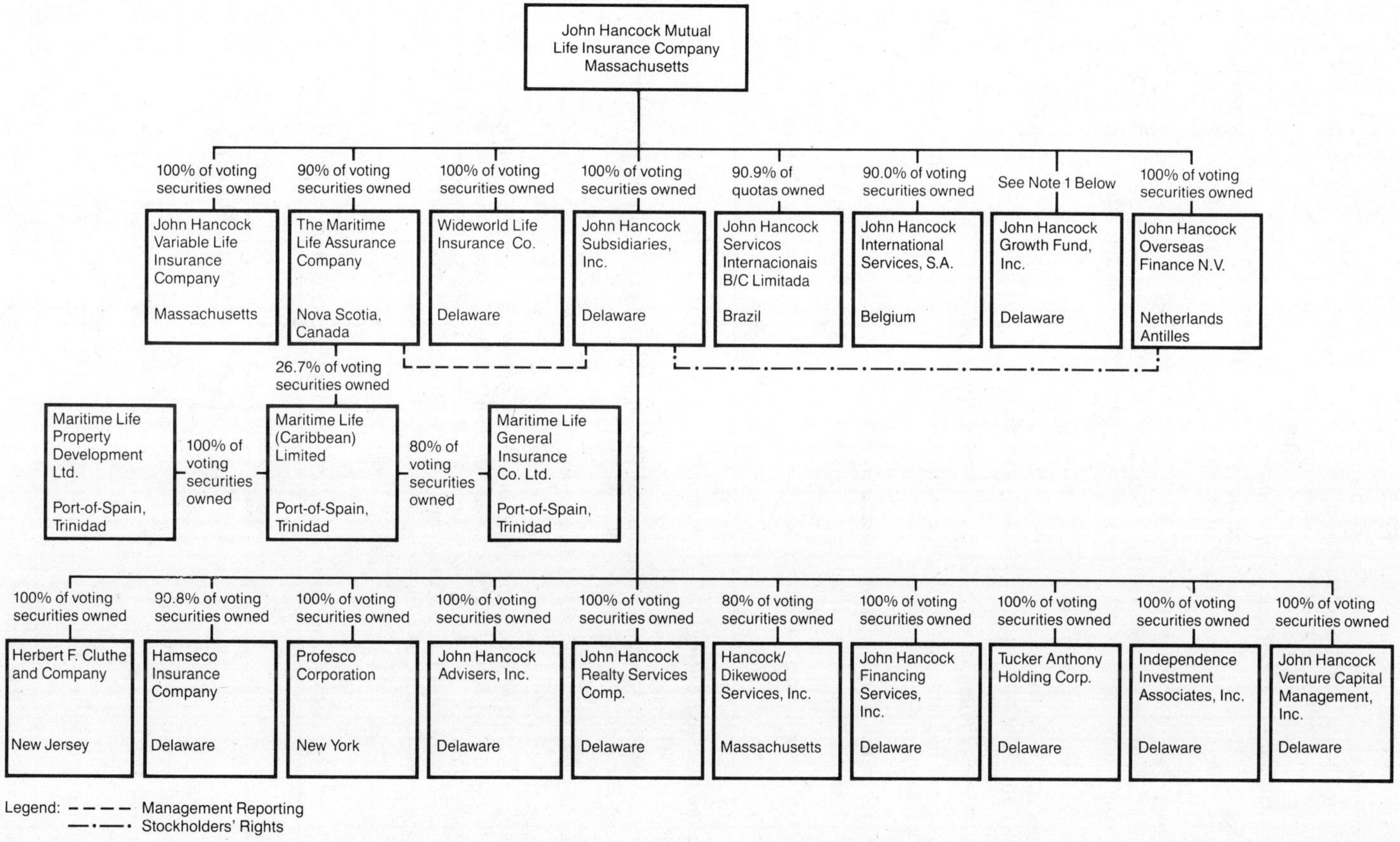

John Hancock Mutual Life Insurance Company
Massachusetts

100% of voting securities owned — John Hancock Variable Life Insurance Company — Massachusetts

90% of voting securities owned — The Maritime Life Assurance Company — Nova Scotia, Canada

100% of voting securities owned — Wideworld Life Insurance Co. — Delaware

100% of voting securities owned — John Hancock Subsidiaries, Inc. — Delaware

90.9% of quotas owned — John Hancock Servicos Internacionais B/C Limitada — Brazil

90.0% of voting securities owned — John Hancock International Services, S.A. — Belgium

See Note 1 Below — John Hancock Growth Fund, Inc. — Delaware

100% of voting securities owned — John Hancock Overseas Finance N.V. — Netherlands Antilles

100% of voting securities owned — John Hancock Venture Capital Management, Inc. — Delaware

100% of voting securities owned — Independence Investment Associates, Inc. — Delaware

100% of voting securities owned — Tucker Anthony Holding Corp. — Delaware

100% of voting securities owned — John Hancock Financing Services, Inc. — Delaware

80% of voting securities owned — Hancock/Dikewood Services, Inc. — Massachusetts

100% of voting securities owned — John Hancock Realty Services Comp. — Delaware

100% of voting securities owned — John Hancock Advisers, Inc. — Delaware

100% of voting securities owned — Profesco Corporation — New York

90.8% of voting securities owned — Hamseco Insurance Company — Delaware

100% of voting securities owned — Herbert F. Cluthe and Company — New Jersey

26.7% of voting securities owned — Maritime Life (Caribbean) Limited — Port-of-Spain, Trinidad

80% of voting securities owned — Maritime Life General Insurance Co. Ltd. — Port-of-Spain, Trinidad

100% of voting securities owned — Maritime Life Property Development Ltd. — Port-of-Spain, Trinidad

Legend: – – – – Management Reporting
 –··–··– Stockholders' Rights

163

Exhibit 6   Subsidiaries of John Hancock Mutual Life Insurance Company (JH)

John Hancock International Services S.A., Brussels, Belgium

1968   Incorporated in Belgium. Established to enable the International Group Department of John Hancock to perform the international employee benefit services expected by multinational companies that participate in the John Hancock International Group Program (IGP).

Maritime Life Insurance Co., Halifax, Nova Scotia

1969   Acquired by JH. Reports to Life Company through JH Subsidiaries, Inc. for management reporting purposes. Offers a full range of life insurance products in Canadian markets.

John Hancock Servicos Internacionalis S/C, Ltda., Sao Paulo, Brazil

1973   Organized in Brazil. Established to enable IGP to deliver the same financial results to clients with subsidiaries in Brazil as in all other IGP countries, and to enable funds to be transferred out of Brazil.

John Hancock Variable Life Insurance Co., Boston, Massachusetts

1979   Incorporated in Massachusetts. Provides a vehicle for John Hancock agents to sell individual variable life insurance and universal life insurance products.

John Hancock Overseas Finance N.V., Curacao, Netherlands Antilles

1982   Incorporated in Netherlands Antilles. Raises funds outside the United States and lends such funds to John Hancock and its affiliates.

John Hancock Subsidiaries, Inc., Boston, Massachusetts

1979   Incorporated in Delaware; commenced business in 1980. A downstream holding company organized to provide a means of centralizing the reporting responsibility for the following subsidiaries as a group to coordinate their financial planning and the development of unified policies and strategies.

Subsidiaries of JHSI

Herbert F. Cluthe and Co., Springfield, New Jersey

1968   Acquired by JH.
1980   Acquired by JHSI. Develops total financial plans and group and pension programs for business and trade associations.

John Hancock Advisers, Inc., Boston, Massachusetts

1968   Incorporated in Delaware.
1980   Acquired by JHSI. Manages the portfolios of six open-end investment companies: John Hancock Growth Fund Inc.; John Hancock U.S. Government Securities Fund Inc.; John Hancock Bond Fund Inc.; John Hancock Tax-Exempt Income Trust; John Hancock Cash Management Trust; and John Hancock Tax-Exempt Cash Management Trust, shares of which are sold by its subsidiary broker-dealer, John Hancock Distributors Inc.

Exhibit 7   John Hancock Companies—Assets Under Management ($ in millions)

	1972	1973	1974	1975	1976
General account	$10,377	$10,737	$11,232	$12,071	$13,098
Separate account	818	710	591	730	898
Guaranteed benefit separate account	0	0	0	0	0
Subsidiaries (estimated)*	283	488	462	633	708
Pension advisory accounts	0	0	0	0	19
Total assets under management	$11,478	$11,935	$12,285	$13,434	$14,723

*Subsidiary assets are net of John Hancock parent equity holdings and contain estimated components.
Source: John Hancock Mutual Life Insurance Company Annual Reports.

Exhibit 6 *(continued)*

John Hancock Realty Services Corp., Boston, Massachusetts
1968   Incorporated in Delaware.
1980   Acquired by JHSI. Invests in income-producing real estate; provides commercial real estate brokerage, mortgage placement and servicing, and appraisal services through its susdiary, John Hancock Real Estate Finance Inc. Operations are conducted nationwide through a series of regional offices.

Profesco Corporation, New York, New York
1968   Acquired by JH.
1980   Acquired by JHSI. A nationwide organization of franchised specialists providing complete financial services to the professional and business communities.

HANSECO Insurance Co., Boston, Massachusetts
1971   Incorporated in Delaware.
1980   JH ownership transferred to JHSI. In addition to providing a vehicle for John Hancock agents to sell personal lines of Sentry Insurance, the company is actively involved in the reinsurance business through three wholly-owned subsidiaries.

Hancock/Dikewood Services Inc., Albuquerque, New Mexico
1979   Incorporated in Massachusetts.
1980   Acquired by JHSI. Provides data processing and systems analysis services to health care providers. The company also offers a full range of management services to health maintenance organizations and associations.

John Hancock Financial Services Inc., Boston, Massachusetts
1980   Incorporated in Delaware. Provides equipment leasing and financing (tax- and nontax-oriented) and related financial services to the agricultural, professional, and general commercial markets on a national scale.

Independence Investment Associates Inc., Boston, Massachusetts
1982   Incorporated in Delaware. Provides investment management and advisory and counseling services, principally to pension funds and other institutional investors.

John Hancock Venture Capital Management Inc., Boston, Massachusetts
1982   Incorporated In Delaware. Serves as general partner and manager of the John Hancock Venture Capital Fund, a limited partnership with $148,000,000 of committed capital.

Tucker Anthony Holding Corp., Main Offices: Boston, Massachusetts, and New York, New York
1982   Incorporated in Delaware. A holding company offering, through its subsidiary Tucker Anthony & R.L. Day Inc., a broad range of financial services, including stocks and bonds, money management, corporate finance, and tax-advantaged investments.

1977	1978	1979	1980	1981	1982	1983
$14,101	$15,212	$16,207	$17,263	$17,824	$18,336	$18,708
937	1,016	1,111	1,377	1,448	1,754	2,066
0	0	0	121	671	1,633	2,766
838	1,014	1,269	1,625	2,365	5,400	6,013
24	83	133	161	203	269	398
$15,900	$17,325	$18,720	$20,547	$22,511	$27,392	$29,951

Exhibit 8 Consolidated Summary of Operations and Changes in Policyholders' Contingency Reserves, John Hancock Mutual Life Insurance Company and Subsidiary

	Year Ending December 31,		
	1983	1982	1981
Income			
Premiums, annuity considerations, and pension fund contributions	$2,489.5	$2,573.4	$2,435.6
Investment income	1,818.1	1,668.1	1,491.2
Separate account capital gains (losses)	118.4	132.9	(106.9)
Other	(346.1)	(562.6)	(552.5)
	4,079.9	3,811.8	3,267.4
Benefits and expenses			
Payments to policyholders and beneficiaries:			
Death benefits	513.3	447.0	405.1
Accident and health benefits	423.9	444.5	496.4
Annuity benefits	182.9	25.0	11.6
Surrender benefits	248.9	90.1	79.1
Matured endowments	15.2	11.6	11.3
	1,384.2	1,018.2	1,003.5
Additions to reserves to provide for future payments to policyholders and beneficiaries	1,560.2	1,599.3	1,187.6
Expenses of providing service to policyholders and obtaining new insurance:			
Field sales compensation and expenses	308.9	292.5	285.6
Home office and general expenses	310.6	279.0	262.5
State premium taxes	30.5	32.2	30.2
Payroll and miscellaneous taxes	27.6	25.2	22.7
	3,622.0	3,246.4	2,792.1
Net gain before dividends to policyholders and federal income taxes	457.9	565.4	475.3
Dividends to policyholders	390.5	326.7	314.2
Federal income taxes	36.0	70.1	50.2
	426.5	396.8	364.4
Net gain	31.4	168.6	110.9
Net capital gain or loss and other adjustments	(52.6)	(50.2)	40.4
Less amounts allocated for:			
Increase (decrease) in valuation reserves	(1.2)	(1.2)	1.2
Additional provision for prior years' federal income taxes		13.9	30.0
Other adjustments	16.0	7.0	15.8
Increase (decrease) in policyholders' contingency reserves	(36.0)	98.7	104.3
Policyholders' contingency reserves at beginning of year	1,002.8	904.1	799.8
Policyholders' contingency reserves at end of year	966.8	$1,002.8	$ 904.1

Exhibit 8 *(continued)*

	Year Ending December 31,	
	1983	**1982**
Assets		
Bonds	$ 6,551.5	$ 6,590.2
Stocks:		
Preferred or guaranteed	190.6	197.1
Common	431.3	361.1
Investment in affiliates	342.5	319.4
	964.4	877.6
Mortgage loans on real estate	6,542.0	6,527.3
Real estate		
Company occupied	161.4	148.6
Investment properties	636.2	530.6
	797.6	679.2
Policy loans and liens	2,041.2	1,890.4
Cash items:		
Cash in banks and offices	40.0	12.4
Temporary cash investments	558.8	789.8
	598.8	802.2
Premiums due and deferred	388.8	341.1
Investment income due and accrued	362.8	344.3
Other general account assets	460.9	283.7
Assets held in separate accounts	4,832.1	3,386.2
Total assets	$23,540.1	$21,722.8
Obligations		
Policy reserves	$11,659.7	$11,442.2
Policyholders' and beneficiaries' funds	4,596.4	4,649.3
Dividends payable to policyholders	429.0	359.5
Policy benefits in process of payment	161.2	99.3
Other policy obligations	161.6	148.3
Indebtedness to affiliate—	74.7	74.4
Commercial paper outstanding—	72.6	0
Mandatory securities and other asset valuation reserves	389.3	272.3
Federal income and other accrued taxes	109.5	148.8
Other general account obligations	101.9	158.1
Obligations related to separate account business	4,817.4	3,367.8
Total obligations	22,573.3	20,720.0
Policyholders' contingency reserves		
Special contigency reserve for group insurance	92.6	87.8
General contingency reserve	874.2	915.0
Total contingency reserves	966.8	1,002.8
Total obligations and contingency reserves	$23,540.1	$21,722.8

company by giving insurance agents a larger package of securities to offer. At that time the major objective of a new addition was synergy—or—as Brown described it, "putting more dollars in the agency force." Profit and growth were secondary.

In January of 1980, when the holding company (John Hancock Subsidiaries Inc.) was established, management was charged with the responsibility of overseeing the subsidiary companies and reporting to the Board of Directors of the life company. As control mechanisms, the holding company was to submit to the board quarterly financial statements and yearly presentations on its overall strategy. In addition, various Board committees on organization, finance, compliance, conflict of interest, and auditing could also ask for reports. The individual subsidiaries submitted strategic plans to the board of the holding company. In 1980 the objectives for the subsidiaries had become first profit, followed by growth, and then synergy; and the subsidiaries were expected in the long run to return 15 percent on investment. Brown noted that before this time "profit and return on investment" were not commonplace expectations in the company.

In Brown's view, the major reasons for changing the structure to a holding company were for tax purposes (some subsidiaries were profitable and others were not) and to form more consistent planning and control systems throughout the subsidiaries. Although there were some in the company who felt that various departments should continue to control the subsidiaries, the outcome of the restructuring, according to Brown, was that "there are now clear controls in place with the subsidiaries operating autonomously from day to day."

Each subsidiary has its own board of directors. The holding company decides on the directors and reviews the minutes of meetings. Major capital requirements and any significant change in the type of business performed by a subsidiary also requires approval by the holding company. Personnel selection and compensation

are left completely to the subsidiaries. Subsidiaries are welcome, but not required, to use the staff facilities at the life company (for example, EDP, Accounting, Public Relations). Brown stated that, on the average, he visits the subsidiaries once a month. With the major objectives of profitability, growth, and synergy clearly stated, the approach used to run the subsidiaries is, according to Brown, "Now, go do it!"

Mr. Brown commented on the future of the John Hancock:

> Profit and return on investment were not common words in the company. In the long run I see us adopting GAAP (Generally Accepted Accounting Principles) instead of statutory accounting and defining profit centers throughout the Life Company as we do in the Holding Company. This is a step toward becoming in the long run a stock company where we can purchase with stock as opposed to cash and offer stock incentives to management and tie a bonus to profits and growth. If in the long run this is where we are headed, the only way to do it is the profit center concept.

The addition of the holding company in 1980, along with the different systems used to measure performance, added a new dimension to the John Hancock and its way of operating. This became clear as people discussed the changes that had taken place inside the Hancock over the past 16 years and the future in the changing financial services industry.

Structure, Culture, and Systems

A major concern in the company was the fact that two different entities operate under the name John Hancock Mutual Life Insurance Company. Furthermore, two distinct cultures evolved as a result of defining the subsidiaries as profit centers in 1980 and evaluating them based on profit and return on investment. That change in structure and systems in essence created a new way of operating and, to some extent, a new breed of manager.

Phyllis Cella was president and chief executive officer of Hanseco, a subsidiary spawned in 1971 from within the Hancock and staffed originally with Hancock employees. The expressed purpose of starting Hanseco was to provide products for the Hancock agents. In 1983, Hanseco had approximately $750 million in assets under its management. Up until 1980 they had operated within the Hancock structure. Cella described some of the thinking that went on inside Hanseco as the subsidiary grew. In the beginning:

> Hanseco was run according to the Hancock style, and we were all on the Hancock payroll. As we got bigger and began to understand our own business, we began to change that. Having grown up in it you learn how to deal with it, but you also understand how time consuming it is and that you don't always get the answer you want because it is a bureaucracy. Even before the Holding Company officially was formed, we saw ourselves as running a company that was now different from and, in our minds, separate from the John Hancock, even though we were still on the John Hancock payroll. In our minds the paycheck was the only connection. When the world turned [introduction of the subsidiary structure] and the primary objective now became profit, it strengthened the fact that you really are a completely separate entity—it has now been blessed—and you are your own employer.

In 1984 Hanseco had its own payroll that was processed, not on the John Hancock computers, but by the First National Bank of Boston. The subsidiary set its own salaries and had its own retirement plan. According to Cella, the attitude at Hanseco was: "If I can get it cheaper downtown, then I'm going to do that—it's my bottom line. There are still people in the organization that don't understand or accept that fact that maybe we will buy their services—but maybe we won't. There is no question that there now exists two different cultures."

Hanseco's 40th-floor offices are a modular arrangement as opposed to the traditional open concept of the Hancock. Cella's office was on the outside corner of the glass building overlooking the Charles River and the Boston Common. She remarked that she had consciously chosen the modular design and had had to fight for it.

Once you get a taste of it (the profit center concept), I don't think it would be possible to go back and work in the other framework—not at this level or an officer level. Partly because of the size—we still have only 225 employees but are growing every day—but partly because of the need. We all participate very heavily in this organization—all of the officers. We have eight officers, so it is not hard to get eight people together, hammer things out, let everyone have his say, have everyone really go at it, and wide open. How do you do that in the Hancock? You don't—it is impossible. It is much more fun here. A bigger challenge, a lot more sleepless nights than you ever had in the other big organization, but you cannot match the excitement and satisfaction of it and the gratification when it works.

Although officers of the life company were quite aware of the differences, some, like Frank Irish, Vice-President, Corporate Analysis and Planning, viewed the subsidiaries "as indistinguishable from the parent company from the point of view of management control. Standards should be applied equally to subsidiaries and parent company. A lot of my efforts have been designed to achieve this goal, and I think we are close to that."

In response to the issue of transforming units of the life company into profit centers, Irish went on to say: "I can only say that we are very seriously considering it. We obviously can. We know we can." He also had some doubts, however, as to whether the change would accomplish what the Hancock wanted and if, in fact, that change was consistent with their policyholders. "When managing a participating insurance business you are not supposed to be profit maximizing—so why have a profit center concept. There is a conflict."

Phyllis Cella felt as Steve Brown did: "Theoretically, they (the units of the life company) ought to be profit centers and have a bottom line." There was some concern, however, from a practical point of view as to the difficulty of actually getting to the bottom line of some of the units within the life company that really do not have income.

There was also some concern among middle managers within the Life Company concerning the somewhat different nature of the business conducted within the holding company and the way the holding company managers were being compensated. As Irish commented:

> What is at this point different about the subsidiaries is their attitude toward things like personnel policies, tenure, compensation, that sort of thing. Not only have they been decentralized, but in theory the subsidiary personnel are working in a more highly rewarded, more risky business than the parent company. . . . I'm not sure how top management views it—and I usually know top management. I know how many middle managers view it—very critically. Subsidiary managers are paid better and have more freedom and have greater opportunities. That's how some people view it, and it's a problem we are going to have to work with. I don't know what the answer is. . . . The other is that you are generally dealing with the kinds of operations where you need risk takers. . . . I think the problem is perhaps made worse by the obvious fact that, despite the statements about profit responsibility, some of the subsidiaries have not produced an adequate rate of return.

Becoming a Stock Company

A related issue was the Hancock's financial restructuring to a stock company. Although this issue was much broader, it related directly to the existing culture within the Hancock. As noted previously, Steve Brown saw the Hancock, in the long run, taking on the structure of a stock company. On that particular issue, Frank Irish pointed out that the thinking had been dominated in the past by having to generate capital internally and that that way of doing things takes away certain possibilities in the way of financial dealings. However, there is less pressure in a mutual company to sacrifice long-term objectives for short-term profit growth.

Irish went on to say that there are other advantages and disadvantages to both forms of business. Some feel mutual companies have more leeway in pricing their products. By adjusting the dividends, mutual companies may much more closely reflect the actual cost of the service provided than their stock company counterparts. Stock companies are constrained to charge whatever the market will bear to achieve the highest possible level of profit for their stockholders.

As insurance companies extend themselves into broader areas of financial service, there is a tendency for firms to make use of holding companies for the management of their subsidiaries. Stock companies typically employ upstream holding companies. An upstream holding company is perched at the top of a corporate organization. The shareholders own it and it owns the subsidiaries. Mutual companies are constrained to use downstream holding companies. A downstream holding company is positioned midway down the corporate hierarchy and is wholly or partially owned by the mutual company. Because the parent mutual company is governed by state insurance laws, the management of a downstream holding company is often more complex than that of an upstream holding company.

As noted earlier, a stock company can raise capital by selling stock. A mutual company does not have this equity option. It may earn revenue from its operations, receive income from its investments, and acquire debt. A stock company may use its stock to acquire other organizations and in merger situations. Frank Irish contends that many of the older and larger mutual companies were able to experience immense growth because at their outset they were not pressured by shareholders to achieve high levels of profitability. Instead, management chose to pursue growth as the company's main objective.

It is possible for a mutual company to convert into a stock company and vice versa. Both processes are complicated, time consuming, and expensive. Conversion from a mutual company to a stock company would typically require the calculation of a policyholder's share of the company and transference of that share to shares of stock. In some instances a stock company, usually motivated by the fear of a takeover, may attempt to mutualize. This conversion would require approval by the company's board, the state insurance commissioner, the stockholders, and the policyholders. All the stock must be purchased and canceled by the company before it can mutualize. According to the *1983 Life Insurance Fact Book,* "In the past 16 years, five companies have converted from the status of a mutual company to a stock company and two stock companies have converted to mutual."[23]

Phyllis Cella commented on moving from a mutual to a stock company:

> I think that it is essentially a good idea, because then the whole company has to have a bottom line. Right now mutuals do have a net gain from operations. A stock company has a very different attitude and culture because they have the stockholder that wants a rate of return. But just doing it is not the answer. Just because you become a stock company doesn't suddenly make everything perfect. The old culture is still there.

The Future

Given the recent announcement of a merger agreement with Buckeye Financial Corporation and the 1982 purchase of Tucker Anthony in addition to the other ten subsidiaries, the Hancock has taken some major steps toward competing in the FSI. The strategic thrust behind such moves was that they would result in synergies along such dimensions as offering more products for the sales force, developing multiple service relationships with individual customers,

---

[23]*1983 Life Insurance Factbook,* (Washington, D.C.: The American Council of Life Insurance, 1983), pp. 88–89. Of the seven companies that converted, the council has identified six. Those converting from mutual to stock were: National Heritage Life-Insurance (1966), Brooking International Life Insurance (1966), Viking Life Insurance (1972), West States Insurance Company (1973), and Equitable Beneficial Mutual Life Insurance Company (1977). Farmers and Traders Life Insurance converted from stock to mutual in 1974.

and management synergy—they "knew how to manage financial services."

For E. James Morton, President and Chief Operations Officer and Vice-Chairman of the Board, the question of measuring performance in the life company was at the heart of what he considered one of the Hancock's major problems. What had been done in the past could not be readily identified as bottom-line. They essentially had no measures of profit and had only inconsistent measures of growth. Size as indicated by assets under management had also become difficult to measure. According to Morton: "We have always had some kind of measures that we have tried to be tough about. But I'm not sure they have been the right ones and the ultimate kinds of measures. And they haven't been the kinds of measures that you can really compensate people on."

Morton had some reservations about moving to the profit center concept. He noted that at times they had the feeling that they were a generation behind and that the profit center idea was becoming outmoded. He referred to management journals that indicated that managers spent too much time worrying about short-term results, thus sacrificing long-term objectives.

Part of the problem of moving to the profit center concept was the method of accounting used in mutual life insurance companies. Morton felt, however, that another big piece of the problem was attitude:

> Maybe the attitude was not so bad in the days when all we were was a mutual life insurance company being operated with the primary purpose to supply insurance at cost to our policyholders. But now that we are trying to compete in a broader financial services industry we can't do that anymore. We have to operate with the same kinds of efficiencies as our competition.

Morton felt that they had to change the way management and essentially all of the employees of the company look at what the objectives are.

> If we do that, we are going to benefit our policyholders a lot more than perhaps we have in the

past. We will be forced to cut costs, run things efficiently, be market-driven, and expand the base that expenses can be spread over, resulting in lower consumer costs. We think we are headed in the right direction. But that is not to say that for the first 100 years things were done the wrong way. The times have changed.

Demutualizing, or moving to a stock company, is a very complex issue because of having to deal with 50 state insurance commissions and agreeing on whether a mutual company has equitably treated its existing policyholders.

For Jack McElwee, this was also a complex issue but one that he related to the future environment of the Hancock.

A lot of people feel that it is too complex but you can't possibly afford to feel that way. If the reality of the future is that only a corporation which is the form of a stock company will be able to survive, then you'd better find a way to be a stock company, or at least have all the legal and regulatory characteristics that a stock company has.

Even though the future of the FSI is questionable, there should also be all kinds of opportunities. McElwee noted that capitalizing on those opportunities means "managing ourselves properly. That's what this exercise is all about—it's called management."

Jim Morton expanded on the role of the John Hancock in the FSI:

I am not sure what one-stop financial shopping means. What we hope to do is attract clients. If we attract a client in one piece of the organization, we hope to make that client a target for the other pieces of the organization. I think it would be unrealistic to think that there are going to be a lot of people that get all their financial services from us. We want to see a lot of cross-selling. We want to have plenty of clients in all the sectors and hopefully the rest will take care of itself.

Morton felt that to succeed in the FSI, the important step is to fill out the product line. He went on to say:

That is why we so badly need a bank. If we can't buy the bank, let's find that out in a hurry because

we have to make other arrangements. There is no way we can be a large financial services organization without offering banking services. If you can't do it by owning a bank, you have to do it some other way.

Morton went on to discuss the future of the John Hancock:

We want to end up with an organization that, when people look at it they say, "That's a financial services organization." And if you ask the man on the street, "What is the John Hancock?" he will say that "it is a financial services organization where I can go to do almost anything. I can buy stocks and bonds, house insurance, securities, and tax shelters. I can also get a mortgage for my house and banking services. Furthermore, I get a statement on everything once a month." . . . That is what we would like to be in 1990, and I think we have a reasonably good chance of doing it. There will be maybe 50 large financial organizations at that time and that is the list we want to be on. In order to do that we have to internally become customer-driven, profit-oriented, entrepreneurial, and all those good things you are supposed to be if you are a healthy, growing business. We know what we need to do. The trick is to do it.

It was also clear to Jim Morton that in the next five to ten years the composition of the businesses of the Hancock was also going to change. The assets in the nontraditional ventures were going to become bigger than those in the traditional ventures. According to Morton, "If we succeed in buying the bank that is another billion dollars of assets. Clearly, the nontraditional ventures are where the growth is."

To complicate management tasks in the environment of an evolving FSI, McElwee also had to deal with what he considered an intriguing question, namely, "What is beyond the financial services industry?" To this end he recently put together a study group focusing on the time frame of 2025 and the major questions of "What are the directions that the Hancock should move?" and "To what extent do those directions influence what we do in the way of financial services today?"

Appendix A

Officers

John G. McElwee

John G. McElwee was elected chairman and chief executive officer of John Hancock Mutual Life Insurance Co. effective January 1, 1982. McElwee entered the John Hancock administrative training program in 1945 and subsequently served as administrative assistant and in a series of line management responsibilities prior to his election as second vice-president in 1961. He became executive vice-president and secretary in 1974. McElwee then served as president and chief operations officer from January 1, 1979, to his election as chairman. He has been on the Board of Directors since March 1976.

E. James Morton

E. James Morton was elected president and chief operations officer of John Hancock Mutual Life Insurance Co. effective January 1, 1982. Morton entered the company as an actuarial student in 1949. He subsequently held a variety of line assignments within the actuarial area prior to his election in 1967 as vice-president and actuary. In 1971, he was elected senior vice-president, technical operations, and in 1974 executive vice-president, corporate operations. Morton has been on the Board of Directors since March 1976.

Stephen L. Brown

Stephen L. Brown was elected executive vice-president of financial operations of the John Hancock Mutual Life Insurance Co. in December 1981, to the Hancock Board of Directors in January 1982, and served as president and chief executive officer of John Hancock Subsidiaries Inc. until February 1984. Brown joined the company in 1958. He subsequently held various assignments within the actuarial department and was elected second vice-president in 1970 and vice-president in 1973. In 1975, he became vice-president at the Treasury Department and in 1977 was named senior vice-president and treasurer.

Phyllis A. Cella

Phyllis A. Cella of Boston is president, chief executive officer, and director of Hanseco Insurance Co., a subsidiary formed for the reinsurance of Sentry Insurance Co. policies sold by John Hancock representatives. She is also chairman of the board of Hanseco (U.K.) Insurance Company Ltd. and a director of John Hancock Subsidiaries Inc. Cella joined the parent company as a statistician. She advanced to statistical consultant in 1963 and served as assistant to the senior vice-president of field management and marketing from 1968 to 1970, when she was named general director of special projects and research. Cella was elected second vice-president in January 1972, vice-president in February 1975, and senior vice-president in December 1979.

Frank S. Irish

Frank S. Irish was promoted to vice-president, corporate analysis and planning, at John Hancock Mutual Life Insurance Co. in January 1979. Irish joined the company in 1963 as an assistant actuary. He was promoted to associate actuary in 1966 and in 1971 joined the Corporate Analysis and Planning Department in that capacity. Irish was elected second vice-president, corporate analysis and planning, in 1972.

Case 5 Update*

To Our Policyholders and Customers

Nineteen eighty-seven . . . fulfilling the promise. This year, more than any other year in the history of John Hancock, was a year of measuring up to the promises made over the past ten years. Promises of a responsive, thoughtful and customer-driven organization that would deliver to the marketplace those products and services our customers needed—and delivering them in a competitive, yet quality-conscious way.

"Real life, real answers" has been the continuing theme in our advertising and our marketing. We have assessed the real-life requirements of the financial services marketplace and have, in 1987, driven toward fulfilling those needs with real answers.

In real life, the lives we all live, there were events that shaped our way of doing business. There were events that shook the financial services world. And events that clearly pointed toward pressing needs among the many publics that we serve.

The continuing plight of many senior citizens, who are living longer and facing destitution rather than dignity after many years of hard work, the shocking stock market tumble of October 19th, the growing concern over the spread of AIDS, and the globalization of American business. Diverse events on the surface, yet linked together in our awareness of the real world we live in.

ProtectCare, a new insurance product that is specifically geared to the senior market, was introduced in 1987. Expectations are high that this product will distinguish John Hancock as an industry leader in the provision of long-term health care coverage.

*Source: Excerpts from John Hancock Mutual Life Insurance Company 1987 annual report, pp. 2–3, 24–27.

To say we were unaffected by the events of October 19th would be unrealistic. Yet, because of John Hancock's approach to the funds under our management, our diversified strategy for investments lessened the impact of the stock market crash on Hancock customers.

John Hancock introduced AIDS Case Management, a humane, caring program that provides our employee benefits customers with a cost-effective way of helping those stricken by this catastrophic disease. And does it with compassion.

To remain competitive in a spreading global marketplace, John Hancock is now the majority owner in a life insurance company in Indonesia, P.T. Asuransi Pensiun Bumiputera John Hancock. Augmenting our presence in Asia, we completed establishment of a fully operational regional office in Hong Kong, John Hancock International Services (Hong Kong) Ltd. And as of January 1, 1988, our regional office in Brussels, originally established to coordinate activity of the International Group Program®, also will be involved in acquisitions. In addition, John Hancock Advisers formed a wholly owned subsidiary, John Hancock Advisers International, Ltd. (London), which provides international investment advice for its mutual funds. We also introduced an international index fund for pension clients.

There were other promises to keep in 1987. John Hancock undertook a major restructuring of its internal organization. Three marketing sectors were established with direct-line responsibility for those areas given to sector presidents, and the post of Chief Financial Officer was created. A reevaluation of our personnel requirements was necessary. In the first quarter of 1987, through a voluntary retirement program, 696 employees left the Company. Additional work force reductions over the year brought that number to 964.

The increased emphasis on profit center and cost center management brought about further reductions in expenses. There emerged, in 1987, a heightened sense of responsibility; an individual sense that each Hancock employee mattered and could contribute. And those contributions would be felt and recognized immediately.

Responding to Our Customers' Needs

ServiceLine, initiated in 1986 on a test basis, was continued throughout 1987. ServiceLine puts John Hancock management personnel in direct contact with customers who call the home office for assistance. Your President and members of the Management Committee, as well as other senior managers, have spent time speaking directly to, and handling inquiries of, customers who call.

We have increased the tempo of management training at John Hancock. Since 1985, more than 1,300 managers from the home office and field organizations have attended a week long Management Training Program that stressed the responsibility of the individual to our customers and prospects. The second phase of this ongoing program is already under way. Called The Excellent Manager Program, it will continue to stress individual responsibility and responsiveness to the needs of our customers.

1987 Results

Assets under management increased more than 9 percent to nearly $46 billion in 1987. Earned Product and Service Income (PSI), a comparative measure of each product's value and contribution to growth, totaled $1.6 billion for the entire complex, of which our non-life subsidiaries accounted for $462 million.

The further development and implementation of the GAAP (Generally Accepted Accounting Principles) system took place throughout the Company. GAAP results have helped us compare ourselves to other diversified financial services companies, not just life insurance companies. Through this comparison, we are able to evaluate our strategies in the real world of financial services. It has helped us focus on the needs of our customers and the viability of the products and services we offer them. It has proven very valuable in restructuring the Company, as well as evaluating the products and services being delivered.

Hancock as a Corporate Citizen

Just as we must evaluate ourselves as a profitable provider of financial services to our customers, we grade John Hancock as a corporate citizen and member of our communities. We have continued to support the improved quality of the Boston public schools system through HEART (Hancock Endowment for Academics, Recreation and Teaching) with a self-perpetuating grant of $1 million. The youngsters of Boston and the surrounding communities have benefited from the running and fitness clinics established in conjunction with our sponsorship of the Boston Marathon. In all, John Hancock contributed $3 million to 1,500 community charities and services nationwide in 1987.

Because of our concern about the spread of AIDS, the Company has taken an active role in education about this fatal disease. Of these efforts, Larry Kessler, Executive Director of the AIDS Action Committee of Massachusetts, said, "I applaud John Hancock's leadership in the corporate community advocating education and support for persons with AIDS." Hancock has contributed to seven Boston health and human services organizations for their respective AIDS education programs; we cosponsor an annual 10-kilometer AIDS "Walk for Life" that raised $750,000 in 1987; conducted forums to help educate employees on AIDS prevention, many during the Company's observance of AIDS Employee Education Month; and held a community forum bringing teenagers together with experts who answer their questions.

Responding to the Real World

In 1987 we took major internal restructuring steps that brought your Company to a state of readiness to deal with the real world problems and opportunities in our marketplace. Not just for 1987 but for many years to come. We now have a new organization, a new line of customer

responsive products coming into being, and a renewed sense of purpose. We are becoming a part of the real life of our customers by providing them with real answers through better products and services than ever before.

E. James Morton
Chairman of the Board and
Chief Executive Officer

Stephen L. Brown
President and
Chief Operations Officer

Consolidated Statement of Financial Position
John Hancock Mutual Life Insurance Company and Subsidiary

	Year ended December 31 (In millions)	1987	1986
Assets			
	Bonds	$ 9,365.8	$ 9,471.3
	Stocks:		
	Preferred or guaranteed	95.3	134.0
	Common	103.1	241.2
	Investments in affiliates	415.0	436.7
		613.4	811.9
	Mortgage loans on real estate	8,687.7	8,563.4
	Real estate:		
	Company occupied	193.6	193.6
	Investment properties	1,271.9	1,151.1
		1,465.5	1,344.7
	Policy loans and liens	2,256.1	2,301.4
	Cash items:		
	Cash in banks and offices	131.8	370.0
	Temporary cash investments	942.2	465.5
		1,074.0	835.5
	Premiums due and deferred	398.1	359.7
	Investment income due and accrued	458.9	483.0
	Other general account assets	955.1	796.7
	Assets held in separate accounts	2,936.3	2,840.8
	Total Assets	$28,210.9	$27,808.4

Obligations and Policyholders' Contingency Reserves

Year ended December 31 (In millions)	1987	1986
Obligations		
Policy reserves	$20,374.6	$19,863.9
Policyholders' and beneficiaries' funds	2,323.8	2,232.0
Dividends payable to policyholders	409.9	456.2
Policy benefits in process of payment	201.8	171.1
Other policy obligations	225.6	220.2
Long-term debt—Note 3	103.3	180.4
Mandatory securities and other asset valuation reserves	473.0	426.2
Federal income and other accrued taxes—Note 2	.0	158.3
Other general account obligations	177.1	274.6
Obligations related to separate account business	2,911.0	2,820.4
Total Obligations	27,200.1	26,803.3
Policyholders' Contingency Reserves		
Special contingency reserve for group insurance	119.2	113.4
General contingency reserve	891.6	891.7
Total Contingency Reserves	1,010.8	1,005.1
Total Obligations and Contingency Reserves	$28,210.9	$27,808.4

Certain 1986 amounts have been reclassified to permit comparison.
The accompanying notes are an integral part of the consolidated financial statements.

Consolidated Summary of Operations and Changes in Policyholders' Contingency Reserves
John Hancock Mutual Life Insurance Company and Subsidiary

Year ended December 31 (In millions)	1987	1986	1985
Income—Note 8			
Premiums, annuity considerations and pension fund contributions	$4,916.8	$4,571.1	$4,388.0
Investment income—Note 5	2,320.7	2,276.3	2,178.8
Separate account capital gains (losses)—Note 2	(117.2)	100.5	277.7
Other—net	(1.9)	(27.6)	(188.2)
	7,118.4	6,920.3	6,656.3
Benefits and Expenses—Note 8			
Payments to policyholders and beneficiaries:			
Death benefits	679.7	635.2	608.2
Accident and health benefits	453.8	402.5	427.3
Annuity benefits	692.6	580.3	480.6
Surrender benefits and annuity fund withdrawals	3,418.5	2,787.2	2,163.2
Matured endowments	21.2	23.4	20.7
	5,265.8	4,428.6	3,700.0
Additions to reserves to provide for future payments to policyholders and beneficiaries	738.4	1,253.2	1,688.5
Expenses of providing services to policyholders and obtaining new insurance:			
Field sales compensation and expenses	364.2	351.7	329.9
Home office and general expenses	319.0	352.9	311.4
State premium taxes	35.3	35.0	28.2
Payroll and miscellaneous taxes	34.1	34.7	32.1
	6,756.8	6,456.1	6,090.1
Gain before dividends to policyholders and federal income taxes	361.6	464.2	566.2
Dividends to policyholders	357.3	410.7	394.8
Federal income taxes (credits)	(135.9)	(63.9)	89.1
	221.4	346.8	483.9
Net Gain	140.2	117.4	82.3
Other increases (decreases) in policyholders' contingency reserves:			
Net capital losses and other adjustments—Note 6	(177.4)	(124.1)	(93.5)
Valuation reserve changes	(3.7)	.5	(3.1)
Prior years' federal taxes	(12.7)	63.2	(73.6)
Other reserves and adjustments—Note 4	59.3	(9.5)	1.0
Net Increase (Decrease) in Policyholders' Contingency Reserves	5.7	47.5	(86.9)
Policyholders' Contingency Reserves at Beginning of Year	1,005.1	957.6	1,044.5
Policyholders' Contingency Reserves at End of Year	$1,010.8	$1,005.1	$ 957.6

Certain 1986 and 1985 amounts have been reclassified to permit comparison.
The accompanying notes are an integral part of the consolidated financial statements.

Consolidated Statement of Changes in Financial Position
John Hancock Mutual Life Insurance Company and Subsidiary

Year ended December 31 (In millions)	1987	1986	1985
Additions			
From operations:			
Net gain	$ 140.2	$ 117.4	$ 82.3
Summary of operations items not affecting cash and temporary cash investments:			
Increase in aggregate reserves for all policies	503.3	1,399.9	1,542.6
Increase (decrease) in policyholders' and beneficiaries' funds and general liabilities	(34.3)	(336.9)	186.3
(Increase) decrease in premiums due and deferred and investment income due and accrued	(20.6)	34.9	48.3
Provision for depreciation	45.8	43.9	33.2
Accrual of discount and amortization of premium on bonds and mortgage loans—net	(39.1)	(45.7)	(47.0)
Total from Operations	595.3	1,213.5	1,845.7
Proceeds from issuance of long-term debt	.0	98.5	.0
Net carrying value of long-term investments upon disposal:			
Bonds	3,362.6	2,127.0	1,936.9
Stocks	392.0	248.4	293.0
Mortgage loans on real estate	934.2	778.3	590.5
Real estate	111.6	77.8	88.2
Policy loans and liens	359.0	325.4	316.5
	5,159.4	3,556.9	3,225.1
Net capital gains (losses) realized for general account upon disposal of long-term investments	(58.8)	78.8	(58.7)
	5,695.9	4,497.7	5,012.1
Deductions			
Acquisition of long-term investments:			
Bonds	3,192.2	2,126.7	2,584.5
Stocks	301.2	213.3	261.7
Mortgage loans on real estate	1,093.4	1,404.7	1,278.6
Real estate	244.8	279.8	256.4
Policy loans and liens	313.7	373.4	407.1
	5,145.3	4,397.9	4,788.3
Other—net:			
Increase in other assets	103.8	36.5	169.5
Increase in assets held in separate accounts	95.5	248.6	355.4
Repayment of commercial paper	75.0	.0	.0
Miscellaneous	37.8	80.4	22.4
	5,457.4	4,763.4	5,335.6
Increase (Decrease) in Cash and Temporary Cash Investments	238.5	184.3	(323.5)
Cash and temporary cash investments at beginning of year	835.5	651.2	974.7
Cash and Temporary Cash Investments at End of Year	$1,074.0	$ 835.5	$ 651.2

Certain 1986 and 1985 amounts have been reclassified to permit comparison.
The accompanying notes are an integral part of the consolidated financial statements.

CrossLand Savings, FSB

After a decade of upheaval, 1990 was expected to be a watershed in history of the U.S. thrift industry. Declining spreads profitability because of rising competition, combined with high level of savings withdrawals, were anticipated to force more thrifts out of business. Of the 3000 federally insured thrift institutions that existed in 1989, only 1200 were expected to survive by the year 1993.

This case focuses on CrossLand Savings, FSB, and its search for a sustainable competitive advantage in the volatile environment of the savings and loan segment of the thrift industry. The case describes the profile of the thrift industry and the evolution of CrossLand's strategy. The case highlights the challenge even the most innovative thrift organizations must address: How can an institution develop and maintain a distinctive competence to insulate itself from the evergrowing adversity of the competitive environment?

In 1988, CrossLand Savings and its consolidated subsidiaries ("CrossLand") was the eleventh largest thrift institution in the U.S. with $14.8 billion assets. CrossLand consisted of a savings bank insured by the Federal Deposit Insurance Corporation (FDIC) located in New York with 41 branches ("CrossLand [FDIC]"); a savings bank insured by the Federal Savings and Loan Insurance Corporation (FSLIC) headquartered in Utah, with 50 branches in Florida, Utah, Oregon, Virginia, California, Washington

This case was prepared by Karen Jones and Shaker A. Zahra of George Mason University. Reprinted with permission.

and New Jersey ("CrossLand [FSLIC]"); and a mortgage banking company with offices throughout the United States ("CrossLand Mortgage").

The U.S. Thrift Industry

CrossLand's predominant operations were in the thrift industry. This industry, which was created by the Home Owner's Loan Act in 1933 to provide a source of funding for mortgage housing, has undergone many changes in the 1970s and 1980s. Prior to this time, thrift institutions primarily obtained funds from savers at fixed interest rates and lent the money to home owners at rates which guaranteed them a profit. Inflation and rising interest rates in the 1960s and 1970s made thrift institutions unable to retain the funding necessary for liquidity. In the 1970s, this loss of funds became even greater with the creation of money market funds which paid investors the going market yields with only little additional risk.

Reacting to rising losses, in 1978 Congress allowed thrifts to offer money market certificates tied to Treasury Bill rates. In 1980 Congress passed the Depository Institutions Deregulation and Monetary Control Act (DIDMCA) which provided for the phasing out of ceilings on deposit rates within six years. Responding to intensifying competition from the money market funds and to the inability of the thrifts to earn market rates on their loan portfolios, Congress passed the Garn-St. Germain Act in 1982. This Act empowered thrifts to offer money market accounts, thereby significantly broadening the investment powers of thrifts. The Act also allowed thrifts to make adjustable rate loans.

This new economic environment and the resulting deregulation altered the thrift industry significantly. For the first time thrifts were forced to compete for funds and for investments. Profits were no longer guaranteed and interest rate risk and credit risk had to be better managed. Many thrifts failed during the 1980 through 1982 recession as interest rates skyrocketed and thrifts were unable to earn enough on their assets to cover the cost of their liability. Under the increased investment powers permitted by the Garn-St. Germain Act and allowed by some states to the state chartered thrifts, some institutions increased the level of their investment in riskier commercial loans in order to earn higher rates. Largely as a result of the excess risk and the subsequent collapse of the economy in certain areas of the country, thrifts were increasingly failing at the highest rate in their history.

The current historical level of failing thrift institutions and the insolvency of FSLIC has attracted considerable attention to the industry. In February 1989 President Bush proposed a plan to rescue the industry. This plan included bringing the Federal Home Loan Bank Board (FHLBB) under the control of the Treasury Department. The plan also required the FDIC to take control over the FSLIC. These actions were expected to result in stricter regulations over the thrift industry which, under the FHLBB and the FSLIC, has enjoyed more freedom than commercial banks have under the FDIC. Furthermore, President Bush's plan called for the raising of $50 billion to cover the costs of shutting down insolvent thrifts.

There were three additional major issues the industry had to address: regulation, undifferentiated products and sensitivity of earnings to interest rates. Historically, the industry had been subject to many regulations that were intended to ensure efficiency of operations and institutional stability. The Federal Home Loan Bank Board (FHLBB) and FSLIC played a major role in this regard. FHLBB, for instance, functioned as a policeman, central banker, and deposit insurance administrator. FSLIC, on the other hand, supervised compliance with capital requirements of the Bank Board. FSLIC had the authority to manage those institutions that failed to meet these standards.

In terms of the second issue, undifferentiated products, some considered the industry's products to be commodities. These products were distinguishable only in their terms and interest rates. While some innovations, such as adjustable mortgage rates, were introduced, product offerings in the 1980s remained the same.

History

CrossLand was chartered as a New York savings bank in 1860 under the name East Brooklyn Savings Bank. Later, it changed its name to Metropolitan Savings Bank. In 1985 the name CrossLand was adopted in order to reflect the bank's expanding nationwide scope of the business.

The bank grew by acquiring two financial institutions in 1970 and 1978. But, until 1981, the institution operated as a home mortgage lender and deposit gatherer primarily in its own backyard.

In 1981, CrossLand began an aggressive strategy of growth through acquisitions by acquiring three local savings banks which nearly tripled its size. This strategy continued throughout the 1980s with an acquisition of a mortgage banking company in 1982 (which was sold in 1985), acquisitions of two Florida thrifts and two Virginia thrifts in 1983, a mortgage banking company and a commercial credit company in 1986, a Utah savings and loan in 1987 (which had licenses to operate in ten states) and a New Jersey savings and loan in 1988.

All of the thrift acquisitions, with the exception of two in 1981 and a 1983 Florida thrift purchase, were completed in regulatory assisted transactions. For instance, the acquisitions of one of the New York banks in 1981 and one of the Florida banks and the two Virginia banks in 1983 were accompanied by subsidies and yield coverage provided by regulators. Likewise, the acquisitions of the Utah and New Jersey institutions in 1986 and 1987 were also regulatory assisted transactions but little assistance was provided. CrossLand acquired these institutions primarily as a way to enter markets forbidden to them under the limitations on interstate banking. Later, the New York institutions were merged into one institution which was insured by the FDIC, and all other institutions were regrouped into one institution which was insured by the FSLIC.

In 1985, CrossLand (FDIC) became a federally chartered institution and went public, thereby raising $116 million. Subsequent offerings to the public of preferred stock and debt raised additional capital in excess of $1 billion. Because 5.5 percent capital (as a percentage of assets) had been maintained to meet FDIC requirements, these funds also represented capital which CrossLand was able to use to leverage its growth.

Exhibit 1 summarizes the growth of CrossLand as a result of its acquisitions and financing activities since November 1981.

Data in Exhibit 1 indicated that CrossLand had the following annual compound growth rates of various balance sheet line items: 19 percent assets; 25 percent net loans; 65 percent borrow-

Exhibit 1   Crossland Savings, FSB: Significant Acquisition and Financing Activities

Year	Event	Increase[1] in Assets	Total[2] Assets at Year End
1981	Acquired Greenwich Savings Bank in New York in an FDIC assisted merger	$2,015	
	Merged with the Brooklyn Savings Bank in New York	1,558	$5,712
1983	Acquired one Florida thrift and two Virginia thrifts in FSLIC assisted merger	247	
	Acquired First City Federal in Florida	897	7,432
1985	Sold mortgage banking subsidiary for a net profit	90	
	Sold common stock	116	
	Sold two issues of callable preferred stock (2)	150	
	Sold collateralized floating rate notes	100	8,023
1986	Acquired a mortgage banking company	339	
	Acquired a finance company	99	
	Sold preferred stock	123	
	Sold two issues of callable preferred stock (2)	150	
	Sold Senior Subordinated Capital Notes	169	10,096
1987	Acquired Western Savings and Loan Association in an FSLIC assisted merger	445	
	Sold preferred stock	238	
	Sold two issues of callable preferred stock (1)	150	13,775
1988	Acquired Reliance Savings and Loan Association in an FSLIC assisted merger	82	15,144

[1]All figures are in $ million.
[2]Represents Dutch Auction Rate Transferable Securities, a form of adjustable rate preferred stock sold through finance subsidiaries and fully collateralized. Although they do not qualify as capital, their high credit rating makes them a cheap form of financing.

ing; and 37 percent common shareholders equity.

CrossLand's Financial Position

Exhibit 2 presents a summary of CrossLand's financial performance for the five years ending December 31, 1988.

Operating earnings (income before income taxes, extraordinary items, cumulative effect of accounting change, and gains on sales of assets) were considered a key measure of ongoing profitability from operations. Data in Exhibit 2 show that CrossLand's operating earnings have steadily improved during the period from 1984 through 1988. During the same period operating

Exhibit 2 CrossLand Savings, FSB: Five-Year Summary Financial and Other Data

	As of December 31, ($ millions)				
	1988	**1987**	**1986**	**1985**	**1984**
Statements of Operations Data					
Interest income	$ 1,251	$ 952	$ 803	$ 753	$ 747
Interest expense	977	709	599	637	707
Net interest income	274	243	204	116	40
Provision for possible loan losses	25	18	8	8	3
Other operating income:					
Gains on asset sales	26	26	25	156	119
Other	97	65	47	52	48
Other operating expenses	245	199	152	160	162
Income before taxes, cumulative effect and extraordinary items	127	117	116	156	42
Income tax provision (benefit) (1)	22	21	75	49	(1)
Extraordinary items (1)	—	—	58	34	1
Cumulative effect of accounting change (2)	(90)	—	—	—	—
Net income	15	96	100	141	44
Preferred dividends	41	21	8	—	—
Net income available to common shareholders	(26)	75	92	141	44
State of Condition Data					
Total assets	15,143	13,747	10,073	8,001	7,932
Loans—net	13,109	11,709	8,298	5,996	5,005
Investment securities	500	645	556	737	1,308
Goodwill	445	540	512	540	573
Deposits	8,791	7,748	6,876	6,971	7,262
Borrowing	4,785	4,268	1,962	411	392
Senior Subordinated Capital Notes	170	170	169	—	—
Callable Preferred Stock	300	450	300	150	—
Stockholders equity	874	922	620	400	139

[1]Net operating loss carryforwards (NOLs) used to offset the income tax provision were recorded as extraordinary items for fiscal years 1986 and prior and were netted against the income tax provision in 1987 and 1988 (due to the adoption of SFAS 96).
[2]Represents the NOLs realized in 1987 and 1988 which arose from the sale of assets acquired in business combinations. Under SFAS 96 these NOLs must be applied as a reduction of goodwill instead of the income tax provision.

earnings (losses) were ($78), $0, $92, $92 and $100 million, respectively. In 1986 and 1987 CrossLand's operating earnings (or core earnings) to average assets well exceeded the industry and CrossLand's peer groups' averages as shown in Exhibit 3.

The operating losses in 1984 and 1985 were directly attributed to the excess of interest earning liabilities over interest earning assets. Further, as Exhibit 4 shows, the interest rate spread—

defined as the difference between the yield earned on interest earning assets over the rate paid on interest bearing liabilities—was generally positive. However, the net yield earned on interest earning assets was significantly lower than the interest rate spread in 1984 and 1985. This was due, perhaps, to the fact that the level of interest bearing liabilities significantly exceeded the level of interest earning assets; i.e., although the rate paid on liabilities was 2.44 percent lower than

Exhibit 3   Profitability: Core Earnings to Average Assets (%)—Most Recent Four Years

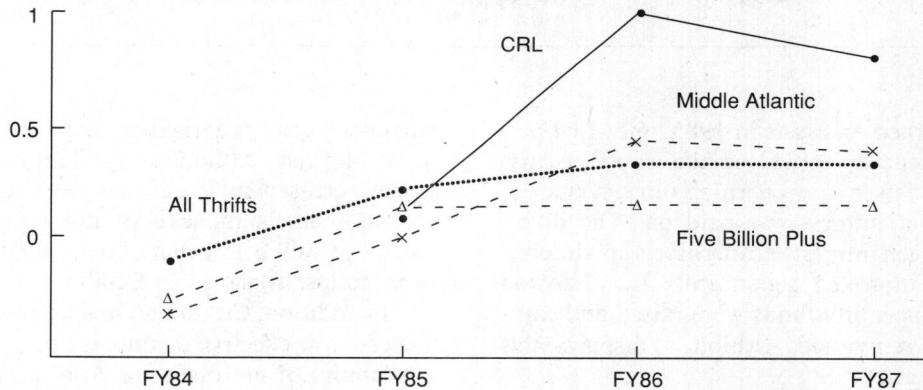

Exhibit 4   Spread: Net Interest Income to Average Assets (%)—Most Recent Four Years

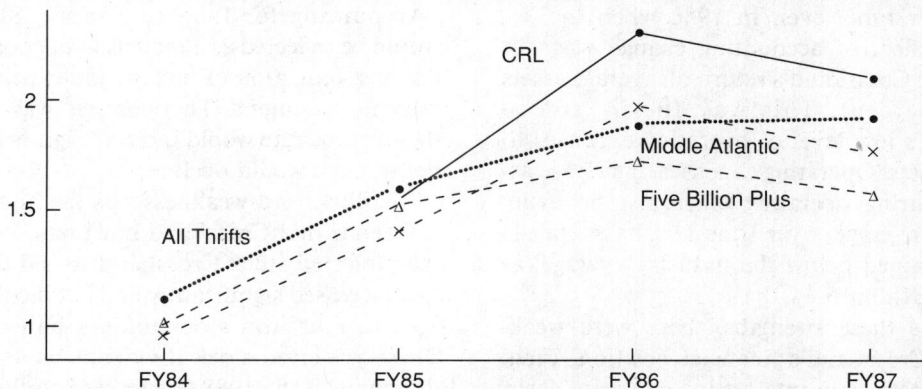

Exhibit 5   Overhead: Operating Expenses to Average Assets (%)—Most Recent Four Years

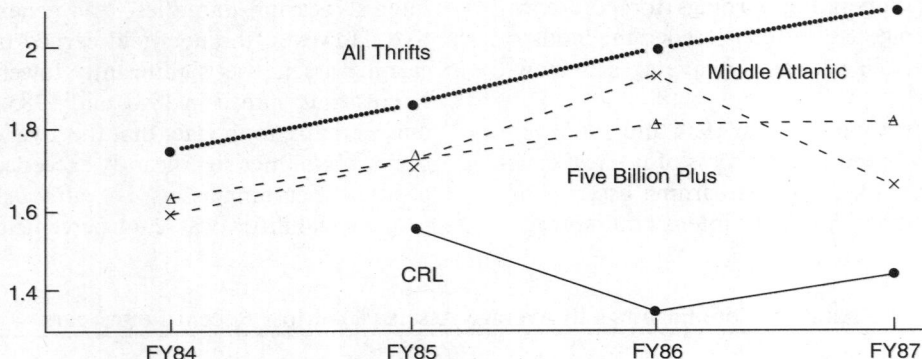

the rate earned on assets in 1985, only 1.64 percent was actually earned on the assets because there were fewer assets earning interest than liabilities that interest was paid on. The differential between interest earning assets and interest liabilities improved significantly in 1986 and thereafter as equity funds were raised and earnings were reinvested. Exhibit 4 displays this improvement.

The long-term industry average for return on average assets (net income divided by average assets) was 65 to 70 basis points (a basis point equals one-hundredth of a percent). CrossLand compared favorably to this measure of performance over time, even in 1988 when the cumulative effect of accounting change was not considered. CrossLand's return on average assets was .75 percent. This was due in part to CrossLand's low level of operating expenses to average assets. Operating expenses to average assets, measuring operating efficiency, have declined, on average, over time and have consistently remained below the industry average, as shown in Exhibit 5.

Despite these strengths, there were weaknesses in CrossLand's financial position. First, revenues other than interest income were desirable as they helped to insulate a thrift from the narrowing spreads earned on assets and from interest rate risk. Although CrossLand's other income increased sufficiently to keep up with the growth in assets, the level of other operating income was well below that of the industry and its peer groups, as shown in Exhibit 6.

In addition, CrossLand had traditionally expected a low effective income tax rate due to the availability of net operating loss carryforwards (NOLs) to offset income tax expense. As of December 31, 1988, CrossLand had $260 million of NOLs remaining. However, of these, $208 million represented acquired NOLs which, under State of Financial Accounting Standards 96 "Accounting for Income Taxes" (SFAS 96), would be reflected as a reduction of goodwill and not as a reduction of income tax expense in the income statement. Therefore, it was expected that income rate would increase significantly and net income would decline.

Still, a third weakness was the high level of dividends that CrossLand must pay. Because of the preferred stock CrossLand issued dividends had increased significantly and net income available to common stockholders had declined. These preferred stock dividends were expected to remain at the 1988 level of $41 million unless some of the outstanding shares were liquidated

Exhibit 6   Loan Fees and Other Income to Average Assets (%)—Most Recent Four Years

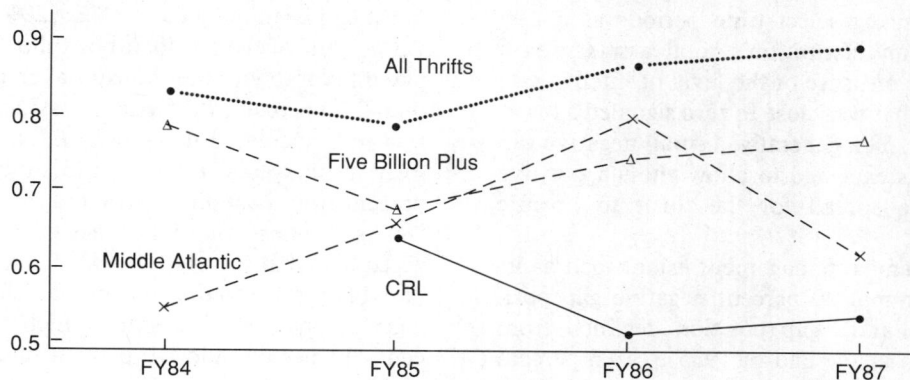

or additional shares were issued. The payment of these dividends, combined with the low level of net income and the dividends paid on common stock in 1988, caused the first decline in CrossLand's stockholders equity since 1983.

Another factor which has kept CrossLand's earnings from being even greater was Cross-Land's increasing reliance on borrowing as a source of funds. Borrowing—including the senior subordinate debt and the Callable Preferred Stock—as a percentage of liabilities increased from 5.0 percent in 1984 to 36.8 percent at the end of 1988. In addition, CrossLand's cost of borrowing was 125, 157 and 172 basis points higher than its cost of deposits in 1988, 1987 and 1986, respectively. This relatively high level of borrowing, combined with the greater cost, was a major cause of the decline in the net yield earned during this period. But CrossLand had one of the lowest cost of funds of any public thrift. This was primarily due to its strong presence in Brooklyn and Queens where depositors continued to invest in low interest bearing passbook accounts.

CrossLand's long-term strength was reflected in its equity position. CrossLand (FDIC) was insured by the FDIC and was required to maintain 5.5 percent primary capital require-

ments (6.0 percent in total capital must also be maintained). In determining whether the capital requirement was met, the FDIC required that any goodwill be deducted from total capital. For CrossLand, this greatly influenced the level of capital as goodwill as significant as a result of its acquisitions. Despite this, CrossLand had always been in compliance with the requirement. In addition to meeting FDIC capital requirements, CrossLand was subject to FHLBB regulations and also had to meet the FHLBB capital requirements. The FHLBB capital requirements were substantially less stringent than those of the FDIC, primarily because goodwill did not have to be deducted from capital and the percent of capital that had to be maintained was lower. As of December 31, 1988, CrossLand exceeded its FHLBB capital requirements of $465 million by $606 million.

CrossLand's Interest Rate Risk and Credit Risk Exposure

One of the most significant risks that thrift institutions faced in the 1980s was interest rate risk. This occurred when risk when interest earning assets matured or "repriced" (i.e., the interest rate was adjusted) at times other than interest bearing liabilities. The gap position, measured by the difference in the repricing of assets and liabilities during select time periods as a percentage of an institution's total assets, was a widely used measure of the level of interest rate risk. A gap that was close to zero signaled a lower level of risk. Yet, generally, a small negative gap position was expected to allow enough positive interest rate spread for the thrift to operate profitably.

CrossLand's management established as its target an annual 20 percent negative gap position. CrossLand's gap position declined from 52.8 percent at the end of 1985 to 19.6 percent at the end of 1988. CrossLand succeeded in lowering its gap position through the implementation of an interest rate risk management program which included the origination of loans with adjustable rates or short-term maturities, increasing the maturities of borrowing, and using hedging activities to extend the repricing term of its liabilities. Despite its success in meeting its 20 percent annual target position, CrossLand's executives believed that the gap position was still significantly greater than that of its peers and the industry. In fact, CrossLand expected to reprice nearly $3 billion more liabilities than assets in 1989.

Industry-wide effort to minimize interest rate risk had been at the cost of net interest income. Earlier in the 1980s, the industry enjoyed higher interest rate spreads because thrifts received a premium for accepting longer term assets and holding shorter term liabilities. This trend changed in the late 1980s. In order to counteract the narrowing spreads earned on their investments, thrifts increased the credit risk they would accept in return for greater yields. As Exhibit 7 shows, CrossLand did not assume a significant amount of risks, with the great majority of its loan portfolio—over 70 percent in 1988— being concentrated in residential real estate mortgages or in mortgage backed securities. Furthermore, on December 31, 1988, over 25 percent of CrossLand's total loan portfolio was in government insured loans. Also, CrossLand's nonaccrual and renegotiated loans for which interest had been reduced totalled $209 million or 1.5 percent of the net loan portfolio. This compared favorably to the industry average of more than 3.00 percent. Likewise, CrossLand had significantly increased its allowance for loan losses over recent years, totalling $45 million or .34 percent of outstanding loans and .46 percent of "at-risk" loans (total loans less government insured loans) at the end of 1988. This, too, compared favorably to the level of loan chargeoffs as a percentage of average loans, which was .08 percent, .15 percent and .10 percent in 1988, 1987 and 1986, respectively. Overall, it appeared that CrossLand's relatively low level of credit risk helped to keep its earnings high because there was not a significant level of nonearning loans or loan losses.

CrossLand's Products and Markets

The 1988 annual report stated that "CrossLand is a group of financial service companies managed to enhance stockholder value through sustained profitability. We expect to accomplish this by generating quality assets, particularly real estate loans and interest, using least cost funding sources and carefully controlling operating costs. Lines of business and geographic diversification will be emphasized as strategies to achieve these objectives. CrossLand will seek to enhance its profitability, maintain a strong capital base and pursue a national presence as a premier banking institution."

CrossLand's primary operations were in the thrift industry, as in Exhibit 8. Its major source of funds was deposits and it primarily invested these funds in loans. CrossLand's thrift operations were located throughout the country, as shown in Exhibit 9.

CrossLand's average outstanding deposits per branch of $97 million were well above the industry average. This was attributable to the high deposit base in the New York branches; the

Exhibit 7 CrossLand Savings, FSB: Select Financial Ratios

Item	As of December 31 (%)				
	1988	1987	1986	1985	1984
Interest rate spread	2.19	2.50	2.83	2.44	1.66
Net yield	2.06	2.34	2.53	1.64	.59
Return on average equity	1.61	12.79	18.21	61.12	32.35
Return on average assets	.10	.84	1.10	1.79	.58
Equity to assets	5.77	6.71	6.16	5.00	1.76
Operating expense to average assets	1.61	1.73	1.68	2.02	2.12
Operating income to average assets	.63	.57	.52	.66	.62

Exhibit 8 CrossLand Savings, FSB: Composition of Loan Portfolio

Item	As of December 31 (%)		
	1988	1987	1986
Residential mortgages	37.6	26.0	36.5
Commercial or industrial loans	22.1	22.7	17.7
Mortgage backed securities	33.0	45.5	38.5
Consumer loans	2.5	2.3	2.9
Commercial business loans	2.9	3.4	4.4
High yield securities	1.9	.1	—
Gross loan portfolio	100.0	100.0	100.0

Exhibit 9 Dispersion of CrossLand's Operations

State	Number of Branches	Outstanding Deposits ($ million)	Average Deposits per Branch ($ million)
New York	41	$7,256	$177
Florida	33	1,069	32
Oregon	6	154	26
Utah	4	130	32
New Jersey	2	75	37
Virginia	2	26	13
Washington	2	56	28
California	1	24	24
Total	91	$8,790	$ 97

other states had average deposit levels which were below the industry average. The Florida branches included seven full service "minibranches" which operated in Winn Dixie supermarkets. The bank had plans to open 28 additional supermarket branches in Oregon and Washington. The bank originated commercial real estate and construction loans through the New York branch offices and through 13 offices in 10 states. In addition, residential mortgages were originated through 34 offices in 16 states.

Despite its nationwide retail presence, as indicated by its high level of mortgage backed securities and borrowing, CrossLand operated much more as a wholesale bank than the average thrift. Mortgage backed securities represented 29 percent of assets, and borrowing constituted almost 35 percent of assets. In addition, a significant part of CrossLand's loan activity was in the purchase and sale of loans. Exhibit 10 shows CrossLand's loan activities for 1986, 1987 and 1988. CrossLand's high level of wholesale operations had contributed, in part, to its low operating cost ratio (the cost of obtaining funds was less) but interest rate spreads were typically less on wholesale funds due to transaction costs.

Exhibit 10 Crossland Savings, FSB: Loan
Activity*

Type	1988	1987 (in millions)	1986
Loans originated	$4,095	$3,061	$1,682
Loans purchased	1,579	5,512	5,129
Loans acquired through merger	42	249	426
Loans sold	1,749	2,914	2,946
Loans satisfactions and amortization	2,560	2,533	2,038
Net loan activity	$1,407	$3,375	$2,253

*Data for the year ended December 31.

CrossLand also provided nontraditional thrift services directly to depositors and through its subsidiaries which included the following:

CrossLand Mortgage Corp. This was the mortgage banking subsidiary which originated and sold loans for CrossLand and for others, serviced loans for CrossLand and others and conducted secondary mortgage marketing activities.

CrossLand Premium Funding Corp. This subsidiary financed insurance premiums for corporate customers.

CrossLand Credit Corp. This finance company made equipment leasing loans and wholesale floor plan loans.

Specialized Management Support, Inc. This data processing company provided accounting, tax reporting and other financial services to real estate attorneys and brokers, title insurance companies and other businesses.

CrossLand Insurance Agency, Inc. This company provided life, health, accident, property, and casualty insurance and tax-deferred annuities to customers.

Perhaps, the largest source of noninterest in-

come from subsidiaries came from CrossLand Mortgage Corp. loan servicing fees. With a loan servicing portfolio of $3.9 billion, $1.1 billion which was for banks other than CrossLand, CrossLand Mortgage was in the top 20 percent of mortgage banking companies in the United States.

CrossLand also offered life insurance in New York through Savings Bank Life Insurance Fund of New York and offered discount brokerage in five branches in New York and Florida in a joint venture with First Institutional Securities Corp. In addition, CrossLand had entered into joint ventures engaged in real estate activities. All of these activities contributed to noninterest income which helped to lessen CrossLand's reliance on interest income and were in line with CrossLand's strategy to expand fee-based services. This expansion was evidenced by the increase in other operating income of 40 percent in 1987 and 48 percent in 1988.

CrossLand's attempts to cross sell its services have been successful as 74 percent of its savings customers had some other relationship with the bank. Nevertheless, Crossland's primary focus was on its retail operations. In the 1988 annual report, CrossLand indicated that its strength was in the retail banking and lending franchise, and that its primary focus was to expand this franchise and focus on cross selling products and services to the retail customers. CrossLand intended to develop a full menu of diversified offerings, providing product and sales training to employees, using incentive programs for branches which met or exceeded sales goals and by offering new products. One of the first new products was introduced in 1988. Known as CrossLand, it represented a package of services that tied the checking, savings and loan products.

CrossLand's Competition

Over the past decade, competition in the thrift industry increased significantly. This was due to the introduction of money market mutual funds, the effects of deregulation, the advent of interstate banking, the increased marketability of mortgage backed securities and the increasing sophistication of the typical thrift customer.

CrossLand competed for its deposits with other thrift institutions, commercial banks, money market funds and credit unions. It primarily competed based on the deposit rates offered, the service provided and the convenience of its retail locations. Most directly, CrossLand competed with other thrift institutions in the areas in which it had its retail locations.

In New York, CrossLand faced stiff competition from five major savings banks: American, Apple, Carteret, CityFed and Dime. These New York institutions were financially healthy and thus could afford to compete more heavily on rates. To avoid direct competition with these banks CrossLand concentrated its branches outside Manhattan. Of its 41 New York branches, 14 were in Brooklyn, 9 were in Long Island, 10 were in Manhattan, 3 were in Queens, 2 were in Westchester County, 2 were in Rockland County and 1 was in Staten Island. In particular, the Brooklyn and Queens branches have a high concentration of passbook savings accounts which are low cost at 5.5 percent and stable deposits.

The competition within Florida was more wide ranging, because many of the larger California and New York thrifts had operations in Florida. In response, CrossLand increased convenience by opening the supermarket branches.

CrossLand's competition for real estate, commercial business and consumer loans came from other thrift institutions, commercial banks, mortgage banking companies, insurance companies and other institutional lenders. The introduction of mortgage backed securities increased the market for mortgages as the liquidity of the securities allowed nonfinancial institutions to own mortgages. In addition, the increased lending powers granted to the thrift institutions in 1980 and 1982 made the distinction between thrifts and banks narrower and increased the

competition for commercial loans. Because CrossLand originated loans throughout the United States it has no significant direct competitors. Competition for loans is primarily based on rates and availability.

CrossLand's Management

CrossLand's Chairman of the Board and Chief Executive Officer until October 1988 was Luke Baione who served with the company for 42 years. Mr. Baione was credited for initiating and leading the changes that took place in CrossLand in the 1980s that made the company among the top thrifts in the United States.

In 1988 Mr. Baione was replaced by Maurice Reissman, 42, the then President and Chief Operating Officer. Mr. Reissman has been with the bank 21 years and served as the President since 1985.

Other key members of the top management team and their functions (following a reorganization in 1989) were as follows:

- Frank Dellomo, 55, was the Vice Chairman of the Board and was responsible for retail banking, consumer lending, administrative services and marketing. He joined Brooklyn Savings Bank in 1951 and was its President when it was merged into CrossLand in December 1981.

- Thomas Eschmann, 52, was an Executive Vice President and Chief Lending Officer. Mr. Eschmann joined CrossLand in 1985. He served with Chase Manhattan Bank for 10 years (1975–1985).

- Ramesh Gupta, 41, was the Executive Vice President and Chief Financial Officer, having previously served as the Chief Investment Officer. Mr. Gupta joined CrossLand in 1984 and previously was employed by Goldome Savings Bank.

- Donald White, 47, was the Executive Vice President in charge of Bank Operations, having previously served as the Chief Financial Officer. Mr. White joined CrossLand in June 1983 when the bank acquired Ralph C. Sutro Co. where he served as Senior Vice President and Chief Financial Officer for the previous six years.

The management team had considerable experience in the thrift and financial services industry and a significant portion of that experience had been with CrossLand itself. Messrs. Baione, Reissman, and Dellomo basically spent their careers with the bank. This was noteworthy because while many of competitors' management teams were unable to adapt successfully to the rapidly changing thrift environment brought about by deregulation, CrossLand enjoyed long-term stability among its highly skilled and innovative senior executives.

Major Opportunities Available to CrossLand

Because of the intense level of competition and the nature of operations within the financial services industry, it was difficult for CrossLand to be distinctive. Yet, two aspects of CrossLand's operations provided it with major opportunities which were not available to competitors.

CrossLand had a significant advantage through its retail network. CrossLand operated in several states. This advantage did not extend, however, to all markets in which CrossLand participated. CrossLand did not have a significant presence in New York and Florida, and suffered from a lack of name recognition. In addition, because of the high cost of participating in local automated teller machine (ATM) networks, it was not worthwhile for CrossLand to join these local networks until a sufficient number of branches were open. By not being able to provide convenience through a large number of branches and by not belonging to a local ATM network, deposits in these areas did not reach their potential.

The retail network not only provided CrossLand with its major source of funds but also provided opportunities for cross selling,

nondeposit related services. CrossLand took advantage of this somewhat by offering, to a limited extent, discount brokerage and insurance services.

Another strength of CrossLand was its mortgage banking company. Having offices throughout the United States enabled CrossLand to obtain loans from different areas and, therefore, it could minimize its exposure to any one area. The impact of this was significant when considering the effect of the recession in the "energy" states which caused many thrifts to fail. In addition, the mortgage company provided a major source of CrossLand's noninterest revenues by earning service fees on its service portfolio. The service portfolio also had significant value that was not reflected on the balance sheet and could easily be sold.

Major Threats Facing CrossLand

Perhaps the major threat facing CrossLand was a threat which afflicted its entire industry. Although 89 percent of thrift institutions holding 90 percent of total industry assets were solvent, there had been a significant amount of press coverage of the remaining thrifts which were not solvent. In addition, the industry as a whole lost $9.4 billion in the first three quarters of 1988 and FSLIC, the industry insurer, itself was reported to be insolvent. This resulted in a campaign for stricter regulations and monitoring of the industry; the Bush Plan was proposed in response to this campaign. If the Bush Plan was adopted, it was expected to increase the capital requirements for CrossLand and its competitors not only under FSLIC but also under FDIC standards. These increased requirements potentially could cause CrossLand to shrink in order to meet the minimum capital requirements.

A more direct threat to CrossLand was its high level of borrowing which caused the cost of funds to be higher than it would be expected. In fact, on December 31, 1988, CrossLand's borrowing was equal to 60 percent of deposits, as shown in Exhibit 11. The average cost of these borrowings was 8.42 percent as opposed to the average cost of deposits of 7.11 percent. In addition, CrossLand's major source of borrowing, Federal Home Loan Bank Board advances, was not without limit. Dollar repurchase agreements and securities sold under agreements to repurchase, the second largest source of borrowing, were collateralized financing transactions whereby CrossLand sold mortgage backed securities and agreed to repurchase the same or substantially identical securities. Because the transaction was collateralized, these borrowing arrangements typically were cheaper than other borrowing sources; however, they generally had terms of one month or less and therefore were very sensitive to interest rate changes.

Still, CrossLand's overall exposure to interest rate changes posed another threat. On December 31, 1988, the level of interest bearing liabilities due to reprice within a year exceeded the level of interest earning assets due to reprice by $3 billion. This was expected to result in nearly a $30 million reduction in net interest income for every 1 percent increase in rates. This was particularly significant in light of the increasing interest rates in the first part of 1989. As a result of the Federal Reserve Board increasing its discount rate—intended to control inflation—the prime rate was increased from 10.50 percent on January 1, 1989, to 11.50 percent on April 30, 1989. Although the Federal Reserve Board was not expected to raise the discount rate further, this possibility could not be eliminated.

CrossLand was not able to cover its dividend payments with earnings in 1988, primarily due to the cumulative effect of change in accounting procedures. But the bank was experiencing financial difficulties. For instance, CrossLand paid dividends in 1988 of $52.5 million, and of these $41.3 million were fixed dividends on preferred stock. Given the effect of rising interest rates causing narrowing spreads and the effect of SFAS

Exhibit 11 CrossLand Savings, FSB: Outstanding Borrowing

Items	Balance* (in millions)	% of Total*
Federal Home Loan Bank advanced	$2,762	52.6
Repurchase agreements	1,695	32.2
Callable preferred stock	300	5.7
Senior subordinated debt	170	3.2
Other borrowing	328	6.3
Total borrowing	$5,255	100.0

*As of December 31, 1988.

96 limiting the NOLs used against income tax expense, CrossLand's net income was expected to decline and may not be sufficient enough to cover dividends.

The Future

CrossLand's executives were well aware that the thrift industry was fraught with risk. With the industry-wide risk of insolvency rising, these executives were pondering options to create and sustain a distinctive competence for CrossLand. Still, they felt compelled to examine the bank's very concept of business. As they reflected on their potential choices, executives recognized the fact that there were four types of thrift institutions. The first was the "traditional" thrift which originated single family residential loans and obtained funds from retail deposits. The second group consisted of thrifts whose strategy centered on investing in mortgage backed securities and obtaining funds from the wholesale markets. The third group included thrifts which elected to become more like commercial banks with investments in nonresidential loans and a heavier emphasis on commercial checking. The final, and fourth, group included thrifts which branched into alternative services such as mortgage banking. CrossLand's executives felt pressured to reposition their bank to take advantage of the many opportunities in the 1990s.

With their growing geographic expansion, CrossLand's executives faced another crucial choice. How can branches be integrated economically? Did CrossLand have the appropriate organizational structure and managerial expertise to deal with demands of this geographic dispersion? Should the bank continue its expansion? Has the firm reached its optimal size? CrossLand was being challenged to rethink the very foundation of the strategy which has served it so well over the past turbulent decade.

Case 7

Cineplex Odeon

Garth Drabinsky, Chairman and CEO of Cineplex Odeon, has never been known to shy away from a fight. On June 30, 1989, he was true to his reputation as he faced a group of unsettled shareholders at the company's annual meeting in a downtown Toronto theater. Drabinsky had burly guards posted at the entrances and exits, instructed his public relations staff to keep their lips sealed, and did not allow reporters to bring in any electronic equipment.

The firm stance reflected a hardball approach to business that had earned Drabinsky the nickname Darth, after the screen super-villain Darth Vader. But this reputation was based on more than just an aura of toughness and a knack for brilliant deals. It was founded on significant accomplishments in the movie industry. Through a combination of innovative theater formats, bold acquisitions, and strong financial alliances, Drabinsky had developed Cineplex Odeon into the second largest theater chain in North America (see Exhibit 4). In the process, Drabinsky had single-handedly changed the face of film exhibition, rejuvenating what had become a stagnant part of the industry.

As long as Drabinsky continued to pile success upon success, his aggressive style and disregard for conventions were tolerated. His dominance over all aspects of Cineplex Odeon had

This case was prepared by Joseph Lampel, New York University, and Jamal Shamsie, McGill University, and is intended for use as a basis for class discussion. It is drawn entirely from published sources. The authors wish to acknowledge the assistance of Xavier Gonzalez-Sanfeliu. Copyright 1990, by the authors. Reprinted with permission.

been deemed necessary for the pursuit of his unique and ambitious vision. But now, with doubts being raised about the financial health of Cineplex Odeon (see Exhibit 1, including footnotes), Drabinsky's reputation as a brilliant strategist was being subjected to increased scrutiny. Drabinsky was also facing strong resistance, and had suffered serious setbacks in his recent attempts to gain a controlling interest in his company. All of these developments had created an unusually high level of anxiety and anticipation among the audience that had gathered for the company's annual meeting.

But the mounting pressure could hardly mute Drabinsky's forceful style. He ruled the meeting with an iron hand, disdainfully rejecting any attacks from the audience, and defiantly reaffirming his faith in the future of Cineplex Odeon. "I am completely sanguine" he remarked, "that the company will continue to grow."[1] As far as Drabinsky was concerned, this was not the first time that he had found himself in a tight corner.

The Early Years

A Consuming Passion

Garth Drabinsky's determination to beat the odds began early in life. Struck by polio at the age of three, he spent most of his childhood checking in and out of hospitals. After a long period of infirmity he was able to walk without a brace, although he has a pronounced limp to this day. The same willpower and concentration that Drabinsky used to confront his illness were later applied to other parts of his life. Although he excelled in a wide variety of activities, it was the silver screen that truly captured his passion.

But it was with his law studies at the University of Toronto in the early 1970s, that Drabinsky began to make movies his life's work. He took a keen interest in the emerging field of entertainment law, and later wrote a textbook on the subject that became a standard reference source. His studies, however, did not prevent him from producing a half-hour TV show starring William Shatner, and launching a movie magazine that was given away free at cinemas.

In 1976, Drabinsky made a foray into movie production. His first film featured Donald Sutherland but it was never completed. The following year, he teamed up with producer Joel Michaels to form a film production company that remained active for several years. Among the movies that the company produced were "The Silent Partner" with Christopher Plummer, "The Changeling" with George C. Scott, and "Tribute" with Jack Lemmon. Although acclaimed critically, none of these films did well at the box office.

A Multiplex Strategy
In 1979, Garth Drabinsky joined forces with Nathan Taylor, an industry veteran who had long believed in the concept of theaters with multiple screens. Drabinsky found the idea appealing, and together the two formed Cineplex. Their first multiplex theater was located in Toronto's Eaton Centre, a newly developed shopping centre. It contained as many as eighteen separate theaters, each with a seating capacity ranging between 60 to 150 people.

Cineplex saw itself as a niche player. It countered the trend in the industry that saw exhibitors using their large theaters to get the potentially lucrative releases from the Hollywood distributors (see Appendix). Instead, the newly developed multiplex chain used its small screens to show specialty movies, in particular foreign films and art films that could not be shown profitably in large theaters. As Taylor put it, Cineplex was not out to challenge the major chains, but to complement them:

> We are seeking to develop a market that to some extent doesn't exist. We are taking specialized markets and filling their needs. It's a latent market and a different niche than the major chains go after.[2]

In addition, Cineplex sought to obtain the successful U.S. films after they had completed their run with the larger theater chains. It was commonly known that the share of the box office receipts accruing to the distributor decreased with the run of the movie. Although this allowed exhibitors to keep more of the revenues, the inevitable decline in attendance ordinarily forced large theaters to discontinue exhibition once the number of empty seats exceeded a certain level. It was at this point that Cineplex could pick up the films, and by virtue of its small theaters keep most of the seats full.

The advantages of the multiplex concept were primarily due to a carefully planned use of shared facilities. All the theaters in a location were served by a single box office and a single concession stand. The use of advanced projection technology made it possible for a handful of projectionists in a centralized projection booth to screen films in several theaters at once. Show times were staggered in order to avoid congestion. Even advertising costs were lowered by using a single ad for all the films playing at a particular location.

The success of the multiplex concept spurred Cineplex to expand its operations across Canada. The company also made an entry into the large U.S. market with the development of a fourteen-screen theater complex in the Beverly Hills section of Los Angeles. By the end of 1982, the company had inaugurated almost 150 screens in as many as twenty different locations.

A Close Brush with Bankruptcy
The rapid rate of expansion brought Cineplex face to face with financial and market realities which its owners had not anticipated. During its

expansion the company had amassed $21 million in debt, mostly in high and floating interest rates. This came in the midst of an economic recession that cut deeply into the company's earnings. To make matters worse, U.S. distributors were increasingly reluctant to supply Cineplex with the hit films for fear of alienating the two large Canadian exhibition chains, Famous Players and Canadian Odeon. Without the revenues of major U.S. releases the company's future was bleak.

Only drastic measures could avert imminent bankruptcy. Thus, Cineplex took steps throughout 1983 to reduce its debt and improve its cash flow by selling off some of the company's assets, raising funds through the public offering of more shares, and persuading the banks to extend further credit. But these measures did not address the company's blocked access to major releases. To break through the barrier, Drabinsky sought government intervention. Using his legal training, Drabinsky marshalled the evidence and managed to convince the Canadian government that strong grounds existed for launching an investigation into the existence of a conspiracy aimed at depriving Cineplex of access to major releases.

In the face of government investigation, and possible sanctions, the U.S. distributors modified their stand and agreed to a system of competitive bidding that would ensure all had equal access to their films. With this hurdle surmounted Drabinsky was able to secure more firm financial backing, particularly from institutional investors. A large investment came from Claridge, a holding company owned by the Bronfmans, one of Canada's most powerful business families.

To Drabinsky, the close brush with bankruptcy had also revealed a basic flaw in his company's position. He became acutely aware that his small theaters generated insufficient revenues to bid for early runs of the most lucrative U.S. films. So when the principal owner of Canadian Odeon passed away, Drabinsky saw an opportunity that was not to be missed. Canadian Odeon had been greatly weakened by the new bidding system that Drabinsky had helped to bring about. Alarmed by Odeon's poor performance, the heirs finally accepted Drabinsky's offer of little over $22 million for the entire chain.

The acquisition of Canadian Odeon in the spring of 1984, at what many viewed as a bargain basement price, ended a remarkable turnaround for a company which just two years earlier had faced bankruptcy. Now, with over 450 screens in as many as 170 different locations, Cineplex was a major player in the industry. Drabinsky relished his comeback, and was not above taking a passing shot at his detractors: "A lot of people who were waiting for me to go under were disappointed. Well they didn't get their jollies."[3]

A Blockbuster Strategy

A Larger than Life Experience

The formation of Cineplex-Odeon crowned Drabinsky's comeback from the verge of bankruptcy, but he was not content to rest on his laurels. Now that he controlled one of North America's major theater chains he set out to transform the movie going experience itself. With the advent of pay-television channels and prerecorded video cassettes, it was becoming increasingly difficult to lure moviegoers from the comfort of their homes.

Drabinsky aimed to change the public's perceptions by renovating the theaters, beginning with the physical format. Cineplex Odeon discarded the uniformly drab design common in most theater chains in favor of artwork in the lobbies, lush woolen carpets spread over marble floors, and coral-and-peach color coordinated walls. The screening auditoriums featured scientifically contoured seats, digital background music, and state of the art projection systems. As a final touch, the company reintroduced real buttered popcorn in the concession stands, and cafes that offered freshly made cappucino.

The metamorphosis was completed with the unveiling of a new company logo in the form of a curved bowl that was reminiscent of a Greek amphitheater. Furthermore, in choosing colors for the logo, Drabinsky decided on a combination of imperial purple and fuschia. For him, the logo was no mere representation, it was intended to make people sit up and take notice. As Drabinsky put it: "I felt that this would be more of a bravado kind of statement. I don't think anyone was ready for that."[4]

Cineplex Odeon's new format differed sharply from the prevailing industry response to the threat posed by pay television and take-home video cassettes. Most theater chains sought to cut their fixed costs by slicing old movie palaces into tiny cinemas, and eliminating many services that were deemed inessential. Drabinsky, on the other hand, believed that the movie going experience was not confined to what was shown on the screen. As the customer entered the theater he was meant to leave behind mundane existence, and gradually move into a different reality. In the words of Drabinsky:

> We are determined to give back to our patrons the rush and excitement and anticipation and curiosity that should be theirs when they leave the techno-regimented world of their daily lives for the fantasy world of escape that is the movies.[5]

Managing Costs

The transformation of reality is however very costly. Cineplex Odeon spends almost $3 million on a typical six-screen multiplex, a third more than the average for the industry. But as far as Drabinsky is concerned, the additional investment bears fruit not only at the box office, but at the concession counter as well. The classier upscale atmosphere is meant to entice customers into spending more time in the theaters before and after the movie, resulting in higher sales at the concession counter. Indeed, the concessions at Cineplex Odeon's theaters usually generated almost $2 per moviegoer, which is close to twice the industry average.

The additional revenues generated by higher concession sales covered only a small fraction of the fixed costs of a typical Cineplex Odeon thea-

ter. In an effort to reduce costs, Drabinsky has imposed stringent cost controls throughout his organization. Odeon's management was Drabinsky's first target. Upon acquisition, Drabinsky dismissed about two-thirds of Odeon's head office staff, and cut the pay of the remaining personnel by 10 percent. He also cancelled their company credit card as an incentive to frugality. As he put it at the time: "When you make people use their own money they think hard about the justification they'll have to provide when filing their expense claims."[6] The cost cutting campaign has not left any facet of the company's operations untouched. Even the traditional cardboard containers used to sell popcorn have been replaced with bags, a move that has saved Cineplex Odeon close to $1 million per year.

In spite of these measures, Drabinsky has also been forced to search for other sources of revenues. He raised admission fees well above the competition in most markets, and began to show commercials before the screening of the main feature. Both moves were highly unpopular. Irate patrons have expressed their anger in a number of cities, sometimes by protesting outside Cineplex Odeon's theaters. The most publicized of these protests occurred in New York City, where Mayor Ed Koch joined picketers in a call for a boycott of the chain because of its price increase.

The criticisms against Drabinsky were tempered by his use of promotional gimmicks. Most significant among these is the lower admission prices that are offered on Tuesdays which are designed to make movies more accessible to the general public. Attendance at Cineplex theaters has climbed substantially for these Tuesdays, generating additional revenues as well as much needed goodwill among customers.

A Powerful Competitor

With Drabinsky at the helm, Cineplex Odeon launched a major expansion into North America's main movie markets. By and large, this expansion was based on a series of acquisitions in the United States (see Exhibit 3). In an industry known for tough negotiators and agile deal makers, Garth Drabinsky has gained a reputation as a tenacious and abrasive businessman. He uses his stamina and his adversarial style of bargaining to wear his interlocutors down, and then in a burst of energy he clinches the deal. His biggest acquisition involved the Plitt theater chain, which had almost 600 screens in over 200 locations.

Drabinsky is implacable to his competitors. In every market he has entered he has used all the means at his disposal to gain market share, and keep the competition on the defensive. He has pursued Famous Players, his long-standing rival in Canada, with special vengeance. In 1986, for example, Drabinsky seized an opportunity to lease part of a building in Toronto that housed the Imperial Theatre, a six theater complex operated by Famous Players. Since his part of the building contained the main entrance to all of the theaters in the complex, Drabinsky could now move to deny Famous Players public access. He used barbed wire and security guards with Doberman pinschers to enforce the blockade. Ultimately, Famous Players was forced to close down and sell this key location to Cineplex Odeon, but not before it extracted a public apology from Drabinsky, and a commitment that the facility will never be used to show motion pictures.

Drabinsky has also tried to use the size of his chain to obtain added clout with film studios and distributors. He has consistently used this clout to obtain potential hits on more favorable terms, but his insistence on having his way has created tensions in his relationships with suppliers. The tensions erupted into the open in 1987 when Columbia Pictures rejected Drabinsky's demand that Bernardo Bertolucci's oriental epic "The Last Emperor" be made available for wide release during the Christmas period. In retaliation, Drabinsky refused to exhibit another of the studio's films that was slated for Christmas release. The episode created tensions in the ex-

isting relationship with Columbia, resulting in more of the studio's films being diverted to other chains, such as Famous Players, Drabinsky's major Canadian competitor.

Drabinsky's readiness to challenge industry conventions has upset many who feel that he does not play by the rules. Walter Senior, the president of Famous Players, considers Drabinsky's tactics as ultimately destructive. As he put it in the aftermath of the Imperial Theatre affair: "We all learn in school that when you set out to destroy someone, it becomes a weakness."[7] Myron Gottlieb, Cineplex Odeon's Chief Administrative Officer, believes that much of the harsh treatment meted out to Drabinsky in the press reflects his impact on the industry, rather than simply his style:

> There's been a lot of press about Garth, and some of it's been negative up until now. Some of it has been because of his aggressiveness, but more of it is because of the antagonism to the waves he's created in the industry.[8]

Vertical Moves

In 1982, at a time when Cineplex was still a small company screening foreign and art films, Drabinsky moved to consolidate and expand the company's other film related activities. These consisted mainly of a film making subsidiary originally started by Nathan Taylor, and a film distribution arm launched by Drabinsky in 1979.

The film making subsidiary was one of Canada's largest and was located just north of Toronto. Its facilities were rented out to various groups for film and television production. These included two sound stages, dressing and wardrobe rooms, a carpentry mill, a plaster shop, and editing and screening rooms. The distribution arm had been originally created by Drabinsky to provide foreign and art films to the newly developed Cineplex chain. It quickly developed into one of the largest distribution companies in Canada, acquiring the right to distribute films to theaters and on video cassettes, as well as for use on network and pay television.

In 1986, Drabinsky increased the involvement of his company in film making through the acquisition of the Film House. The Toronto-based facility consisted of a large film processing laboratory, and a fully equipped post-production sound studio. Subsequent to its purchase, Cineplex Odeon increased the capacity of the film laboratory and constructed new upgraded sound facilities.

Meanwhile, Drabinsky expanded the film production and distribution activities of his company into the United States. With the move into this larger market, Cineplex Odeon was able to step up its level of participation in film making. It began to contribute towards the production of small budget films such as Paul Newman's "The Glass Menagerie," and Prince's rock concert film "Sign 'O' the Times."

Finally, Drabinsky entered into a collaborative venture with MCA, a large U.S. entertainment conglomerate. The two companies have agreed to jointly develop and operate a large film studio and theme park in Orlando, Florida, that would compete with Disney World. The move reflects Drabinsky's determination to make Cineplex Odeon into a corporation that straddles every part of the movie industry. As he put it:

> It's an amalgamated company with revenue from theaters, distribution, production, the studio, and, down the road, live theater. People aren't buying a share in this company just to have a share in a motion picture. They're getting a share in a vertically integrated entertainment corporation.[9]

A One Man Show

Cineplex Odeon is firmly under the control of Drabinsky, who has concentrated power in his hands over the years. He became President of the company in 1980, added the title of Chief Executive Officer in 1982 and was confirmed as Chairman of the Board in 1986. The titles reflect Drabinsky's total involvement with the company and it is well known that no one else is allowed to speak on behalf of the company.

In both deed and word Drabinsky attempts to communicate to his employees the total commitment that is expected of them. The managers who work in close proximity to Drabinsky find his driving energy both exhilarating and exhausting. Lynda Friendly, Vice President of Marketing and Communications since 1982, sits in on all of Drabinsky's interviews with the press and is inspired by his stamina and drive:

> Garth is so bloody energetic. I don't know how he does it. It's mind over matter. He stretches people to their absolute limit. He is a teacher, a mentor—a leader.[10]

Other officers, however, are finding Drabinsky's energy difficult to emulate. They do not appreciate the midnight phone calls they regularly receive from Drabinsky, nor do they agree that they must be ready to sacrifice all to their work. As a former Cineplex Odeon executive described it, the pressure that Drabinsky puts on managers is relentless:

> He works seven days a week and doesn't believe in holidays. Holidays are a disloyalty to the corporation and he *is* the corporation. He is tireless and he expects the same amount of dedication and effort from everyone else.[11]

Some of Drabinsky's immediate subordinates may have found his drive for total control unacceptable. His consolidation of power has been accompanied by a significant turnover among the top executives of the company. Several of the present executive officers have been appointed since 1986 (see Exhibit 5). Those who survived the transition are for the most part people with close personal ties to Drabinsky. Lynda Friendly, for example, has known Drabinsky since they attended synagogue together as teenagers. One of the most important loyalists is Myron Gottlieb who has financially supported Drabinsky since the starting days of the company. Gottlieb's career in Cineplex Odeon closely dovetails that of Drabinsky. He became the Vice-Chairman of the Board in 1982, and was appointed to the position of Chief Administrative Officer in 1985.

Operating Philosophy

By January 1, 1989, Cineplex Odeon was the second largest motion picture exhibitor in North America with just over 1,800 screens in 500 different locations (see Exhibit 4). Almost two-thirds of the company's screens were located in the U.S. and were spread out over twenty different states. The remaining one-third of these screens are situated in six different Canadian provinces. Cineplex Odeon theaters could be found in virtually all major population centers, from New York to Los Angeles in the United States, and from Toronto to Vancouver in Canada. Close to 90% of the chain's theaters, however, were located in leased premises, with rent calculated as percentage of box office receipts subject to a minimum.

As of early 1989, the company had close to 13,000 employees. These include film projectionists, cashiers, concession workers, ushers, and ticket takers. However, the bulk of these employees are hired on a part-time basis during seasons of high demand, and they are paid the minimum wage. Only about 15% of the employees are represented by unions. For each theater, the information obtained from its computerized box office terminals is used to schedule the minimal amount of staff for any given show. In addition to staff employed to operate the theater, Cineplex Odeon employs as many as 100 full-time architects, engineers, and draftsmen, all used for design and renovation of theaters.

The Cineplex Odeon chain of theaters is divided into districts, with each district under the control of a supervisor. The task of a district supervisor is to ensure that all theaters follow guidelines set by head office. He also regularly inspects theaters and reports the results to head office. His report is contrasted with information provided by an independent agency whose representatives visit each theater on a random basis. In addition to this information, head office relies on weekly reports supplied by the theater's manager detailing market conditions, competitors' activities, and audience response to advanced screening.

The centralization of information is matched by a consistent effort to centralize purchasing and accounting. All supplies and services are purchased centrally in order to maximize economies and reduce spoilage and waste. The computerized box office allows the company to monitor ticket sales, as well as exercise stringent controls on the handling of cash.

Cineplex Odeon puts a great deal of emphasis on a set of standards and practices which are set forth in staff orientation and training manuals. These standards are often drafted by Drabinsky who goes to great lengths to ensure that they are followed to the letter. He visits theaters regularly, often dropping by unannounced to talk with cashiers or ushers. He also phones or sees twenty or twenty-five theater managers a week.

All of this reflects Drabinsky's conviction that he must know everything that goes on in his theaters, and be always on the lookout for problems that need correcting. He has been known to deliver a silent but none-too-subtle reprimand to ushers by bending down in front of them to pick up a single piece of spilled popcorn. An employee who has observed Drabinsky in action observed: "Anything that is not absolutely perfect drives him crazy. He leaves people with a lasting impression when they screw up."[12]

Financial Structure

As of January 1, 1989, Cineplex Odeon had 23.9 million common shares and 23.6 subordinate restricted voting shares outstanding. The company made the transition from private to public financing in 1982 when it was listed on the Toronto Stock Exchange. The total value of its equity has been estimated at $375 million (see Exhibit 2).

A large block of shares, representing just over 30% of the company's total equity, have been in the hands of Claridge, a holding company. For the most part, Claridge handles the investments of the Bronfman family who own the Seagram liquor business. The investment was made in 1983 to help Cineplex out of its early difficulties. Claridge had backed the development of the Eaton Centre, in the basement of which Cineplex had opened its first theaters.

In a subsequent deal Drabinsky sold a large block of shares to MCA, a U.S. entertainment conglomerate which owns Universal Studios. The deal allowed MCA to purchase up to 50% of the company's outstanding shares. However, MCA's control of Cineplex Odeon was restricted to 33% by Canadian law which limits voting shares by foreign companies. MCA's total ownership is therefore represented by specially created subordinate restricted voting shares.

In 1987 Cineplex Odeon consummated its first offering of shares in the U.S., and was listed on the New York Stock Exchange. In spite of this substantial enlargement of the company's equity base, most of the financing during 1987 and 1988 was through the use of debt. Not surprisingly, the price of Cineplex Odeon's shares has fluctuated. It reached a high of almost $25 a share (Canadian) around the time of the MCA purchase, but has dropped considerably since then. In spite of the decline, Drabinsky continues to defend his gross margins and insists that his chain boasts the highest return on equity among major exhibition chains. The fault, Drabinsky has claimed on one occasion, is to be found in the brokerage industry, and not in the performance of Cineplex Odeon:

> The brokerage industry is just full of people who like to hear themselves speak, but there's not a lot of substance there. This company is complete substance from top to bottom.[13]

Future Horizons

Relentless Growth
In spite of growing financial constraints, Cineplex Odeon has not slowed the pace of its expansion. The company continues to construct new theaters and to refurbish existing ones. At the present rate of expansion Cineplex Odeon will have twenty-one hundred screens in North

America alone by 1992. For Drabinsky the expansion has a dual purpose. First, he would like to surge past his competitors and capture an increasing share of the North American market. Second, Drabinsky believes that only a larger Cineplex Odeon can force the major distributors to give the chain the big budget movies at more favorable terms.

But several other large exhibition chains that compete with Cineplex Odeon are also on the move, building new multiscreen theaters, and acquiring smaller chains (see Exhibit 4). Many in industry fear that the proliferation of screens will not be matched by a corresponding increase in movie attendance. If anything, the strong likelihood of a major recession may aggravate the situation. It will also increase the reliance of exhibitors on the limited supply of major Hollywood releases.

Drabinsky's critics contend that costly acquisitions and expensive theaters are making Cineplex Odeon especially vulnerable to an industry slowdown. For his part, Drabinsky has sought to allay the fears of shareholders by insisting that the growth of Cineplex Odeon is neither haphazard nor reckless:

> I want you to appreciate that everything we do is part of a thoroughly studied, painstakingly thought out game plan. We're not expanding for the sake of expanding.[14]

Plans for the expansion of theaters are not confined to the North American continent. Drabinsky has recently unveiled plans to spend around $100 million to develop over 100 screens in the United Kingdom by the end of 1990. He believes that better theaters and a faster release of major U.S. films can reverse the decline in attendance and reinvigorate the British market.

In addition to theater expansion, Drabinsky has been getting his company increasingly involved in film production since it has the capacity to both distribute and exhibit movies. During 1988, Cineplex Odeon helped to finance and distribute movies by such noted directors as

John Schlesinger and Oliver Stone. The company has also negotiated a joint production agreement with small production companies headed by Robert Redford and Taylor Hackford. But Drabinsky has frequently stated that Cineplex Odeon will restrict itself to a few low budget films, and will not become involved in the risky business of producing big budget movies.

Drabinsky has also extended his production activities to other entertainment areas. Cineplex Odeon had financed the run of some lavish Broadway musicals in Toronto during 1988. At present the company is converting the Toronto theater it wrestled from the Famous Players chain into a 2,100 seat center for the performing arts. The theater, a vaudeville palace in its previous incarnation, will be restored to its former glory, and then used to stage the Canadian Production of Andrew Lloyd Webber's "The Phantom of the Opera." The musical is scheduled to open in the fall of 1989, and it is estimated that its initial production cost will total over $6.5 million.

A Performance under Scrutiny

Drabinsky's unrelenting drive for growth has been putting pressure on the company's finances. During 1988, Cineplex Odeon asked the banks to boost its line of credit by another $175 million to $750 million. More recently, the company sold off 50% of the Film House, its film production operation in Toronto, and most of its share in the Florida theme park to a British entertainment firm. The company has also been raising capital by selling off some of its theaters, and then leasing them back.

In the opinion of a number of industry observers the true financial position of Cineplex Odeon is masked by the company's liberal accounting practices (see footnotes to Exhibit 1). In 1986, the company extended the period over which it would depreciate its properties and its goodwill, resulting in much higher values of its total assets. The company's operating profits are also believed to be overstated because of the inclusion of one-time sales of assets as part of operating revenue.

The financial uncertainty has created apprehension among the company's stockholders who can still recall his narrow escape from bankruptcy six years earlier. Drabinsky, however, denies that he is undermining Cineplex Odeon by involving the company in activities it can ill afford. He frequently reiterates his conviction that he must at all times be ready to take advantage of emerging opportunities. When asked in a recent interview to predict the company's future development, he had this to say:

> If you asked me five years ago what Cineplex would look like today, I wouldn't have predicted what we have today. So when you ask me today what Cineplex will look like in five years, I can't tell you exactly.[15]

Publicly, Drabinsky has rebuffed his critics, and has sought to allay shareholders' fears. In private, he and his close associates have recently sought to gain control of Cineplex Odeon by making an offer to buy the 30% stake held by Bronfman's holding company. Taken together with the 8% stake that is already owned by Drabinsky and Gottlieb, they would have had enough shares to outvote and outflank MCA who was restricted to a 33% limit on voting rights.

But MCA moved swiftly to obtain an injunction preventing the deal from going through, even as Drabinsky and Gottlieb were putting on the finishing touches. A financial analyst attempted to explain the reasons for MCA's reaction:

> No one understands what Drabinsky and Gottlieb are up to. They pulled out of the Florida deal, they sold off Film House, they are taking bigger risks in film production, and now the Bronfmans are getting out. From MCA's point of view there are probably lots of reasons to stop Garth from getting control.[16]

MCA eventually managed to get the court to rule that the offer that had been made by Drabinsky and his associates should be extended to all of Cineplex Odeon's outstanding shareholders. This has forced Drabinsky to scramble for over $1 billion of financing in order to back such an offer. It is now widely speculated that if he is not able to raise this required amount, he could be forced out of the company that he has always considered to be his own.

Notes

1. *Report on Business Magazine*. The Perils of Drabinsky. July 1989.

2. *Financial Post*. Cineplex Getting in the Big Picture. June 14, 1980.

3. *Report on Business Magazine*. Upwardly Mogul. December 1985.

4. *Macleans*. King of the Silver Screen. September 28, 1987.

5. *Macleans*. Big Money at the Movies. July 28, 1986.

6. *Report on Business Magazine*. December 1985.

7. *Macleans*. September 28, 1987.

8. *Canadian Business*. A Czar is Born. October 1984.

9. *Business Journal*. Movie Mogul. October 1982.

10. *Macleans*. September 28, 1987.

11. *Report on Business Magazine*. Tough Bosses. December 1987.

12. *Business Week*. A New Hollywood Legend called—Garth Drabinsky? September 23, 1985.

13. *Financial Times*. Drabinsky's Movie Machine. August 26, 1985.

14. *Toronto Globe and Mail*. Market Apathy the Real Culprit, Drabinsky says. May 13, 1988.

15. *Financial Times*. 'Darth' plays Movie Hardball—and Wins. December 28, 1987.

16. *Financial Post*. Clash of the Movie Titans. April 22–24, 1989.

Exhibit 1   Income Statements

| | in millions of U.S. dollars for the year ended December | | | | |
	1984	1985	1986	1987	1988
Revenues					
Admissions	$42.7	$85.0	$230.3	$322.4	$355.6
Concessions	12.3	24.9	71.4	101.6	114.6
Distribution and Other	9.3	7.8	30.8	61.2	156.4*
Sales of Properties#	2.8	6.6	24.4	35.0	69.2
	$67.1	$124.3	$356.9	$520.2	$695.8**
Expenses					
Operating Expenses	48.7	89.5	258.3	371.9	464.3
Cost of Concessions	3.7	6.0	13.7	18.8	21.6
Cost of Sold Properties	0.9	2.7	11.7	21.6	61.8
General and Administrative	3.5	5.7	15.3	18.0	26.6
Depreciation and Amortization+	2.1	3.7	14.3	24.0	38.1
	$58.9	$107.6	$313.3	$454.3	$612.4
Other Income	0.1	0.3	—	—	3.6
Interest Expenses@	2.5	4.0	16.2	27.0	42.9
Income Taxes	2.2	5.0	6.3	4.3	3.7
Extraordinary Items	5.6	2.3	1.4	—	—
Net Income	$9.2	$10.3	$22.5	$34.6	$40.4

*shown as part of operating revenue
+depreciation schedule changed from 1986 to lower this charge
@excludes interest costs that have been capitalized
#includes proceeds from sale of 49% interest in Film House
**later changed to $648.0 million to exclude proceeds from sale of Film House
Source: Cineplex Odeon Annual Reports

Exhibit 2   Balance Sheets

	in millions of U.S. dollars for the year ended December				
	1984	**1985**	**1986**	**1987**	**1988**
Current Assets					
Cash and Receivables	5.2	10.0	20.1	42.3	151.5
Distribution Advances	3.8	5.3	9.0	21.3	36.9
Inventories and Prepaid Expenses	3.0	4.6	11.0	13.3	13.0
Property Investments	—	—	16.6	22.7	25.6
Fixed Assets					
Properties and Equipment	49.2	53.3	208.9	261.5	296.7
Leaseholds	17.4	26.9	324.1	490.2	594.4
Accumulated Depreciation*	4.3	7.2	19.6	40.2	66.3
Other Assets					
Long-term Investments	2.7	6.2	14.3	50.0	130.3
Goodwill*	0.6	0.6	40.9	52.6	54.0
Deferred Charges	0.8	1.7	6.6	12.0	27.1
	$78.4	$101.4	$631.9	$925.7	$1,263.2
Current Liabilities					
Bank Loans	—	4.8	0.1	20.7	21.7
Payables and Accruals	10.0	13.5	47.7	74.9	129.5
Income Taxes	—	0.4	1.9	4.6	5.7
Mature Long-term Debt	2.1	1.1	6.3	6.0	10.8
Long-term Debt	36.1	40.7	317.6	449.7	663.8
Other Liabilities					
Lease Obligations	—	—	15.9	14.6	14.9
Deferred Income Taxes	0.8	4.2	11.1	13.3	10.4
Pension Obligations	—	—	3.7	4.0	6.3
Minority Interest	—	—	—	—	25.1
Shareholders' Equity					
Capital Stock	39.5	37.1	212.1	289.2	283.7
Translation Adjustment	—	—	(3.6)	1.9	13.4
Retained Earnings	(10.1)	(0.4)	19.1	46.8	77.9
	$78.4	$101.4	$631.9	$925.7	$1,263.2

*As of 1986, depreciation rates were reduced to 2.5% from 5.0% straight-line for buildings and to 6.7% from 10.0% straight-line for equipment.
*As of 1986, goodwill is being amortized over forty years instead of over twenty years.
Source: Cineplex Odeon Annual Reports

Exhibit 3   U.S. Theater Acquisitions

1985	Plitt Theaters Los Angeles, California 574 screens / 209 locations
1986	Septum Cinemas Atlanta, Georgia 48 screens / 12 locations
1986	Essaness Theaters Chicago, Illinois 41 screens / 13 locations
1986	RKO Century Warner Theaters New York, New York 97 screens / 42 locations
1986	Neighborhood Theaters Richmond, Virginia 76 screens / 25 locations
1986	SRO Theaters Seattle, Washington 99 screens / 33 locations
1987	Walter Reade Organization New York, New York 11 screens / 8 locations
1987	Circle Theaters Washington, D.C. 80 screens / 22 locations

Source: Cineplex Odeon

Exhibit 4 Theaters in Operation

	1988		1987		1986		1985		1984	
	Screens	Locations	Screens	Locations	Screens	Locations	Screens	Locations	Screens	Locations
United Artists	2,677	686	2,048	485	1,595	437	1,124	329	1,063	344
Cineplex Odeon	1,832	502	1,644	492	1,510	495	1,117	394	439	170
American Multi-Cinema	1,614	278	1,528	277	1,336	263	956	182	800	156
General Cinema	1,400	321	1,358	332	1,275	342	1,163	333	1,083	331
Loews	822	221	310	87	300	85	232	66	215	66
Carmike	701	213	669	220	674	236	435	168	432	182
Hoyts	550	120	275	55	240	52	103	22	105	25
National Amusements	552	91	404	77	393	88	345	84	314	84
Mann	456	109	447	110	456	126	350	110	325	98
Famous Players	448	148	427	147	466	176	469	196	466	199

Source: Variety

Exhibit 5 Management Profile

	G.I. Drabinsky	M.I. Gottlieb	J.M. Banks	A. Karp	L. Friendly	C. Bruner	E. Jacob
Title(s)	Chairman of Board; President; Chief Executive Officer	Vice-Chairman of Board; Chief Administrative Officer	Senior Executive Vice-President, Corporate Affairs	Senior Executive Vice-President	Executive Vice-President, Marketing and Communications	Senior Vice-President; Treasurer	Senior Vice-President; Chief Financial Officer
Age	40	45	57	48	39	31	35
Previous Positions	Director since 1978	Director since 1980	Director 1983–1986	—	Senior V.P., Marketing and Communications	Assistant Treasurer	V.P. and Corporate Controller
Year of Entry	1980	1985	1987	1986	1982	1985	1987
Previous Employment	Law firm	Investment firm	Law firm	Law firm	Not Available	Public Accounting Firm	Electronics Firm

Source: Cineplex Odeon Form 10-K

Appendix
The Movie Industry

Supply of Movies

The number of movies available for exhibition has grown significantly over the past few years. Most of this growth in supply has resulted from the increased activities of smaller independent distribution companies. The number of feature length films released over the last five years were as follows:

	1984	1985	1986	1987	1988
Major Distributors	169	149	142	133	159
Smaller Distributors	210	271	296	354	330
Total	379	420	438	487	489

Source: Variety

In spite of the growing number of suppliers, the bulk of the revenues still comes from the films that are distributed by the nine major companies that have dominated the industry for more than fifty years. Based in Hollywood, these companies include Paramount, Warner Brothers, Disney, Universal, and Columbia. In 1988, the 159 films that were released by these firms accounted for more than 90% of the box office dollars in the U.S. and Canada.

The relative success of the major distributors stems in large part from their greater supply of capital. The typical Hollywood studio spent, on the average, almost $16 million for each of the films that it produced during 1988. Another $4 to $6 million was usually spent to market or advertise the movie and up to $2 million can be spent on making sufficient copies of the film so that it can be released to a wide number of theaters.

The movies of the smaller distributors are usually budgeted at under $5 million and frequently lack the major stars or production values that can increase their chances of striking it rich at the box office. In fact, an industry publication recently reported that more than half of the movies that are offered by the smaller distributors do not ever play in theaters, but are released directly into the video cassette market.

Although the major distributors continue to dominate the industry, they have long abandoned their practice of binding the most attractive movie directors and stars to long term employment contracts. Most of the Hollywood movies are now typically made through contractual arrangements with thousands of smaller production outfits. The major distributor may either fund a movie from start to finish or provide a portion of the financing in return for a share of the subsequent box office receipts.

As a result of lackluster financial results, some of the smaller distributors have either folded their operations or merged with other distributors. Even some of the major distributors have merged together, such as the amalgamation of MGM with United Artists. These trends indicate that in the future, fewer major distributors will control the total number of movies that are available to theaters for exhibition.

Exhibition of Movies

Recent surveys have indicated that a large segment of the population—up to 45 percent in recent years—has stopped going out to see movies. Consequently, there has been a growing emphasis upon improving the quality of theaters in order to entice more people into visiting them. This has resulted in large scale renovations of existing theaters as well as the construction of new ones. During this process, hundreds of smaller independent theaters have been forced to sell out to the larger chains that could more easily afford to make the necessary investments.

Industry estimates indicate that there were over 23,000 screens in the United States and Canada by the end of 1988. Almost fifty percent of these were collectively held by the top ten exhibition chains. Over the past decade, some of the major movie distributors have also begun to buy up theater chains. These distribution companies have argued that by owning theaters, they can guarantee the public a higher quality presentation of their movies.

The major distributors had been forced to divest themselves of their theaters at the peak of the growth of the movie industry. In the late 1940s, the U.S. Justice Department had ruled that the same companies could not make, as well as show movies. The legislation was a result of allegations that the movie distributors were restricting their movies to their own theaters and engaging in fixing prices. However, the attitudes towards restrictions on the ownership of movie theaters have become more relaxed in recent years. In part, this has been made possible by clearer and more stringent laws that provide fairer access to movies by all exhibitors.

Revenues from Theaters
There is a widespread debate about the effects of recessions on movie attendance. Some financial analysts have recently shown that box office receipts decreased during the early 1930s and during the early 1970s. In fact, ticket sales in 1971 dipped to 820 million before picking up again.

For the most part, however, annual ticket sales have been relatively stable at around one billion admissions per year for almost thirty years. The audience for movies in theaters has been heavily dominated by younger individuals, particularly below thirty years of age. But recent evidence has suggested that the traditional drop in attendance after the age of thirty has been lessening.

Box office receipts have risen considerably over the years, largely as a result of increases in the prices of tickets. There is considerable variation in ticket sales over the year, with almost

half of the sales coming between late May and early September as well as between late November and early January. The box office totals for the U.S. over the past five years are as follows:

1984	$4.0 billion
1985	$3.8 billion
1986	$3.7 billion
1987	$4.2 billion
1988	$4.4 billion

Source: Variety

The average ticket price had risen to $4.11 in 1988, up from $3.36 in 1984. Theater owners are generally reluctant to raise ticket prices more rapidly than inflation for fear of losing viewers. Increasingly, however, they have come to rely upon the lobby concession stand to make their profits. Once inside the theaters, moviegoers become a captive market for popcorn, soft drinks, and candy that is sold at inflated prices. Recent surveys indicate that exhibition chains may derive as much as 20% of their revenues from high profit items that are sold at their concessions.

Splitting of Revenues
There has been considerable wrangling between the distributors and exhibitors over the distribution of box office revenues. The distributors have tried to use their new sources of revenue from video cassettes and pay TV to reduce their dependence on the theaters.

In spite of the growing availability of these new channels, distribution companies reach more people through exhibiting their movies in theaters. More significantly, the values of their movies on video cassettes and pay TV are heavily dependent upon a respectable theatrical run. A successful movie will create more demand for pay TV as well as for video cassette rentals.

In recent years, the exhibitors have been able to use the increased supply of movies to negotiate a larger share of the box office receipts. But the observed increase in the total number of screens across the continent may allow the distributors to regain the advantage. Several growing exhibition chains may have to compete with each other to get the potential hit movies which still tend to come from a few large Hollywood studios.

Typically, the distributor and the exhibitor split the box office revenue equally with each other. The distributor eventually passes on to the producers and investors about 20% of the revenues of a movie. The remainder is retained by the distributor to cover its own distribution and advertising costs.

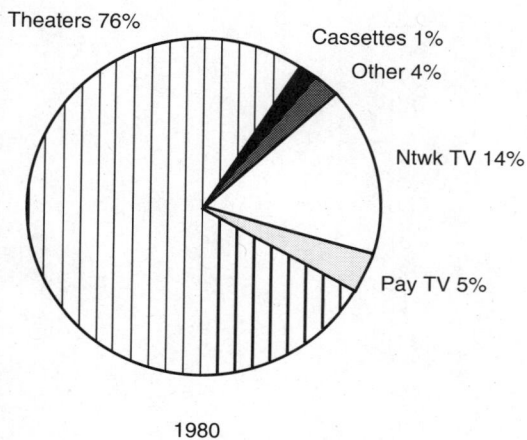

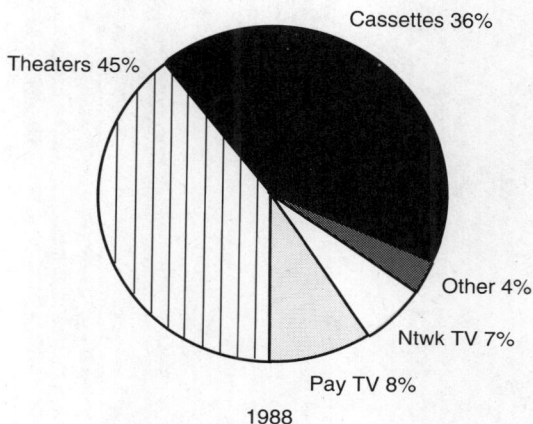

Theaters 76%
Cassettes 1%
Other 4%
Ntwk TV 14%
Pay TV 5%
1980

Theaters 45%
Cassettes 36%
Other 4%
Ntwk TV 7%
Pay TV 8%
1988

Source: Variety

Case 8

Blockbuster Video: America's Family Video Store

Blockbuster Entertainment Corporation Corporate Profile

Blockbuster Entertainment Corporation is the world's leading video retailer within the videocassette rental industry. Its operations consist of 1,079 stores of which 561 are company-owned stores and 518 are franchise-owned stores. Its markets are located throughout the United States, the United Kingdom, Canada, Puerto Rico and Guam.

The success of Blockbuster Entertainment Corporation is based upon the Superstore concept. The focus of this concept consists of a greater number of copies of popular rental titles, greater selection opportunities, longer store operating hours and time-saving computerized check-in/check-out procedures. Blockbuster stores also have Kids' Clubhouses in which children can play and watch videos, a unique concept within the market. In addition, Blockbuster does not carry X-rated movies and has initiated a Youth Restricted Viewing Program which enables parents to maintain control over what videos children under seventeen may view. Blockbuster also features a community service section which offers a wide selection of public interest videos which can be checked out and viewed at no charge.

Blockbuster has been nicknamed "the King

of Video" by *Fortune* magazine (6/4/90), p. 208, Companies to Watch, Meet the King of Video). When referred to as the McDonald's of the videocassette rental industry, Tom Gruber, Blockbuster marketing head who spent 19 years with McDonald's, most recently as vice president of international marketing, suggests "Any similarity is purely on purpose. . . . Our target audience is very similar to the target at McDonald's" (*Fortune*, 6/4/90, p. 208). It should be noted that Luigi Salvaneschi, the company's president, spent 23 years with McDonald's Corporation and five years with Kentucky Fried Chicken where he was in charge of real estate acquisition and was instrumental in the tremendous growth experienced by those companies (News release, Blockbuster Video, 6/22/90, p. 3). What supermarkets did to the corner green grocer and waste management to the local garbage hauler, Blockbuster Entertainment hopes to do to video rental (*Forbes*, 5/2/88, p. 54).

Total company revenue grew from $119,000 in 1985 to $402,538,000 in 1989, with total revenue composed of rental revenue, product sales, royalties, and other fees. Further, earnings per share rose from $(.44) in 1985 to $.57 in 1989.*

Historical Summary

Blockbuster Entertainment Corporation, formerly Cook Data Services, Inc., was incorpo-

Case prepared by Dorothy E. Brawley, Brian Cone, Linda Kobel, Jody Prentice, and Jeffrey Sowell, Kennesaw State College. Copyright © 1990 by Dorothy E. Brawley. Reprinted with permission.

*Sources: 1989 Annual Report, p. 1.
1989 Form 10-K, p. 3, 4.

rated in the State of Delaware in December, 1982. From its inception until July 1985, the company had been engaged in the business of providing software and remote computing services to businesses within the oil and gas industry. In July, 1985, the company discontinued its software and computing activities; sold its operating subsidiary, DPC & A, and successfully executed its plan to redeploy its assets from the depressed and cyclical oil and gas industry into the rapidly growing consumer entertainment market (AR, 1986, p. 1).

Blockbuster opened its first "Superstore" in Dallas, Texas, in 1985. In 1986, 18 more stores were added, with a total of 133 stores by year end of 1987 and a total of 415 Superstores by December 31, 1988. There were 1,290 stores in the system as of June 22, 1990.

The dramatic growth of Blockbuster has been achieved under the leadership of H. Wayne Huizenga, Chairman and Chief Executive Officer. He brought in much needed cash and an aggressive expansion strategy. In April, 1987, the original Blockbuster management team relinquished control to an investor group headed by Mr. Huizenga.

During 1987, Blockbuster moved its headquarters from Dallas, Texas, to Fort Lauderdale, Florida. While bringing the system to its present size, Mr. Huizenga complemented its management team by adding top senior executives with Fortune 500 experience in franchising operations and in marketing to carry out a restructured growth plan that called for rapid nationwide expansion. This was accomplished through both internal growth and acquisitions.

At the same time, the company decentralized its operations into eight regions while centralizing its financial control to better manage its rapid growth; adopted the strategy of increasing the ratio of company-owned stores to about 50 percent of the system; and obtained the necessary equity and financing (a $125 million five year unsecured revolving line of credit) to fund its aggressive development program.

Under Mr. Huizenga's guidance, Blockbuster became the industry's revenue leader within three years of its entry into the video retail industry.

In June, 1987, Blockbuster acquired the 29 store, St. Louis based Movies To Go and in March, 1988, the 42 store Video Library chain headquartered in San Diego, California, followed by the acquisition of Major Video Corporation in 1989. On August 25, 1989, the company moved closer to its goal of 60% company-owned stores, with the completed acquisition of its largest franchise, Video Superstore Master Limited Partnership, which at the time operated 104 Blockbuster Video Superstores in the Chicago, Milwaukee, Atlanta, Detroit, and Minneapolis metropolitan areas.

In February, 1989, the company entered the United Kingdom market with its first store in London, England, and became a joint venture partner in developing and franchising Major Video stores in Canada. The joint venture had 39 stores at the end of 1989.

Both company-owned and franchised stores in the Major Video Corp. system are being systematically converted to the Blockbuster concept as they meet Blockbuster criteria and their owners choose that affiliation. In July 1990, Blockbuster joined forces with Miami sports and entertainment impressario Zev Bufman to build amphitheaters in Phoenix and Charlotte.

Blockbuster has regional offices in its headquarters city, Fort Lauderdale, Florida, and in Chicago, Illinois; St. Louis, Missouri; as well as San Francisco, Los Angeles, and San Diego, California; Dallas, Texas; and New York City. In Dallas, the company maintains its computer center, warehousing, distribution center, and its training center, Blockbuster University.

Blockbuster Entertainment Corporation's common stock was traded over the counter (NASDAQ) from April 15, 1986, until April 27, 1989. It began trading on the New York Stock Exchange under the symbol "BV" in 1989. The company became the first in history to declare two 2-for-1 stock splits in less than 20 weeks, doing so in March and August of 1988. The company announced its third 2-for-1 split as a 100% stock dividend since March, 1988, at its annual meeting on May 9, 1989, and became the first company to split its stock three times within 14 months.

Exhibit 1 summarizes key events in the company's history. Exhibits 2, 3, 4, 5, and 6 present an overview of the Blockbuster Entertainment Corporation.*

Mission and Goals

The Blockbuster Entertainment Corporation seeks:

▪ To consolidate markets within the videocassette rental industry and become the "McDonald's" of video stores through name recognition, uniformity of product, consistency of service, and carefully chosen locations.

▪ To increase market share within the home video industry beyond the 6% level reached in 1989, through continued expansion in existing markets as well as penetration of new markets while the industry continues to grow.

▪ To add an additional 160 company-owned and 240 franchise-owned stores in 1990, ending the year with approximately 1,500 stores systemwide.

▪ To increase the ratio of company-owned stores to about 50 percent of the system.

▪ To further expand its international market. Blockbuster is currently evaluating opportunities in Puerto Rico, Australia, the Pacific Rim, and Western Europe.

▪ To continue channeling energies into programs and philosophies that will further enhance Block-

buster's standing in the industry, both in terms of financial growth and the service provided to their customers.

▪ To strengthen ties with Hollywood and find new ways to enhance the mutually shared interest in movies.

▪ To benefit from the experience of Blockbuster's franchise owners.

▪ To remain committed to a deep sense of corporate responsibility and the development of innovative programs that respond to the needs of the customers and communities Blockbuster serves.*

Competition

Analyzing Blockbuster's competitive positioning is a difficult process. The company must compete for every dollar of disposable income the consumer is willing to spend on entertainment and leisure time activity. In this sense, Blockbuster must view any source which is seeking the consumer's disposable income in the entertainment area as a competitor.

Blockbuster Entertainment Corporation does not have a national competitor in terms of the total number of stores it has positioned throughout the United States and internationally. Its closest competitors on the national level are West Coast Video and Erol's, Inc. West Coast Video has approximately 666 stores located primarily on the east coast and Erol's, Inc. has 189 stores. In addition to these competitors, Blockbuster faces local competition from smaller mom-and-pop video stores, grocery stores, pay-per-view cable television and theatres.

Blockbuster Entertainment Corporation is the largest videocassette rental chain in the United States and has created a niche for itself as a recognized name in the home videocassette rental market. Their ability to outrun their com-

*Sources: 1989 Annual Report, p. 3, 7.
News Release, Blockbuster Entertainment Corporation, April 27, 1990.
News Release, Blockbuster Entertainment Corporation, 06/22/90, p. 1, 2.

*Sources: AR, 1989, p. 7, 11, 15, 19, 23, 27.
News Release, Blockbuster Video, June 22, 1990, p. 1, 3.
Florida Trend, April 1990.

Exhibit 1 Time Line

	1985	1986	1987	1988	1989
	Blockbuster Entertainment Corp. formed from Cook Data Services.	Equity position enhanced with public common stock offering, raising $4,000,000. Opened 25,000 square foot distribution center.	600% increase in number of stores to 133. 481% increase in revenues. H. Wayne Huizenga appointed CEO. Aquired Movies to Go.	212% increase in number of stores to 415. Declared two 2-for-1 stock splits. Aquired Video Library.	Acquired Major Video Corp, Video Superstore Master Limited Partnership. Cox Cable announced $15 million equity investment in Blockbuster. Opened 1,000th store. (1,211 year end) Announced third 2-for-1 stock split. United Kingdom/Canada

Total revenues company (actual)	$119,000	$7,438,000	$43,228,000	$136,893,000	$402,538,000
*Total Revenues System Wide	$8,587,000	$24,586,000	$98,218,000	$283,691,000	$663,475,000
* (Company)	$4,499	$15,100	$55,560,000	$179,779,000	$402,538,000

Establishment	*Equity Financing*	*Leadership Market Development*	*Leadership Horizontal Integration Acquisition Growth*	*Horizontal Integration Acquisition Growth International Market Development*

* Adjusted to reflect acquisitions.

*Quote adjusted to reflect acquisitions.
Source: AR '89, p. 2.

Exhibit 2   Blockbuster Entertainment Corporation Company Overview 1989*

General Information

Name:	Blockbuster Entertainment Corporation 901 East Las Olas Boulevard Fort Lauderdale, Florida 33301 (305) 524-8200
Regional Offices (8):	Dallas, Texas (Distribution Center) Chicago, IL; St. Louis, MO; San Francisco, Los Angeles, San Diego, CA; New York, NY.
Trading Symbol:	BV
Trading Exchange:	New York Stock Exchange
SIC Numbers:	5735, 6794, 7841
Industry:	Prerecorded videocassette rental/retail
Date Incorporated:	1982
Date Public:	March 1985
Distribution:	National, International
Business Sector:	Services (Rental, Retail)

Strategy/Structure

Strategy of Growth:	Single Business
Vertically Integrated:	Yes
Competitive Strategy:	Differentiation/Broad market focus
Process of Growth:	Number of Stores (Company owned vs franchises) (Exhibit 3) External Growth—acquisitions (Exhibit 4)
Structure:	Functional (Exhibit 5)

*All 1989 data refers to the fiscal year ended December 31, 1989, unless otherwise specified.
Sources: 1989 Annual Report.
1988 Annual Report.
1986 Annual Report.
Datext.
Wall Street Journal, December 31, 1989.
Wall Street Journal, December 31, 1987.

petition is primarily based upon their unique Superstore concept.

The business strategy of Blockbuster Entertainment Corporation is to provide product differentiation through wide selection opportunities and high quality operational consistency. These objectives are embodied in their Superstore concept.

Blockbuster currently dominates the industry for the following reasons:

- They have acquired all of their national competitors and are in a league by themselves.

- Their warehousing facility allows them to purchase prerecorded videocassettes in bulk and repackage and ship them to stores more efficiently.

- Their stores are bigger in terms of square footage than any other video rental stores.

- They offer a wider selection (10,000) of videos per store in 33 separate categories.

- They utilize computerized check-in/check-out procedures, emphasizing convenience and efficiency for their customers.

- Family-oriented environment.

- Large kids' rental section.

- They target community service issues by providing cassettes which address such concerns as smoking and breast self examination.

- Point locations in high volume traffic areas.

- Aggressive domestic and international expansion plans.

- Nationwide marketing program based upon name recognition.

- Their technologically advanced inventory management system allows them to track customer preferences and rental trends.

- They have a single focus which is to be America's family video store.*

*Sources: *Computer World*, August 21, 1989.
1989 Annual Report.
Palm Beach Post, February 8, 1988.

Exhibit 3 Blockbuster Entertainment Corporation
Number of Stores

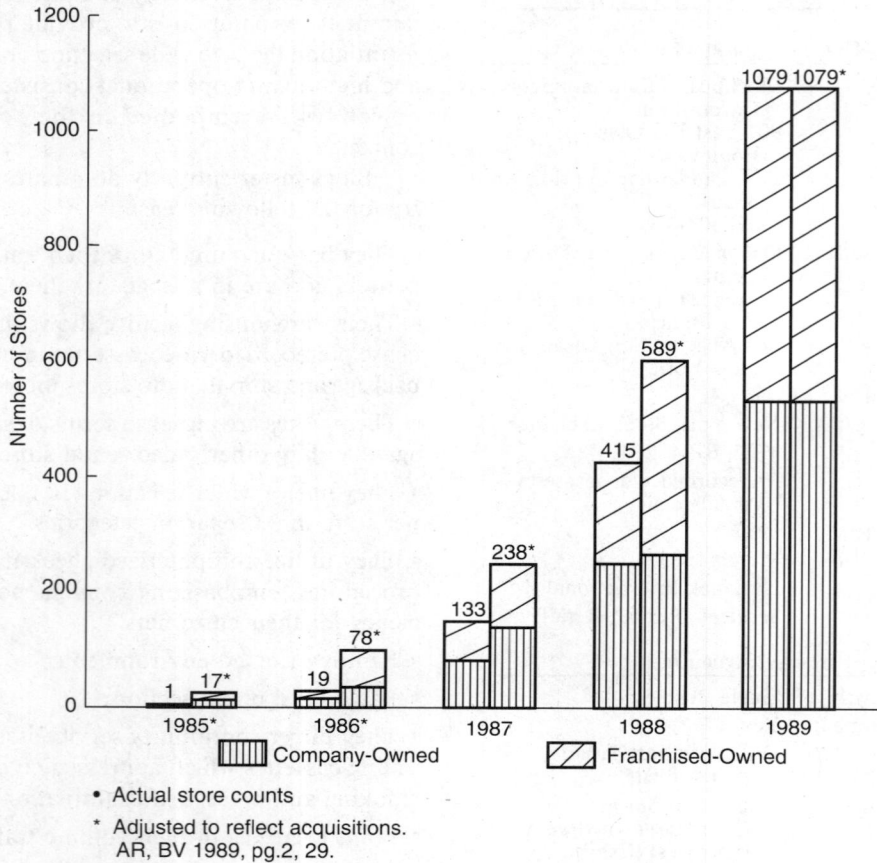

- Actual store counts
* Adjusted to reflect acquisitions.
  AR, BV 1989, pg.2, 29.

Source: AR, BV 1989, p. 2, 29.

Blockbuster Entertainment Corporation continues to expand in the United States and abroad. They have a competitive edge in these new regions based upon their name recognition and familiarity of the Superstore concept. Blockbuster's continued primary competition will come from those smaller stores in more remote locations throughout the United States. Up to this point, Blockbuster has focused its expansion into large, metropolitan areas and it has not yet

branched out into smaller, less populated regions.

Exhibit 7 suggests estimated market share for Blockbuster and its key competitors.

Exhibits 8 and 9 graphically suggest how Blockbuster Entertainment Corporation is positioned among its competitors within the video-cassette rental industry. With its high growth and market share it would be a "STAR" on the BCG portfolio and would be positioned between

Exhibit 4 Blockbuster Entertainment Corporation Acquisitions (1987–1989)

Company:	Date Acquired:
Southern Video For 321,840 shares, acquired net assets. Based in San Antonio, TX.	March 1987
Movies to Go For $14,500,000 in cash, notes & warrants, acquired 29 stores. Based in St. Louis, MO.	May 1987
Video Library For 885,508 shares and $6,380,861 in cash, acquired 42 stores. Based in San Diego, CA.	March 1988
Major Video Corp. 39 co-owned, 136 franchises. For 4,207,052 shares, acquired all stores operated. Based in Las Vegas, NV.	January 17, 1989
Oklahoma Entertainment, Inc. United Texas Entertainment, Inc. For 108,474 shares, acquired all stores operated.	January 1989
Three Times Prime, Inc. For 144,632 shares, acquired all stores operated.	January 1989
Marketplace Video, Inc.	February 1989
Vibrant Video, Inc. For 215,181 shares, acquired net assets and franchise rights.	February 1989
Video Superstores Venture L.P. Vector Video, Inc. For 146,906 shares, acquired all stores operated.	February 1989
Video Superstores Master L.P. For 7,875,573 shares, acquired 106 stores.	August 1989

Total Companies Acquired 12
Total Stores Acquired .... Over 352
Total Shares Issued 13,905,166
Total Cash Outlay $20,880,861

Moody's Industrial Manual, 1989, p. 2644.

growth and maturity on the industry life cycle.

Forces Driving Competition

The state of competition in a particular market depends on five basic forces which are the threat of new entrants, the bargaining power of customers, the bargaining power of suppliers, the threat of substitute products or services, and jockeying for position. The collective strength of these forces determines the ultimate profit potential of an industry.

Threat of New Entrants. To discourage entries, Blockbuster has successfully bought out their major competitors (Movies To Go, Inc., Major Video, and VSMLP). In addition, they have taken advantage of economies of scale by expanding throughout the United States and abroad. Blockbuster has grown from approximately 1 store in 1985 to 1,079 in 1989. With respect to product differentiation, Blockbuster is a recognized name as well as the leader in the United States of home videocassette rental tapes. These two factors act as a deterrent for new entrants into the market. Blockbuster operates under the belief that funds generated from both company-owned and franchise-owned stores, as well as its $125 million line of credit, will be sufficient to fund its operating needs and anticipated capital expenditures for its planned expansion. Success of new entrants in the industry would be limited to their capital requirements and the ability to expand into the market as rapidly as Blockbuster has. In addition, Blockbuster has its own distribution facility, its videocassette warehouse in Dallas, Texas. New entrants in the industry would need to secure a distribution channel similar to that of Blockbuster. This could be a major deterrent to new entrants.

Powerful Suppliers and Buyers. Blockbuster Entertainment Corporation has established a good supplier-buyer relationship with distributors of videocassettes. Blockbuster purchases prerecorded videocassettes directly from both distrib-

Exhibit 5 Blockbuster Entertainment Corporation
Organizational Chart

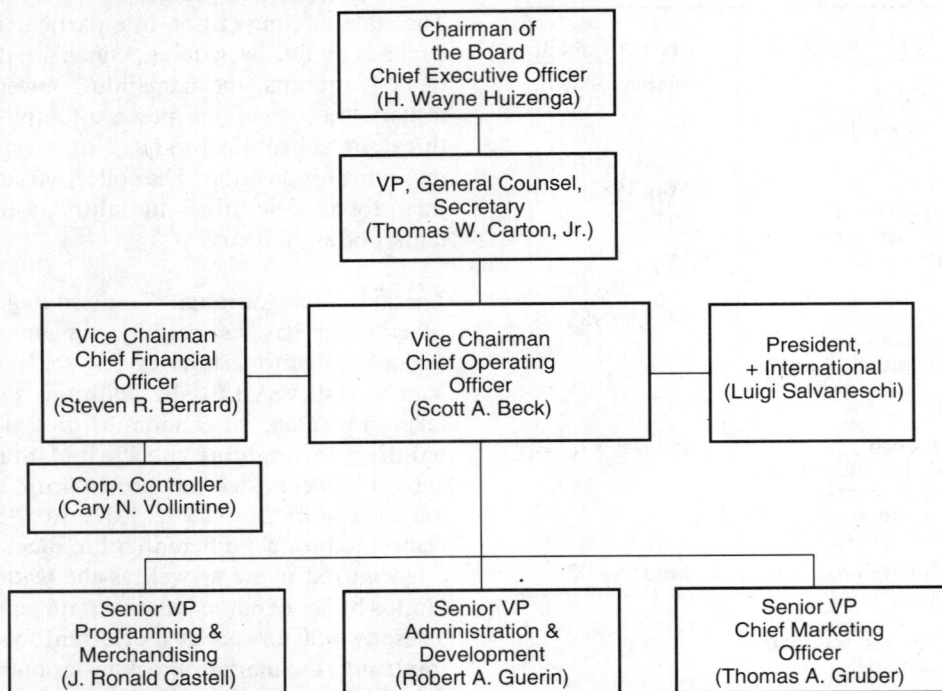

```
                    ┌──────────────────────┐
                    │     Chairman of      │
                    │      the Board       │
                    │ Chief Executive Officer │
                    │  (H. Wayne Huizenga) │
                    └──────────────────────┘
                               │
                    ┌──────────────────────┐
                    │  VP, General Counsel, │
                    │      Secretary       │
                    │ (Thomas W. Carton, Jr.)│
                    └──────────────────────┘
                               │
   ┌──────────────┐  ┌──────────────────┐  ┌──────────────┐
   │ Vice Chairman│  │  Vice Chairman   │  │  President,  │
   │ Chief Financial│ │ Chief Operating  │  │ + International│
   │   Officer    │──│     Officer      │──│(Luigi Salvaneschi)│
   │(Steven R. Berrard)│ │  (Scott A. Beck) │  └──────────────┘
   └──────────────┘  └──────────────────┘
          │
   ┌──────────────┐
   │Corp. Controller│
   │(Cary N. Vollintine)│
   └──────────────┘

   ┌──────────────┐  ┌──────────────────┐  ┌──────────────┐
   │  Senior VP   │  │   Senior VP      │  │  Senior VP   │
   │ Programming &│  │ Administration & │  │Chief Marketing│
   │ Merchandising│  │  Development     │  │   Officer    │
   │(J. Ronald Castell)│ │(Robert A. Guerin)│ │(Thomas A. Gruber)│
   └──────────────┘  └──────────────────┘  └──────────────┘
```

Sources: 1989 10K, p. 49–52.
1989 Annual Report, p. 57.
Personal Interview, May, 1990; July 1990

utors and producers. Due to the large number of videocassette titles used in their Superstores, the company has been able to negotiate favorable volume purchasing terms from their suppliers. In addition, current industry practices allow the company to return videocassettes purchased for resale to distributors with exchange privileges up to a predetermined amount of videocassette purchases. In addition to purchasing prerecorded videocassettes from both distributors and producers, Blockbuster stocks its warehouse in Dallas, Texas, with videocassettes it supplies to its own stores. This distribution channel between suppliers and buyer ensures conformity, familiarity, and consistency within each Blockbuster store. This in turn enhances customer satisfaction as customers are secure in knowing they can obtain a variety of videocassettes from certain categories in any Blockbuster store they choose to visit.

Substitute Products. Blockbuster's substitute products are limited in scope as there is no comparable direct substitute for prerecorded videocassettes. The one exception to this might be the laser disc. Blockbuster is currently test marketing this disc in some of its stores. Sales of laser disc players may increase in the future as consumers

Exhibit 6 Blockbuster Entertainment Corporation and Subsidiaries Consolidated
Balance Sheet at December 31*

	(In thousands, except share data)				
	1989	1988	1987	1986 (restated)	1985
Assets					
Current Assets:					
Cash and cash equivalents	$ 39,790	$ 8,959	$ 7,168	$ 3,402	$ 7,690
Accounts receivable less allowances	15,954	5,617	2,596	1,264	150
Notes receivable from shareholders	—	—	7,919	—	—
Merchandise inventories	29,455	17,901	8,440	3,153	—
Refundable income taxes	—	—	—	890	218
Other	7,393	6,359	1,357	148	125
Total Current Assets	92,592	38,836	27,480	8,857	8,183
Videocassette Rental Inventory, Net	133,041	60,294	16,389	3,076	567
Property and Equipment, Net	132,544	47,284	14,998	4,228	589
Intangible Assets, Net	38,509	24,754	12,149	—	—
Other Assets	20,628	5,599	3,169	936	264
	$417,314	$176,767	$74,185	$17,097	$ 9,603
Liabilities and Shareholders' Equity					
Current Liabilities:					
Current portion of long-term senior debt	$ 19,030	$ 3,139	$ 2,812	$ 1,400	$ —
Accounts payable	42,564	34,131	10,587	2,306	334
Accrued liabilities	11,140	8,108	2,546	647	—
Income taxes payable	3,724	189	445	—	33
Advance payments from franchise owners	6,899	3,653	489	2,000	—
Total Current Liabilities	83,357	49,220	16,879	6,353	367
Long-Term Senior Debt, Less Current Portion	24,218	21,303	14,797	—	—
Subordinated Convertible Debt	93,729				
Other Non-Current Liabilities	7,821	1,293	451	264	—
Deferred Income Taxes	—	3,167	60	—	—
Shareholders' Equity:					
Preferred stock, $1 par value; authorized 500,000 shares; none outstanding	—	—	—	—	—
Common stock, .10 par value [1989 authorized 100,000,000 shares; issued and outstanding 71,736,058 and 67,519,891 shares, respectively]	7,174	2,574	900	534	217
Capital in excess of par value	140,348	84,086	41,472	14,410	10,262
Retained earnings (deficit)	60,667	15,124	(374)	(4,464)	(1,243)
Total Shareholders' Equity	208,189	101,784	41,998	10,480	9,236
	$417,314	$176,767	$74,185	$17,097	$ 9,603

*Note: Unrevised. Figures do not include adjustments and revisions as a result of acquisition activity.   *(continued)*
AR 88, p. 26
AR 89, p. 40
AR 87, p. 19, 20
AR 86 p. 17

Exhibit 6 (*continued*) Blockbuster Entertainment Corporation and Subsidiaries Consolidated Statements of Operations for the Years Ended December 31

	(In thousands, except per share data)				
	1989	1988	1987	(restated) 1986	1985
Revenue:					
Rental revenue	$283,933	$ 87,299	$19,009	$ 2,893	$ 84
Product sales	101,268	41,452	21,546	4,247	35
Royalties and other fees	17,337	8,142	2,673	298	—
	402,538	136,893	43,228	7,438	119
Operating Costs and Expenses:					
Cost of product sales	71,391	31,343	15,923	3,511	27
Operating expenses	207,760	63,638	16,429	5,152	1,081
Selling, general, and administrative	47,246	15,567	4,162	2,093	542
Operating Income (Loss)	76,141	26,345	6,714	(3,318)	(1,531)
Equity in Loss of an Affiliate	—	—	—	(954)	(442)
Interest Expense	(11,039)	(2,066)	(569)	—	—
Interest Income	1,283	626	456	228	737
Other Income, Net	3,380	92	104	—	—
Income (Loss) from Continuing Operations before Income Taxes	69,765	24,997	6,705	(4,044)	(1,236)
Provisions for Income Taxes	25,613	9,499	2,615	(823)	(285)
Income (Loss) from Continuing Operations	$ 44,152	$ 15,498	$ 4,090	$(3,221)	$ (951)
Discontinued Operations, Net	—	—	—	—	625
Net Income (Loss)	44,152	15,498	4,090	(3,221)	(326)
Net Income per Common and Common Share Equivalent Continuing Operations	$ .57	$ .58	$ 1.12	$ (1.36)	$ (.44)
Discontinued Operations	—	—	—	—	.29
Net Income (Loss) per Common and Common Share Equivalent	.57	.58	1.12	(1.36)	(.15)

*Note: Unrevised. Figures do not include adjustments and revisions resulting from subsequent acquisition activity.
AR 86, p. 17
AR 87, p. 19
AR 88, p. 25
AR 89, p. 39

become acquainted with the technology. If this occurred, Blockbuster would devote space in its stores for the rental and sale of laser discs.

Some additional potential influences on the industry include pay-per-view cable television and other types of television programming.

Jockeying for Position. Blockbuster's immediate competitors include West Coast Video and Erol's Inc. In addition, mom-and-pop rental stores and convenience stores also compete with Blockbuster for their proportionate share of the market. Blockbuster utilizes the following strategies to jockey for position.

Exhibit 7   Blockbuster Entertainment Corporation
Estimated Market Share

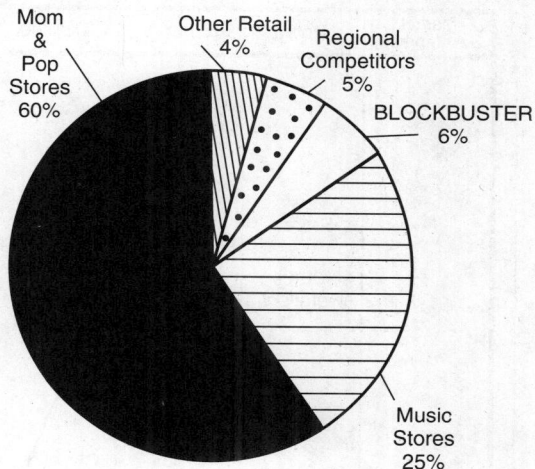

- Mom & Pop Stores 60%
- Other Retail 4%
- Regional Competitors 5%
- BLOCKBUSTER 6%
- Music Stores 25%

Exhibit 8   Blockbuster Entertainment Corporation
Competitive Portfolio

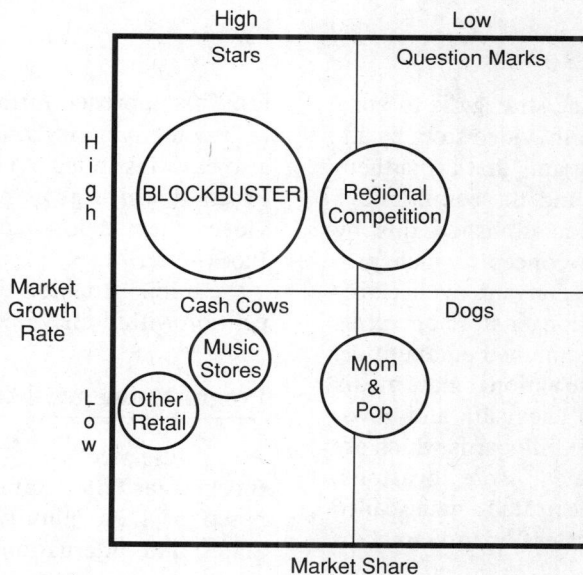

High — Low

Stars — Question Marks

BLOCKBUSTER — Regional Competition

Market Growth Rate

Cash Cows — Dogs

Music Stores — Mom & Pop

Other Retail

High — Low

Market Share

Exhibit 9   Blockbuster Entertainment Corporation
              Industry Life Cycle

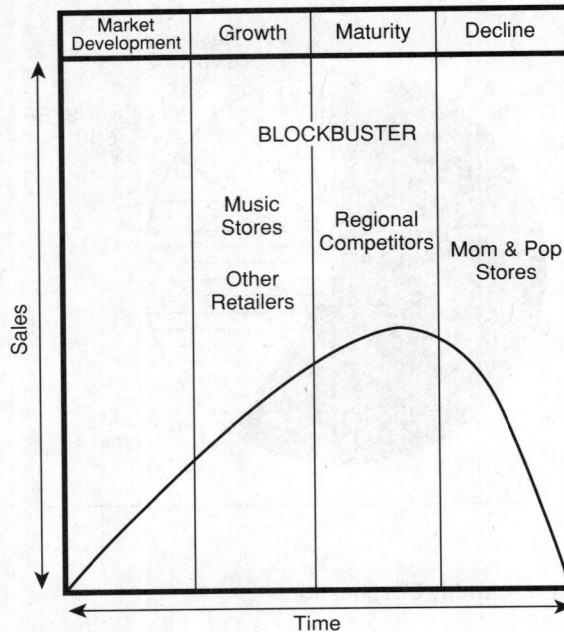

Blockbuster's marketing strategy is to position itself as America's family video store by adhering to policies and programs that bring them closer to their customers and the communities they serve. They have accomplished this by adopting their Superstore concept, which provides greater title selection, convenient check-in/check-out procedures and longer store operating hours. Their prices have remained competitive. They also have an extensive national mass media campaign, which includes television and newspaper advertising and large billboards which are positioned strategically near store locations. Blockbuster has recently instituted a game called the "$10,000,000 Blockbuster Video Game" as a new promotional tool.

Blockbuster further appeals to its customers by using two approaches that are unique. Unlike other video stores, they do not rent X-rated mov-

ies. This approach further supports their intent to become America's family video store. They also have instituted a Youth Restricted Viewing Program which gives parents control over the videos their children under 17 can rent from Blockbuster.

Exhibit 10 depicts the forces that drive competition within the videocassette rental market.*

Programming and Merchandising

Product/Service
Blockbuster Entertainment Corporation is composed of 1,200 plus stores across the United States and internationally, which rent prerecorded videocassettes to their customers for

*Sources: 1989 Form 10-K.
1989 Annual Report.

Exhibit 10 Forces Driving Competition
             Home Rental Videocassette Industry

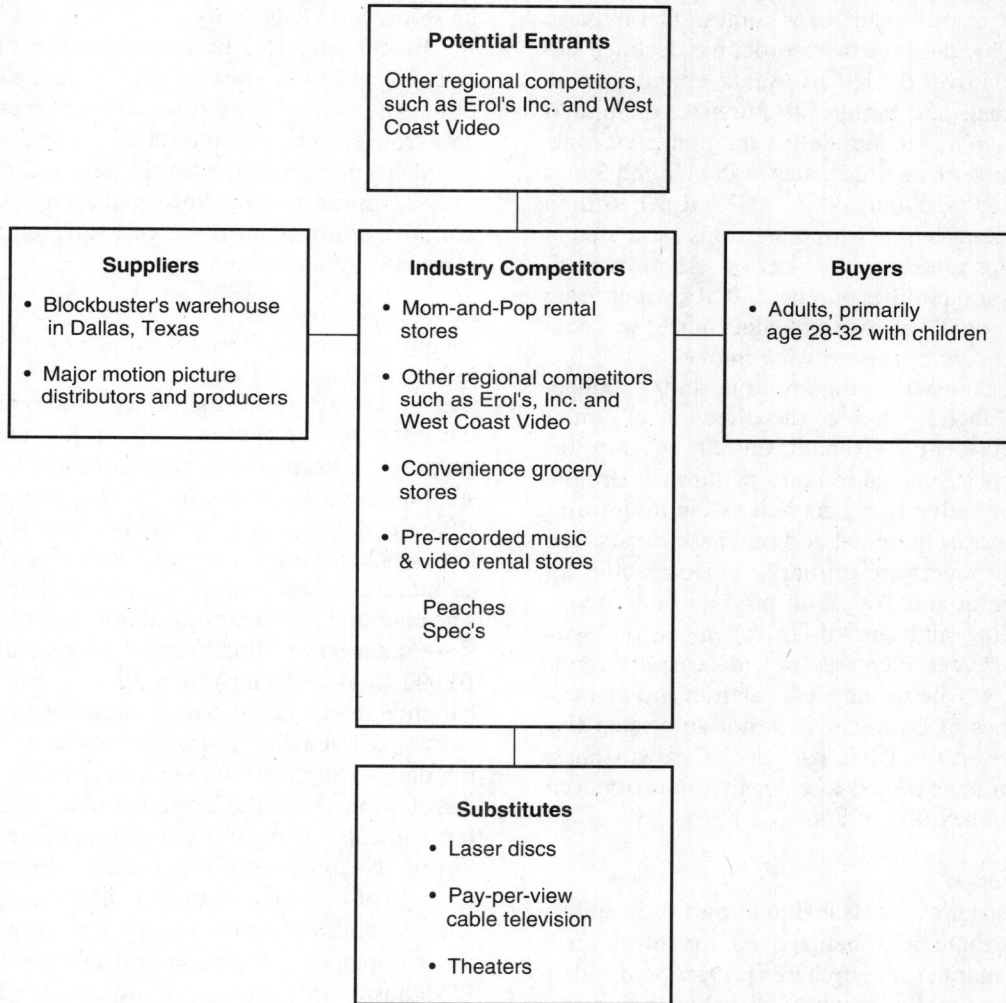

Potential Entrants

Other regional competitors, such as Erol's Inc. and West Coast Video

Suppliers

- Blockbuster's warehouse in Dallas, Texas

- Major motion picture distributors and producers

Industry Competitors

- Mom-and-Pop rental stores

- Other regional competitors such as Erol's, Inc. and West Coast Video

- Convenience grocery stores

- Pre-recorded music & video rental stores

    Peaches
    Spec's

Buyers

- Adults, primarily age 28-32 with children

Substitutes

- Laser discs

- Pay-per-view cable television

- Theaters

home viewing. In addition, Blockbuster also sells prerecorded videocassettes to its customers. Blockbuster realized a niche in this market in 1985 when it determined that the rental of videocassettes was a fragmented market without a leader in sight. Blockbuster determined that existing video stores did not provide a large title selection or transaction convenience in renting videocassettes. As such, they set out to develop their Superstore concept which provided a greater number of copies of popular rental titles, greater selection opportunities, longer store operating hours, and time-saving computerized check-in/check-out procedures.

Customers/Markets

Blockbuster's primary market consists of individuals and families who own and utilize videocassette recorders in their homes. The average price of a videocassette recorder has declined significantly over the last five years, enabling more individuals and families to purchase them, and in turn, rent videocassettes for home viewing. Videocassette recorder sales in the United States were $12,000,000 in 1989 with VCR penetration among households with televisions estimated at 67.6% for the same time period. As more individuals and families purchase VCRs, penetration in homes will increase and Blockbuster will continue to service this growing market.

Blockbuster's programming and merchandising functions, under the direction of Senior Vice-President J. Ronald Castell, support the company's Superstore concept through promotions and advertising, as well as the monitoring of videocassette rental and purchase trends. The firm's products are primarily videocassettes for both rental and sale. Both product lines are experiencing high growth in revenues, but with more sizeable increases in videocassette rental revenues. Due to the close relationship of these two types of products, it is not surprising that both are in the latter part of the growth phase and can be expected to enter the maturity cycle over the next five years.

Distribution

Blockbuster's success is due in part to its ability to distribute and manage its inventory in a timely manner. It purchases prerecorded videocassettes directly from both distributors and producers. After the videocassettes are purchased, they are shipped to its distribution center in Dallas, Texas. The distribution center has the capacity to house 400,000 videocassettes in its 80,000 square foot facility. It is here that the videocassettes are received, packaged, electronically coded and shipped to its company-owned and franchise-owned stores. When the videocassettes arrive at the stores, they are already sorted alphabetically within categories and are ready to be placed on the display shelves. With its own distribution center, Blockbuster is able to service its stores more efficiently.

Blockbuster also utilizes its own computer software within its stores. This software package utilizes a laser bar code scanner which reads key data from each rental videocassette and from the member's identification card. This technologically advanced system allows management to assess such information as videocassette rental patterns and inventory management.

Information Systems

Owing to its origins from a company which provided programming and remote computer services, it is no surprise that Blockbuster employs the latest technology and top professionals to support its information systems. Most of the substantial franchise fee Blockbuster charges its store operators goes to cover the computer system which provides inventory control and management assistance applications to each store. The potential and flexibility of this system allows store managers to track rentals of each of over 10,000 titles and more than 30 categories. The bar-code readers ensure that check-in/check-out is easy, convenient, and quick, while collecting the data to support inventory decisions. At the distribution level, the central warehousing system controls the incoming inventory of tapes and directs the shipping of the needed titles to each store location. State-of-the-art information systems capabilities support many of the aspects of the company's Superstore concept and allow Blockbuster to maintain its dominance in the dynamic home videocassette rental/sales industry.

Franchising

Blockbuster has assembled a staff of members who have expertise in franchise development as part of the company's plan to penetrate franchise markets. This staff is headed by Douglas M. Kinney, vice president, franchise development. In order to pursue its expansion objectives, the company has employed a strategy of developing Superstores through a combination of company and franchise development. The balance between company-owned and franchise-owned stores is determined by such factors as resource availability and operating efficiency.

Blockbuster currently operates under two different forms of franchise relationships with its franchise owners. Beginning in January, 1988, the company initiated its current form of franchise agreement. The current agreement requires an initial fee of up to $55,000 for the right to operate under the Blockbuster Video service mark. In addition, a fee of up to $30,000 is charged prior to opening a store for the required proprietary software, with a continuing monthly payment of $500 to $650 for maintenance of the software. The franchise owner is also charged $5,000 in advance as a development fee for each store to be developed during the term of the agreement.

In addition, franchise owners must pay a continuing royalty and service fee equal to a certain percentage (between three and eight percent) of store gross revenue. They must also pay the company a certain percentage of gross revenue for development of the company's advertising and marketing programs and a further one percent of revenue for national advertising.

Under the company's current franchise agreement, franchise owners are required to purchase a minimum of 5,000 tapes of the 7,000 required for opening, directly from the company.

The monetary commitment required to open a store is between $425,000 and $650,000. These figures are exclusive of any franchise or development fees. The company does not assist potential franchise owners in obtaining financing, but states that it carefully screens potential franchise owners.*

---

*Sources: 1988 Annual Report.
1989 Annual Report.
Datext.
Computer World, August 21, 1989.
1989 Value Line.

Finance

The uniqueness of Blockbuster's Superstore concept is without question a major key to the company's success, but this concept employed without sufficient financial resources would have little chance of survival. From the beginning, access to large amounts of working capital has allowed the company to plan on a large scale and secure the top market share in a fragmented industry. At the start it seemed Blockbuster would have trouble securing the additional capital needed for ongoing expansion. Its first public offering was practically over before it began, due to an unfavorable report from an analyst. Now its stock is commonly regarded as quite appealing. Currently, Blockbuster's finance organization, under the direction of Steven R. Berrard, one of the youngest of the company's executives, has accomplished such feats as securing a five-year, unsecured $125 million line of credit, retiring most of its existing indebtedness, and issuing a series of Liquid Yield Option Notes due in 2004 which netted the company about $90 million. The year 1989 has also seen the third 2-for-1 stock split in the company's short history. Blockbuster's combination of aggressive positioning and top quality executive leadership carries over into its financing operations. This leadership should continue to manage the resources needed for ongoing expansion of the company to the satisfaction of both shareholders and top management. The next challenge facing this department, and the company as a whole, is the transition from the role of prospector to that of defender. This combined with early signs of a slowing economy may prove formidable concerns in the next decade for Blockbuster.

Exhibit 11 represents a condensed, common size, comparative Balance Sheet for the fiscal years 1987,* 1988,* and 1989. This comparison illustrates:

---

*The 1987 and 1988 figures have been adjusted to reflect acquisitions.

▪ The decrease in the amount of current assets as compared to total assets, reflecting the expansionary trend of Blockbuster's operations. As the number of store openings stabilizes, this percentage should also stabilize.

▪ The decrease in the relative amount of merchandise inventories. These represent the cost to purchase and prepare products for in-store use at company owned locations. With greater experience and expertise gained over time, the company apparently has managed to bring these costs down.

▪ An increase in the relative importance of long term debt consistent with Blockbuster's expansion.

▪ An increase in the percentage of liabilities matched with a decrease in the percentage of equity, highlighting the company's move towards debt based financing rather than issuance of more equity.

Exhibit 12 represents a common-size, comparative Income Statement for the fiscal years 1987,* 1988* and 1989. In this exhibit all items are presented as a percentage of total revenue. This comparison illustrates:

▪ The relative importance of rental revenue, product sales, and royalties and fees remained proportionate over all three periods.

▪ An overall decrease in all operating costs over all three periods occurred.

▪ The gross margin on product sales exhibited a decrease from 26.1% in 1987 to 25.1% in 1988, however it increased to 29.5% in 1989. This increase in the profitability of product sales contributes to the overall improvement of the financial position of the firm.

▪ An increase to nearly 11 cents out of every dollar as net income occurred in 1989.

Exhibit 13 is a financial ratio analysis for Blockbuster for the years 1987,* 1988* and 1989.

*The 1987 and 1988 figures have been adjusted to reflect acquisitions.

No industry comparison is presented due to Blockbuster's enviable status as the lone national operator in a fragmented industry.

After only five years of operation, Blockbuster's financial position has never been stronger. Shareholders' equity was $208,189,000 on December 31, 1989, an increase of nearly 68% from the previous year. Net earnings for 1989 were reported at $44,152,000 up almost 152% from 1988. Revenues increased by about 124% to $402,538,000. In June, 1989, the company entered into a five year, unsecured $125 million line of credit, and in October, 1989, Blockbuster completed the offering of Liquid Yield Option Notes netting the company approximately $90 million. During the year the company also initiated its third 2-for-1 stock split.

Blockbuster Entertainment Corporation's good profit margin, upward trends in total asset turnover, return on investment, and return on equity in 1989, depict a strong financial position as displayed in Exhibit 14.**

Leadership

There are fourteen executives, officers, and directors which make up the senior management team of Blockbuster. Messrs. Huizenga, Beck, Berrard, and Salvaneschi are members of the Executive Committee. Together, these gentlemen are the major decision makers for Blockbuster. A brief biography of Blockbuster's executives and directors is listed below.

Inside Directors
Mr. H. Wayne Huizenga, *Chairman of the Board and Executive Committee and Chief Executive Officer.* Mr. Huizenga became a Director of Blockbuster in February, 1987, and was elected as Chairman of the Board and Executive Committee and CEO in April, 1987. Mr. Huizenga served as President of Blockbuster until June, 1988. He is a co-founder of Waste Management, Inc., where he served in various capacities in-

**1989 AR, 10K.

Exhibit 11   Blockbuster Entertainment Corporation Common Size Comparative Balance Sheet

	(Dollars in Thousands)					
	FY 1987	Common Size %	FY 1988	Common Size %	FY 1989	Common Size %
Assets						
Current Assets:						
Cash and Equivalents	$ 7,168	9.66%	$ 15,366	6.55%	$ 39,790	9.53%
Accounts Receivable, Net	2,596	3.50%	8,151	3.47%	15,954	3.82%
Notes Receivable from Shareholders	7,919	10.67%	0	0.00%	0	0.00%
Merchandise Inventories	8,440	11.38%	20,678	8.81%	29,455	7.06%
Other	2,399	3.23%	9,935	4.23%	7,393	1.77%
Total Current Assets	$28,522	38.45%	$ 54,130	23.06%	$ 92,592	22.19%
Videocassette Rental Inventory, Net	16,389	22.09%	82,928	35.33%	133,041	31.88%
Property and Equipment, Net	14,998	20.22%	63,990	27.26%	132,544	31.76%
Intangible Assets, Net	12,149	16.38%	25,356	10.80%	38,509	9.23%
Other Assets	2,127	2.87%	8,294	3.53%	20,628	4.94%
Total Assets	$74,185	100.00%	$234,698	100.00%	$417,314	100.00%
Liabilities and Shareholders' Equity						
Current Liabilities:						
Current Portion, Long Term Debt	$ 2,812	3.79%	$ 9,332	3.98%	$ 19,030	4.56%
Accounts Payable	10,587	14.27%	39,272	16.73%	42,564	10.20%
Accrued Liabilities	2,546	3.43%	11,385	4.85%	11,140	2.67%
Current Deferred Income Taxes	445	0.60%	189	0.08%	3,724	0.89%
Advance Payments from Franchisees	489	0.66%	3,303	1.41%	6,899	1.65%
Total Current Liabilities	$16,879	22.75%	$ 63,481	27.05%	$ 83,357	19.97%
Long Term Debt, Senior Debt	14,797	19.95%	39,488	16.83%	24,218	5.80%
Subordinated Convertible Debt	0	0.00%	0	0.00%	93,729	22.46%
Other Non-Current Liabilities	451	0.61%	7,671	3.27%	7,821	1.87%
Deferred Income Taxes	60	0.08%	0	0.00%	0	0.00%
Total Liabilities	$32,187	43.39%	$110,640	47.14%	$209,125	50.11%
Shareholders' Equity:						
Common Stock and Excess Paid-in-Capital	42,372	57.12%	107,543	45.82%	147,522	35.35%
Retained Earnings (Deficit)	(374)	−0.50%	16,515	7.04%	60,667	14.54%
Total Shareholders' Equity	$41,998	56.61%	$124,058	52.86%	$208,189	49.89%
Total Liabilities and Equity	$74,185	100.00%	$234,698	100.00%	$417,314	100.00%

Note: Numbers for 1987 and 1988 are revised to reflect acquisitions.
AR 1989 p. 40.

Exhibit 12   Blockbuster Entertainment Corporation Common Size Comparative Income Statement

	(Dollars in Thousands)					
	FY 1987	Common Size %	FY 1988	Common Size %	FY 1989	Common Size %
Revenue						
Rental Revenue	$30,399	54.71%	$127,023	70.66%	$283,933	70.54%
Product Sales	22,880	41.18%	46,460	25.84%	101,268	25.16%
Royalties and Other Fees	2,281	4.11%	6,296	3.50%	17,337	4.31%
Total Revenue	$55,560	100.00%	$179,779	100.00%	$402,538	100.00%
Operating Costs and Expenses:						
Cost of Product Sales	16,915	30.44%	34,784	19.35%	71,391	17.74%
Operating Expenses	26,894	48.41%	90,103	50.12%	207,760	51.61%
Selling, General and Administrative	6,536	11.76%	25,076	13.95%	47,246	11.74%
Total Operating Costs	$50,345	90.61%	$149,963	83.42%	$326,397	81.08%
Operating Income	$ 5,215	9.39%	$ 29,816	16.58%	$ 76,141	18.92%
Interest Income	843	1.52%	1,213	0.67%	1,283	0.32%
Interest Expense	(1,035)	−1.86%	(3,711)	−2.06%	(11,039)	−2.74%
Other Income, Net	521	0.94%	1,026	0.57%	3,380	0.84%
Income before Taxes	$ 5,544	9.98%	$ 28,344	15.77%	$ 69,765	17.33%
Provision for Taxes	2,372	4.27%	10,818	6.02%	25,613	6.36%
Net Income	$ 3,172	5.71%	$ 17,526	9.75%	$ 44,152	10.97%

AR, 1989, p. 39.
Note: Numbers for 1987 and 1988 are revised to reflect acquisitions.

cluding President, CEO, and Director. He believes Blockbuster is the leading company in the home video rental business. Mr. Huizenga has a strong work ethic; he normally works 12–14 hours a day. He believes the success of Blockbuster is attributed to the people of the organization. Mr. Huizenga owns 4,861,346 shares of Blockbuster stock. He is 52 years of age.

Mr. Scott A. Beck, *Vice-Chairman and Chief Operating Officer.* Mr. Beck became Vice-Chairman and Chief Operating Officer of the company in September, 1989. From March, 1986, to August, 1989, Mr. Beck was managing partner of VSMLP. Blockbuster acquired VSMLP, formerly the company's largest franchise owner, in August, 1989. Mr. Beck is 31 years of age.

Mr. Steven R. Berrard, *Vice-Chairman and Chief Financial Officer.* Mr. Berrard joined

Blockbuster in June, 1987, as Senior Vice-President, Treasurer, and Chief Financial Officer. He became a Director of the company in May, 1989, and was appointed Vice-Chairman of the Board in November, 1989. From April, 1985, until he joined Blockbuster, he served as President of Waco Services which is a leasing company. He owns 161,600 shares of stock and is 35 years of age.

Mr. Luigi Salvaneschi, *Director and President.* Mr. Salvaneschi joined the company in January, 1988, as Executive Vice-President, and was elected President of the company in June, 1988, and became a director of Blockbuster in May, 1989. From August, 1960, until 1988, he held various positions including Vice-President of Corporate Real Estate at McDonald's Corporation and Senior Vice-President of Real Es-

Exhibit 13 Blockbuster Entertainment Corporation Financial Ratio Analysis

	FY 1987	FY 1988	FY 1989
Liquidity			
Current	1.69:1	.85:1	1.11:1
Quick	1.05:1	.37:1	.67:1
Working Capital (in thousands)	$11,643	($9,351)	$9,235
Leverage			
Debt/Assets	.43:1	.47:1	.50:1
LTD/Equity	.35:1	.32:1	.57:1
Activity			
Asset Turnover	.75 Times	.77 Times	.96 Times
Fixed Asset Turnover	1.22 Times	1.00 Times	1.24 Times
Videocassette Inventory Turnover	1.85 Times	1.53 Times	2.13 Times
A/R Turnover	21.40 Times	22.06 Times	25.23 Times
Avg. Collection Period	17.05 Days	16.55 Days	14.47 Days
Profitability			
Return on Revenue	5.71%	9.75%	10.97%
Return on Investment	4.28%	7.47%	10.58%
Return on Equity	7.55%	14.13%	21.21%
Gross Profit Margin (Product Sales)	26.07%	25.13%	29.50%
Gross Operating Margin	9.39%	16.58%	18.92%

1989 Annual Report.
Note: 1987 and 1988 figures reflect revision as a result of acquisition activity.

tate, Construction, and Architecture/Engineering of Kentucky Fried Chicken. Mr. Salvaneschi is 60 years of age and owns 106,863 shares of stock.

Mr. Thomas A. Gruber, *Senior Vice-President and Chief Marketing Officer.* Mr. Gruber joined Blockbuster in October, 1987, in his current position. From October, 1967, to January 1987, he served in various positions for McDonald's Corporation, including Director of Marketing and Vice-President of International Marketing. From February, 1987, to July, 1987, Mr. Gruber was Executive Vice-President and Chief Marketing Officer of Jerrico, Inc., the operator of 1,500 Long John Silver's Seafood Restaurants. Mr. Gruber is 49 years of age.

Mr. J. Ronald Castell, *Senior Vice-President of Programming and Merchandising.* Mr. Castell was hired in February, 1989, in his current po-

sition and serves as an officer of Blockbuster. From October, 1985, until he was hired by Blockbuster, he was Vice-President of Marketing and Merchandising of Erol's, Inc., one of Blockbuster's major competitors. Mr. Castell is 52 years of age.

Mr. Robert A. Guerin, *Senior Vice-President of Administration and Development.* Mr. Guerin was appointed to his present position in October, 1989. He is an officer of the company. He joined Blockbuster in March, 1988, as Vice-President. From March, 1986, to March, 1988, he served as Vice-President and Region Manager of Waste Management of North America, Inc. From June, 1982, to March, 1986, he served as President of Wells Fargo Armored Service Corporation. Mr. Guerin is 46 years of age.

Mr. Gary N. Vollintine, *Corporate Controller.* Mr. Vollintine joined the company in Feb-

Exhibit 14 Blockbuster Entertainment Corporation
DuPont Financial Analysis—1989

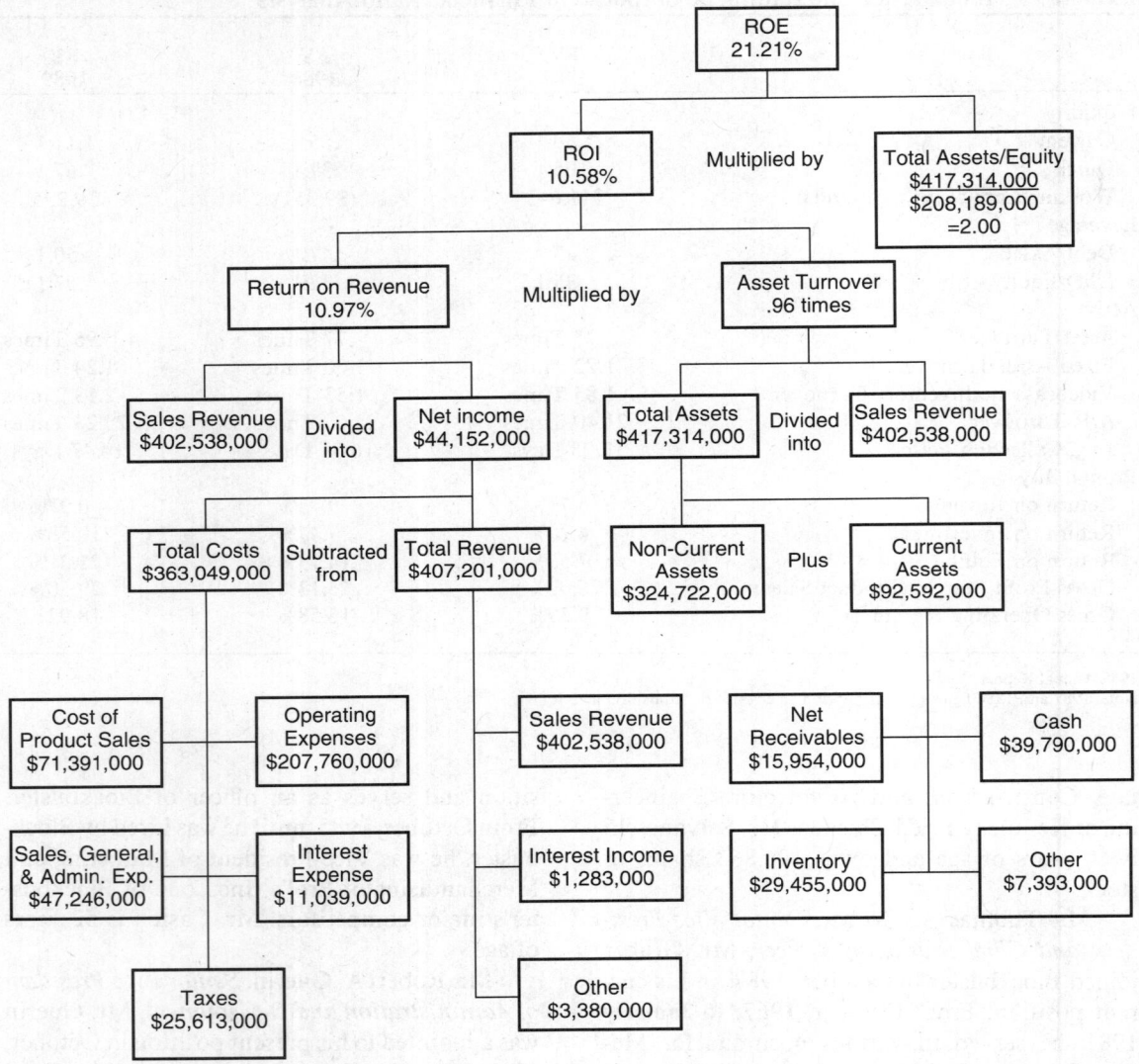

```
                                    ┌─────────────┐
                                    │     ROE     │
                                    │   21.21%    │
                                    └─────────────┘
                    ┌─────────────┐              ┌──────────────────────┐
                    │     ROI     │ Multiplied by│ Total Assets/Equity  │
                    │   10.58%    │              │    $417,314,000      │
                    └─────────────┘              │    $208,189,000      │
                                                 │       =2.00          │
                                                 └──────────────────────┘
        ┌──────────────────┐              ┌──────────────────┐
        │ Return on Revenue│ Multiplied by│  Asset Turnover  │
        │     10.97%       │              │    .96 times     │
        └──────────────────┘              └──────────────────┘
```

Sales Revenue $402,538,000	Divided into	Net income $44,152,000		Total Assets $417,314,000	Divided into	Sales Revenue $402,538,000

Total Costs $363,049,000	Subtracted from	Total Revenue $407,201,000		Non-Current Assets $324,722,000	Plus	Current Assets $92,592,000

Cost of Product Sales $71,391,000	Operating Expenses $207,760,000		Sales Revenue $402,538,000		Net Receivables $15,954,000	Cash $39,790,000

Sales, General, & Admin. Exp. $47,246,000	Interest Expense $11,039,000		Interest Income $1,283,000		Inventory $29,455,000	Other $7,393,000

Taxes $25,613,000			Other $3,380,000			

ruary, 1989, as Controller. He currently serves as an officer of the company. Prior to this date, he had been managing partner of the Ft. Worth, Texas, office of Arthur Andersen & Company for more than five years. Mr. Vollintine is 47 years of age.

Mr. Thomas W. Carton, Jr., *Vice-President, General Counsel, and Secretary*. Mr. Carton joined Blockbuster in October, 1988, in his present position. From August, 1987, until October, 1988, he was employed by Kalmar A/C Group, Inc., in a similar position. From February, 1981, through July, 1987, Mr. Carton was Assistant General Counsel and Assistant Secretary of Wendy's International, Inc. He is 41 years of age.

Outside Directors

Mr. Donald F. Flynn, *Director*. In February, 1987, Mr. Flynn became a director of the company. He currently serves as director of Waste Management, Inc., Chemical Waste Management, Inc., Wheelabrator Technologies, Inc., and Psychemedics Corporation. Mr. Flynn is 50 years of age and owns 1,700,044 shares of Blockbuster stock.

Mr. A. Clinton Allen, III, *Director*. Mr. Allen became a director in July, 1986, and is Chairman of the Compensation Committee. Since October, 1988, he has served as Chairman of A.C. Allen & Company, a financial services firm. Prior to 1988, Mr. Allen was Executive Vice-President of Advest, Inc., an investment banking firm. He is 46 years of age and owns 52,100 shares of stock.

Mr. John W. Croghan, *Director*. In July, 1987, Mr. Croghan became a director of Blockbuster and owns 130,000 shares of the company's stock. He currently serves as Chairman of the Audit and Finance Committee. For more than five years he has been Chairman of Lincoln Capital Management Company, an investment advisory firm. Mr. Croghan is 59 years of age.

Mr. Carl F. Barger, *Director*. Mr. Barger became a director of the company in November, 1988, and is chairman of the Nominating Committee. He has been a partner in the law firm of Eckert, Seamans, Cherin & Mellot since 1962 and currently serves as managing partner. Since 1987, he has also served as President and Director of Pittsburgh Baseball, Inc. He owns 15,000 shares of stock and is 59 years of age.

Mr. Gene W. Schneider, *Director*. Mr. Schneider became a director of the company in November, 1988. He served as President, Chief Executive Officer, and Chairman of the Board of United Cable Television Corporation from 1982 through May, 1989. In May, 1989, Mr. Schneider

became a director and chairman of the board of United Artists Entertainment Company. He currently serves as a director of Turner Broadcasting Systems, Inc., The Fashion Channel Network, Inc., and Sillerman MaGee Communications Management Corp. He owns 15,000 shares of stock and is 63 years of age.

Each director holds office until the next annual meeting of shareholders and until his successor has been elected and qualified. Officers are elected by the Board of Directors and serve at its discretion. The Board of Directors meets quarterly.*

Corporate Culture/Values

Insights to the culture of Blockbuster Entertainment Corporation include:

▪ One middle manager of Blockbuster was quoted as saying "Wayne (Mr. Huizenga) works harder than anyone else. He's usually in the office from 6:30 a.m. till 8:30/9:00 p.m. every night."

▪ Employees are considered to be one of Blockbuster's major assets. Mr. Huizenga was paraphrased as saying "If it costs ten or fifteen thousand more to get the right person, get the right person. Good people are our answer."

▪ One of the major strategies of Blockbuster is a deep sense of corporate responsibility to the needs of its customers and the communities it serves. Mr. Huizenga personally donated over a million dollars in 1989 to various charities, especially those that benefit children and animals.

▪ Loyalty, dedication, and hard work are strong company values. One employee was quoted as saying "If you don't come in on Saturday, don't show up on Monday."

---

*Sources: 1989 Form 10-K.
Personal Interviews, May, 1990.
Washington (D.C.) Times, June 29, 1989.
Virginian Pilot, June 18, 1989.
Business First of Buffalo, August, 1989.

▪ Employees perceive Blockbuster as a fast track and wonderful place to work.

▪ Training is a strength of the company. There are two major training centers for management and field training. In Dallas, Texas, the company maintains its training center, Blockbuster University.

▪ Reward systems such as the annual "Chairman's Award" for best all-around franchise owner are used to reinforce the value of employees to Blockbuster.

▪ The company supports an entrepreneurial spirit.

▪ On July 4, 1989, the company launched a nationwide community service program that offers the free use of special family-oriented videotapes. This is another example which illustrates management's sense of responsibility to its customers.*

---

*Sources: Personal Interviews, May, 1990.
1989 Annual Report.
Times and News Leader, January 25, 1988.
Florida Trend, April, 1990.
News Release, Blockbuster Video, April, 1990.

Case 9

The Restructuring of Ramada Inc.

History

The Ramada chain was started by a Chicago restaurateur, Marion Isbell. When in his 40s, Isbell sold a Chicago-based food service business and retired to Arizona. He grew restless in retirement and soon began building roadside motels around Phoenix and Flagstaff, using the name Ramada.

By 1959 Isbell and his partners owned 14 motels and were encouraged by the rapid expansion of Holiday Inn. In 1962, the partners began competing directly with Holiday Inn as both firms developed units along the interstate highway system. Like Holiday Inn, Ramada established design, construction, and purchasing divisions, so that the company became a one-stop shopping center for hotel developers and operations. Potential franchisees could look to Ramada for help in site selection, building site designs, and the provision of everything needed for operation (e.g., supplies and a reservation network).

In addition to the franchise network, Ramada was also building inns on its own as fast as the highway system expanded. By 1969, however, the interstate system was completed and new sites became harder to find.

In the 1970s, Ramada expanded its operations through the purchase of existing hotels and resorts and attempted to diversify by getting into the car rental business and into the ownership and management of campgrounds. However, the

company was not successful in either venture. At this time Ramada also expanded overseas into Europe and entered into hospital management in California.

In 1974 Bill Isbell, Marion Isbell's son, assumed control of the company. At about the same time, the Arab oil embargo raised energy prices, which adversely affected the tourism industry. Ramada's earnings fell from $15.3 million in 1973 to $1 million in 1975. Instead of continuing to expand and/or diversify, the company began to streamline its operations. Ramada renovated its units and encouraged its franchisees to do likewise. The refurbishing program occurred at an opportune time. As the program was being completed, industry sales rose and Ramada's earnings were in excess of $17.5 million by 1980.

Also in the 1970s, Ramada became interested in owning and operating a casino. The company purchased a 7 percent stake in Del Webb, which operated the Mint and the Sahara in Las Vegas. Del Webb also owned casinos in Reno, Lake Tahoe, and Laughlin, and had purchased a site in Atlantic City. Due to its ownership position, Ramada expected to gain a seat on Del Webb's board of directors. One was never given and, subsequently, Ramada sold the stock in Del Webb for a sizable profit. Soon thereafter, Ramada purchased the Ambassador Hotel in Atlantic City, which had become defunct. Ramada's intention was to completely renovate the hotel. Unfortunately for Ramada, New Jersey officials were encouraging new construction rather

235

than renovations. Eventually, Ramada was able to renovate the Ambassador but, due to government delays and the effects of the salty ocean air, the project was far over budget.

During the time that Ramada was waiting for regulatory approval on the Ambassador Hotel, Nevada gaming officials approached the company to purchase the Tropicana. The Tropicana had a history of trouble and the Nevada regulators hoped that Ramada would stabilize the hotel/casino operations. Ramada bought the Tropicana Hotel and Casino in 1979. The Atlantic City casino, now called Tropicana Hotel and Casino, opened in 1981.

Between 1976 and 1982, Ramada decreased its chain by 35 percent, selling the units to raise cash to enter the gaming business or to get rid of unprofitable properties. Earnings from the Atlantic City casino hit an all-time high, with revenues from the hotel/casino greater than the revenues of the entire hotel division in 1982. Ramada continued with its system of selling older hotels and replacing them with newer properties.

Changes under CEO Snell

President and chief executive officer Richard Snell was elected Chairman of the board for Ramada in 1981. Snell was for 25 years associated with the Phoenix law firm of Snell & Wilmer. He was elected president of Ramada in 1982. Bankers drafted Snell to manage the financially distressed company, for which he served as legal counsel until 1981. According to various sources, he joined Ramada reluctantly and expected to leave in a few months. The company's nervous bankers persuaded him to stay on until the company was healthy.

In his first three years as CEO he sold 69 hotels, cut staff, and pumped up Ramada's balance sheet. Long-term debt had reached 79 percent of total capital in 1982. This was mostly a function of costs overruns at the Atlantic City casino hotel. Snell arranged a sale–lease back of the facility and reduced debt in 1985 to 58 percent. His feelings on Ramada's performance for 1987 and 1988 are presented in Exhibit 1, a letter to shareholders. Results of Ramada Inc.'s operations are presented in Tables 1a through 1e.

Exhibit 1   Annual Letter to Shareholders from the Chairman of the Board

In last year's letter to you I expressed confidence that our plan to reposition Ramada's hospitality products would lead to appreciable earnings gains as we moved toward the end of the decade. At the same time, I was cautious in my assessment of the company's 1987 prospects. As things turned out, that caution was well-deserved for the reasons discussed further on.

Nonetheless, 1987 was a year of significant progress toward our goal of transforming Ramada from a company whose product mix had low growth prospects into one whose upgraded mix offers excellent growth potential. Our development programs, notably those in hotels and gaming, will soon be far enough along to make measurable contributions to income. But the nature and timing of these programs were such that they diluted earnings of the two groups in 1987.

In the hotel group, the operating results for 1987 were about as expected. The year-over-year decline in

operating income was occasioned by the planned sale of older hotel properties that had limited growth opportunities. In their stead, we have been opening hotels in markets selected to broaden our representation and to provide higher levels of profit. But the immaturity of most of these hotels, in relation to start-up expense and fixed costs, limited their profit contribution.

Within the gaming group, we anticipated that the huge expansion project at the Atlantic City Tropicana would have a disruptive effect on casino and food and beverage operations at the property. That situation proved to be worse than we had expected and contributed to a decline in the property's, and the gaming group's, performance for the year.

A disappointment in 1987 was the contribution from the restaurant group. Marie Callender's, operating in an industry characterized by intense compe-

Exhibit 1 *(continued)*

tition, experienced severe pressure on revenues and margins which produced weak full-year earnings.

These circumstances, along with a higher tax rate and an extraordinary loss, contributed to lower net income in the year just ended.

While 1987 was not a banner year from a financial standpoint, it was not without some important achievements that have moved Ramada into position to attain significantly improved results from its three business units beginning in 1988.

Our hotel group made tremendous progress in extending the reach of the company's lodging products and more clearly defining the market niches of our hotel brands.

Owing to aggressive domestic and international development programs, we added more new Ramada and Renaissance rooms to the company's worldwide hotel system than in any other year in Ramada's history.

Through the mid-year acquisition of the Rodeway inn chain we added several thousand more rooms. Equally important, the Rodeway purchase gave us a strong foothold in the economy, limited-service lodging tier, sharpened the focus of our brand strategy and provided a new product for expansion through franchising.

The year just ended saw our activity on company-developed hotel projects move into full swing. The opening of several new domestic and international properties contributed to an improving image for Ramada's lodging products and further anchored our presence in the global marketplace.

In 1987, our gaming group moved within sight of its goal of establishing a portfolio of highly profitable, themed casinos in the primary U.S. gaming markets.

The Las Vegas Tropicana, the first property to be themed as part of a major expansion two years ago, came into its own and delivered an impressive operating performance in 1987.

During the year, the gaming group also guided the $200 million expansion of the Atlantic City Tropicana through its first year of construction on budget and on schedule for opening by early 1989, and perhaps sooner given the progress to date. This project will clearly position the Tropicana, to be renamed TropWorld when the expansion is completed, as one of the first of a new generation of gaming megafacilities in the Atlantic City market.

Through an active program of geographic expansion, the gaming organization completed its entry into a third gaming jurisdiction, Reno, Nevada, and began construction on a fourth gaming property, a hotel casino in the dynamic and fast-growing Laughlin, Nevada, market.

The restaurant group devoted considerable resources to the tasks of seizing new development opportunities for Marie Callender's and implementing measures to respond to the competitive pressures in its industry.

The group made measurable progress against its development agenda, opening a number of new Marie Callender's restuarants in both established territories and new markets. In the face of a tough competitive environment, Marie Callender's management assigned a top priority to sales and marketing initiatives to increase on-premises sales at individual restaurants.

Throughout the Ramada organization, we remained on course toward our goal of positioning Ramada's hotel, gaming and restaurant properties as the service leaders in their industries. In 1987, our business units embarked on a number of programs to strengthen service delivery. Noteworthy among these efforts is the hotel group's "You're Somebody Special" program through which employees at company-operated and franchised hotels are working together to give our guests the finest service available in our markets.

With the programs and plans I've discussed, we enter 1988 confident in our ability to realize substantially higher levels of profitability in the years immediately ahead, assuming reasonably decent economic conditions. Our development programs are now nearing the point where they will make an important contribution to earnings. We also expect a reorganization completed last year to provide real savings in corporate expense and business unit overhead. Future income should also benefit from other expense reduction measures already taken and a lower effective tax rate.

The thousands of employees who represent Ramada and its hospitality products around the world are fully committed to achieving higher levels of performance and, in the process, enhancing the value of your investment in our company.

Richard Snell
Chairman of the Board and President

Annual Report, Ramada Inc., 1987, 3–6.

Table 1a   Financial Highlights, 1984–1988

FINANCIAL HIGHLIGHTS
Ramada Inc. and Subsidiaries
For the Five Years Ended December 29, 1988
(in thousands, except per share data and number of shareholders)

	1988	1987 (Restated)	1986 (Restated)	1985 (Restated)	1984 (Restated)
Revenue	$476,645	$407,622	$383,712	$344,163	$334,023
Operating income	$ 39,961	$ 30,686	$ 37,970	$ 31,296	$ 44,422
Corporate expense	(10,236)	(10,871)	(14,532)	(13,957)	(17,361)
Interest expense (net of capitalized interest)	(24,813)	(18,103)	(12,951)	(12,367)	(18,443)
Other, net	(6,692)	(9,898)	(8,163)	(3,269)	(4,410)
Income/(Loss) from continuing operations before income taxes and extraordinary items	(1,780)	(8,186)	2,324	1,703	4,208
(Provision)/Benefit for income taxes	15	1,422	(3,087)	(1,750)	(3,653)
Income/(Loss) from continuing operations before extraordinary items	(1,765)	(6,764)	(763)	(47)	555
Discontinued operations	(3,898)	13,041	11,038	13,840	4,150
Extraordinary items	563	(1,365)	—	3,414	4,116
Net income/(loss)	$ (5,100)	$ 4,912	$ 10,275	$ 17,207	$ 8,821
Earnings per share:					
Income/(Loss) from continuing operations before extraordinary items	$ (.04)	$ (.17)	$ (.02)	$ —	$ .02
Discontinued operations	(.10)	.32	.29	.37	.11
Extraordinary items	.01	(.03)	—	.09	.11
Net income/(loss)	$ (.13)	$ .12	$ .27	$ .46	$ .24
Dividends declared: None					
Weighted average shares outstanding	39,751	39,727	38,705	37,209	37,205
Position at end of year:					
Total assets	$705,035	$663,142	$535,933	$471,576	$450,983
Long-term debt	$275,863	$258,584	$131,276	$109,448	$117,872
Shareholders' equity	$295,659	$300,326	$301,532	$268,706	$248,753
Equity per share	$ 7.43	$ 7.56	$ 7.59	$ 7.22	$ 6.69
Number of shareholders of record (at February 1 of the subsequent year)	30,536	34,389	37,346	39,990	44,801

Source: Ramada Inc. 1988 Annual Report, p. 1.

Table 1b Consolidated Statements of Operations, 1986–1988

RAMADA INC. AND SUBSIDIARIES
Consolidated Statements of Operations
For the Years Ended December 29, 1988, December 31, 1987 and January 1, 1987
(in thousands, except per share data)

	1988	1987 (Restated)	1986 (Restated)
Revenue:			
Casino	$358,295	$302,565	$289,053
Rooms and related services	68,677	58,645	51,049
Food and beverage	68,537	60,477	56,440
Other	22,436	21,076	21,492
	517,945	442,763	418,034
Less promotional allowances	(41,300)	(35,141)	(34,322)
Net revenue	476,645	407,622	383,712
Operating expenses:			
Casino	127,991	117,878	109,547
Rooms and related services	41,222	35,036	30,629
Food and beverage	63,660	55,924	51,948
Other operating expenses	96,217	74,852	68,718
Property operations	23,670	19,287	18,172
Lease rentals	59,331	55,582	51,141
Depreciation and amortization	24,593	18,377	15,587
Total operating expenses	436,684	376,936	345,742
Operating income	39,961	30,686	37,970
Corporate expense	(10,236)	(10,871)	(14,532)
Interest expense, net	(24,813)	(18,103)	(12,951)
Equity in unconsolidated partnerships' losses	(5,982)	(5,958)	(5,455)
Minority interests	(710)	(3,940)	(2,708)
Income/(Loss) from continuing operations before income taxes and extraordinary items	(1,780)	(8,186)	2,324
(Provision)/Benefit for income taxes	15	1,422	(3,087)
Income/(Loss) from continuing operations before extraordinary items	(1,765)	(6,764)	(763)
Discontinued operations	(3,898)	13,041	11,038
Extraordinary items	563	(1,365)	—
Net income/(loss)	$ (5,100)	$ 4,912	$ 10,275
Earnings per share assuming no dilution:			
Income/(Loss) from continuing operations before extraordinary items	$ (.04)	$ (.17)	$ (.02)
Discontinued operations	(.10)	.32	.29
Extraordinary items	.01	(.03)	—
Net income/(loss)	$ (.13)	$ .12	$ .27
Weighted average shares outstanding assuming no dilution	39,751	39,727	38,705

The accompanying Financial Review is an integral part of these financial statements.

Table 1c   Consolidated Balance Sheets, 1987 and 1988

RAMADA INC. AND SUBSIDIARIES
Consolidated Balance Sheets
December 29, 1988 and December 31, 1987
(in thousands)

	1988	1987 (Restated)
ASSETS		
Current assets:		
Cash	$ 23,875	$ 38,730
Accounts and notes receivable, net	28,129	26,391
Refundable income taxes	12,015	—
Inventories	5,388	3,355
Prepaid expenses and other	5,488	5,356
Total current assets	74,895	73,832
Net assets of discontinued operations	179,902	217,025
Property and equipment:		
Buildings and equipment, net	237,301	56,550
Land	63,281	71,728
Construction in progress	4,894	112,871
Leased under capital leases, net	20,143	21,704
	325,619	262,853
Investments and long-term receivables:		
Investments in and advances to unconsolidated partnerships	20,904	22,368
Notes receivable and other investments	76,719	69,345
	97,623	91,713
Other assets	26,996	17,719
	$705,035	$663,142
LIABILITIES AND SHAREHOLDERS' EQUITY		
Current liabilities:		
Accounts payable and accruals	$ 35,410	$ 40,865
Accrued payroll and employee benefits	23,490	14,557
Accrued interest payable	13,496	6,932
Current portion of long-term debt	28,100	18,915
Total current liabilities	100,496	81,269
Long-term debt, net	275,863	258,584
Other long-term liabilities	23,701	16,235
Deferred income taxes	7,044	4,906
Contingencies and commitments		
Minority interests	2,272	1,822
Shareholders' equity:		
Common stock	3,978	3,973
Paid-in capital	224,556	224,245
Foreign currency translation adjustments	1,443	1,291
Retained earnings	65,682	70,817
Total shareholders' equity	295,659	300,326
	$705,035	$663,142

The accompanying Financial Review is an integral part of these financial statements.

Source: Ramada Inc. 1988 Annual Report.

Table 1d Consolidated Statements of Cash Flows, 1986–1988

RAMADA INC. AND SUBSIDIARIES
Consolidated Statements of Cash Flows
For the Years Ended December 29, 1988, December 31, 1987 and January 1, 1987
(in thousands)

	1988	1987	1986
CASH FLOWS FROM OPERATING ACTIVITIES:			
Cash provided by continuing operations before extraordinary items	$ 13,458	$ 14,101	$ 15,493
Extraordinary items	563	(1,365)	—
Items not using/(providing) cash:			
Decrease in deferred mortgage expense		1,015	—
Tax benefit of capital loss carryforward	(563)	—	—
Cash used by extraordinary items	—	(350)	—
Cash provided by continuing operations after extraordinary items	13,458	13,751	15,493
CASH FLOWS FROM INVESTING ACTIVITIES:			
Payments on notes receivable	610	928	66,352
Proceeds from sales of property and equipment	12,000	—	—
Reduction in invested funds	6,603	131,111	3,602
Purchases of property and equipment	(129,111)	(107,071)	(27,815)
Increase in invested funds	—	(96,519)	(44,313)
Additions to other long-term assets	(13,504)	(8,528)	(14,741)
Cash used in investing activities	(123,402)	(80,079)	(16,915)
CASH FLOWS FROM FINANCING ACTIVITIES:			
Proceeds from issuance of common stock	316	157	21
Net borrowings under line-of-credit agreements	(30,000)	11,000	29,000
Proceeds from issuance of long-term debt	108,067	130,127	91
Principal payments on long-term debt	(19,900)	(13,922)	(12,173)
Redemption of Ramada New Jersey Holdings Corporation preferred stock	(295)	(18,918)	—
Cash provided by financing activities	58,188	108,444	16,939
Cash flows from discontinued operations	36,901	(27,135)	(31,742)
Net increase/(decrease) in cash	(14,855)	14,981	(16,225)
Cash at beginning of year	38,730	23,749	39,974
Cash at end of year	$ 23,875	$ 38,730	$ 23,749

The accompanying Financial Review is an integral part of these financial statements.

Source: Ramada Inc. 1988 Annual Report.

Table 1e Financial Review, 1985–1987

Revenue and operating income by industry segment are as follows (in thousands):

	1987	1986	1985
HOTEL			
Revenue:			
Room and related services	$121,504	$136,453	$138,210
Food and beverage	58,319	65,863	63,534
Other	46,823	37,584	36,462
	226,646	239,900	238,206
Cost and expense:			
Room and related services	35,438	40,152	41,251
Food and beverage	49,216	51,797	49,621
Other (including undistributed operating expenses and fixed charges)	129,737	127,188	128,942
	214,391	219,137	219,814
Operating income (excluding gains on property dispositions)	$ 12,255	$ 20,763	$ 18,392
GAMING			
Revenue:			
Casino	$302,565	$289,053	$272,470
Room and related services	45,225	39,232	27,391
Food and beverage	38,756	35,317	24,330
Other	20,297	19,770	17,623
	406,843[a]	383,372[a]	341,814[a]
Cost and expense:			
Casino	117,878	109,547	110,328
Room and related services	35,036	30,629	25,299
Food and beverage	55,924	51,948	43,485
Other (including undistributed operating expenses and fixed charges)	168,098	153,618	133,755
	376,936	345,742	312,867
Operating income	$ 29,907	$ 37,630	$ 28,947
RESTAURANT			
Revenue:			
Food and beverage	$104,542	$ 58,895	
Other	8,517	4,459	
	113,059	63,354	
Cost and expense:			
Food and beverage	73,539	41,140	
Other (including undistributed operating expenses and fixed charges)	30,758	15,104	
	104,297	56,244	
Operating income	$ 8,762	$ 7,110	

[a]Total promotional allowances netted against revenue were $35,141, $34,322 and $39,020 in 1987, 1986 and 1985, respectively.
Source: Ramada Inc. 1988 annual report.

Reasons behind the Restructuring

In a marked shift of corporate strategy, Ramada management decided in October 1988 to shed its hotel and restaurant divisions leaving it with only its four casino hotels. This sale of assets moved Ramada closer to its objective of managing assets instead of owning them. Financial factors, a potentially damaging lawsuit by the firm's second largest shareholder, takeover threats, and a major deal that fell through may have led to the decision.

Results of operations in the hotel and restaurant group had been disappointing. The hotel group had a pretax profit of $749,000 for the first half of 1988 compared to $6.8 million the year before. Restaurant pretax profit fell from 5.3 million to 2.1 million.

Management felt increased pressure to reorganize when the Pritzker family offered Ramada $371 million for the company. The Pritzkers, who owned 7.2 percent of the company, indicated if the company refused to discuss a sale they might attempt a hostile takeover. Rumor had it that the Pritzker family had talked internally and with third parties about a possible acquisition or restructuring of Ramada. The Pritzkers owned Hyatt Corporation, and with its casino in Lake Tahoe they could expand gaming operations into Las Vegas, Reno, Laughlin, and Atlantic City.

Ramada operated in three areas of the hospitality industry before its restructuring began: hotel, gaming, and restaurants. Ramada's hotel group operated a system of midpriced domestic and international hotels, restaurants, and resorts. Further, Ramada licensed the use of the Ramada name and provided services to its licensees. The company's activities in the gaming group consisted of four casino hotels, three in Nevada and one in Atlantic City. Ramada was consequently divided into three divisions—hotel group, gaming group, and restaurant group.

The hotel group conducted its business through a network of company-owned, leased and licensed hotels located throughout the U.S., Puerto Rico, and over 20 foreign countries. The hotel group was run by Jerry Manion, an executive vice president. He was the fourth president of the hotel group in six years. Prior to his joining Ramada in February 1985, Manion was president of Economy Motor Inns. In addition, he was senior vice president, director of franchise, for Quality Inns International from 1977 to 1980. Manion discussed Ramada's goals in an interview reproduced in Exhibit 2.

April 1989 marked the completed sale of the hotel group.

The restaurant group was established in 1986 through the acquisition of Marie Callender's, a California-based chain of family-style restaurants. Tom Martin was the executive vice president in charge of the restaurant group. Prior to heading up the restaurant division, Martin served in various executive positions with Ramada. In 1979 Martin was appointed senior vice president and chief financial officer, and in 1982 he was appointed executive vice president, finance and administration.

Ramada announced in March 1989 that the restaurant group had been sold to Wilshire Restaurant Group Inc. Marie Callender's is a midpriced restaurant operation that has 152 franchised or company-owned restaurants. These units were primarily concentrated in California and other western states. Operating income had been deteriorating steadily since Ramada purchased Marie Callender's. Management attributed this to the tough industrial market the group was in.

Former owner and founder of Marie Callender's, Donald Callender, had been suing Ramada. He claimed the units had been mismanaged. According to Callender, the deal to sell the chain didn't "pass the smell test." He further stated that the Wilshire group had an "inside track" because it promised to "keep all the incompetent management" Ramada had installed at Marie Callender's. Michael Hayes, chairman of Hayes Financial, indicated that Wilshire had

Exhibit 2   An Interview with the Hotel Group President about Ramada's Goals

Jerry Manion, president of the Ramada Hotel Group, discussed [Ramada's] goals with the hotel editor of *Travel Weekly*.

TW: Let's talk about the overall state of the company. Analysts have said that Ramada has been underperforming for years; that its profitability is low and its development is behind that of its major competitors. What is your estimation of the company's financial health?

Manion: It's true that the company has been under-performing in the past number of years. I think everybody realizes we had serious problems. Since the new management took over in 1981 under [chairman] Richard Snell, the company has been in a restructuring position.

In the past several years, we have come out of the doldrums and are now back in the mainstream of the hospitality industry.

We have development going throughout the world—probably more in the international area than any other company has been able to achieve in the last four years.

In the U.S., we have a considerable number of developments, not only company investment in our new Ramada Inns, but also in the franchising opportunities. We have put together probably the finest franchising development teams in the industry. This started about three years ago and is now producing quite well.

We have restructured the management of the hotel group, the marketing areas, the financial areas and the franchise operations area, which was and is responsible for the quality of our product.

We have eliminated several hundred Ramada properties from our system over the past four or five years.

We have been replacing those on a steady basis, a very slow, direct program where we look for properties that can be financially successful for the owners and for Ramada.

We are not looking for numbers. We are looking to be a very healthy company again, and we are very rapidly achieving that.

TW: What were your goals when you took over? How far have you gone toward realizing them?

Manion: My goal was really to restructure Ramada, bring it back as a well-performing hotel company.

Ramada has always been a large company; it has probably been the third largest hotel company for a number of years and still is.

However, it was not a performing company.

Franchise relations were at an all-time low when I joined the company. The health of the company-owned properties, the management group for the company-owned properties, the attitude of the employees left a lot to be desired. There wasn't a service attitude to any great degree.

I think that when the company got very successful and then went into various other areas that had nothing to do with the travel industry, it lost sight of what its main objective was: to run a fine hotel company.

While we are heavily franchised, we can help the licensees make money in their own investments.

TW: What were the reasons for the slump, in terms of the company's performance?

Manion: It didn't happen overnight. It built over a number of years from about mid-1970.

I believe that in '74, when the crash hit the hospitality industry, Ramada found itself injured considerably.

And there was a change in management where Marion Isbell, the founder of the company, stepped aside and his son took over. It's apparent the company started going downhill at that time and was not able to reverse itself.

It then invested in the gaming business, buying the Tropicana in Las Vegas and then starting the Tropicana in Atlantic City.

Those two ventures caused some serious financial distress from operating losses in Las Vegas and a tremendous overbudget drain in Atlantic City to finish that property.

That, along with the fact that the money was being taken out of the other hotels to feed these investments, continued to take Ramada on a downward slide.

Our properties weren't renovated. If you don't put money back into a hotel every year, it becomes tired very, very quickly because of the massive use.

The company also lost direction in terms of the quality control of its licensee group. The licensees had a negative attitude toward Ramada as things continued to go downhill, and this continued to build. It is just a domino effect.

Finally, in '81, the board saw fit to make a management change, at which time Dick took over to see if there was a way to save the company.

It takes a considerable amount of time to change a company of this size and scope. It's also very difficult

Exhibit 2   *(continued)*

to grab 500 licensees and say, "OK, guys, we're back in the boat now. Get behind us and spend the money to renovate your properties, and let's get it rolling immediately."

You just can't turn the switch that fast. It's a matter of working individually with owners to help them find ways to invest in their property to bring it back.

Ramada invested $65 million in the company-owned properties we elected to keep. We completed that renovation in about three years.

All of the company properties have been totally refurbished. They are all first class operations. Most of the licensee properties have now been totally renovated.

Today we only have 30 properties in our licensee group that do not meet our minimum standards. We still have a number of properties, roughly 100, in some phase of renovation.

These will soon be completed, and 30 properties is not a disastrous number for us.

At the same time the operational reorganization of the company has been going on. We have eliminated a tremendous amount of bureaucracy.

TW: You have eliminated positions?

Manion: Yes, in our headquarters here in Phoenix. Ramada, at one time, had a tremendous number of company-owned properties. As these were sold, the headquarters was not shrunk in size.

In January '85, we had roughly 700 people at our headquarters. We dropped that down to just less than 400 people over the 2½-year period since I arrived.

We eliminated positions that were not necessary. The people were all pretty good, but the jobs weren't necessary for the products we had.

TW: So it was really a streamlining?

Manion: It was a reorganization to take away what you might call interference in the operation of the company.

There were so many people here that when a licensee called to have a question answered no one knew who to give it to. This we eliminated.

We gave each of the executives who were responsible for major functions the authority to make decisions. We made them viable executives who could utilize their ability to bring the company around.

Within a year from the time I arrived, we had brought a service attitude to all areas of our operations. We had put together some of the basic framework to start rebuilding in terms of marketing and advertising

and the product we had to offer.

We have come out with our "new concept" Ramada Inns. We had five open and six more under construction, with another 15 under contract ready to start.

At this stage of the game, Ramada is prepared to take on this over-built industry we are operating in and survive. As our new product comes on line and as those new products mature, the profits on them will [have an] impact on the bottom line of Ramada.

This year the hotel group has exceeded its budget and its bottom-line profit performance for the first time—considerably so—and we anticipate this will continue.

TW: Do you think, as some people have said, that Ramada is a takeover target? There have been rumors, and the Pritzker family, owners of Hyatt Hotels, has purchased a 6 percent stake in the company. Are you nervous about that purchase? Do you view it as a threat or is it viewed merely as an investment?

Manion: I think Ramada is a takeover target. It's a very healthy company today, and in the next three or four years we are going to see the return of our efforts to rebuild this organization.

We are at the threshold of really showing improved bottom lines. So therefore, I think Ramada is a good target.

It is a company I think a lot of people would like to have their hands on.

Ramada is an international hotel company with representation in most of the major markets today with fine new properties, inns, hotels and Renaissance properties.

We have over 100 properties right now operating internationally. That has grown from 32 in 1984—tremendous growth. We will open 18 more properties internationally this year. So the future is very good for Ramada.

Do the Pritzkers want to own it? I don't know. They have said they want to invest in our stock, and that very likely is what they are doing. We have had no other contact with them on that.

TW: Your strategy now is to transform the company from one that owns property into a management company. Is this an outgrowth of the effort to reduce your debt?

Manion: It happens to be what most other hotel companies are doing to get out of asset management. The returns are much higher in a nonasset com-

(continued)

Exhibit 2 *(continued)*

pany where you do not have to invest huge sums of monies into your facilities.

The effort is to use other people's money to build the properties and take a reasonable management fee or the licensee franchise fee and supply those investors with what they need to manage a hotel, run the international marketing organization, the reservations system, support systems, etc. That gives you your best return on your investment.

TW: Will you still own a certain number of hotels?

Manion: Yes. As a matter of fact we are building a number of company-owned properties right now.

These properties are 150 to 180 rooms and run $10 million to $12 million.

TW: These are residential-style properties, similar to the Courtyard by Marriott?

Manion: Yes. We took advantage of a lot of their research and improved it in some areas. But yes, they are very similar.

TW: They are also similar to Howard Johnson's Park Square Inns and Hilton's Hillcrest. Why the decision to build this sort of property? It's got a lot of competition.

Manion: We have always been in the midpriced market. That's what we know best. This property fits that market.

Marriott is actually after our market. They found it to be a very profitable type inn to build, what the traveling public is looking for today, and they started building it.

We, of course, came along a little later. We were not able to venture into these new developments at that time, partially because of the financial problems the company had gone through.

But in 1984 our new concept inn was conceived and we opened our first one in 1986 in Naperville, just outside of Chicago. We now have five open with another five under construction.

So, the reason we did it? It's our market, the midprice market. And we also needed to come up with a new so-called prototype that licensees could build and develop themselves. We needed to make it cost effective so that in today's market—a very overbuilt market and a very difficult time in which to finance new hotels—we can have one that has a good chance of getting financing and of being profitable.

TW: Marriott gave its property a different name. Hilton did the same and so did Howard Johnson. How do you at Ramada market your new inn as something new and appealing, when it still bears the Ramada Inn name?

Manion: Ramada has, as I said, always been in the midprice market. Marriott is trying to get into that market. The Marriott name didn't fit the midprice market, so I am sure that's why they chose a different name.

But we market this as Ramada Inn. We have, while we are developing this, totally rehabbed and rebuilt our Ramada system so that our properties out there are viable, long-term investments.

The existing Ramada Hotels that are in the field have been refurbished; are first class. They compete with anyone else in the market on an equal or better basis and they compete with this hotel.

TW: I understand the company's philosophy is keep everything under the Ramada umbrella.

How does Rodeway [purchased last year] fit in with that philosophy of keeping the same name? This would be a first for Ramada wouldn't it, in terms of having a segment under a different name?

Manion: That is correct. It is a first for Ramada in having something that doesn't have the Ramada name on it.

We chose it because, in our decision to go into the limited service tier, we did not want to confuse the Ramada customer who is used to having a midprice inn or hotel right here, knowing roughly what they are going to get and what they are going to spend and then ending up with another Ramada Hotel down the road that is a limited service, no restaurant, no meeting space, much lower price.

So we say, let's keep them separate, and we looked for a chain that had a name that could fit into the tier. We also wanted to pick up a company that had some distribution so we weren't starting from scratch.

TW: What are your plans for Rodeway?

Manion: Our plans are to take the Rodeway company and make it very aggressive and hard hitting in the marketing area of the limited service tier; to expand it as a franchise company, and to give it the necessary support it hasn't had in the past because of its financial problems.

Exhibit 2 *(continued)*

TW: In terms of your development, is it true you are dropping franchise licenses at a faster rate than you are picking up new license agreements? Does that pose a problem for the company's growth at this time?

Manion: Ramada basically held its own with no growth for three or four years as we eliminated a lot of not only franchise properties but company-owned properties that no longer fit with what we were trying to bring the company back to. So there was a rather stagnant number of properties and number of rooms for three to four years.

In 1986, we increased for the first time the number of rooms in the system. And in 1987, we increased it considerably over the previous year. We now have open and operating in Ramada, roughly 110,000 rooms.

If you will look back to past years, you will find that the replacement properties we brought in have usually been larger properties, particularly in the national marketplaces. So that most properties on the average are coming in roughly at 200 or more rooms where it was much lower before.

So while we have the same number of properties, roughly, the number of rooms was continuing to grow.

We will probably always be at a base of about 30 company-owned properties in the U.S., give or take 3 or 4 over one year or the other, and roughly 30 properties in the international marketplace, not wholly owned international but joint ventures or leases.

TW: In light of the Tax Reform Act and its effect in slowing development, last October's stock market crash and the overbuilt nature of many markets, what do you think the prospects are for development at this time?

Manion: The climate for development right now is not good. But at the same time, that doesn't mean it's not good for the hotel industry. We were tremendously overbuilt. We are still overbuilt. That's not going to change in a period of a year or two.

However, the fact that it is more difficult to develop means there will be fewer properties built and therefore those properties that are in existence will have a chance to come into a more profitable structure. This way they can survive and give the service that is necessary to satisfy the traveling public.

Source: Robin Amster, "Manion Sees New Vitality and Worldwide Role for Ramada Inns," *Travel Weekly,* March 10, 1988. Reprinted with permission from Travel Weekly.

no plans for management changes and hoped to keep on Thomas Martin as CEO.

Proceeds of the sale were to go toward a $7 cash dividend payment to shareholders. Though the terms were not announced, financial analysts estimated that Ramada would fetch no more than $60 million for Marie Callender's Pie Shops Inc. Ramada purchased the chain for $57 million and 2.5 million shares of stock in 1986.

Gaming Group Potential

The gaming group competes in the gaming industry with the operation of four casinos. It is headed by Paul Rubeli, who is also an executive vice president. Rubeli joined Ramada in 1979 as group vice president, industrial operations, and was named executive vice president, gaming, in 1982. Prior to joining Ramada, Rubeli was an industrial engineer. Despite his relative lack of experience in gaming, Rubeli is highly thought of not only in Ramada but also in the gaming industry.

The casino group for Ramada continued to be a major factor. The newly expanded Atlantic City hotel and casino was in 1985 the largest in the city. It features a 90,000-square-foot casino and 1,000 hotel rooms. This $200 million addition to the Atlantic City casino hotel included a two-acre theme park (indoor), a 508-room guest tower, a 26,000-square-foot convention center, and 37,000 square feet of additional casino space. The completion of the expansion plus the improved infrastructure of Atlantic City (Atlantic City is expanding its airport, widening the freeway system, and implementing a street traffic control system) should greatly improve Ramada's gaming revenues.

In 1984 Ramada invested over $70 million to expand and transform its Las Vegas Tropicana into a world-class resort and convention center. This work, completed in 1986, included a new 806-room guest tower and a five-acre tropical theme water park.

The Ramada casino in Reno, Nevada, incorporates a 1950s theme into an existing gaming facility. The building consists of a 35,000-square-foot casino but does not include hotel rooms. The casino opened in 1987 and was named Eddie's Fabulous 50's Casino.

In addition, Ramada owns a casino in Laughlin, Nevada, which it developed into a 406-room hotel, a 30,000-square-foot casino, five restaurants and lounges, and a 1,500-car parking facility in 1988. It was named the Ramada Express Hotel and Casino.

Some analysts felt that Ramada could quadruple its net income in 1989 and 1990 through its gaming group, which had been labeled the jewel in Ramada's crown.

Merck: Strategy Making in "America's Most Admired Corporation"

Merck and Company is, perhaps, America's best kept corporate secret. Selected by Fortune 1000 executives—for four consecutive years—as "America's Most Admired Corporation," Merck is hardly a household name. But, Merck knows how to compete effectively and how to do the right things right. Merck is driven by an ambition to be on the cutting edge of research and development in its industry and by an obsession with building quality into its products. This dual goal pervades every aspect of the firm's culture, managerial decision making, and organizational structure. Guided by an innovative (or more appropriately, a visionary) chief executive officer (CEO), Merck is determined to remain the leading pharmaceutical company in the United States.

What does it take to build "America's Most Admired Corporation"? This case provides some clues to the secret of one of the most successful companies in modern American history. This case shows how carefully crafted strategies, orchestrated by a visionary and dedicated leader, can pay off. But, to understand Merck's secrets, let us first examine how the company came into existence.

History

Merck's roots can be traced as far back as 1668 when the Merck family bought an apothecary in

Case prepared by Shaker A. Zahra, Robert Lewis, Richard Hubbard, Jr., and William D. Schulte, Jr. of George Mason University. Reprinted with permission.

Darmstadt, Germany. More than 150 years later the Merck family decided to complement their apothecary by manufacturing their own drugs. In 1827 this decision became a reality when they opened a manufacturing operation in Darmstadt, Germany. The Merck family brought their drug manufacturing expertise to the United States in 1887 by opening a branch in New York. Shortly thereafter, in 1891, the Merck & Company partnership was formed in New York. Merck started manufacturing drugs and specialty chemicals in Rahway, New Jersey in 1903. In 1908, Merck & Company incorporated in New York and later, in 1919, they sold stock to the public for the first time. By 1941 Merck & Company had established manufacturing facilities throughout the United States.

As Merck & Company was growing throughout the U.S., another competitor, Sharp & Dohme, was following close behind. In 1845 Sharp opened an apothecary in Baltimore and later in 1860 formed a partnership with Dohme. While Merck was building expertise in manufacturing, Sharp and Dohme concentrated heavily on research. Today's Merck & Company was formed in 1953 by a merger with Sharp & Dohme. Other acquisitions and divestments followed, but this merger established Merck's current philosophy, excellence in research and manufacturing of pharmaceuticals and specialty chemicals. Indeed, Merck defines its business as "a world-wide, research-intensive health products company that discovers, develops, produces, and markets human and animal health products and specialty chemicals" (Annual Report, 1988).

Industry Groups and Businesses

Merck competes primarily in two industry segments: Human and Animal Health products, and Specialty Chemicals. The contribution to sales for 1988 for each of these segments is presented in Exhibit 1.

Specialty Chemicals

This group offers a wide variety of products that include: xantham gum, a biogum with various uses including oil field applications; Epi-Lock and Synthaderm, polyurethane wound dressings; and several water treatment related products including pHreeGUARD, BoilerGUARD and POL-E-Z. In addition, the group provides special software applications to maximize the efficiency of water treatment facilities.

Specialty Chemicals products are used in a wide variety of applications. The most common uses are water treatment, food processing, and skin care. Merck entered the specialty chemicals market in 1968 when they acquired Calgon Corporation. Calgon's main business was the manufacturing of water treatment products and providing related services. In 1972 Merck strengthened its position in specialty chemicals by acquiring the Kelco company. Kelco mainly produced alginates and xantham gum. Today, Merck's specialty chemical products come from the Kelco Division, Calgon Vestal Labs, and Calgon Water Management Division.

Products and services from the Specialty Chemicals group are sold in channels of trade including industrial users, distributors, wholesalers, municipalities, and utilities. The group has been making steady gains in its segment. Exhibit 2 reflects sales of the group over the last couple of years.

Human and Animal Health Products

Most of Merck's income comes from the Human and Animal Health products segment. Within this segment Merck's products can be grouped into eight primary categories, as illustrated in Exhibit 3 which lists their contributions to company sales in 1988.

Merck's human products include therapeutic and preventive preparations, generally sold by prescription. Merck sells prescription drugs through its professional representatives to drug wholesalers and retailers, physicians, veterinarians, hospitals, clinics, government agencies, and other institutions. Merck prides itself on the knowledge and competence of its detail men. A new sales recruit can expect to be in training for two years, which includes technical training equivalent to that provided by many medical schools.

The cardiovascular medications, particularly Vasotec, are the flag ship products of the Merck line. Vasotec, originally developed as a blood pressure reducer, was approved in 1988 for treatment of congestive heart failure patients. Sales in 1988 for Vasotec alone were nearly $1 billion. Mevacor and Zocor, which have not received FDA approval, are two additional cardiovascular products with billion dollar futures. Both are medications used to reduce cholesterol levels, and analysts expect that these two drugs will contribute in excess of a billion dollars a year by 1990.[1]

Pepcid, a once a day treatment for peptic ulcers, had made great strides on the once sacred grounds of SmithKline's Tagamet. Pepcid now contributes well over $100 million in annual sales, and is being prescribed more often than Tagamet and Glaxo's Zantac.[2]

Antibiotic medications are another area where Merck's commitment to research is paying off. The product Primaxin currently has the broadest spectrum of antimicrobial activity of any antibiotic yet marketed.

Overall, Merck has 15 drugs currently producing annual revenues in excess of $100 million each.

Financial Performance

The pharmaceutical industry tends to be somewhat immune to most economic conditions. Rather, demographics and public interest in health related issues, such as cholesterol reduction, have a greater influence on the industry.

In the late '70s and early '80s Merck lost its number one position in the industry to Bristol-Myers because several of their drugs came off patent protection.[3] Merck maintained a focus on long-term strategies rather than on the short-term, by spending a significant amount of both time and money to develop new products. This long-term view is credited with bringing Merck through the difficult times of the early '80s and back to the top of the pharmaceutical industry. Table 1 presents selected financial data for the period 1978–1988.

In addition to excellent financial performance, Merck has managed to maintain an impressive rate of growth in sales in recent years, as shown in Exhibit 4.

Between 1981 and 1985, Merck's profits grew by an average of only 8 percent; the rest of the industry enjoyed rates in excess of 15 percent.[4] The reason for this gap between Merck and industry performance was simple; some of Merck's cash cow drugs were coming off patent and the company was losing sales to increasing generic competition both domestic and abroad. Rather than seeking a "quick-fix" Merck stepped up R&D to protect its long term survival. As a result, Merck's earnings have made a strong comeback and currently lead the industry. Exhibit 5 depicts Merck's progressive growth and recent surge in earnings. Clearly, Merck's ROI also has far outpaced the industry average in recent years. Exhibit 6 compares Merck and the pharmaceutical industry as a whole.

In addition to classic measures of performance, such as earnings growth, ROI and net profit margin, Merck has been "America's Most Admired Corporation" four years running in *Fortune* magazine's annual feature of the same title. *Fortune* polls 8,000 top executives and financial analysts and asks them to rank companies in their industry in eight categories:

- quality of management;
- quality of products or services;
- innovativeness;
- long-term investment value;
- financial soundness;
- community and environmental responsibility;
- use of corporate assets; and
- ability to attract, develop, and keep talented people

For the fourth consecutive year, Merck has received the highest cumulative score compared to the 300 largest corporations in America.

Foreign Trade Contribution

The pharmaceutical industry as a whole, and Merck in particular, have a favorable impact on the burgeoning U.S. trade deficit. Historically, Merck has had large favorable trade balances and in 1988 Merck had a favorable balance of approximately $850 million. This can be attributed to Merck's aggressive global push for growth, and the recent weakening of the dollar. Exhibit 7 shows both domestic and foreign sales for 1988.

Management

The current style and attitude of management at Merck & Company can be attributed directly to the efforts of the CEO, Dr. P. Roy Vagelos. Ironically, Vagelos grew up working at his parent's luncheonette that was located within walking distance from the Merck plant in Rahway, New Jersey. Listening to the scientists' discussions over lunch inspired Vagelos to seek a career in medicine. Vagelos worked as an intern in Merck's labs while attending medical school at Columbia University. After completing medical school he spent the next 20 years in basic research and teaching. In 1976 he joined Merck & Company as head of the research division.

When Vagelos joined Merck, the research division was not productive and "the company had not produced a big winner for a decade or more."[5] Vagelos determined that this lack of production was due to a lack of direction. Scrapping dubious projects, Vagelos began financing only major programs directed at discovering drugs that would cure known diseases.[6]

After pointing the research division in the right direction he sought to perfect it by hiring the most talented people money could buy. He proceeded to recruit eminent university scientists. To entice these scientists, Vagelos created a "campus like" atmosphere and offered outstanding salaries. His background as a scientist at Washington University and his other academic credentials made him credible to those he wanted to hire. Vagelos also made sure that researchers had first rate facilities which was rare in private industry. Vagelos sums up his recruiting philosophy as follows: "We don't always get our man, but we have never missed hiring someone we wanted because of money."[7]

Vagelos became the CEO of Merck in 1985. His management practices then spread from the research division to the entire company. Vagelos refuses to rest on his string of successes. After the news on September 1, 1987, that the FDA approved the Merck drug Mevacor, Vagelos phoned the scientist that had developed Mevacor to congratulate him. In the same conversation he also asked the scientist how they were coming on possible substitutes. "Instead of running Merck defensively, avoiding risks and letting its current successes carry it along, he is driving the company just as hard today as he did when he became research chief 12 years ago. For all Merck's momentum, Vagelos is making sure it runs scared."[8]

The most significant feat that Vagelos has accomplished at Merck was gaining the respect of his employees. The employees realize that Vagelos is both a capable scientist and manager. As a result, they do not spend time second guessing strategic decisions; instead, they concentrate their efforts on supporting and implementing the decisions. A significant indication of his appropriate style and capabilities as a CEO is the aforementioned fact that Merck has been "America's Most Admired Corporation" four years in a row. When the top executives from America's 300 largest corporations rate your quality of management at the top of all industries four years in a row, that indicates that you are doing something right![9]

Human Resources

Excellence in management and development of their employees worldwide is of strategic importance to Merck. Vagelos' strategy is to, "Hire the best, provide the best training, and encourage professional growth."[10] Merck's managers and supervisors have the responsibility to establish and maintain work environments where people receive appropriate responsibility for their jobs, understand their objectives, and feel they are treated fairly.

Research is the lifeblood of Merck, and recruiting and retaining of top researchers is key to the continuing success of Merck. Merck has worked very hard to set up their labs and research divisions to erase the stigma most academics usually associate with moving from academia to industry.[11] Merck's research labs employ over 3320 people, representing more than 10% of the company's total work force. The researchers and scientists working in these labs enjoy a casual atmosphere, moving around the lab grounds in white coats and jeans, and have one of the best compensation packages in the industry. Vagelos places recruiting of top researchers at the top of his priority list. For example, to recruit Leslie Iversen, a British biochemist, and one of the world's leading researchers in Alzheimer's and other neurological diseases, Merck built a 122-person neuroscience research center in Harlowe, Essex, a short distance from Iversen's home.[12]

In addition to active pursuit of the best employees available, Merck also takes progressive approaches to ensure their employees' job satisfaction. The turnover rate at Merck averages only 5 percent. Flexible schedules, day care facilities, and work-at-home arrangements are a few examples of what Merck does to create a pleasant working environment for their employees. In particular, Merck has adopted changes in policy to reflect the changing demographics of the work force, more specifically the two worker family, and the resulting need for quality day care. For example, Merck will hold a position for new mothers and fathers who go on unpaid leave for up to 18 months after the birth of a child, six times longer than most other companies. At the company's main facilities in Rahway, N.J., employees can get day care for their infants at facilities started by Merck, for a price based on the employee's salary level.[13]

Merck has also developed a fair performance appraisal system. In response to declining company performance during the early eighties, Merck created a task force to identify factors responsible for these problems. The major conclusion of the task force was the overwhelming employee dissatisfaction with the company's current performance appraisal system and salary administration programs. In fact, the biggest single complaint was the lack of real reward distinction between the outstanding performers and the average performers.

To remedy the situation, Merck implemented a new appraisal system that evaluates employees' performance in three categories: specific job measures and ongoing duties, planned objectives, and management of people.[14] The third category, management of people, was added because employees and managers at all levels of the company felt that managers were primarily rewarded for their technical abilities, but that their managerial abilities were ignored. This is a common problem in technically driven companies, that are managed by technicians.

A distribution target for performance ratings was established to help managers rate the em-

ployees in relation to their peers. This essentially produced a two-step evaluation process; first, an employee's performance is measured against objectives and ongoing duties, and then his/her performance is compared with the performance of other employees in the same area of the company.

Salary guidelines have also been established that define salary ranges for each position, and the level and frequency of increase that may be given for each category of performance.

Organization and Structure

Merck & Company is divided into several divisions. Merck Sharp & Dohme (MSD) is responsible for the marketing and administration of Merck's human pharmaceuticals. This division employs approximately 2500 people. The majority of these employees are Merck's Professional Representatives who present Merck's product line of human pharmaceuticals to physicians, pharmacists, and hospitals.

MSD's counterpart for the animal health markets is MSD AGVET. MSD AGVET is responsible for marketing and administration of agricultural products in addition to animal health products.

Merck Sharp and Dohme Research Laboratories is the division responsible for the discovery and development of compounds for both MSD and MSD AGVET.

Merck Pharmaceutical Manufacturing Division (MPMD) is the manufacturing arm of Merck & Company. This is the largest division, employing 5400 people.

Merck & Company shows signs of backward integration in their Merck Chemical Manufacturing Division (MCMD), which produces bulk chemicals used by MPMD, in addition to making chemicals for sale to the public. Merck has a few smaller subsidiaries, such as Calgon Corporation, but the divisions outlined above represent the major business of Merck & Company.

Merck's divisions and departments interact

frequently with each other. This is no accident. Because Merck's dedication to research is the gospel according to Vagelos, the company has a unique informal structure. Vagelos purposely instituted a free atmosphere so that his scientists would not be restricted by formal authority. For example, a research team must sell their idea to functional groups from whom they need assistance on their projects. These functional groups, or units, are allocated development money to invest in projects of their choice. "The idea is to gain greater collegiality and unity of purpose. As a consensus develops around a project, it gains support intellectually and financially from the team's members."[15] The flexibility and freedom of Merck's structure are what make their research department, and thus the whole company, thrive.

A second important area that a research project must gain support from is the marketing function. In fact, marketing is second in importance only to research at Merck. With the advent of new products and the continued success of existing products, Merck has added sales personnel and restructured their sales force. Prior to 1988, Merck had 1600 sales representatives divided into two groups. However, Merck soon realized that this organization was not adequately promoting their products. As a result, in 1988 they increased their sales force by one-third and created three general groups of 550 representatives and a fourth group of 430 representatives to specialize in hospital products. Each representative in the general groups has one to three products to sell. This permits salespeople to develop thorough knowledge of their products.

Manufacturing and Operations

As mentioned above, Merck has two manufacturing divisions, MCMD and MPMD. MCMD is responsible for producing specialty chemicals for the market and bulk chemicals used by the MPMD. Merck believes in quality. The MCMD facilities are "state of the art." For example, the

Elkton, Virginia plant uses robotic technology to ensure high quality. "This system guides a product sample through testing and returns the results electronically to the plant floor, minimizing response time and handling errors."[16] Safety is another important issue at Merck. The MCMD was recognized by the Chemical Manufacturing Association for having the best safety record of all firms having over 20 million hours of exposure.

This same commitment to quality and safety also applies to the MPMD. The MPMD produces products for direct human consumption; therefore, quality control is imperative. Since the MPMD receives almost all of its raw materials from the MCMD, management believes it is imperative that both divisions produce a quality product. The MPMD also ensures quality through "state of the art" technology. As an example, Merck's plant at West Point, Pennsylvania, uses a unique Vision System. This system uses computer imaging to measure the accuracy of labeling. The MPMD is starting to design new packaging techniques to make them more consumer oriented. Merck has also instituted modular designs in both manufacturing divisions so they can be used to produce more than one product.

Merck has consistently invested large amounts of capital in their manufacturing divisions, resulting in model facilities. However, this financial commitment has apparently peaked. Merck feels that their facilities are the best available and, therefore, are starting to turn their financial attention to their research laboratories and new administrative offices. Their facilities are now completely modular and therefore can be more productive and adaptive to changes in the market. Also, the new high potency medicines do not require the complex production facilities of the past, primarily because they do not require as many different raw materials. For these reasons, management believes that reductions in capital expenditures on plant facilities without compromising their productive output are possible.

Merck's manufacturing focus in the future

will center on five objectives. First, Merck will still ensure that preventative maintenance occurs where necessary. Second, the company will provide expansion to support new products after careful review of existing plant capacities. Third, they will maintain their commitment to a clean environment and employee safety. Fourth, they will continue to look for ways to increase productivity through advances in process technology. Last and most important, they will continue their dedication to producing the highest quality products possible.

Major Competitors

The pharmaceutical industry is very competitive; no single company holds a dominant market share position. In this industry, it appears that gaining market share is not directly correlated to an increase in profitability. But, gaining market share is the result of successful product differentiation.

Merck's major domestic competitors include Abbott Labs, American Home Products, Eli Lilly, Johnson & Johnson, Squibb, Warner-Lambert, Syntex, and Schering-Plough. In particular, Merck is currently engaged in fierce competition with Squibb in the anti-hypertensive market. Merck's Vasotec competes head to head with Squibb's highly successful Capoten. Capoten sales continue to grow at about 26% per year; Vasotec sales are accelerating and are expected to exceed Capoten's level of sales.[17] The outcome of this battle is particularly crucial for Squibb since Capoten accounts for more than 40% of its sales. Both drugs have exceeded the billion dollar mark in annual sales, a feat accomplished by only three other drugs.

The primary competition from outside the U.S. comes from Glaxo Holdings, Hoescht, Ciba-Geigy, each with about 3% of the global market, and from Sankyo, a Japanese firm. Merck's current goal is to expand its global market share, but each of the above firms uses the Merck formula, which consists of plenty of R&D and successful product differentiation.

In 1989, the pharmaceutical industry in which Merck competed was fiercely competitive. Exhibit 8 shows that the top four companies accounted for nearly 25% of industry sales.

Exhibit 9 illustrates the correlation between market share and profitability, as measured by return on investment (ROI).

Instead of building market shares within the pharmaceutical industry, key competitors opted to diversify into the related health care industry. Many of these companies believed that they could better serve "the changing health care industry as a diversified supplier of health aids, from drugs to equipment."

The push for diversification among pharmaceutical companies began in the 1970s, intensified throughout the 1980s, and was expected to continue well into the 1990s.

In the '70s pharmaceutical companies began purchasing consumer products companies in an effort to diversify. For example, Warner-Lambert bought Entenmann's, a bakery products company, and American Optical, an eyeglass manufacturer, and Squibb purchased Lifesavers, a candy manufacturer. Toward the '80s, after displaying a dismal record of success with their consumer products acquisitions, many of the companies began shedding these units and investing in companies in other health care type businesses. For example, Warner-Lambert shed Entenmann's and used the proceeds to purchase IMED Corp., a medical technology firm.[18]

Finally, in the mid '80s the pharmaceutical companies began divesting their unprofitable attempts at diversification, and funneling the proceeds back into their strengths, R&D and new product marketing. Divesting these units left many companies with large cash reserves. A survey of estimated cash and liquid reserves of major pharmaceutical companies at the end of 1986 included: Merck with $1.5 billion, Bristol-Myers with $1.3 billion, Pfizer with $1.4 billion, and Eli Lilly with $800 million.[19] This enabled these companies to invest heavily in R&D and marketing. Yet, these cash reserves, coupled with the industry's historically high profit margins, also made these companies targets for takeover bids. As a result, many companies instituted stock repurchase plans as a defensive measure.

A summary of key acquisitions and divestitures in this time period is listed below:

1985—GD Searle Corp. is bought by Monsanto
  —Sterling Drugs is bought by Eastman Kodak
  —Richardson Vicks is bought by Procter & Gamble
  —Bristol-Myers buys Genetic Systems Corp., a developer of diagnostic and therapeutic products
1986—Warner-Lambert sells off 3 medical equipment businesses
  —Squibb sells off its Charles of the Ritz cosmetic and fragrance unit
1987—Eli Lilly sells off its Elizabeth Arden cosmetics unit, and announces stock repurchase plan
  —SmithKline Beckman repurchases 12.6 million of its outstanding shares

What is the effect of these mergers, acquisitions, and divestments on the structure of the industry? Experts do not expect significant changes in the level of concentration in the industry. Rather, they predict that these companies will have to compete differently.

Product Differentiation

Fierce competition in the industry is in many ways a manifestation of product differentiation, through R&D spending and marketing activities.

Research and Development

Exhibit 10 depicts the strong positive association between R&D spending and corporate ROI. While not perfectly linear, the exhibit shows that spending on R&D is associated with superior corporate financial performance.

Table 2 presents data on R&D spending by major companies in the industry. During the pe-

riod from 1983 to 1987, Merck consistently ranked first among the leading 16 companies in terms of R&D spending.

Statistics on R&D indicated that spending by pharmaceutical companies was one of the highest among U.S. major industries, rising from 11.3% as a percent of sales to 15.1% over the past decade. Statistics also show that about 70% of drug R&D in this country was funded directly by domestic pharmaceutical manufacturers, 10% by colleges and universities (often in conjunction with leading drug companies), and 20% by government and other sources.[20] These percentages translate to $5.4 billion spent in R&D in 1987 up from $1.4 billion in 1978.

Industry experts considered R&D spending to be essential for effective, sustainable product differentiation. Being the first to introduce new drugs yielded a rewarding financial performance.

In addition, Ronald Bond and David Lean (1977) concluded that the original seller's "persistent dominance in the face of competition from cheaper, more highly-promoted substitute drugs would suggest that the product differentiation advantage of being first with a 'breakthrough' is very substantial."[21]

Exhibit 11 illustrates the number of new drugs that received FDA approval over the last 13 years. These approvals represented a major milestone by companies achieving them, and often served as a barrier to entry.[22]

Marketing and Advertising

Advertising is important in the pharmaceutical industry to build brand recognition with the public for proprietary drugs and to build brand recognition and loyalty with physicians for ethical drugs. In a study in 1981, Mier Statman concluded that physicians had come to identify the drugs with specific brand names so that the original seller maintained most of its prior market position even after patent expiration.[23]

Pharmaceutical companies accomplished brand loyalty for ethical drugs mainly through direct sales, which built strong relationships with physicians. These salesmen, called "detail men," were a valuable source of information for physicians. In fact, the Kefauver committee challenged the pharmaceutical industry's selling expenses claiming that they were too high and recommended that they be reduced to provide a savings for the consumer. The industry countered that significant expenditures went into training the detail men sufficiently to serve as a reliable resource to physicians. The physicians stood behind the industry by testifying that the detail men provided important information and that the physician relied heavily on the detail men to stay abreast of the changes in available drugs.

These marketing efforts comprise approximately 20% of sales.[24] "Traditional product advertising in scientific journals accounts for 24% of advertising efforts, direct mail about 6%, and detail staff for another 20%."[25] Table 3 presents data on advertising expenditures by the leading 15 pharmaceutical companies during the 1983–1987 period.

Industry Performance and Outlook

During 1975–1985, industry revenues grew at an annual average rate of 8%, as illustrated in Exhibit 12. Exhibit 13 compares industry performance, measured by return on equity (ROE), to the average achieved by all U.S. industries during the 1983–1988 period. Exhibit 14 compares the pharmaceutical industry to all other industries using net profit margin as a measure of performance.

Merck faces several major threats in the industry. First, as mentioned, the industry is fiercely competitive. In recent years, foreign companies have posed the greatest threat to Merck. Foreign companies are not only active in marketing and distributing their products in the U.S., but they are also involved in joint ventures that will solidify their competitive position.

Second, since 1984 the government has undertaken many steps that may weaken industry innovativeness. The effect of government actions was to reduce the time span of patent protection, thus making it easier for other firms to manufacture generic drugs.

Third, the ever rising growth of the generic drug industry is a major threat facing the industry. Firms in this industry (a few of which may also produce branded drugs) make copies of unpatented drugs and sell them under a generic name at a lower price than the branded drugs. The branded only drug firms are vehemently opposed to generic drugs and claim that many of the generic drugs are not bioequivalent to the branded drug. In fact, "the FDA has acknowledged that, of the 6000 marketed generic drugs listed in its Approved Drug Products with Therapeutic Equivalence Evaluations, about 20 percent have not been determined by the Agency to be therapeutically equivalent to the pioneer products."[26] Despite the controversy, the generic drug industry is capturing an increasingly larger share of the prescription drug market without having to spend any significant amount of money in research and development. Currently generic drugs account for about 23% of all prescriptions.[27]

Opportunities

The above threats notwithstanding, Merck is positioned to explore many promising opportunities in the U.S. and abroad. Continuing its tradition of extensive R&D, Merck can target specific market groups, such as senior citizens, or continue its current strategy. Additionally, Merck's excellent reputation makes it an attractive candidate for strategic alliances in the U.S. or abroad. Opportunities appear limitless for Merck. Still, the question Merck's executives must answer in the 1990s is: how much emphasis should the firm give its pharmaceutical core business?

Notes

1. Byrne, John, "The Miracle Company," *Business Week*, October 19, 1987, pp. 84–89.

2. Annual Report, p. 28.

3. Staff Writer, "Merck; admirable, but . . .," *The Economist*, Jan 17, 1987, pp. 61–62.

4. Eklund, Christopher, and Green, Cynthia, "A Research Whiz Steps Up From the Lab," *Business Week*, Jun 24, 1985, pp. 87–88.

5. Quickel, Stephen, "The Drug Culture," *Business Month*, December 1987, p. 36.

6. Ibid.

7. Ibid.

8. Quickel, Stephen, "Merck & Company—Sheer Energy," *Business Month*, December 1988, p. 36.

9. Schultz, Ellen, "America's Most Admired Corporations," *Fortune*, January 18, 1988, p. 36.

10. Annual Report, p. 34.

11. Staff Writer, "Giving Free Rein to Merck's Best and Brightest," *Business Week*, Oct 19, 1987, p. 90.

12. Quickel, Stephen, "The Drug Culture," *Business Month*, December 1987, p. 36.

13. Staff Writer, "The Flexible Work Force; What Organizations Think," *Personnel Administrator*, Aug 1986, pp. 36–40.

14. Wagel, William H., "Performance Appraisal With a Difference," *Personnel*, Feb 1987, pp. 4–7.

15. Byrne, John, "The Miracle Company," *Business Week*, Oct 19, 1987, p. 86.

16. Annual Report, p. 22.

17. Benway, Susan, "Don't Look Back, Squibb–A Giant is Gaining on You," *Business Week*, Oct 10, 1988, pp. 68–71.

18. Ibid.

19. Staff Writer, "Prospects Continue Strong," *Standard & Poor's Industry Surveys*, Apr 1987, p. H19.

20. Staff Writer, "Industry Has Prescription for Success," *Standard & Poor's Industry Surveys*, June 1988, p. H19.

21. Comanor, William S., "The Political Economy of the Pharmaceutical Industry," *Journal of Economic Literature*, Vol. XXIV, Sep 1986, p. 1188.

22. Pharmaceutical Manufacturers Association, "Pharmaceutical Research: Delivering Value in the Cost Containment Era," 1988, p. 27.

23. Comanor, William S., "The Political Economy of the Pharmaceutical Industry," *Journal of Economic Literature*, Vol. XXIV, Sep 1986, p. 1189.

24. Kangilaski, Joan, "Drug Companies Reach into Mixed Marketing Bag," *Advertising Age*, Oct 24, 1985, p. 35.

25. Ibid.

26. Mossinghoff, Gerald J., "Generic Drugs," Pharmaceutical Manufacturers Association.

27. Ibid.

Bibliography

Benway, Susan, "Don't Look Back, Squibb–A Giant is Gaining on You," *Business Week*, Oct 10, 1988, pp. 68–71.

Byrne, John, "The Miracle Company," *Business Week*, October 19, 1987, pp. 84–89.

Colford, Steven W., "CBS Readies for Prescription Drug Ads," *Advertising Age*, Nov 11, 1985, p. 12+.

Colford, Steven W., "New Rx for Drug Ads," *Advertising Age*, Aug 7, 1985, p. 1+.

Comanor, William S., "The Political Economy of the Pharmaceutical Industry," *Journal of Economic Literature*, Vol. XXIV, Sep 1986, pp. 1178–1217.

Davenport, Carol, "America's Most Admired Corporations," *Fortune*, Jan 30, 1989, pp. 68–82.

Eckholm, Erik, "River Blindness—Conquering an Ancient Scourge," *The New York Times Magazine*, Jan 8, 1989, pp. 1–6.

Eklund, Christopher, and Green, Cynthia, "A Research Whiz Steps Up From the Lab," *Business Week*, Jun 24, 1985, pp. 87–88.

Kangilaski, Joan, "Drug Companies Reach into Mixed Marketing Bag," *Advertising Age*, Oct 24, 1985, pp. 35–36.

Liebenau, Jonathan, "Innovation in Pharmaceuticals: Industrial R&D in the Early Twentieth Century," Research Policy, Vol. 14, 1985, pp. 179–187.

McCabe, E.F., "Merck Responds to Market Changes: A University Learns its Lessons," *Management Review*, Jan 1987, pp. 56–60.

Mossinghoff, Gerald J., "Generic Drugs," Pharmaceutical Manufacturers Association.

Schultz, Ellen, "America's Most Admired Corporations," *Fortune*, Jan 18, 1988, p. 36.

Smith, Lee, "Merck Has an Ache in Japan," *Fortune*, March 18, 1985, pp. 42–46.

"Merck; admirable, but . . .," *The Economist*, Jan 17, 1987, pp. 61–62.

"Giving Free Rein to Merck's Best and Brightest," *Business Week*, Oct 19, 1987, p. 90.

"The Flexible Work Force; What Organizations Think," *Personnel Administrator*, Aug 1986, pp. 36–40.

"Drugs Need New Boffins," *The Economist*, July 16, 1988, p. 12.

"Profit Outlook Remains Favorable," Standard & Poor's Industry Surveys, Jan 1975, pp. H13–H19.

"Steady Growth in Shipments Likely," Standard & Poor's Industry Surveys, July 1980, pp. H12–H18.

"Wall Street High on Drug Firms," Standard & Poor's Industry Surveys, March 1986, pp. H17–H24.

"Prospects Continue Strong," Standard & Poor's Industry Surveys, April 1987, pp. H17–H24.

"Industry Has Prescription for Success," Standard & Poor's Industry Surveys, June 1988, pp. H17–H27.

Quickel, Stephen, "Merck & Company—Sheer Energy," *Business Month*, December 1988, p. 36.

Quickel, Stephen, "The Drug Culture," *Business Month*, December 1987, p. 36.

Wagel, William H., "Performance Appraisal With a Difference," *Personnel*, Feb 1987, pp. 4–7.

Waldholz, Michael, "Merck and Johnson & Johnson to Form Venture for Over-The-Counter Medicines," *The Wall Street Journal*, March 29, 1989, p. A4.

Value Line Industry Profile, "Drug Industry," *Value Line*, Feb 10, 1989, p. 1253.

Additional Sources

"About Merck" (Internal Publication).

Merck's 1988 Annual Report.

"Manufacturing Strategy," *Merck World* (Internal Publication).

Pharmaceutical Manufacturers Association, "Facts at a Glance," May 1987.

Pharmaceutical Manufacturers Association, "Fulfilling the Promise," 1987.

Pharmaceutical Manufacturers Association, "Pharmaceutical Research: Delivering Value in the Cost Containment Era," 1988.

Pharmaceutical Manufacturers Association, "Reporters' Handbook for the Prescription Drug Industry," 1989.

Industry Analyses

Bagemary, Anne, "Drugs," *Forbes*, Jan 2, 1984, pp. 245–246.

Fritz, Michael, "Health," *Forbes*, Jan 12, 1987, pp. 141–142.

Fritz, Michael, "Health," *Forbes*, Jan 11 1988, pp. 140–142.

Fritz, Michael, "Health," *Forbes*, Jan 9, 1989, pp. 150–151.

King, Ralph, "Health," *Forbes*, Jan 13, 1986, pp. 154–155.

"Health Care," *Forbes*, Jan 14, 1985, pp. 154–155.

Table 1 Financial Ratios

	1988	1987	1986	1985	1984	1983	1982	1981	1980	1979	1978
Sales / Total assets	96.93	89.10	80.87	72.36	77.54	77.01	83.79	88.31	94.02	90.01	86.98
Total debt / Total assets	2.33	2.94	3.28	3.48	3.90	9.14	9.22	7.26	7.27	8.06	9.27
Net income / Sales	20.30	17.90	16.40	15.20	13.80	13.90	13.60	13.60	15.20	16.00	15.50
Net income / Total assets	20.40	16.80	13.50	11.40	11.20	11.50	11.90	12.80	15.00	15.50	14.40
ROE	42.26	42.82	26.59	20.70	19.57	18.71	19.04	20.13	22.56	23.21	21.41
Mktg exp / Sales	31.61	33.23	30.76	28.44	26.56	27.88	29.13	28.58	27.90	28.06	27.99
R&D exp / Sales	11.26	11.18	11.62	12.02	11.04	10.97	10.45	9.36	8.56	7.89	8.15

Table 2 R&D Expenditures

	1983 $	1983 Rank	1984 $	1984 Rank	1985 $	1985 Rank	1986 $	1986 Rank	1987 $	1987 Rank	Average $	Average Rank
Merck	356.0	1	393.1	1	426.3	1	479.8	1	565.7	1	444.2	1
Eli Lilly	293.6	2	341.3	2	369.8	2	427.0	2	466.3	2	379.6	2
SmithKline Beckman	264.7	3	279.2	3	309.6	3	376.9	3	423.7	3	330.8	3
Pfizer	227.2	5	252.3	5	286.7	4	335.5	4	401.0	4	300.5	4
Upjohn	229.2	4	258.2	4	284.1	5	314.1	5	355.5	6	288.2	5
Bristol-Myers	185.3	7	212.4	8	261.7	6	311.1	6	341.7	7	262.4	6
American Cyanamid	214.7	6	236.8	6	250.6	7	278.3	8	313.6	8	258.8	7
Abbott Labs	184.5	8	218.7	7	240.6	8	284.9	7	361.3	5	258.0	8
American Home Prods.	161.2	10	183.7	10	217.3	9	227.1	9	247.3	10	207.3	9
Warner-Lambert	175.0	9	194.9	9	208.2	10	202.3	11	231.8	11	202.4	10
Schering-Plough	144.7	11	163.6	11	175.4	11	212.1	10	250.7	9	189.3	11
Squibb	141.7	12	150.6	12	165.7	12	163.0	12	221.4	12	168.5	12
AH Robins	40.7	13	43.4	13	52.4	13	51.8	15	58.4	15	49.3	13
Marion Labs	21.6	16	32.2	14	42.7	14	52.8	14	81.5	14	46.2	14
Rorer Group	25.7	14	29.5	15	17.9	16	69.7	13	81.8	13	44.9	15
Bausch & Lomb	23.6	15	18.2	16	21.5	15	25.7	16	26.5	16	23.1	16

Table 3　Advertising Expenditures

	1983		1984		1985		1986		1987		Average	
	$	% sls	$	% sls	$	% sls	$	% sls	$	% sls	$	% sls
Abbott Labs	70.3	2.4	77.5	2.5	87.2	2.6	94.4	2.5	135.3	3.1	92.9	2.6
AH Robins	64.2	11.4	72.8	11.5	86.8	12.3	95.5	12.1	109.7	12.8	85.8	12.1
American Home Prods.	409.9	8.4	412.0	9.2	408.1	8.7	441.3	9.0	447.3	8.9	423.7	8.8
Bausch & Lomb	27.8	4.9	29.3	5.5	36.5	6.2	40.1	5.7	77.3	9.2	42.2	6.5
Bristol-Myers	651.4	16.6	743.8	17.8	775.9	17.5	820.4	17.0	918.7	17.0	782.0	17.2
Eli Lilly	47.6	1.6	49.5	1.6	47.6	1.5	49.4	1.3	29.9	0.8	44.8	1.3
Marion Labs	23.2	12.8	28.2	12.5	41.4	14.0	58.8	14.7	62.5	10.5	42.8	12.6
Merck	97.4	3.0	101.3	2.8	102.8	2.9	145.4	3.5	202.0	4.0	129.8	3.3
Pfizer	166.5	4.4	161.6	4.2	158.0	3.9	170.6	3.8	181.8	3.7	167.7	4.0
Rorer Group		n/a	22.4	4.3	19.3	5.7	40.0	4.7	49.4	5.3	32.8	5.3
Schering-Plough	206.5	11.4	211.9	11.3	224.5	11.6	262.4	10.9	321.9	11.9	245.4	11.5
SmithKline Beckman	160.1	5.6	179.3	6.1	176.0	5.4	236.5	6.3	250.8	5.8	200.5	5.9
Squibb	105.6	6.0	111.0	5.9	119.5	5.9	117.6	6.6	151.1	7.0	121.0	6.3
Upjohn	71.8	3.6	87.3	4.0	94.1	4.7	101.4	4.4	123.7	4.9	95.7	4.3
Warner-Lambert	592.0	19.0	607.0	19.2	630.8	19.7	692.8	22.3	797.5	22.9	664.0	20.7

Compustat Data System, 1983–1988

Exhibit 1　Merck Sales by Segment

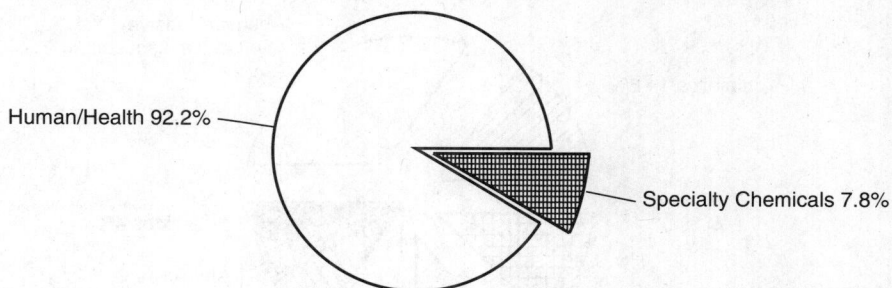

Source: Annual Report, 1988

Exhibit 2 Sales Trend in Specialty Chemicals Segment

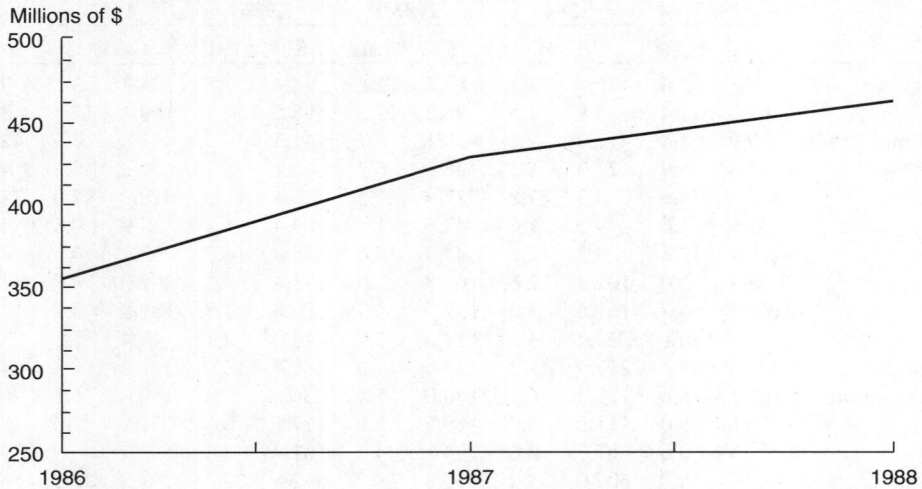

Source: Annual Report, 1988

Exhibit 3 Product Contribution to Human and Animal Segment Sales

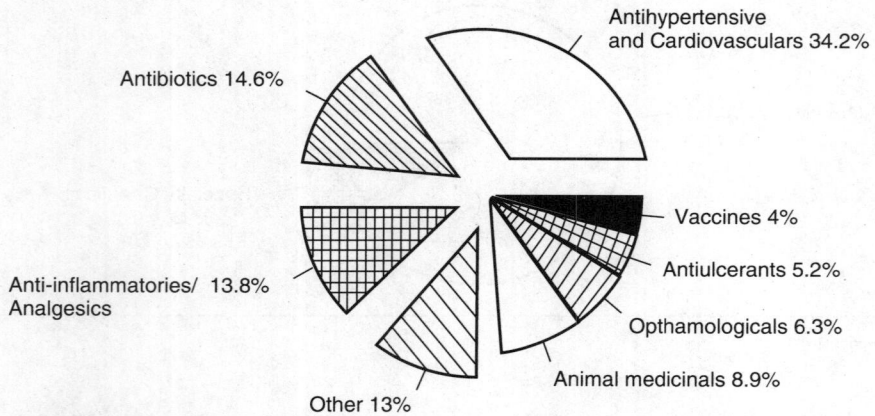

Source: Annual Report, 1988

Exhibit 4   Sales

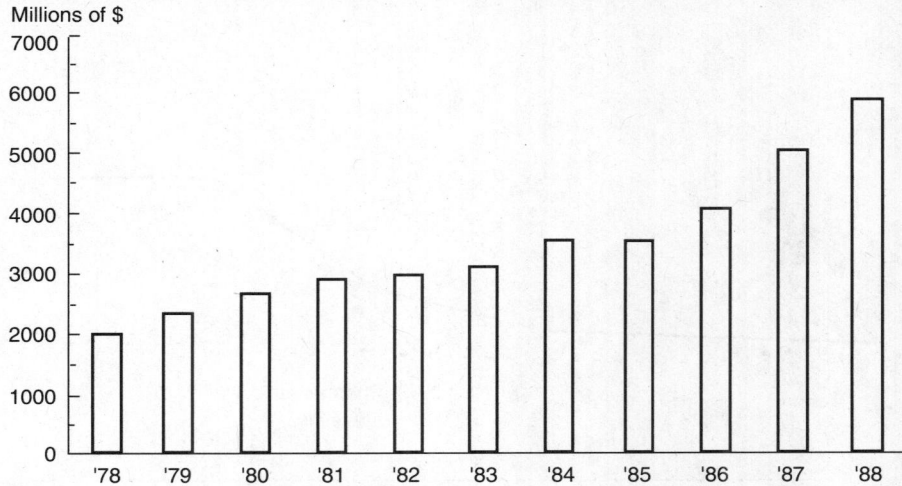

Source: Annual Report, 1988

Exhibit 5   Earnings per Share

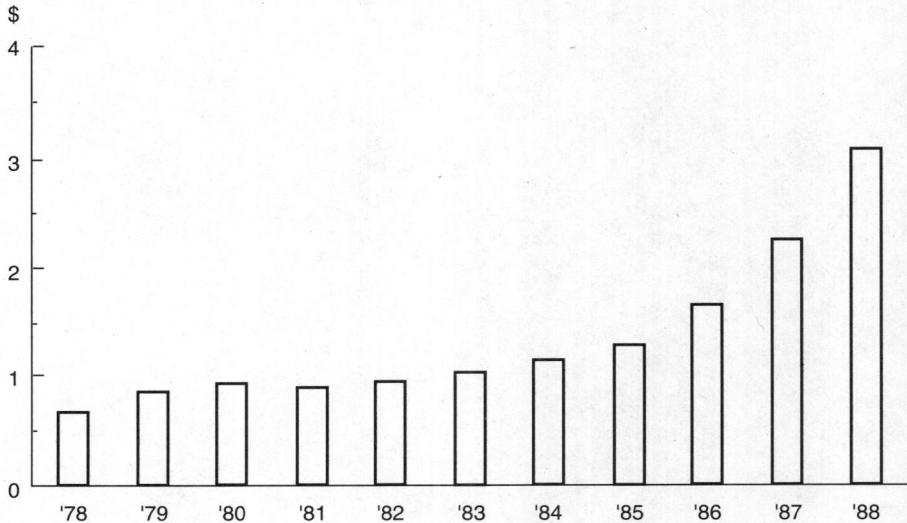

Source: Annual Report, 1988

Exhibit 6   ROI

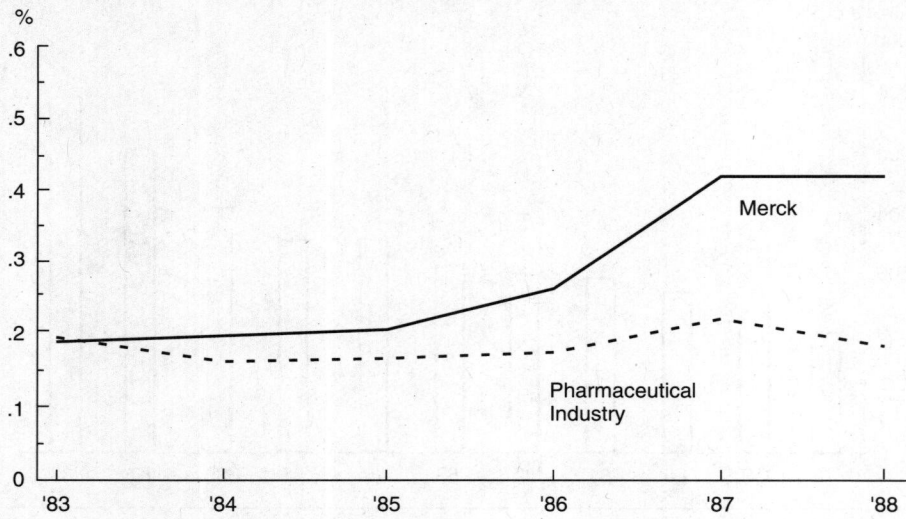

Source: Pharmaceutical Manufacturers Association, Facts at a Glance, 1987

Exhibit 7 Percentage of Sales—Domestic and Foreign

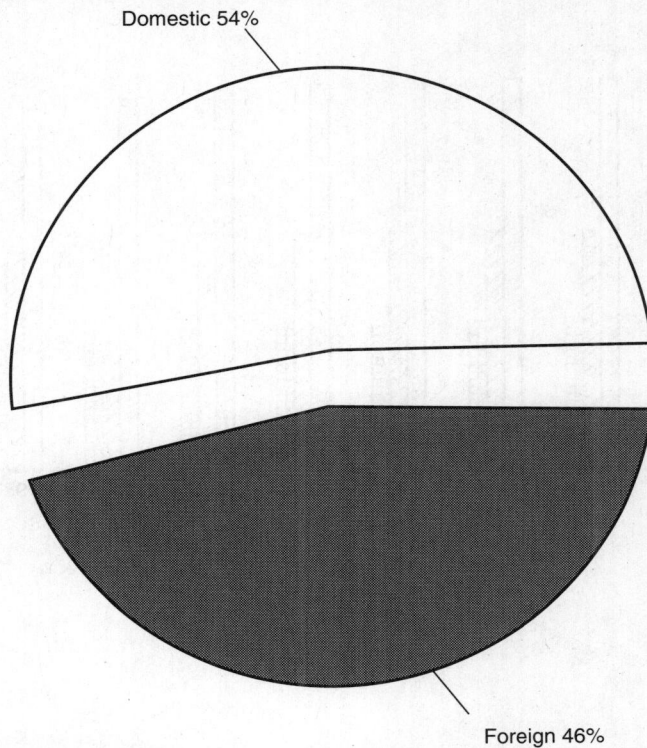

Domestic 54%

Foreign 46%

Source: Annual Report, 1988

Exhibit 8 Concentration Ratio

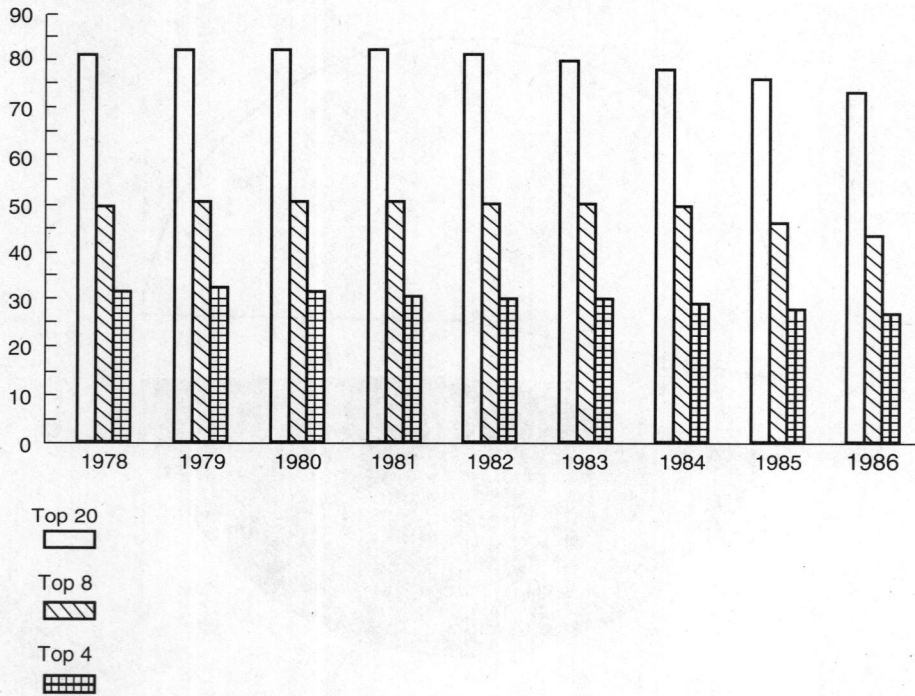

Top 20

Top 8

Top 4

Source: Pharmaceutical Manufacturers Association, Facts at a Glance, 1987

Exhibit 9 Market Share vs. ROI

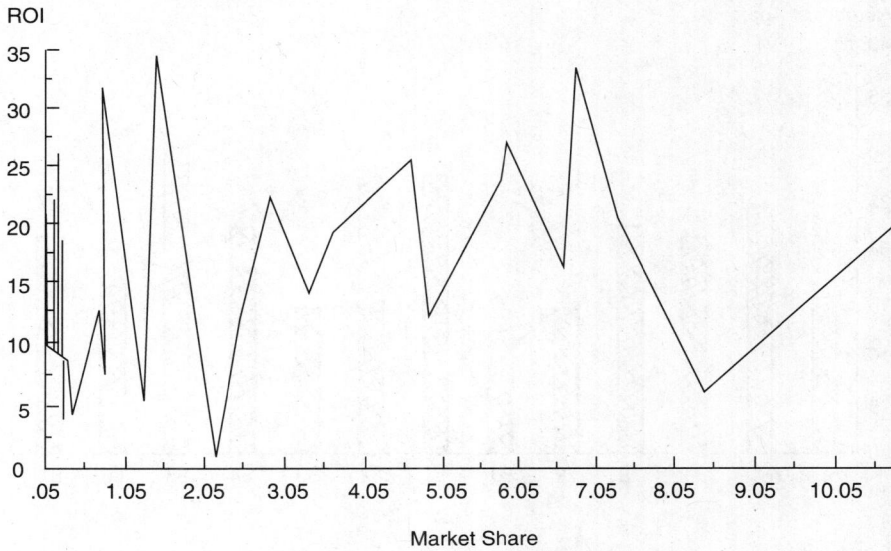

Source: Compustat

Exhibit 10 R&D Expenditures vs. ROI

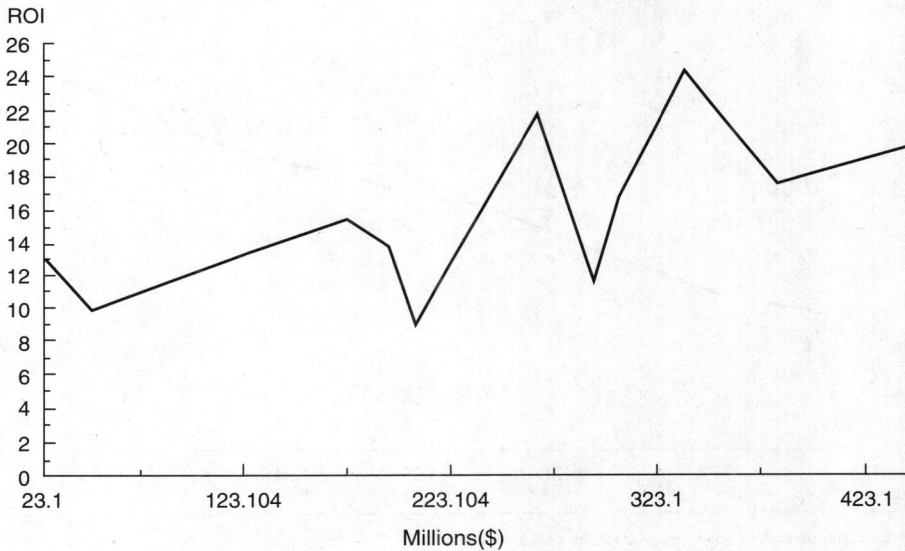

Source: Compustat

Exhibit 11   U.S. New Drug Approvals

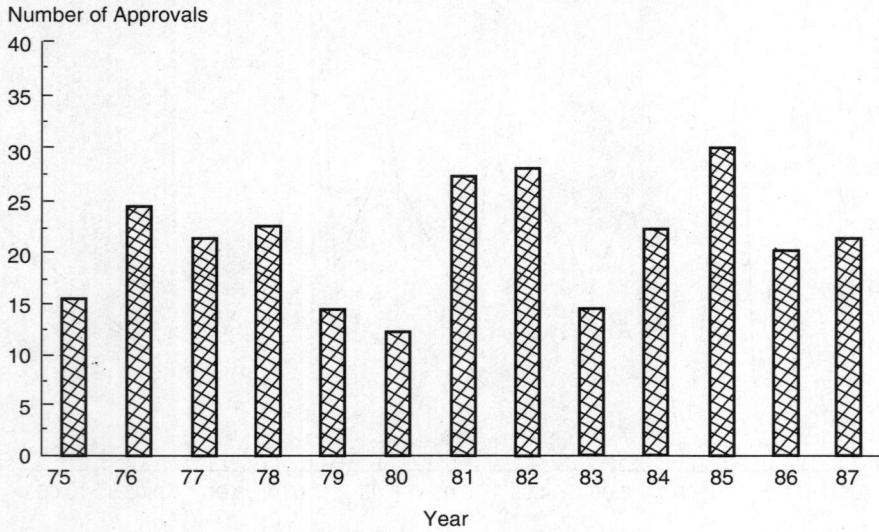

Number of Approvals

Source: Pharmaceutical Manufacturers Association, Facts at a Glance, 1987

Exhibit 12   Sales Growth

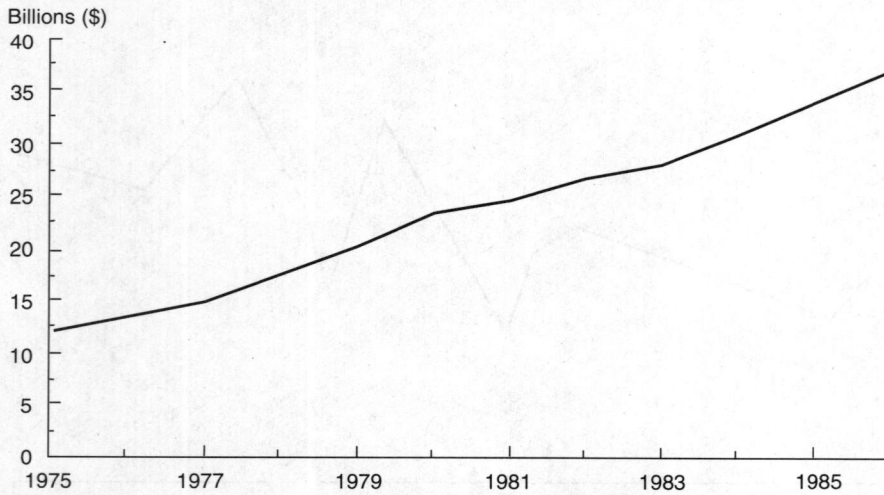

Billions ($)

Source: Pharmaceutical Manufacturers Association, Facts at a Glance, 1987

Exhibit 13   Return on Equity

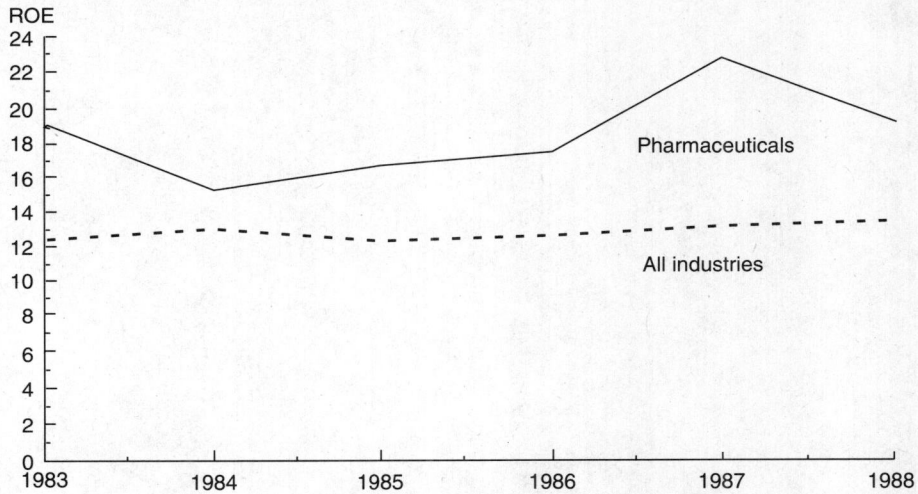

ROE

```
24
22
20
18                                                    Pharmaceuticals
16
14
12                                                    All industries
10
 8
 6
 4
 2
 0
   1983      1984      1985      1986      1987      1988
```

Source: Forbes Industry Analyses, 1984–1989

Exhibit 14   Net Profit Margin

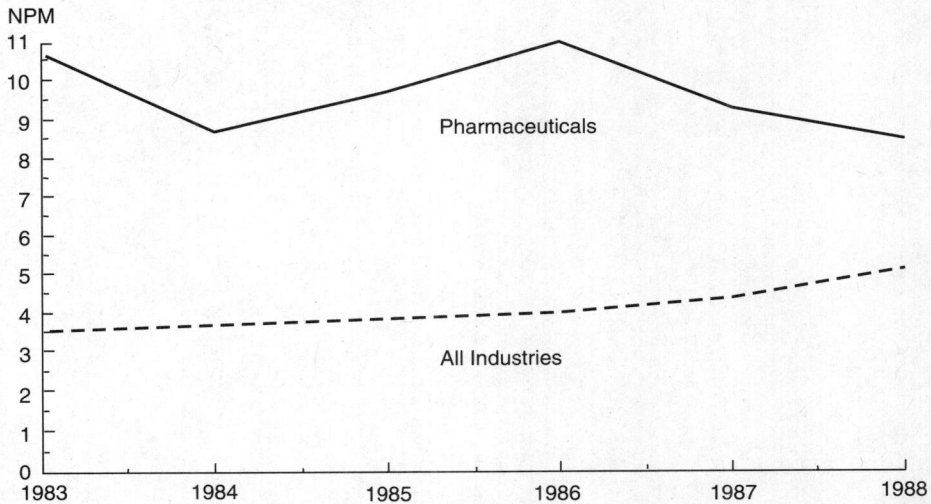

NPM

```
11
10
 9                                                    Pharmaceuticals
 8
 7
 6
 5
 4
 3                                                    All Industries
 2
 1
 0
   1983      1984      1985      1986      1987      1988
```

Source: Forbes Industry Analyses, 1984–1989

Case 11

The Airline Industry

Since the first scheduled passenger service of the 120-mile distance between Los Angeles and San Diego, the airline industry has undergone dramatic changes. Today, the U.S. airline industry employs more than 355,000 people, operates over 4,500 aircraft, and serves over 380 million passengers.

Tremendous growth has occurred in the industry, as evidenced in Table 1. Flying, once a glamorous experience, has become today's mass transportation. Since 1975, the number of available seat-miles (one airline seat transported one mile) has increased by 80 percent, and the number of passengers has increased 85 percent. Capacity utilization has improved, with load factors rising from 53.7 percent to 61.4 percent. With the exception of a slight dip in 1982, passenger revenues have steadily increased.

Net operating profit has followed a more erratic course, with the 1978 record profits exceeding $1 billion in sharp contrast to the red ink that flowed in the 1981–83 time period. The industry returned to profitability in 1984, and earned profits in excess of $860 million in 1985.

This industry note will concentrate on domestic operations of passenger airlines, and as such, will not focus on air cargo or international operations. International operations are subject to regulation by both the U.S. and foreign governments, thus adding a degree of complexity beyond the scope of this discussion. Although a secondary source of revenue for the scheduled passenger airline, air cargo remains a somewhat unique operation served by a small group of specialized carriers.

The Competitors

Airlines are classified into three principal groups—majors, nationals, and regionals. The majors (sometimes referred to as trunks) have annual revenues exceeding $1 billion. Nationals are those carriers with annual revenues between $75 million and $1 billion. Regional airlines' revenues are less than $75 million.

The term *national* is somewhat misleading, as the operating territory of these airlines is normally regional. The nationals typically operate shorter segments and may serve smaller cities than the majors do. Aloha, Braniff, and Southwest are examples of national carriers.

Selected 1985 statistics are provided in Table 2 on the top 12 airlines in operating revenues (airlines with more than a billion dollars in revenues).

The intense competition which has occurred since deregulation has contributed to the erratic performance of several major carriers. Table 3 compares the net operating profit or loss for 11 major carriers between 1985, 1986, and the first quarter of 1987.

The Pre-Deregulation Era

Government action has impacted the structure of the industry since its earliest days. In the industry's infant days, postal service air mail subsidies served to promote development. In the 40

This case was developed by Patricia P. McDougall, Georgia State University. © Patricia P. McDougall, 1988. Reprinted with permission.

Table 1 1975–1985 Highlights—U.S. Scheduled Airlines

	1975	1976	1977	1978
Traffic—scheduled service:				
Revenue passengers enplaned (000)	205,062	223,318	240,326	274,719
Revenue passenger-miles (000)	162,810,057	178,988,026	193,218,819	226,781,368
Available seat-miles (000)	303,006,243	322,821,649	345,565,901	368,750,530
Revenue passenger load factor (%)	53.7	55.4	55.9	61.5
Passenger revenue ($000)	12,353,501	14,265,947	16,273,355	18,806,247
Freight and express revenue ($000)	1,309,779	1,497,123	1,718,529	1,986,820
Mail revenue ($000)	303,022	320,121	390,762	386,639
Charter revenue ($000)	489,856	572,580	644,381	578,285
Total operating revenues ($000)	15,355,921	17,501,215	19,924,800	22,883,955
Total operating expenses ($000)	15,228,042	16,779,282	19,016,760	21,519,092
Operating profit ($000)	127,879	721,933	908,040	1,364,863
Interest expense ($000)	402,041	371,634	373,206	538,642
Net profit ($000)	(84,204)	563,354	752,536	1,196,537
Revenue per passenger-mile (c)	7.6	8.0	8.4	8.3
Rate of return on investment (%)	3.1	8.5	10.2	6.5
Operating profit margin (%)	0.8	4.1	4.6	6.0
Net profit margin	(.5)	3.2	3.8	5.2
Employees	289,926	303,006	308,068	329,303

Source: Air Transport Association of America, Washington, D.C.

Table 2 Top 12 Airlines in 1985 in Operating Revenues

Airline	Total operating revenues ($000)	Passengers (000)	Break-even*	Net profit (loss) ($000)
American	$5,859,334	41,229	47.8	$ 322,640
United	4,920,132	38,101	56.5	(88,223)
Eastern	4,815,070	41,766	56.8	6,310
Delta	4,738,168	39,805	44.9	156,775
Trans World	3,860,695	20,871	60.0	(193,092)
Pan American	3,156,988	13,040	54.4	40,474
Northwest	2,650,008	14,538	51.5	72,961
USAir	1,749,126	19,278	47.7	109,850
Republic	1,734,397	17,442	NA†	177,006
Continental	1,731,054	16,143	NA	64,280
Piedmont	1,366,641	18,053	46.6	66,710
Western	1,306,546	11,908	51.4	67,134

*Percent of capacity that must be sold to cover all expenses.
†NA = not available.
Source: *Air Transport 1986* (the Annual Report of the U.S. scheduled airline industry).

1979	1980	1981	1982	1983	1984	1985
316,863	296,903	285,976	294,102	318,638	344,683	380,024
262,023,375	255,192,114	248,887,801	259,643,870	281,829,148	305,115,855	335,897,966
416,126,429	432,535,103	424,897,230	440,119,206	464,537,979	515,323,339	546,994,334
63.0	59.0	58.6	59.0	60.7	59.2	61.4
22,791,390	28,048,689	30,722,629	30,549,719	32,744,618	36,939,345	39,235,809
2,211,321	2,431,926	2,596,850	2,437,703	2,592,567	2,859,419	2,680,715
452,021	610,996	653,996	688,675	653,129	712,070	889,575
520,916	1,160,524	1,175,154	1,085,537	1,075,428	1,112,050	1,279,812
27,226,665	33,727,806	36,662,555	36,407,635	38,953,672	43,825,047	46,664,414
27,026,610	33,949,421	37,117,325	37,141,070	38,643,262	41,673,536	45,238,150
199,055	(221,615)	(454,770)	(733,435)	310.410	2,151,511	1,426,264
618,446	967,719	1,209,461	1,384,084	1,482,352	1,540,377	1,588,306
346,845	17,414	(300,826)	(915,814)	(188,051)	824,668	862,715
8.7	11.0	12.3	11.8	11.6	12.1	11.7
6.5	5.3	4.7	2.1	6.0	9.9	9.8
0.7	(0.7)	(1.2)	(2.0)	8.0	4.9	3.1
1.3	1.3	(0.8)	(2.5)	(0.5)	(1.9)	1.8
340,696	340,696	360,517	330,495	328,648	345,079	355,113

years between 1938 and 1978, the Civil Aeronautics Board (CAB) was given broad power in regulating entry, exit, subsidy allocation, route structure, pricing, mergers and acquisitions, and quality of service. Unlike other regulatory agencies such as the Interstate Commerce Commission, the CAB had the explicit responsibility not only for the regulation of the air transport industry, but also for its promotion and development. The CAB was not given responsibility for safety, as this was and still is, the province of the Federal Aviation Administration (FAA) formed in 1958. Since the formation of the Department of Transportation in 1966, the FAA has been housed within the DOT.

Under regulation, airlines operating in interstate markets were required to obtain a certificate from the CAB that they had been found "fit, willing, and able" to provide air transportation. In its 40 years of regulation, the board did not approve a single one of scores of proposals to form new carriers to serve major markets. The only significant entry into scheduled service came when the board certified the local service carriers after World War II. Although several local service airlines were later permitted to serve major markets, they initially were granted certificates only to replace the trunks in providing subsidized service to smaller communities.

During regulation, a carrier's route map was among its most valuable assets. Route competition was tightly controlled by the CAB through issuance of route certificates. Some routes were highly competitive, while others were protected and became the virtual property of one or two carriers. In assigning routes, the CAB often sought to maintain the status quo of the industry. A financially weak carrier was often awarded a profitable route. This type of action maintained

Table 3 Major Carrier Performance

| | Net profit (loss) ($000) | | |
Carrier	1985	1986	1987—1st quarter
American	$322,640	$ 529	$25,210
Continental	64,280	(13,626)	(97,835)
Delta	156,775	(6,375)	27,076
Eastern	6,310	(110,626)	2,098
Northwest	72,961	(16,445)	(25,981)
Pan American	40,474	(125,274)	(87,690)
Piedmont	66,710	(6,918)	5,662
TWA	(193,092)	(169,363)	(54,813)
United	(88,223)	(107,284)	(35,120)
USAir	109,850	(10,360)	18,701
Western	67,134	10,883	(15,795)

Source: U.S. Department of Transportation.

competition and avoided bankruptcies. When an airline was forced to service unprofitable routes, the CAB often assigned a more profitable route as well.

Mergers were also used to maintain status quo in the industry and to avoid disruption in passenger services. Financially weak carriers were often allowed to merge in order to avoid bankruptcy.

Since deregulation virtually removed competition on pricing and routes, the various carriers competed principally on scheduling convenience and service.

Deregulation

Limited competition and the refusal of the board to permit new carriers into the industry provoked complaints from entrepreneurs who wanted to enter the industry, and from critics who argued that the industry had developed into an oligopoly that charged consumers higher prices than were necessary and offered few price or service options. Proponents of deregulation cited the lower fares of smaller, unregulated intrastate operators such as Southwest Airlines operating in Texas, and Air California and Pacific Southwest Airlines operating in California.

In light of the protected environment to which carriers had become accustomed, it was not surprising that the Airline Deregulation Act of 1978 transformed the industry. The act removed almost all market entry barriers and price controls. However, the government did retain control of safety and controlled air traffic through the Federal Aviation Administration (FAA).

With deregulation new airlines entered the industry, and with the aid of a deep recession, recruited experienced airline personnel and purchased aircraft at bargain prices. Unencumbered by union wage contracts, the new entrants operated on a lower cost basis, and in turn were able to cut fares below those of the majors. A major shakeup of the industry followed.

Costs

Labor. As shown in Table 4, labor represents the single largest expense. During regulation, fare increases were typically passed on to the consumer in fare increases. Following deregulation, the new entrants operated with significantly lower wage costs. This disparate situation was created by a number of conditions. The new entrants entered the industry at a time when there was a surplus of airline personnel, the new entrants

Table 4 Principal Elements of Airline
Operating Expenses

	Percent of total operating expense	
	1982	1983
Labor	35.8%	36.6%
Fuel	27.8	25.0
Traffic commissions	6.2	6.9

were encumbered with union wage contracts, and their employees had no seniority. The starting pay of an airline pilot at a new airline was about $30,000, whereas the average union pilot's wage was about $71,000 per year. New entrant People Express was able to operate on a cost basis of 5.3 cents per seat mile, compared to an 11 cents average for major carriers.

Airlines with comparatively low operating costs became the industry's price leaders, forcing the higher cost carriers to lower costs so they could reduce prices. Western Airlines and Pan American both received 10 percent wage cuts from its employees, with workers receiving company stock in exchange. Some airlines drastically cut their work forces and sought higher productivity. For example, United pilots increased their flying time 15 percent. More extreme measures occurred at some airlines. With Continental's bankruptcy in 1983, Chairman Lorenzo reduced pilots' salaries of $89,000 to $43,000 and flight attendants' salaries dropped from $29,000 to $15,000.

As airline executives attempted to rachet down wages, the controversial two-tier wage system developed. The economic recovery and resultant expansion in the industry changed a labor surplus into a tight labor market, and by the mid-1980s, the two-tier systems began to be modified or eliminated. New entrants were forced to increase wages to retain their personnel. Industry giants, as well, found themselves subject to wage competition. A 29-day strike by United pilots in 1985 prevented the carrier from achieving its objective of permanent lower wages. American,

finding its pilot salary scales lagged United, hastened to match United. American abandoned its two-tier wage scale for mechanics and proposed to abandon it for flight attendants.

Fuel. Fuel costs represent the second most significant cost to the carrier. Carriers have attempted to reduce fuel costs through the purchase of more fuel efficient aircraft, speed reduction, and weight reduction. Lighter seats and carpets, the elimination of 125 to 450 pounds of exterior paint, a change from glass to plastic minibottles, and carrying a reduced quantity of drinking water have all contributed to weight reduction. Even small reductions in speed bring large fuel savings. For example, a reduction of 14 miles per hour on a DC-8 in a flight from Chicago to Los Angeles saves 164 gallons of fuel, but adds only 4 minutes of flight time.

Following deregulation, fuel costs skyrocketed. The average price per gallon in 1978 was $.392; in 1979 it rose to $.578. It continued to rise in 1980 to $.894, and by 1981 was $1.042. For some airlines, fuel costs escalated to more than one third of operating expenses. The reaction of some major carriers of purchasing more fuel efficient aircraft and selling off older, less fuel efficient aircraft, created a glut of airplanes. New entrants purchased these aircraft at fire-sale prices and were able to offset their higher fuel costs with lower labor costs. People Express purchased seventeen 737s for only $62 million. That same amount would have purchased only four new 737s.

The drop in fuel costs since the early 1980s and the fuel conservation measures have benefited the industry. From June 1985 to June 1986, aviation fuel costs plummeted 35 percent to $.52 a gallon—one half the 1981 cost. Each one cent change in the price of jet fuel affects operating costs by about $100 million.

Barriers to Entry

Hub and Spoke System. In the hub and spoke system an airline uses connecting flights to and from smaller spoke cities to generate traffic for flights from hubs in larger cities. This ability to feed passengers from one flight to another has allowed large airlines to dominate traffic at major airports, reaping economies of scale and enormous market clout. For example, US Air, Inc., in Pittsburgh and TWA in St. Louis control more than 80 percent of the flow through these hubs.

The spoke flights may be flown by the carrier's own planes, or increasingly, major carriers are linking with smaller, commuter lines to generate traffic for flights from hubs in larger cities. The advantages of the system are numerous: a large number of points are connected without having to schedule individual flights between them; lightly traveled point-to-point segments are avoided; the passenger is retained in the system for a longer distance without interlining; and the carrier has a centralized location for maintenance, control, and crew base.

Facilities. Sufficient facilities (air traffic control personnel and airports) have not kept pace with the increased air traffic following deregulation. The 1981 Professional Air Traffic Controllers Organization (PATCO) strike added additional pressure to the system. New entrants and airlines wishing to expand often find that established carriers already control terminal facilities such as ticket counters and gates at congested airports. Landing slots may be allocated by the FAA.

Antitrust immunity has been granted to establish airlines for meetings to allocate slots and gates. With demand exceeding supply, agreements have been difficult to reach, and their allocations have not pleased new entrants and small commuters. No easy solution is seen in the short term as additional airports and massive additions to the air traffic control system require a long lead time.

Computer Reservation Systems. The unfairness of computer reservation systems (CRS) have long been argued by the small carriers. These systems handle approximately 90 percent of flights booked by travel agents. The systems are available to all carriers for a fee. In response to charges that the systems offered unfair advantages to the host company in methods of display and ticketing, the CAB adopted anti-bias rules in 1984. Even so, Delta Air Lines complained to the Transportation Department that American Airlines, who owns the largest CRS, had "abused its CRS market power to the detriment of air transportation."[1] American has denied the charge.

Five CRS systems are currently in operation. These are owned by American, United, TWA-Northwest, Texas Air, and Delta. American's Sabre and United's Apollo, together, account for about 70 percent of the market. The CRSs have become an important source of revenues for their owners. Some of the systems have been extended to other kinds of reservations, such as hotels and rental cars.

Frequent Flier Programs. Frequent flyer programs have probably become the most widely used and successful marketing effort in the industry. These plans offer points for various totals of mileage which can then be traded for free airline tickets. The plans are designed to build carrier loyalty among customers. Since the programs were introduced in 1981, airlines have issued about 30 million memberships. Julius Maldutis, an airline analyst with Salomon Brothers, estimates that if the rewards were claimed, the potential lost revenue would amount to over $300 million for the industry. Triple award programs increase the potential for lost revenue to $940 million. As seen in Table 5, the potential revenue lost to American, the program's innovator and largest member, is $190 million.

Wall Street analysts, who try to predict the financial performance of the industry, contend that the airlines don't have a consistent method of accounting for the value of frequent-flier re-

---

[1]"Is Deregulation Working?" *Business Week,* December 22, 1986, p. 53.

Table 5 Frequent-Flyer Programs

Airline	Membership (millions)	Extra potential revenue loss* (millions)
American	6.3	$190
Continental/Eastern	3.0	170
Delta	4.0	140
Northwest	3.0	90
Pan Am	1.0	30
TWA	4.0	15
United	6.0	215
USAir/Piedmont	3.0	90
Total	30.3	940

*Includes direct losses (cost of meals, baggage handling, etc.) and potential lost ticket sales if members cashed in their miles.
Source: Salomon Brothers, Inc., estimates.

wards. One of the Financial Accounting Standards Board (FASB) proposals for measuring frequent flyer liabilities called for airlines to set aside 10 percent of their revenues to cover potential losses from the reward programs. Such an accounting change could have a devastating impact on earnings.

Code Sharing—New Opportunity for the Commuters and Regionals

Deregulation allowed the major carriers to abandon lower-density routes they were previously required to serve, thus abandoning service to many smaller cities. This created opportunities for the commuter and regional carriers. In the first five years following deregulation, they increased their service from less than 175 cities to over 850 cities. Airplanes belonging to this group typically accommodate about 19 passengers, although a small percentage hold more than 30 passengers. The number of cities they serve has remained fairly constant since this time, as the majors have, for the most part, completed their route abandonments.

Recent growth for the commuters and regionals has resulted primarily from marketing agreements with major carriers. Table 6 lists some of the larger airlines and their partners. The commuters or regional airline feeds traffic from smaller cities into the major's hub airport, and in return the smaller airline code-shares the major's flight schedule. In code-sharing the smaller carrier's flight schedule is listed with that of the

Table 6 Major Airlines' Code-Sharing Agreements (as of March 1987)

American Airlines	Air Midwest, AV Air, Chaparral, Command Airways, Executive Air Charter, Metro Airlines, Simmons Airlines, Wings West
Continental Airlines	Air New Orleans, Britt Airways, Colgan Airways, Emerald Airlines, Gull Air, Mid Pacific Air, PBA, Presidential Airways, Rocky Mountain Airlines, Royale Airways, Trans-Colorado
Delta Air Lines	Atlantic Southeast, Business Express, Comair, Skywest
Eastern Air Lines	Air Midwest, Atlantis Airlines, Aviation Associates, Bar Harbor, Britt Airways, Metro Airlines, Precision Valley Aviation
Northwest Airlines	Big Sky Airlines, Express Airlines, Fischer Brothers, Mesaba Aviation, Simmons Airlines
Pan American	Air Atlanta, Pan Am Express (Ransome), Presidential Airways
Piedmont Aviation	Brockway Air, CCAir, Henson Aviation, Jetstream International
Trans World Airlines	Air Midwest, Piedmont, Resort Air, Resort Commuter
United Airlines	Air Wisconsin, Aspen Airways, Westair Commuter
USAir	Air Kentucky, Chautauqua Airlines, Crown Airlines, Pennsylvania Airlines, Pocono Airlines, Southern Jersey Airways, Suburban Airlines

Source: *Travel Weekly.*

Table 7   Concentration among Carriers Increasing

1986 Rank	Company	Market share	1985 Rank	Company	Market share
1.	Texas Air System	19.6%	1.	American	13.3%
2.	United	16.4	2.	United	12.5
3.	American	14.1	3.	Eastern	10.0
4.	Delta	11.7	4.	TWA	9.6
5.	NWA	10.1	5.	Delta	9.0
6.	TWA	8.2	6.	Pan Am	8.1
7.	USAir	7.1	7.	NWA	6.7
8.	Pan Am	6.0	8.	Continental	4.9
9.	Southwest	2.0	9.	People Express	3.3
10.	America West	0.9	10.	Republic	3.2
	Others	3.9		Others	19.4

Source: Department of Transportation and S&P.

larger carrier in the commuter reservation system. The smaller carrier may also benefit from shared advertising and the handling of flights at the larger airline's gate. The larger carrier benefits by the added development of their hub operation at a minimal cost. Passengers can be carried beyond the major hub airport without the cost of providing support operations at the smaller city.

Airline Oligopoly—The Reconcentration of the Industry

The fierce competition by new entrants which followed deregulation appears to be about over as the industry returns to the conditions which brought on regulation in the first place. With more than half of the airlines operating in 1978 and two thirds of the new entrants having failed, the industry is dominated by six megacarriers controlling 80 percent of the market, versus 73 percent in 1978. Ten airlines control 96 percent of the market. Airlines consultant Lee Howard of Airline Economics, Inc., predicts a share of more than 90 percent by 1990. Market shares of the 10 largest carriers for 1985 and 1986 are shown in Table 7.

Industry analysts cite the following seven major factors as contributing to this reconcentration:

1. Hub and spoke development by major national airlines.

2. Marketing alliances between large and regional/commuter airlines.

3. Control of traffic by such mechanisms as computerized reservation systems and code-sharing.

4. Innovative marketing plans such as bonus miles for frequent flyers.

5. Control of airport access gates, landing slots, ticket counters, and hangars.

6. Mergers and acquisitions.

7. Bankruptcies.[2]

As indicated from Table 8, 19 of the 36 scheduled carriers operating before deregulation are no longer in operation, having either been acquired, merged, or declared bankrupt. The operating percentages of the other categories are

[2]Frank A. Spencer and Frank H. Cassell, "Airline Oligopoly Reemerges from Deregulation," *Airline Pilot* 56, no. 5 (1987), pp. 10–14.

Table 8 Airline Attrition under Deregulation, October 1978–December 31, 1986

Category	Total	No longer operating	Currently operating	Percent operating
Certified prior to regulation	36	19	17	47%
Former intrastate	4	3	1	25
Former supplemental charter	10	10	0	0
Former commuters	59	38	21	36
New entrants	119	84	35	29
Former all cargo	6	5	1	17
Total	234	159	75	32%

Source: Frank A. Spencer and Frank H. Cassell, "Airline Oligopoly Reemerges from Deregulation," *Airline Pilot* 56, no. 5 (1987), p. 13.

even lower. Of the four former intrastate carriers, only one remains in operation. All 10 of the former supplementals have ceased operation. Thirty-eight of the 59 former commuters have disappeared. Of the new entrants, 84 of the 119 have fallen from the industry. The six all-cargo lines have been reduced to one.

Rampant merger activity characterized the industry in the 1980s. The 22 mergers shown in Table 9 represent over $7 billion spent in pursuing concentration. Texas Air, which has accounted for much of the activity, has combined Continental Airlines, New York Air, Eastern, People Express, and Frontier Airlines to become the largest airline in the free world.

The increased importance of the hub and spoke system has been an impetus for merger activity, as a merger is often viewed as the cheapest and most efficient manner to enter a market dominated by a competitor's hub. Delta's acquisition of Western added a valuable western hub in Salt Lake City to Delta's major hub in Atlanta.

Declining Service, Concern for Safety, and Reconcentration Foster the Move toward Re-regulation

The American public's increasing concern with flight safety and the declining quality of service

has made re-regulation at some minimum level more amenable. Complaints by passengers to the Department of Transportation, flight delays, and the bumping of passengers from overbooked flights have increased.

Reports of near midair collisions involving at least one commercial airliner jumped 48 percent in 1987. Airline pilots filed 487 reports of near collisions with the Federal Aviation Administration (FAA) in 1987, compared with 329 in 1986. Sixty-six of these were classified as critical; that is, the planes passed within 100 feet of each other.

Many pilots believe the air traffic control system has not fully recovered from the 1981 Professional Air Traffic Controllers Organization Strike, and that the federal government has failed to provide sufficient facilities to handle the increased traffic. FAA officials dismiss the charges that the system is not back up to standards. The FAA is quick to note that despite the record number of near miss reports, the actual number of in-flight collisions dropped from 27 in 1986 to 21 in 1987.

Unprecedented fines have been levied by the FAA on American Airlines, Continental, and Eastern Air Lines for maintenance violations. To correct faulty maintenance practices which earned Eastern $9.5 million in fines in 1985, the airline increased its spending on maintenance to

Table 9 Merger/Acquisition Activity,
1980–1987

Year	Companies	Price ($ millions)
1980	Pan Am-National	373.7
	Republic-Airwest	38.5
1981	Texas Air-Continental (50 percent)	80.8
1985	Southwest-Muse	61.8
	People Express-Frontier	309.0
	United-Pan Am Pacific Routes	750.0
	Texas Air-Continental (19 percent)	81.1
1986	Northwest-Republic	884.0
	Texas Air-Eastern	607.5
	Trans World-Ozark	224.0
	People Express-Britt	36.0
	People Express-PBA	UNK
	Delta-Western	860.0
	Alaska-Jet America	19.8
	Texas Air-People/Frontier (September 16)*	298.0
	Texas Air-Rocky Mountain Airways	3.0
	American-AirCal (November)	225.0
	Alaska-Horizon	68.0
	USAir-PSA	400.0
1987	USAir-Piedmont	1,600.0
	Total	7,365.2

*Note: Texas Air later reduced its offering for People Express from
$138.4 million to $113.7 million, a decrease of about $25 million. A
proposed $146 million merger of Frontier and United Airlines was
aborted because of lack of agreement on Frontier pilot pay after ab-
sorption into United.
Source: Frank A. Spencer, "The Creeping Shadows of Re-regulation,"
Airline Quarterly, April 1988, p. 8.

$500 million in 1987. Maintenance problems on aircraft may entail serious safety concerns which are not apparent to the consumer. For instance, American was fined for a leaky toilet, a problem more than merely hygienic. Water escaping to the outside of the plane formed a chunk of ice that knocked off an engine in midflight.

Calls for some form of reregulation are being heard from diverse quarters. Alfred E. Kahn, former chairman of the CAB and considered to be deregulation's granddaddy, has expressed serious concerns about anticompetitive side effects of deregulation. In a June 1987 speech, Robert Crandall, chairman and president of American Airlines, suggested that the government should allocate airport capacity. New entrants, as well, are beginning to suggest a return to regulation as they find it more and more difficult to protect themselves in the concentrating industry. Code-sharing is seen by many of the commuters as a form of domination by the majors in which the commuter airline is forced to lose its independence in order to survive in an oligopolistic market. Environmentalists want greater regulation in noise and particulate emissions.

Just as the industry appears to be returning to some stability, many industry analysts predict that the Department of Transportation or Congress may be forced to return the airline industry to some form of regulation.

Airline Industry, 1988

Fundamentals for the airline group appear to be reasonably positive, at this juncture. Indeed, we're optimistic that the industry has evolved to the point where the fare structure will no longer be as vulnerable to collapsing as it once was. Still, earnings prospects are mixed. 1988 is shaping up as a record year. But next year may well be another story, given our forecast of a mild recession in the June and September interims.

In our view, there are currently few interesting investment opportunities within the Air Transport Industry. A number of these stocks, however, are suitable for inclusion in risk-tolerant portfolios that are focusing on capital gains to the early Nineties.

The Evolving Marketplace

The airline group has endured tumultuous times since deregulation occurred a decade ago and, for the most part, industrywide profitability has been disappointing over this period. Two external factors were responsible for a good deal of the poor bottom-line performance—the sharp rise in fuel prices and the walkout by the air traffic controllers. But throughout this evolution—which is still ongoing—industry players have grappled with the problem of fares. This shouldn't have been surprising; ticket prices, as well as market entry and/or withdrawal, had previously been controlled by the federal authorities. Suddenly, not only were carriers freed to set fares and redeploy assets at their own discretion, but restrictions on the number of players in the marketplace were also removed.

Indeed, the post-deregulation era was initially characterized by a rash of new entrants

*Source: Marilyn M. McKellin, "AIR TRANSPORT INDUSTRY," *Value Line Investment Survey*, September 30, 1988, pp. 251–252. Copyright © 1988 by Value Line, Inc.; used by permission.

which weren't burdened with seniority and unionized work forces; and these upstart carriers were able to profitably price their services below those of the major airlines. Thus, in order to maintain market share, the established companies found they had to slash prices. The resulting lower fare structure, plus the surge in fuel prices, pushed the industry into the red. But the older players fought back by seeking ways to differentiate their service and reduce costs. This led to the development of hub-and-spoke flying (to carry more passengers from origin to destination by offering connecting opportunities at a central location), and frequent flyer programs (to establish a base of loyal customers). Ploys used by one airline to distinguish itself from its competitors were quickly copied by the other carriers, however. Seats became pretty much a commodity product, and fare discounting ran rampant.

The combination of declining oil prices, a strong economy, and a lengthy strike by United's pilots (which proved to be a boon for all other industry players) helped the bottom line in '84 and '85. But consistent profitability remained elusive, and the established carriers finally realized that market share couldn't be secured by pricing alone. The strategy eventually embraced was one of "critical mass". The theory here was that maximizing revenues required control of a reasonably good flow of traffic which, in turn, necessitated a wide base of loyal customers. In order to build the latter, an airline had to be able to satisfy a great proportion of travelers' needs, and this pretty much required an extensive domestic route network. So, the industry entered a phase of consolidation, as the now-major carriers scrambled to expand their domain by acquiring more vulnerable players as quickly as possible.

Composite Statistics: Air Transport Industry*

1984	1985	1986	1987	1988	1989	© Value Line, Inc.	91-93E
39743	42803	38885	46684	**55000**	**58000**	Revenues ($mill)	**75000**
57.8%	55.3%	57.9%	60.0%	**58.0%**	**57.0%**	Load Factor	**57.0%**
11.7%	10.3%	10.7%	10.4%	**10.5%**	**11.0%**	Operating Margin	**12.0%**
2455.0	2693.5	2773.7	2848.3	**2775**	**2950**	Depreciation ($mill)	**3700**
827.8	438.3	39.6	129.8	**1000**	**1250**	Net Profit ($mill)	**1750**
45.0%	47.9%	NMF	NMF	**30.0%**	**33.0%**	Income Tax Rate	**34.0%**
2.1%	1.0%	.1%	.3%	**1.8%**	**2.2%**	Net Profit Margin	**2.3%**
10919	13734	15402	16827	**21000**	**22000**	Long-Term Debt ($mill)	**25000**
8851.4	10704	11432	13199	**13750**	**14700**	Net Worth ($mill)	**19750**
7.1%	4.4%	2.6%	3.1%	**5.5%**	**6.0%**	% Earned Total Cap'l	**6.5%**
9.4%	4.1%	.4%	1.0%	**7.5%**	**8.5%**	% Earned Net Worth	**9.0%**
8.3%	2.4%	NMF	NMF	**6.5%**	**7.5%**	% Retained to Comm Eq	**8.0%**
23%	47%	NMF	NMF	**20%**	**16%**	% All Div'ds to Net Prof	**15%**
12.8	42.8	NMF	NMF	Bold figures are		Avg Ann'l P/E Ratio	**11.0**
1.19	3.48	NMF	NMF	Value Line		Relative P/E Ratio	**.90**
.8%	.8%	.8%	.7%	estimates		Avg Ann'l Div'd Yield	**.7%**

*Excludes Airborne Freight, Air Express Int'l, British Airways, Emery Air Freight, Federal Express, KLM, Tiger Int'l.

By now, merger mania has just about run its course, and a vastly different marketplace has emerged. To better understand the change the industry has undergone, consider this: Of the carriers covered by Value Line in the early 1980s, Eastern, Frontier, Ozark, Pacific Southwest, People Express, Piedmont, Republic, and Western are no longer independent. Indeed, about 80% of the market is now dominated by six companies—*AMR, Delta, NWA, Texas Air, UAL,* and *USAir.* Importantly, fare restructuring has been one of the major consequences of this transformation. To be sure, discount traffic still accounts for about 90% of the total. But the majors that survived deregulation have all developed sophisticated computerized systems to maximize revenues by coordinating flight demand and the sale of reduced-fare tickets. The absence of new entrants, and the fact that marginal carriers have either been grounded or acquired, has also helped the industry to establish restrictions that make it difficult for the typically price-insensitive business traveler to qualify for the discount fares.

At this juncture, a return to the destructive fare wars of the early '80s appears unlikely. That's not to say that discounting will abate. Indeed, we think the cut-rate ticket is here to stay. But, given that the industry is dominated by only a half-dozen megacarriers, it seems probable that a reasonable fare structure will prevail. That's largely because fewer players frequently mean less competitive pressures. Witness Northwest's near-monopoly in its major markets at Minneapolis-St. Paul, Detroit, and Memphis, USAir's dominance at Pittsburgh, and the benefits *Delta* is reaping from the problems of its main competitor—Eastern. Additionally, our optimism is in part due to the fact that the individual carriers are focusing more on profits these days; but it also assumes that *Texas Air* continues with its strategy of upgrading service and attempting to raise revenue per passenger mile at Continental.

We're further encouraged because quality of service—as measured by the now-publicized reports of on-time performance and number of passenger complaints—is fast becoming a major weapon in the airlines' marketing arsenals. Though better service does take its toll on the cost side of the ledger, we think such a move away from price-only considerations will be a definite positive over the longer haul.

How Fundamentals Are Holding Up

There are four critical variables for the airline group—yield (revenue per passenger mile), traffic, fuel prices, and labor-related expenses. As discussed above, the yield picture is looking reasonably bright. The other major factor that influences these companies' revenues is traffic. Gains in revenue passenger miles are running at good levels in view of the recent upturn in yields. Moreover, we don't look for a marked weakening over the next year or so since comparisons will not be against a particularly strong base. The story on the expense side doesn't give rise to too much concern either. True, there will be substantial—but manageable—capacity additions next year, as United ramps up its expansion plans and Airbus and McDonnell Douglas catch up on aircraft deliveries to American. And for the time being, we're not estimating any spike up in jet fuel prices over the near term. As usual, on the labor front there are pluses and minuses. The recent spate of takeovers has exacerbated these issues. *NWA's* negotiations with its pilots are stalled, as the groups from Northwest and Republic struggle to come up with a combined seniority list. *USAir* faces similar difficulties as it seeks to assimilate the work forces of PSA and Piedmont. *UAL* has yet to resolve differences with its pilots. *Pan Am* seems to be making little headway in getting its unions to accept more competitive contracts. Finally, Eastern's unions have taken their grievances to both the FAA and the courts. We doubt that *NWA* or *USAir* will face serious difficulties in reaching satisfactory

Figure 11A Relative Strength (Ratio of Industry to Value Line Comp.)

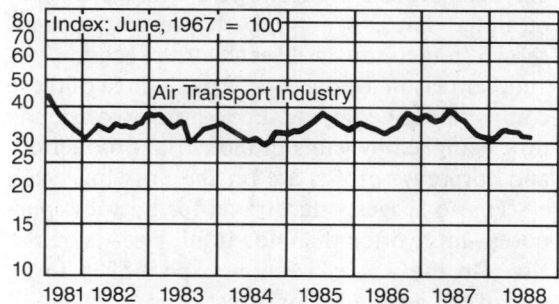

Source: "AIR TRANSPORT INDUSTRY," *Value Line* (Sept. 30, 1988): 251.

settlements. We're less optimistic about the situation at *UAL*. As far as Eastern is concerned, we think management's current proposal will be rejected and that at some point mediators will start the clock ticking on a 30-day cooling off period. If so, odds would seem to favor a strike by machinists. On the plus side, *AMR* and *Delta,* along with regional carriers like *Southwest,* have no potentially confrontational labor discussions looming on the horizon. On balance, then, though we foresee employee-related expenses gradually drifting up as the two-tier wage scale is eventually merged into one, we don't see any sharp departure from the status quo in the near term.

Earnings Prospects This Year and Next

Postings in the past couple of quarters have generally been stronger than had been expected. We think the better results are due to a number of factors—some of which are discussed above. Higher yields, in our opinion, are the major reason for the improvement. Though discounting ebbs and flows, the pricing structure is such that the typical all-important business traveler has difficulty qualifying for a reduced-fare ticket. As we've mentioned, this happy situation is probably the result of a somewhat less competitive marketplace. Yield management systems are also playing a big role in limiting the damages of promotional fares. We think the recent strength shown in the industrial sector of the economy is another reason for the good growth most of these companies are enjoying. Economic expansion is now being led by gains in industrial production, and corporate profits are on the upswing. Such a scenario suggests that travel for business purposes—more often than not at full-fare—is on the rise. On the whole, we now expect 1988 to be one of the airline sector's best ever.

Prospects of a mild recession along about mid-1989 dampen our enthusiasm for next year. Although at this juncture we only expect a modest downturn in the second and third interims, this could well be enough to trigger deeper fare discounts, particularly in view of the industry's planned capacity additions. To be sure, we think the staying power of the group's major players, plus the yield management expertise that all six have demonstrated, will prevent the degree of erosion in revenue per passenger mile that characterized the early Eighties. Still, the downward pressure on yield and traffic that would be precipitated by even a mild recession would not go unnoticed. Accordingly, we aren't looking for more than modestly improved share net next year from most of the airlines under review here. An exception, in our opinion, would be *NWA*, which should have most of its post-merger difficulties behind it. *Texas Air's* losses should narrow substantially, too, assuming that the impasse with Eastern's employees can be satisfactorily resolved before midyear.

Investment Considerations

The Air Transport Industry remains in the lower third of Value Line's industry rankings for relative market performance in the upcoming six to 12 months. That's not to say, however, that there are not investment opportunities here. Indeed, we think a number of these equities offer 3- to 5-year capital gains potential that's greater than that of the typical issue. In selecting long-term holdings, however, we recommend that investors focus on the stocks of companies that can be characterized by the following: a strong domestic route system or market niche, solid finances, some flexibility in capital spending plans, a management team with a proven track record, access to a computerized reservations system, an efficient fleet, and a history of reasonably good labor relations. At present, the companies that appear to fit this bill are *AMR*, *Delta*, *NWA*, *Southwest*, and *USAir*.

Case 12

USAir's Competitive Response to Deregulation: Key Policy and Tactical Choices of the CEO*

Abstract

There are few American domestic airlines that have managed to follow a successful and profitable course of action since the deregulation of the U.S. domestic airline industry in 1978. During this decade of freedom, the industry has experienced a period of major restructuring. Most carriers have experienced difficulty developing viable competitive strategies that were consistent with the rapidly changing nature and market structure of this industry. The evidence is the loss of stockholders' value, the continuing failure of both large and small industry participants, massive consolidation, and some would say an inevitable movement toward unchecked market power by the remaining few "mega carriers."

One important exception to this development has been USAir, Inc., now a wholly owned subsidiary of USAir Group, Inc., which began

This case was prepared by Jon G. Kalinowski, Department of Management, College of Business Administration, Mankato State University and Charles R. Klasson, Department of Management Sciences, College of Business Administration, University of Iowa.

*This material represents the authors' interpretation of available published information about the economic development of this airline in response to the industry's deregulation. The materials were reviewed by corporate officers. It is not intended to illustrate either effective or ineffective administrative procedures or policies.

the decade of change as a small regional carrier, Allegheny Airlines, and ended as one of the most profitable and least leveraged carriers in the industry. It produced the highest profitability of any major carrier during the period 1982–1987. This case presents an analysis of (1) how this firm managed itself throughout the deregulation process, (2) what key policy choices its top management made, and (3) how its management formulated and implemented an adaptive competitive strategy. This expost case study provides an excellent example of competitive behavior under conditions of free and contestable markets as described in the emerging new theory of "industrial organization." Part One provides an overview of the carrier's overall development. Part Two traces the historical development of the carrier's competitive strategy along with major policy and tactical choices of its CEO that produced one of the outstanding competitors in the air transport industry today.

Part One: A Major Competitive Move

On October 31, 1987, the Assistant Transportation Secretary Matthew Scocozza ruled that the requested merger of USAir Group, Inc. and Piedmont Aviation be approved. He reversed an administrative law judge, Ronnie Yoder, by saying that the action would not likely "reduce competition substantially in any relevant market." Yoder's concern was that the merger posed potential serious problems in East Coast markets where the two carriers offered service at more than 50 common cities. The two locations most seriously affected were La Guardia and Washington National airports.

The initial rejection of the proposed merger with Piedmont was called incomprehensible by USAir's management. They felt prior mergers had far more potential antitrust, customer, and labor negative side effects that the USAir-Piedmont merger proposal. Consequently, Edwin I. Colodny, USAir's Chairman of the Board, escalated the debate to a public forum to gain more favorable exposure and treatment of the request.

Final approval of this proposed merger, one of some twenty-two in this industry since 1980, signalled a major change in the competitive structure of the U.S. domestic airline industry. USAir Group Inc., through the leadership of its CEO Edwin I. Colodny, had managed to strategically position itself as a financially strong and widely respected major U.S. domestic carrier capable of becoming a dominant airline in a very competitive and economically transformed industry.

Challenging the Mega-Carriers

The operational merger of the two carriers when finalized in late 1989, would make USAir the seventh largest domestic carrier in the United States with a 7 percent market share. This was considered to be the minimal size for the combined carriers to compete successfully with other large established airlines like United and American. This meant that the existing large carriers in the so-called "mega-carrier" category could then be challenged on a market by market basis. This competitive capability would hence serve the public's best interest. Specifically, the new unit could compete effectively east of the Mississippi River while building market share to the West Coast on additional transcontinental routes. USAir had earlier purchased Pacific Southwest Airlines (P.S.A.) which served West Coast markets. This link created a coast-to-coast

system that opened new transcontinental markets that could be served from its established East Coast hubs. In the East, the USAir unit operated major hubs in Pittsburgh and Philadelphia while providing service to 77 markets in 31 states. The Piedmont unit then had hubs in Charlotte, North Carolina, Dayton, Ohio, and Baltimore, Maryland and serviced 87 airports in 26 states.

The Competitive Impact of a USAir-Piedmont Merger

The merged carriers would not share a common hub or primary base of operations. USAir headquartered at Washington, D.C., while Piedmont based their operations from Winston-Salem, North Carolina. Piedmont's presence was strong in the Southeast while USAir's presence was strong in the Northeast. This combination would solidify USAir's position in the Eastern United States. Although more than fifty cities were served by both carriers only six were not provided with service by other major or commuter airlines. Both USAir and Piedmont served different destination points. Both location of hub cities and the routes flown by the merged carriers were important criteria—measures of market power—used by the Department of Transportation to assess the competitive impact of such a merger. The D.O.T. wanted to determine if (1) competition would be lessened and fares increased above competitive levels and/or (2) service to the public would be reduced below competitive levels or eliminated. Their determination was that there would be no adverse impact from this action.

Unfair Competitive Advantage

The chairman and CEO of America West alleged that his company would ask a federal court to issue a stay of decision. This was necessary since the merger would allow the dominant carriers to achieve a monopoly position and preclude their entry into these markets. They claimed the problem involved the two airports in question—La

Guardia and Washington National. If USAir would agree to sell several of its landing slots, America West said it would drop its objections. The absence of available slots was considered to be the major barrier to entry into these markets. The denial to force the sale of slots as a condition for approving the USAir-Piedmont merger was based upon the notion that it would be discriminatory. The argument stated that if slots should be taken away from anybody at those airports, it should be on a nondiscriminatory basis in which case all new entrants and incumbent carriers would be requested to present their own cases to the D.O.T. for official review.

Integrating the Merged Carriers

While the USAir Group acquired controlling interest of Piedmont on November 4, 1987, the merger plans called for a transition period before the two carriers became fully integrated as so-called "mirror images." The $1.56 billion acquisition called for Piedmont to operate as a separate subsidiary for at least nine months flying with their own name and paint. Colodny wanted to avoid the labor and customer service problems that plagued other merged carriers. He wanted to implement a "go-slow policy" approach to merging the two organizations and was actively involved with various merger activities. Colodny recognized that his management team would face a difficult task of integrating two companies that had followed different competitive strategies and utilized different operational practices for providing air services. Piedmont followed an aggressive market expansion strategy. They grew by external acquisitions even though in secondary markets. On the other hand, USAir had built market strength around its Pittsburgh hub through primarily internal growth and the use of joint marketing programs with independent commuter operators.

USAir acquired controlling interest in the California based Pacific Southwest Airways in May of 1987. This strategic move represented one step in the process of implementing the firm's expansion objective of becoming a major U.S. carrier while retaining their historical performance record of strong profits. This was accomplished with the acquisition of first P.S.A. and then the Piedmont organization. And because of excellent labor relations in both acquired companies, similar fleet configurations, and excellent performance records, Colodny felt USAir's management team would be successful in their integration and implementation of these acquisitions.

Planning for the Piedmont Merger

To start the merger off in the right direction, Colodny agreed to so-called "labor protective provisions" which provided the employees of the acquired firm with assurances on critical matters like job seniority. While no employee groups opposed the proposed merger, the presence of seniority issues and differential compensation systems would present Colodny a real challenge in making this a smooth and profitable merger. But the carrier's management had worked hard to both plan for and communicate with its employees about the new emerging organization.

Few layoffs were anticipated except for overlapping jobs of headquarters staffs. USAir employed 16,000 employees compared to Piedmont's 22,000. Colodny's objective was to maintain their existing image as a high quality service carrier. He wanted to achieve a smooth transition and to avoid any image of poor customer service and safety as had plagued both Northwest Orient and Texas Air's Continental and Eastern units after their acquisition efforts. The public was becoming increasingly hostile about the abuses they were receiving from domestic carriers as an apparent result of deregulation. He did not want to encounter stiff opposition to his anticipated merger plans as a result of the poor service levels then being experienced by the public. USAir had a history of strong labor relations since they operated in the heavily unionized Northeast with Pittsburgh as their primary operating hub. Mr. Colodny had established a reputation for building and maintaining high employee morale.

Positioning the Carrier. USAir Group Inc.'s market and financial performance during this post-deregulation period (1978–1987) provided clear evidence that the earlier strategic positioning choices made by Colodny had in fact produced the intended competitive results. He had readied the carrier for increased competition through two strategic acquisitions. First, he made further market penetration into their established primary hubs. Second, market extension choices were made that permitted the transformed regional L.S.A. carrier to start exercising its expanded market presence as a "new emerging major carrier" in the industry. These acquisitions can be seen as the result of two clear strategic choices.

Strategic Choice One:
The Opportunity to Grow

In 1978, management realized that future growth opportunities would be seriously limited by its regional orientation. Several threats existed. First, with freedom of entry into markets, carriers would undoubtedly start to expand their scope of operations. Markets would be contested. Capacity would be expanded. Both excess capacity and severe price competition would surely result. This could adversely impact USAir's performance in their established markets. Consequently, market forces were in part responsible for the carrier's decision to expand operations. Second, the value of their Eastern franchise could be protected with market links to the West Coast in addition to actions aimed at strengthening their primary hub operations. As pointed out by Robert E. Dunn, USAir's Vice President of Economic Research, USAir's expansion was as much a market driven event as the concrete deliberate choices of its management. So to grow the regional carrier into a new major carrier, the strategic objective of doubling its share of market to seven percent from three percent was accom-

plished through mergers with Pacific Southwest Airlines and Piedmont Airlines. The apparent emerging competitive strategy called for (1) increased market penetration in its well established Eastern markets—a defensive position—and (2) transcontinental market development through its link with the acquired regional carrier P.S.A.—an offensive move.

Strategic Choice Two:
Select Merger Partners Carefully

Anticipated industry consolidation was delayed until the early 1980s due to the air controllers' strike, a recession, and the effects of high priced fuel apart from the many competitive moves from established and new entrants to the industry. But once the consolidation movement began, smaller carriers who wished to grow by this route had to exercise considerable care in the process of identifying other carriers that would provide needed strategic resources and capabilities. The carriers acquired by USAir each had comparable operating philosophies, sound employee relations, established customer images for high quality service, and a history of high performance management. There was a good "fit" of their capabilities with those present in the existing USAir organization. Beyond careful identification of appropriate merger partners, serious attention was paid to the need to effectively integrate the acquired strategic capability into the existing USAir organization. It had to work or otherwise the strategic significance of the decision would be lost.

Part Two: Historic Growth and Development of USAir

The Formative Years: 1937–1977

USAir began as a mail carrier on March 5, 1937 under the name of All American Aviation Inc. serving Pennsylvania and West Virginia. When it started carrying passengers, it changed its name to All American Airways on September 20, 1948, and then to Allegheny Airlines on January 2, 1953. They acquired a route to Boston from Washington, D.C., in 1960 which started the expansion of this certified local service airline. A major shift to jet aircraft began with the acquisition of Lake Central Airlines on July 1, 1968, and Mohawk Airlines on April 12, 1972.[1] Prior to these acquisitions, and as a federally subsidized carrier, Allegheny was restricted to short haul local routes. The incentive for merging was to acquire new and longer routes which otherwise were difficult to receive through the route award procedures then used by the C.A.B.

The solution was to associate with smaller nonregulated commuter feeder carriers that could assume some of Allegheny's subsidized routes. These feeders could handle Allegheny's less profitable routes by using smaller propeller equipment, providing more frequent flights, and providing passenger feeds to Allegheny's routes through use of its reservation system. The sharing of Allegheny's ground facilities for a small fee also made this joint marketing approach economically attractive.[2] Finally, Allegheny scheduled its flights to make convenient connections for commuter airline passengers.

The concept of joint marketing with smaller nonscheduled commuter airlines produced what is now called the "Allegheny Commuter System." The system started operations on November 15, 1967. In order to qualify as an Allegheny commuter, an operator had to meet operations and maintenance standards set by Allegheny Airlines that were more stringent than those set by the F.A.A. for non-Allegheny commuters. The extensive use of commuters provided visibility for Allegheny in markets too small to serve and a stream of passengers for their on-line flights. After Allegheny became USAir, it owned outright the two largest units in the system—Pennsylvania and Suburban Airlines (all stock acquired in 1986). By 1986, this system consisted of nine commuters which operated 594 daily flights and provided USAir with a significant number of feed passengers.[3] This marketing al-

liance concept gradually became widely adopted in the industry. It continued to grow and by 1980, commuter enplanements accounted for 5 percent of the total U.S. enplanements at 618 airports, up from 3 percent in 1972.

By 1977, Allegheny had managed to reposition itself as a large regional L.S.A. carrier who was ready for its next stage of development. The C.A.B. had been convinced of the economic advantages for permitting this firm and other L.S.A.s to expand their operations to longer regional routes. This successful repositioning was credited to E.I. Colodny who joined the company in 1957 and was placed in charge of the acquisition of new route approvals from the C.A.B. He knew that two ingredients made for a successful airline: (a) knowing what made a good airline market and what did not and (b) knowing how to get an application approved by the C.A.B. Even though the carrier had become a large regional L.S.A. carrier, it had a major image problem in the marketplace. Known then as "Agony Airlines" for its late and unreliable service, Colodny did not believe that bigger was better—the popular public notion of a good airline. However, he apparently did have several tactics in mind designed to enhance the profitable development and growth of Allegheny.

Tactic One: Prepare Yourself for Expansion

Colodny knew how to shed the carrier of unprofitable routes while strengthening its core business. This was accomplished by engaging in joint marketing with commuter carriers and acquiring entry into new markets through service expansion to existing cities and strategic mergers. This was the quickest alternative given the C.A.B.'s existing route regulations.

Tactic Two: Move from a Position of Strength

Colodny paid increasing attention to building a strong market presence at the Pittsburgh hub. He followed a conservative expansion policy for entering new regional markets while maintaining a strong dominant position in his core Eastern marketplace. He would not seek gains in market share at the expense of weakening his primary Eastern presence.

Deregulation of the Domestic Airline Industry: 1978

With the Airline Deregulation Act of 1978, Allegheny came to accept the realities of an industry soon to be faced with revolutionary change and the need to map out a competitive strategy in light of the changing structure of the air transport industry. One of the first decisions focused upon how to position the carrier relative to the moves of large trunk operators. Historically, these trunk carriers provided service to large population markets using large jet aircraft. In contrast, Allegheny utilized smaller jets which permitted them to operate flexibly in short to medium haul markets. Their geographical location in the East and Midwest permitted them to take advantage of the air travel patterns of Americans who flew shorter routes because of the location of markets. Cities were close together. This produced efficient aircraft utilization and greater employee productivity. And it provided a unique locational competitive advantage.

By October 1979, the carrier had improved its capital structure, market image, and began to shed its regional image and renamed itself USAir Airlines. This ended a 26 year period as a smaller local service airline operator who had grown systematically through this early period of economic transformation of the airline industry. After the first full year of deregulation, USAir had captured a 2.26 percent market share.[4]

Tactic Three: Creating a New Identity

The company had readied itself for systematic growth by creating a new image for the renamed carrier called USAir. The former L.S.A. unit had prepared itself to participate as a major player as evidenced by its global new name. Market entry applications would be automatically approved by the C.A.B. starting January 1980. It

had found a new way to enter trunk markets on a competitive basis with a clear consumer identity.

The Emerging Strategy of USAir: Financial Strength

Because of their entrenched market position, new focus upon customer service, and the relaxing of pricing guidelines, the firm was able to sustain a profit even though the industry was experiencing operating losses. A conservative attitude toward route expansion and fleet modernization produced an improvement in their balance sheet. By 1984, the firm had dramatically improved their capital structure over 1975 by achieving a ratio of 35 percent debt to 65 percent equity.

But the very foundation of the firm's competitive strategy was (1) to control route expansion consistent with acquiring sound financing and (2) to build strong financial statements with which to exercise yet unseen market opportunities. Building this financial strength started in 1972 when the firm established a strong and successful relationship with the investment banking firm Shearson Lehman Brothers. Then the brokerage firm arranged the carrier's market quotations. Since then Shearson has advised and managed 26 transactions for the carrier including two major debt for equity conversions in 1987. William M. Kearns Jr., Managing Director of Shearson Lehman Brothers, served the carrier for 15 years and indicated that his firm functioned like the carrier's own finance department.

Three policy decisions by Colodny, according to Kearns, served the carrier well during this period of development. They included the decision not to buy large jets, the decision not to expand randomly into large city markets all over the country after entry restrictions were removed, and the decision to manage the debt/equity ratio in a conservative manner. Even after the P.S.A. acquisition in 1986, which required over $400 million, the ratio remained a safe 30/

70. The forecasted capital structure requirements called for it to return to 50/50 at the turn of the decade.

The competitive importance of the capitalization decision during the early days of deregulation was strategic. It related to USAir's ability to conserve its operating capital in order to endure the strong price competition it anticipated from (a) new upstart rival carriers like People Express and (b) counterattacks from large trunk carriers protecting their market presence from intruders. It would have the capacity to match prices from an aggressive entrant on a market by market basis and to retaliate by service expansion if necessary. The competitive result was success in disciplining both price and service competition and sustaining market share in contested markets. However, the firm never implemented a marketing/sales program which was driven primarily based upon market share objectives. While important, it was but one of several competitive goals operating.

Finally, Blake Thompson, Senior Vice President of Finance, summed up their strategy. He stated "we held off fleet replacement as long as we could to build a strong equity base. The more you borrow, the higher passenger load you need to break even, and the more difficult it is to fill the seats you need to break even, and the more you are driven to discount fares, and that drives your breakeven point higher."[5] For this reason the firm did not buy wide body jets which required 400 passengers to fill their seats. The criticism that smaller aircraft (BAC-111) were less efficient than the DC-9 or Boeing 737 was answered by Colodny when he said that it cost less to fly smaller planes and it requires fewer passengers to break even.[6]

Another Reorganization:
Formation of USAir Group, Inc.

On February 1, 1983, USAir, Inc., became a wholly owned subsidiary of USAir Group, Inc., a newly established holding company. By then USAir had managed to gain a 3.14 percent market share or an increase of 39 percent over the preceding year. Colodny described this growth as a by-product of their main objective—profitability. Management noted that they managed from a yield standpoint. It was a three legged stool—cost, yield, and load factor were all important. Then the firm had achieved a yield of 19 cents per each revenue passenger mile flown compared to the industry average of 11.68 cents. Then USAir, Inc., generated 97 percent of the parent company's revenue and enjoyed a strong balance sheet position. By December 31, 1985, USAir generated 99.5 percent of its parent's revenues.[7] The strategy of selective expansion stayed in effect. Colodny's policy of market extension required (1) profitable entry and (2) a fit with the carrier's overall route structure game plan. Because market entry decisions were well thought out, the carrier had experienced relatively few withdrawals from its new market entries.

By the end of 1984, the carrier had achieved five years of profitability since the 1978 deregulation. In fact a net profit of $18.5 million in the fourth quarter of 1984 was the highest earned in the company's history. This seemed to reflect the results of Colodny's earlier strategy of conservative expansion and control of route extensions along with efforts to achieve a strong financial position. He stated in May of 1984 that "our basic mission is still in the short to intermediate stage lengths because that's the way the country is built east of the Mississippi River .... That is where the cities are in relation to each other, and you cannot change them, and we are not going to become a long-haul carrier except insofar as it's a key part of our hub operation."[8]

According to Civil Aeronautics Board data, by 1984 almost two-thirds of all domestic market travel was on trips under 1,000 miles in length. And almost 40 percent of the passengers were taking trips under 500 miles in length. Colodny stated that since deregulation, the average pas-

senger trip length on USAir flights was steadily
climbing. However, it was still only 480 miles—
the shortest of any major carrier. The average
distance between stops was only 375 miles. But
the carrier had moved west of the Mississippi
River and by 1984 had begun new service to 24
cities. Of the carrier's top 25 traffic generating
cities, 14 had been started after 1978.

Randall Malin, USAir's Executive Vice
President of Marketing, explained that they try
to fit new markets into their primary hubs and
have a strong presence in one of the two markets
they enter. Then they flew to 69 airports serving
94 cities in 27 states. The allied commuters
added another 82 flights a day serving 51 airports
and feeding a third of their 2.1 million passengers
to USAir. Management had been reluctant to enter the transatlantic market in a major way for
the same reason they avoided rapid domestic expansion. The long-standing policy of running the
airline for profits and not merely market share
growth guided the organization's sales and marketing decisions.

Further Acquisitions

To solidify their regional strength and to support
their hub and spoke route strategy, several acquisitions were made. In May of 1985, USAir
Group, Inc., acquired Pennsylvania Airlines.
The local commuter feeder carrier increased the
number of on-line passengers carried by the parent airline. Later that same year, a new USAir
Group subsidiary was formed called USAir Leasing, Inc. This unit provided a range of aviation
related services including the ownership and
leasing of aircraft. They also reached agreement
to acquire Suburban Airlines which was another
Pennsylvania based Allegheny commuter airline.
Despite these acquisitions and development of
new organizational units, as of December 31,
1985, USAir generated 99.5 percent of its parent's revenues, was classified as a major carrier
by the D.O.T., provided regularly scheduled air
service through 74 airports to more than 100 cities, and carried 19 million passengers.

Tactic Four: Build Market Power

Build a feeder system that maximizes the capacity of available equipment on major short haul
routes thereby providing your passengers with
point-to-point service while avoiding interlining
with other airlines.

Entry into Domestic Transcontinental Markets

By 1986, USAir Group, Inc., had established its
U.S. presence in eastern markets as being one of
the strongest and most profitable carriers. This
was measured by the percentage of passenger enplanements they held at major markets and the
profitability of these markets. The cost of de-
fending these markets from entry and competition would rise even though the carrier had
gained control over a critical barrier to entry
which was the availability of limited station gates
and landing slots. The next competitive move
then seemed to be major expansion into transcontinental markets. At that time, the carrier already had service from Pittsburgh to Los Angeles. The key decision was which markets to
enter. The West Coast market was a logical one
because of its high passenger density and because
of the existing demand from their own East
Coast passenger base. The two existing West
Coast carriers that might be acquired were P.S.A.
and Alaskan Airways. So in December of 1986,
USAir and Pacific Southwest Airlines (P.S.A.), a
national carrier, announced that they had entered into an agreement to join forces. USAir
would pay about $17 per share for a total of $400
million to acquire this established West Coast
carrier. Based upon 1986 statistics, the combined
carriers would rank sixth in terms of annual enplanements (30 million passengers) and seventh
in terms of passenger revenue miles flown (14.9
billion). The plan called for the linking up of
these West Coast markets served by P.S.A. (Los
Angeles, Phoenix, San Diego, San Francisco, and
Tucson) with USAir's strong Pittsburgh hub.
P.S.A.'s long-standing reputation as a high quality operation servicing the short and medium
haul markets represented a key strategic move

by Colodny's management group. Gaining West Coast gateway cities like Los Angeles would provide needed collection points from P.S.A.'s feeder cities. Both carriers had followed similar strategies as short haul regional market airlines. Both being well managed, operating similar midrange and new fuel efficient aircraft, following innovative marketing programs, and having established customer franchises, meant that their integration should be relatively smooth and synergetic. The plan called for P.S.A. to operate as a wholly owned subsidiary for a reasonable transition period in order to achieve an effective integration of the two organizations. This also provided USAir with an opportunity to observe the competitive reactions to this step toward further consolidation of the industry.

Tactic Five: Control External Growth

When implementing a service extension merger, acquire similar operating organizations to facilitate their timely, efficient, and effective integration.

Protection from Unfriendly Takeover Bids

With the acquisition of P.S.A., the grand strategy of USAir Group, Inc., was becoming clear. The next step had to be the acquisition of another carrier that could bring established capacity, a favorable operating capability, sufficient resources with which to enter a new competitive group (the top five major carriers) and additional experience in servicing transcontinental domestic markets. But the P.S.A. acquisition would require time and capital for integration if it was to be successful. Consequently, management stated that "the airline should not be vulnerable to hostile takeover." The board then approved a plan to give shareholders the right to buy common stock at half the market price. The purchase rights could only be exercised if a person or group acquired 20 percent or more of USAir Group's common stock or announced a tender offer for 30 percent or more of its common stock. Finally, it amended its certificate of incorporation to re-

quire that holders of 80 percent of its shares instead of half, approve any acquisition in which the acquirer failed to comply with certain procedural requirements. But a stockholder's effort staged by the California Public Employees Retirement System almost overturned this antitakeover provision in favor of (1) a direct redemption of the shares or (2) a direct stockholder vote on the issue.[9]

Tactic Six: Block and Parry

This action—the anti-takeover effort—provided top management with a tool to protect their stockholders' vested interests regarding their implementation of the grand strategy being pursued by Colodny. This was a critical step in view of the large number of acquisitions that had occurred in the industry. During the period 1980–1987, a total of 22 major mergers occurred estimated at a value of $7.365 billion. Any carrier trying to position itself for long term growth in this rapidly changing industry had to guard against unfriendly takeover attempts.

USAir Group, Inc.'s Competitive Position: 1986

From 1976 forward, this carrier had experienced considerable annual growth in markets, personnel, equipment, share of markets, competitive know-how and in earnings per share. In a word, they had been "successful." This transformed carrier had achieved its development objectives through the implementation of its intended competitive strategy. It is interesting to speculate why this was the case as revealed by the operational and competitive consequences of these major policy and tactical choices made by this firm's top management.

Routes. The firm believed that it could best compete with routes of less than 1,000 miles. They developed the distinctive competency to serve these carefully selected markets.

Hubs. The firm had competed effectively utilizing secondary hub markets like Pittsburgh and

Philadelphia. It had avoided large hubs dominated by major competitors like United, Eastern, Delta, and American Airlines. However, at some large hubs the firm had maintained a market presence; but the game plan seemed to call for gaining large market shares in strategic secondary hub cities.

Interlining with Commuters. Cooperative behavior had been strongly practiced by USAir with the Allegheny Commuter Association. This produced profitable and competitive advantages for both parties.

Market Extension. The carrier believed that strong earnings and financial capacity were more important than achieving mere market share objectives. It had generated one of the highest returns on owners' equity in the industry. Consequently, it had required that the marginal value of new route opportunities be assessed in terms of their overall economic impact upon the existing route structure of the carrier.

Yield Management. A yield driven pricing policy was effectively implemented. They were the high priced carrier in the industry. Even though the average yield in the industry had been reduced, USAir was able to maintain their basic pricing policies without following the growing trend toward deep discounting and promotional pricing in the industry. This did not mean the carrier was not responsive to the pricing behavior of their competitors.

Barriers to Entry. By servicing secondary and hence shorter haul routes, the firm had been able to gain a large share of these less competitive routes. USAir had managed to acquire a strategic number of gates and landing slots at the airports they served—a key competitive advantage. However, the carrier competed with at least one major carrier on all of its major routes. This did cause them to follow a "meet the competition price policy" on a market by market basis throughout their system.

Distribution System. Travel agents issued tickets to approximately 68 percent of USAir's passengers. Most of the country's 30,000 travel agents (by 1987) used one or more of the five major computer reservation systems (C.R.S.) to book client travel arrangements. Clearly, this was a key distribution and competitive tool for the major carriers—American, United, Delta, and Eastern. Competition had been intense among the top owners of these systems (1) to attract travel agent subscriptions for these services and (2) to establish joint-venture participation with other domestic and international carriers for the operations of these critical distribution systems.

Clearly, the lack of its own C.R.S. would have operated to USAir's competitive disadvantage. Distribution could be a major barrier that could lock USAir out of their markets. But this problem was solved when USAir Group, Inc., purchased 11.3 percent interest in Allegis' Apollo booking system for $113.1 million.[10] It was to be called Covia Partnership since four other European firms also purchased into the system for $386.7 million. Randall Malin, USAir's Executive Vice President for Marketing, said the purchase accomplished the carrier's long-standing objective to acquire access to a major travel distribution system.

Operations. For the period 1976–1986, the carrier experienced a 12.3 percent annual rate of growth in its revenue passenger miles flown. Other major competitors only experienced a 4 percent annual growth rate. But besides this strong performance, the carrier remained one of the high cost carriers as measured by cost per available seat mile flown. This was not due to inefficient operations, but rather because of the nature of the short haul routes they flew. They had differentiated their service successfully and proved that a high cost/high revenue strategy could work.

Labor Relations. They had been effective at the carrier. Even though they tried to minimize exposure to unions by organizing separate subsidiaries distinct from their airline operations, the firm still managed to avoid taking a strike. They settled with their pilots in 1987 for a three year contract that established a two-tier pay scale with a conditional merger of pay scales after six years. Negotiated pay increases amounted to slightly higher ones than those awarded in the 1987 United Airline contract. Bringing their labor costs into line with other low cost carriers was a necessary move by company management. This left the industry with seven major carriers utilizing two-tier pay systems.[11] As of January 1987, USAir employed 14,970 employees with approximately 54 percent covered by five collective bargaining agreements. Average salary with benefits amounted to $45,197 annually. Total labor costs amounted to 41.7 percent of operating expenses. This was about 6 percent above the industry average.

The Results. By 1986 it was clear that USAir had become a transformed domestic carrier. It had achieved outstanding results from its deliberate transformational policy and tactical choices. Its positioning strategy in response to the Airline Deregulation Act of 1978 worked. Its actual transitional operating and financial results were outstanding compared to average industry financial performance as shown in Exhibits A and B. And its ability to implement systematically the adopted proactive strategy of becoming a "major domestic carrier" through a period of major restructuring of the U.S. domestic airline industry was impressive. Perhaps the most impressive observation was the "steady-firm hands on approach" taken by CEO Edwin Colodny. He demonstrated the true art of executive leadership while being a master strategist through this all. Many carriers failed to survive let alone prosper during this period of industry turmoil, change, and consolidation.

The Next Move

Both the financial community and CEOs of other major carriers were speculating about the next move or set of moves that this carrier would likely make given its new position as a major and profitable industry carrier. One speculation focused upon their need to establish themselves in their new markets as a viable competitor. They had just made entry into a new strategic group. They would now have to work their clearly identified competitive strategy. Could they effectively compete with the large established players in the industry? How would these carriers respond to the emerging competitive threat of USAir? Another view speculated about their need to move quickly into international markets in a major way. Air transportation was in the process of globalization with deregulation and liberalization taking place around the world. They had several Atlantic overseas flights and operated into Canada. Could they afford to delay such a move especially since there were several targets of opportunity available? One scenario involved the gradual buildup of transatlantic routes in order to participate in the marketing alliances then occurring among other major U.S. carriers and foreign carriers. Another scenario would be to acquire routes from an established carrier like T.W.A. who needed a strong partner. Or Pan Am was faltering and could become another means to expand into the international market. Yet, perhaps the best move would be "strategy implementation." This would entail the consolidation of USAir's new route structure and organizational delivery system. But the competition could bet on the idea that whatever future choices Chairman Edwin I. Colodny would make, USAir Group, Inc., would be a formidable competitor in the U.S. domestic airline marketplace.

Specific Information Sources
1. *Moody's Transportation Manual*, 1985.

2. "It Wasn't Done with Mirrors," *Forbes*, June 15, 1973.

3. "Allegheny Commuter Sets the Pace for Marketing Agreements," *Air Transport World*, March 1986.

4. James P. Woolsey, "USAir: First in Pittsburgh, First in the U.S., and First in the World," *Air Transport World*, June, 1983.

5. Thomas G. Donlan, "U.S. Bucks Powerful Industry Headwinds," *Barrons*, July 19, 1982.

6. Ibid.

7. James P. Woolsey, "USAir: First in Pittsburgh, First in the U.S., and First in the World," *Air Transport World*, June, 1983.

8. Carole A. Shifrin, "USAir's Business Strategy Succeeds in Deregulation," *Aviation Week and Space Technology*, May 14, 1984, p.42.

9. "USAir Holder Vote to End Poison Pill Narrowly Defeated," *Wall Street Journal*, May 12, 1988, p.6.

10. Robert L. Rose, "Allegis to Sell Half of Apollo Booking System," *Wall Street Journal*, May 3, 1988, p.4.

11. "USAir Management, Pilots Agree to Establish Two-Tier Pay Scale," *Aviation Week and Space Technology*, November 25, 1985.

General Information Sources About Airlines and the U.S. Airline Industry

12. Order 87-3-58, United States of America, Department of Transportation, March 20, 1987, Application of USAir Group, Inc., for the Expedited Approval of a Voting Trust under Section 408 of the Federal Aviation Act, Docket 44719.

13. Order 87-3-70, United States of America, Department of Transportation, March 25, 1987, Application of USAir Group, Inc., for Expedited Approval of a Voting Trust under Section 408 of the Federal Aviation Act, Docket 44719.

14. Air Transport Association's Annual Reports, 1976–1986.

15. James F. Molloy, Jr., *The U.S. Commuter Airline Industry*, Lexington Books, Lexington, Massachusetts, 1985.

16. Elizabeth E. Bailey, et al, *Deregulating the Airlines*, The M.I.T. Press, Cambridge, Massachusetts, 1985.

17. Jonathan L.S. Byrnes, *Diversification Strategies for Regulated and Deregulated Industries: Lessons from the Airlines*, Lexington Books, Lexington, Massachusetts, 1985.

18. First Boston Research, Piedmont Aviation, Inc. (PIE), Progress Report, July 30, 1984.

19. Annual Report of the Regional/Commuter Airline Industry, 1987, Regional Airline Association, Washington D.C.

20. Ed Bean, "Piedmont Makes It Big in Small Cities," *Wall Street Journal*, June 23, 1986.

21. Henry Lefer, "Piedmont Played the Game and Won," *Air Transport World*, January, 1985.

22. William E. O'Connor, *An Introduction to Airline Economics,* Praeger Press, New York, 1985.

23. Standard and Poor's Industry Surveys, "Aerospace and Transportation Basic Analysis," 1976–1986.

24. *Moody's Transportation Manuals*, 1976–1985.

25. "Consolidation: Is it a Threat to the Industry" *Air Transport World*, November, 1985.

26. "Piedmont Shuttle Targets Florida Business Market," *Air Transport World*, January, 1986.

27. Civil Aeronautics Board Report to Congress, "Implementation of the Provisions of the Airline Deregulation Act of 1978," January 31, 1984.

28. Civil Aeronautics Board (1976–1984), *Air Carrier Statistics*, Washington D.C., Government Printing Office.

29. William J. Curtin, "Airline Deregulation and Labor Relations," *Monthly Labor Review*, June 1986 (29–30).

30. J.A. Donoghue, "Talking to Employees: Airlines Discover Internal Communications," *Air Transport World*, August 1986 (20–28).

31. Joan M. Feldman, "CRS Controversy Grows as Systems Become More Powerful," *Air Transport World*, August 1986 (33–41).

32. Pacific Southwest Airlines, Inc., Report on Special Meeting of Shareholders, March 1987.

33. "World Airline Fleets," *Air Transport World*, May 1986.

34. "Allegheny Commuter Sets the Pace for Marketing Agreements," *Air Transport World*, March 1986.

35. "USAir's Business Strategy Succeeds in Deregulation," *Aviation Week and Space Technology*, March 1986.

Exhibit A   Selected Financial Data: USAir Group, Inc.

	1987	1986	1985	1984	1983	1982	1981	1980	1979	1978	1977
Income Statement											
Operating Revenues	$3,001	$1,835	$1,765	$1,630	$1,432	$1,273	$1,110	$ 972	$ 729	$ 567	$ 492
Operating Expenses	2,682	1,666	1,597	1,438	1,304	1,194	1,052	880	677	533	467
Operating Income	$ 319	$ 169	$ 168	$ 192	$ 128	$ 79	$ 58	$ 92	$ 52	$ 34	$ 25
Net Income	$ 195	$ 98	$ 117	$ 122	$ 81	$ 59	$ 51	$ 60	$ 33	$ 32	$ 16
Fully Diluted Earnings per Share	$ 5.27	$ 3.33	$ 3.98	$ 4.46	$ 3.22	$ 2.88	$ 2.66	$ 3.59	$ 2.24	$ 2.82	$ 1.77
Dividends per Common Share	$ .12	$ .12	$ .12	$ .12	$ .12	$ .12	$ .12	$ .09	$ –	$ –	$ –
Balance Sheet											
Total Assets	$5,257	$2,147	$1,951	$1,621	$1,318	$1,062	$ 881	$ 715	$ 553	$ 404	$ 387
Long-Term Debt	$,1870	$ 454	$ 474	$ 430	$ 350	$ 334	$ 303	$ 236	$ 184	$ 144	$ 237
Stockholders' Equity	$1,895	$1,058	$ 956	$ 737	$ 615	$ 459	$ 353	$ 272	$ 216	$ 167	$ 75
Shares of Common Stock Outstanding	43.2	27.3	26.9	23.0	22.8	19.8	17.1	12.0	11.9	9.9	6.0
Book Value per Share	$43.90	$38.77	$35.44	$31.89	$26.77	$22.89	$20.34	$18.43	$13.85	$11.82	$10.69

Source: Annual Report, 1987

Exhibit B Operating Statistics: USAir, Inc.

	1987	1986	1985	1984	1983	1982	1981	1980	1979	1978	1977
Revenue Passengers (Millions)	24.8	21.7	19.3	17.0	16.2	14.6	13.4	14.2	14.1	12.8	11.7
Average Passenger Journey (Miles)	527.7	513.5	504.8	480.5	446.5	415.2	404.6	385.3	359.1	318.1	312.6
Revenue Passenger Miles (Millions)	13,072	11,155	9,732	8,191	7,245	6,078	5,424	5,476	5,049	4,083	3,643
Available Seat Miles (Millions)	20,014	18,254	16,433	14,098	12,235	10,666	9,383	8,992	7,853	6,721	6,568
Passenger Load Factor	65.3%	61.1%	59.2%	58.1%	59.2%	57.0%	57.8%	60.9%	64.3%	60.8%	55.5%
Revenue per Passenger Mile	14.91¢	14.93¢	16.71¢	18.57¢	18.42¢	19.51¢	18.93¢	16.26¢	12.88¢	12.29¢	12.05¢
Cost per Available Seat Mile	8.90¢	8.74¢	9.45¢	9.98¢	10.50¢	11.07¢	11.07¢	9.65¢	8.46¢	7.67¢	6.95¢
Average Distance between Stops (Miles)	425.2	405.8	395.4	374.3	354.5	339.3	325.6	306.1	284.2	242.6	235.2
Breakeven Load Factor	57.3%	56.4%	54.2%	51.7%	54.6%	54.1%	54.9%	55.6%	60.2%	56.9%	54.7%
Gallons of Fuel Consumed (Millions)	463	435	404	367	327	301	276	273	262	239	228
Cost Per Gallon of Fuel	54.74¢	53.85¢	79.74¢	84.80¢	89.08¢	97.30¢	103.14¢	86.74¢	55.83¢	39.65¢	37.15¢
Number of Employees at Year End	16,509	14,976	13,789	12,524	11,899	11,046	10,765	10,379	9,741	8,745	8,067
Aircraft Fleet at Year End	162	149	143	133	127	119	106	95	90	93	94

Source: Annual Report, 1987

Letter to the Stockholders

Nineteen eighty-nine was a difficult year for our company, a year in which record earnings of $116 million for the first half of the year were overshadowed by record losses of $180 million in the second half. The net loss for the year was $63 million. The loss applicable to Common Stock was $76 million after preferred stock dividends. This performance can be attributed to the combination of deteriorating industry fundamentals and unexpected merger-related problems.

Last year, the domestic airline industry experienced generally flat traffic, competitive pressure on yields, and, toward the end of the year, rapidly escalating fuel prices. In addition, USAir's results were uniquely affected by the costs in the third and fourth quarters associated with the Piedmont merger. This was the largest airline merger in history, joining more than 22,000 Piedmont employees with 27,000 USAir employees, and combining Piedmont's fleet of 205 aircraft with USAir's 226 jets.

Although the formal merger date was August 5, it was not until February 1, 1990, that a truly merged airline became a reality. Full integration was delayed until necessary labor agreements had been finalized.

Less than satisfactory reliability in our on-time performance was a negative factor during the last half of 1989. That, in turn, triggered many customer service problems. I am pleased to report that overall operating performance has steadily improved in the past few months as a result of numerous programs implemented to restore our reputation for quality service.

Continued emphasis on service occupies the highest priority on management's agenda. We cannot afford to jeopardize our revenue stream with less than superior customer service.

New fuel-efficient and quieter aircraft, improved airport facilities, additional maintenance facilities, and employee training programs are all vital to meeting our service objectives. We are committed to investing the funds and effort required.

We added 32 new jets in 1989—17 new Boeing 737-400s, seven Boeing 737-300s, and eight Fokker 100s—the latter aircraft type being new to our fleet. Aircraft on order and option total 241 and are valued at $6.8 billion.

Among our new facilities are a new 723,000-square-foot Charlotte maintenance base, which will open this year and employ 925 maintenance personnel, and a $10 million renovation of airport terminal facilities in San Diego.

Work continues on schedule for the Pittsburgh Midfield Terminal, due to open in early 1993. This state-of-the-art facility will allow significant expansion of USAir's service at Pittsburgh.

In May 1989, we unveiled a new wordmark and a red, white, and blue color scheme that better represents the major, nationwide airline that USAir has become. We will initiate a new aircraft interior design program this year.

USAir introduced first-class cabin service on all flights on June 15, 1989. The USAir Club network, one of the largest in the nation, now offers 27 club rooms at 24 airports.

Our controlled-growth program continues to focus on expanding our hubs, adding flights linking eastern and western cities, expanding operations in the Caribbean, and developing new major markets, such as Kansas City.

We are also continuing limited international expansion. Nonstop Pittsburgh-Frankfurt service will begin June 15, complementing our Charlotte-London service. Other European destinations are being considered for 1991 and beyond.

While USAir's balance sheet remains one of the best in the industry, it is essential that we return to profitability at an early date to maintain our vigorous programs for growth and modernization.

In the third quarter, we took several steps to further stockholder and employee interests. We improved the preferred share purchase rights plan. A new series of convertible preferred stock was issued to Berkshire Hathaway, a committed, long-term investor. We also initiated an employee stock ownership plan, which is geared to the Company's earnings performance. In addition, the Board of Directors authorized the repurchase of up to 9.4 million shares of Common Stock. By year-end, the Company had repurchased 2.1 million shares.

We are beginning to see significant benefits from the PSA and Piedmont mergers as we capitalize on the expanded scope of our revenue base. With the mergers behind us, our objective is to return USAir to its historic position as one of the nation's most profitable airlines. This calls for a renewed focus on customer service, as well as improved productivity and lower unit costs. We are well along with these efforts.

USAir has a reputation as a good place to work and enjoys good employee relations. In an election concluded in January 1990, fleet service employees voted not to have union representation. We believe that this election result reflects the confidence our employees have in USAir.

As a service business, we depend on the performance of our people. I wish to take this opportunity to thank our employees for their professionalism and dedication.

An Office of the Chairman was established in early 1989. In July, the Board of Directors elected Randall Malin and Seth E. Schofield to the Board and named them Vice Chairmen.

As a final note, after 37 years of service, Paul A. Schoellkopf retired from the Board of Directors last year. His many contributions are greatly appreciated.

Edwin I. Colodny
Chairman of the Board and
President

March 2, 1990

USAir Group, Inc.
CONSOLIDATED INCOME STATEMENTS

Years Ended December 31, *(in thousands except per share amounts)*	1989	1988	1987
Operating Revenues:			
Passenger transportation	$5,809,048	$5,273,955	$2,775,581
Other	442,511	433,037	225,503
Total operating revenues	6,251,559	5,706,992	3,001,084
Operating Expenses:			
Personnel costs	2,277,018	1,944,428	1,039,471
Aviation fuel	775,997	638,453	377,602
Travel agency commissions	433,563	382,718	203,623
Rentals and landing fees	604,881	510,740	200,397
Aircraft maintenance	387,087	337,564	155,782
Depreciation and amortization	253,827	229,729	127,630
Other	1,497,694	1,229,768	577,361
Total operating expenses	6,230,067	5,273,400	2,681,866
Operating Income	21,492	433,592	319,218
Other Income (Expense):			
Interest income	5,773	12,573	22,474
Interest expense, net of capitalized interest	(104,058)	(123,206)	(88,828)
Writedown of BAC 1-11 aircraft and spares	—	(33,000)	—
Other	4,749	(20,445)	3,501
Total other income (expense)	(93,536)	(164,078)	(62,853)
Income (loss) before taxes and equity in net income of Piedmont	(72,044)	269,514	256,365
Provision (credit) for income taxes	(8,868)	104,510	101,080
Income (loss) before equity in net income of Piedmont	(63,176)	165,004	155,285
Equity in net income of Piedmont	—	—	39,364
Net Income (Loss)	$ (63,176)	$ 165,004	$ 194,649
Earnings (Loss) Per Common Share	$ (1.73)	$ 3.81	$ 5.28
Shares Used For Computation	44,051	43,304	37,728

See accompanying Notes to Consolidated Financial Statements.

USAir Group, Inc.
CONSOLIDATED BALANCE SHEETS

December 31,	1989	1988
(dollars in thousands)		
ASSETS		
Current Assets:		
Cash and cash equivalents	$ 14,936	$ 78,000
Receivables, net	378,041	381,127
Income tax refund receivable	89,994	—
Materials and supplies, net	347,604	265,310
Prepaid expenses	105,823	97,088
Total current assets	936,398	821,525
Property and Equipment:		
Flight equipment	3,764,820	3,117,121
Ground property and equipment	941,266	824,230
Less accumulated depreciation and amortization	(936,069)	(778,100)
	3,770,017	3,163,251
Purchase deposits	457,083	405,448
Property and equipment, net	4,227,100	3,568,699
Other Assets:		
Goodwill, net	606,873	623,889
Other intangibles, net	179,014	189,678
Other assets	119,603	145,087
Total other assets	905,490	958,654
	$6,068,988	$5,348,878
LIABILITIES AND STOCKHOLDERS' EQUITY		
Current Liabilities:		
Current maturities of long-term debt	$ 75,067	$ 85,643
Accounts payable	495,220	371,146
Traffic balances payable and unused tickets	385,388	318,883
Accrued expenses	622,036	433,381
Total current liabilities	1,577,711	1,209,053
Long-Term Debt, Net of Current Maturities	1,468,319	1,332,872
Deferred Credits and Other Liabilities:		
Income taxes	356,131	340,769
Deferred gains and other liabilities	416,176	396,672
Total deferred credits and other liabilities	772,307	737,441
Commitments and Contingencies		
Redeemable, Convertible Preferred Stock,		
358,000 shares issued, no par value	358,000	—
Stockholders' Equity:		
Common stock, par value $1 per share, authorized 75,000,000 shares, issued 46,909,000		
shares and 44,411,000 shares, respectively	46,909	44,411
Paid-in capital	1,189,853	1,068,958
Retained earnings	899,914	982,904
Common stock held in treasury, at cost, 2,754,000 shares and 635,000 shares, respectively	(123,914)	(20,643)
Deferred Compensation	(120,111)	(6,118)
Total stockholders' equity	1,892,651	2,069,512
	$6,068,988	$5,348,878

See accompanying Notes to Consolidated Financial Statements.

USAir Group, Inc.
CONSOLIDATED STATEMENTS OF CASH FLOWS

Years Ended December 31,	1989	1988	1987
(dollars in thousands)			
Cash and Cash Equivalents at Beginning of Year	$ 78,000	$ 232,577	$ 336,158
Cash Flows from Operating Activities:			
Net income (loss)	(63,176)	165,004	194,649
Adjustments to reconcile net income to cash provided by operating activities:			
Depreciation and amortization	253,827	229,729	127,630
Deferred income taxes	15,362	(3,739)	57,294
Writedown of BAC 1-11 aircraft and spares	—	33,000	—
Equity in net income of Piedmont, net of dividends	—	—	(37,508)
Loss (gain) on sale of property	(9,910)	2,119	(6,184)
Other	9,057	3,299	9,339
Changes in certain assets and liabilities net of effects of purchase of subsidiaries:			
Decrease (increase) in receivables	(86,908)	(37,957)	64,512
Decrease (increase) in materials, supplies and prepaid expenses	(88,203)	(43,483)	(7,028)
Increase (decrease) in traffic balances payable and unused tickets	62,710	21,398	(37,530)
Increase (decrease) in accounts payable and accrued expenses	306,461	139,209	(8,915)
Net cash provided by operating activities	399,220	508,579	356,259
Cash Flows from Investing Activities:			
Payment for purchase of subsidiaries, net of cash acquired:			
Piedmont	—	—	(1,476,705)
PSA	—	—	(313,291)
Additions to flight equipment and purchase deposits	(460,205)	(414,691)	(249,665)
Additions to other property	(222,353)	(229,302)	(225,781)
Proceeds from disposition of property	207,352	564,433	353,607
Investment in Covia Partnership	7,146	(113,133)	—
Other	2,196	(15,285)	19,052
Net cash used in investing activities	(465,864)	(207,978)	(1,892,783)
Cash Flows from Financing Activities:			
Issuance of debt	338,606	127,241	1,905,450
Repayment of debt	(575,406)	(591,510)	(965,085)
Issuance of common stock	4,616	14,302	517,268
Issuance of preferred stock	358,000	—	—
Treasury stock	(102,422)	—	(20,043)
Dividends	(19,814)	(5,211)	(4,647)
Net cash provided by (used for) financing activities	3,580	(455,178)	1,432,943
Net increase (decrease) in cash and cash equivalents	(63,064)	(154,577)	(103,581)
Cash and Cash Equivalents at End of Year	$ 14,936	$ 78,000	$ 232,577

See accompanying Notes to Consolidated Financial Statements.

USAIR GROUP NYSE-U

RECENT PRICE	27	P/E RATIO	NMF	(Trailing:NMF Median: 8.0)	RELATIVE P/E RATIO	NMF	DIV'D YLD	0.4%	VALUE LINE	266

TIMELINESS 4 Below Average (Relative Price Performance Next 12 Mos.)	High:	12.5	19.3	26.1	36.5	39.9	35.0	38.5	41.0	53.5	40.1	54.8	33.8		Target Price Range 1993 1994 1995
	Low:	6.5	6.5	11.0	10.0	25.9	22.0	27.3	30.1	26.0	28.0	30.6	24.8		

SAFETY 3 Average (Scale: 1 Highest to 5 Lowest)

BETA 1.25 (1.00 = Market)

1993-95 PROJECTIONS
	Price	Gain	Ann'l Total Return
High	75	(+180%)	29%
Low	50	(+85%)	17%

Insider Decisions
	S	O	N	D	J	F	M	A	M
to Buy	1	0	1	0	1	1	0	0	0
Options	1	0	0	0	0	0	0	0	0
to Sell	1	0	0	0	0	0	0	0	0

Institutional Decisions
	3Q'89	4Q'89	1Q'90
to Buy	56	54	49
to Sell	90	91	76
Hld's(000)	34329	29265	30288

Percent shares traded: 30.0 / 20.0 / 10.0

5.0 x "Cash Flow" p

Relative Price Strength

Options: PACE

© VALUE LINE PUB., INC.

1974	1975	1976	1977	1978	1979	1980	1981	1982	1983	1984	1985	1986	1987	1988	1989	1990	1991		93-95 G
62.74	61.94	72.88	81.79	57.20	61.12	80.67	65.04	64.19	62.68	70.74	65.61	67.32	69.52	130.37	141.58	150.55	158.90	Revenues per sh A	175.00
3.65	1.23	3.69	5.89	5.64	5.53	8.32	5.55	5.69	6.30	8.16	7.22	7.02	7.46	9.02	4.32	5.50	8.55	"Cash Flow" per sh	12.80
.66	d1.64	.67	2.62	2.75	2.64	4.71	3.13	3.35	3.49	4.92	4.05	3.34	5.28	3.81	d1.73	d1.20	1.50	Earnings per sh B	6.50
--	--	--	--	--	--	.09	.12	.12	.12	.12	.12	.12	.12	.12	.12	.12	.18	Div'ds Decl'd per sh C	.20
39.16	39.34	45.12	46.22	39.96	37.86	45.61	43.21	45.60	54.34	64.57	65.24	74.80	95.25	99.30	116.93	119.10	126.65	Gross Equipment per sh	135.00
9.41	7.52	9.81	12.43	11.82	13.89	18.47	20.34	22.89	26.77	31.89	35.45	38.76	43.90	47.28	42.86	41.25	42.15	Book Value per sh	52.35
5.87	6.02	6.02	6.02	9.91	11.92	12.05	17.07	19.83	22.85	23.04	26.91	27.26	43.17	43.78	44.16	44.50	45.00	Common Shs Outst'g D	50.00
9.5	--	8.2	1.8	3.1	3.4	2.6	5.6	5.5	9.3	5.9	8.2	10.6	8.0	9.2	--	Bold figures are		Avg Ann'l P/E Ratio	9.5
1.33	--	1.05	.24	.42	.49	.35	.68	.61	.79	.55	.67	.72	.53	.76	--	Value Line estimates		Relative P/E Ratio	.80
--	--	--	--	--	--	.7%	.7%	.7%	.4%	.4%	.4%	.3%	.3%	.3%	.3%			Avg Ann'l Div'd Yield	.3%

CAPITAL STRUCTURE as of 3/31/90
Total Debt $1859.4 mill. **Due in 5 Yrs** $858.0 mill.
LT Debt $1783.9 mill.   **LT Interest** $165.0 mill.
Incl. $222.6 mill. capitalized leases.
Incl. $.6 mill. 6% sub. debs. ('93) each cv. into 18.1 shs. at $55.25.
(Interest not earned)

(45% of Cap'l)
Leases, Uncapitalized Annual rentals $450.2 mill.
Pension Liability None in '89 vs. None in '88
Pfd Stock $358.0 mill.   **Pfd Div'd** $33.2 mill.

(9% of Cap'l)
Common Stock 44,155,000
(50.1 million fully diluted shares)

(46% of Cap'l)

	971.8	1110.5	1273.0	1432.3	1629.7	1765.1	1835.2	3001.1	5707.0	6251.6	6700	7150	Revenues ($mill) A	8750
	61.2%	58.1%	57.2%	59.5%	58.6%	59.2%	61.1%	65.3%	61.3%	60.5%	59.0%	60.0%	Load Factor F	61.5%
	13.9%	9.3%	10.5%	13.4%	15.0%	13.9%	14.3%	14.9%	11.6%	4.4%	4.3%	7.5%	Operating Margin	11.0%
	43.4	45.3	54.4	63.5	66.4	77.2	93.2	127.6	229.7	253.8	260	285	Depreciation ($mill)	310
	60.4	51.1	59.1	80.6	121.6	117.1	98.4	194.7	165.0	d63.2	d15.0	100	Net Profit ($mill)	330
	31.6%	25.8%	39.0%	34.0%	40.4%	33.5%	42.1%	39.4%	38.8%	--	NMF	42.0%	Income Tax Rate	42.0%
	6.2%	4.6%	4.6%	5.6%	7.5%	6.6%	5.4%	6.5%	2.9%	NMF	NMF	1.4%	Net Profit Margin	3.8%
	221.0	280.6	315.8	331.8	414.8	451.4	425.0	1798.2	1332.9	1468.3	1800	2400	Long-Term Debt ($mill)	2400
	271.8	353.4	459.1	615.1	737.3	955.5	1058.0	1894.9	2069.5	2250.7	2200	2250	Net Worth ($mill)	2600
	14.4%	9.2%	9.4%	10.0%	12.0%	9.6%	8.0%	6.6%	6.9%	.5%	1.0%	3.5%	% Earned Total Cap'l	8.0%
	22.2%	14.5%	12.9%	13.1%	16.5%	12.3%	9.3%	10.3%	8.0%	NMF	NMF	4.5%	% Earned Net Worth	12.5%
	25.0%	13.7%	12.4%	12.7%	16.2%	11.9%	9.0%	10.0%	7.7%	NMF	NMF	3.0%	% Retained to Comm Eq	12.0%
	8%	7%	5%	4%	2%	3%	3%	2%	3%	NMF	NMF	41%	% All Div'ds to Net Prof	3%

CURRENT POSITION
(MILL.)	1988	1989	3/31/90
Cash Assets	78.0	14.9	14.6
Receivables	381.1	378.1	412.4
Inventory (Avg Cst)	265.3	347.6	349.2
Other	97.1	195.8	182.8
Current Assets	821.5	936.4	959.0
Accts Payable	371.2	495.2	431.4
Debt Due	85.6	75.1	75.5
Other	752.3	1007.4	1105.6
Current Liab.	1209.1	1577.7	1612.5

ANNUAL RATES
of change (per sh)	Past 10 Yrs.	Past 5 Yrs.	Est'd '87-'89 to '93-'95
Revenues	5.5%	11.5%	7.5%
"Cash Flow"	2.0%	0.5%	11.0%
Earnings	-1.0%	-9.0%	17.5%
Dividends	--	--	9.0%
Book Value	13.5%	10.5%	2.5%

QUARTERLY REVENUES ($ mill.) A
Calendar	Mar.31	Jun.30	Sep.30	Dec.31	Full Year
1987	465	620	791	1125	3001
1988	1248	1493	1483	1483	5707
1989	1485	1735	1531	1501	6252
1990	1537	1735	1730	1698	6700
1991	1610	1850	1850	1840	7150

EARNINGS PER SHARE A B E
Calendar	Mar.31	Jun.30	Sep.30	Dec.31	Full Year
1987	.81	2.33	1.66	.62	5.28
1988	d.43	2.14	1.58	.52	3.81
1989	.35	2.29	d1.86	d2.49	d1.73
1990	d1.05	.05	.05	d.15	d1.20
1991	Nil	.90	.60	Nil	1.50

QUARTERLY DIVIDENDS PAID C
Calendar	Mar.31	Jun.30	Sep.30	Dec.31	Full Year
1986	.03	.03	.03	.03	.12
1987	.03	.03	.03	.03	.12
1988	.03	.03	.03	.03	.12
1989	.03	.03	.03	.03	.12
1990	.03	.03			

BUSINESS: USAir Group, Inc. operates USAir, the 7th largest domestic carrier. Major hubs at Pittsburgh, Philadelphia, and Charlotte. PSA acquired 5/87. Piedmont Aviation, 11/87. Revenue mix: passenger, 95%; other, 5%. Combined fleet: 44 B-727s, 74 DC-9s, 31 MD-80s, 21 BAe-146s, 212 B-737s, 45 F-28s, 6 B-767s, 8 F-100s. On firm order: 5 B-767s, 51 B-737s, 20 MD-82s, 23 F-100s. Fuel: 13% of revenues; labor, 36%. '89 depreciation 4.9%. Est'd fleet age: 9 years. Has 53,700 employees, 22,400 shrhldrs. Directors own 1% of common; ESOP, 5%. Berkshire Hathaway holds preferred stock that is convertible into 12% of common. Chrmn. & Pres.: E.I. Colodny. Inc.: DE. Address: 1911 Jefferson Davis Highway, Arlington, VA 22202. Telephone: 703-892-7224.

USAir's profits have been hurt by a weak pricing environment. Rival Eastern is still discounting aggressively in a desperate attempt to regain market share after being shut down last year. USAir has been the biggest victim of these bargain fares, because about 22% of its route system overlaps with Eastern's. Since these Northeast-to-Florida routes primarily appeal to price-sensitive, leisure travelers, USAir has had little choice but to match these fares. Revenue per passenger mile (yield) also has been hurt by Midway's presence at USAir's Philadelphia hub and by fierce rivalry among the major carriers in the San Francisco/Los Angeles corridor. As a result, yields declined almost 6% in the March period, and we estimate they will slide another 2% in the June quarter. The cost picture, meanwhile, appears to be improving. Earnings have been decimated in the past three quarters by expenses relating to USAir's merger with Piedmont last August, the standardization of pay scales at the two carriers, and a sharp spike in jet fuel prices earlier this year. In the past several months, though, the price of kerojet has declined about 20%. The airline also is beginning to reap productivity benefits from the implementation in February of a new and fully integrated flight itinerary. As a result, we expect unit costs to gradually fall over the next 12 to 18 months.

On balance, we estimate a loss of more than $1 a share in 1990 and a small profit in 1991. Although costs are falling, declining yields and load factors will heavily penalize profits for the balance of the year. Looking to 1991, we figure USAir will chalk up a profit of $1-$2 a share, assuming this carrier's pricing recovers moderately, merger-related costs subside, and management is successful in refining its new route system. We'd steer clear of these shares for now, at least until this carrier returns solidly to the black. Over the 3- to 5-year haul, however, we think a strong market position and emerging economies of scale will help propel earnings to record levels, thereby rewarding shareholders with lofty capital gains. We calculate the stock's downside potential as $25 a share, which is roughly equal to its tangible book value.
Paul A. Graham, Jr. *June 29, 1990*

(A) Includes Pacific Southwest Air beginning 6/87; Piedmont beginning 11/87. (B) Primary egs. Incl. profits and losses from sale of operating equipment. Excl. extraord. gain: '78, $1.31. — Next egs. report due late July. Next div'd goes ex about July 10. Next div'd mtg. about Sept. 27. Approx. div'd payment dates: Jan. 31, April 30, July 31, Oct. 31. (D) In millions. — (E) Quarterly egs. don't total in 1987 and 1989 due to changing number of shs. outstanding. (F) USAir only, prior to 1989; incl. Piedmont thereafter. (G) Fully diluted 3 to 5 years hence.

Chronological History—USAir

March, 1936	First demonstration airmail pickup at Coatsville, Pennsylvania.		Initiated service at: Erie, Pennsylvania; Cleveland, Ohio; and Parkersburg and Huntington, West Virginia.
May, 1939	All American Aviation is founded by Richard C. du Pont to provide airmail pickup service to isolated locations.		Colonel Robert Love becomes Chairman of the board of directors. Leslie O. Barnes becomes the new president of Allegheny.
	The Post Office Department grants All American Aviation a one year experimental contract.	1956	Communities served: 50. Fleet: 6 Martin 202s, 15 DC-3s. Stock listed with the American Stock Exchange.
May 12, 1939	First official airmail pickup flight performed by three out of a total fleet of five Stinson Reliant SR-10 aircraft in Latrobe, Pennsylvania.	1959	Allegheny becomes the first airline to put Convair 540 turboprops into service.
May 13, 1940	Experimental contract with the Post Office Department expires.		Initiated shuttle service between Pittsburgh and Philadelphia.
July 22, 1940	The Civil Aeronautics Board (CAB) issues its first Certificate of Public Convenience and Necessity to All American Aviation.	1960	Service initiated to several New England cities.
		1963	Fleet profile: 23 Convair 440s. 15 Martin Executives.
1942	Richard du Pont leaves All American Aviation to help the US Army Air Corps establish a glider program. Major Halsey R. Bazley becomes president of All American Aviation.		Maintenance, engineering, flight operations and flight control personnel were moved from Washington to larger facilities at Pittsburgh International Airport.
1945	Wartime glider equipment research and manufacturing contracts ended. Substitute business ventures sought.	1966	Allegheny purchases its first jet, a McDonnell Douglas DC-9.
	Major Bazley became vice-president and Colonel Robert Love became the new president.	1967	Allegheny Commuter formed to provide service to smaller localities. Fleet consisted of 37 DC-9s, 31 BAC 1-11s, and 40 Convair 580s.
	All American Aviation entered the manufacturing arena. Items that were manufactured included machine castings, roof rafter systems, and toy airmail pickup models.	July 1, 1968	Allegheny merged with Indianapolis based Lake Central Airlines. Service provided to 70 airports.
1946/1947	Manufacturing division and airmail pickup service experience losses.	1972	Allegheny and New York based Mohawk Airlines merged. Employees: 7,100. Cities served: 150. Fleet: 37 DC-9s 31 BAC 1-11s 40 Convair 580s. Ranking: 6th largest passenger carrying airline.
Feb., 1948	The CAB gives All American Aviation one year to phase out its pickup service and issues a Certificate of Public Convenience and Necessity to transport persons, property, and mail in Maryland, New Jersey, the District of Columbia, Pennsylvania, Delaware, New York, West Virginia, and Ohio.	1974	Removed from the federal subsidy program.
1953	All American Airways becomes Allegheny Airlines. Total fleet size: 13 DC-3s.	1974	Reversals: High fuel costs. Unstable economy.

(continued)

Chronological History—USAir *(continued)*

	Losses of 9.9 million. Sharp cuts in capacity. Employee furlough.		Initiated service to Los Angeles and San Francisco.
1975	Leslie O. Barnes retires. Edwin I. Colodny becomes new president.	1984	The Boeing 737-300 is introduced.
1978	Airline Deregulation Act is passed. Deregulation contributed to growth in passenger volume on all US airlines. All-jet fleet. Stock listed on the New York Stock Exchange. Initiated service to Houston, Orlando, Tampa, and West Palm Beach.	May 1987	Purchase of Pacific Southwest Airlines (PSA) was approved by the Department of Transportation (DOT). Acquired for $4 million.
		Nov. 1987	Department of Transportation grants permission to acquire Piedmont Airlines.
		April 9, 1988	Pacific Southwest Airlines (PSA) operations were merged with USAir.
Oct. 28, 1979	Allegheny Airlines changes its name to USAir in order to reflect its new size and scope.	August 5, 1989	Merger of USAir and Piedmont. Hubs added: Charlotte; Baltimore/Washington; Dayton; and Syracuse.
1983	Reorganization: USAir Group holding company formed. Subsidiaries include USAir and Piedmont Aviation, four regional airlines, aviation overhaul and supply companies, an aircraft, and a leasing company.		Fleet size: 400+ jet aircraft. Passengers boarded: 60+ million. Cities served: 300.

Adapted from USAir (1989) 50 Years of Flying High

Chronological History—Piedmont

1939	Thomas Davis principal shareholder and vice-president of Camel City Flying Service, a distributer of Piper and Stinson aircraft and provider of aircraft overhaul and maintenance, flight training and aircraft rental.	Dec. 12, 1947	The Civil Aeronautics Board (C.A.B) grants Piedmont Aviation a Certificate of Public Convenience and Necessity to operate a local service passenger, mail and cargo route.
July 2, 1940	Davis changes Camel City Flying Service's name to Piedmont Aviation, Inc.	Jan. 1, 1948	Airline division of Piedmont Aviation is formed.
1941	17 new Piper and Stinson dealer outlets established. Sold 100 planes. The first fully certified aircraft and engine overhaul shop to be approved by the Civil Aeronautics Administration.	1949	Employees: 273 Passengers boarded: 39,370 Cities Served: 20
		1951	Passengers boarded: 189,831 Revenue: $1,332,943.20 Profits: $53,317,728
		1955	The C.A.B grants Piedmont a permanent Certificate of Public Convenience and Necessity.
1943	Thomas Davis becomes president of Piedmont Aviation. Provided flight training for the military during World War II.	Nov. 1958	Eight F-27 aircraft acquired for six million dollars.
		1961	17 404 skyliners are acquired for 6.5 million.

Chronological History—Piedmont *(continued)*

	Passengers Boarded: 664,000		Thomas Davis retires; William K. Howard becomes president.
Feb. 20, 1963	Last commercial DC-3 flight.		
1967/68	Jets put into service:		Salsbury, Maryland, based Henson Aviation merges with Piedmont.
	Fairchild Hiller 227s.		
	Boeing 727s.		
	Boeing 737s.	1984	Revenues: $1.3 billion
1969	Employees: 3,191	1985	Merger with Charlotte, N.C., based Sunbird Airlines.
	Cities Served: 78		
	Passengers Boarded: 2 million+		Piedmont Shuttle began serving 12 cities in Florida.
	Gross Revenues: $70 million		
1972	Record profits: Over 3 million.	1986	Mergers with:
1975	63% increase in fuel costs.		Jet Stream Airlines; Ohio based.
	10% reduction in flights.		Brockway Airlines; New York based.
	Gross Profit: $204,293.		Empire Airlines; New York based.
1978	Piedmont stock traded on the New York Stock Exchange.	Feb. 1987	USAir offers to buy Piedmont for a $71/share stock swap.
1979	Unsuccessful takeover attempt by Air Florida.	March 9, 1987	Edwin Colodny and William Howard announce that the two firms would merge to become the seventh largest carrier in the U.S.
1978	Initiated service to Miami and Tampa, Florida, and Boston, Massachusetts.		
Oct. 1978	Airline Deregulation Act.	August 1987	William Howard resigns and William G. McGee becomes the new president.
1981	First hub established at Charlotte, N.C.		
	Norfolk Southern offers to buy Piedmont for $68/share or $1.8 billion.	1988	William McGee joins Braniff and Thomas E. Schick becomes president.
1983	Initiated hubs at:	August 5, 1989	Merger of USAir and Piedmont.
	Dayton, Ohio		
	Syracuse, New York		
	Baltimore/Washington.		

Adapted from USAir (1989) 50 Years of Flying High

Case 13

America West Airlines

Introduction

America West Airlines Inc. was incorporated September 4, 1981, and began flight service to five cities with three used Boeing 737-200s on August 1, 1983. By early 1989 the airline had grown to 70 aircraft serving 47 cities. Foremost among the cities served are Phoenix, the airline's base of operations, and Las Vegas. Since October 1984, America West has had the largest market share in Phoenix. From just four gates at its inception, the airline has expanded to 21 gates and 42 percent of all passengers boarded in Phoenix. By contrast, Southwest Airlines, the primary competitor in the Phoenix hub, has just over 21 percent of the market share of enplanements. By the end of 1986, America West had also become the number one carrier in Las Vegas. America West routes are shown in Exhibit 1.

Along the way, the rapid expansion of the America West system has also had a few changes. One of the air carrier's first scheduled destinations, Kansas City, was subsequently removed from the schedule in October 1984. Similarly, flights to Tulsa and Oklahoma City, which were begun in December 1983, were canceled in October 1984. Also in October 1984, America West moved its flight to San Francisco, which had begun only four months earlier, to Oakland. Finally, the service to Palm Springs, which began in February 1984, was discontinued in March 1985. Meanwhile, the airline was expanding to areas in the Midwest having little competition, such as Lincoln, Grand Junction, Durango,

Sioux City, Cedar Rapids, Springfield, Pueblo, and Moline/Quad Cities. Many of these routes have low landing fees and gate costs, which serve to make them some of the more profitable destinations flown by America West. The servicing of these various noncompetitive destinations was one of the initial strategies conceived by the airline's management.

Beginning in 1985, America West expanded flights dramatically to Las Vegas, and instituted flights from Las Vegas to a number of other destinations apart from Phoenix. By the end of 1986, this service had created a second hub city, with direct flights to 18 destinations, excluding Phoenix. Together, the Phoenix and Las Vegas airports comprise a newly conceived superhub, whereby schedules are integrated to common cities in order to maximize both direct and connecting services between points on one side of either hub and points on the other side. This is accomplished with more than 20 daily round trips between Phoenix and Las Vegas. Outside of these flights, America West has 167 daily departures from Phoenix and 92 daily departures from Las Vegas. The locations of gates in Phoenix and Las Vegas are shown in Exhibit 2.

America West has little competition on most of its Midwest routes and serious competition on its flights to Denver, New York, and Chicago, but California is by far the most popular destination for Arizona travelers. Therefore, the company focuses on service to and from California as an essential element in its hub and spoke system. Nearly 70 percent of the airline's passengers travel through the Phoenix hub from other destinations, which underscores the importance of linking California with the Midwest. Although

Exhibit 1   America West Routes in 1989

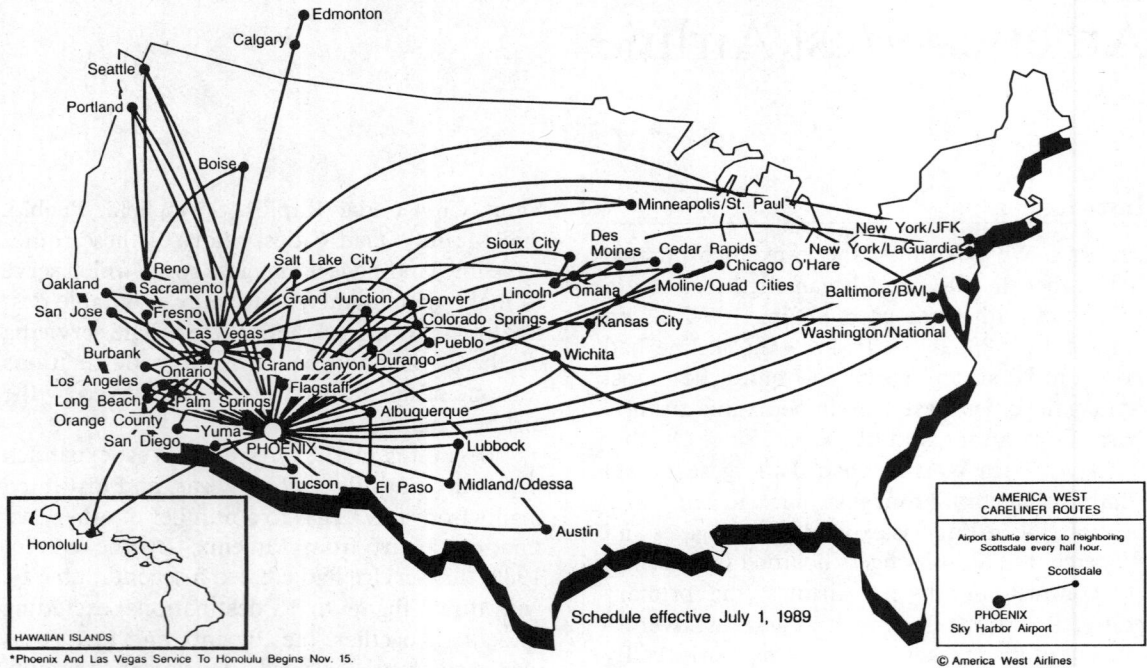

Source: America West Airlines

the California routes are an important ingredient in the success of America West, they are highly competitive and not as lucrative. However, the airline has been successful in these markets as a result of its dominance of the Phoenix market and its overall low costs.

The airline has also experienced success in its Las Vegas and Phoenix flights to New York because there are few direct flights from these cities to New York. The threat of direct competition from a major carrier remains on these routes. America West is inviting competition in the opinion of Gerald Grinstein, former chairman of Western Airlines, who believes that America West has "succeeded so far through anonymity."[1]

[1]Stewart Toy, "This Upstart Could Be Flying a Bit Too High,"*Business Week*, June 15, 1987, 76.

A chronological history of America West is presented in Exhibit 3.

Air Fleet

From its inception, America West has centered its aircraft needs on the fuel-efficient, twin-engine, two-pilot Boeing 737. More recently, two-pilot 757s and Boeing de Havilland Dash 8s have been added for short haul routes. The efficiency of these aircraft is enhanced through the use of slim-line seats, which have enabled the company to substantially increase passenger capacity. Through its reliance for most flights on a single plane (the 737), the company has endeavored to minimize parts inventory and maintenance expense. As of February 1989, America West had a fleet of Boeing 737 aircraft, 7 Boeing 757 aircraft, and 3 Boeing de Havilland Dash 8s. The

Exhibit 2   America West's Superhub Gate Connections

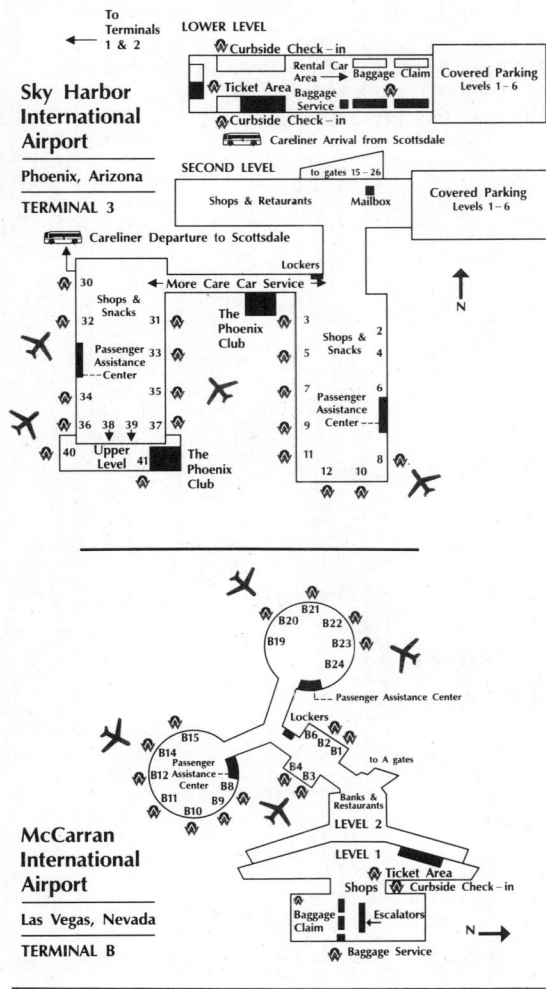

Source: America West Airlines

airline offers both economy and first-class service on its 757s. All other service is economy.

The average age of the fleet is six years, which is young by industry standards. Together with future planned deliveries of new aircraft, America West will have one of the youngest fleets by far in the airline industry.

Initial Marketing Strategy

America West has consistently pursued a well-conceived marketing strategy designed to have broad-based appeal to air travel customers. To attract the individual discretionary traveler, the airline offers consistently low fares and only one seating class on its 737s. To attract the business traveler, America West offers complimentary copies of *The Wall Street Journal* and *USA Today*, assigned seating, complimentary alcoholic beverages, a frequent flier program, larger overhead bins for carryon luggage, interline ticketing and baggage transfer, and the participation in travel agent automated reservation systems. America West believes that it is presently the only airline in its service areas that provides this exact combination of services.

As previously noted, America West's principal route strategy was to link less competitive Midwest markets with California flights through the Phoenix hub. As is evident from the history of the airline, this strategy underwent some revision with the cancellation of flight service to the more competitive Midwest markets of Tulsa, Oklahoma City, and Kansas City. More recently, however, the air carrier began flights to Denver, Chicago, New York, Baltimore, and Washington, which appears to signal a willingness to enter more competitive markets. With the future delivery of more large aircraft, the entry of America West into increasingly competitive markets appears inevitable. In its short history of operations, the airline has altered its initial route strategy, which was committed to serving the western United States, to direct service from Phoenix to various major East Coast destinations. Although these distant destinations will be more competitive, America West will be the only air carrier with direct service from Phoenix.

Current Marketing Strategy

America West's marketing strategy is centered around the motto, "What we serve is you,"

Exhibit 3 Chronological History

Sept. 1981	Incorporated as America West Airlines, Inc.
Nov. 1981	Issued a certificate to engage in domestic scheduled air transportation by the Civil Aeronautics Board
Feb. 1983	First public offering of 2,500,000 shares of common stock at $7.50 with two subsequent equity transactions raising $33 million for preoperating and start-up
Aug. 1, 1983	Revenue service established from Phoenix hub with three Boeing 737s

Aug. 1, 1983 (cont.) — Initiated service at:
  Colorado Springs, Colorado
  Kansas City, Missouri (Discontinued 10/28/84)
  Los Angeles, California
  Phoenix, Arizona
  Wichita, Kansas

Aug. 1, 1983 **Phoenix**
  Daily Departures: 9
  Employees: 280
  Total Fleet Size: 3 Boeing 737s
  Cities Served: 5

Oct. 1, 1983 Initiated service at:
  Omaha, Nebraska
  Ontario, California

Oct. 30, 1983 Initiated service at:
  Las Vegas, Nevada
  Las Vegas
  Daily Departures: 3

Dec. 1, 1983 Initiated service at:
  Albuquerque, New Mexico
  Des Moines, Iowa
  Oklahoma City, Oklahoma (Discontinued 10/28/84)
  San Diego, California
  Tulsa, Oklahoma (Discontinued 10/28/84)

Dec. 31, 1983 **Phoenix**
  Daily Departures: 31
  Employees: 806
  Total Fleet Size: 10 Boeing 737s
  Cities Served: 13
  Las Vegas
  Daily Departures: 4

Feb. 1, 1984 Initiated service at:
  Palm Springs, California (Discontinued 3/15/85)

Mar. 13, 1984 Western Savings & Loan Association of Phoenix purchased $15 million of Series B 10.5% convertible preferred stock.

Mar. 30, 1984 Second public offering of 1,000,000 shares of common at $9.50

June 1, 1984 Initiated service at:
  Austin, Texas
  Durango, Colorado
  San Jose, California
  Tucson, Arizona

July 15, 1984 Initiated service at:
  San Francisco, California (Switched service from SFO to OAK 10/28/84)

Sept. 14, 1984 Initiated service at:
  Burbank, California

Oct. 26, 1984 Expansion at Phoenix Sky Harbor Airport from 3 to 9 gates

Exhibit 3 *(continued)*

Oct. 28, 1984	Initiated service at: Oakland, California
Nov. 1, 1984	Initiated service at: Calgary, Alberta, Canada

Nov. 15, 1984	Initiated service at:
	   El Paso, Texas
	   Salt Lake City, Utah

Dec. 8, 1984	Initiated temporary service at: Montrose, Colorado (Special ski flights Saturday only through April 8, 1985.)
Dec. 15, 1984	Initiated service at: Grand Junction, Colorado
Dec. 31, 1984	**Phoenix** Daily Departures: 78 Employees: 1650 Total Fleet Size: 21 Boeing 737s Cities Served: 22 **Las Vegas** Daily Departures: 7
Mar. 15, 1985	Initiated service at: Edmonton, Alberta, Canada

Apr. 1, 1985	Initiated service at:
	   Orange County—John Wayne Airport—Santa Ana, California
	   Sacramento, California

Apr. 11, 1985	Third public offering of 3.8 million shares of common stock at $7.00
July 1, 1985	Initiated Air Cargo Service
July 1, 1985	Opened a Satellite Reservations Center in Colorado Springs, Colorado
July 15, 1985	Initiated service at: Lincoln, Nebraska
Aug. 6, 1985	Public offering of $69,000,000 7¾% Convertible Subordinated Debentures; due 2010
Aug. 23, 1985	Expanded existing corporate office space with an additional building. The new facility, called the Madison I Building, 606 Madison, Tempe, houses the airlines' warehouse, engine shop, purchasing department, quality assurance, technical publications, and sales department.
Nov. 15, 1985	Initiated service at: Pueblo, Colorado
Dec. 5, 1985	Expansion at Phoenix Sky Harbor Airport from 9 to 18 gates
Dec. 31, 1985	**Phoenix** Daily Departures: 118 Employees: 2527 Total Fleet Size: 32 Boeing 737s Cities Served: 26 **Las Vegas** Daily Departures: 16
Jan. 24, 1986	Initiated service at: Sioux City, Iowa

Feb. 15, 1986	Initiated service at:
	   Cedar Rapids, Iowa
	   Scottsdale, Arizona (Complimentary shuttle bus service to and from Sky Harbor)

Mar. 19, 1986	Public offering of $80,000,000 7½% Convertible Subordinated Debentures. Due 2011

(continued)

Exhibit 3 *(continued)*

Mar. 28, 1986	Office space expanded with an additional building at 618 Madison, called Madison II, housing Corporate Marketing, Properties & Facilities, Legal, Air Cargo offices, and Operations Management
Apr. 27, 1986	Initiated service at: Springfield, Missouri (Discontinued 2/29/88)
July 1, 1986	Initiated Las Vegas "Nite Flite" service to seven cities: Albuquerque Oakland Phoenix Los Angeles Ontario Salt Lake City Tucson
July 15, 1986	Initiated service at: Chicago Midway, Illinois (Discontinued 1/5/88)
Sept. 3, 1986	Purchased three de Havilland Canada Dash 8s with options to purchase three additional turboprop airplanes
Sept. 11, 1986	A ground-breaking ceremony held at Sky Harbor commemorating the beginning of construction for the new America West Airlines Technical Support Facility
Nov. 15, 1986	Initiated service at: Denver, Colorado Reno, Nevada
Dec. 15, 1986	Initiated service at: Portland, Oregon Seattle, Washington
Dec. 31, 1986	**Phoenix** Daily Departures: 145 Employees: 4596 Total Fleet Size: 46 Boeing 737s Cities Served: 35 **Las Vegas** Daily Departures: 54
Jan. 15, 1987	Initiated service at: Midland/Odessa, Texas Moline/Quad Cities, Illinois
Feb. 4, 1987	Purchased six Boeing 757 aircraft from the Boeing Company with a commitment for an additional three to be delivered in fall 1989
Feb. 27, 1987	Received delivery of first Boeing de Havilland Dash 8
Mar. 2, 1987	Initiated service at: Yuma, Arizona (Boeing de Havilland Dash 8 service)
May 1–22, 1987	Received delivery of four Boeing 757s
May 16, 1987	Received delivery of two Boeing de Havilland Dash 8s
May 20, 1987	Initiated service at: Chicago O'Hare, Illinois Flagstaff, Arizona (Boeing de Havilland Dash 8 service) Grand Canyon, Arizona (Boeing de Havilland Dash 8 service) Mesa, Arizona (Discontinued 1/31/88 (Complimentary shuttle bus service to and from Mesa, Arizona)
May 20, 1987	Expansion at Phoenix Sky Harbor Airport from 18 to 21 gates
June 1, 1987	Initiated service at: Long Beach, California
June 1, 1987	Opened a Satellite Reservations Center in Reno, Nevada
June 3–12, 1987	Received delivery of two Boeing 757s

Exhibit 3 *(continued)*

July 1, 1987	Initiated service at: New York/JFK, New York Baltimore/Washington International, Maryland
Aug. 11, 1987	Ansett Airlines of Australia invests in 20% of America West's common stock (newly issued shares—3,029,235 shares at $10.50 per share). Total value of stock transaction—$31,806,967
Sept. 15, 1987	Opened new VIP lounge, the Phoenix Club, near Gate 40 in Terminal III at Sky Harbor International Airport. Available to members only, providing separate television and bar areas, a library with a personal computer and copy machine, and a conference room
Nov. 15, 1987	Initiated service at: Lubbock, Texas
Dec. 1, 1987	Initiated nonstop service between: Oakland—Calgary
Dec. 13, 1987	Received delivery of the seventh Boeing 757
Dec. 14, 1987	Grand opening of AmeriWest Vacations (tour packaging division)
Dec. 31, 1987	**Phoenix** Daily Departures: 167 Employees: 7800 Total Fleet Size: 59 Boeing 737s 7 Boeing 757s 3 Boeing de Havilland Dash 8s Cities Served: 45 **Las Vegas** Daily Departures: 102
Feb. 16, 1988	Opening of "Fast Check" drive-through terminals east of Terminal III at Sky Harbor International Airport offering full check-in services. Passengers may proceed directly to the airplane after utilizing "Fast Check."
Feb. 23, 1988	America West Airline's Hangar and Technical Support Facility ribbon-cutting press conference
Apr. 13, 1988	America West unveils new laser baggage system at Sky Harbor International Airport. The $2.5 million system works similar to automated grocery store checkout stands and allows America West to handle baggage with high speed and accuracy.
May 1, 1988	Initiated service at: Minneapolis-St. Paul, Minnesota
May 15, 1988	America West Airlines joins the International Air Transport Association (IATA).
June 23, 1988	America West Airlines is announced as the official carrier for the Phoenix Cardinals (National Football League). America West agrees to charter the Cardinals to all road games and launches a major advertising campaign utilizing the Cardinals as a vehicle to tell the America West story.
June 27, 1988	America West Airlines receives a Federal Aviation Administration (FAA) contract to train FAA pilot-inspectors on the Boeing 737 aircraft. The contract is valued at $894,415.
Sept. 11, 1988	Initiated service at: Kansas City, Missouri
Oct. 16, 1988	Initiated service at: Boise, Idaho Initiated daytime service at: Minneapolis-St. Paul, Minnesota
Dec. 10, 1988	Initiated new service at: Palm Springs, California
Dec. 12, 1988	Opened second luxury lounge (Phoenix Club) at Sky Harbor Airport in Phoenix on the connector between the two America West concourses in Terminal III. The lounge offers complimentary cocktails, beverages, and snacks; two conference rooms, a library

(continued)

Exhibit 3   *(continued)*

	complete with a personal computer, copier, and facsimile machine; free local phone calls; credit card telephones, and separate television and bar areas.
Dec. 13, 1988	America West announced the order of 15 new Boeing 737-300s and 10 new Boeing 757s at an estimated purchase amount of $800 million. Options for 10 Boeing 737-300s and 15 757s were also announced. Delivery date of the 25 firm orders begins in 1992.
Dec. 17, 1988	Initiated new service at: Steamboat Springs, Colorado (3 round trips/week)
Jan. 19, 1989	Announced the signing of a two-year maintenance agreement with Odyssey International Airlines of Canada in which America West will provide the heavy maintenance on Odyssey's 757s. Contract could produce revenue in excess of $3 million.

Feb. 1989

Phoenix
Daily Departures: 167
Employees: 8000
Total Fleet Size: 60 Boeing 737s
       7 Boeing 757s
       3 Boeing de Havilland Dash 8s
Cities Served: 47

Las Vegas
Daily Departures: 92
"Nite Flite" cities served: 30

Apr. 4, 1989	DOT begins hearing for route authorization to Sydney, Australia.
Apr. 11, 1989	America West filed with the DOT for the authority to serve Tokyo, Japan with service from Honolulu, Hawaii.
May 3, 1989	Announced the offer of $726 million for the Eastern Shuttle and ten Boeing 757 aircraft. Included in the Eastern Shuttle were 21 Boeing 727s. (America West withdrew offer on May 24, 1989.)
May 11, 1989	Announced purchase of four 747-200 aircraft from Amsterdam based KLM Royal Dutch Air to be delivered in the 4th quarter of 1989 and the 1st quarter of 1990.
May 11, 1989	Announced new non-stop service from Phoenix and Las Vegas to: Honolulu, Hawaii (beginning November 16,1989.)
May 25, 1989	Announced new service from Phoenix to: New York LaGuardia, New York (beginning July 1, 1989) Washington National, District of Columbia (beginning July 1, 1989) Both New York LaGuardia and Washington National will be served via Omaha, Nebraska and Wichita, Kansas.
May 31, 1989	Announced new non-stop service from Las Vegas to: Fresno, California (beginning July 1, 1989)
June 1, 1989	Introduced a special new offer, "Passport to Paradise," which provides FlightFUND members with the opportunity to earn a free award certificate and two upgrade discount certificates for a round trip to Honlulu, Hawaii. (Complete details are available upon request.)

June 1989

Phoenix
Daily Departures: 181
Employees: 9000
Total Fleet Size: 63 Boeing 737s
       7 Boeing 757s
       4 Boeing de Havilland Dash 8s
Cities Served: 46
Las Vegas
Daily Departures: 104
"Nite Flite"cities served: 31

Source: "Chronological History," America West Airlines, February 1989, June 1989.

which is central to its "More Care" service commitment. The airline has tried to set itself apart from the typical discount airline. Its pricing policy is to offer more low-fare seats than the competition. This is intended to stimulate traffic by developing and increasing air travel among four groups:

1. Frequent business travelers

2. Current passengers who may travel more frequently due to better service at low fares

3. Automobile, bus, and train travelers who may switch to air travel

4. Nontravelers who may fly as an alternate expenditure of discretionary income

The airline's "More Care" strategy is described in Exhibit 4.

America West is currently listed in the APOLLO, PARS, SABRE, and SYSTEM I central reservation systems, but it does not own even a portion of any of these CSRs.

Personnel

The management at America West is both young and experienced. The CEO and founder of the firm, 52-year-old Edward Beauvais, was a partner in a consulting firm for ten years prior to founding America West. His specialty was route selection. Beauvais also completed a long-range planning study for the never consummated Continental–Western merger. Prior to 1971, Beauvais served as the assistant vice president of research and development for Bonanza and Hughes Air West. His position prior to that was as an accountant for Frontier Airlines.

The current president of America West is Michael Conway. Conway, who is 43 years old, was named president in 1984 after the company's first president, Michael Roach, resigned. From 1981 to 1984, Conway was the executive vice president of America West. His previous experience was as vice president and controller for Continental Airlines. The other officers are also

Exhibit 4 "More Care" Service: Amenities Offered by America West to Attract the Frequent Traveler

1. Assigned seating
2. Knowledgeable and well-trained personnel dedicated to the company's goals of personalized service
3. High-quality complimentary alcoholic beverages
4. King-size overhead baggage bins for storage of carryon baggage
5. Quality seats in each aircraft designed for passenger comfort and maximum legroom
6. Interline agreements that provide baggage handling for connecting flights to final destinations
7. Complimentary copies of *The Wall Street Journal* and *USA Today*
8. Efficient ticketing procedures to reduce waiting time at airports and facilitate faster access to flights
9. A frequent flyer program (FlightFUND) whereby credit accrual is measured by the fares paid, as well as actual miles flown. Credit may be gained through the use of various FlightFUND partners.
10. Complimentary round-trip shuttle service between the popular resort area of Scottsdale, Arizona, and Phoenix Sky Harbor International Airport
11. Members-only V.I.P. airport lounges (Phoenix Club) at Sky Harbor Airport. Offer complimentary snacks and beverages, library (complete with personal computer, copy machine, and facsimile machine) and conference room, as well as separate television and bar areas
12. Seatfone Service, an inflight telephone system by GTE Airfone Inc., available on all America West Boeing 757s. These credit card telephones will be available in each seatback in first class and the center seatback of each row in coach.
13. A "Fast Check Drive-Thru" satellite terminal located just east of Terminal III at Phoenix Sky Harbor Airport. Full check-in services are offered without leaving the car.

Source: "Fact Sheet," America West Airlines, March 1989, 6.

young and have substantial experience with large airlines.

By April 1989, America West had grown to over 8,000 employees. The airline's labor force is entirely nonunion, which effectively reduces the overall cost of operations. These savings enable America West to cross-utilize staff. For example, most flight attendants double as ticket agents and baggage handlers. In addition to increasing productivity, cross-training increases employee value and encourages promotion from within.

The emphasis placed on employee development is also illustrated by the creation of various employee advisory boards, whereby the staff is able to interact with all levels of management. A further example of employee involvement is the fact that over 16 percent of the issued and outstanding common shares of the company are held by the staff and management of the airline; the percentage of the airline owned by the employees has steadily grown from just over 11 percent at the end of 1983. Much of the stock was purchased voluntarily, but the airline mandates that employees acquire stock at a 15 percent discount from market amounting to 20 percent of their first year's salary. The entrepreneurial culture at America West is emphasized through the payment of annual profit sharing of 15 percent of pretax profits. This amounted to over $1.8 million in 1988.

America West offers its employees an attractive benefit package. In addition to comprehensive medical, dental, and life insurance benefits, the company offers unusually liberal travel benefits. Employer-sponsored child care is the newest of the benefits. The company is attentive to the well-being and interests of its personnel. *Working Mother* magazine rated it one of the top 50 companies in the country from the standpoint of the needs of working mothers.[2] Some comments made by employees about worklife at America West are given in Exhibit 5.

Phoenix Base

An important part of the initial strategy of America West was its decision to be based in Phoenix.

---

[2]Darla Morgan, "Flying Right," *Arizona Trend*, December 1988, 63.

Exhibit 5   Personal Comments of Employees on America West's Fifth Anniversary

"As one of the very first employees, it has been my distinct privilege and a unique experience to witness the company's growth from the dream to the reality . . . a true caterpillar-to-butterfly story in not-so-slow motion. Our top management has genuine compassion for their fellow employees, and I am proud to work with the thousands of delightful people who make up our company."—*Evelyn Daurio, Director, Human Resources*

"I had come from the coolness of Alaska to listen to 'the man,' Ed Beauvais, despite the 110-degree temperature in Phoenix. This natural leader unfolded the America West business plan with solid, in-depth knowledge, maturity, vision and charisma. The 'risk' I envisioned as part of a start-up airline reversed itself. Now, how could I pass up the opportunity of a lifetime? I didn't . . . based on 'the man' and his presentation, I accepted a captain's position in the first pilot class of 1983."—*Pat Helfrich, Captain*

"As we reach our fifth year of operation at America West Airlines, I can only say how proud and thankful I am to have been a part of starting our airline. The road has been rough at times for all of us, but we have stuck together, sharing pride, positive thinking, love and above all, respect for each other."—*Edward Gonzales, Customer Service Representative*

"In five years, this company has gone from no aircraft and a handful of employees to an airline of substantial proportions. People say that it has changed. In some ways, that is true, but the basic fiber, the thing that holds it all together, is still intact. It has made me realize the awesome power of a right idea coming to fruition at the right time."—*Greg Gibbs, Manager, Aircraft and Facility Appearance*

"I first started as an aircraft technician and then became a supervisor. I am now a shift manager at the new hangar. I am filled with pride as I walk through the hangar door and see how professional and sophisticated we have become."—*Fritz Warnstedt, Shift Manager, Hangar*

"I have found that at America West you can grow as much as you would like, both personally and professionally. There are no limits!"—*Doug Karolak, City Manager/Yuma*

Source: "Welcome Aboard," *America West Airlines Magazine*, August 1988, 7.

Much of the initial success achieved at America West results from the decision to concentrate air service in points to and from its Phoenix base. Phoenix is the ninth largest metropolitan area in the United States and has consistently been one of the most rapidly growing cities in recent years. Between 1983 and 1987 Phoenix was the fastest growing air transportation center among the 20 largest cities in the United States, with passenger levels growing at more than 70 percent (Table 1). It moved up in rank from 14 to 11, surpassing Miami, Las Vegas, and Honolulu. In addition to the obvious benefits of being based in a high-

growth area, the generally good weather conditions in Phoenix and the lack of congestion at the airport promote timely and consistent service.

America West at present maintains its headquarters in downtown Tempe, Arizona. The airline opened its new four-plane-bay airline hangar and technical support facility in February 1988. As previously noted, it maintains 21 gates at Phoenix Sky Harbor International Airport. The airline committed to accept all 30 to 35 gates in the new Terminal 4 in Phoenix, scheduled for completion in 1990.

Table 1   Air Transportation Demand in 20 Largest U.S. Cities, 1983–1987

City	1983 O&D Passengers[a]	Passenger Rank 1983	1984	1985	1986	1987	1987 O&D Passengers[a]	Growth Absolute	Percent
New York	41,308,580	1	1	1	1	1	44,098,850	2,790,270	6.8%
Los Angeles	21,081,410	2	3	3	2	2	27,200,860	6,119,450	29.0%
Chicago	19,379,030	3	2	2	3	3	26,179,350	6,800,320	35.1%
Dallas/Ft. Worth	15,430,250	4	4	4	4	5	18,019,620	2,589,370	16.8%
San Francisco	15,263,620	5	5	5	5	4	18,140,940	2,877,320	18.9%
Washington, DC	13,610,370	6	6	6	6	6	17,352,260	3,741,890	27.5%
Boston	13,002,030	7	7	7	7	7	16,982,980	3,980,950	30.6%
Houston	11,580,550	8	8	8	10	9	13,004,100	1,423,550	12.3%
Atlanta	9,293,670	9	10	10	9	8	14,321,270	5,027,600	54.1%
Denver	9,016,800	10	9	9	8	10	12,134,260	3,117,460	34.6%
Miami	8,286,010	11	11	11	13	12	11,053,340	2,767,330	33.4%
Las Vegas	7,324,770	12	15	17	16	15	10,011,800	2,687,030	36.7%
Honolulu	7,006,010	13	14	18	21	23	6,481,970	(524,040)	−7.5%
Phoenix	**6,926,100**	**14**	**12**	**13**	**11**	**11**	**11,818,270**	**4,892,170**	**70.6%**
Detroit	6,875,510	15	13	12	14	14	10,807,880	3,932,370	57.2%
Seattle	6,706,410	16	20	20	12	17	9,052,280	2,345,870	35.0%
Philadelphia	6,174,350	17	17	16	18	16	9,179,700	3,005,350	48.7%
Minneapolis	6,093,870	18	16	15	17	19	8,190,830	2,096,960	34.4%
Tampa	6,016,930	19	19	19	20	20	8,116,020	2,099,090	34.9%
San Diego	5,849,630	20	21	21	19	18	8,643,460	2,793,830	47.8%
	236,225,900						300,790,040	64,564,140	27.3%

[a]Air transportation demand is measured in terms of annual origin/destination (O&D) passengers from the ongoing Department of Transportation 10 percent sample.
Source: "The Economic Impact on Phoenix," America West Airlines Inc., 1988, p. 6.

Aircraft

America West's aircraft fleet as of November 1988 is described in the table that follows. The total number of aircraft was 70, and the average age of the fleet was six years.

Aircraft Type	Status	Number of Aircraft	Average Age (years)	Average Remaining Lease Term (years)
DHC-8	Leased	3	2	8
737-100	Owned	1	19	—
737-200	Owned	6	11	—
737-200	Leased	24	11	8
737-300	Owned	7	1	—
737-300	Leased	22	2	10
757-200	Leased	7	2	17

Source: Proxy Statement, America West Airlines Inc., November 1988, 38.

Financial Data

America West operating and financial highlights for the past several years are presented in Table 2. After America West achieved break-even results in the last quarter of 1984, positive earnings results were achieved until 1987, when the company lost over $45 million. During 1986, the airline expanded to nine new cities and increased its staffing to be poised for further similar expansion in 1987. The result was increasing operating costs as a percentage of sales, despite a 34.1 percent drop in fuel prices from 1984 to 1988. Were it not for a $9.8 million gain from the sale of six used aircraft and the early termination of two leases, America West would have posted a loss for 1986. Also adversely affecting the company during 1986 was a nearly 5 percent decline in passenger yield due to steep industry-wide airfare discounts.

America West's operating efficiencies have made up for the costs resulting from the extremely high leverage of the air carrier. Inclusive of operating lease obligations, effective debt was over 15 times equity in early 1988. Leverage rose to new highs in 1989 as the result of new asset acquisitions. Despite this high leverage, return on equity has been nominal as a result of low earnings levels. Partially offsetting the risk of the higher leverage has been the use of roughly $151 million in convertible subordinated debentures. It should also be noted that the airline has steadily experienced infusions of equity through its employee stock plan. Additionally, the company has consistently maintained large cash balances and a good positive working capital position, which reduces the risk of an immediate liquidity crisis.

Because of America West's high leverage and the increasingly large fixed costs of the infrastructure, the airline appears extremely vulnerable to cyclical economic downturns (which it has never experienced), rising interest rates (nearly $100 million in debt in floating rate obligations on December 31, 1986), and predatory pricing from competing airlines.

Although America West prides itself on its ability to maintain costs below the industry average, operating costs have steadily risen as a percentage of sales as a result of the toll of increasingly rapid expansion. The resulting nominal operating pretax earnings underscore the risks of combining high leverage with rapid expansion.

In 1987 America West received 30 million in cash from Ansett Airlines of Australia. This company, 50 percent owned by billionaire Rupert Murdoch, received a 20 percent stake in America West and a seat on the board. America West subsequently applied to fly to Australia via Hawaii, one of four airlines in contention for this potentially profitable route. Flights from the United States then may feed into Ansett's domestic system. The seat on America West's board is held by Tibor Sallay, New York–based general council for the TNT/Ansett Group. Sallay has commented, "We think it [America

Table 2 America West Operating and Financial Highlights, 1984–1988

OPERATING HIGHLIGHTS	1988	1987	1986	1985	1984
Revenue Passengers Enplaned	12,746,499	11,231,607	7,140,160	5,125,710	2,397,953
Available Seat Miles (000)	12,200,104	10,318,096	5,296,100	3,657,560	2,373,833
Revenue Passenger Miles (000)	7,120,084	5,785,814	3,233,085	2,283,806	1,247,134
Passenger Load Factor (%)	58.4	56.1	61.0	62.4	52.5
Break-Even Passenger Load Factor (%)	56.7	59.6	60.2	57.5	56.2
Average Passenger Revenue Per Passenger Mile (¢)	10.44	9.66	9.90	10.41	9.71
Average Passenger Revenue Per Available Seat Mile (¢)	6.09	5.42	6.05	6.50	5.10
Operating Expense Per Available Seat Mile (¢)	6.21	5.92	6.14	6.09	5.52

FINANCIAL HIGHLIGHTS (In thousands except per share amounts)	1988	1987	1986	1985	1984
Passenger Revenues	$743,261	$559,181	$320,179	$237,805	$121,062
Total Operating Revenues	775,675	575,447	328,926	241,307	122,565
Operating Income (Loss)	18,141	(35,355)	3,957	18,674	(8,564)
Income (Loss) Before Income Taxes and Extraordinary Items	(12,247)	(45,675)	3,088	11,436	(15,441)
Income Taxes	—	—	1,482	5,313	—
Income (Loss) Before Extraordinary Items	(12,247)	(45,675)	1,606	6,123	(15,441)
Extraordinary Items (1)	21,608	—	1,421	5,261	—
Net Income (Loss)	9,361	(45,675)	3,027	11,384	(15,441)
Per Average Share of Common Stock	0.51	(3.85)	0.11	1.01	(3.26)
Cash and Short-Term Investments	68,448	26,049	76,600	42,270	5,904
Total Assets	639,477	572,255	385,406	237,686	157,515
Long-Term Debt	384,819	369,232	254,762	121,269	87,212
Net Stockholders' Equity	57,983	45,870	57,933	65,048	28,129
Working Capital (Deficiency)	(7,606)	1,583	50,177	29,442	(15,094)

(1) Include gains of $21,608,000 in 1988 resulting from the purchase and retirement as well as exchange of convertible subordinated debentures and, in 1986 and 1985, the utilization of net operating loss carryforwards amounting to $1,421,000 and $5,261,000, respectively.

Source: Annual Report, America West Airlines Inc., 1988, inside front cover.

West] is going to be a good investment. . . . We think its strengths are a modern, up-to-date fleet, employees who are stockholders, very good management. And it fills a niche in Arizona and California that has been missing."[3]

Industry observers quoted in a March 1988 *Business Week* believed that America West had less than a fair chance of survival.[4] America West's management insisted that the reports of the airline's demise were exaggerated. According to CEO Beauvais, "We are not very impressed with [it]. Things are not as bleak as they said."[5] Helane Becker of Shearson Lehman Hutton wrote in August 1988, "We had all but given up on the company, but management has been able to turn the company around."[6]

The year 1988 marked a return to profitability for America West. Sales reached the $775 million mark and profitability per share reached a new all-time high of 51 cents. This was achieved by slowing expansion, improving load factors, improving on-time performance, and increased employee productivity. Beauvais credited the company's employees: "The support from our employees was a vital factor in turning the airline around. It was tough on them. They did a terrific job—unlike the employees at Eastern who are battling their management every step of the way."[7]

The airline reported first quarter 1989 traffic up 19.8 percent compared to the previous year, while available seat miles remained flat.

Competition from Southwest Airlines

In Phoenix, airfare competition was largely with Southwest Airlines, which serves nearly 50 per-

[3]Morgan, "Flying Right," 63.
[4]"The Last of the Upstarts May Be Falling," *Business Week*, March 14, 1988, 35–36.
[5]Morgan, "Flying Right," 62–63.
[6]Morgan, "Flying Right," 63.
[7]Morgan, "Flying Right," 63.

cent of America West's destinations. Southwest's steep fare discounts seemed intended to raise its market share of Phoenix enplanements while keeping the earnings level depressed for America West. However, in December 1986, Southwest raised the fares on most Phoenix departures by as much as 30 percent. Analysts perceive this move to be the result of a need to increase Phoenix passenger yield while the air carrier is competing with Continental in its Houston market.

Then, in November 1987, Southwest slashed fares in markets in which the airline competed with America West. (A map of Southwest flights is reproduced as Exhibit 6.) Fares were as low as $19 from Phoenix to Los Angeles. In 1988 the airline had 104 departures a day from Phoenix, a 27 percent increase. Highlights of Southwest performance in 1988 and 1989 are presented in Table 3.

Southwest initiated a large advertising campaign in Phoenix criticizing America West. These ads contended that Southwest had lower fares, more accessible gates, and more punctual flights than America West. America West CEO Edward Beauvais said, "This kind of competition is designed to drive us out of business. It's more aggressive and tenacious than most airlines deal with."[8]

Southwest employs a point-to-point method of scheduling instead of the more common hub-and-spoke strategy employed by America West. The point-to-point strategy enables the company to offer a large number of convenient daily departures between nonstop city pairs. This keeps ground time and total flight time to a minimum. The airline feels this best serves the short-flight business traveler.

Other more noticeable differences exist between the two airlines. Southwest is considered a no-frills airline. No meals are served and passengers are not given assigned seats. America

[8]Morgan, "Flying Right," 62.

Exhibit 6 Southwest Airlines Flight Routes in 1989

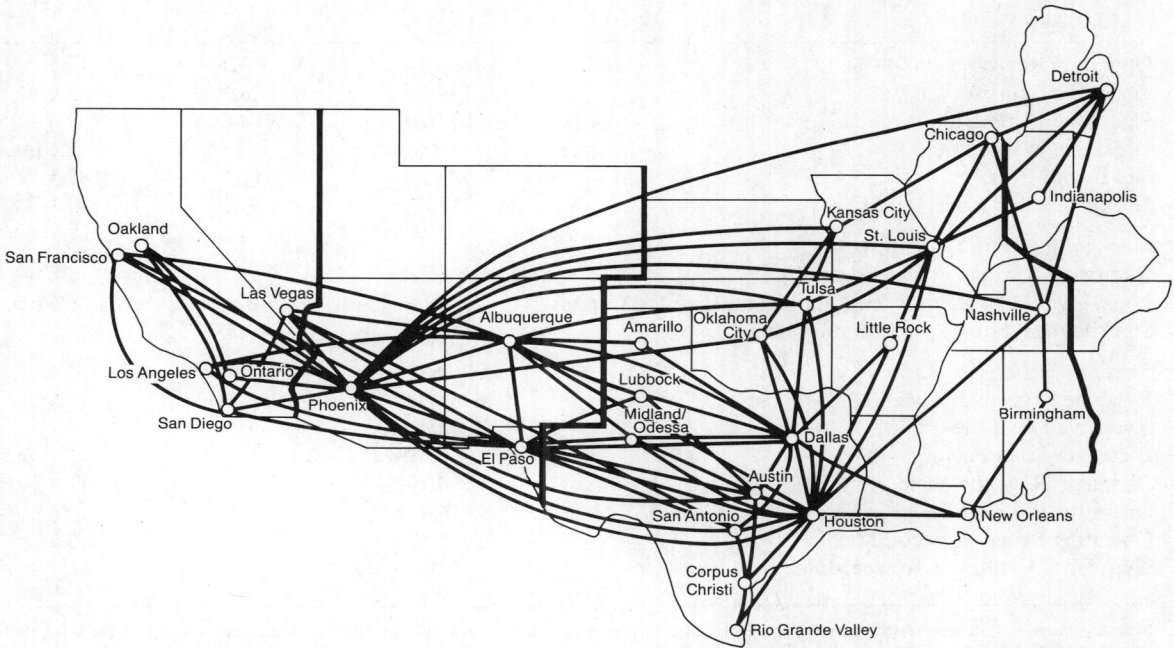

Source: Southwest Airlines

West offers all the traditional services and more, as described in Exhibit 4.

Southwest continues to be a big threat to America West. It earned almost $60 million in 1988. Its debt is low and it has a strong cash position. Growth in Phoenix seems inevitable. Southwest is seeking to increase from 9 gates to 12 in Phoenix. In addition, it has opened a reser-vation center. Its total work force in Phoenix in 1989 exceeded 1,000.

Even with this increase in direct competi-tion, Ed Beauvais is confident of America West's success: "America West will be one of the great-est stories written in our industry."[9]

[9]Morgan, "Flying Right," 62.

Table 3 Southwest Airlines Performance Highlights, 1987–1988

	1988	1987	Percent Change
Operating Revenues (000)	$860,434	$778,328	10.5
Operating Expenses (000)	$774,454	$747,881	3.6
Operating Income (000)	$ 85,980	$ 30,447	182.4
Operating Margin (000)	10.0%	3.9%	6.1 pts.
Net Income (000)	$ 57,952	$ 20,155	187.5
Net Income per Common Share	$1.84	$.63	192.1
Stockholders' Equity (000)	$567,375	$514,278	10.3
Return on Average Stockholders' Equity	10.8%	4.0%	6.8 pts.
Long-Term Debt as a Percentage of Total Invested Capital	39.4%	32.8%	6.6 pts.
Stockholders' Equity per Common Share	$18.15	$16.43	10.5
Revenue Passengers Carried	14,876,582	13,503,242	10.2
Revenue Passenger Miles (RPM) (000s)	7,676,257	7,789,376	(1.5)
Available Seat Miles (ASM (000s)	13,309,044	13,331,055	(.2)
Passenger Load Factor	57.7%	58.4%	(.7) pts.
Passenger Revenue Yield per RPM	10.79¢	9.65¢	11.8
Operating Revenue Yield per ASM	6.47¢	5.84¢	10.8
Operating Expenses per ASM	5.82¢	5.61¢	3.7
Number of Employees at Year-End	6,467	5,765	12.2

Note: Operating income and related operating data include the results of TranStar through June 30, 1987. After that date TranStar decided to cease its operations and liquidate its assets and liabilities and, accordingly, is excluded from operations.
Source: Annual Report, Southwest Airlines Inc., 1988, inside front cover.

Case 14

Hanson—1989

*It is our true policy to steer clear of permanent
alliance with any portion of the foreign world.
[George Washington (1732–1799), Farewell
Address, September 17, 1796]*

If you have recently eaten a Ball Park hot dog
or a Burger King Whopper, drunk Carnation
milk, exercised on a Spartan weight training machine, used Glidden paint, or relaxed in a Jacuzzi, you were contributing to the profits of a
foreign firm. Many of the products with which
we are familiar are no longer produced by American controlled firms.

In business, no country is an island. Over
the past ten years, global trade has grown at an
annual rate of 6.8 percent.[1] Next year it is expected to increase 13 percent and, thereafter, at
10 percent per annum. The globalization of business is not restricted exclusively to the trade of
goods and services. It also includes the acquisition of foreign firms. In 1983 the acquisition
value of foreign firms by U.S. firms was $1.4
billion.[2] By 1988 the value had increased to $6.5
billion. Foreign acquisition of U.S. firms increased even more dramatically. Between 1983
and 1988 the value of the acquisitions soared
from $2.1 billion to $60.8 billion. Against this

background of increasing foreign penetration
into the U.S. industrial base this case study concentrates on Hanson, a British based multinational company that has made numerous acquisitions in the U.S.

Ranked by sales, Hanson is the world's
ninety-fifth largest industrial corporation.[3]
Ranked by profits, it is fifteenth. Hanson is an
aggressive acquirer of undervalued, marginally
profitable firms in mature, low-tech industries.
After acquisition, some activities are spun-off to
recoup the original investment. The retained activities are then made into profitable contribu-
tors to the funds that provide cash for the next
acquisition. This case study describes five of
Hanson's recent takeovers, two of which are British and three of which are American. The main
focus is on the U.S. acquisitions of SCM and
Kidde.

Foreign Acquisitions in the U.S. (1980–1989)

Since 1984 there has been a reversal in the net
balance of U.S. investment abroad and foreign
investment in the U.S. (see Table 1a). Foreign
investment in the U.S. is increasing.[4] Some direct
foreign investment, aimed at building new manufacturing facilities, is usually welcomed. In fact,
politicians in some states have been actively
seeking such investment. They have extolled
their state's virtues of inexpensive land, eco-

This case was prepared by Richard Reed, Washington
State University, and is accepted and forthcoming in
David, F.R. *Strategic Management* (3rd ed.), Columbus,
OH, 1990; and David, F.R. *Cases in Strategic Manage-
ment*, Merril, Columbus, OH, 1990. Copyright © Richard
Reed, 1989. Reprinted with permission.

[1]*Business Week*, October 16, 1989.

[2]*Mergers and Acquisitions*, May–June, 1989

[3]*Fortune*, July 31, 1989.

[4]For a fuller discussion see *Time*, September 14, 1987,
pp.52–62.

Table 1   International Investment Position of the United States

a. Net International Investment Position (1980–1988)

($ billion)	1980	1981	1982	1983	1984	1985	1986	1987	1988
U.S. Foreign Assets (of which)	607	720	825	874	896	950	1,071	1,168	1,267
Direct investment	215	228	208	207	211	230	260	309	329
Securities	63	63	75	84	89	113	133	147	159
Foreign Assets in U.S. (of which)	501	579	688	784	893	1,061	1,341	1,536	1,769
Direct investment	83	109	125	137	165	185	220	262	304
Securities	90	94	119	148	185	290	400	423	493
Net Investment	106	141	137	89	4	−111	−269	−368	−502

Source: World Economic Survey, United Nations, 1989.

b. Foreign and U.S. Acquisitions by Country (1988)

Countries Most Active in U.S.

Country	Transactions	Value
Great Britain	188	$23.6 bn.
Canada	46	9.7 bn.
Japan	45	11.9 bn.
West Germany	27	1.2 bn.
France	26	3.0 bn.
Total	332	$49.4 bn.

Countries Attracting U.S. Buyers

Country	Transactions	Value
Canada	49	$4.4 bn.
Great Britain	36	1.0 bn.
West Germany	7	*
Australia	7	0.1 bn.
Italy	7	*
Total	109	$5.5 bn.

* < $0.1 billion

Source: Mergers and Acquisitions, May–June, 1989.

nomic infrastructure, and available work force, in film presentations and expenses-paid visits for foreign executives. Other investment, aimed mainly at real estate purchase and the acquisition of U.S. industrial assets, is generally less welcomed. Table 1b shows who is buying American assets. British acquisitions now exceed $100 billion.[5]

Many of the names involved in the acquisitions are familiar. Sony (Japanese) has bought CBS Records, Nestle (Swiss) bought Carnation, and Grand Metropolitan (British) bought Pills-

bury, who owns Burger King. Unilever (joint Anglo-Dutch) has bought Chesebrough-Pond's, British Petroleum now has Sohio, Bridgestone (Japanese) acquired Firestone, Hoechst (West German) took over Celanese, Marks and Spencer (British) bought Brooks Brothers, Seagram (Canadian) acquired Tropicana Products, Total Cie (French) bought CSX Oil and Gas, and Heileman Brewing agreed to be bought out by the (Australian) Bond Corporation. Amid the continuing list Hanson acquired SCM, Kaiser Cement, and Kidde.

There are obvious things like political stability and size of market that have made the U.S.

[5]*CNN*, November 2, 1989.

attractive to foreign investors. But, these have existed for some time and do not explain the surge of foreign takeovers. More recent events have brought about the dramatic increase. First is the decreased value of the U.S. dollar. While this curbs imports and boosts exports, it also means that American domestic assets appear to be low-priced in terms of the Japanese yen, the British pound, the German mark, and others. Real estate is considered a "snip" and, despite the existence of bull markets between 1982 and 1989, some company stocks remain a good buy for foreign firms seeking acquisitions. Second, is the continuing trend toward the globalization of business. Through their hugely successful export activities, Pacific rim countries have accrued earnings at the same time as they've become familiar with American culture and business. Consequently, they are now able to acquire and operate U.S. companies with relative equanimity. Others, like the Swedish home appliance maker, Electrolux, and their Italian subsidiary, Zanussi, have saturated European markets and have seized growth opportunities in the American marketplace.[6]

A third factor which indirectly fueled foreign investment in the U.S. was the recession in the early 1980s. Increased European acquisitions of U.S. firms resulted from the shakeout effects that the recession had in more marginal economies. Some firms were forced to adopt imaginative strategies, such as stock buybacks. Others rationalized and cut away unproductive fat and then aggressively pursued longer term gains through acquisition. Only the better managed and more cost effective companies survived. These lean and aggressive survivors see firms in the U.S. that would "benefit" from their hard-learned management skills. The American firms targeted for acquisition usually have some potential for increased profitability. They are firms

that have never had the pressing economic need to fully develop the skills necessary for strict control of costs. They are also firms who have not been prepared to look beyond their traditional domestic boundaries for new opportunities and growth.

Background and History of Hanson

Hanson is a firm that knew the secret of efficient operation coupled with growth by takeover long before the last recession forced other firms into using the same strategy. By making judicious acquisitions, strictly controlling capital expenditures, and keeping efficiency high, Hanson has come a long way since its humble beginnings twenty-five years ago. James Hanson (now Lord Hanson) and Gordon White (now Sir Gordon White) are the people primarily responsible for building the Hanson empire. Lord Hanson and Sir Gordon White first met in the 1950s. Lord Hanson was then involved in the family trucking business and Sir Gordon sold advertising space in magazines published by his father. Their first business venture was a greeting card firm which they sold in 1963.[7] 1964 found them in charge of the Wiles Group, a relatively small British company. It was based in Yorkshire, in the north of England, and sold fertilizer. That year saw two key events occur that would initiate the transformation of the company into the Hanson of today. First, Wiles became a quoted company on the London Stock Exchange, thus providing facilities for increasing capital. Second, they acquired Oswald Tillotson Ltd., another small British company engaged in commercial vehicle distribution. Lord Hanson, who was a director of the acquired company, became chairman of the Wiles Group in the following year, 1965.

Under Lord Hanson's direction the Wiles Group embarked upon a series of acquisitions that were also concentric diversifications. In 1967, a construction equipment and distribution

---

[6]In the mid-1980s Electrolux bought White Industries, a major U.S. home-appliance maker. In response, Whirlpool has entered a joint-venture with Philips NV to market its products in Europe, and Maytag has acquired Hoover which has strong sales in Britain.

[7]For a fuller discussion of their histories and lives see *Business Week*, August 15, 1989, and *Fortune*, November 7, 1988.

company was purchased for 0.7 million pounds (nearly $1.7 million). Table 2 provides exchange rates between the U.K. pound and the U.S. dollar. An agricultural sack rental company was purchased for just over 3 million pounds in mid-1968 and, at the end of that year, a brick manufacturer was acquired for nearly 5 million pounds. In 1969, the company's name was changed to Hanson, Ltd. and further acquisitions followed in construction equipment distribution, brick manufacturing, and engineering. Hanson's obvious strategy of acquiring companies in low-technology but stable industries was now well established. It was allied to an equally obvious rationalization program that produced improved levels of profit from the acquired assets. Between 1964 and 1973, before-tax profit climbed from 0.14 million pounds to 8.2 million pounds, a fifty-eight fold increase in ten years.

In 1973, Sir Gordon White left England with the aim of establishing Hanson in the U.S. The company entered the U.S. with an initial equity investment of only $3,000.[8] Sir Gordon's first major acquisition was Seacoast Products, a producer of animal feedstuffs and edible oil. The acquisition was achieved through a leveraged buyout with assets of the target company being used as collateral against loans. Seacoast was purchased for $32 million. From the first year, Seacoast produced a cash flow which helped facilitate other acquisitions. A textile company, Indian Head (now Carisbrook Industries), was acquired in 1975 and was followed by Hygrade Foods in 1976. Interstate United (food services), Templon (textiles), and McDonough (building materials) were acquired over the period 1977–1981. In total, Hanson spent over $0.3 billion in acquisitions in the first eight years of its U.S. operation. From this small beginning Hanson has balanced its U.S.-U.K. portfolio to the extent that, by 1988, U.S. operations provided about 43

Table 2 Currency Exchange Rates (1967–1989) for U.S. Dollars & U.K. Pounds

Year	One U.S. Dollar in U.K. Pounds	One U.K. Pound in U.S. Dollars
1967	0.4155	2.4067
1968	0.4194	2.3843
1969	0.4166	2.4004
1970	0.4174	2.3959
1971	0.4091	2.4442
1972	0.3999	2.5008
1973	0.4080	2.4510
1974	0.4273	2.3403
1975	0.4501	2.2216
1976	0.5541	1.8048
1977	0.5731	1.7449
1978	0.5212	1.9184
1979	0.4712	2.1224
1980	0.4300	2.3258
1981	0.4940	2.0243
1982	0.5721	1.7480
1983	0.6597	1.5159
1984	0.7482	1.3366
1985	0.7707	1.2974
1986	0.6813	1.4677
1987	0.6098	1.6398
1988	0.5914	1.6910
1989	0.6452	1.5500

Source: *Statistical Abstract for the United States* and *Wall Street Journal.*

percent of sales and profits. To Sir Gordon's dismay only 15 percent of Hanson's 200,000 shareholders are American.[9] Hanson has become one of the largest British investors in the U.S. and, in the process, has earned Sir Gordon White the reputation of being a top corporate raider.[10] Sir Gordon was the model for the British corporate raider who outmaneuvered the character Gor-

[9]*Fortune*, November 7, 1989.

[10]*Fortune*, September 28, 1987, carries an article on the top twelve corporate raiders in which Sir Gordon White, along with Sir James Goldsmith and Carl Icahn, receives the highest (most aggressive) rating on a "shark fin" rating scale of one fin to four fins.

[8]Due to currency exchange regulations, $3000 was the maximum sum that could be transferred from the U.K. for foreign investment. This rule no longer applies.

don Gekko in the film *Wall Street*.[11] However, Sir Gordon prefers to see himself as an "industrialist."[12]

Structurally, Hanson reflects the geographic split in its operations. Lord Hanson is overall company chairman and chairman of the British operations. U.K. operations are controlled by the chief operating officer, A.G.L. Alexander. American operations, Hanson Industries, Inc., has Sir Gordon White as chairman. The control of Hanson Industries is delegated to its president, David H. Clarke, who joined Hanson via the acquisition of Seacoast Products. In April, 1988, Martin G. Taylor joined Derek N. Rosling, CBE, as a vice-chairman of Hanson. Martin Taylor, who is a member of the Confederation of British Industry and is on the Panel for Takeovers and Mergers, has been with Hanson since 1969. He is the main contact at Hanson for securities analysts and the business press. He is also involved in Hanson's strategy formulation and is seen as a likely successor to Lord Hanson and Sir Gordon White when they retire (at age 70), in 1992.[13]

Hanson has maintained a rate of growth that has made it into one of the top performing British firms and has elevated Hanson Industries (the U.S. operations) to a rank of 67 in the Fortune 500. Hanson's ten year record for 1980—1989 is shown in Table 3. Between 1980 and 1988, sales increased over twelve fold. Gross profit increased twenty-two fold and earnings per share increased over eight fold. The phenomenal growth that has been achieved is due, in part, to the continued policy of acquisition. This has led to both conglomeration and diversification. Because the diversifications have moved beyond being related, to become unrelated, there has been a smoothing effect on earnings. Also, by operating in both the U.K. and the U.S. the diversification effect has been increased. The 1985 financial results were not as good as earlier years,

but currency exchange rates worked in Hanson's favor when U.S. earnings were translated into U.K. pounds. 1986 saw a return to real growth which continued through 1988 and, from quarterly results, it is estimated that Hanson will produce the equivalent rates of growth for 1989 (see Table 3).

Organization and Control

In 1984 Hanson described itself as "an industrial management company."[14] This statement, which is still accurate in 1989, reflects the company's policy of maintaining a "hands off" attitude to the operational activities of its subsidiaries. To quote Sir Gordon, "I don't even know all the presidents of our companies. I know their names but I've never been to any of our plants. . . . There's no need for me to. It's best for me to keep away and give Hanson's company presidents their autonomy. Autonomy as managers and as human beings."[15]

The hands off approach means ignoring operational synergies between subsidiaries. For example, no attempt is made to integrate distribution activities for firms producing similar products in the same geographic area. Hanson is quite happy to have separate fleets of delivery trucks covering the same routes. Sir Gordon White argues that the costs of administering combined delivery can be as much as the savings it generates. Or worse, customers do not receive goods because responsibility for deliveries is unclear. Integration of activities to release synergy also reduces the flexibility to make divestments at will. Hanson satisfies itself with the financial synergy gained from internal capital markets.

The essence of the Hanson's philosophy is to provide "essential goods and services to proven markets, with definable future prospects."[16] In the U.S., Hanson operates in the ma-

[11]*The Economist*, March 11, 1989.

[12]*Fortune*, November 7, 1989.

[13]*Wall Street Journal*, April 21, 1988.

[14]Hanson *Annual Report* and Accounts, 1984.

[15]*Fortune*, November 7, 1988.

[16]Hoare Gosset Limited (Analysts), October, 1986.

Table 3 Hanson Review (1980–1989)

U.K. Pounds (million)	1989[a]	1988	1987	1986	1985	1984	1983	1982	1981	1980
Income										
Sales	7,742	7,396	6,682	4,312	2,674	2,382	1,484	856	684	605
Profit (before tax)	1,242	880	741	464	253	169	91	60	50	39
Earnings per Share[b]	21.0	15.9	14.0	10.7	7.9	5.7	3.5	2.8	2.5	1.9
P/E Ratio	8.1	7.2	11.8	12.9	12.4	15.0	13.2	9.5	8.7	5.9
Assets Less Liabilities										
Tangible Assets	n.a.	1,476	1,183	1,074	603	685	289	211	129	92
Investments	n.a.	178	178	40	187	17	11	4	4	6
Current Assets	6,728	6,158	5,014	5,551	2,062	1,443	962	547	458	216
Current Liabilities	2,553	2,272	1,966	2,486	907	754	565	323	196	142
Financed By										
Share Capital	1,102	1,014	1,043	814	500	164	106	55	27	27
Reserves	1,808	1,235	836	774	625	247	323	134	138	94
Long Term Debt	2,065	2,124	1,727	1,972	640	797	186	188	191	42
Liability Provisions	1,063	886	686	619	180	183	82	62	39	9
Total	6,038	5,259	4,292	4,179	1,945	1,391	697	439	395	172
Assets per Share[b]	70	57	48	40	39	23	25	14	12	9

[a]Estimates from results of the first three quarters, and from Value Line.
[b]In pence (one hundred pence = one U.K. pound), fully diluted.
Source: Hanson Annual Report and Accounts, 1988, 1986; Value Line, Oct 20, 1989.

ture, low technology areas of food products, building products, office furniture, pigments, lighting, and consumer products (cookware, sports equipment, toys, kitchen appliances, and so forth). The U.K. activities remain in equally basic and mature industries; tobacco products, battery manufacture, retailing, yarns and threads, engineering, heating appliances, and building products. With the acquisition of London Brick for 245 million pounds in 1984, and its existing subsidiary, Butterley Building Materials, Hanson became the largest brick manufacturer in the world.[17] Table 4 gives a breakdown of activities by operating divisions for both the U.S. and the U.K.

Hanson has very few corporate staff. SCM had 230 corporate staff when it was acquired by Hanson Industries in 1986, U.S. Industries (ac-

quired 1984) had 180, and Kidde, acquired in 1987, had 200. Hanson Industries had 30 staff. Post-acquisition rationalizations have reduced the total number of head office staff for all four to just 120.[18] Major responsibilities at the corporate level include financial control and a constant search for attractive takeover candidates. Hanson's affinity for leanness at the top has become a major factor in their impressive stretch of profitability.

David Clarke, president of Hanson Industries, has a team of seven people who are responsible for agreeing budgets and targets with the presidents of the 150 U.S. subsidiary companies.[19] Stock options are used to encourage managers to think as shareholders, and thus im-

---

[17]Hanson Trust *Annual Report* and Accounts, 1984.

[18]*Fortune*, November 7, 1989.

[19]Because Hanson is so active in buying and selling companies, this figure is approximate.

Table 4 Hanson Divisional Activities (1987–1988)

	(In U.S. $ million[a])			
	1988		**1987**	
	Sales	**Profit**	**Sales**	**Profit**
U.S.				
Consumer Products	1,360	105	893	75
Smith-Corona typewriters, word processors, supplies; Farberware cookware, kitchen appliances; Tucker housewares; Rexair vacuum cleaners; Spartus clocks; artificial flowers; Tommy Armour sports equipment; Universal gym equipment; Valley pool tables; Bear archery equipment; Ertl toys.				
Building Products	1,084	123	690	96
USI commercial and residential lighting; Kidde lighting; Kaiser cement and aggregates; Duke City lumber; Superlite masonry products, aluminum windows and patio doors; MW windows and doors; Ames tools; Brown Moulding and wood trim; Jacuzzi baths, spas, and pumps.				
Industrial	2,257	298	1,048	137
SCM pigments and chemicals; Office Group furniture and office supplies distribution; Grove cranes and aerial access equipment; Weber Aircraft seating, galleys, and lavatories.				
Food	710	35	673	34
Hygrade processed meat products: Ground Round family restaurants	5,411	561	3,304	342
U.K.				
Consumer Products	5,394	382	5,411	353
Imperial Tobacco cigarettes, cigars, and tobacco products; British Ever Ready dry cell batteries; Allders department stores and duty- and tax-free shops.				
Building Products	523	163	416	124
Hanson Brick (London Brick, Butterley Bricks)—fletton and non-fletton bricks.				
Industrial	858	174	634	145
Lindustries electrical, automotive, engineering, and gas products; Barbour Campbell textile products; SLD construction services; Berry Magicoal and Robinson Willey heating appliances.				
Food	321	22	308	20
Seven Seas health products; Elizabeth Shaw confectionery.				
	7,096	741	6,769	642
	12,507	1,302	10,073	984
Businesses owned in 1987 and sold in 1988	—	—	1,226	76
Other income less central expense	—	186	—	193
	12,507	1,488	11,299	1,253

[a]All information restated at 1.6910 dollars to the pound.
Source: Hanson Annual Report, 1988.

prove profits and return on capital. While Hanson pays salaries that are below average, its managers can earn up to an additional 60 percent depending upon the performance of their unit. Beyond the budgeting process, responsibility for operations is wholly decentralized. The zero interference approach to operations does not, however, extend to capital expenditures. Any expenditure greater than $1,000 requires corporate approval. This maximizes profit and discourages waste. Some managers argue that it also discourages investment for future growth.[20] But, Hanson's decision in August, 1989, to spend $67.5 million on its titanium dioxide operations in Ohio suggests that where real profits can be made, real investments will also be made.

Hanson's Takeover Strategy

In the early days, the company's acquisitions had the potential to generate profit without the need for substantial reinvestment. Takeovers were usually agreed for family tax reasons, or to ensure profitability, or even survival. Where possible, original managements were kept intact after acquisition. With increasing size there has been a subtle but distinct change in Hanson's policy for acquisition and post-acquisition control. Targets now include firms with untapped earnings potential and tactics for takeover have become more aggressive. Where possible, managements are still retained but profitability is instilled into the culture through managerial performance and appraisal criteria.

The objectives of Hanson have remained constant over the past 25 years: ". . . to expand profitability while achieving careful expansion through acquisition."[21] There is also the objective "to increase earnings per share and dividends annually . . ."[22] The strategy for achieving this is to locate the target, make the acquisition

(often for cash), streamline the operations, and then let it run as a separate profit center with an expectation of growth in profits. A good example of this is Hanson's acquisition of Berec (formerly Ever Ready).[23] After the takeover in 1981, Berec's name was changed to the British Ever Ready Company to reflect its original name and the product for which the company was famous: batteries. In a very short time Hanson turned Berec around from a position of declining profitability to one of strength through the simple expedient of improving efficiencies and divesting nonprofitable activities. Corporate staff and research activities were reduced to manageable proportions and direction was refocussed on the core activity of dry cell batteries. In contrast to the 1981 pre-acquisition profits of 10 million pounds on sales of 241 million, the company produced 1985 profits of 31 million pounds on sales of 128 million. British Ever Ready still produces two-thirds of the zinc batteries sold in Britain.

Lord Hanson and Sir Gordon White are deal makers. They will only buy if the price is right. But they will also sell anything if the price is right. Selling off nonprofitable or marginal assets from its new acquisitions has been used to great effect by Hanson. In the U.S., in 1981, McDonough (tools, shoes, building materials) was bought for $185 million and $53 million was immediately recouped from the sale of its cement manufacturing activities. While these assets accounted for almost 28 percent of the total cost, they were responsible for only 10 percent of profits. In addition to releasing $53 million for further acquisitions, McDonough's ROI was instantly improved by 25 percent. Today's net asset value for McDonough's remaining activities (Ames Tools, Endicott Johnson, and others) is estimated to be $450 million.[24] Obviously, this figure includes some inflationary effects, but it also reflects improved operations and profits.

[20]*Business Week*, August 15, 1988.
[21]Hanson *Annual Report* and Accounts, 1988.
[22]Hanson *Annual Report* and Accounts, 1986.

[23]Not related to Ever Ready Batteries, U.S.A.
[24]*Fortune*, November 7, 1988.

The 33 company conglomerate of U.S. Industries Inc., purchased in 1984 for $532 million, has been similarly improved. Nine companies were sold for a total of $225 million. The estimated net asset value of the remaining 24 companies is now $1.8 billion.[25] SCM, the Imperial Group, Kaiser Cement, Kidde, and Hanson's latest acquisition, Consolidated Gold Fields, are all going through the same process of divestitures and improvements to profitability.

SCM

The Battle for SCM

Hanson's biggest takeover battle occurred with the acquisition of SCM. On August 22, 1985, Hanson announced a $755 million ($60 per share) tender offer for any or all shares of SCM. Hanson's offer could have been covered by its cash reserves but, instead, they chose debt as a means of financing the purchase. Favorable borrowing rates in the U.S. made the obtaining of loans an attractive proposition. In this way, the company remained flexible enough to consider other takeovers.

Merrill Lynch was called in to act as SCM's financial advisor. On August 25, SCM announced that "golden parachutes" had been previously voted into effect. These golden parachutes would richly compensate any existing SCM executive who left the company up to two years after an outside party had acquired 20 percent or more of the company's stock. On August 29, SCM and Merrill Lynch announced plans to initiate a $70 per share ($868 million) joint LBO of SCM. Hanson responded on September 4 by raising their offer to $72 per share. Experts did not expect the bidding to go much higher and conceded that SCM had achieved its goal of increasing the common stock price.[26]

Merrill Lynch acted as white knight for SCM. On September 11, Merrill made a $74 per share, two-thirds LBO offer. SCM's management instantly accepted. Normally, this would have signalled the end of the contest but within a matter of hours Hanson retracted their $72 bid and acquired approximately 25 percent of SCM's common stock from large institutional investors for $73.50. This move entailed wide-ranging legal implications. SCM charged that in purchasing the stock on the market Hanson had made an illegal tender offer and violated federal law. A temporary restraining order was won against Hanson prohibiting any further purchases of SCM shares and, as security, the 3.1 million shares that had been acquired were held in escrow. It was disclosed that the LBO planned by SCM and Merrill Lynch was, in fact, a "poison pill" and contained a "crown jewel lock-up" option. Upon the accumulation of one-third of SCM shares by a hostile suitor, the most valuable divisions of SCM would immediately be sold to Merrill Lynch at a substantial discount.

On October 2, the U.S. Federal District Court ruled in favor of Hanson and its September buy-up of SCM stock. The judge ruled that the purchases were legal because they were made from sophisticated investors who, unlike the general market, were aware of the implications of their actions.[27] Merrill Lynch prepared to exercise the lock-up option but, first, they had to determine whether Hanson had acquired one-third of SCM's stock. This new controversy centered around the question of the level of diluted or undiluted SCM stock. Hanson filed suit claiming that SCM and Merrill Lynch unlawfully conspired to obtain and exercise the previously described lock-up option. On October 9, Hanson made a new offer of $75 for SCM stock. The bid was made in response to Merrill Lynch's move to exercise the $74 lock-up option after the courts ruled that Hanson did hold one-third of SCM's common stock. The matter was finally resolved

[25]Ibid.

[26]*Wall Street Journal*, September 4, 1985.

[27]*Wall Street Journal*, October 2, 1985.

Table 5 SCM Review (1976–1985)

$ million	1985	1984	1983	1982	1981	1980	1979	1978	1977	1976
Income										
Sales	2,175	1,963	1,663	1,703	1,761	1,745	1,628	1,406	1,289	1,244
Net Profit	58	42	27	29	57	54	47	38	37	30
Earnings per Share[a]	n.a.	4.05	2.45	2.88	5.44	5.17	4.59	3.75	3.70	3.04
Assets and Debt										
Total Assets	1,391	1,362	1,113	1,124	1,078	1,009	980	845	768	740
Tangible Assets	561	563	406	436	404	350	327	305	279	251
Working Capital	413	417	430	351	361	369	362	279	285	288
Long Term Debt	336	260	277	240	238	229	245	190	201	210
Book Value per Share[a]	n.a.	54.3	52.7	52.7	51.7	47.5	43.4	40.4	37.4	34.2
Other Data										
No. of Employees[b]	n.a.	20.9	24.5	25.5	27.6	27.4	28.6	27.4	25.5	27.1
U.S. Index of Inflation[c]	.955	.964	.984	1.000	1.041	1.136	1.289	1.443	1.546	1.645

[a]In dollars, fully diluted.
[b]In thousands.
[c]Purchasing power of the dollar, in producer prices; 1982 = $1.
Source: SCM Annual Report and Accounts, 1984; Value Line, 1985; and, *Statistical Abstract for the United States.*

in the courts in January 1986. A ruling that the lock-up option was valid was overturned in appeal. Hanson finally acquired SCM for $930 million ($75 per share).

SCM: The Company
In 1985 SCM was a 22 business conglomerate with just over $2 billion in sales and a net profit of $58 million (see Table 5). Activities and products included chemicals, Glidden Paints, Smith-Corona typewriters, Allied Paper, and Durkee Foods. As shown in Table 6, the chemicals division led SCM with 1985 sales over $538 million and an operating income of nearly $74 million. Coatings and resins operations were second with sales and operating profits $687 million and $50 million respectively. While paper products and foods turned in profits of only $23 million each, on sales of $361 million and $422 million, they performed better than the typewriter division which had losses of $47 million on $176 million sales.

Paul H. Elicker, chairman and CEO, had been restructuring SCM when Hanson started its bid for takeover. SCM had recently acquired additional titanium oxide operations from Laporte Industries. Titanium oxide is used in the manufacture of paints, plastic packaging, vinyl siding, vinyl pipes, and numerous rubber products. Technology was upgraded in pigment plants at Ashtabula, Ohio, and Stallingborough in England. Smith-Corona was also being restructured to concentrate on electric typewriters and personal word processors. Manual machines were being deemphasized. Employment in the typewriter division was reduced by over 2,000 and the asset base was being reduced from a high of $149 million to less than $100 million. Paul Elicker's restructuring plan was possibly well conceived, but it was insufficient and too late to avoid SCM becoming a good buy for Hanson.

After the Acquisition
By November, 1988, Hanson had recouped

Table 6 SCM Divisional Results (1982–1985)[a]

	(Amounts in $ million)			
	1985	1984	1983	1982
Chemicals				
Net Sales	538.9	360.7	250.6	248.6
Operating Income	73.7	36.9	15.1	22.4
Return on Sales (%)	13.7	10.2	6.0	9.0
Depreciation	NA	15.0	16.8	10.7
Capital Expenditures	NA	49.7	9.6	29.8
Total Assets	NA	316.9	266.6	272.7
Coatings and Resins				
Net Sales	687.3	654.6	575.8	552.0
Operating Income	49.9	51.4	36.7	32.2
Return on Sales (%)	7.3	7.8	6.4	5.8
Depreciation	NA	8.6	9.3	7.6
Capital Expenditures	NA	16.1	9.8	16.9
Total Assets	NA	348.9	330.0	311.2
Paper Products				
Net Sales	361.7	351.7	315.9	327.8
Operating Income	23.1	21.0	15.3	33.3
Return on Sales (%)	6.4	6.0	4.9	10.2
Depreciation	NA	10.1	9.8	8.7
Capital Expenditures	NA	10.9	12.4	14.3
Total Assets	NA	167.5	155.1	146.7
Foods				
Net Sales	422.1	393.3	354.8	389.9
Operating Income	23.0	17.2	28.6	18.2
Return on Sales (%)	5.4	4.4	8.1	4.7
Depreciation	NA	4.7	3.8	3.9
Capital Expenditures	NA	10.0	9.8	6.0
Total Assets	NA	160.3	145.9	148.1
Typewriters				
Net Sales	176.3	198.5	164.3	177.4
Operating Loss	47.4	15.9	11.6	23.8
Return on Sales (%)	—	—	—	—
Depreciation	NA	6.6	6.2	6.6
Capital Expenditures	NA	6.8	6.4	7.5
Total Assets	NA	149.1	148.6	148.6

[a]Excludes income (expenditure) and profit (loss) from other unspecified sources.
Source: SCM Annual Report, 1985.

$1.26 billion from the sale of SCM subsidiaries and hidden assets like the $36.5 million worth of Park Avenue real estate.[28,29] Glidden Paints was sold to Imperial Chemical Industries PLC[30] for $580 million, and Durkee Foods was sold to the U.S. arm of Unilever for $185 million. This left Hanson Industries with the highly profitable chemicals division and the restructured Smith-Corona typewriter division. The net asset value of the chemicals division is now estimated to be in excess of $2 billion. SCM's chemicals operations are a substantial cash generator and fit well in Hanson's cash cow portfolio. By 1989 Smith-Corona was producing operating margins of 18 percent on sales of $493 million and, in July, Hanson sold off 53 percent of Smith-Corona in a $21 per share market issue. This generated about $300 million in cash and expanded Hanson's acquisition war chest to $3.2 billion.[31]

Two weeks after the issue, Smith-Corona announced that soft sales were forcing it to lay off 10 percent of its workers. Smith-Corona's stock which had been as high as $23.375 dropped to $16.375. Some investors were upset and threatened legal action on the grounds that the prospectus had not revealed that the firm had high inventory levels—a fact discovered by Smith-Corona's chairman at the end-of-month meeting.[32] Hanson may or may not get embroiled within a legal battle. Much depends on Smith-Corona's performance. By November 1989, Smith-Corona's stock stood at $17.75, and the

[28]The Economist, March 11, 1989.

[29]Wall Street Journal, November 1, 1988; Fortune, November 7, 1988.

[30]Imperial Chemical Industries (ICI) is a British firm with (approximately) 350 subsidiaries, worldwide. ICI produces general, specialty, agricultural, and petro-chemicals plus pharmaceuticals, fibers, explosives, fertilizers, colors and paints.

[31]Wall Street Journal, June 6, 1989.

[32]Business Week, August 28, 1989.

earnings forecast for 1990 are $2.20 per share (a 22 percent increase).[33]

The Imperial Group

On December 6, 1985, while still fighting for control of SCM, and in anticipation of a successful outcome, Hanson started moves to rebalance its U.S. and U.K. operations. These moves were aimed at the Imperial Group PLC—a large British conglomerate, with sales of 4.9 billion pounds ($6.5 billion) and more than 90,000 employees. Imperial's activities included tobacco, brewing, food, hotels, restaurants, and retail.

The Imperial Group was in the midst of negotiating a merger with the food company, United Biscuits PLC, when Hanson started its acquisition. Both United Biscuits and Imperial responded with a caustic attack against Hanson, arguing that Hanson's increases in profits came from acquisition rather than returns from capital investment programs. During the ensuing weeks, roles were modified and, in effect, United Biscuits became Imperial's white knight. Hanson gained control of the Imperial Group in April 1986. The cost of the acquisition was 2.5 billion pounds ($3.7 billion), of which 126.5 million pounds ($188 million) was in cash and the remainder in issued stock, convertible unsecured loan stock, and loan notes.

One of the first actions after completion of the takeover was to defray some of the purchase cost and restore the cash balance by selling off Imperial's relatively unprofitable retailing division, its hotels, and restaurants. Two of Imperial's subsidiaries, U.S.-based Lea and Perrins and the British-based HP Foods, were sold to BSN, a French food group, for $91 million. BSN paid a substantial premium so that it could enter the U.S. and U.K. markets with well known brands. By July of 1988, Hanson had recouped 2.23 billion of the 2.5 billion pounds paid for the Imperial Group. Among other things, this leaves

Hanson with the tobacco products division which generated over 50 percent of the Imperial Group's 1985 profits.[34]

Kaiser Cement

The California-based Kaiser Cement Corporation produced Portland cement, sand, gravel, and ready mixed concrete, and had a decidedly lacklustre performance. Sales hovered around $240–250 million, and profits were poor. For the three years prior to Hanson's ($250 million) purchase in March 1987, Kaiser Cement had incurred losses of $5 million and $52 million, and made a profit of $16 million.[35]

By the end of 1988, Hanson had recouped $283 million from the sale of Kaiser's assets.[36] Sales included the Lucerne Valley CA cement plant with a capacity of 1.6 million tons, which was sold to the Japanese Mitsubishi Mining and Cement Company for $195 million.[37] Like the sale of Imperial's Lea and Perrins and HP Foods to the French BSN, the price for the Lucerne Valley plant included a substantial premium that Mitsubishi Mining was prepared to pay to gain access to U.S. markets. Among other Kaiser assets, Hanson still retains its largest cement plant at Permanente, California, 3,500 acres of real estate in Silicon Valley, and 400 acres in Hawaii.

Kidde

The Acquisition

Kidde's financial performance into the 1980s was not impressive and the value of its stock had languished. So, in May, 1986, the chairman, Fred R. Sullivan, retained the investment bankers La-

---

[33]Ibid.

[34]Data obtained from the prospectus for Hanson's offer for Kidde, September 25, 1987, which also provides information on the Imperial Group.

[35]*Moody's Industrial Manual*, 1987.

[36]*Fortune*, November 7, 1988.

[37]*Wall Street Journal*, February 9, 1988.

zard Freres and Bear Stearns to help produce a plan for restructuring Kidde.[38] Based on Kidde's assets, the investment bankers concluded that the firm's stock was undervalued. Three options were suggested: recapitalization, a leveraged buyout, or sale of the company. In the interim, Hanson had accumulated 2.2 percent of the undervalued stock.[39] Chairman Sullivan learnt of this in July, 1986, and immediately put Kidde up for sale and invited bids from five leveraged buyout firms and conglomerates. Among these was Hanson. Hanson's bid of $60.10 cash per share and a seven year warrant to buy one Hanson ADR[40] for $18 prevailed. Hanson had to decide whether to dig into its $5.8 billion mountain of cash, or whether to finance the deal by borrowing. The $1.6 billion deal to acquire Kidde was finalized August 4, 1987, and was approved by Kidde shareholders in January, 1988.[41] Unlike the SCM acquisition, the Kidde takeover was not hostile.

Kidde: The Company

Kidde's inflation-adjusted sales and operating profits peaked in 1979. From that point on, the firm had been treading water. It had been making efforts to reduce its long term debt since 1983. Kidde's ten year record up to 1986 is shown in Table 7. Although a conglomerate, like Hanson, Kidde was not an aggressive buyer and seller of firms. It made occasional acquisitions, like the 1984 purchase of the British firm, Grove Cranes, but made very few divestments. Once a company was acquired it was as likely as not to remain within the Kidde portfolio. This suggests that Kidde was looking toward internally generated growth. However, the 1980–1986 increases in

capital expenditure did not even keep up with inflation.

Before the takeover, Kidde had 108 subsidiaries. Table 8 shows the breakdown of income by activity. Products included Farberware cookware and electrical appliances, Spartus clocks, Rexair vacuum cleaners, Jacuzzi baths and spas, Ertl toys, Bear archery equipment, Universal gym equipment, PGA/Tommy Armour golf equipment, Weber aircraft seats and toilets, and Kidde fire extinguishers. The fire extinguisher business was Kidde's original base of business. In 1986 fire protection and safety still produced over 20 percent of revenues but the consumer and recreation activities (lighting and home products, and housewares and leisure products) had become the new core businesses. Jointly, they produced 40 percent of sales and 50 percent of profits and received the bulk of reinvestment. Kidde also had financial services, office supplies, nursing services, semiconductor products, computer products, and much more.

The management and control of Kidde and of SCM exhibit distinct similarities prior to acquisition (compare divisional performances for Kidde and SCM, Tables 6 and 8). Kidde fits Hanson's target profile well.

After the Acquisition

It has been suggested that when Sir Gordon White paid $1.6 billion for Kidde, it was an expensive buy at 25 times earnings.[42] Although Barry Nelson of Louis Nicoud and Associates said "... If they [Hanson] think it is worth $60 a share, the odds are pretty good that it will be worth more than $90 a share later on."[43] The usual treasure trove of hidden assets was discovered at Kidde. One of Kidde's companies owned three corporate jets, a hunting lodge, and a collection of art and antiques. All were sold except one jet, which Hanson Industries has kept. Kidde's headquarters in New Jersey were

[38]*Business Week*, August 17, 1987.

[39]*Wall Street Journal*, August 6, 1987.

[40]ADRs are American Depository Receipts—the means by which the stock of foreign firms can be traded on U.S. stock markets.

[41]The final figure for Kidde varies between $1.5 billion (*Fortune*, November 7, 1989) and $1.8 billion (*Wall Street Journal*, November 11, 1987). $1.6 billion corresponds to $60.1/share for the 26.7 million shares outstanding.

[42]*Fortune*, November 7, 1989.

[43]Ibid.

Table 7 Kidde Review (1977–1986)

$ million	1986	1985	1984	1983	1982	1981	1980	1979	1978	1977
Income										
Sales	2,356	2,165	2,087	1,864	1,900	2,037	1,934	1,778	1,454	1,128
Net Profit	25	72	79	73	84	99	87	84	69	57
Earnings per Share[a]	1.04	3.18	3.50	3.15	3.60	4.22	3.71	3.39	2.68	2.35
Assets and Debt										
Fixed Assets	421	313	324	293	410	380	324	288	233	216
Current Assets	1,137	1,145	1,010	1,108	1,215	1,306	1,115	1,107	952	737
Current Liabilities	533	460	470	506	562	648	481	516	324	240
Capital Expenditures	72	66	63	70	92	89	72	63	38	30
Long Term Debt	425	448	492	504	514	468	450	433	433	383
Book Value per Share[a]	n.a.	32.9	29.4	27.5	35.1	32.7	29.3	25.8	22.6	20.7
Other Data										
U.S. Index of Inflation[b]	.969	.955	.964	.984	1.000	1.041	1.136	1.289	1.443	1.546

[a]In dollars, fully diluted.
[b]Purchasing power of the dollar, in producer prices; 1982 = $1.
Source: Kidde Annual Report and Accounts, 1986; Value Line 1985; and, *Statistical Abstract for the United States.*

closed down to eliminate the duplication of personnel functions. The two Theurer truck manufacturing plants were rationalized on to one site to eliminate the duplication of operations. As a result, the work force was reduced by 425. By the beginning of 1989 Hanson had recouped over $500 million from the sale of a few of Kidde's subsidiaries. Among these were the security personnel firm and the fire protection equipment (excluding fire extinguishers). Kidde Credit's U.S. operations were sold to the Concord Commercial Corp., a subsidiary of the Hong Kong and Shanghai Banking Corp., and the Canadian credit operations were sold to Bruncor Inc. of St. John, New Brunswick.

Consolidated Gold Fields

For 18 months after buying Kidde, Hanson sold companies but did not buy. Over the 12 months up to June 1989, Hanson spun off more than $1 billion of assets. In November, 1988, they obtained permission from stockholders to increase borrowing power 69 percent up to $20 billion.

Then, nothing happened. Lord Hanson wrote to stockholders in May, 1989, saying ". . . the time has not been right for us to make a major acquisition at today's inflated [stock] prices."[44] Hanson had been on the periphery of several possible takeovers. Two desultory excursions into banking (a 3.3 percent stake in Morgan Grenfall PLC, and a 5.2 percent stake in Midland Bank PLC) resulted in nothing more than a very modest profit on the investment. Hanson also held an 8.8 percent stake in Cummins Engines which it sold for a 15 percent profit in July, 1989, one month after the bid came for Consolidated Gold Fields.[45]

The Acquisition
Early in the morning of June 23, 1989, Hanson offered 3.1 billion pounds ($4.83 billion, $22.25/ share) for the British firm Consolidated Gold Fields. On news of the bid Consolidated Gold's stock jumped 16 percent, and Hanson's ADRs

---

[44]*Wall Street Journal*, June 23, 1989.
[45]*Wall Street Journal*, July 18, 1989.

Table 8   Kidde Divisional Results
(1984–1986)[a]

	(Amounts in $ million)		
	1986	**1985**	**1984**
Lighting and Home Products			
Net Sales	486.9	457.6	446.5
Operating Income	35.7	33.9	31.2
Return on Sales (%)	7.3	7.4	7.0
Depreciation	9.7	9.1	8.3
Capital Expenditures	14.1	11.1	19.6
Total Assets	306.5	311.3	277.2
Housewares and Leisure Products			
Net Sales	468.3	451.7	455.9
Operating Income	43.6	34.8	52.3
Return on Sales (%)	9.3	7.7	11.5
Depreciation	16.1	14.3	13.2
Capital Expenditures	27.3	25.9	17.1
Total Assets	334.5	301.2	301.3
Safety, Security, and Protection			
Net Sales	505.5	460.5	439.6
Operating Income	31.8	30.4	30.3
Return on Sales (%)	6.3	6.6	6.9
Depreciation	8.5	8.0	6.5
Capital Expenditures	7.4	7.3	7.1
Total Assets	236.6	248.1	237.9
Office Supplies and Services			
Net Sales	446.0	394.6	339.4
Operating Income	24.9	24.6	22.6
Return on Sales (%)	5.6	6.2	6.7
Depreciation	4.6	3.8	3.0
Capital Expenditures	4.9	6.2	4.1
Total Assets	163.4	152.0	127.4
Transportation and Other Equipment			
Net Sales	449.5	400.5	405.6
Operating Income	22.6	27.2	33.4
Return on Sales (%)	5.0	6.8	8.2
Depreciation	15.9	11.0	10.3
Capital Expenditures	18.0	15.3	9.7
Total Assets	293.4	267.6	232.8

[a]Excludes income and profit from other unspecified sources.
Source: Kidde Annual Report, 1986.

increased 5 percent. Consolidated Gold Fields is the largest gold mining concern outside South Africa, and controls 49.3 percent of the largest U.S. gold mining firm, Newmont Mining. Newmont's stock rose nearly 15 percent. Hanson's vice-chairman, Martin Taylor, said that the bid for Consolidated Gold would not affect the ability to make other acquisitions.[46] At this point, Hanson's acquisition potential (cash and borrowing) was over $23 billion.

When the Hanson bid came, Consolidated Gold had just spent 30 million pounds fighting off a takeover bid by the South African controlled Minorco. Minorco's bid had been blocked by legal action in the U.S. because of Consolidated Gold's holdings in Newmont Mining. Minorco still controlled 29.9 percent of Consolidated Gold's stock and promised the shares to Hanson. This put the pressure on Consolidated Gold to accept the Hanson bid. After talks between Hanson and Consolidated Gold Field executives, Hanson raised its bid to 3.5 billion pounds. In August, 1989, Hanson revealed that it had won control of 57.3 percent of Consolidated Gold's stock and that the offer to purchase all the shares would remain open.

And After (?)

Hanson is expected to recoup the entire investment for Consolidated Gold within three years of the purchase.[47] After acquisition, Hanson immediately sold three-fourths of Consolidated Gold's 38 percent stake in Gold Fields South Africa to the South African controlled Rembrandt Group. This recouped 368 million pounds. Hanson is expected to sell off most of Consolidated Gold's mining operations. The U.S. Gold Fields Mining subsidiary and the U.S. part of Consolidated Gold's ARC building materials subsidiary may be sold to Minorco S.A. for up to $1.6 billion. However, Alabama-based

[46]*Wall Street Journal*, June 24, 1989.

[47]Ibid.

Vulcan Materials, Beazer PLC (British), and Tarmac PLC (British) are also interested in buying the U.S. part of ARC. The Canadian firm, American Barrick Resources, is interested in acquiring the U.S. Gold Fields Mining subsidiary and the 49.3 percent stake in Newmont Mining.[48] During 1989 gold had been down to $358 an ounce but, by November, had climbed to $388 on nervousness about the stock market and the strength of the U.S. economy. The price was expected to go higher.[49]

What Next for Hanson?

As 1989 heads rapidly towards 1990, the question must be asked: where does Hanson go from here and can it sustain its growth? It has been rumored that Hanson may be considering Xerox and B.F. Goodrich for acquisition.[50] Another rumor is that Sir James Goldsmith (famous in the U.S. for his hostile bid for Goodyear) will drop his attempted takeover of BAT Industries because of the market's low confidence in junk-bonds, and Hanson with its incredible purchasing power will step in.[51] Yet another rumor is that Hanson is looking to acquire the conglomerate Canadian Pacific.[52] The Canadian government is unlikely to let this happen given the firm's importance to the Canadian economy. Hanson's portfolio of firms is again weighted toward Britain. It therefore seems likely that some sort of rebalancing will occur with a sizable acquisition in North America.

There is no evidence to suggest that Hanson intends to change its strategy. The size of its acquisition war chest, which is still around $20 billion, suggests the reverse. How much is $20 billion? To put the figure in perspective $20 billion is greater than the market value of Mobil, which is ranked fifth in the Fortune 500.[53] It is more than the market value of Procter and Gamble, RJR Nabisco, Dow Chemical, Boeing, or 3M. It is more than the value of Chrysler and Texaco combined. These are unlikely targets for Hanson. They do not fit the profile of undervalued, marginally profitable firms, operating in low-tech industries. However, Weyerhaeuser or American Brands may be more in keeping with Hanson's requirements.

Hanson needs acquisitions; it improves their stock value. Unlike most firms, Hanson's stock rises on the news of a new acquisition. Between acquisitions the stock price tends to be flat. In the quiet period between buying Kidde and Consolidated Gold, the flat stock price led Hanson to flirt with the idea of a 10 percent stock buyback. If the period between acquisitions is too long, Hanson's own stock may become attractive to a corporate raider. Prior to the acquisition of Consolidated Gold, Hanson's market value was as low as $10 billion. The breakup value of the assets was estimated at $16-19 billion.[54] To quote from *The Economist*:

> . . . Breaking [up] Hanson is one of those games that investment bankers love to play. It has always been a hypothetical one because there is no one around to do the breaking up. Few outside companies have the credibility to mount a hostile takeover; in public, Hanson itself has always remained open to offers ("If a bidder offered enough money, we'd send round a car to pick him up"). In private, though, the top managers are against the idea.[55]

Another rhetorical question concerns the onslaught of foreign acquisitions. Will it continue? Unless American business invests more abroad and competes with foreign firms in their own markets, the answer has to be yes. The high leverage of many U.S. firms limits their ability to make foreign takeovers, so improving export

---

[48]*Wall Street Journal*, August 15, 1989.

[49]*Wall Street Journal*, November 3, 1989.

[50]*Wall Street Journal*, June 24 and July 18, 1989.

[51]Ibid.

[52]*Forbes*, October 16, 1989.

[53]*Fortune*, April 24, 1989.

[54]*The Economist*, March 11, 1989.

[55]Ibid.

abilities may be the best way to fight back. But, paradoxically, while U.S. output per hour worked increased more than 6 percent between 1980 and 1986, the international competitiveness of U.S. companies (measured in terms of worldwide market share) declined by the same amount. In other words, not enough is being done. The best defense against foreign (or domestic) takeovers is a high stock value that is derived from the efficient use of assets and high profitability and growth expectations. Whether the reawakening philosophies of efficiency, quality and innovation, and looking toward foreign markets will reach the majority of American companies in time, and stem the tide of foreign takeovers, remains to be seen. Perhaps the final word on this should go to Sir Gordon White.

The following is taken from an article in *Time* magazine in which Sir Gordon was interviewed:

> . . . New managers like Sir Gordon White are giving their American troops a pep talk. Says he: "In the U.S., you haven't got the drive to export. It's often very difficult to convince managers in companies we've bought that they should flog [sell] their products in Britain. They say 'Why go to all of that trouble when I can sell in the U.S.?' . . . White would be only too happy to discover more American corporations that need to be taken over and set straight. . . . With all those tempting troves of undervalued wealth in view, it is small wonder that Sir Gordon and his many foreign imitators still want to buy, buy, buy.[56]

---

[56]*Time*, September 14, 1987, p. 62.

Case 15

Xerox's Competitive Dilemma in the High-End, Nonimpact Printer Industry

At midyear 1989, the market for high-end printers was heating up. Major U.S. manufacturers, specifically Xerox and IBM, contemplated new product and marketing initiatives. They wanted to forestall incursions into their domestic markets by foreign producers, such as Siemens of West Germany. Despite a respected and well-earned reputation for leading edge products, top management of Xerox's printer group faced serious challenges to its ability to attract and retain customers. Xerox has had difficulty transferring its success in the copier business into other product markets, including printers. In areas where its efforts have been less than successful, the firm has reorganized structurally and dropped unprofitable product lines. Industry observers were beginning to speculate that Xerox needed to consolidate its efforts in printers in this dynamic market. Without such changes, it was rumored that Xerox could become a takeover target. Xerox's high-end, nonimpact printers were targeted as a primary source of revenues in its redefined mission for the future. However, a number of strategic issues confront the top management of Xerox's printer business:

This case was prepared by Michael W. Lawless, Linda Finch Tegarden, and Howard D. Feldman, Graduate School of Business, University of Colorado at Boulder. Distributed by North American Case Research Association. All rights reserved to the authors and the North American Case Research Association. Permission to use the case should be obtained from the authors and the North American Case Research Association. Reprinted with permission.

• How should Xerox position itself relative to its competitors in high-end, nonimpact printers? One of Xerox's new strategies is to focus its document processing systems in a few information-intensive industries. This requires expertise, not only in high-end printers, but in industry-specific information needs and software requirements. Does Xerox have this expertise? Will they be able to maintain (or increase) their current market share in high-end printers with this focus strategy?

• How will growing demand for complete information processing system solutions (data processing, data storage, and document generation) affect both Xerox and competitors' strategies in high-end, nonimpact printers? An emerging opportunity in the industry is the increasing demand for solutions to organizational information needs. Integration of data processing, report and document report generation, and data storage issues all need to be addressed at a broader level. How will this affect Xerox's focus on document processing systems?

• Can Xerox sustain a leadership position in its niche with its present high-end, nonimpact printer strategy? While Xerox has historically commanded price premiums for new products be being first with technological features, will they be able to continue? Japanese and German high-end printer products are viewed as an increasing threat because of their quality. Their low price-driven strategies have already proven effective in other markets. Xerox's large market share in the U.S. market was also an inviting target for these global competitors, not to mention its principal domestic competition, IBM. Is Xerox's high-end printer (and copier) technology still a competitive advantage and if so, how much longer will it last?

Xerox Corporation

Overview

Xerox Corporation encompasses both business products and systems activities (developing, manufacturing, marketing, and servicing a complete range of document processing products and systems designed to make offices more productive) and financial services (see Figure 1 for a description of Xerox's businesses).

Since its initial success in copiers, Xerox Corporation has continually expanded into technologically related areas: electronic typewriters, printers, computers, workstations and telecommunication services, including supporting software. To finance these new ventures, Xerox Corporation has acquired financial service-oriented businesses that are both cash and profit-generators. However, most of the new business product ventures have failed to meet expectations. Over the last two decades, the company has tried selling mainframes, personal computers and telecommunication services, but none of these ventures was successful. In fact, Xerox Corporation continues to have performance problems. Business product equipment revenues remained flat through most of the 1980s, and profit margins are still lower than desired.

Some say the company has not solved the long-run problem of defining itself, nor can it shake its reputation as a supplier of less exciting office products such as copiers and typewriters. While Xerox's technological leadership in product development is generally undisputed, the company seems to have problems marketing their new products. This may be the primary reason for the most recent retrenchments, which include closing its medical imaging business, scaling back production of electronic typewriters, and writing off its workstation hardware business. Such failures have convinced some analysts that Xerox will be hard-pressed to duplicate its earlier successes anytime in the near future.

Performance

Xerox Corporation reported total revenues of $16.44 billion in 1988, up from $15.11 billion in 1987. Net income declined 33 percent from $578 million in 1987 to $388 million in 1988. Profit margins (operating income to revenues—not including Xerox Credit Corp.) have steadily declined from 30.6% in 1978 to 13.3% in 1987.[1] Industry segment contributions, reported in Table 1 for 1988, show that Xerox's financial services businesses provide 89% of Xerox's total profits. (Refer to Tables 2–5 for detailed financial data.)

Copiers account for about 75% of Xerox's business product profits. Despite all expansion efforts, however, business product revenues overall have been flat through most of the 1980s at about $8 billion. Profit margins in this segment are still small, partially due to severe price competition. While high-end, nonimpact printers generate $1 billion in revenues, this business activity is falling short of profit expectations.

As business products continue to lag financial services in profitability, Xerox took a $275 million pretax write-off in 1988 to reduce nonperforming assets—closing the unprofitable medical imaging business, scaling back an electric typewriter plant, writing off its workstation hardware business, improving the flow of research ideas into new products, and cutting 2% of its workforce. Xerox also intends to put more emphasis on computer-related technologies, such as printers and scanners that support document processing, and on selling software to run on other makes of computers.

---

[1]Source: Standard & Poor's NYSE Reports, Volume 56, No. 45, p. 24.

Figure 1 The Business of Xerox[1]

Business Products and Systems

Corporate Research Group: Performs research and exploratory development to enable the transfer of technologies to the Development and Manufacturing Organization.

Development and Manufacturing Organization: Plans, develops, and manufactures Xerox products and systems, including copiers, duplicators, laser printers, professional workstations, network systems, software, and supplies.

Marketing and Customer Operations:

(1) U.S. Marketing Group: Handles direct sales and service of Xerox products and systems to major accounts and commercial customers.

(2) Integrated Systems Operations: Markets integrated document processing systems for both government and commercial customers, using products and technologies from Xerox and other sources.

(3) Information Products Division: Markets and services entry-level and specialized products through agents, dealers, distributors, OEM manufacturers, value-added resellers, and telemarketing.

(4) Engineering Systems Division: Markets and services wide-format plotters, engineering reprographic and systems, and computer-aided design products widely used in the engineering industry.

(5) Americas Operations: Markets and services Xerox business products and systems through subsidiaries or distributors in Canada and more than 40 countries in North, South, and Central America, the Caribbean, the Middle East, and North Africa.

(6) Rank Xerox: Markets and services all Xerox business products and systems in more than 80 Eastern Hemisphere countries.

Xerox Financial Services

(1) Crum and Forster, Inc.: Provides property and casualty insurance protection, including reinsurance and specialty coverages, for businesses, auto and home through independent agents and brokers.

(2) Xerox Credit Corporation: Provides financing for customers buying Xerox products and systems, as well as financing and leasing for third parties. Also engages in truck and auto leasing.

(3) Van Kampen Merritt, Inc.: Offers fixed-income investment products such as unit investment trusts and mutual funds, and provides asset management and capital market services.

(4) Furman Selz: Provides equity-oriented research, sales and trading, investment banking, asset management, arbitrage and other institutional financial services.

(5) Xerox Life: Provides investment-oriented life insurance products, including single-premium life and single-premium deferred and immediate annuities.

FAR EAST AFFILIATE

Fuji Xerox: Develops, manufactures, and markets a full range of business equipment; operates in Japan, Indonesia, South Korea, the Philippines, Taiwan, and Thailand.

[1]Source: Xerox Annual Report, 1988, pp. 12–13.

Xerox's Printing Business

Since 1986, Xerox has devoted much of its energies to document processing. The company defines this market as almost any activity in which information is put on paper. It is projected to be a multi-billion dollar market for the 1990's. The current focus is on selling integrated publishing solutions, and offering products that cover the entire publishing spectrum, from PC software to

Table 1

Business	Revenues	Profit (ROS)
Business products & systems	68%	11%
Financing of Xerox equipment	3%	27%
Insurance & other financial services	29%	62%

dedicated systems complete with scanners, workstations, specialized software, local-area networks (LANs), and high-end nonimpact printers. Xerox focuses efforts on five paper-intensive industries in particular: pharmaceutical, insurance, aerospace, defense contracting, and utilities. To penetrate these markets, Xerox recently reorganized its operations and now offers customized processing systems to these industries through its Integrated Systems Operations (ISO). This group was formed as a marketing center for all document processing business in North America and Europe. The restructuring was done with an eye toward improving the competitive position of the high-end, nonimpact printer division vis-a-vis IBM and Siemens.

Xerox's competence in new product development gives it an acknowledged technical edge. The company has spent heavily on new product development, particularly in recent years, to recapture customer acceptance lost to competitors, primarily IBM, Siemens, and several Japanese firms. While product development is a strength, its ability to successfully market its new offerings is questionable. Xerox has restructured both marketing and sales to better support customer printing needs: this is an attempt to follow a new marketing approach. For example, they recently revamped the direct sales force by converting product specialists into general-line sales representatives. Two separate sales forces resulted from the restructuring. The Special Markets Group, with 100 to 150 representatives, now handles products distributed through third-party channels, such as dealers, original equipment manufacturers (OEMs), and distributors. The Custom Systems Division, with 50 to 70 sales representatives, services the federal government and other large noncommercial accounts, including states and educational institutions. Despite these changes, Xerox has difficulty releasing software for its printers in anything less than two years. The problems result from the company's attempt to support an expanding range of printer functions, and their push toward IBM-compat-

ibility. Therefore, efforts have been made to shorten the product development cycle. For example, Xerox restructured its research and development and manufacturing functions in an attempt to better support the new marketing strategies.

A recent policy memorandum called customer satisfaction the number one objective at every level of the organization: every employee would now be a "marketer" of Xerox products. The extent to which they have been successful in achieving this goal, however, is debatable. While technological leadership allows them to use a premium pricing strategy, Siemens is going after its market by providing better service—a key area where Xerox has been criticized in recent years.

Xerox High-End Printers

Xerox has built a $1 billion business in cutsheet (separate pages) laser printers, and is considered the industry leader. Unlike several of their competitors, however, Xerox has no fanfold (continuous sheet) machines. This currently reduces some customers' choices for printing solutions and excludes Xerox from a major market segment. However, Xerox is expected to continue improving its cutsheet technology, and is testing multi-purpose machines based on scanner (digital) technology. Potential substitution and possible obsolescence in the current product line because of new technology are a concern of both Xerox and its competitors.

Xerox's printer is also distinctive for its greater processing power, giving customers off-line printing capability that the competition does not offer. Its distributed approach puts a microprocessor capable of prioritizing jobs and managing workflow right at the printer. It reduces throughput times for printing, and is a major selling point. However, it has the disadvantage that the printer does not communicate with the central processing unit (CPU) as effectively as IBM's host-computer approach to printing.

Xerox is continually enhancing its high-end

printers by offering automated pre- and post-printing procedures that reduce operational costs. For example, document finishing devices like cutters can trim a large sheet of paper into smaller units, and stuff and seal envelopes with the cut documents. These features do not substantially add to current prices. Product enhancement prices range from $1,300 to $8,600 as opposed to printer prices of $140,000 to $400,000. Xerox continues to be the value-added leader in printers with new features and technological advancements. Its printers feature higher resolution relative to competitors' products. In addition, plans call for two-color printing that will help users cut the costs of producing stationery. These differences allow higher prices than rivals, although some customers contend that Xerox prices are too high. Others complain of poor service from their Xerox field representatives. Its recent reorganization, as well as expected order increases for both copiers and high-end laser printers, may improve Xerox's performance. But as Xerox assesses its strategic options for the '90s, and waits to see the results of its changes, the rest of the high-end, nonimpact printer industry continues to move forward at a rapid pace.

High-End, Nonimpact Printer Industry: 1989

High-end printers are used in medium to large information processing systems to create paper documents ranging from reports to labels and envelopes. Because of their speed, high-end printers are typically used in operations where volume is very high. Figure 2 shows their essential characteristics. The term "high-end" defines the range of printers operating at speeds from 50 pages per minute (ppm) to 220 ppm. These high production rates are achieved with nonimpact technology such as the laser, where entire pages are printed at one time using photoelectric means. Traditional impact technology is limited to printing a line at a time, or even a character

Figure 2 High-End, Nonimpact Printer Characteristics

Types	Cutsheet
	Fanfold
Speeds	50–220 pages per minute
Price	$140,000–$400,000
Printing Technology	Laser, Light Emitting Diode

at a time (a physical device actually strikes the paper). For the remainder of the discussion, high-end printers are synonymous with high-end, nonimpact printers.

The high-end printer market is divided into two types: fanfold and cutsheet. Fanfold printers use continuous paper sheets that are either perforated for separation into individual pages or are cut into separate pages after the page is printed. Cutsheet printers input separate pages, much like standard copying machines. In general, fanfold printers are faster than cutsheet, operating at the high end of the speed range (220 ppm). In contrast, 140 ppm is the highest speed attained by current cutsheet printers. Prices range from $140,000 to $400,000, and are directly related to printing speed.

Compatibility, in respect to both hardware and software, is essential for high-end printer products, since a printer serves as an output function to an entire information system. Thus, each competitor must conform to some degree on product standardization or be completely out of step. At one extreme, IBM's system design requires both software and hardware compatibility. At the other, decentralized printing systems, such as that offered by Xerox, must still communicate with other elements of the processing system within an installation. Few printing activities can completely stand alone.

Opportunities in the High-End, Nonimpact Printer Market

Annual market growth for high-end printers in the U.S. is estimated to be about 20%, with world-wide sales running slightly higher. Future growth potential is estimated to be greatest in cutsheet printer sales, although fanfold printers will continue to coexist in large data processing centers. Competition in the industry is primarily concentrated in three rivals—IBM, Xerox, and Siemens—who directly influence each other's revenues and related profits. One industry analyst noted that IBM is the leader in fanfold printers in the U.S., with Siemens "right behind." Siemens is the leader in fanfold in Europe with IBM second. Xerox is the leader in cutsheet printers in both markets. While there is some market growth opportunity, the high-end printer market is perceived by major competitors as a zero-sum game, where each one's actions directly affect the distribution of industry profits.

Mid-range printers are consistently cited as a major opportunity. Growth in printer sales to mid- and small-size data processing shops, and the enormous growth expected in remote or decentralized computing, provide sales opportunities for mid-range printers. However, the expansion of personal computer (PC) networks is viewed as contributing to the rise in sales in this market. The current focus of the largest competitors is on meeting the needs of large data processing shops.

To date, printers are sold without educating customers about printing and printing systems and the ways they evolve. Opportunities exist for companies that can assist businesses contemplating purchases of new equipment by informing them about advantages and disadvantages of various technologies. Increased customer service that eases the adoption of new technologies may provide avenues to competitive advantage. Paper-intensive service and information industries—insurance, banking, auto parts, aerospace, legal, and pharmaceutical—offer additional opportunities for sales. Color is reported as a possible opportunity, that excites some customers, within the next four to five years. On the other hand, development costs and cost-per-page copy-

ied will be too high for most customers. Other opportunities are graphics, inplant publishing, and magnetic ink character recognition (MICR) printed documents.

Competitor Comparisons: IBM and Siemens

Aside from Xerox, the only serious competitors in the U.S. market are IBM and Siemens. Both are described below.

Strategy

IBM's strategy is to provide complete information processing solutions. Its primary thrust is to sell mainframes and supporting software, with printers included in a total system solution. IBM succeeds as a result of its marketing strength and a large installed customer base.

Siemens' strategy is to become a global competitor in high-growth electronics markets, including high-end printers. It is focusing mostly on the U.S., comprising 30% of world demand. However, Siemens' name and products are relatively unknown in the States. Its printer strategy focuses on offering a superior IBM-compatible product at a lower price in order to generate increased market share.

Printer Technology

IBM offers a range of both cutsheet and fanfold printers that link to IBM central processing units (CPUs) through a common controller interface called Advanced Function Printing (AFP). Unlike Xerox, IBM's printers are "dumb," requiring two-way communication with the host computer to operate. This approach gives centralized control over printing functions while reducing duplication of data throughout an installation. IBM's printers are known for their reliability and lower maintenance costs, but they also have fewer features than their competitors. Siemens is attempting to exploit this situation by offering a better product at a lower price. As part of a package solution, IBM dictates prices on printers and relies on software to retain its market share.

IBM's weaknesses in the high-end printer market are related to its emphasis on mainframes and its use of original equipment manufacturers (OEMs) to produce its printer engines. For instance, its nondedicated sales force does not have the printer expertise of Xerox's and Siemens' dedicated sales forces. Sales reps must manage a wide variety of computer-related products, rather than specialize in only printer-related products and services. In addition, IBM's reliance on OEMs for most of its printer engines leaves its machines behind both Xerox and Siemens technology. But in order to interface with IBM systems, competitors are required to develop IBM-compatible equipment interfaces. IBM tries to lock in customers with software, the heart of its integrated systems. To attract customers in the IBM environment, competitors must support Advanced Function Printing (AFP) controller interfaces with their IBM customers. IBM's printers are considered by many to be high-priced with more product limitations than any of their competitors'.

Siemens' IBM-compatible printers are considered to be superior in quality and reliability to IBM's own equipment. They were developed specifically to overcome many of IBM's shortcomings, and are superior according to a number of industry analysts. Both fanfold and cutsheet printers are offered, and an aggressive pricing strategy is used to consistently undercut IBM prices.

Marketing and Sales

IBM's sales force is responsible for a full computer product line. Its marketing and sales functions are considered among the best, utilizing extensive resources and a system solution approach. But IBM sales personnel, in a sense product line generalists, are seen in an unfavorable light when compared to the printer specialists of Xerox and Siemens. IBM representatives are

sometimes perceived as less knowledgeable and responsive to their customers.

IBM succeeds by brute strength (size), aggressive selling style, and a large customer base. Its sheer size (market share leader in all IS areas) provides distinctive capabilities that contribute to its competitive position in the high-end printer market. In addition, IBM offers customers a wide range of products, virtually supplying a customer's complete computing needs. Thus, customers are assured compatibility when purchasing products from IBM.

IBM promotes competitiveness, especially in selling mainframe computer systems, which continue to be its most profitable equipment segment. Its new strategy, promotion of mainframe-based network hubs for database management in large systems, reemphasizes this dedication to mainframes.

IBM's image is that of a large, visible, aggressive leader. Even though mainframe sales growth slowed considerably in the second half of the 1980s, IBM continues in a leadership position for information system products. It also intensively pursues acceptance of its technology and systems as industry standards. IBM is a formidable power in the industry, particularly given its large existing customer base.

Siemens is a leader in electronic products throughout Europe, and is making tremendous strides in other areas, primarily in U.S. markets. For example, its recent acquisition of Rolm (1988), gives it a leadership position in U.S. telecommunications. With an ample supply of cash, Siemens has concentrated on investments in electronics, especially microelectronics research and development. The company has long been considered a leader in technology, generating superior products in many electronics markets.

Siemens' present thrust into U.S. markets is hindered primarily by lack of name recognition. It is concentrating on "buying" market share, which to date has not been profitable. To succeed in the long run, these weaknesses must be overcome. Thus, expansion and name recognition campaigns are currently under way in the U.S. One initial move has been to create 15 U.S. branch offices to sell and service printers. Their sales force, like Xerox's, is dedicated to printers. Since the company lacks a U.S. customer base, Siemens is currently targeting sales to both IBM and Xerox customers. A second move has been to initiate a brand image campaign to increase consumers' awareness of Siemens. Marketing personnel are committed to Siemens' expansion in the U.S. and voice their excitement for the company's strategic moves. They are confident that their product is superior and their strategy appropriate.

Strategic Variables

Strategic variables affecting profitability are divided into "maintenance" and "leverage" types. Maintenance variables are factors or characteristics a firm must have to compete in a specific market. Like entry requirements, all viable competitors must at least have parity with rivals in regard to these variables. However, they are generally not a means to enhance a position. They directly affect revenues, which in turn affects profitability. On the other hand, leverage variables differentiate one rival from others, and contribute directly to profitability. For example, by allowing a firm to charge higher prices, they enable it to earn above normal profit margins. They generally are unique to a particular firm, and offer value to customers not duplicated by other competitors. Maintenance and leverage variables for the high-end printer market are summarized in Figure 3.

Maintenance Variables
The minimum firm size needed to support required investments in production scale economies and new product development is very large. The top three competitors are very large organizations with sales in the billions of dollars.

Figure 3 Strategic Variables for the High-End Printer Market

Maintenance Variables
Firm size
Geographic scope
Established sales and service resources
Firm image/reputation
Joint ventures

Leverage Variables
Installed base of related products
Know-how about printer products and printing systems
Market niches/specialization
Customer switching costs
Product features, value-added

They have ample capital to support the investments required to compete in the high-end printer market. IBM's size provides production efficiencies, a large customer base and a large, established sales and service force with supporting resources. Xerox routinely supports major R&D and new product development investments. Siemens' large size allows it to sustain low profits caused by startup investments and below-profit pricing while it becomes established in the U.S. market.

All three major competitors' markets are global, indicating a large minimum revenue requirement to support economies of scale in production unit costs and investments. While IBM and Xerox are well-established in international printer markets, Siemens is currently focusing on increasing its U.S. market share.

Another industry requirement is an established sales organization with strong expertise in printers and printing systems, and with supporting hardware and software. In addition, high-end printers and printer systems require service in the form of maintenance, enhancements, and repair on an ongoing basis. Both IBM and Xerox have extensive sales and service support. Siemens' current expansion of sales and service locations in the U.S. is necessary to be a major competitor. Additionally, Siemens intends to approach Xerox customers with better service to gain market share.

All competitors must create a product brand image and reputation, most likely related to proven reliability and durability. Reputations must be established, not only with printers, but with the system in which a printer is integrated. IBM's product brand image comes from its data processing system capability. For Xerox, it comes from its printing system capability and superior products. Siemens' reputation is improving based on its superior products and service.

All three competitors are expanding their alliances with other firms. IBM is contracting to offer full product lines to customers, and reducing its traditional competitive posture against venture partners. Xerox has publicly announced a willingness to be a subcontractor for systems integrators to generate printer sales. Siemens' drive to penetrate U.S. markets in electronics has been dominated by alliances, in both acquisitions and joint venture agreements designed to increase market share and to improve its technological position. These alliances indicate movement by high-end printer manufacturers to expand their range of activities beyond current organizational boundaries.

Leverage Variables

Different combinations of leverage variables, those on which above-normal profits are based, are used by the top three competitors. While it can be argued that none of the three has an exclusive hold on any leverage variables, it is the individual firm's emphasis on each that determines its strategic importance in generating profits.

An installed base of related products is IBM's means to a distinct market position. Existing mainframe customers are its ready-made audience for related products, including printers. Buyers' integrated software solutions require IBM-compatible equipment.

Know-how about printer products and systems is leveraged by Xerox and Siemens. Both have dedicated sales and service forces that focus exclusively on printers. Xerox, the cutsheet leader, concentrates on printer solutions. The recent formation of Integrated Systems Operations is based on the belief that know-how can be transferred from noncommercial to commercial applications. Siemens specializes in printer technology know-how, and specifically addresses IBM's product/service weaknesses, offering IBM-compatible printers at a lower price.

Both IBM and Xerox leverage on market niches or specialization. IBM's focus is on mainframes, targeting the larger data processing operations. Customer preference for one-vendor solutions gives IBM a competitive advantage with its own mainframe customers. Xerox targets paper-intensive industries like insurance and aerospace to concentrate on meeting specific customer needs.

IBM creates switching costs for its existing customers. An IBM customer requires IBM-compatible equipment, reducing the number of potential providers. By staying with IBM, customers are assured that printers are compatible, and will be serviced and maintained under the IBM umbrella.

Both Xerox and Siemens leverage product features. Xerox's product enhancements, like post-processing features, enable it to tailor systems to better meet customer printing requirements. Meanwhile, Siemens' investment in new product features is leading to a corporate image of the innovative producer in the IBM environment.

Table 2 IBM and Siemens Revenue
Comparison for 1986–1987[1]
($ in millions)

	IBM	Siemens
1987 Total Revenue	$54,217.0	$28,615.7
1987 Net Income	5,258.0	709.4
1987 Total Information Systems Revenue	50,485.7	5,703.0
1986 Total Information Systems Revenue	47,685.0	4,383.3
IS Revenue Change 1986–87	5.9%	30.1%
1987 Net Income/ Total Revenue	9.7	2.5
1987 IS Revenue/Total Revenue	93.1	19.9
1987 Return on Assets	8.3	2.0[2]
1987 World Rank— IS Revenue	1	7
1986 World Rank— IS Revenue	1	8

[1]Source: Datamation, 6-15-88.
[2]Source: Compact Disclosure.

Table 3 Competitor 1987 IS Sources of
Revenues [Datamation, 6–15–88]
($ in millions)

Revenue Sources	Xerox	IBM	Siemens
Mainframe	—	$11,193.0	$ 695.5
Software	—	6,836.0	550.8
Peripheral	$1,560.0	8,725.0	1,502.3
Datacom	—	1,507.0	1,402.1
Service[1]	3,310.0	9,360.0	1,000.0

[1]Source: Computerworld, 12–19–88.

Table 4 Competitor 1987 IS Revenue Source
Market Share [Datamation, 6–16–88]

	Xerox	IBM	Siemens
Mainframe Market Share	—	41.6%	2.6%
Software Market Share	—	40.2	3.2
Peripheral Market Share	2.9%	16.4	2.8
Datacom	—	10.0	9.3

Table 5 Competitor Comparison on 1987
Financial Information

	Xerox	IBM	Siemens
Profitability			
Net Inc./Net Sales	0.05	0.10	0.02
Net Inc./Total Assets	0.05	0.08	0.02
Net Inc./Common Equity	0.13	0.14	0.08
Relative Expenditures			
R & D	0.07	0.10	0.12
Direct Costs	0.50	0.45	0.49
Productivity			
Net Sales/Working Capital	6.75	3.07	1.91
Net Sales/Plant & Equip.	4.32	2.14	3.83
Net Sales/Current Assets	2.44	1.75	1.30
Net Sales/Total Assets	0.94	0.85	0.94
Liquidity			
Quick Ratio	0.85	1.47	1.28
Current Ratio	1.56	2.32	3.14
Receivables Turnover	5.16	4.25	5.62
Inventories Turnover	7.72	6.27	2.20
Leverage			
Total Liab./Total Assets	0.47	0.40	0.70
Long Term Debt/ Equity	0.28	0.10	1.59
Total Debt/Equity	0.28	0.10	2.37
Total Assets/Equity	2.09	1.66	3.37

Source: Compact Disclosure, Datamation, and Moody's.

Case 16

Robert F. Ramsey, Inc. and Ramsey Paint Manufacturers, Inc.

Introduction

It was after 9 p.m. when Robert F. Ramsey locked the warehouse door behind him and stepped into the employee parking lot. He had just finished his nightly ritual of checking all the sales invoices for the day and signing all the accounts payable checks. As he pulled on his motorcycle helmet, Mr. Ramsey thought he should be very content: the new store opened on schedule, the operating results this year looked very good, and all three of his children were working with him at the paint company. Few men 62 years of age had as much to be grateful for as he did. But as his Harley-Davidson roared to life, Robert Ramsey still had the same sense of uneasiness that had plagued him for the past several months: "Is the company doing as well as it should?" His companies manufactured, wholesaled, and retailed paint, and he had competed successfully against industry giants for years. But he thought the family was working too hard for the money the company was making. "What do we need to be doing to ensure the future success of the company? If we are going to expand, how do we do it? And what is the value of the company?" As the traffic light beside the store turned green, Robert Ramsey put these thoughts away and slipped the Harley into gear, merging into the evening traffic.

The Paint and Allied Products Industry

At year end 1987, the entire paint and allied products industry had over 1,000 firms and directly attributable sales of approximately $10.2 billion. Additional industry data are found in Exhibit 1.

The major divisions of the industry are architectural coatings, product finishes for original equipment manufacturers (OEMs), and special purpose coatings. Architectural coatings are stock or shelf-type goods for general application and are the largest, most mature segment of the industry. OEM coatings are proprietary and are dependent upon new technologies and environmental restrictions. Special purpose coatings are stock or shelf-type goods for specific applications such as extreme temperatures, corrosive conditions, etc.

The industry is highly fragmented with high transportation costs representing the business's most competitive factor. Smaller players remain profitable, for example, by keeping operations close to their consumers. These high costs not only create intense competition but also keep foreign substitutes to a minimum. Imports, almost invisible before 1986, grew slowly through 1986 and 1987 to $187 million. Exports only became

This case was prepared by Michael D. Atchison, Stewart C. Malone, and Sandra L. Schmidt, McIntire School of Commerce, Monroe Hall, University of Virginia, Charlottesville, Virginia 22903.

This case was written for the McIntire Commerce Invitational, sponsored by the General Electric Foundation. Copyright 1989 by McIntire School of Commerce Foundation. All rights reserved. Reproduced with permission. Note: this is a disguised case. The authors gratefully acknowledge support from the General Electric Foundation and the McIntire School of Commerce.

noticeable in 1987, when they rose 22 percent to about $305 million—still only about 2 percent of total industry sales. The industry is in a mature stage; therefore, growth comes from product innovation, market penetration, and acquisition of competitors' shares of the market. The maturity of the industry is also evidenced in the heavy price competition. The top 10 companies in the industry control only 40 percent of the market. There are no clear price or technological leaders.

Paints and coatings are commodity items— mostly standardized products produced by a large number of firms. Distribution for architectural coatings and automotive refinishes is achieved through retail channels, distributors, and sales forces. OEM and special purpose coatings are distributed mainly through direct sales because of the higher level of technical assistance required in the products' use.

Sales for the industry have been quite scattered over the last several years. Sales fell to a low in 1980, then grew slowly through 1981 as the industry financed its growth with more debt. The years 1982 and 1983 saw the industry recover as sales grew at their sharpest pace in five years. This was followed by slow expansion through 1987.

The business is material intensive, with ingredients making up as much as 75 percent of cost of goods sold. This relationship has declined through the second half of the decade to a level of about 64 percent in 1987. Profits have also followed a similar path, although the highs and lows of net income growth are more extreme. Profits dipped drastically in 1982, but recovered quickly and grew through 1987.

Liquidity management for the paint and allied products industry has become increasingly more difficult since the late 1970s. There appears to be a steady downward trend on the quick and current ratios, illustrating the industry's propensity toward less conservatism and the acceptance of more financial risk. The industry's highly price-competitive environment has forced

a steady increase in capital expenditures (such as plant modernization), research and development costs, and advertising expenses, all leading toward less liquidity.

Architectural coatings sales are linked to the residential and PPE (nonresidential) portions of investment. As new housing starts or residential resales increase, demand for paint necessarily increases. OEM coatings sales are tied to PPE investment because, as productivity increases, the demand from OEMs goes up.

Another factor substantially affecting the industry is seasonality. Professional paint contractors, as well as individual do-it-yourselfers, paint mostly when the weather allows—the spring through fall. The industry therefore suffers during the winter months.

The final determinant of industry performance in the economy is the presence of environmental regulations, typically those aimed at reducing emissions of organic compounds. These regulations have forced new technology to turn toward solventless paints, high solids coatings, waterborne-based coatings, powder coatings, and radiation-curable coatings. These categories all show room for high growth rates.

Brief Description

Robert F. Ramsey, Inc. (RFR) and Ramsey Paint Manufacturers, Inc. (RPM) are privately owned corporations, with Robert F. Ramsey, Jr. owning 100 percent of the common stock of each company. RFR consists of three retail locations and a wholesaling operation. The retail operations include paint and sundries, wall coverings, paint spray equipment, automotive paint finishes, artists' supplies, and a full range of window treatments. The wholesale operation distributes paint, paint sundries, and arts and crafts supplies. RPM produces paint for trade sales and industrial use. Management believes that the companies deliver better service and price/value to their customers than their competitors.

History

Robert F. Ramsey, Inc.

RFR was established in downtown Roanoke, Virginia, in May 1936 by Robert F. Ramsey, Sr., with three employees (Main Street Store). From 1936 until 1978, the company experienced strong growth. In 1978, the company expanded locations and opened another retail store located in a Roanoke shopping center, Waterlick Plaza East. In 1982, the company opened a new headquarters in a 50,000 square foot sales and office complex on Carter's Mountain Road.

With the new headquarters came a change in retailing philosophy. For the new showroom and decorating center, the company employed a unique concept in the merchandising of paint and related items. The retail showroom was specifically designed to operate more as a department store than as a typical paint store. It featured skylights, indoor planters, color-corrected lighting, and other amenities to help the customer feel comfortable with the shopping experience. The showroom was designed by Jon Greenberg and Associates of Berkley, Michigan, one of the nation's foremost designers of paint and wallpaper stores.

What started as a place to buy paint has evolved into something much more. RFR is Roanoke's largest retail and wholesale paint business, comprising a full line of automotive paint and spray equipment for supply to professional body shops. It is also Roanoke's largest art supply center, a decorating center with over 1,000 books of wall coverings; it carries a full range of window treatments from miniblinds to vertical blinds to custom draperies and several lines of paint (predominantly Blue Kay, manufactured by RPM). The wholesale division for arts and crafts distributes to over 500 stores in Virginia and North Carolina. RFR also has a wholesale division of paint and paint sundries. (See Exhibit 2 for sales figures by department.) The company operates under a philosophy of "good advice, good service, and quality products at competitive prices." The work force consists of approximately 60 employees.

In April 1988 the Main Street store closed because of a sales decline caused by population shifts. The company recently opened a new store in the growing suburb of Vinton.

Ramsey Paint Manufacturers, Inc.

RPM was founded in 1955 by Robert F. Ramsey, Sr. In 1968, the company built a 29,300 square foot facility on Carter's Mountain Road, containing 26,300 square feet of manufacturing and warehouse space and 3,000 square feet of office space. RFR later built a sales/office complex adjacent to this facility. The manufacturing and warehouse space is divided into three separate areas: raw materials, production, and finished goods.

RPM is divided into a Trade Sales Division and an Industrial Paint Division. The Trade Sales Division distributes consumer paints through approximately 35 dealers in Virginia and North Carolina who carry Ramsey's Blue Kay paint. The Industrial Paint Division sells product finishes (for application to manufactured products such as automobiles, shelving, or doors) and metal protective paints designed specifically to protect ferrous or steel surfaces such as bridges, tanks, or structural steel.

The company produces approximately 400,000 gallons of paint a year and has the space and equipment capacity to produce 475,000 gallons. Additional equipment could be added in the 15,000 square feet that is included in square footage to RFR, currently being leased for $45,000 per year. This would expand capacity to 750,000 gallons a year.

In 1983, Mr. Ramsey, disappointed with the previous five years' stagnant sales, replaced both the firm's general manager and its chemist with Clyde Johnson and Kris Alexander. The result was a dramatic increase in sales (see Exhibit 3 for the financial statements) attributed to Clyde's sales ability and the increase in the formulation and sales of metal protective paints. These products take a great deal of expertise to formulate and quite a bit of field testing to prove their worth. The company's goal is to get its product approved by every state east of the Mississippi River, thus gaining wide acceptance from steel fabricators, who would be able to use one product on just about any state bridge project that comes through their shops.

Location

Roanoke is located in the heart of South Central Virginia and is easily reached by road and rail. The area is serviced by two railroads, CSX Transportation and Norfolk-Southern. Twenty-three trucking companies have terminals in the Roanoke area, and it is served by hundreds of other carriers. It is accessed by Interstate 81 to the north and south and four-lane U.S. 460 to the east and west.

The population is growing at 1.3 percent and the unemployment rate is 4.7 percent. The outlook for the community and surrounding area is extremely positive.

Competition

RFR

Locally, RFR maintains the number one position in the Roanoke market in terms of total paint and decorating sales to consumers.

The Ramsey family considers the following companies as their chief competitors. Mr. Ramsey subscribes to an investment service for information on his competitors, but does not provide information on RFR or RPM. The information below represents the family's assessment of competition.

Retail Paint, Wallpaper, Window Coverings

J K Shaw—oldest paint store in Roanoke. Has two locations, one in Roanoke and one in Bedford, Virginia. Major paint lines are Benjamin Moore and Coronado. Employs approximately 15 people in both locations. Has strong contractor trade. Competes primarily on price. Is considered by the Ramsey family to be their main competitor.

Suburban Paint—has one location in Roanoke. In 1988 closed a retail location in Vinton. Major paint lines include Pittsburgh and Duron. About 75 percent of its business is contractor trade. Employs eight people.

Roanoke Paint Center—has one location and employs three people. Major paint lines are Pittsburgh and Blue Ridge. About 75 percent of its business is contractor trade.

Sherwin Williams—has one store. Not in a good location to be considered a major competitor.

Discount Department Stores—include K-Mart, Roses, and the leading paint distributor, Sears.

Window Treatment

Custom Design Verticals—the major competitor in this department. Manufacture their own blinds, which tend to be lower priced than RFR's but also of lower quality. Sell national brands of miniblinds and pleated shades at competitive prices. Are aggressive in their sales. Employ four people. Actively target new construction.

Wallpaper and Window Treatments

Designs on You—has two employees and sales of approximately $150,000. Sells only special order wall coverings.

Complements of the House—employs six in-house decorators. Upscale customers. Also sells furniture, floor coverings, and draperies.

Other competitors include J.C. Penney and Sears.

Automotive

Seven Hills Auto—located in central Roanoke. Employs six people. Carries automotive parts, in addition to the finishing products that RFR carries. Has good delivery service.

Automotive Paint and Supply—not located in Roanoke, Virginia, but has a Roanoke sales representative. Sells wholesale to body shops, and its prices are better than RFR's. Sells in volume only.

Wholesale Paints/Sundries

Lancaster—located in Pauline, South Carolina. Much larger than RFR's wholesale division. Employs six outside sales representatives. Major distributor in RFR's territory. Employs 25.

D.P.G.—located in Tennessee, but services North Carolina. Prices comparable to RFR.

Sanders Brothers—located in Richmond, Virginia. The oldest distributor in the area. Employs 18. Not considered a threat.

Arts and Crafts Wholesale Division

Craft World in Westminster, Maryland, American Arts in Winston-Salem, North Carolina, and Craft and Hobby in Greensboro, North Carolina. However, RFR is the only true "art supply" store in the area.

RPM's Trade Sales Division's Main Competition for Blue Kay Line of Paint

Competitors included Blue Ridge Paint, Sampson Paint, Bruning Paint, and Glidden.

Industrial Paint Division

Competitors are Southern Coatings, Valspar (see Exhibit 4 for Valspar's Financial Statements), and Carolina Paint.

Descriptions by Key Personnel of Their Responsibilities

RFR

Robert F. Ramsey, Jr., President—Age 62. Mr. Ramsey began working in the business as a teenager and was familiar with every aspect of both companies. He had been running the business for 14 years when his father died. He became president in 1968. According to Mr. Ramsey, his major responsibilities center on RFR operations. However, he does oversee the management of RPM.

Looking to the future, Mr. Ramsey is concerned that his retirement may cause major disruptions in the business. "It would be hard if anything happened to me. They [Mark and Bobby] could do it, but it would be hard." Mr. Ramsey owns RFR's building on Carter's Mountain Road personally and leases it to the corporation.

Mark T. Ramsey, Vice President—Age 36. The eldest son of Robert F. Ramsey, Mark received a BA in Speech and Communications in 1974 and a law degree in 1977. Choosing not to practice law, he started full time with the company in 1977.

Mark states that he spends about 10 percent of his time working on personnel matters, especially performance evaluations. Another 20 percent of his time is spent in advertising (copy, scheduling, production, etc.). Some current projects would occupy about 20 percent of his time. Examples of current projects would be the opening of the Vinton store, a labeling project for RPM, or plans for revising other store layouts. The balance of his time is spent on day-to-day administrative matters. Examples of these routine tasks include approval of all outgoing letters and handling all requests for company contributions.

Mark sees the development of key mid-level managers as a critical factor in the future success of the company. Additionally, he sees his job in five years as a marketing director not only for RFR-Retail, but also RFR-Wholesale and RPM. He further states that his community connections (for example, with the Roanoke Art Alliance) give him an entree for future sales that he has yet to exploit.

Robert F. Ramsey, III, Corporate Secretary—Age 25. The owner's youngest son received his BS in business in 1985 and began working for the company in that year. Bobby describes his job as the manager of the wallpaper/window treatment departments, which includes setting policies, systems (that is systems to order, check, and pay for the wallpaper), product lines, pricing, etc. If there is a problem, it doesn't go to Jerry Simpson, (store manager, Carter's Mountain Road); it comes to him (paint problems go to Jerry). Bobby is the designated supervisor for four wallpaper clerks, two art clerks, and two window-treatment installers. This includes setting schedules, vacations, etc. Additionally, he reviews and approves all related invoices to the window/wallpaper department. The company is frequently billed incorrectly and invoices are checked for errors. (It probably takes about six hours a month to do this.) He organizes the wholesale catalog once a year and the flyers (specials) six to eight times a year. Additionally, he does about four "how to hang" wallpaper clinics with about 100 people attending each clinic.

According to Bobby, "One of the things I do, and probably should do more of, is the commercial jobs. I do handle all the sales, pricing, ordering, and general follow-up of the commercial wallpaper/window treatment jobs. I know we could get more commercial jobs if I spent more time at this.

"The future direction should entail several things. One is to hire more middle managers so the Ramsey family can turn their attention to more planning and less detail work. There has to be more communication such as store department meetings for training and product knowledge.

"Growth probably should come in retail stores. Maybe opening one a year could be a goal. Vinton went very smoothly and is doing quite well. On the wholesale side, I really see it stabilizing—maybe pooling orders with three other distributors to take advantage of the discounts. Dad is looking into this now.

"I see myself doing something at Ramsey Paint, but I'm not sure what. I really don't know much about the manufacturing plant. Dad and I haven't discussed my involvement with the plant. I don't know what would happen if Dad retired. We really haven't talked about the structure without Dad."

Hope Dawson—Age 32. The owner's daughter received a BS in business in 1978 and a MS in chemical engineering in 1983. She has been employed with the company since 1986. Hope is responsible for the art supply departments at Carter's Mountain Road and Waterlick Plaza. This means she is responsible for taking the inventory, placing orders, and handling returns and price changes (which come at least once a year from each supplier). She orders from their own warehouse and from fifteen other companies. The time-consuming part is special orders. "Since we are service oriented, we find the product a customer wants—whatever it is. Getting a price quote is time-consuming because we only order from many of these companies once in two years, and the prices change frequently." The art department takes up 70 percent of her time.

The other 30 percent of Hope's time is spent in wallpaper and windows. Drapery sales are handled by a salesperson, who calls directly on the customer. At the time of the sale, all window measurements are taken. Hope then works with the salesperson to determine exactly what is needed based on the measurements and determines the price of the job. Hope handles all contacts with the supplier: "I take care of all the problems. In some cases I've hung the drapes myself."

Hope is in charge of stock wallpaper, ordering new products and discontinuing products, and taking advantage of restocking programs.

Personnel is another major responsibility. Hope is responsible for making the floor run smoothly. She supervises two clerks, one of whom works in both art and blinds.

In the next five years, Hope would like to have a floor manager so she does not have to deal with personnel problems. She would like to work with large commercial jobs, in particular wallpaper and draperies. Hope has no interest in the manufacturing of paint. Even though she has the background (chemical engineering), she prefers a cleaner environment. She has worked as a chemical engineer before but did not like it and does not want to go back to it.

RPM

Robert F. Ramsey, Jr., President

Clyde Johnson, Vice President and General Manager—Age 47. Clyde had a background in journalism and a past history with Porter Paint Company and Pruf Coat in trade sales. He joined RPM in 1983. Clyde oversees the operations of the plant, including sales, office, technicians, and purchasing. He reports to Mr. Ramsey. He is also responsible for the company's catalogue, the specifications for all highway projects, and advertising and promotional material.

According to Clyde, "The future appears to be in protective coatings. Product finishes have some potential, but I don't see how we will be very effective once we expand past the Carolinas and perhaps Tennessee. I can't see that we will make any significant improvement in trade. Protective coatings seem to be our niche."

Clyde states, "I'm not sure what will happen in five years. I like Roanoke and I like working here at Ramsey. However, Mr. Ramsey could retire in five years and then I'm not sure about the future. We really need to look at everyone's talents; we don't seem to be using them now. Maybe we need a different structure or a different communication process."

Kris Alexander, Technical Director and Chief Chemist—Age 48. Previously employed by Iowa Paint as a chemist, Kris joined RPM in 1984. His primary responsibilities include reformulation of paint lines, development of new products, quality maintenance, and field work with customers.

"Currently, we are working to make the solvents meet air pollution requirements. Each state is different, and even within a state, the requirements could change. We are also working on converting to water-based coatings instead of the solvent-based ones.

"There are two new projects we are working on. One is with a large national manufacturer of oil filters to develop a coating without aluminum. Aluminum is a fire hazard, and this company has asked us to develop a pigment to look like aluminum. Also, we are investigating a high solids coating to use with railroad freight cars.

(Also, see RFR's and RPM's organizational charts, Exhibit 5 and Exhibit 6.)

Store Descriptions

The Carter's Mountain Road outlet is the flagship store, with 8,000 square feet of retail space. It is located across from Roanoke's largest regional shopping center. This building also has 39,000 square feet of warehouse space and 3,000 square feet of office space. It has been leased from Robert F. Ramsey, Jr., for $14,250 per month. Of this, $4,560 goes toward the retail space. The lease expires December 1, 1996.

The Waterlick Plaza outlet is in a small shopping center in southern Roanoke. The building was built in 1978, and RFR has a lease agreement for one year. The rent is $1,610 per month for 6,440 square feet.

The Vinton outlet is located in the River James Shopping Center, approximately 15 minutes from the Carter's Mountain Road store. Other stores in the shopping center include K-Mart, Krogers, and a few specialty stores. The rent is $1,860 per month for 3,200 square feet.

All stores operate 61 hours per week (7:30

a.m.–6 p.m. Monday–Friday; 7:30 a.m.–4 p.m. on Saturday).

Financial Condition

RFR is a privately held corporation with Robert F. Ramsey, Jr., owning 100 percent of the stock. RPM, however, was set up as a Subchapter-S Corporation in 1987. Thus, the income for RPM is considered the personal income of the owner and is taxed to Robert F. Ramsey, Jr. This structure was elected because S corporations are not subject to the accumulated earnings tax. S corporations' income can be accumulated without restrictions and paid out later to shareholders tax free, to the extent of their stock and debt basis.

The companies have financed virtually all of their expansion by internally generated funds, and cash balances increased to a high in December 1987 of $857,166 on RPM's books (see Exhibit 7). This excess cash was invested short term and earned between 6 and 7 percent. Sales are seasonal, with spring the peak season and fall the second highest season. The Ramsey family strives for 10 percent sales growth per year. Both companies have low amounts of debt. The note payable on RFR's books (see Exhibit 7 for financial statements) is to RPM and Robert F. Ramsey, and the note payable on RPM's books is the result of an agreement with the previous general manager. Mr. Ramsey does not see any future financial problems.

RFR does not own any of its stores. The company had owned the Main Street store but is currently leasing all of the other facilities.

Because the stock is not publicly traded, Mr. Ramsey and his children have little idea of the value of the two companies and have had difficulties assessing the progress the firms are making. This problem is causing some anxiety for the family. Industry numbers were obtained in 1987 from the National Paint and Coatings Association (see Exhibit 8 for excerpts and Exhibit 1 for SIC code data); however, Mr. Ramsey is not sure how valid the comparisons are since RFR and RPM are family-owned businesses.

The family, therefore, has continued to operate the two firms without being sure how good or bad a job they are doing.

RFR Operations

Each store has a store manager who reports to Mark Ramsey, and the managers are closely watched by the Ramsey family. Retaining good employees, however, has been a problem for the company. As Mark Ramsey states, "We must have trained most of the paint store managers in Roanoke." Geographic expansion of the retail stores has been limited by the workload each store has placed on the family.

The problems with developing top personnel also extend to personnel working the sales floor. Hope Dawson says, "Clerks don't care about the business the way we do. We want things done right. We have trouble trusting people to handle things. Whenever there is a problem, the customer always wants to talk to Robert Ramsey." As a result, all of the Ramsey family are heavily involved in the day-to-day operations of the stores.

The only exception to the intense family involvement is in the wholesale arts and crafts department. William Winn was hired to run this department and is considered an expert in the field. Wholesale arts and crafts are primarily sold to craft shops and 18 college bookstores in Virginia. The sales breakdown by state is North Carolina, 18 percent; Virginia, 75 percent; and other, 7 percent. Of the Virginia sales, RFR accounted for 9 percent.

Exhibit 2 shows the sales by store and department. Exhibit 9 shows the approximate retail markup per department. The retail business could be expanded through new stores or new departments within stores. Each department, however, has unique problems and/or attributes. Paint, for instance, has one of the lower profit margins but the highest sales level. Paint brings in the customers and also allows the markup on sundries to be one of the highest. A customer may come in to get a deal on paint but may not want to take the time to go to another retailer for brushes, drop cloths, etc. The wallpaper department takes up a large amount of space because of the large number of books. Also, RFR has to purchase the books from the manufacturer. Many times customers will pick out patterns, then order the paper from discount outlets. Window treatments require the employment of an installer, who also makes house calls with the sample books. This personalized treatment brings in customers, and this department is operating smoothly. Mark Ramsey feels, however, that the automotive department does not afford the cross-selling opportunities that the other departments do. It services professional auto body shops; therefore, the other departments are not utilized.

Retail employees are paid on an hourly basis plus a 1 percent commission. The commission amounts to approximately $60 per week per employee. Mr. Ramsey feels the commission adds an incentive to keep the employees from standing around.

The Vinton store was designed as a prototype store; it contains 3,200 square feet. The costs associated with opening a new store are approximately $50,000. If retail expansion is pursued this would be the standard design.

The warehouse for wholesale is divided into two sections: paint and paint sundries, and arts and crafts. Each area employs its own work crews. Because of the large number of small items it handles, the arts and crafts area has been computerized as to location and quantity. The paint and paint sundries area is not computerized. The key to success in both areas has been speedy deliveries. Because speed is considered of primary importance, two separate work crews specializing in their respective areas provide the most efficient use of these employees.

RFR Marketing

There are basically two markets served by RFR—the professional contractor and the do-it-yourselfer. Mark states, "We do not have as much of the professional contractor business as we should

or as we'd like. We do have a large share of the do-it-yourself segment."

RFR advertises more heavily than any of its competitors in the Roanoke area. Their vendors pay for about 65 percent of all advertising through cooperative advertising funds. RFR uses all media forms, with expenditures of 40 percent on newspaper, 25 percent on radio, 25 percent on television, and 10 percent on outdoor.

Most products have "sale periods" during the year. The schedule of 1988 sales is included as Exhibit 10.

The arts and crafts wholesale division has two salespeople on the road calling on 500 active accounts. Approximately 1,200 companies in Maryland, Virginia, North Carolina and South Carolina list themselves as arts and crafts retailers.

The wholesale paint and sundry division has four salespeople, as well as an in-house sales manager. They call on approximately 400 active accounts. They also handle the Blue Kay accounts from RPM. All salespeople are paid on commission plus expenses. The salaries for the four road salespeople were $43,000, $30,000, and two at $21,000 last year.

RPM Operations

As general manager of RPM, Clyde Johnson has been a major force in the success of the company: "I've been in the business for 25 years and I've got a gut feeling for things," he says. One threat Clyde foresees for Ramsey is in the area of computer-aided manufacturing (CAM). Ramsey Paint is produced in batches of 275 gallons by twelve employees. Each batch is then taken to the assembly line where each can is filled, labeled, and boxed. All assembly is done by hand. Larger companies, however, are in the process of computerizing production in trade sale for large batches of standard colors. "If they get the bugs worked out," says Clyde, "the big companies could put the small manufacturer out of business." Clyde thinks that a CAM system would allow Ramsey to produce the same amount of products with one or two employees that they produce with twelve now. However, Mr. Ramsey wonders: "I do know that our overhead is about $1 a gallon and that some companies who use computer-aided manufacturing can get it down to about $.20 a gallon. However, we would have to be manufacturing a completely standard product. It would be very hard for us." Although Clyde has spent a considerable amount of time learning various programming languages, he has been limited in this regard by his other duties: "When I find a program that does what I want, I can't understand it." The computer system at RFR and RPM is limited to accounting and order placement.

Clyde states, "There seems to be a shrinking market in paints. The new wave is in powders, but the costs seem prohibitive." Company estimates put the investment necessary to get into powders at approximately $1.5 to 2.0 million. Powders are highly labor intensive to develop and sell. Each customer's requirements are unique, and extensive formulation and testing are required before a sale can be completed. Clyde might spend two years courting a customer before closing the sale. Therefore, he says, "I don't have a desire for the powders. I like the metal protective side of the business because you have a stock product." Ramsey Paint now has state approval for bidding on jobs for its zinc coatings for highway and bridge work in every state from Virginia to Maine.

The only waste disposal problem is the disposal of solvent. RPM does recycle solvent and is able to salvage 45 gallons of solvent from every 50 gallons of dirty waste solvent. It costs RPM $.90 a gallon to buy the clean solvent, but $6.00 a gallon to get rid of the waste.

The pigment used in paint is titanium dioxide. In 1988 a shortage of this raw material occurred, and, if the shortage continues, expansion of sales will be difficult. RPM manufactures high quality paint, and the amount of titanium dioxide is a determinant of the paint quality. However, Mr. Ramsey finds that it is difficult to demonstrate paint quality to the customer.

RPM Marketing

RPM has its own marketing plan, separate from RFR's. In the trade sales division, the company has an advertising and promotional package they send to their dealers at the end of each year to be used for the following year. RPM offers them cooperative advertising as well as several promotional buying periods. In the industrial paint division, the company has one road salesperson who calls directly on industrial accounts.

The percentage of sales accounted for by each market segment is product finishes 39.69%, trade sales 29.11%, and protective coatings 31.20%. The largest customers are located in Virginia, West Virginia, and North Carolina, with the exception of their second largest customer, which is located in Pittsburgh, Pennsylvania. RFR is their largest customer and accounts for approximately 20 percent of sales.

Conclusion

Mr. Ramsey, Mark, Bobby, and Hope are all concerned about the future direction the companies should take. Mr. Ramsey is the only family member heavily involved in RPM, and he works closely with Clyde Johnson. RPM faces two possible expansion areas: computer-aided manufacturing and new product development (in particular, powders). RFR's most likely expansion path is retail store expansion, but another possibility is to manufacture some of the products for which RFR has been the retailer or distributor, for example, miniblinds for windows.

The biggest problem in planning is finding time to do it. As Bobby states, "We have an owner and family who have too much to do to talk about what to do next." Mr. Ramsey confirms, "We're too busy with the day-to-day activities."

Exhibit 1   Paints, Varnishes, Lacquers

Fiscal Year End	87	86	85	84	83
Sales Performance					
Dollars of Sales	107.3	94.7	95.2	90.9	81.3
Change from Prior Year ($)	12.6	(0.5)	4.3	9.7	7.2
Change from Prior Year (%)	13.36	−0.55	4.72	11.88	9.74
Sales per Employee (Thousands)	1.40	1.28	1.22	1.16	NA
Profitability Performance					
Income before Extraordinary Items and Discontinued Opers	6.0	5.2	4.8	4.8	3.8
Change from Prior Year ($)	0.8	0.4	(0.0)	1.0	1.2
Change from Prior Year (%)	16.09	7.33	0.72	26.70	43.56
Return on Sales (%)	5.58	5.45	5.05	5.32	4.70
Return on Equity (%)	17.81	16.50	15.74	16.13	13.88
Interest Expense after Tax	1.16	1.03	0.79	0.70	0.70
Minority Interest	0.06	0.11	0.03	0.02	0.02
Return on Assets (%)	7.48	7.28	7.44	8.11	6.81
Return on Invested Capital (%)	NA	NA	NA	NA	NA
Gross Profit to Sales (%)	36.55	36.21	34.65	33.63	32.26
SG & A Expense to Sales (%)	22.53	21.95	21.71	20.46	20.54
Asset Management					
Sales to Assets	1.31	1.24	1.41	1.44	1.38
Sales to Current Assets	2.81	2.75	3.12	3.08	2.99
Sales to Net Plant	3.09	2.75	2.98	3.12	2.92
Inventory Turnover—COGS	4.58	4.05	4.72	4.97	5.08
Inventory Turnover—Sales	7.22	6.35	7.22	7.48	7.50
Days COGS in Inventory	79.64	90.15	77.33	73.50	71.86
Sales to Accounts Rec.	6.23	6.24	7.26	7.13	7.06
Average Collection Period	58.63	58.49	50.29	51.17	51.67
Financial Management					
Total Liab. to Equity	1.37	1.33	1.27	1.01	1.05
Total Assets to Equity	2.37	2.33	2.27	2.01	2.05
Current Liabilities to Equity	0.63	0.57	0.52	0.48	0.48
Long-Term Debt to Equity	0.46	0.50	0.51	0.33	0.37
Sales to Equity	3.10	2.89	3.19	2.90	2.82
Net Plant to Equity	1.00	1.05	1.07	0.93	0.97
Interest Expense to Sales (%)	1.85	1.92	1.48	1.36	1.45
Times Interest Earned	6.20	6.14	7.09	7.93	6.53
Liquidity Management					
Current Ratio	1.76	1.84	1.95	1.98	1.97
Quick Ratio	1.07	1.04	1.11	1.16	1.19
Sales to Cash	27.98	36.77	34.28	28.72	22.70
Capital Expenditures ($)	1.46	1.46	1.45	4.82	1.01
Advertising Expense to Sales (%)	1.04	1.01	1.10	1.06	1.06
R&D Cost to Sales (%)	2.90	3.00	2.63	2.30	2.20
Rental Expense to Sales (%)	1.67	1.62	1.71	1.62	1.64

(continued)

Exhibit 1 *(continued)*

	87	86	85	84	83
Assets	$82	$76	$68	$63	$59
as a Percentage of Assets	100.0	100.0	100.0	100.0	100.0
Cash and Equivalents	4.7	3.4	4.1	5.0	6.1
Receivables	21.0	19.9	19.4	20.2	19.5
Inventories	18	19.5	19.5	19.3	18.4
Other Current Assets	2.7	2.3	2.2	2.3	2.2
Percentage of Total Current Assets	46.6%	45.1%	45.2%	46.9%	46.1%
Plant—Gross	76.0	78.4	80.8	79.3	81.7
Less: Accum. Depr.	33.6	33.3	33.5	33.1	34.5
Plant—Net	42.4%	45.1%	47.3%	46.2%	47.2%
Construction in Progress	NA	NA	NA	NA	NA
Land	NA	NA	NA	NA	NA
Buildings	NA	NA	NA	NA	NA
Equip. & Machines—Net	NA	NA	NA	NA	NA
Natural Resources	NA	NA	NA	NA	NA
Leases	NA	NA	NA	NA	NA
Unconsolidated Subs.	1.9	1.7	1.6	1.4	1.3
Other Investments	0.5	0.5	0.4	0.4	0.4
Intangibles	1.9	2.1	2.0	1.7	1.6
Other Assets	6.8	5.7	3.4	3.3	3.5
Deferred Charges	1.5	1.4	0.0	0.0	0.0
Total Assets	100.0%	100.0%	100.0%	100.0%	100.0%

Exhibit 1 *(continued)*

	87	86	85	84	83
Liabilities and Net Worth					
Debt in Current Liabs.	7.3	5.6	4.2	3.6	3.3
Income Taxes Payable	0.9	0.9	1.0	1.1	1.1
Accounts Payable	8.9	9.2	9.7	9.6	9.8
Other Current Liabs.	9.4	8.7	8.2	9.4	9.2
Total Current Liabilities	26.5%	24.5%	23.1%	23.7%	23.4%
Debt Structure					
Convertible	0.7	0.8	0.0	0.2	0.3
Subordinated	2.4	2.6	2.3	2.5	2.2
Notes	7.8	7.7	9.9	6.2	6.5
Debentures	2.3	2.9	3.8	4.2	4.5
Other Long-Term Debt	6.2	7.6	5.8	3.8	3.8
Cap. Lease Oblig.	0.8	0.8	1.2	1.5	1.6
Less: Debt (1 yr)	1.1	1.6	0.9	1.9	1.1
Total Long-Term Debt	19.4%	21.3%	22.4%	16.6%	18.1%
Other Liabilities	4.6	3.6	3.6	3.6	3.8
Deferred Taxes & ITC	6.2	6.4	5.7	5.5	5.0
Minority Interest	1.1	1.2	1.0	0.9	0.8
Redeemable Pref. Stock	0.0	0.0	0.0	0.0	0.1
Total Liabilities	57.8%	57.1%	55.9%	50.3%	51.2%
Equity Structure					
Preferred Stock	0.1	0.1	0.0	0.0	0.1
Common Stock	4.9	3.5	3.7	3.1	5.6
Capital Surplus	−8.0	−2.8	−2.1	5.3	4.0
Retained Earnings	45.2	42.1	42.6	41.2	39.1
Common Equity	42.0%	42.8%	44.1%	49.6%	48.7%
Total Stockholders' Equity	42.2%	42.9%	44.1%	49.7%	48.8%
Total Liabs. & N.W.	100.0%	100.0%	100.0%	100.0%	100.0%

(continued)

Exhibit 1 *(continued)*

	87	86	85	84	83
Sales ($ Million)	$107	$95	$95	$91	$81
as percent of Sales:	100.0%	100.0%	100.0%	100.0%	100.0%
Cost of Goods Sold	63.4	63.8	65.3	66.4	67.7
Selling, General, and Admin.	22.5	22.0	21.7	20.5	20.5
Operating Income	14.0%	14.3%	12.9%	13.2%	11.7%
Depreciation and Amort.	3.5	3.5	3.2	3.2	3.2
Interest Expense	1.9	1.9	1.5	1.4	1.5
Interest Capitalized	NA	NA	NA	NA	NA
Non-Oper. Income (Exp.)	0.8	0.9	0.5	1.0	1.3
Special Items	0.2	0.2	0.2	−0.2	−0.3
Pretax Income	9.6%	9.9%	9.0%	9.4%	8.0%
Income Taxes:					
Income Tax (Fed.)	NA	NA	NA	NA	NA
Invest. Tax Cred.	NA	NA	NA	NA	NA
Income Tax (St.)	NA	NA	NA	NA	NA
Deferred Taxes	NA	NA	0.6	NA	0.5
Minority Interest	0.1	0.1	0.0	0.0	0.0
Income before Extraord. and Discontinued Operations	5.6%	5.4%	5.0%	5.3%	4.7%
Extraordinary Items	−0.0	0.0	0.1	0.0	0.0
Discontinued Operations	−0.0	0.1	−0.0	0.1	0.0
Net Income	5.5%	5.5%	5.1%	5.4%	4.7%
Preferred Dividends	0.7	0.4	0.1	0.3	0.7
Available for Common:					
Before Adjustments	5.6	5.4	5.0	5.3	4.7
After Adjustments	5.6	5.4	5.0	5.3	4.7

Exhibit 1 *(continued)*

	87	86	85	84	83
Per Share (adjusted)					
EPS (Primary)					
Excluding Extraordinary and Discontinued Items	$2.28	$1.96	$1.75	$1.73	$1.37
Including Extraordinary and Discontinued Items	2.25	1.99	1.76	1.76	1.37
EPS (Diluted)					
Excluding Extraordinary and Discontinued Items	2.26	1.94	1.74	1.71	1.36
Including Extraordinary and Discontinued Items	2.23	1.97	1.76	1.75	1.36
Dividends Per Share	0.74	0.65	0.58	0.52	0.45
Common Shares Out (Primary)	262	263	275	280	278
Common Shares Out (Diluted)	NA	NA	NA	NA	NA
Supplementary Items					
Advertising Expenditures	1.0	1.0	1.1	1.1	1.1
Amortization of Intang.	0.0	0.0	0.0	0.0	0.0
Capital Expenditures	1.4	1.5	1.5	5.3	1.2
Capitalized Interest	NA	NA	NA	NA	NA
Depletion Expense	NA	NA	NA	NA	NA
Depreciation Expense	NA	NA	NA	NA	NA
Excise Taxes	0.0	0.0	0.0	0.0	0.0
Foreign Currency Adj.	NA	NA	NA	NA	NA
Interest Exp. on LT Debt	NA	NA	NA	NA	NA
Interest Income	0.1	0.1	0.1	0.2	0.2
Labor Expense	NA	NA	NA	NA	NA
Pension and Retire. Exp.	0.0	0.1	0.4	0.7	1.0
Research and Development	2.9	3.0	2.6	2.3	2.2
Unconsol Subsids. (EQ)	0.2	0.2	0.1	0.1	0.2

Exhibit 1 *(continued)*

	Price	Beta	EPS
De Soto Inc.	$31	$ .95	$2.15
Grow Group Inc.	8	1.25	NA
PPG Industries Inc.	40	1.35	3.51
Pratt & Lambert Inc.	17	1.05	1.56
RPM Inc.—Ohio	16	1.00	.95
Sherwin-Williams Co.	30	1.20	2.26
Tyler Corp.	13	1.10	1.21
Valspar Corp.	26	1.00	1.88

Note: The price is quoted as of March 1988.

Exhibit 2 Robert F. Ramsey, Inc.

			Sales by Store			
	1983	1984	1985	1986	1987	June 30 1988
Carter Mt. Road						
Paint	506,604	640,687	907,837	956,298	1,014,546	609,328
Wallpaper	119,431	163,496	229,689	238,399	271,382	166,742
Automotive	400,118	475,848	461,372	455,103	502,219	288,031
Spray Dept.	176,579	253,175	268,782	248,540	357,598	152,944
Window Treatment	62,409	61,276	117,932	140,196	178,007	102,070
Art Materials	169,827	179,274	223,669	248,484	270,276	145,233
Paint Sundries	165,527	203,147	249,653	262,697	339,680	207,976
	1,600,495	1,976,903	2,458,934	2,549,717	2,933,708	1,672,324
Main Street						
Paint	432,478	466,852	420,819	395,162	338,624	58,008*
Wallpaper	11,676	12,746	11,022	5,788	3,569	972*
Automotive	89,574	85,092	63,488	42,562	40,028	5,994*
Spray Dept.	17,328	11,584	11,267	6,677	7,239	2,043*
Window Treatment	3,649	2,896	4,536	2,863	546	0*
Art Materials	19,903	9,800	4,543	3,505	3,875	578*
Paint Sundries	95,332	108,215	104,167	104,443	108,526	23,024*
	669,940	697,185	619,842	561,000	502,407	90,619*
Waterlick						
Paint	206,051	239,743	234,456	249,953	251,366	132,499
Wallpaper	53,899	49,439	72,320	76,977	75,104	41,611
Automotive	53,389	64,708	66,284	56,425	63,958	33,004
Spray Dept.	2,417	6,145	3,057	1,086	1,801	1,451
Window Treatment	15,005	11,966	5,905	15,204	25,419	12,768
Art Materials	12,887	10,771	6,559	7,241	8,392	3,599
Paint Sundries	68,414	84,385	81,122	90,901	99,784	54,321
	412,062	467,157	469,703	497,787	525,824	279,253
Wholesale Arts and Crafts						
Sold by Paint Sundries Sales Reps.	302,448	313,815	346,313	349,814	383,852	133,367
Sold by Arts/Crafts Reps. and Craft Department	273,122	431,619	421,028	535,456	460,899	273,620
Wholesale Paints/Sundries	756,519	780,209	975,011	1,012,966	1,092,301	752,477
Does *not* include Blue Kay paint sold by RPM.						
"House" Sales: noncommissioned wholesale sales, no sales rep. paid	137,720	77,986	49,992	75,982	160,994	31,834
Total Sales	4,152,306	4,744,874	5,340,823	5,582,722	6,059,985	3,233,494

*Through April 15, 1988.

Exhibit 3 Ramsey Paint Manufacturers, Inc.

	Balance Sheets 1983–1988						
	Oct. 31 1983	Oct. 31. 1984	Oct. 31 1985	Oct. 31 1986	Dec. 31 1986	Dec. 31 1987	June 30 1988
Assets							
Current Assets							
Cash	345,741	486,964	492,645	381,907	418,186	857,166	631,201
Accts. Rec.	175,860	206,743	334,705	446,160	247,506	236,973	370,421
Inventories	260,429	192,872	202,070	221,220	322,713	247,232	517,920
Other	15,003	16,402	1,386	1,441	4,227	608	216
Total Current Assets	797,033	902,981	1,030,806	1,050,728	992,632	1,341,979	1,519,758
PP&E							
Land	20,834	20,834	20,834	20,834	20,834	20,834	20,834
Building	368,606	368,606	368,606	368,606	368,606	369,952	369,952
Machinery and Equipment	154,523	175,759	254,724	275,925	275,925	305,057	306,744
Autos and Trucks	32,625	25,435	25,435	24,599	24,599	28,312	40,905
Less Accum. Depr.	389,073	405,000	440,096	464,068	471,071	517,697	517,697
Net PP&E	187,515	185,834	229,503	225,896	218,893	206,458	220,738
Other L-T Assets	79,460	42,600	95,680	141,820	141,820	127,060	127,060
Total Assets	1,064,008	1,131,415	1,355,989	1,418,444	1,353,345	1,675,497	1,867,556
Liabilities							
Current Liabilities							
Accounts Payable	14,646	0	23,594	30,970	48,964	2,170	116,680
Note Payable	14,000	14,000	34,997	34,997	203,118	188,152	188,152
Accrued Salaries	118,023	87,000	45,500	52,500	0	0	0
Accr. Profit Shrg. Contr.	17,812	16,000	21,000	21,000	0	28,000	0
Income Taxes Payable	−26,593	−11,577	65,101	−16,146	−16,223	51,800	0
Total Current Liabilities	137,888	105,423	190,192	123,321	235,859	270,122	304,832
Stockholders Equity							
Common Stock (1100 Par)	44,000	44,000	44,000	44,000	26,300	26,300	26,300
Retained Earnings	974,600	1,074,472	1,241,086	1,370,412	1,091,186	1,379,075	1,536,424
	1,018,600	1,118,472	1,285,086	1,414,412	1,117,486	1,405,375	1,562,724
Less Treasury Stk. (850 Shs)	92,480	92,480	119,289	119,289	0	0	
Total Liabilities and Equity	1,064,008	1,131,415	1,355,989	1,418,444	1,353,345	1,675,497	1,867,556

(continued)

Exhibit 3   *(continued)*

	Income Statement						
	Oct. 31 1983	**Oct. 31 1984**	**Oct. 31 1985**	**Oct. 31 1986**	**Dec. 31 1986**	**Dec. 31 1987**	**June 30 1988**
Net Sales	1,828,552	1,956,360	2,728,823	2,977,132	278,380	3,131,273	1,650,323
Cost of Sales	941,410	1,008,937	1,528,934	1,631,999	143,371	1,716,111	864,632
Gross Profit on Sales	887,142	947,423	1,199,889	1,345,133	135,009	1,415,162	785,691
Other Operating Income	0	0	0	0	0	0	0
Operating Expenses							
Advertising	22,787	24,374	34,869	29,754	2,247	41,337	
Bad Debt Expense	0	0	0	18,389	0	6,818	
Delivery Truck Expense	2,145	2,586	3,758	2,428	245	2,562	
Depreciation	21,555	23,289	36,993	39,829	7,002	49,946	
Donations	10,049	7,447	19,036	12,256	0	550	
Dues & Subscriptions	11,112	11,138	13,582	15,127	624	17,650	
Lab Expense	0	0	4,549	9,336	1,056	3,861	
Factory Expense	17,407	18,780	19,278	33,318	3,666	28,913	
Heat, Lights, and Water	17,845	18,894	20,852	23,139	4,871	24,652	
Office Expense	0	0	5,381	12,500	6,954	7,336	
Insurance	13,539	19,385	41,935	49,456	3,345	75,823	
Interest Expense	881	1,252	991	1,998	2,756	18,028	
Label Expense	3,659	9,985	10,683	19,036	4,570	14,997	
Legal Fees and Acctg.	3,221	5,879	4,487	3,179	3,710	22,987	
Payroll Taxes	21,498	26,637	28,311	33,755	5,870	37,306	

Exhibit 3   *(continued)*

	Income Statement						
	Oct. 31 1983	Oct. 31 1984	Oct. 31 1985	Oct. 31 1986	Dec. 31 1986	Dec. 31 1987	June 30 1988
Profit Sharing Expense	17,812	16,000	21,000	21,000	0	28,000	
Salaries and Wages	438,567	451,385	461,141	585,200	73,847	581,393	
Sales Commission	70,485	76,174	113,794	105,779	13,808	110,867	
Stationery and Office	4,591	4,282	3,052	7,691	200	5,171	
Taxes and Licenses	12,188	16,008	14,964	9,774	47	11,723	
Telephone	4,993	7,807	8,704	6,952	2,012	2,042	
Travel Expense	24,940	29,022	16,083	17,428	2,713	22,338	
Life Insurance	−910	−1,337	−1,481	−1,327	309	−2,521	
Medical Expense	0	0	0	763	0	0	
Repairs to Machinery	2,442	5,735	14,843	31,999	5,018	27,413	
Commission—W.H. Woodhouse	367	83	0	0	0	0	
Research and Development	15,594	40,967	57,350	35,362	4,745	28,811	
Operating Expenses	736,767	815,772	954,155	1,124,121	149,615	1,168,003	481,528
Income (loss) from Operations	150,375	131,651	245,734	221,012	−14,606	247,159	304,163
Other Income	33,572	37,020	45,622	30,916	6,334	76,828	22,257
Other Deductions	0	0	0	0	0	0	0
Income (loss) before Taxes	183,947	168,671	291,356	251,928	−8,272	323,987	326,420
Taxes	62,174	43,517	73,713	102,434	0	0	0
Net Income (loss)	121,773	125,154	217,643	149,494	−8,272	323,987	326,420

Exhibit 4 Ratio Report: Valspar Corp

Fiscal Year End	87	86	85	84	83
Sales Performance					
Dollars of Sales	448.9	345.2	347.2	224.2	161.6
Change from Prior Year ($)	103.7	(1.9)	122.9	62.6	9.8
Change from Prior Year (%)	30.04	−0.55	54.82	38.77	6.49
Sales per Employee (Thousands)	167.08	162.78	157.52	94.89	139.42
Profitability Performance					
Income before Extraordinary Items and Discontinued Opers.	18.1	14.8	11.5	11.4	10.2
Change from Prior Year ($)	3.3	3.2	0.1	1.2	3.1
Change from Prior Year (%)	22.22	28.08	1.23	12.06	43.89
Return on Sales (%)	4.02	4.28	3.32	5.08	6.29
Return on Equity (%)	23.02	20.32	16.52	18.77	20.82
Interest Expense after Tax	3.50	2.82	3.47	1.14	0.39
Minority Interest	0.00	0.00	0.00	0.00	0.00
Return on Assets (%)	9.01	8.97	6.73	8.70	13.12
Return on Invested Capital (%)	16.26	15.71	9.70	12.16	18.89
Gross Profit to Sales (%)	30.58	28.83	26.88	30.56	32.52
SG&A Expense to Sales (%)	20.02	18.46	17.98	18.94	20.21
Asset Management					
Sales to Assets	1.90	2.10	2.11	1.26	1.92
Sales to Current Assets	3.20	3.13	3.22	1.88	2.35
Sales to Net Plant	6.01	6.65	6.39	3.89	11.53
Inventory Turnover—COGS	4.55	5.23	5.35	2.95	5.84
Inventory Turnover—Sales	6.55	7.35	7.32	4.24	8.65
Days COGS in Inventory	80.30	69.76	68.20	123.91	62.51
Sales to Accounts Rec.	7.35	7.80	7.73	4.31	8.26
Average Collection Period	49.68	46.80	47.24	84.61	44.18
Financial Management					
Total Liabilities to Equity	1.75	1.32	1.22	1.72	0.50
Total Assets to Equity	2.75	2.32	2.22	2.72	1.50
Current Liabilities to Equity	0.97	1.14	0.68	0.75	0.41
Long-Term Debt to Equity	0.68	0.09	0.48	0.95	0.07
Sales to Equity	5.23	4.86	4.67	3.44	2.88
Net Plant to Equity	0.87	0.73	0.73	0.88	0.25
Interest Expense to Sales (%)	1.39	1.48	1.77	0.94	0.44
Times Interest Earned	6.15	6.23	4.33	11.02	27.18
Liquidity Management					
Current Ratio	1.69	1.36	2.13	2.43	2.97
Quick Ratio	0.86	0.78	1.20	1.36	2.16
Sales to Cash	338.83	26.61	33.03	21.41	5.89
Capital Expenditures ($)	10.03	4.81	4.06	4.89	2.38
Advertising Expense to Sales (%)	0.79	1.02	0.68	1.26	1.76
R&D Cost to Sales (%)	3.80	4.31	4.46	3.57	3.23
Rental Expense to Sales (%)	0.85	1.06	1.07	1.51	1.73

Exhibit 5 Robert F. Ramsey, Inc.

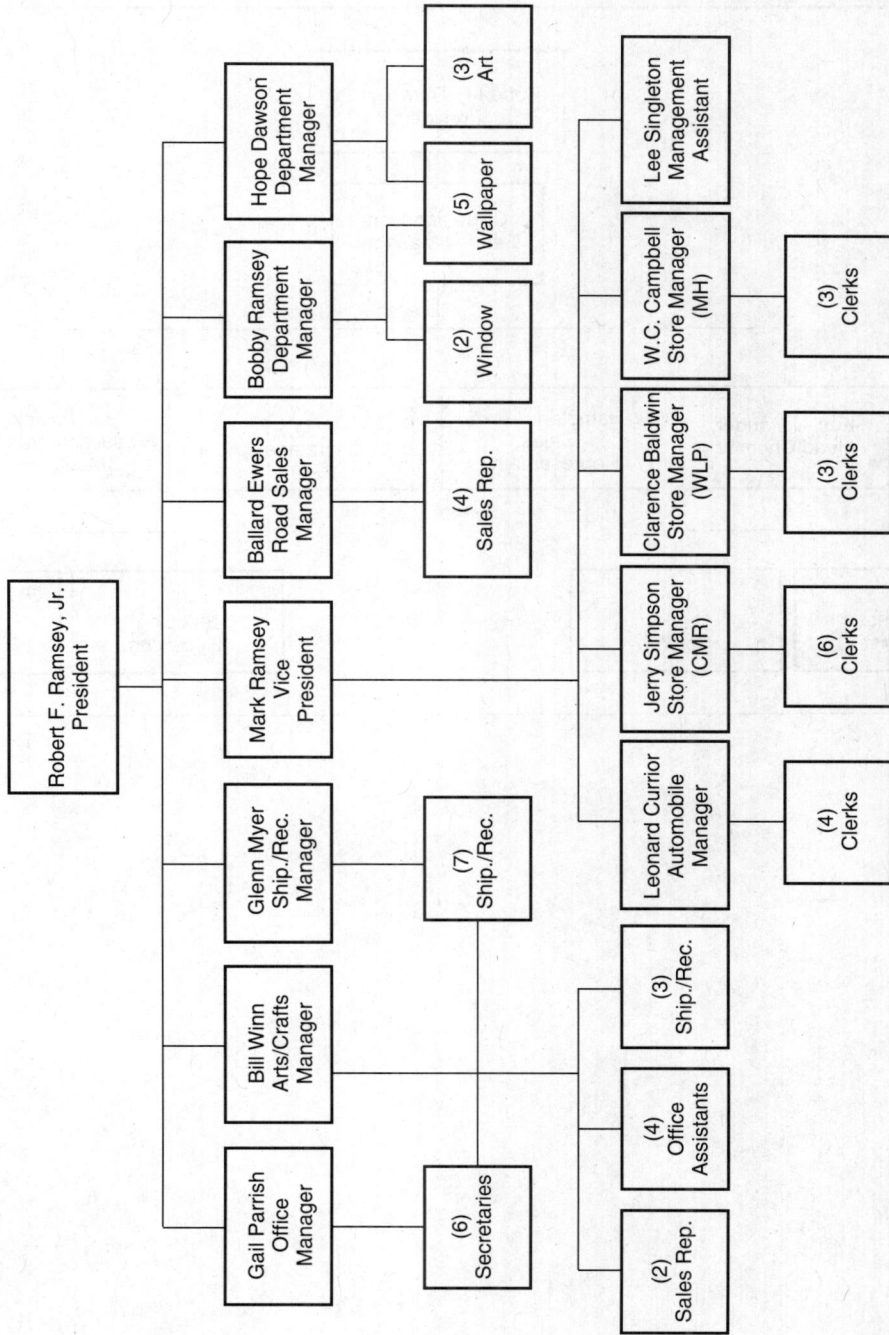

Exhibit 6   Ramsey Paint Manufacturers

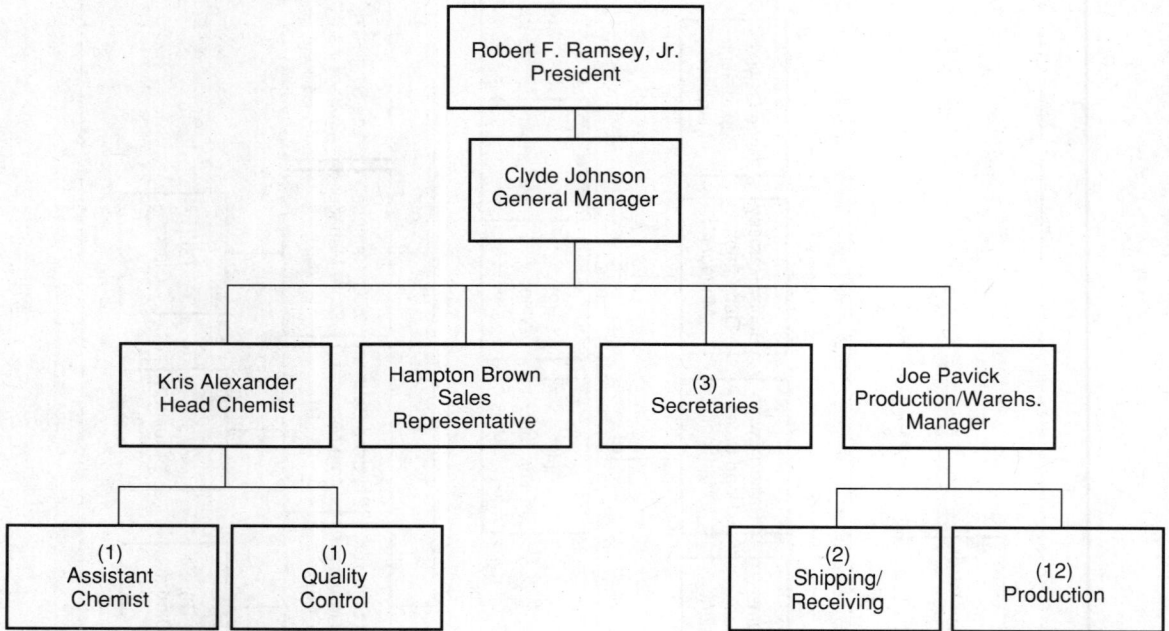

```
                        ┌─────────────────────┐
                        │ Robert F. Ramsey, Jr.│
                        │      President       │
                        └─────────────────────┘
                                   │
                        ┌─────────────────────┐
                        │    Clyde Johnson     │
                        │   General Manager    │
                        └─────────────────────┘
                                   │
        ┌──────────────┬───────────┴────────────┬──────────────────┐
┌───────────────┐ ┌──────────────┐ ┌──────────────┐ ┌──────────────────┐
│ Kris Alexander│ │Hampton Brown │ │     (3)      │ │   Joe Pavick     │
│  Head Chemist │ │    Sales     │ │  Secretaries │ │Production/Warehs.│
│               │ │Representative│ │              │ │     Manager      │
└───────────────┘ └──────────────┘ └──────────────┘ └──────────────────┘
        │                                                    │
   ┌────┴─────┐                                      ┌───────┴──────┐
┌──────────┐ ┌──────────┐                    ┌──────────────┐ ┌──────────┐
│   (1)    │ │   (1)    │                    │     (2)      │ │   (12)   │
│Assistant │ │ Quality  │                    │  Shipping/   │ │Production│
│ Chemist  │ │ Control  │                    │  Receiving   │ │          │
└──────────┘ └──────────┘                    └──────────────┘ └──────────┘
```

Exhibit 7   Robert F. Ramsey, Inc.

	Balance Sheets 1983–1988					
	Dec. 31 1983	Dec. 31 1984	Dec. 31 1985	Dec. 31 1986	Dec. 31 1987	June 30 1988
Assets						
Current Assets						
Cash	18,890	72,547	45,245	107,096	164,855	396,482
Accts. Recv.	284,611	321,174	387,409	384,706	510,646	574,035
Inventories	609,580	626,335	802,295	815,696	680,641	808,998
Other	18,367			22,543		3,630
Total Current Assets	931,448	1,020,056	1,234,949	1,330,041	1,356,142	1,783,145
PP&E						
Land	15,000	15,000	15,000	15,000	15,000	15,000
Building	44,465	44,465	44,465	44,465	44,465	44,465
Furniture & Fixtures	301,529	301,941	308,146	312,857	316,241	317,424
Autos & Trucks	48,940	61,700	53,078	67,900	71,888	85,298
Less Accum. Depr.	227,474	277,241	314,232	382,272	393,925	393,925
Net PP&E	182,460	145,865	106,457	57,950	53,669	68,262
Other L-T Assets	62,879	67,050	91,290	85,250	91,485	87,855
Total Assets	1,176,787	1,232,971	1,432,696	1,473,241	1,501,296	1,939,262
Liabilities						
Current Liabilities						
Accounts Payable	144,326	187,002	365,995	278,163	285,608	492,291
Note Payable—Affiliate	40,000	0	0	93,000	75,000	75,000
Notes Payable—Stockholder	180,000	150,000	100,000	84,000	30,000	30,000
Accrued Salaries	1,500	1,500	2,000	0	0	0
Accr. Profit Shrg. Contr.	5,000	16,000	27,000	22,000	34,000	0
Income Taxes Payable		23,178	16,486		7,609	−16,341
Total Current Liabilities	370,826	377,680	511,481	477,163	432,217	580,950
Stockholders Equity						
Common Stock ($100 Par)	165,000	165,000	165,000	80,000	80,000	80,000
Retained Earnings	755,711	805,041	870,965	916,078	989,079	1,278,312
	920,711	970,041	1,035,965	996,078	1,069,079	1,358,312
Less Treasury Stk. (850 Shs)	114,750	114,750	114,750	0	0	
Total Liabilities and Equity	1,176,787	1,232,971	1,432,696	1,473,241	1,501,296	1,939,262

(continued)

Exhibit 7 *(continued)*

| | Income Statement | | | | | |
	Dec. 31 1983	Dec. 31 1984	Dec. 31 1985	Dec. 31 1986	Dec. 31 1987	June 30 1988
Net Sales	4,152,306	4,744,874	5,340,823	5,582,722	6,059,985	3,233,494
Cost of Sales	2,998,028	3,365,689	3,785,101	3,899,537	4,206,037	2,153,507
Gross Profit on Sales	1,154,278	1,379,185	1,555,722	1,683,185	1,853,948	1,079,987
Other Operating Income	72,585	64,549	84,505	116,745	139,238	
Operating Expenses:						
Officers' Salaries	67,517	78,273	109,413	81,800	178,229	
Salaries and Wages, Other	637,674	696,474	796,332	830,174	879,246	
Payroll Taxes	56,493	64,164	70,119	76,465	81,215	
Taxes and Licenses	10,013	11,204	11,736	12,943	12,931	
Rental Expense—Stores	140,275	172,814	154,506	141,293	184,632	
Travel Expenses	42,972	47,564	55,647	58,730	66,319	
Truck Lease Expense	23,699	16,516	8,069	13,316	13,335	
Store Delivery Expense	21,775	17,966	0	0	0	
Telephone	32,308	40,440	41,602	43,934	39,389	
Depreciation	60,495	61,773	63,988	68,040	30,567	
Insurance, General	11,395	16,366	28,593	36,340	30,941	
Group Insurance	27,994	22,598	32,358	31,936	39,998	
Advertising, Net of Refunds	3,341	10,800	13,137	48,941	73,068	
Office Equip., Maintenance	5,792	7,066	4,055	5,696	5,469	
Office Equip., Rental	5,667	4,114	2,107	1,419	216	
Office Supplies	5,432	3,393	3,923	5,352	4,939	
Stationery, Forms, & Catalogs	14,168	21,623	16,284	28,353	41,453	
Store Expenses	14,510	18,930	39,385	33,534	33,167	
Postage	9,303	9,963	11,641	12,359	12,629	
Utilities	30,179	30,594	30,263	32,055	29,207	
Bad Debts	26,732	8,270	14,659	40,399	11,650	
Legal and Acctg. Expenses	5,859	6,918	7,351	5,758	9,375	
Dues and Subscriptions	6,151	4,377	2,558	2,676	3,404	
Contributions	325	3,767	9,044	40	21,732	
Auto and Truck Expenses	0	0	10,459	9,729	9,364	
Collection Fees	0	0	0	1,243	35	
Miscellaneous	213	2,671	0	10,833	2,343	
Operating Expenses	1,260,282	1,378,638	1,537,229	1,633,358	1,814,853	880,898
Income (loss) from Operations	−33,419	65,096	102,998	166,572	178,333	199,089
Other Income	25,912	49,563	54,859	52,690	59,681	90,144
Other Deductions	28,421	42,151	52,207	38,504	52,804	
Income (loss) before Taxes	−35,928	72,508	105,650	180,758	185,210	289,233
Taxes	−18,367	23,178	39,726	46,455	56,674	
Net Income (loss)	−17,561	49,330	65,924	134,303	128,536	289,233

Exhibit 8   Selected Items for the Years 1983–1986 (Median Percentages of Net Sales)

All Companies with Sales between $3 and $5 Million

Items	1983	1984	1985	1986
Total Cost of Manufactured Products (%)	69.4	69.5	72.4	71.6
Total Selling Expenses (%)	15.5	13.0	15.5	12.7
Shipping and Finished Goods Warehouse Expenses (%)	1.8	1.3	1.0	.5
Office, Administrative and General Expenses (%)	11.2	10.5	9.1	11.0
Net Profit before State and Federal Income Taxes (%)	3.6	3.1	2.5	2.2
Net Profit after State and Federal Income Taxes (%)	3.0	2.3	2.0	1.6
Pension & Benefit Costs (%)	3.5	3.8	2.5	3.7
Annual Turnover Rate of Accounts Receivables (Times)	7.6	7.2	7.6	8.2
Sales Per Employee ($)				
Total	103,893	115,147	113,182	126,600
Architectural Coatings	64,416	38,450	59,161	35,373
Product Coatings—OEM	73,436	81,293	86,398	80,494
Special Purpose Coatings	26,264	33,084	51,172	30,271
Net Profit after Taxes to Total Net Worth (%)	12.1	7.2	7.6	4.7
Net Profit after Taxes to Net Working Capital (%)	13.4	9.9	10.3	8.8
Average Saleperson's Sales ($)				
Total	615,536	580,000	670,926	590,500
Architectural Coatings	414,960	267,341	NA	NA
Product Coatings—OEM	537,586	606,170	NA	NA
Special Purpose Coatings	155,146	NA	NA	NA
Annual Turnover Rate of Manufactured Finished Goods (Times)	7.2	9.0	14.4	7.4
Annual Turnover Rate of Raw Material Inventory (Times)	7.2	5.9	8.4	7.9

All Companies

Items	1983	1984	1985	1986
Total Cost of Manufactured Products (%)	67.1	66.4	67.6	64.7
Total Selling Expenses (%)	17.0	15.9	16.7	17.6
Shipping and Finished Goods Warehouse Expenses (%)	1.6	1.2	1.6	1.2
Office, Administrative, & General Expenses (%)	9.3	8.9	9.0	9.6
Net Profit before State and Federal Income Taxes (%)	4.6	4.8	4.4	5.1
Net Profit after State and Federal Income Taxes (%)	3.1	3.2	3.1	3.1
Pension & Benefit Costs (%)	3.3	3.5	3.2	3.1
Annual Turnover Rate of Accounts Receivables (Times)	8.0	7.9	7.9	8.0
Sales Per Employee ($)				
Total	109,961	120,000	116,603	126,637
Architectural Coatings	76,040	65,346	84,700	96,909
Product Coatings—OEM	86,335	102,064	87,908	100,882
Special Purpose Coatings	17,000	22,590	31,542	36,649
Net Profit after Taxes to Total Net Worth (%)	11.9	13.8	11.5	12.1
Net Profit after Taxes to Net Working Capital (%)	14.0	16.1	12.6	12.9
Average Saleperson's Sales ($)				
Total	621,000	691,325	716,064	729,769
Architectural Coatings	477,400	419,747	504,213	475,000
Product Coatings—OEM	657,139	837,298	863,698	863,443
Special Purpose Coatings	394,000	312,000	578,503	571,494
Annual Turnover Rate of Manufactured Finished Goods (Times)	7.4	7.9	7.8	7.4
Annual Turnover Rate of Raw Material Inventory (Times)	7.3	7.7	8.3	7.8

(continued)

Exhibit 8   *(continued)*

Companies Using LIFO Method of Inventory Accounting

Companies Included: 65
Companies Using: LIFO, 65; FIFO, 0
Companies with Store Operations: 21

	Percentage of Net Sales			
Summary	**Lower**	**Average**	**Median**	**Upper**
Net Sales	100.0	100.0	100.0	100.0
Cost of Goods Sold	71.5	65.5	64.4	59.1
Gross Profit	28.4	34.5	35.6	40.9
Selling Expenses	24.2	18.5	19.1	13.1
Office, Administrative, and General Expense	12.6	9.7	8.3	5.6
Total Selling & Administrative Expense	35.0	28.3	28.6	23.0
Operating Gain	2.5	6.2	5.8	9.2
Other Expenses	2.9	2.1	1.4	.2
Other Income	.1	.9	.6	1.2
Net Profit before State and Federal Income Tax	2.0	5.0	5.2	7.7
Net Profit after State and Federal Income Tax	1.4	2.6	3.1	4.6
Net Sales				
Net Sales	100.0	100.0	100.0	100.0
Manufactured Product Sales	88.9	91.8	98.2	100.0
Resale Product Sales	11.1	8.2	1.8	.0
Cost of Goods Sold—Manufactured Products				
Raw Materials	53.8	47.1	46.9	40.5
Packages	6.5	4.3	4.3	2.5
Direct Labor	5.9	4.7	4.2	3.0
Manufacturing Overhead	10.0	8.0	7.2	4.8
Control Laboratory	1.2	1.0	.8	.3
Total Cost of Manufactured Products	73.9	65.0	63.2	57.4
Gross Profit on Manufactured Products	26.0	35.0	36.8	42.5
Cost of Goods Sold—Resale Products				
Cost of Resale Products	71.7	66.9	68.3	63.0
Gross Profit on Resale Products	28.3	33.1	31.6	36.9
Selling Expenses				
Total Selling Expenses	23.9	18.2	18.8	13.3
Salespersons Comp. & Travel Exp.	6.4	5.3	4.9	3.2
Salesmanager Comp. & Travel Exp.	1.8	1.1	.8	.0
Advertising & Promotion Expense	2.0	1.7	1.0	.1
Technical Service	.9	.7	.2	.0
Research & Development Laboratory	4.1	2.4	2.3	.6
Freight Out	2.9	1.9	1.3	.2
Shipping & Finished Goods Warehse.	3.2	1.8	1.6	.7
A. At Manufacturing Site	2.7	1.8	1.7	.8
B. Nonplant Site	.4	.5	.0	.0
Other Selling Exp. Including Store Exp.	4.9	3.4	1.2	.0

Exhibit 8 *(continued)*

All Companies with Sales between $3 and $5 Million

Companies Included: 17
Companies Using: LIFO, 6; FIFO, 9
Companies with Store Operations: 3

Summary	Percentage of Net Sales			
	Lower	Average	Median	Upper
Net Sales	100.0	100.0	100.0	100.0
Cost of Goods Sold	75.5	70.2	71.6	64.7
Gross Profit	24.5	29.8	28.4	35.3
Selling Expenses	19.2	14.3	13.3	10.1
Office, Administrative, and General Expense	16.0	12.0	11.0	8.6
Total Selling & Administrative Expense	29.4	26.3	26.8	21.6
Operating Gain	1.7	3.5	4.0	5.8
Other Expenses	2.6	1.5	.9	.1
Other Income	.0	.7	.4	1.0
Net Profit before State and Federal Income Tax	.6	2.3	2.2	4.9
Net Profit after State and Federal Income Tax	.6	1.3	1.6	3.1
Net Sales				
Net Sales	100.0	100.0	100.0	100.0
Manufactured Product Sales	94.7	93.8	100.0	100.0
Resale Product Sales	5.2	6.2	.0	.0
Cost of Goods Sold—Manufactured Products:				
Raw Materials	54.0	51.9	52.1	47.9
Packages	6.4	4.4	5.1	1.8
Direct Labor	6.9	5.8	6.3	4.4
Manufacturing Overhead	11.4	6.6	6.2	3.0
Control Laboratory	3.0	1.6	1.2	.3
Total Cost of Manufactured Products	75.5	70.4	71.6	67.7
Gross Profit on Mfgd. Products	24.5	29.6	28.4	32.3
Cost of Goods Sold—Resale Products				
Cost of Resale Products	79.5	57.7	64.4	32.5
Gross Profit on Resale Products	20.5	42.3	35.6	67.4
Selling Expenses				
Total Selling Expenses	19.1	14.0	12.7	10.5
Salesperson Comp. & Travel Exp.	9.0	6.9	6.0	3.9
Salesmanager Comp. & Travel Exp.	2.8	1.3	.5	.0
Advertising & Promotion Expense	1.0	.5	.2	.1
Technical Service	.5	.3	.0	.0
Research & Development Laboratory	2.9	1.8	1.8	.0
Freight Out	2.0	1.5	.8	.1
Shipping & Finished Goods Warehse.	1.5	.9	.5	.0
A. At Manufacturing Site	2.9	1.5	1.0	.5
B. Nonplant Site	.0	.0	.0	.0
Other Selling Exp. Including Store Exp.	1.0	.8	.0	.0

Exhibit 9 Estimated Gross Profit Percentages
(Based on Selling Price)

Retail	
Paint	40%
Wallpaper	40
Automotive	33
Spray	30
Window	45
Art	55
Sundries	50

Wholesale	
Paint	25–28%
Sundries	33
Arts/Crafts	33

Exhibit 10 Robert F. Ramsey, Inc.

1988 Sales—January–June

1. Art Supply Clearance	January 18–January 30	18. Cabot Stains	June 27–July 16
2. Designer Wallpaper 25%	February 15–February 27	19. Designer Wallpaper 25%	July 11–July 23
3. Del Mar 60%	February 29–March 12	20. Storewide "Blue Kay" Paint Sale	July 18–August 6
4. Wallpaper 20%–40%	March 14–March 26	21. Summer Paint Sale	August 8–August 20
5. Art Supply Specials—3 days	April 7, 8, 9	22. Olympic Specials	August 21–September 10
6. Fuller O'Brien Paint	March 28–April 16	23. Fuller O'Brien Labor Day Paint	August 29–September 10
7. Del Mar 60%	April 11–April 23	24. Cabot Stains	August 29–September 10
8. Stock Wallpaper 20%	April 25–May 7	25. Back-to-School Art Supplies	September 12–September 24
9. Blue Kay "Microwave" Sale	May 4–May 21	26. Stock Wallpaper 20%	September 19–October 1
10. Del Mar 60%	May 16–May 28	27. Blue Kay Get Ready for Winter Paint	September 26–October 8
11. Olympic Specials	May 16–June 4	28. Wallpaper 20%–40%	October 10–October 22
12. Fuller O'Brien Memorial Day Paint	May 23–June 4	29. Del Mar 60%	October 24–November 12
13. Cabot Stains	May 23–June 4	30. Let Us Lend You a Hand Sundries	November 7–November 19
14. Art Supply 40%–3 days	June 9, 10, 11	31. Art Gifts for Christmas	November 25–December 31
15. Blue Kay "Early Summer" Paint Sale	June 13–June 25		
16. Industrial Air Specials	June 17–July 16		
17. Fuller O'Brien Independence Day Paint	June 27–July 9		

1989 Sales

1. Art Supply Clearance	January 23–February 4

Paint–Wallcoverings–Art Materials–Spray Equipment–Automotive Paint

Case 17

GENICOM CORPORATION

GENICOM CORPORATION

Curtis W. Powell, President of GENICOM COR-PORATION, faced the morning of June 18, 1985 with uncertainty. His upcoming meeting with the labor union at the firm's Waynesboro, Virginia facility was one which raised some disturbing questions about the company's future, and even its past.

Prior to today's meeting, GENICOM had proposed wage and benefit reductions, which resulted in increasing confrontation with union representatives. Mr. Powell pondered what strategic alternatives the company should pursue if the union did not accept the proposed reductions. And even if the union did make the concessions needed, what strategy should GEN-ICOM follow in the competitive computer printer market over the next 3 to 5 years?

Background

GENICOM was founded in June 1983, as a result of a leveraged buy-out of General Electric's (GE) Data Communication Products Business Department in Waynesboro, a relatively self-contained entity which produced computer printers and relay components. The department operated as one of GE's strategic business units.

This case was prepared by Per V. Jenster, IMD, Lausanne, Switzerland, John M. Gwin, and David B. Croll. McIntire School of Commerce, University of Virginia, Charlottesville, Virginia 22903. This case was used in the fifth McIntire Commerce Invitational (MCI V) held at the University of Virginia on February 13–15, 1986. We gratefully acknowledge the General Electric Foundation for support of the MCI and the writing of this case. Copyright © 1986. Reprinted with permission.

GE came to Waynesboro, a small town in Central Virginia, in 1954 as part of a major decentralization effort which also included establishing facilities nearby in Lynchburg and Salem, Virginia. Between 1954 and 1974, the Waynesboro plant produced a wide variety of highly sophisticated electro-mechanical devices such as process controls, numerical controls, and aircraft controls, many of which are now produced by other GE divisions.

Products once manufactured in the Waynesboro facility accounted for several hundred million dollars in annual sales revenues for GE. As a result, the Waynesboro factory had a long-standing reputation for its skill in electro-mechanical design and engineering and for its ability to solve difficult design tasks in its highly vertically integrated facilities.

The first electro-mechanical printer was created by GE in Waynesboro as a result of the firm's own dissatisfaction with the performance of the Teletype 33 printers. The new GE printer was three times faster than the Teletype 33 and gained quick popularity. In 1969, a send-receive printer was introduced with such success that it evolved into one of GE's fastest-growing product lines. Other products were added using the same technology, and by 1977 the business in Waynesboro had attained annual revenues of $100,000,000 while being very profitable.

In 1980, GE changed corporate leadership. The new GE Chairman, John F. Welch, initiated a major review of the corporation's businesses to determine which ones were critical to GE's future strategies. Businesses with products which did not rank number one or number two in their served industries or did not have the technological leadership to become first or second required special review. The Waynesboro products did not rank number one or number two in their served industry, nor were they critical to GE's long-term strategies, and in 1981, the department's Strategic Planning process investigated the possibility of divestiture as an alternative course of action.

During 1981, the then current General Manager resigned and Curtis Powell, the Financial Manager and long-term GE employee, was appointed the new General Manager.[1]

During the same time frame the printer business' line of reporting was dismantled; the General Manager, the Division Manager and his superior, the Group Vice President, left GE and the Executive Vice President and Sector Executive retired. As a result, there were no administrative levels between the Waynesboro facility and a newly appointed Sector Executive. Mr. Powell received the dual task of (1) positioning the business for divestiture and (2) making it viable if no acceptable buyers could be found. To accomplish these two objectives, Mr. Powell implemented programs to improve the competitiveness of the Department's printer products and productivity programs to reduce the cost of operations. To support aggressive new product design efforts, funding of research and development activities were increased by $1.0MM per year. The first product, the new 3000 Series printer, was introduced in the latter part of 1981. By 1982, the 3000 Series product had received an excellent reception in the marketplace. Variable cost had been reduced by 28%, primarily as a result of the relocation of 300 jobs from Waynesboro to the Department's Mexican facility, fixed costs had been reduced by 25% and

net assets in the business had been reduced by $14.0MM. Despite the successful introduction of the new printer product and rapidly increasing orders, GE was still interested in divesting the business.

After several months of meetings with potential acquirers, GE had not received an acceptable offer. During the fourth quarter of 1982, Mr. Powell and a group of plant managers offered to purchase the Waynesboro based business from GE.

The Buy-Out Of GENICOM

During early 1983, GE agreed to sell the business as a leveraged buy-out, but required a substantial cash payment. In order to complete the transaction, the Management team was joined by two New York based venture capital firms who provided the financial resources needed to purchase the business.

The price agreed upon for the business was net depreciated value plus $8.0MM (note that the business had been in Waynesboro since 1954 and the net depreciated value was significantly less than the appraised value). The purchase price amounted to less than six months sales revenue.

The assets purchased included every printer ever designed by the Waynesboro facility, all customers and contracts, all patents and cross licenses, tools, and buildings, as well as the Relay business. The purchase agreement was signed October 23, 1983, at which time GE received approximately 75% of the purchase price in cash and subordinated notes for the balance. The purchase amount was financed through sale of shares to the venture capital firms and to local management (approximately 45 of the top managers received stock or stock options). Twelve million dollars were borrowed against fixed assets in the business, and a revolving credit line was secured against equipment leases, receivables, and selected inventory. Given the assessed value of the firm, GENICOM had not exceeded 65% of its borrowing capacity.

[1]In this respect, it is important to understand GE's organizational structure. GE was organized as follows: The chairman, three vice-chairmen, seven industry sectors, numerous groups and divisions, each containing many departments. The Waynesboro factory was a department.

The GENICOM Corporation

By 1983, GENICOM was one of the larger independent computer printer companies which manufactured teleprinters (i.e., keyboard send/receive units), dot-matrix printers, and line printers. These printers were primarily industrial grade, and thus were not widely used for personal computer output. They served a wide variety of data processing and telecommunication needs, with printing speeds ranging from 60 cps (characters per second) in the teleprinter version to 400 lpm (lines per minute) in their line printer series. GENICOM was also the industry leader in crystal relays sold to defense, space, and other industries where there was a need for highly reliable electrical switches.

GENICOM was also a multi-national company with production facilities in Waynesboro (1300 employees) and Mexico (700 employees). Approximately 20% of the 1984 sales revenue of $140.0MM was derived from International customers, primarily Original Equipment Manufacturers (OEM's). GENICOM was in the process of establishing its own sales affiliates in the United Kingdom, France, Germany, and Sweden in order to further serve its foreign customers.

Prior to the change in ownership, GENICOM's management negotiated a comprehensive benefits package which was essentially the same as GE's. Furthermore, a new agreement with the Union was settled, and customers and suppliers were briefed. All but fifteen current employees were offered positions with GENICOM at the same salary and similar benefits as provided by GE and all accepted.

According to Mr. Powell, "Everything considered, the buy-out went extremely well. 1984 was an excellent year, a very successful year for GENICOM. We are still trying to change the culture we inherited from GE, where people feel they have unlimited resources to a small company climate, a climate in which costs must be contained. Some of our people in Waynesboro believe that the success we had in 1984 will continue forever. They don't realize that in our industry product life cycles are short and even if your products are doing well today, you need to prepare for tomorrow. This transition from GE to GENICOM has been difficult."

"When we were a part of GE all employees were paid GE wages and salaries. Other firms in our industry and other firms in Waynesboro paid considerably less than GE rates." As part of the two largest employers in Waynesboro, GENICOM's actions when dealing with its employees became public very soon. "We have a very quality conscious work force in Waynesboro and quality has always been extremely important to us. But in our competitive market quality is not enough, we must be cost competitive also."

Management and Structure

GENICOM's management inherited an organizational structure and an information system which reflected GE's standards and procedures. Consequently, GENICOM was probably the most vertically integrated printer company in the world (largely encouraged by GE's capital budgeting and performance evaluation system), making almost everything in-house from tools to printer ribbons to sales brochures. This high degree of vertical integration enabled GENICOM to respond quickly to specific requests for redesign of products to suit individual customer needs.

The firm's information system was also aligned with GE's reporting system, which led one outside observer to conclude that he "had never seen an organization with such a sophisticated information system which used it so little." As an illustration, Exhibit 1 shows GENICOM's MIS budget *vis-a-vis* industry averages. Exhibit 2 compares GENICOM's data processing department with a similar organization in the industry. According to Coopers and Lybrand, a consulting firm retained by GENICOM, the cost problem, highlighted in these two exhibits, could

Exhibit 1 MIS Budgets: Industry Averages and Genicom, 1983–1984

	Manufacturing (electronics, electrical)			Genicom		
	Thousands of Dollars[a]	Percent of Revenue	Percent of MIS Budget	Thousands of Dollars[a]	Percent of Revenue	Percent of MIS Budget
Total revenue	$75,590	100.00%	n/a	$165,000	100.00%	n/a
MIS operating budget	723	1.01	100	2,567.4[b]	1.56	100.0%
Personnel	308	0.43	42.5	1,271.0	0.77	49.5
Hardware	208	0.29	28.4	400.6[c]	0.24	15.6
System software	21	0.03	3.1	27.5	0.02	1.1
Application software	36	0.05	4.9	76.5	0.05	3.0
Supplies	57	0.08	7.8	110.3	0.07	4.2
Outside services	36	0.05	7.8	559.0	0.34	21.8
Communications	21	0.03	3.3	19.8	0.01	0.8
Other	36	0.05	5.0	102.7[d]	0.06	4.0

[a]Average amounts reported in source survey.
[b]Genicom's IS&S actual expenses, January-May 1985, have been annualized and have been modified to (1) remove office services expenses and (2) add estimated hardware depreciation expense and estimated occupancy expense in order to correlate with survey figures.
[c]This category includes equipment rental, maintenance, and depreciation expense. Depreciation expense is drawn from Genicom's fixed asset register and includes annual depreciation (book) for all assets acquired through December 1984.
[d]This category includes occupancy expense, estimated at 4% of total MIS expense budget.
Sources: Infosystems 25th and 26th Annual Salary Surveys, June 1984 and June 1983. A survey of 642 firms conducted for Datamation and published March 15, 1985, shows that firms averaging $200 million in revenue employ an average of 20.1 people in data processing (equivalent to IS&S at Genicom without office services), for an index of average revenue of $9,950,200 per data-processing employee.

Exhibit 2 MIS Characteristics, Genicom and a Similar Organization, 1985

	Genicom	Other Firm
Hardware	5 H-P 3000s	4 H-P 3000s
Number of data centers	1 current	2
	1 planned	
Annual revenues	$165,000,000	$500,000,000
	(1985 budget)	
Type of business	Manufacturing	Manufacturing
Number of employees in MIS	34[a]	44[b]
Salary expense	$1,051,300	$1,075,200 [c]
Processing characteristics	In-house plus heavy use of remote computing service	In-house plus heavy use of remote computing service
Company revenues per MIS employee	$4,852,900	$12,500,000

[a]Includes staff at one data center.
[b]Includes staff at two data centers.
[c]1984 budget plus 5%.

also be found in other areas: Finance, Materials, Shop Operations, Manufacturing Engineering, Quality Control, Marketing, Product Engineering, and Relays.

The management team of GENICOM (April 1985) consists of the following members:

Curtis W. Powell, President/Chief Executive Officer: Mr. Powell graduated from Lynchburg College, Lynchburg, Virginia in 1961 with a BA Degree in Business Administration - Economics. Prior to the purchase of the Waynesboro business by GENICOM, Mr. Powell had served 22 years in various General Electric assignments; the last two as Department General Manager of the Waynesboro business.

John V. Harker, Executive Vice President: Mr. Harker was responsible for the Sales and Marketing functions, including Product Planning, Market and New Business Development, Marketing Administration, Customer Service, Domestic Sales and International Operations. He formerly held positions as Senior Vice President for Marketing and Corporate Development at Dataproducts, Vice President of Booz, Allen, and Hamilton, Inc., a Management Consulting firm, and with IBM in various Marketing capacities. Upon joining GENICOM, he initiated the hiring of six new Marketing and Sales Executives from the computer peripherals industry.

Robert C. Bowen, Vice President & Chief Financial Officer: Mr. Bowen has served in various financial capacities with GE since 1964, and with Genicom's predecessor for the past ten years.

W. Douglas Drumheller, Vice President of Manufacturing: Mr. Drumheller joined GE's Manufacturing Management Program in 1970 and was appointed Vice President at GENICOM in 1983.

Dennie J. Shadrick, Vice President of Engineering: Mr. Shadrick recently joined GENICOM after seventeen years with Texas Instruments, where he served in a variety of Engineering and Management positions in the terminal and printer business unit.

Charles A. Ford, Vice President of Relay Operations: Mr. Ford has had a long career with GE and GENICOM serving in the areas of Manufacturing, Engineering, and General Management.

Robert B. Chapman, Treasurer: Mr. Chapman has been with GENICOM since 1984, after holding positions with Centronics Data Computer Corporation, Honeywell, Inc., and the Datapoint Corporation, where he was Assistant Treasurer.

"Part of our GE heritage was a strong Engineering and Manufacturing orientation and this is a valuable asset. However, as a new and independent company, we needed to establish a Marketing presence, we needed a new and aggressive approach to our Marketing and Sales Activities. One of our first action items was to recruit the best Marketing and Sales executives we could locate. GENICOM's strategy for developing marketing strengths has been to bring experienced and capable people from other firms in the computer peripherals industry."

Financial Statements

The 1984 financial statements and footnotes are included in Exhibits 3-7. Due to the time period constraints associated with any financial statements, GENICOM's balance sheet for December 30, 1984 did not include the subsequent private placement of stock that took place on January 3, 1985. GENICOM sold 353,000 shares of its unissued common stock for $5 per share. If these shares had been issued at December 30, 1984, unaudited *pro forma* stockholders' equity would have been $16,993,000.

Exhibit 3 Genicom Corporation and Subsidiaries Consolidated
Balance Sheet, 1984 (in thousands of dollars)

	December 30, 1984	January 1, 1984
Assets		
Current assets		
Cash	$ 451	$ 3,023
Accounts receivable, less allowance for doubtful accounts of $958 and $483	21,224	22,459
Inventories	26,917	24,343
Prepaid expenses and other assets	1,368	356
Total current assets	$49,960	$50,181
Property, plant, and equipment	27,821	27,314
Other assets	239	180
Total assets	$78,020	$77,675
Liabilities and Capital		
Current liabilities		
Current portion of long-term debt	$ 1,600	$11,841
Accounts payable and accrued expenses	16,104	15,682
Deferred income	1,519	1,359
Income taxes (note 8)	5,579	
Total current liabilities	$24,802	$28,882
Long-term debt, less current portion	36,400	44,500
Deferred income taxes	1,590	504
Redeemable preferred stock, $1 par value; 32,000 shares issued and outstanding at January 1, 1984; stated at liquidation value of $100 per share	-0-	$ 3,200
Stockholders' equity		
Common stock, $0.01 par value; 20,000,000 shares authorized; shares outstanding: December 30, 1984, 10,995,500; January 1, 1984, 8,575,000	$ 110	$ 86
Additional paid-in capital	9,297	772
Retained earnings (deficit)	5,821	(269)
Total stockholders' equity	$15,228	$ 589
Total liabilities and stockholders' equity	$78,020	$77,675

The accompanying notes are an integral part of the financial statements.

The two period comparisons used in the financials entitled "December 30, 1984" and "January 1, 1984" are not true comparisons since the time periods covered are not equal. The first column for the year ending December 30, 1984 represents a 12-month period, but the second column for the year ending January 1, 1984 represents only a two-month, ten-day period.

The remaining statements and ten footnotes are complete and self-explanatory. The strong fi-

Exhibit 4 Genicom Corporation and Subsidiaries Consolidated Statement of Income, 1984 (in thousands of dollars except per share amounts)

	Year ended December 30, 1984	October 21, 1983, to January 1, 1984
Net sales	$136,661	$26,752
Cost of goods sold	90,647	20,403
Gross profit	$ 46,014	$ 6,349
Expenses		
Selling, general, and administration	$ 22,442	$ 3,965
Engineering, research, and product development	4,795	890
Interest	6,900	1,386
Total expenses	$ 34,137	$ 6,241
Income before income taxes	$ 11,877	$ 108
Income tax expense (note 8)	5,787	377
Net income (loss)	$ 6,090	$ (269)
Net income (loss) per common share and common share equivalent		
Primary	$ 0.61	$ (0.03)
Fully diluted	$ 0.59	$ (0.03)
Weighted average number of common shares and common share equivalents		
Primary	9,967	8,753
Fully diluted	10,292	8,892

The accompanying notes are an integral part of the financial statements.

nancial orientation of the management is evident in the statement presentation.

Cost Accounting

A major cost accounting issue was that GENICOM's product costs were well above those of their competitors. GENICOM's willingness to customize their products to meet their customers' individual needs allowed them to charge a premium price. The costs that seemed disproportionately high were salary and hourly wages. GENICOM's salary and wage structures were established over many years while it was a part of GE. General Electric traditionally provided its employees with both a generous base salary and a generous fringe package. As wages and benefits were negotiated with the union on an overall corporate basis, the printer department had avoided serious conflicts with the union.

Consultants from Coopers and Lybrand were hired by GENICOM to evaluate the firm's cost structure. Although the study was not completed, preliminary research had focused on this labor cost problem. The preliminary findings suggested that most areas of the firm seemed overstaffed and salary and wage levels exceeded both industry norms and local community standards (e.g., see Exhibits 1 & 2).

Exhibit 5 Genicom Corporation and Subsidiaries Consolidated Statement of Changes in Capital Accounts for the Year Ended December 30, 1984 and the Period from October 21, 1983 (commencement of operations) to January 1, 1984

	Redeemable Preferred Stock	Common Stock	Additional Paid-In Capital	Retained Earnings
Issued in connection with acquisition:				
32,000 shares of redeemable preferred stock	$ 3,200			
8,000,000 shares of common stock		$ 80	$ 721	
Issuance of 525,000 shares of common stock		5	47	
Exercise of stock options		1	4	
Net loss				$ (269)
Balance, January 1, 1984	$ 3,200	$ 86	$ 772	$ (269)
Issuance of 1,297,000 shares of common stock		13	5,288	
Redemption of preferred stock	$(3,200)	6	3,194	
Exercise of stock options		5	43	
Net income				6,090
Balance, December 30, 1984	—	$110	$9,297	$5,821

The accompanying notes are an integral part of the financial statements.

An interesting point was that GENICOM's wage and salary differential over other local companies was so great that it proved detrimental to some laid-off employees. Other companies in the region had reported that they were hesitant to hire a laid-off GENICOM employee knowing that, as soon as an opening existed, the employee would be lost back to GENICOM.

Union Negotiations

Negotiations with Local 124 of the United Electrical Radio and Machine Workers (UE) of America started on April 23, 1985. Management's primary goal was to reduce the average costs of an applied direct labor hour by four dollars. Included in the employee benefit package were vacation (five weeks maximum), holidays (ten days), comprehensive medical benefits, life insurance, temporary disability, overtime premium, pension, breaks, night-shift bonus, paid sick days/personal time, and job structures which included seventeen pay grades. Appendices 1–6 provide a picture of the negotiations as the confrontation grew.

Earlier in April, a different local of UE in a nearby Virginia town had been involved in an almost identical situation. A former department of Westinghouse which had been sold to outside interests, confronted with wage and benefit structures originally negotiated at the national level, attempted to win major financial concessions from its workforce in order to become cost competitive in its market. The local refused to accept any cutbacks in its package and, after several months of negotiation, went on strike. Two days later the company announced it would begin hiring permanent replacements for the striking workers on the following Monday and placed help wanted ads in the local newspapers. On Sunday afternoon, in a close vote, the union members voted to end the strike and accept management's proposals.

Exhibit 6   Genicom Corporation and Subsidiaries Consolidated Statement of Changes in Financial Position, 1984 (in thousands of dollars)

	Year Ended December 30, 1984	October 21, 1983, to January 1, 1984
Sources of working capital		
From operations		
Net income (loss)	$ 6,090	$ (269)
Charges to income not affecting working capital		
Depreciation	4,664	630
Amortization	49	
Deferred income taxes	1,086	504
Working capital from operations	$ 11,889	$ 865
Issued or assumed in connection with acquisition		
Redeemable preferred stock		$ 3,200
Common stock		801
Long-term debt		57,841
Proceeds from issuance of common stock	8,501	52
Exercise of options	48	5
Other, net	357	(189)
Total sources	$ 20,795	$62,575
Applications of working capital		
Additions to property, plant, and equipment	$ 5,636	$ 918
Noncurrent assets purchased in acquisition		27,017
Reduction of long-term debt	8,100	13,341
Redemption of preferred stock	3,200	-0-
Total applications	$ 16,936	$41,276
Analysis of working capital components		
Increase (decrease) in current assets		
Cash	$ (2,572)	$ 3,023
Accounts receivable	(1,235)	22,459
Inventories	2,574	24,343
Prepaid expenses and other assets	1,012	356
Total	$ (221)	$50,181
Increase (decrease) in current liabilities		
Current portion of long-term debt	$(10,241)	$11,841
Accounts payable and accrued expenses	422	15,682
Deferred income	160	1,359
Income taxes	5,579	
Total	$ (4,080)	$28,882
Increase in working capital	$ 3,859	$21,299
Working capital, beginning of period	21,299	-0-
Working capital, end of period	$ 25,158	$21,299

The accompanying notes are an integral part of the financial statements.

Exhibit 7   GENICOM Corporation and Subsidiaries Notes to Consolidated Financial Statements

1. *Incorporation and Acquisition:*

GENICOM Corporation (the "Company") was incorporated on June 1, 1983 and had no activity other than organizational matters until October 21, 1983 when it acquired substantially all of the net assets of the Data Communication Products Business Department and all of the outstanding common stock of Datacom de Mexico, S.A. de C.V., both wholly owned by General Electric Company ("GE"), a related party. These entities together functioned as a single business unit and were acquired in a purchase transaction for consideration totaling $62.1 million. The consideration was financed by (a) borrowing $41.0 million under a revolving credit and term loan agreement, (b) issuing $16.8 million in subordinated notes to GE, (c) assuming $340,000 of liabilities and (d) selling $800,000 of common stock and $3.2 million of redeemable preferred stock.

The consideration was allocated to working capital ($35.1 million) and property, plant and equipment and other assets ($27.0 million). The allocation of the purchase price to assets acquired and liabilities assumed is subject to adjustment resulting from refinements in the application of purchase method accounting.

If the acquisition is assumed to have been made as of January 1, 1983, unaudited pro forma consolidated net sales, net loss and net loss per share (computed by adjusting historical operations for acquisition financing and purchase method accounting) would approximate the following for the year ended January 1, 1984 (dollar amounts in millions, except per share amounts): net sales—$113.5; net loss—$3.4; net loss per common share and common share equivalent: primary—$.42 and fully diluted—$.42.

2. *Summary of Significant Accounting Policies:*

The Company, one of the largest independent computer printer companies, is a manufacturer and leading supplier of teleprinters, serial dot matrix printers, and line printers serving a wide variety of data processing and telecommunication markets. Additionally, the Company is a recognized leader in the manufacturer and supply of high quality, crystal/can relays, which are used in the Aerospace and Defense industries.

a. Principles of consolidation: The consolidated financial statements include the accounts of the Company and its wholly owned subsidiaries. All significant intercompany accounts and transactions have been eliminated.

b. Fiscal year: The Company's fiscal year ends on the Sunday nearest December 31. Accordingly, the Company is reporting on the period October 21, 1983 (commencement of operations) to January 1, 1984 and for the 52-week period ended December 30, 1984.

c. Inventories: Inventories are stated at the lower of cost or market. Cost is determined on a first-in, first-out basis.

d. Property, plant and equipment: Property, plant and equipment is stated at cost. Depreciation is computed using the straight-line method for financial reporting purposes based on estimates of useful lives at their acquisition date (generally 15 to 25 years for buildings and 3 to 8 years for machinery and equipment). Significant improvements and the cost of tooling are capitalized, while repairs and maintenance costs are charged to operations.

e. Income taxes: Timing differences exist in the computation of income for financial and tax reporting purposes which give rise to deferred taxes. The principal reason for these differences is the use of alternative methods for computing depreciation. The Company accounts for investment tax credits as a reduction of current taxes in the year realized.

f. Research and development: Research and development costs are charged to operations as incurred. The costs were $3,367,000 for the year ended December 30, 1984 and $475,000 for the period October 21, 1983 to January 1, 1984.

g. Foreign currency translation: Through its subsidiary, Datacom de Mexico, S.A. de C.V., the Company operates in a country considered to have a highly inflationary economy. As such, translation adjustments, which are not material, are included in results of operations. The consolidated financial statements of the Company include foreign assets and liabilities of $2,643,000 and $526,000 at December 30, 1984 and $1,291,000 and $96,000 at January 1, 1984.

h. Employee benefit plans: Substantially all of the Company's employees are eligible to participate under the Company's employee benefit plans described in Note 5. These plans are

Exhibit 7 *(continued)*

contributory and each employee must elect to participate and make contributions to the plans. Employee contributions vest immediately.

i. Net income per common share and common share equivalent: Primary net income (loss) per share was computed by dividing net income (loss) by the weighted average number of common shares and common share equivalents outstanding during the period. Common share equivalents include the weighted average number of shares issuable upon the assumed exercise of outstanding stock options and warrants after assuming the applicable proceeds from such exercise were used to acquire treasury shares at the average market price during the period.

Fully diluted net income (loss) per share was based upon the further assumption that the applicable proceeds from the exercise of the outstanding stock options and warrants were used to acquire treasury shares at the market price at the end of the period if higher than the average market price during the period.

3. *Supplemental Balance Sheet Information:*
Inventories consist of:

(Amounts in thousands)	December 30, 1984	January 1, 1984
Raw materials	$10,110	$ 9,897
Work in process	9,781	9,708
Finished goods	7,026	4,738
	$26,917	$24,343

Property, plant, and equipment consist of:

(Amounts in thousands)	December 30, 1984	January 1, 1984
Land	$ 709	$ 709
Buildings	5,383	5,268
Machinery and equipment	25,628	21,760
Construction in progress	1,291	207
	$33,011	$27,944
Less accumulated depreciation	5,190	630
	$27,821	$27,314

Accounts payable and accrued expenses consist of:

(Amounts in thousands)	December 30, 1984	January 1, 1984
Trade accounts payable	$ 6,297	$ 7,881
Accrued liabilities:		
Compensated absences	2,801	2,532
Payroll and related liabilities	1,589	808
Interest	1,337	1,426
Employee benefits	1,830	332
Other	2,250	2,703
	$16,104	$15,682

4. *Long-Term Debt:*
Long-term debt consists of:

(Amounts in thousands)	December 30, 1984	January 1, 1984
Revolving credit notes	$21,000	$27,500
Term loan	12,000	12,000
Subordinated notes payable to GE	5,000	16,841
	38,000	56,341
Less current portion	1,600	11,841
	$36,400	$44,500

On October 21, 1983, the Company entered into a financing agreement with several banks which provides the Company with $31 million of revolving credit and a $12 million term loan.

The revolving credit and term loan bear interest at the price rate (10¾% at December 30, 1984) plus 1½%, payable quarterly. In addition, a commitment fee of ½ of 1% is payable quarterly on the average daily unused portion of the revolving credit borrowing base. The Company is also required to maintain compensating balances of at least 5% of the total outstanding revolving credit and term loan. Withdrawal of the compensating balances is not legally restricted and any deficiency in maintaining such balances is subject to a fee based upon an average borrowing rate on amounts outstanding under this agreement.

The initial revolving loan base of $31 million decreases by $1.55 million beginning on October

(continued)

Exhibit 7 *(continued)*

1, 1986, and continues to decrease by $1.55 million each quarter thereafter and expires on October 1, 1991.

The term loan is payable in quarterly installments of $600,000 beginning October 1, 1985.

All borrowings by the Company under the agreement are collateralized by liens on all of the Company's assets. The agreement requires the Company to meet certain financial ratios related to indebtedness, net worth and current assets and current liabilities. The agreement also limits additional borrowing, purchase of property and equipment, the sale or disposition of certain assets, and restricts the payment of dividends to 50% of retained earnings. Under the most restrictive covenant $2.9 million of retained earnings was available for payment of dividends at December 30, 1984.

In connection with the acquisition, at October 21, 1983, the Company issued subordinated notes to GE in the amount of $16.8 million. These notes bear interest at the prime rate, payable quarterly. During 1984 in accordance with the terms, the Company paid $11.8 million of the notes. The remaining $5 million is payable as follows: October 21, 1985—$1 million; October 21, 1986—$2 million; and October 21, 1987—$2 million.

Maturities of long-term debt for the five fiscal years subsequent to December 30, 1984 are (in millions): 1985—$1.6; 1986—$4.4; 1987—$4.4; 1988—$6.4; and 1989—$8.6.

5. *Employee Benefit Plans:*

Effective January 1, 1984, the Company established a defined benefit pension plan for hourly employees. Employees must elect to participate and the plan is contributory. Employee contributions are 3% of compensation in excess of $12,000 per year. The Company makes contributions to the plan and records as pension expense an amount that is actuarially determined to be sufficient to provide benefits provided for under the plan, including amortization of unfunded liabilities over a maximum of 30 years. For the year ended December 30, 1984, pension expense was $408,000. Details of accumulated plan benefits and net plan assets as of the initial valuation date (January 1, 1984) are as follows:

Actuarial present value of accumulated plan benefits are:

Vested	$ 74,777
Nonvested	28,067
	$102,844
Market value of assets	$ 49,969
Rate of return assumed	7½%

Certain hourly employees have the additional benefit of receiving Unemployment Supplemental Income if their employment is terminated due to reductions in the Company's workforce.

Substantially all salaried employees are eligible to participate in the Company's deferred compensation and savings plan. The plan provides for contributions to be made by employees through salary reductions. The Company makes certain matching contributions which are allocated to the participants and vest as called for by the plan. For the year ended December 30, 1984, the Company's expense under this plan was $1,002,000.

6. *Warrants and Redeemable Preferred Stock:*

In connection with the acquisition the Company issued to GE stock purchase warrants to acquire 2,500,000 shares of the Company's common stock at a price of $.50 per share. The warrants are currently exercisable and expire October 21, 1988.

On December 20, 1984, the Company redeemed all of the outstanding redeemable preferred stock ($3.2 million) by issuing 640,000 shares of common stock. Holders of the redeemable preferred stock waived payment of the cumulative preferred stock dividends for all periods the stock was outstanding.

7. *Restricted Stock Purchase and Incentive Stock Option Plans:*

Under the Company's restricted stock purchase plan, the Company may offer to sell up to 975,000 shares of common stock to employees of the Company at a price per share equal to 100% of the fair market value as determined by the Board of Directors on the date of offer. Purchased shares vest to the employees as provided for under the agreement and, in certain cases, is dependent upon the attainment of annual financial objectives. Shares issued under the plan which are not vested at an employee's termination are subject to repurchase by the Company at the lower of original issue price or their then fair market value.

At December 30, 1984, 200,000 shares of common stock are reserved for future grants under this plan. The following table summarizes the activity of the plan during the respective fiscal periods (fair market value as determined at date of purchase): *see table A.*

Effective October 21, 1983, the Company adopted an incentive stock option plan whereby 1,300,000 shares of unissued common stock was reserved for future issuance. The plan was amended on October 20, 1984 to reduce the number of shares

Exhibit 7   *(continued)*

available under the plan from 1,300,000 to 1,025,000. Stock option activity for the respective fiscal periods is as follows: *see table B*.

The plan provides for the exercise of the outstanding options at 20% per year beginning five years from date of grant. The Company accelerated the exercising provisions of 475,000 options granted, and these options were exercised prior to December 30, 1984. Of these shares issued, 425,000 shares are restricted and subject to certain vesting provisions related to annual financial objectives. Additionally, under the plan, other options granted also become exercisable at earlier dates if these same financial objectives are attained. During the year ended December 30, 1984, such objectives were attained and 45,000 shares of those restricted above accrued to the benefit of the holders and 63,500 options became exercisable of which 58,500 were exercised and shares of common stock issued. The Company must continue to attain certain financial objectives annually in order to continue to have accelerated exercise dates (with respect to options) and continue to vest (with respect to restricted shares). In the event of employee termination prior to full vesting in these shares, the Company may purchase such shares at the lower of fair market value at date of termination or the original option price.

Table A

| | Year ended December 30, 1984 | | October 21, 1983 to January 1, 1984 | |
	Number of Shares	Market Value	Number of Shares	Market Value
Unvested shares outstanding, beginning of period	525,000	$ 52,500		
Shares issued	250,000	95,000	525,000	$52,500
Shares vested	(175,000)	(17,500)		
Unvested shares outstanding, end of period	600,000	$130,000	525,000	$52,500

Table B

| | Year ended December 30, 1984 | | | October 21, 1983 to January 1, 1984 | | |
| | | Option Price | | | Option Price | |
	Number of Shares	Per Share	Total	Number of Shares	Per Share	Total
Outstanding, beginning of period	780,000	$.10	$78,000			
Granted	82,500	$.20–$1.00	46,500	830,000	$.10	$83,000
Exercised	483,500	$.10	48,350	50,000	$.10	5,000
Cancelled	65,000	$.10–$.20	7,250			
Outstanding, end of period	314,000		$68,900	780,000		$78,000
Options exercisable, end of period	5,000	$.10	$ 500			
Options available for future grants	177,500					

(continued)

Exhibit 7   *(continued)*

8. *Income Taxes:*
   Income tax expense consists of:

(Amounts in thousands)	Year ended December 30, 1984	October 21, 1983 to January 1, 1984
Current:		
Federal	$4,788	
State	936	
Foreign	(72)	
	5,652	—
Deferred:		
Federal	73	$ 302
State	1	75
Foreign	61	
	135	377
	$5,787	$ 377

Total tax expense amounted to an effective rate of 48.7% for the year ended December 30, 1984 and 449% for the period October 21, 1983 to January 1, 1984. Income tax expense was different from that computed at the statutory U.S. Federal income tax rate of 46% for the following reasons:

(Amounts in thousands)	Year ended December 30, 1984	October 21, 1983 to January 1, 1984
Tax expense at statutory rate	$5,463	$ 50
Increases (decreases) related to:		
Investment tax credits	(249)	(56)
State income tax, net of federal income tax benefit	515	40
Purchase method accounting for inventories	103	370
DISC income	(70)	
Other, net	25	(27)
Actual tax expense	$5,787	$ 377

Deferred income tax expense results from timing differences in the recognition of revenue and expense for tax and financial statement purposes. The sources of these differences and the tax effect of each are as follows:

(Amounts in thousands)	Year ended December 30, 1984	October 21, 1983 to January 1, 1984
Depreciation	$ 728	$ 497
Inventory valuation	(668)	
Other, net	75	(120)
	$ 135	$ 377

9. *Leasing Arrangements:*
   As Lessee
   The Company leases certain manufacturing and warehousing property. Rent expense included in the consolidated statement of income amounted to $740,000 for the year ended December 30, 1984 and $120,000 for the period October 21, 1983 to January 1, 1984.
   Annual future minimum lease commitments for operating leases as of December 30, 1984 are immaterial.

   As Lessor
   The Company has rental plans for the leasing of printers. Operating lease terms vary, generally from one to 60 months. Rental income for the year ended December 30, 1984 and for the period October 21, 1983 to January 1, 1984 was $18,139,000 and $3,807,000, respectively. Minimum future rental revenues on noncancellable operating leases with terms of one year or longer at December 30, 1984 are (in thousands): 1985—$2,900; 1986—$500; 1987—$400; and 1988—$300.
   At December 30, 1984 and January 1, 1984, the cost of equipment leased was (in thousands) $4,087 and $4,040, which is included in property, plant and equipment, net of accumulated depreciation of $1,072 and $131, respectively.

10. *Related-Party Transactions:*
    The Company presently utilizes GE for various services, such as repair services for customers and data processing, under contracts expiring generally in 1985. The Company also purchases various raw materials from GE. The cost of these materials and services for the year ended December 30, 1984 and the period October 21, 1983 to January 1, 1984, totaled $8.4 million and $1.1 million, respectively.

Exhibit 7 *(continued)*

Sales to GE were $12.4 million for the year ended December 30, 1984 and $3.3 million for the period October 21, 1983 to January 1, 1984. In addition, sales to GE affiliates, who serve as distributors to third party customers in certain markets, and sales of parts for maintenance services to customers amounted to $14.4 million for the year ended December 30, 1984 and $1.7 million for the period October 21, 1983 to January 1, 1984. Accounts receivable from GE were $4.6 million at December 30, 1984 and $5.2 million at January 1, 1984; accounts payable to GE were $.8 million at December 30, 1984 and $.9 million at January 1, 1984.

The Printer Industry

The demand for printer hardware is derived from the demand for computing machinery. As the demand for computing capability shifted from mainframe computers to minicomputers to microcomputers, so did the demand for printing capacity shift from output capability to output quality. Similarly, the attributes of printers which determined their success in the marketplace changed from reliability and performance when dealing with mainframe applications to price and capability when dealing with microcomputer applications. At the same time, as business applications of microcomputers moved into networking situations, where a number of microcomputers are linked to a central database and a single printer, the demands placed on the printer hardware changed from the demands of a stand-alone microcomputer.

In addition to the changes that took place in the printer industry as a result of changes in the computer industry, there was change in the competitive structure of the marketplace. The presence of the Japanese manufacturers had altered the competitive nature of the industry. As had been the strategy in other industries, Japanese manufacturers entered the market at the bottom of the price structure. Because of lower labor rates and efficient production capability, the Japanese products forced extreme price pressure into the market. Once established, the Japanese manufacturers then began to "trade up" through product improvement and brand extension. As a result, the Japanese printer manufacturers became a formidable force in the marketplace, particularly in the microprinter (for personal computer use) segment. This set of competitors was a force all U.S. manufacturers of printers must have accounted for in the formulation of new product introductions and pricing strategies. A number of U.S. manufacturers had licensed "offshore" (Mexican, Korean, Taiwanese, and Japanese) manufacturers to produce price competitive products under the U.S. manufacturer brand names as a means of competing with the Japanese manufacturers.

The Market

The total market for printers of all types was predicted to be $10.44 billion in 1986. The breakdown of sales by printer type is shown in Exhibit 8. The market was segmented by impact (printers which use a printhead that actually strikes the paper) and non-impact (printers which do not strike the paper, but apply ink in some other fashion). Within the impact market, printers were also segmented by dot-matrix (printers which use dots to form the characters printed) and fully formed (printers which print an entire character at once, such as a "daisy wheel" printer). This market was further segmented according to whether a printer was a serial printer (one which prints character by character in a serial fashion) or a line printer (one which prints an entire line at a time—in general, line printers are called "high speed" and print faster than serial printers, but often at a lower quality); finally, the impact market segment was subdivided according to speed of printing. The non-impact segment was divided further according to printer

Exhibit 8 The U.S. Printer Market, 1983 and 1986

	1983				1986			
	Number of Units	Percent Share	Value (millions of dollars)	Percent Share	Number of Units	Percent Share	Value (millions of dollars)	Percent Share
Serial daisy wheel	712,000	25%	1,370	25%	2,000,000	24%	$ 2,400	23%
Serial dot matrix	1,857,000	66	2,280	41	4,600,000	54	4,140	40
Serial non-impact[a]	132,000	5	162	3	1,600,000	19	990	9
Nonimpact page printers[b]	5,200	0	222	4	150,000	2	1,000	10
Fully formed line printers	86,000	3	1,130	21	100,000	1	1,400	13
Dot matrix line printers	31,000	1	318	6	55,000	0	510	5
Total	2,823,000	100%	5,482	100%	8,505,000	100%	10,440	100%

[a]Ink-jet and thermal transfer printers
[b]Laser and similar printers.
[c]Source: Datek Information Services, Inc.

technology (electrostatic, ink jet, laser), and by speed (in characters per second). Certain non-impact printers were also segmented as page printers (those which print a complete page at a time). All non-impact printers were considered to have fully formed characters. A schematic representation of the complete market for printers is shown in Exhibit 9.

Besides print quality, different classes of printers had advantages and disadvantages for end users. Fully-formed character printers, whether daisywheel or band line, offered no graphics capability since they were limited to alphanumeric characters. These printers also were very noisy while printing unless special quietized enclosures were used to surround them. Additionally, daisywheel printers, which were found almost exclusively in offices for word processing applications, were extremely slow.

The primary drawback to dot matrix printers was perceived print quality, although a num-

ber of technological developments had improved their performance. These printers, however, supplied excellent adaptability to applications needs—graphics, spreadsheets, data and word processing, for instance—and prices had been dropping very rapidly in this market segment.

Non-impact printers offered much of the best aspects of performance—quiet operation, flexible application, and outstanding print quality—but drawbacks included high prices, inability to print multiple copies simultaneously (i.e., continuous multipart forms printing), higher cost of operation because of their utilization of consumable supplies such as toner, and some perception of the part of users that non-impact printers, like the copiers their technology was derived from, were less reliable.

As advances in technology decreased the cost of non-impact printers, the growth of sales in these segments was expected to increase. The prices of nonimpact printers were still high rel-

Exhibit 9   Electronic Printer Market Breakdown

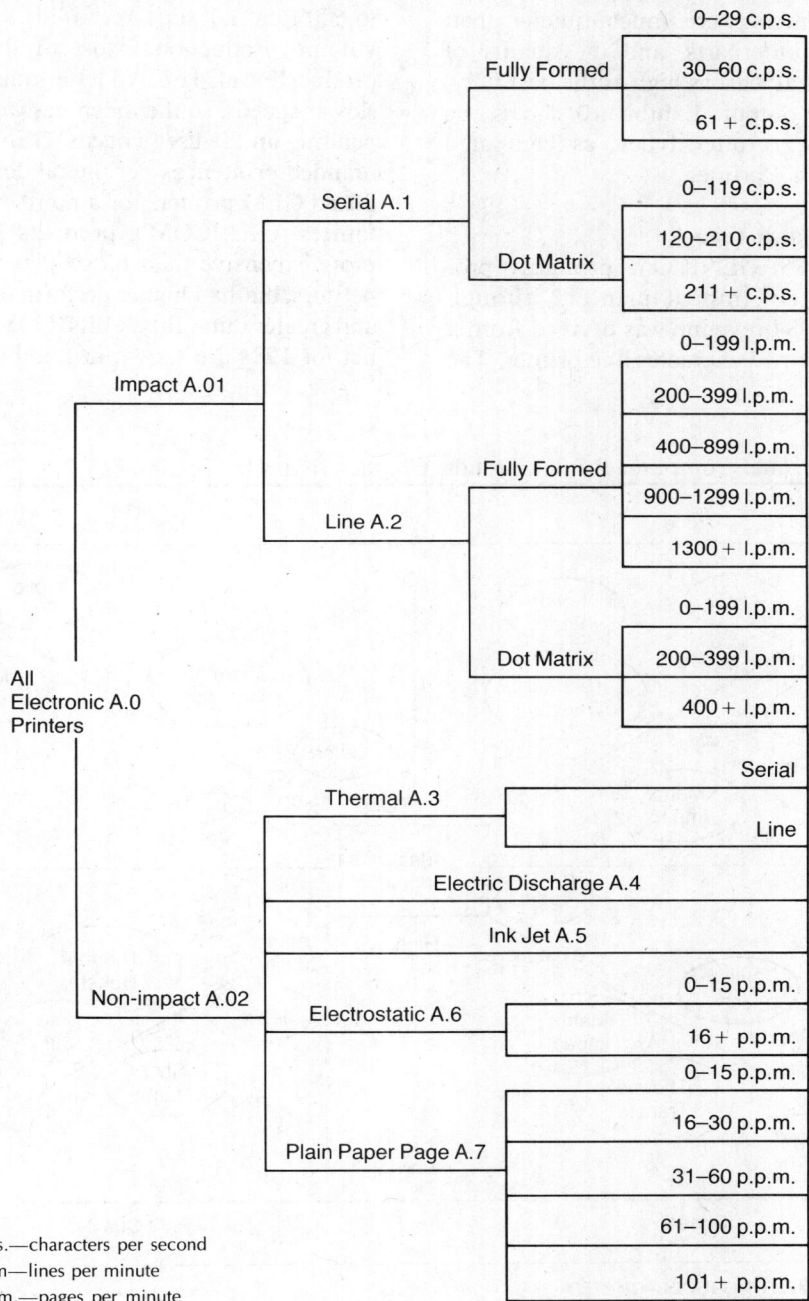

```
                                                                    ┌─ 0–29 c.p.s.
                                                    Fully Formed ───┼─ 30–60 c.p.s.
                                                                    └─ 61 + c.p.s.

                                    Serial A.1 ────┐
                                                    │               ┌─ 0–119 c.p.s.
                                                    Dot Matrix ─────┼─ 120–210 c.p.s.
                                                                    └─ 211 + c.p.s.

                Impact A.01 ───────┤
                                                                    ┌─ 0–199 l.p.m.
                                                                    ├─ 200–399 l.p.m.
                                                    Fully Formed ───┼─ 400–899 l.p.m.
                                                                    ├─ 900–1299 l.p.m.
                                    Line A.2 ──────┤                └─ 1300 + l.p.m.

                                                                    ┌─ 0–199 l.p.m.
                                                    Dot Matrix ─────┼─ 200–399 l.p.m.
                                                                    └─ 400 + l.p.m.
All
Electronic A.0 ─┤
Printers
                                                                    ┌─ Serial
                                    Thermal A.3 ───┤
                                                                    └─ Line

                                    Electric Discharge A.4

                                    Ink Jet A.5
                Non-impact A.02 ───┤
                                                                    ┌─ 0–15 p.p.m.
                                    Electrostatic A.6 ─────────────┤
                                                                    └─ 16 + p.p.m.

                                                                    ┌─ 0–15 p.p.m.
                                                                    ├─ 16–30 p.p.m.
                                    Plain Paper Page A.7 ───────────┼─ 31–60 p.p.m.
                                                                    ├─ 61–100 p.p.m.
                                                                    └─ 101 + p.p.m.
```

c.p.s.—characters per second
l.p.m—lines per minute
p.p.m.—pages per minute

Source: DATAQUEST, Inc.

ative to impact offerings, and the impact printers still enjoyed a speed advantage. However, the non-impact printers were much quieter than their impact counterparts, and the quality of their output was at least as high as the best fully-formed impact output. Exhibit 10 shows the characteristics of printer types, as compared against the "ideal" printer.

GENICOM Product Line

By April of 1985, GENICOM primarily produced dot matrix impact printers, though $6,000,000 in 1984 revenue was derived from a 300 lpm fully formed character line printer. The company produced line and serial printers which could print from 60 cps in an office environment to 600 lpm in a high speed line printer used for volume production. Most of the GENICOM product line also offered letter-quality printing at slower speeds, so the machines were flexible, depending on the user's needs. GENICOM offered branded printers as peripheral devices, and produced OEM printers for a number of major customers. GENICOM's products generally were more expensive than those of their major competitors, but had higher performance capabilities and greater durability. GENICOM sales by product for 1984 are shown in Exhibit 11.

Exhibit 10   Personal Computer Printer Trends: Characteristics by Technology

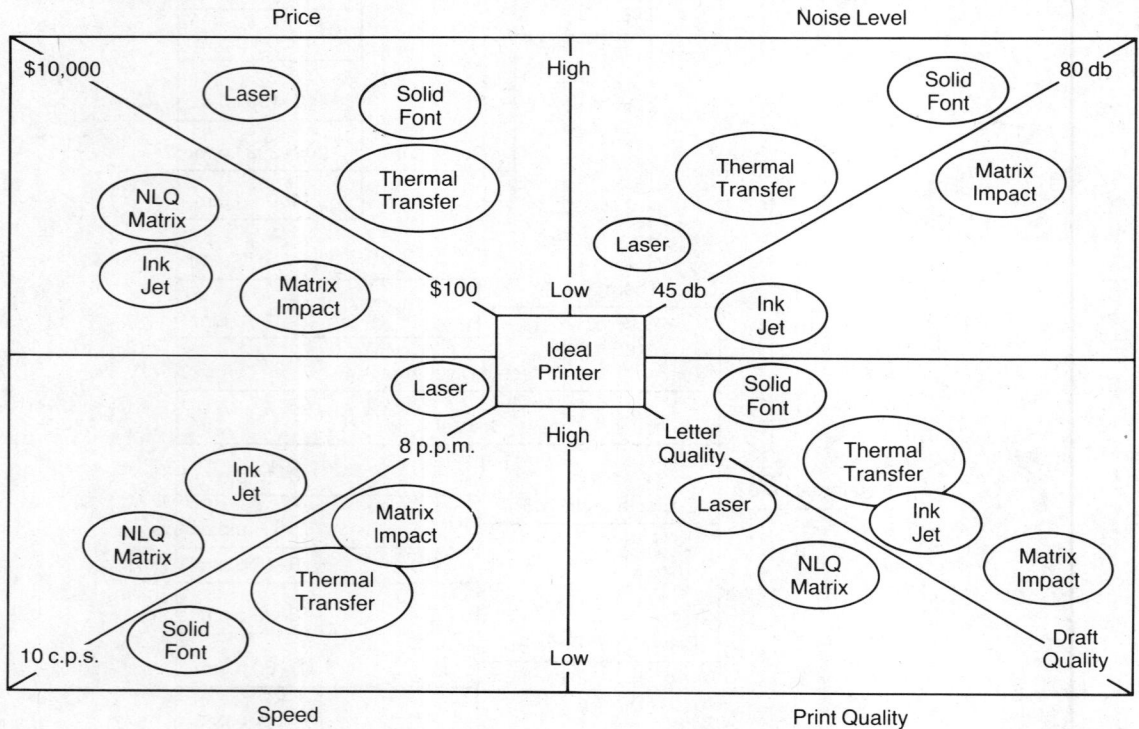

Source: FUTURE COMPUTING INCORPORATED

Exhibit 11   Genicom Sales, 1984

Printers	Thousands of dollars	Number of Units
340/510	$ 5,980	1,749
200	8,564	4,016
2030	6,131	} 9,623
2120	5,011	
3000	30,924	20,495
3014/3024	3,879	5,036
4000	—	—
Other	399	—
Total printers	$ 60,888	40,919
Parts	16,962	
Ribbons	7,846	
Lease	18,140	
Service	9,380	
Total printer business	$113,216	
Relays	23,426	
Total company business	$136,642	

GENICOM Competitors

GENICOM had a number of major competitors in each of the market segments it served. Its two major U.S. competitors were Centronics and Dataproducts, both competing essentially "head on" with GENICOM in almost every market segment. There were other, smaller competitors for special applications and certain of GENICOM's market segments. Exhibit 12 offers market share estimates for major competitors in each major segment.

End User

The end user for GENICOM products was faced with a complex decision process in the choice of a printer. The current products operated faster, printed more legibly, and cost less than those of a few years ago. However, there were more machines to choose from, so the choice needed to be carefully made.

GENICOM Marketing Strategy

GENICOM's general marketing strategy had been one of improving current products and expanding product lines rather than developing entirely new products or diversifying into new technologies. The strategy could have been characterized as "evolutionary" rather than "revolutionary." GENICOM's main distinctive competencies in the market had been flexibility in production and the quality of its products. They had traditionally been on the upper end of price points for similar products and had sought to gain market share by stressing the advantages their machines offered relative to the competition. Each of GENICOM's products offered some distinct advantage—speed, print quality, quietness, or flexibility—which was thought to offset price disadvantages.

GENICOM had an important presence in the OEM market, offering those customers a

Exhibit 12 Market Share, U.S. Printer Markets, 1984 (in units)

U.S. Serial Impact Printer Market, 1984 (market share in units)

Country of Manufacture	Manufacturer	% Share	Fully-formed	Dot Matrix
Japan	Epson	20.1		×
	C. Itoh (TEC)	13.9	×	×
	Okidata	11.4		×
	Star	3.2		×
	NEC	2.4	×	×
	Brother	2.0	×	×
	Ricoh	2.0	×	
	Toshiba	1.1		×
	Canon	0.9		×
	Juki	0.9	×	
	Fujitsu	0.6	×	×
	Subtotal	58.5		
United States	Xerox	3.2	×	
	IBM	3.0	×	
	Texas Instruments	2.2		×
	DEC	2.2		×
	Teletype	2.0		×
	Quae	2.0	×	
	Centronics	1.6		×
	Genicom	1.1		×
	Anadex	0.6		×
	Datasouth	0.4		×
	Dataproducts	1.6	×	×
	Subtotal	19.9		
Europe	Mannesmann	0.9		×
	Facit	0.5	×	×
	Philips	0.3		×
	Hermes	0.2		×
	Subtotal	1.9		
Other		19.7		

U.S. Nonimpact Printer Market, 1984 (market share in units)

Country of Manufacture	Manufacturer	% Share	Page	Thermal	Ink jet
Japan	Canon	17.3	×		×
	Okidata	17.0		×	×
	Star	12.8		×	
	Sharp	8.5		×	×
	Brother	4.5		×	
	Subtotal	60.1			
United States	IBM	8.0	×	×	×
	Hewlett-Packard	4.5		×	×
	Xerox	3.6	×	×	×
	Texas Instruments	2.5		×	
	Subtotal	18.6			
Europe	Siemens	3.5	×		×
	Honeywell	1.0	×		
	Subtotal	4.5			
Other		16.8			

Exhibit 12 *(continued)*

U.S. Line Impact Printer Market, 1984 (market share in units)

Country of Manufacture	Manufacturer	% Share	Fully Formed	Dot Matrix
United States	Dataproducts	31.0	×	
	IBM	23.0	×	×
	Teletype	8.0	×	
	Centronics	7.0	×	
	Hewlett-Packard	6.0		×
	Printronix	6.0	×	×
	Genicom	1.5	×	
	Subtotal	82.5		
Japan	NBC	4.1	×	
	Fujitsu	1.6	×	
	Hitachi	0.7	×	×
	Subtotal	6.4		
Europe	Mannesmann	2.1	×	
Other		8.0		

wide variety of choices regarding specifications for products. The GENICOM presence in the branded printer market was not so strong, though efforts were underway to increase the importance of that market.

The product positioning of the GENICOM line had been for the professional user. Both for data processing and for word processing, the strength of GENICOM's product line had been in the commercial rather than the personal segments. The current product line was more durable, had more capability, and was more expensive than the bulk of the personal printer market. The GENICOM products could be compared to IBM office typewriters; they were generally considered "over-engineered" for the home market. GENICOM was giving some consideration to the personal printer market, to compete with Epson, Okidata, Toshiba and others. It recognized that among other factors a new product line, rather than modification of an existing product, would be necessary to compete in this highly price-competitive market.

Distribution

In early 1985, GENICOM products were distributed through a distributor network which focused on industrial users and on wholesale/retail distributors who serviced end user needs. Consideration was given to entering retail distributorship relations with large companies or with independently owned and franchised chains.

The GENICOM distribution system was not vertically integrated at that time. Although GENICOM had been contemplating expanding the distributor network slightly to effect better geographic coverage of markets, other plans suggested that they develop recognition of authorized dealers through the current distributor network. A schematic representation of the GENICOM distribution system is presented in Exhibit 13.

While prices and margins for dot-matrix impact printers had been dropping as market pressures grew, the future could be said to be nothing but certain. Curtis Powell considered the union negotiations a critical turning point in the firm's history.

Exhibit 13 Domestic Multi-Tier Distribution Channels

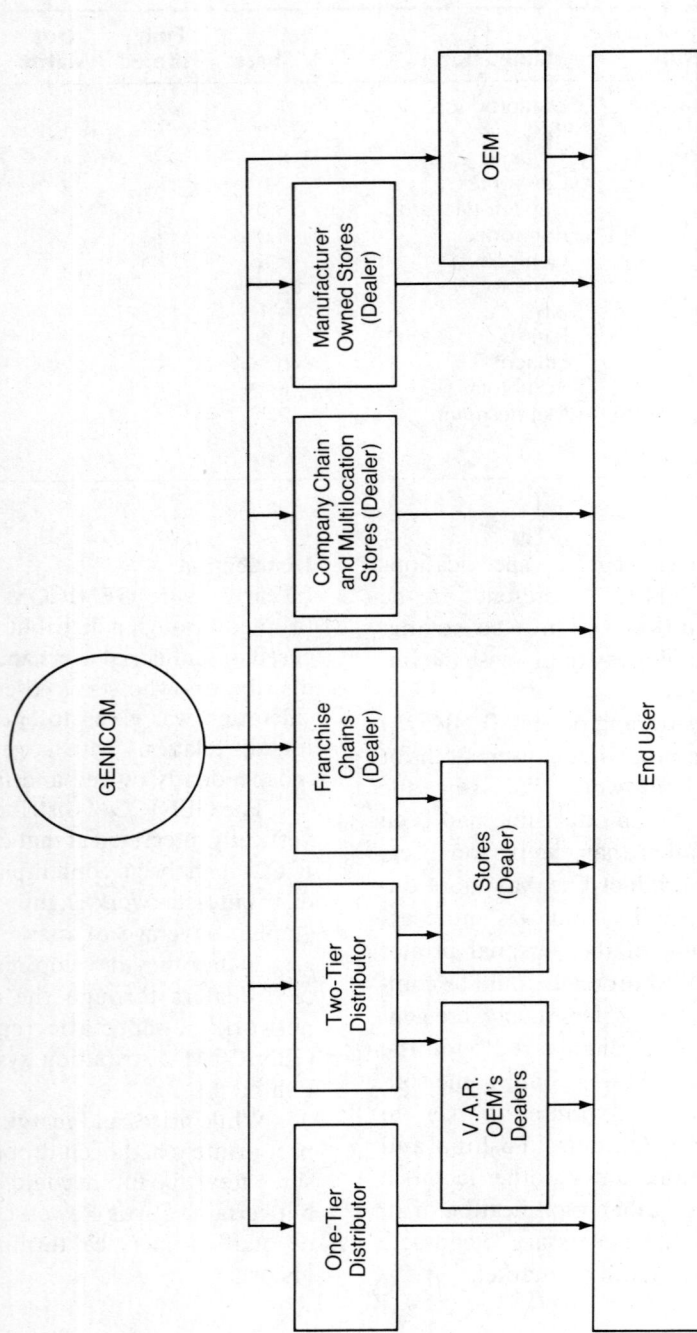

The United Effort

Local 124   Park Station P.O. Box 2245   Waynesboro, Va. 22980

Negotiations Report

On Tuesday afternoon the negotiating committee met with Relations and a lawyer to start contract talks. Right away, without putting any paperwork on the table, this lawyer wanted us to tell him ways management can cut *four dollars an hour* off the cost of labor. According to him, the cost per hour, including wages and benefits, is fourteen dollars an hour and this is, "significantly higher" than other workers are making in Waynesboro and must drop to ten dollars total of wages and benefits. He was even so helpful as to offer selections, like a smorgasbord, if you will, of items from which *we* could decide where to make the cuts.

For our consideration he laid out: rate cuts, night shift differential pay, vacation time cuts and other paid time off, give up bump rights, retraining, premium pay for some overtime, call in pay, medical benefits and the list goes on. All he wants *us* to do is decide where to cut to come up with a four dollar price cut. He pointed out that the wages in the lower job rates are much to high and will have to be cut to make us more comparable with other wage earners in Waynesboro.

Based on the claim that Genicom needs for us to cough up four dollars worth of wages and benefits, we naturally figured the company was going broke so we asked a question about the financial condition of the business. The reply was contrary to what you might suspect based on them wanting cost cuts. It turns out that the company is *making* money but wants to make *more* money and in order to do that they want to get into our pocket.

Just as we figured, when the word got out in the plant, you became furious to think that the company would be so greedy as to come after the wages and benefits you have worked years for and some of you even walked a picket line for a hundred and two days in 1969 to get. There is a growing demand from the union membership to hold work stoppages to protest these unrealistic demands by management and it appears the time will come for that kind of action! The next meeting with management is scheduled for May 6th and Boris "Red" Block will be here for that meeting. We will have a full membership meeting the next day, Tuesday, May 7th, to let you know what is going on and how negotiations are progressing. At that time we will be *led by the membership* about what action you want to take.

After we listened to what management had to say about their thoughts we laid out our proposals and informed them that the list was only a partial list of what we think is needed in a new contract. Some of what we are looking at includes strong job security language, improvement in pensions and downward adjustments in our contributions to the pension plan, a better severance pay clause, insurance coverage to be nothing less than we now have, improvements in S&A benefits, cost of living clause, contract language improvements and a general wage increase. And, as we pointed out, there are other things we are looking at which we will lay on the table later. What happens in negotiations and what we are able to do is directly dependent on you and how much support you are willing to give.

It's your Local and "The Members Run This Union!"

The United Effort

Local 124   Park Station P.O. Box 2245   Waynesboro, Va. 22980

The Members Decide

At the end of the second session of negotiations management still insists on demanding a $4.00 an hour wage and benefit concession from you. They set the record straight so there would be no mistake in anyones mind we were told "we are taking it." We asked time and time again what they would do with the $4.00 if they can take it and we were told rather matter of factly, "we are going to put in in our pockets." It's not that Genicom didn't make a profit last year its just plain and simple they just want to add an additional $3200.00 an hour to their pockets (300 employees × $4.00 per hr. = $3200.00 an hour) at your expense.

At a full house special membership meeting, 1st and 2nd shift, the committee was instructed to take a secret ballot strike vote. We normally keep the meetings to one hour but due to the number of members who wanted to speak, the meeting lasted well over the normal length of time and then a vote was taken, which was in favor of a strike action. As we have said before, this local doesn't have a history of strike action but the workers at Genicom feel they have no choice but to fight on the issues of wages and

working conditions in this plant. Management sometime ago decided to cut the rate of the mold machine operators from R13 to R9 and it seems this only wet their appetite to want to take even more. We filed a grievance and processed it through the required steps of the grievance procedure and we will be taking action on that grievance at the proper time of which you will be notified.

We don't need to tell you how important it is for everyone to support the strike action. The issue is over a rate cut on one job but remember, the bigger issue is now management is saying they are going to cut $4.00 off of everyone in wages and benefits. Whether they can get away with it or not depends on you and everyone in the plant. The stakes are high and it's up to you to decide. Do you just fork over the $4.00 in wages and benefits or do you join your fellow workers and fight?

Shop Steward Election

There will be a meeting at Jim Durcin's desk today, five minutes before the end of lunch break, to nominate and elect a shop steward.

Appendix 3

GENICOM Printer Flash
Date May 31, 1985   No. 85-6

To All Employees:

In response to the excessive amount of publicity in the local press concerning GENICOM's negotiations with the UE Local 124, the following advertisement will appear in tomorrow's Waynesboro News-Virginian and Sunday's Stanton News Leader. We felt you, as GENICOM employees, should be the first to have this information.

What's Really Happening at GENICOM

GENICOM and its negotiations with Local 124 have been the subject of much discussion in our community and among GENICOM employees in recent weeks. All the information to this point has come from the Union. Since so much is at stake for GENICOM, its employees, and our community, we believe management should do its best to assure that the people who may be affected understand what is happening—and why.

GENICOM is a Waynesboro company that is dedicated to remaining a Waynesboro company. That dedication is reflected in GENICOM's proposals to UE Local 124 to establish a wage and benefit program that will allow GENICOM to meet competition while providing GENICOM workers with wages and benefits in line with community standards.

As part of the negotiations process, GENICOM provided wage survey data to Local 124 on both GENICOM's national competition and its Waynesboro neighbors. Reflecting that data, GENICOM's proposal includes job rates from $6.50 to $12 per hour, three weeks paid vacation, eight holidays, medical and dental insurance at a cost of $4 per week to employees, a defined benefit pension plan with limited contributions by employees, as well as company paid life and disability programs.

Starting in 1954, and for nearly 30 years, General Electric Company conducted manufacturing operations at the current GENICOM facility in Waynesboro. Under General Electric, wages were negotiated on a national basis. As a result, Waynesboro wage and salary costs reached levels which are out of line with the electronics industry and with the Waynesboro community. GENICOM Corporation was formed to operate the Business purchased from G.E. GENICOM is now managed by people who are committed to establishing and maintaining a successful and profitable business—because it is our only business. In the 19 months since GENICOM acquired its business, it has been operated on a profitable basis. This was particularly true in 1984, when the market for computers and related equipment was robust. The Business is less profitable now that its market has become much softer and competition for sales of electronic products such as GENICOM's has become very intense. GENICOM management is determined and committed to reducing costs and competing.

These costs reductions can be accomplished either by moving operations to GENICOM's existing lower cost locations or by lowering costs in Waynesboro. GENICOM has decided to stay in Waynesboro. The wage and benefit concessions requested will make Waynesboro a competitive manufacturing location—a manufacturing location with a future. These concessions will not be easy or insignificant for GENICOM workers to accept, but they are not unreasonable. Competitive wages will make operations in Waynesboro much more economically attractive for GENICOM and increase GENICOM's incentive to maintain and expand those operations, thus offering more job security to Waynesboro workers and greater stability to the Waynesboro community.

C.W. Powell
President and Chief Executive Officer
GENICOM Corporation

405

The United Effort
Local 124   Park Station P.O. Box 2245   Waynesboro, Va. 22980

Genicom Should Tell It Like It Is, Instead of Wanting to Pocket 6½ Million Dollars of Its Employees and the Community

Thats what Genicom wants in concessions from the hourly workers. Genicom said thats not all. They are going to get a like amount from the lower paid salary workers and supervisors.

Not once have they said they are going to cut top paid Genicom employees such as Mr. Powell.

Genicom says they are dedicated to remaining in Waynesboro. If that is so, why have they moved over 600 jobs to Mexico, and continue to move jobs out of Waynesboro. They say they need concessions from their employees to do this. But they refuse to put in writing to the Union that these concessions will keep jobs in Waynesboro.

Instead the Company tells us they want to "put the money in their pockets." They go on to say they will use some of this money to buy other plants in other states. This will not bring jobs to Waynesboro. The Company is going to run the plants where they buy them. Not once has the Company said they would brings jobs back from Mexico with the $4 per hour concessions that they want.

The Truth Is!

The Company proposal to the Union means 2 less paid holidays per year, it means that most employees would lose 2 weeks paid vacation per year. All employees would take pay cuts. Some Genicom families would take cuts of $12,000 per year. As for the pensions and the insurance, the proposal is to leave it as it is now. The Company proposal would take away all of the night shift bonus, the few sick days workers have now, and would do away with rest breaks.

If the company really means that they will bring more jobs to Waynesboro. They should be willing to put it in writing.

If the Company really means to have greater stability for the Community they should reinvest the extra profits in the Genicom Waynesboro plant. Not take the money and buy plants in other states.

Genicom would like the Community to believe that GE negotiated the last Union contract. *THAT IS NOT SO. GENICOM NEGOTIATED THE LAST CONTRACT.* Mr. Stoner of Genicom Management was part of the last negotiations and he is part of this negotiations. Mr. Stoner plays a big part in negotiations.

The Company admits in their paid ad that they made money with the last Union Contract. They could make money with the new contract that has no cuts.

Its time for Genicom to put in writing to its employees that the Company will keep jobs in Waynesboro. Genicom is making a profit. They should let the employees keep what they have. There should be NO CUTS. Workers should keep their 6 1/2 Million Dollars. This would keep the money in the Community. Not take it to other States and Mexico.

If Genicom takes this money and "puts it in their pockets." Merchants will lose, taxes for other people in the Community will go up and everyone in the Community will lose.

Only top management like Mr. Powell will gain when they line their pockets with our money at Community expense.

Appendix 5

GENICOM

June 13, 1985
This letter was mailed to all hourly employees on 6/14/85. This copy is for your information.

TO: OUR GENICOM EMPLOYEES AND THEIR FAMILIES

I would like to take this opportunity to express my appreciation for the patience being displayed by the majority of our employees during a very difficult time in which we are negotiating a new labor agreement.

GENICOM and its Management team remain dedicated to the resolution of differences with UE Local 124 and the adoption of a new collective bargaining agreement through the negotiation process. Nevertheless, in reflecting on Local 124's recent newsletter concerning strike preparations, we feel compelled to offer our thoughts on some questions and other appropriate subjects that should be addressed by the Union's lawyer at Sunday's meeting.

QUESTION: Is the Company required to pay wages to strikers during an economic strike?

ANSWER: No, the Company is not required to pay wages to economic strikers.

QUESTION: Is the Company required to pay the premiums to continue health insurance, life insurance and other benefits for strikers during an economic strike?

ANSWER: No, the Company is not required to continue payments for benefits to economic strikers.

QUESTION: Are economic strikers eligible for Virginia unemployment benefits during an economic strike?

ANSWER: No, state law disqualifies employees involved in a "labor dispute."

QUESTION: Is it possible for the UE to guarantee that GENICOM will change its proposals because of strike action?

ANSWER: No, negotiations are a give and take process that may remain unchanged in the face of employee strikes or Company lockouts.

QUESTION: If there is no agreement for a new contract by June 23rd, is the Company required to keep the current contract in effect?

ANSWER: No, at that time the Company may unilaterally implement its final proposal.

QUESTION: Can economic strikers be permanently replaced by new workers if the Company decides to continue operations without them?

ANSWER: Yes, federal law allows a company to continue operations with new employees. The law also does not require the Company to discharge these employees to allow returning strikers to resume their jobs. Replaced strikers who indicate they wish to return to work on the Company's terms may fill open positions if any exist or be placed on a hiring list ahead of non-employees.

Once again let me say we, as GENICOM's Management team, remain dedicated to reaching agreement with UE Local 124 *without* any strike action. However, we are also dedicated to continue the growth of a viable business in Waynesboro. In order to accomplish this, we *must* reduce our cost structure to a level that will allow GENICOM to meet our competition.

Currently, the demand for our printers is poor due to a downturn in the computer market and foreign competition. This market situation, and GENICOM's decision to maintain Waynesboro as our primary production location, demand the changes we have proposed to the UE.

We have furnished wage data on Waynesboro and our national competition to the Union negotiating committee establishing that our proposals are competitive with both Waynesboro and national rates.

Under one proposal, wages would run between $6.00 per hour and $11.50 per hour and benefits would remain at current levels or slightly better. In recognition of the economic impact that such concessions may have, we have offered

alternative proposals such as eliminating sick days, night shift differential and afternoon breaks. These reductions would increase the wage proposal to between $6.50 and $12.00 per hour. All other benefits would remain the same or slightly better.

We hope that our employees, their families and their collective bargaining representatives will consider all these factors before taking any action that could be injurious to both the Employees and the Company.

Sincerely,
Curtis W. Powell
President/Chief Executive Officer

GENICOM SEEKS WORKERS; UNION CLAIMS 'A THREAT'

By SERGIO BUSTOS
Staff Writer

WAYNESBORO—Genicom's advertisement in area newspapers seeking immediate applications for production and maintenance workers was seen as "a threat" Monday by a union representative as negotiations between both sides continue toward a June 23 contract deadline.

The company advertised in two newspapers, including The Daily News Reader today, seeking immediate applications for production and maintenance employees "to fill regular, full-time positions . . ."

The company is advertising "an excellent compensation package, including competitive pay rates, beginning at $6.50 per hour, up to $12 per hour . . ." It also offers medical and dental benefits as well as up to three weeks paid vacation.

"We figure it's a threat—a form of intimidation," said George Stevens, the union representative for United Electrical Radio and Machine Workers local 124. He said he was "not surprised" by management's action.

"We are still a long way apart in negotiations," added Stevens, who said Monday's negotiations saw a change in management's position.

"It's still the same basic proposal of a $4 cut in wages and benefits," said Stevens.

Genicom management officials would not comment when reached Monday.

William Freeman, union president, however, said management's latest move would "intimidate workers" and result in their not joining further work stoppages. He added it "was a definite threat" and "was not expected."

"I imagine it (management's action) would work," said Freeman, who said Monday's negotiation session between the two was "terrible."

"I'm amazed that each offer (from management) is worse than the one made before," said Freeman.

Management's action is similar to the action taken by the McQuay division of Snyder General in April when its workers went on strike.

Following six days of striking, however, McQuay union workers agreed to a three-year contract after management threatened to hire non-union workers.

Negotiations between Genicom management and the union began late in April and will continue until June 23, according to Stevens.

A LEADING MANUFACTURER OF ELECTRONIC EQUIPMENT IS SEEKING IMMEDIATE APPLICATIONS

For Production & Maintenance Employees To FNI Regular, Full-Time Positions Including: janitors, assemblers, machine operators, inspectors, testors, stock keepers, drivers, material handlers, painters, machinists, machine repairers, electricians, electronic technicians, and tool & die makers.

The company offers an excellent compensation package including competitive pay rates, beginning at $6.50 per hour, up to $12 per hour (depending upon skill); substantial medical & dental benefits; company paid life & disability programs; eight paid holidays; up to three weeks paid vacations; and a defined benefit pension plan.

INTERESTED, QUALIFIED
CANDIDATES SHOULD APPLY
BY CALLING
(703)949-7553 or (703) 949-7652

Case 18

Applied CAD Knowledge, Inc.: The "Boom/Splat" Syndrome

Something is seriously wrong with this planet. Look at us. I'm working a hundred and twenty hours a week or more, and not catching up. I've got these two friends—both recently divorced, like me—who aren't working at all: they're living off their girl friends, and loving it. One of them is basking in Hawaii. But here I am, busting my ass and giving my customers problems anyhow.

Some guys go on television and say, "Send money now," and people *do*. I ask my best customer to send $30,000, and he goes bankrupt instead. What's wrong with this picture?

Jeff Stevens, president and 90 percent owner of Applied CAD Knowledge, Inc., was reporting on current sales and production levels to the two business school professors who comprised his Board of Directors. It was late August of 1987, and the three men sat in a booth at Bogie's restaurant. The waitress, Patty, was accustomed to these monthly meetings; she offered another round of Lite beer. "Make mine cyanide," said Stevens. "On the rocks, please."

This case has accompanying videotapes featuring Jeff Stevens, president and owner of Applied CAD Knowledge, Inc., in a question and answer session with an Executive MBA class that can be purchased from Northeastern University, College of Business Administration, Boston, MA 02115.

This case was prepared by John A. Seeger, Bentley College, and Raymond M. Kinnunen, Northeastern University, as a basis for class discussion. Distributed by the North American Case Research Association. All rights reserved to the authors and the North American Case Research Association. Permission to use the case should be obtained from the authors and the North American Case Research Association. Copyright © 1990 by John A. Seeger and Raymond M. Kinnunen. Reprinted with permission.

Applied CAD, a small service bureau which designed electronic circuit boards, was experiencing the highest sales levels in its three-year history. June sales had reached $50,000—leaving a backlog of $90,000; July shipments had set a record at $58,000; August would be nearly as high. The problem facing Stevens through the summer of 1987 was a shortage of good designers to work as part-time freelancers. The surge in business saw Stevens sitting at the computer consoles himself, doing design work on second and third shifts, six or seven days a week. After eight weeks of this schedule, the strain was showing. One director asked about the longer-range sales picture, and Stevens summed it up:

> There's nothing on the books at all for late fall, and not much likely. Every major customer we have is in "busy phase" right now. When these designs are finished, it will be another four to six months before their next generation of product revisions. In the meantime, everybody is burned out. All I'm hoping for right now is a front porch, a rocking chair, a lobotomy, and a drool cup.

The Electronics Industry and Circuit Board Design

The United States electronics industry in 1987 was a sprawling giant, some of whose sectors were growing while others remained in a protracted slump. In 1986, total industry size was variously estimated as $100 billion to $182 billion.

A basic part of nearly every electronic product was the printed circuit board (PCB) to which a variety of electronic components were attached. These components ranged from old-fashioned resistors and capacitors to transistors and the most modern integrated circuit chips. All components needed some sort of platform to sit on, and some way to make connection with other components.

In the 1930s and '40s, circuit boards were made from thin, non-conducting fiberboard with metal pins and sockets attached. Assembly operators wound the wire leads of the circuit's resistors, capacitors, etc. around the proper pins and soldered them in place. By the 1960s, this technology had become highly automated. Numerically-controlled machines positioned the components and connected the pins to one another with wires. By the 1980s both the pins and the wires had disappeared, replaced by electrically conductive lines which were "printed" or plated onto (or under) the surface of the board itself. Wire leads from electrical components are inserted through small holes in the board and soldered on the underside. (Figure 1 shows specimen PCBs.)

The increasing complexity of electronic circuits presented a problem for PCB technology. When connections were made with wires, assemblers simply attached one end, routed the wire over the top of everything between the two pins involved, and attached the other end where it belonged. With printed circuits, however, designers are constrained to two dimensions on a flat board; they must route the line between two pins without touching any other lines. Furthermore, efficient design calls for the components to be tightly packed together, grouped by function. Designers frequently find situations where they cannot lay out a trace from one point to another without interfering with other traces.

"Multilayer" PCBs (see Figure 2) ease this problem by providing "upstairs" layers on the board, allowing the designer to "go over the top." Multilayer boards contain at least three layers of traces, and sometimes more than twenty layers. Skilled designers seek to minimize the number of layers required for a given circuit, in order to reduce manufacturing costs: multilayer PCBs are far more expensive to manufacture.

Board design was made more complicated by increasing density of components, by sensitivity of components to heat (some threw off large amounts of heat, while others would go haywire if their operating temperature was disturbed), and by radio-frequency interference (some components generated static, while others might "hear" the noise and try to process it). The layout of components on the board had tremendous impact on how well the finished product worked, as well as on its manufacturing cost.

In 1983, according to *Electronic Business* magazine, multilayer boards had sales of $900 million, or 25 percent of the PCB market. By 1993, multilayer boards were forecast to reach sales of $5.6 billion, or 41 percent market share. Exhibit 1 shows PCB sales and projections by type of board.

Frost and Sullivan, Inc., a New York market research firm, estimated (in "The Printed Circuit Board Market in the U.S.," July, 1986, quoted by permission) that the total U.S. PCB market reached $3.7 billion in sales in 1985, a decrease of 12 percent from 1984's production. PCBs were projected to grow to a likely $6.5 billion by 1990 and to $10.8 billion in 1995. Multilayer PCBs were expected to be the fastest-growing type, averaging 15.7 percent per year annual growth. A little over half the market was served in 1985 by independent PCB fabricators, as opposed to captive suppliers, Frost and Sullivan said.

Trends in Circuit Board Design Equipment

Originally (and still, for simple circuits), an engineer or technician worked from a "schematic" drawing of the circuit, which showed how the various components were connected. On a large layout table, the PCB designer manually drew in the components and linked them with black tape (or ink), to produce a "photo master" film which was in turn used to manufacture the circuit board. As circuits became more complex, the manual process bogged down.

By the mid 1970s, computer-aided design (CAD) vendors began to offer computer systems specifically for PCB designing. Racal-Redac, Inc., a British firm, was the first to offer a system which permitted PCB designers to interact with the computer, trying various routings of traces to see how they looked on the graphic display. This approach, based on the moderate-price DEC PDP-11, competed well against established CAD systems such as those made by Gerber Scientific or Computervision, whose equipment was priced in the $500,000 class and still lacked interactive design capability.

By 1982, prices for PCB design systems had fallen below $100,000. New CAD equipment makers entered the field with automated routing or documentation features which carried substantial advantages over the established Redac software. Calay and Cadnetix, as examples, introduced strong entries—neither being compatible with the Redac or Sci-Cards or Telesis equipment already in the field. Racal-Redac Ltd. had perhaps taken the greatest strides to tailor its software to run on a variety of computers. Said Ian Orrock, chief executive of Redac's CAD division in England, "We're all going to end up being software houses."

Another important feature of the new CAD equipment was ease of use; the older systems might require months of learning time before a designer became proficient.

Service Bureau Operations

In the late 70s, with high equipment costs and low availability of trained designers, only the largest electronics firms designed and produced their own PCBs. Service bureaus took advantage of the market opportunity, acting as the primary design resource for smaller clients and as peak load designers for firms with in-house capacity. These small service firms specialized in design,

working for electronics companies in the same way an architect works for real estate developers. (Figure 3 shows the relationship between firms in the PCB production process).

When the design phase of a job was finished, the computer tape or disk containing the final output would be carried to a photoplotting service bureau for creation of the precision film needed for manufacturing. The equipment for photoplotting was far more complex and expensive than the computer systems needed for design. Only a few design shops in the New England area had their own photoplotting capability; they performed this work for other service bureaus and for electronics firms' in-house design departments as well as for their own design clients.

The actual production of PCBs might be done by the electronics company itself or by a fabrication shop which specialized in the work. The New England area was home to some 80 to 100 fab shops, many of which offered design as well as manufacturing services. A few large firms (Hadco at $125 million in sales) were equipped to service very large orders—100,000 or more boards of a design—but most fab shops fell in the $1 to $2 million size range, with an average order size of 25 to 30 relatively small boards. One such fabricator estimated its average low-tech PCB was priced at $22 each, with a setup charge of $150. For the most difficult boards, in small quantities with rigid testing requirements, Applied CAD's customers might pay as much as $1,000 each for fabrication.

As electronics firms purchased and began to use the newer CAD systems, they wanted service bureaus to be equipped with similar or compatible machines. A firm with its own Telesis equipment, for example, would favor Telesis-equipped service bureaus for its overload work. Service bureaus felt the pressure to acquire the most up-to-date hardware and software available, in order to qualify as bidders.

When a service bureau invested in CAD equipment, the sheer size of the investment created pressure to use the equipment intensively.

Multi-shift operations were common, but the supply of designers to staff them was severely limited. Typically, a service bureau did not hire permanent staff for all three shifts: the work load was too unpredictable. Service bureaus generally hired moonlighting designers from established electronics firms to staff their second and third shifts.

Printed circuit board design requires a peculiar combination of human skills, primarily in spatial geometry, circuit insight, memory, and persistence. A talented designer—perhaps capable of completing a complex design in three weeks of console time—might be several times more productive than a "journeyman." In the early 1980s, talented designers willing to work odd shifts were earning over $100,000 per year; few of them had college educations.

Most customers requested separate quotations for each board; often, customers asked for bids from several service bureaus. Design clients always ran on tight schedules, Jeff Stevens observed, wanting their work to be delivered "yesterday":

> Circuit board design is usually one of the last steps before a new product goes into production. Our design time may be the customer's time-to-market. It's natural for them to be in a hurry.

For the design of a large, complex, four-layered PCB a client might pay between $10,000 to $15,000. Such a project might require five to six man weeks of labor input (two-thirds of which might be designer's time); it might involve extensive communication between Applied CAD and a wide variety of the client's technical personnel, and it would often require the designer to work through the night at various project stages to make deadlines. Much of the time would be spent sorting out and coordinating conflicting information and directions from different technical people in the client company. Stevens noted,

> Even our clients themselves won't always know completely what they want. When we take their directions to their logical conclusions, problems often occur. Then we have to show them what developed. You spend a lot of time on the phone with clients, sometimes at 3 a.m. Often, I make decisions for the client, so the work can go ahead; later, I have to convince the client the decision was right.

Clients were inclined to stay with their existing service bureaus, unless they were severely burned. Good relationships between service staff and engineering personnel helped minimize communication errors, and availability of the data base from the original job allowed for revisions or modifications at much lower cost. Design reliability remained a key attribute of a service bureau's reputation, since whole product lines (or engineers' jobs) might depend on the PCB design's working properly and on its prompt delivery:

> We had one job, in the old days, where a satellite was literally sitting on the launch pad, waiting for a corrected module design. The engineers had discovered a design flaw. They flew into town with the specs, and then took turns sitting behind the designer at the scope, or sitting beside their hotel room telephone, waiting to answer any questions that might come up. In this business, you have to deliver.

Future Trends in PCB Design

By the end of 1986, a number of vendors had developed PCB design packages to run on personal computers—primarily the IBM XT or AT machines. These software systems, some including automatic routing, were priced as low as a few hundred dollars or as high as $13,000, and varied widely in their features and capabilities. In-house design capability thus became practical for most electronics firms, although many lacked the PCB expertise that still marked the better service bureaus. Freelance designers, too, could now acquire their own equipment. Exhibit 2 compares the features and prices of 24 such software packages.

In the 1980s, as the cost of entering the service bureau business dropped, many new firms appeared. Jeff Stevens observed, "When I started at Redac in 1978, there were three service bureaus in New England. By 1983 there were maybe a dozen. Now there might be seventy-five, and it could reach 100 in another year." In 1987, several competing service bureaus in the area were owned by former employees of Racal-Redac, where Jeff himself had learned the business. Exhibit 3 lists the major competitors in the Northeastern United States in 1986. The small firms in this listing were design specialists like Applied CAD, Stevens noted; the larger firms all supplied finished boards to their customers.

For the longer run, some industry analysts speculated that constant advances in miniaturizing electronic circuits might permit semiconductor technology to reduce certain whole PCBs (such as those developed for computer memory) into a single integrated circuit chip.

Applied CAD Knowledge, Inc.: History

Jeff Stevens had learned the rudiments of circuit board design in his first job after high school graduation, as a technician in a five-person product development laboratory. Here, in 1975, one of his duties was to prepare enlarged prints of circuits, using black tape on white mylar. In another, concurrent job as a technician in an electronics manufacturing firm, he learned how the circuits themselves worked.

In 1977, Stevens left his two technician jobs for an entry-level design position with Racal-Redac in Littleton, Massachusetts. Redac operated a service bureau to complement its sales of DEC hardware and British software. As a pioneer in the field, Redac at the time boasted a near-monopoly in powerful systems dedicated to PCB design. Jeff Stevens, in a training rotation, joined Redac's service bureau as a data-entry technician.

> We had three computer systems—about 20 people altogether. A system then cost about $200,000 and a lot of companies didn't have enough design work to justify buying one.

In data entry, you prepare code to represent all the terminals and components on the board. I refused to code the first job they gave me, and nearly got fired. Finally I convinced them that the job *shouldn't* be coded: the turkey who engineered it had the diodes in backward, and the circuit wasn't going to work. About a week later, they put me in charge of data entry, supervising the guy who had wanted to fire me.

Stevens became a designer, then a lead designer, then operations manager of the service bureau. Under his leadership, the operation dramatically improved its reputation for quality and on-time delivery, as well as its financial performance:

> When I took over in October of 1981, monthly sales were $50,000 and monthly expenses were $110,000. In six months we turned it around: monthly sales were $110,000 and expenses were $50,000. There was a tremendous amount of dead wood. We had a big bonfire with it, and went from 26 people to 16. In some ways, it was a brutal campaign, I guess.

In June 1983, Stevens left Racal-Redac to work as a consulting designer, helping electronics firms with their CAD decisions as well as doing freelance design work. He had developed design and management expertise and established a reputation in industry circles which he could now broker directly to clients who were familiar with his previous work.

In December 1983, Jeff established Applied CAD while still working from his home in Pepperell, Massachusetts. By purchasing used computer equipment and installing it himself in his living room, Stevens was able to hold his initial investment to $35,000; the largest cost element was $28,000 for the software purchased from his former employer. (Financial data on Applied CAD's latest three years of operation are shown in Exhibit 4.)

> The equipment pretty well filled up the living room, and through the summer I couldn't run it during the daytime: we didn't have enough electricity to cool it down. Winter solved that problem, though; the PDP-11 heated the house.

Jeff had sought the help of a business school professor, who lived in Littleton, to negotiate the purchase of software from his former employer. This professor and another, also from a well-known Boston area school, purchased small stock interests as Applied CAD was incorporated and became members of the Board of Directors. By the fall of 1985, the Board met monthly for three to four hours, usually during the first week of the month. At most meetings the Board first discussed the previous month's sales and current levels of cash, accounts receivable, backlog and payables. (Exhibit 5 shows the data recorded in these talks.) Other typical agenda items ranged from the purchase of new equipment and/or software, to marketing, to personnel problems and bank relationships.

In late 1984, Applied CAD leased a 1,000 square foot office suite on the ground floor of a new building near the Merrimack River in Tyngsboro, Mass. Jeff Stevens designed the interior space to hold a central computer room (with special air conditioning), a darkened "console room" for the actual design work, and a large front office. By January of 1985, the computing equipment was installed and operating. The console room was furnished with two Recaro ergonomic chairs (at $1,100 each) for the designers' use; the front office held a large receptionist's desk and a sparse collection of work tables, file cabinets, and spare hardware.

Hardware and Software

After moving into his new quarters, Jeff Stevens located another PDP-11/34 computer—this one for sale at $7,000. Adding it to his shop required purchase of another Redac software package, but the added capacity was needed. Other competing CAD systems were now available, but the decision to stick with Redac seemed straightforward to Jeff:

> Redac systems had several advantages. They were specifically dedicated to PCB design work and they had software that was brutally efficient. They were familiar to most of the freelance designers

in the area. Wide acceptance of Redac's software makes it easier to get overflow work from companies who demanded compatibility with their own equipment. Not to mention that I know this gear backward and forward, and could keep several machines busy at once.

The Redac software was originally developed in 1972, which made it very old by industry standards. Jeff pointed out, however, that because machines were slower in 1972 and had much less memory, their software *had* to be extremely efficient. Having used this software for a long time, he said, "I've been able to make process modifications to improve its efficiency, and I know all its intricacies." Jeff had developed some proprietary software for PCB design work which he believed kept him at the cutting edge of the competition. At times, he wondered about the possibilities of licensing his proprietary software to other PCB design firms. He concluded, however, that the small market for this type of software product would probably not justify the necessary marketing and additional product development costs.

In addition to the original equipment purchased by Jeff in 1983, the company purchased a VAX Model 11/751 and a Calay Version 03 in December of 1985 at a cost of approximately $170,000. (See Exhibit 6 for the cash flow statements prepared for the bank to obtain a loan.) The VAX was intended to be used as a communications and networking device and for developing new software. The Calay was a dedicated hardware system that included an automatic router which could completely design certain less complex boards without an operator. On more complex boards it could complete a major percentage of the board, leaving a designer to do the remainder. Jeff and the Board felt that this automatic routing capability might open a new market for the company for less complex boards. They also felt that the manufacturer of the Calay, as well as the Calay user group, would supply new customer leads. Some of these expectations had been met.

In September of 1986, a software upgrade to

the Calay was purchased for approximately $28,000. Although bank financing was available, Jeff decided to pay cash for this purchase, to avoid raising his monthly fixed expenses. The new purchases gave Applied CAD enough machine capacity to support some $2 million in annual sales.

The VAX, however, was not being fully used as originally intended—to allow hands-off automation of the firm's varied pieces of computing equipment, as well as providing batch data processing capacity. In its ultimate form, the VAX might actually operate the older, more cumbersome systems. It would be able to juggle dozens of design tasks between work stations and autorouters, queuing and evaluating each job and calling for human intervention when needed. One director, visualizing robots sitting in Applied CAD's Recaro chairs, called this the "Robo-Router plan." To carry it out would require an additional investment of approximately $15,000 in hardware and another $10,000 to $20,000 in programming, along with a significant amount of Jeff's time. The investment would result in very substantial cost reductions and reduced dependence on freelance designers, but it would only pay for itself under high volume conditions.

Applied CAD's Organization

Jeff oversaw all operations in his company, did all the high level marketing/sales contact work with clients, and did much of the technical design work as well. Another full-time designer was hired in May of 1985 but had to be terminated in September of 1986 due to persistent personal problems. Steve Jones, Jeff's data manager and former assistant at Redac, became a full-time employee in January, 1986. Among other duties, Steve covered the telephone, coordinated technical work done by freelance contractors in Jeff's absence, and performed various administrative duties. Steve had a B.S. in engineering and, before Redac, had worked for other PCB electronics companies. In April of 1987 Jeff hired John

Macnamara, a former subcontract designer, on a full-time, salaried basis.

In May of 1987 Jeff also hired a part-time person to keep the books, write checks, and handle other office related matters. For her first three months, she focused on straightening out the books and tax-related items. She was also trying to find time to set up an accounting package on the personal computer. The package had been purchased in August of 1986 (at the request of Board members), for the purpose of generating accurate monthly statements. Since the company's founding, the Board had been asking for accurate end-of-month data on sales, accounts receivable, cash balance, backlog, and accounts payable. They also wanted monthly financial statements, although Stevens himself saw little point in them: cash flow projections served his immediate needs. The accounting package was chosen by one of the Board members, based partly on its broad capabilities. For example, it could assist in invoicing and aging receivables.

Jeff had other capable designers "on call"—available for freelance project work when the company needed them. Depending upon the market, there were time periods when Jeff could obtain the services of several contractors to meet peak work loads. In general, design contractors worked on a negotiated fixed-fee basis for completing a specific portion of a design project. In July of 1987, however, (after sales in June reached approximately $50,000 and the backlog reached $90,000) Jeff found it hard to attract contract designers with free time. The backlog consisted of about 15 boards ranging in price from $800 to $15,000. The electronics industry had turned upward and in busy times everyone was busy. Consequently, free-lance designers were committed to their own customers or employers who were also busy. Jeff attempted to fill the production gap by working as a third-shift designer.

At most of its meetings, the Board of Directors spent considerable time discussing the current business climate and the future sales outlook. This usually led to a discussion of hiring someone to take over the marketing and sales function. It was generally agreed that such a person could not only contribute to the company's growth in sales but also free up a considerable amount of Jeff's time that could be devoted to design and operational matters. When Applied CAD was busy, however, Jeff had very little time to devote to finding, hiring, and working with such a person. Even if one were hired, a salesperson would require Jeff's time for introductions to the present customers and for responding to questions about new sales potentials.

When Applied CAD was *not* busy, Jeff's concern over the reliability of future cash flows made him hesitant to make the major salary commitment that a marketing professional would require. He was aware of the contrary pressures: "I can't get out of the 'boom-splat' syndrome," he said.

To Jeff, the "splat" came when backlogs and cash balances fell. The winter of 1987, for example, had felt to him like hitting a wall. (See Exhibit 5 for monthly totals of sales, backlogs, etc. as estimated by Jeff at monthly Board meetings.)

Current Business Options

In August of 1987, Jeff was contemplating the current business climate, his accomplishments with Applied CAD over the past three years, and where the company was headed. His major objective—agreed with the Board—was growth. Jeff had discussed many times with his Board the needs for a marketing person and a promotional brochure for the company. He hoped to attract someone with top management credentials, who could work with him as a peer. On occasion, he had talked with marketing people about the job, but most of these prospective employees lacked the level of skills and PCB experience Jeff hoped to acquire. He had also talked with commercial artists about design of a brochure. Jeff and his Board felt that a "first class" brochure would cost between $5,000 and $10,000.

Marketing in the PCB business, especially among companies with sales of under $1 million, was characterized as informal. Very few companies had full-time people devoted to the marketing task; in most cases it was the owner-president who handled marketing and sales. Most small companies had their own list of faithful customers and new customers tended to come by word of mouth. In the under $1 million segment it was not uncommon for a company when extremely overloaded with work to farm out a board to a competitor. Also, certain other services, such as photoplotting, were done by shops that also did design work. Consequently, there was considerable communication among the competitors; the players seemed to know who got what jobs.

The marketing job at a company like Applied CAD would consist mainly of coordinating the advertising and sales brochure, calling on present customers, and attempting to find new customers. Such a person needed a working knowledge of PCB design which required experience in the industry. People with these qualifications normally made a $40,000–$50,000 base salary plus commissions; frequently their total compensation exceeded $100,000 per year. Of major concern to Jeff was Applied CAD's erratic history of sales and cash balances, and the difficulty of predicting sales volume any further than two months in advance. He balked at taking on responsibility for an executive-level salary, lacking confidence in the future. "This would probably be somebody with kids to feed or send to college," Jeff said. "How could I pay them in slow times?"

Still, marketing appeared to be the function most critical to achieving the growth rates Jeff Stevens and his Board hoped for. It was key, also, in meeting the major potential threat posed by the recent availability of inexpensive software which could enable personal computers (PCs) to design printed circuit boards (see Exhibit 2). Jeff had heard that some of that new software could perform almost as well as the more expensive equipment used by Applied CAD. He wondered how the advent of low-cost software might be turned into an opportunity, not a threat.

Four possible responses had occurred to Jeff and his Board: Applied CAD could ignore the PC software, adopt it, distribute it, or sell its own software to the PC users. Ignoring the new technology might work in the short run, since the complex boards designed by Applied CAD would not be the first affected; in the long run, however, failure to keep up with technology would leave more and more jobs subject to low-cost competition.

By adopting the new software for his next equipment expansion, Applied CAD could take a proactive stance. Jeff could buy a system or two to see how good they were, and hire people to work on the new systems on a freelance basis. Of course, he would need a flow of jobs to experiment with. A variation of this alternative was to sit back and wait while ready to move quickly if he saw something developing.

A third alternative, acting as a distributor for the PC software, would give Applied CAD a product to sell to prospects who insisted on doing their own design. This could establish relationships with people who might later need overload capacity.

Fourth, Applied CAD could proceed with development of its proprietary software, creating a product to sell to PC users. Jeff estimated that his Automated Design Review System could save both time and grief for other designers. In some tasks, it could cut the required design time in half. In all jobs, the capability to check the finished design against the original input automatically and completely could improve quality. ADRS already existed in rough form; it was one of the elements which would make up the "Robo-Router" system, if that were implemented.

Many of these options seemed to require significant marketing skills—strengths—where the company was presently weak. The technical questions could be answered, if Jeff had the time to work on them. But the marketing questions called for a person with extensive industry experience, broad contact, a creative imagination, and the ability to make things happen.

Amid all the other problems facing him as owner of a small business, Jeff was trying to figure out how to shape his business for the long-range future, and how to attract the kind of person he could work with to assure growth—and survival. He looked across the table at Bogie's restaurant, caught the eye of one director, and yawned. Tonight, after this meeting, he hoped to finish the design of a particularly complicated board. His best customer was desperate for this job.

Exhibit 1   Sales and Projections for PCBs by Type of Board

PCB Type	1983			1993	
	Sales in $ Millions	Market Share	Annual Growth Rate	Sales in $ Millions	Market Share
Multilayer	900	25%	20%	$5,600	41%
Double-sided	2,000	56	13	6,700	49
Flexible	353	10	10	916	7
Single-sided	307	9	4	454	3
	$3,560	100%		$13,670	100%

*Source: *Electronic Business,* Feb. 1, 1985, p. 87.

Exhibit 2 Low Cost PC Board Design Software Available, Spring, 1987

TABLE 1—REPRESENTATIVE LOW-COST PC-BOARD LAYOUT PACKAGES

COMPANY	PRODUCT	BASE PRICE	REQUIRED HARDWARE	OPERATING SYSTEM	AUTO-ROUTER	AUTO-ROUTER PRICE	COMPATIBLE NET LISTS	MAXIMUM NUMBER OF COLORS	MAXIMUM NUMBER OF TRACES	MAXIMUM NUMBER OF COMPONENTS	MAXIMUM NUMBER OF LAYERS	PACKAGING TECHNOLOGIES
ABACUS SOFTWARE	PCBOARD DESIGNER	$195	ATARI 520ST OR 1040ST	GEM	●			2	1100 LINES	250	2	SMD
ACCEL TECHNOLOGIES	TANGO-PCB	$495	IBM PC/XT OR PC/AT	MS-DOS	●		ACCEL, OMATION, ORCAD	16	25,000 LINES	1000	9	SMD
APTOS SYSTEMS	CRITERION II	$4000	ARTIST 1 CARD AND IBM PC/XT OR PC/AT	MS-DOS	●	$5000	APTOS, FUTURENET, P-CAD	16	2000 NETS	1000	50	SMD, ECL, ANALOG
AUTOMATED IMAGES	PERSONAL 870	$8000	IBM PC/XT OR PC/AT	MS-DOS			APPLICON, FUTURENET, ORCAD	16			16	SMD, HYBRID
B&C MICROSYSTEMS	PCBDE	$395	IBM PC/XT OR PC/AT	MS-DOS (AND THE AUTOCAD DRAFTING PACKAGE)			B&C	16				
CAD SOFTWARE	PADS-PCB	$975	IBM PC/XT OR PC/AT	MS-DOS	●	$750	FUTURENET	16	4511 NETS	784	30	SMD, FINE-LINE
CASE TECHNOLOGY	VANGUARD PCB	$4250	IBM PC/XE, SUN-3, OR DEC MICROVAX	MS-DOS, UNIX, OR VMS	●	$5500	CASE	16	2000 NETS	1000	256	SMD
DAISY SYSTEMS	PERSONAL BOARDMASTER	$8000	IBM PC/AT OR DAISY PL386	UNIX			DAISY	7	14,000 LINES	14,000	255	SMD
DASOFT DESIGN	PROJECT: PCB	$950	IBM PC/XT OR PC/AT	MS-DOS	●		DASOFT	6			4	SMD
DESIGN COMPUTATION	DRAFTSMAN-EE	$1147	IBM PC/XT OR PC/AT	MS-DOS	●	$2450		16	4000 NETS	300	20	FINE-LINE
DOUGLAS ELECTRONICS	DOUGLAS CADCAM	$395	APPLE MACINTOSH	MACINTOSH				2				SMD, ANALOG
ELECTRONIC DESIGN TOOLS	PROCAD	$2495	IBM PC/XT OR PC/AT AND 80800 COPROCESSOR	MS-DOS	●	$2495	ELECTRONIC DESIGN TOOLS	16	10,000 NETS	3000	56	SMD, CONSTANT-IMPEDANCE
ELECTRONIC INDUSTRIAL EQUIPMENT	EXECUTIVE CAD	$11,000	IBM PC/XT OR PC/AT	MS-DOS	●		ELECTRONIC INDUSTRIAL EQUIPMENT	16			4	SMD, ECL
FUTURENET	DASH-PCB	$13,000	IBM PC/AT AND 32032 COPROCESSOR	UNIX	●		FUTURENET	4			10	FINE-LINE
HEWLETT-PACKARD	EGS	$7000	HP 9000	HP-UX			HP	15			255	HYBRID
KONTRON	KAD-286	$10,400	IBM PORT	MS-DOS			KONTRON	64	5300 LINES	3200	256	ECL, SMD, HYBRID
PERSONAL CAD SYSTEMS	PCB-1	$6000	IBM PC/XT OR PC/AT	MS-DOS	●	$6000	P-CAD, FUTURENET	16	1000 NETS	300	50	SMD
RACAL-REDAC	REDBOARD	$12,000	IBM PC/XT OR PC/AT	MS-DOS	●		RACAL-REDAC	16	1900 NETS	511	16	SMD
SEETRAX (IN US, CIRCUITS AND SYSTEMS)	RANGER	$5000	IBM PORT	MS-DOS	●	$2000	SEETRAX	16	10,000 LINES	1400	16	SMD
SOFTCIRCUITS	PCLOPLUS	$1024	COMMODORE AMIGA 1000	AMIGADOS				16				
VAMP	McCAD	$395	APPLE MACINTOSH	MACINTOSH	●	$995	VAMP	2	32,000 LINES	32,000	6	SMD, METRIC
VISIONICS	EE DESIGNER II	$1875	IBM PC/XT OR PC/AT	MS-DOS	●	$1475		16		900	26	SMD
WINTEK	SMARTWORK	$895	IBM PC/XT OR PC/AT	MS-DOS	●		WINTEK	3			6	SMD
ZIEGLER INSTRUMENTS (IN US, CADOM)	CADDY ELECTRONIC SYSTEM	$2495	IBM PC/XT OR PC/AT	MS-DOS	●	$2500	ZIEGLER	16			128	ANALOG

Exhibit 3   PC Design Service Bureaus in New England

Design Houses by Sales Volume

0–1 Million Dollars/Year

Abington Labs.
Berkshire Design
Cad Tec
Cadtronix, Ltd.
Computer Aided Circuits, Inc.
Dataline PCB Corp.
Design Services
Energraphics
Graphics Technology Corp.
Herbertons, Inc.
HET Printed Circuit Design
High Tech Cad Service Co.
Jette Fabrication
LSI Engineering
PC Design Company
Pac-Lab, Inc.
Packaging for Electronics
PC Design Services
Point Design, Inc.
Power Processing, Inc.
Product Development Co.
Qualitron Corp.
Quality Circuit Design, Inc.
Research Labs, Inc.
Scientific Calculations, Inc.
Tracor Electro-Assembly Inc.
Winter Design

1–2 Million Dollars/Year

Automated Images, Inc.
Automated Design, Inc.
CAD Services, Inc.
Antal Associates
Multiwire of New England
Teccon
Tech Systems & Design
Kenex, Inc.
Alternate Circuit Design Technology
Photofabrication Technology, Inc.

2–5 Million Dollars/Year

Tek-Art Associates
Stratco Reprographix
Altek Co.
Eastern Electronics Mfg. Corp.
Datacube, Inc.
Owl Electronic Laboratories

5–10 Million Dollars/Year

Triad Engineering Co.
Photronic Labs, Inc.

10+ Million Dollars/Year

Algorex Corp.
ASI Automated Systems, Inc.
Augat Interconnection Group
Racal-Redac Service Bureau
Synermation, Inc.

Source: Beacon Technology, "New England Printed Circuit Directory." Copyright © 1985. Reprinted by permission.

Exhibit 4   Financial Statements of Applied CAD Knowledge, Inc.

	Balance Sheet		
	1985	**1986**	**1987**
Assets			
Current assets:			
Cash	$128,568	$ 14,148	$ 33,074
Accounts receivable, trade	18,865	15,375	14,250
Prepaid taxes and other current assets	4,853	1,200	5,074
Total current assets	152,286	30,723	52,398
Property and equipment	174,079	190,079	203,079
Less accumulated depreciation	48,697	86,357	124,062
Total property and equipment	125,382	103,722	79,017
Total assets	$277,668	$134,445	$131,415
Liabilities and Stockholders' Equity			
Current liabilities:			
Accounts payable, trade	$127,685	$ 9,025	$ 21,823
Current maturities of long-term debt	13,300		
Income taxes payable	4,008		2,303
Other current liabilities	5,000	5,373	70
Total current liabilities	149,993	14,398	24,196
Long-term debt, less current maturities	41,121	83,247	53,663
Stockholders' equity:			
Common stock, no par value; authorized 15,000 shares, issued and outstanding 1,000 shares	25,000	25,000	25,000
Retained earnings	61,554	11,800	28,556
Total stockholders' equity	86,554	36,800	53,556
Total liabilities and stockholders' equity	$277,668	$134,445	$131,415
Statement of Income and Retained Earnings			
Net revenues	$328,262	$232,540	$346,627
Cost of revenue:			
Salaries, wages and outside services	134,686	116,835	209,998
Research and development	14,154	7,551	13,731
Software costs	65,131	18,864	
Total cost of revenue	$213,971	$143,250	$223,729
Gross profit	114,291	89,290	122,898
Selling, general, and administrative expenses	72,320	143,051	77,732
Operating profit	41,971	(53,761)	45,166
Bad debt expense			(28,660)
Interest income (expense), net	2,331	3,176	(10,103)
Income before income taxes	44,302	(50,185)	6,403
Income taxes	4,508	0	0
Net income	39,794	(50,185)	6,403
Retained earnings, beginning of year	21,760	62,385	22,154
Retained earnings, end of year	$ 61,554	$ 11,800	$28,557

Exhibit 5 Monthly Sales and Month-End Receivables, Backlogs, Cash Levels (All in $000's)

	A/R	Sales	Backlog	Cash
January 1986	$18	$20	$20	$98
February	*	10	*	*
March	18	10	12	62
April	18	10	20	28
May	24	20	26	26
June	*	10	*	*
July	14	25	*	18
August	70	50	30	15
September	90	40	*	8
October	50	30	*	26
November	19	5	10	17
December	24	10	18	14
January 1987	13	3	*	7
February	40	21	*	8
March	35	28	22	6
April	32	22	37	11
May	25	22	50	5
June	50	50	90	10
July	90	58	30	10

*Information not available

Exhibit 6 Applied CAD Knowledge, Inc.: Cash Flow Projections as of December 16, 1985

	Dec 1985	Jan 1986	Feb 1986	March 1986	April 1986	May 1986	June 1986	July 1986	Aug 1986	Sept 1986	Oct 1986	Nov 1986	Dec 1986	Total $(000s)
Sales	25	30	30	30	30	30	30	30	30	30	30	30	30	360
Expenses[6]	20	24	29.5	29.5	29.5	29.5	29.5	29.5	29.5	29.5	29.5	29.5	29.5	348.5
Profit	5	6	.5	.5	.5	.5	.5	.5	.5	.5	.5	.5	.5	11.5
Opening Cash	141	148	102	102.5	88	88.5	89	89.5	90	90.5	91	91	91.5	
Receivables	37	17	30	30	30	30	30	30	30	30	30	30	30	
Disbursements[5]	30	24[1]	29.5[3]	29.5	29.5	29.5	29.5	29.5	29.5	29.5	29.5	29.5	29.5	
Taxes[4]		29[2]		15										
Closing Cash	148	102	102.5	88	88.5	89	89.5	90	90.5	91	91	91.5	92	

1. Includes loan payment of 4K/mth.
2. 25% of equipment costing 156K.
3. Includes new employees at 66K/yr.
4. Taxes based on the following assumptions: 1985 Profit of 150K; 50K software expense on new equipment; 20K depreciation on new equipment; 10K misc. expenses; investment tax credit of 15K.
5. Figures do not include depreciation which would only influence total profit.
6. Expenses include rent, heat, light, power, salaries, contract work, telephone, etc. This level of expenses will support sales double those projected.

Figure 1

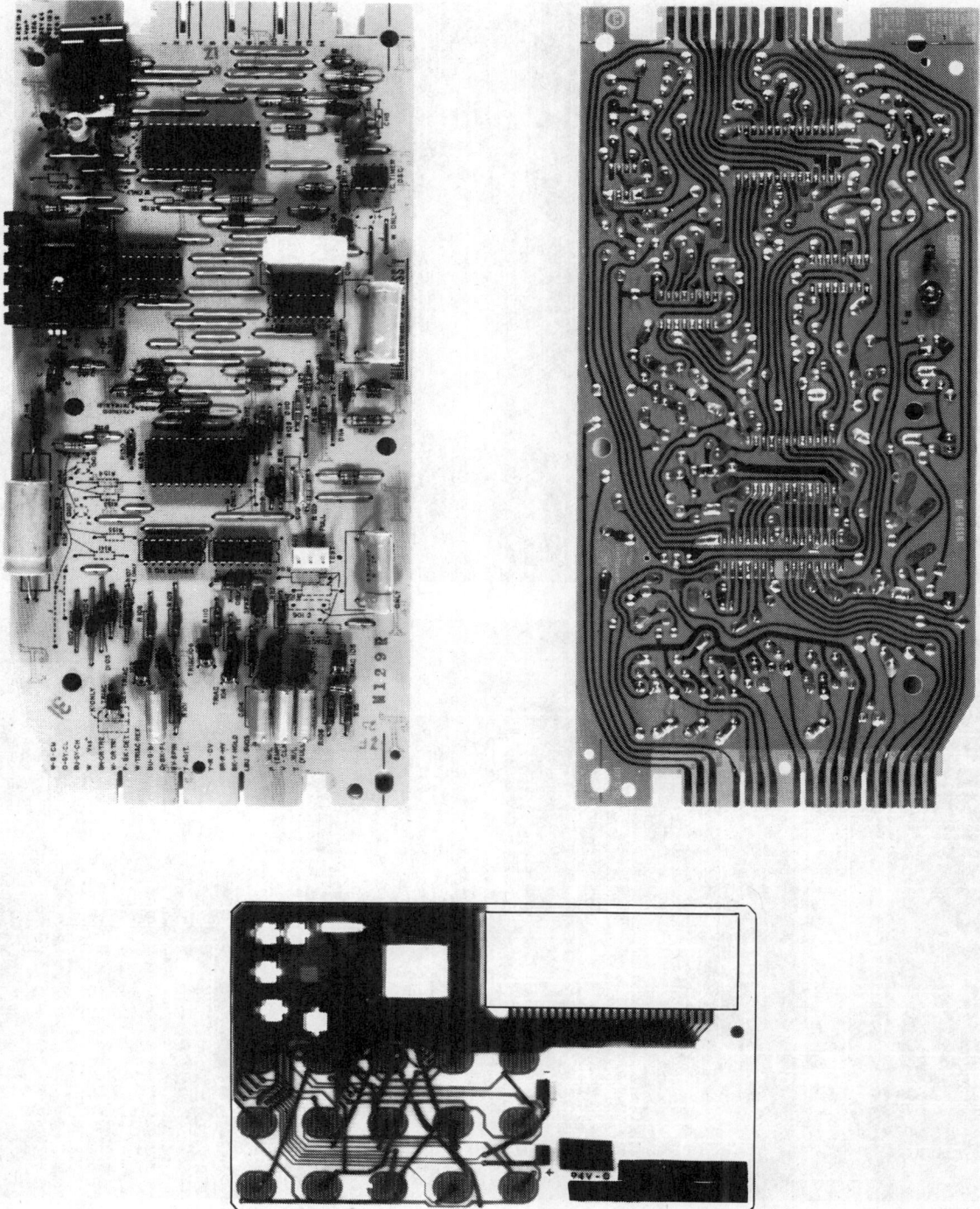

(Above): Top and bottom views of a fully assembled circuit board, taken from a Kenmore washing machine. Electronic components are visible in the top view (left); their soldered connections are visible in the bottom view (right). (Left): Circuit board for a ten-key hand calculator. This board is made of transparent plastic; both the top and bottom levels of traces are apparent.

Figure 2

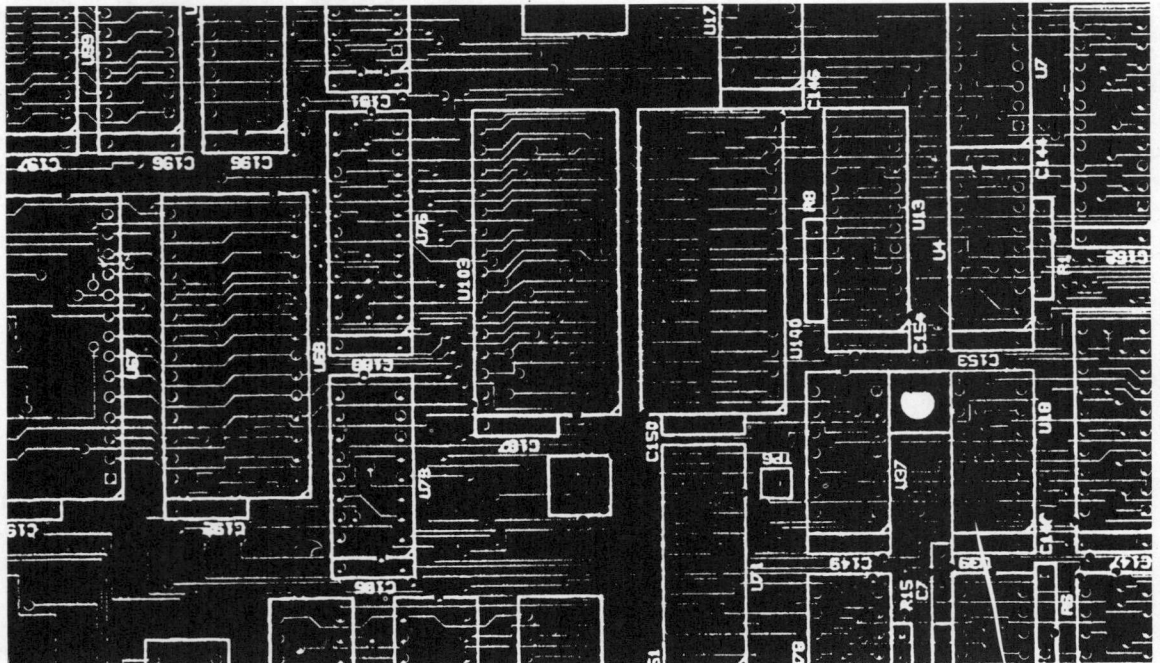

Sections of the top surface (above) and the bottom surface (below) of a four-level circuit board designed by Applied CAD Knowledge for the maker of a communications controller. The entire board measures $10\frac{1}{2}$ x 15 inches.

Figure 3   Work Flow between Firms in Production of Printed Circuit Boards

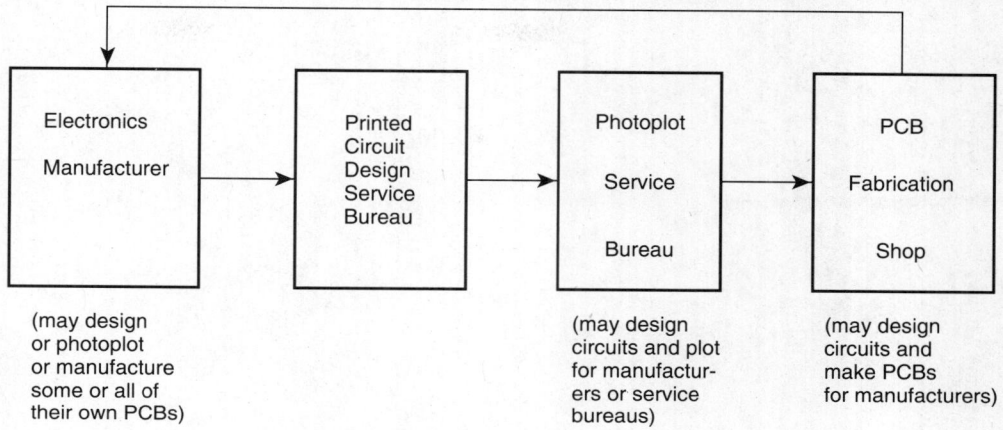

Electronics
Manufacturer

Printed
Circuit
Design
Service
Bureau

Photoplot
Service
Bureau

PCB
Fabrication
Shop

(may design
or photoplot
or manufacture
some or all of
their own PCBs)

(may design
circuits and plot
for manufactur-
ers or service
bureaus)

(may design
circuits and
make PCBs
for manufacturers)

Case 19

Applied CAD Knowledge, Inc. (B)

In September of 1987, as the summer rush slowed, Jeff Stevens began to talk seriously with Jerry King, Regional Sales Manager of Calay Systems, Inc., about the marketing problems of Applied CAD Knowledge, Inc. Stevens wanted someone to become in effect a co-owner and officer of the small firm. King had been a principal in his own service bureau in the very early days of automated PCB design, and retained friendships and contacts with high level personnel in many electronics firms. (Exhibit 1 shows King's resume.)

After a month of conversations and negotiations, including a meeting with the Board of Directors, the two men reached tentative agreement on employment terms which would give King a 3% commission on all company sales, a car allowance, and a base salary of $40,000 per year. Since the marketing person would be influential in pricing many jobs, it was important to preserve his regard for profitability; King was offered a stock interest in Applied CAD, contingent on the bottom line at the end of 1988. With a handshake of agreement, Stevens set out to re-

This case has accompanying videotapes featuring Jeff Stevens, president and owner of Applied CAD Knowledge, Inc. in a question and answer session with an Executive MBA class that can be purchased from Northeastern University, College of Business Administration, Boston, MA 02115.

This case was prepared by Raymond M. Kinnunen, Northeastern University, and John A. Seeger, Bentley College, as a basis for class discussion. Distributed by the North American Case Research Association. All rights reserved to the authors and the North American Case Research Association. Permission to use the case should be obtained from the authors and the North American Case Research Association.

Copyright © 1988 by Raymond M. Kinnunen and John A. Seeger. Reprinted with permission.

duce the terms to an employment contract letter.

The following night, Jerry King called Stevens to express his regret that he would be unable to accept the Marketing VP position, after all: he had just received an offer from AT&T, to set up Australian operations for a new venture. It was simply too good an offer to refuse, King said. A dejected Jeff Stevens reported the development at the next Board meeting; "We're back to square one," he said. "And the next 'splat' is just about to arrive."

Applied CAD's monthly sales dropped to half their mid-1987 level, and the backlog dropped to near zero. On December 8, however, Jerry King called Jeff to say he had just decided against Australia, and would like to apply again for the Marketing Vice President position, if it was still open. Jeff agreed, and the next day Jerry presented to Jeff and the Board a plan for reaching $1 million in sales in 1988, and for growing by $1 million per year in the following two years. (This plan is partially reproduced in Exhibit 2.) Concerned with the timing of cash flows, one of the directors asked how long it would take to generate enough new sales to cover their added marketing expenses. King responded, "If I couldn't provide more than enough sales to cover my pay, I wouldn't take the job."

Although not officially joining Applied CAD until January 4, Jerry spent the rest of December in joint calling, with Jeff, on customers where Calay and Applied CAD shared some interests. In these first weeks, the "chemistry" Jeff Stevens had hoped for became readily apparent. The two men's skills complemented each other well: this would be a highly effective team, Stevens felt.

As 1988 began, King and Stevens continued

to work closely together. Since Applied CAD's office layout did not provide the privacy needed for telephone prospecting, Jerry worked out of his home, joining Jeff several times per week on joint sales calls. At the January 8 meeting of the Board of Directors, the two men presented detailed sales projections for the first quarter and broader estimates for the entire year (see Exhibit 3). One account alone—California PrinCo—held the promise of some $250,000 in sales over the next four months. An old and steady customer of Applied CAD, PrinCo was nearing a decision on a major expansion in their use of circuit boards.

January sales totalled only $6,000 but many prospects seemed close to signing for large orders. At the February 19 Board meeting, Jeff and Jerry predicted sales of $100,000 per month for February and March; it appeared a 1988 sales goal of $1,000,000 might still be reachable. (Exhibit 4 shows monthly sales and backlogs through January, 1988.)

Exhibit 1   Resume

Jerry King

Married
Four Children
Excellent Health

EDUCATION:

FAIRLEIGH DICKENSON UNIVERSITY, Madison, New Jersey
Major: Business Administration

U.S. NAVY, Electronics "A" School, Pearl Harbor, Hawaii

CONTINUING EDUCATION, including numerous seminars and workshops in Corporate Finance, Power Base Selling, Territory Time Management, The Art of Negotiating, Computer Graphics in Electronics, Sales Management and Marketing Techniques.

EXPERIENCE:

GENERAL BUSINESS MANAGEMENT: Establishing policies and procedures for high volume cost efficient business operations, planning promotions for new business development, hiring, training and supervising personnel, including management level, designing and conducting management, sales, marketing and CAD/CAM training seminars internationally.

TECHNICAL BACKGROUND: Twenty one years of direct Printed Circuit Design, Fabrication and Electronics CAD/CAM marketing experience. Helped to create detailed business plans for three start-up companies including a high volume printed circuit design service bureau and raised five million dollars in venture capital used to purchase state-of-the-art CAD/CAM systems and other related equipment. Managed the development and marketing of a PCB Design Automation turn-key system which was sold exclusively to Calma/GE in 1977 and integrated with their GDS1 TRI-DESIGN system. Very strong market knowledge in Computer Aided Engineering (CAE), Computer Aided Design (CAD), Computer Aided Test (CAT), and Computer Aided Manufacturing (CAM).

ACCOMPLISHMENTS:

Particularly effective in areas of personnel management, motivation and training, thereby increasing sales volume production flow, productivity and employee morale. Significant career accomplishments in customer relations, marketing and sales leadership and management.

EMPLOYMENT HISTORY:

1986–Present   Calay Systems Incorporated, Waltham, Massachusetts
                SENIOR ACCOUNT MANAGER
Responsible for a direct territory consisting of Northern Massachusetts, Vermont, New Hampshire, Maine and Quebec.

1985–1986   Automated Systems Incorporated, Nashua, N.H.
                EASTERN REGIONAL SALES MANAGER.

Exhibit 1   (continued)

Responsible for regional design and fabrication service sales with a regional quota in excess of $5 million.

1981–1985   Engineering Automation Systems, Inc., San Jose, California.
              WESTERN REGIONAL SALES MANAGER.

Responsible for new Printed Circuit Design CAD/CAM system. Set up regional office, hired and trained sales and support staff of twelve people. Western regional sales were in excess of fifty percent of the company's business.

              September 1984   PROMOTED TO NATIONAL SALES MANAGER.

1978–1981   Computervision Corporation, Bedford, Massachusetts
              NATIONAL PRODUCT SALES MANAGER.

Responsible for all electronic CAD/CAM system sales and related products. Provided direct sales management and training to the national field sales team, conducted sales training internationally, assisted in developing competitive strategy, technical support and new product development. Reported to the Vice President of North American Division.

              March 1980   PROMOTED TO MANAGER, CORPORATE DEMONSTRATION and
              BENCHMARK CENTER.

Managed team of 38 people who performed all corporate level demonstrations and benchmarks. Supported field offices with technical information and people worldwide. Reported to the Vice President of Marketing Operations. THIS WAS A KEY MANAGEMENT POSITION FOR THE COMPANY.

1966–1978   King Systems, Inc., San Diego, California (A Printed Circuit Design CAD/CAM and NC
              Drilling Service Bureau.)
              FOUNDER, PRESIDENT, CHAIRMAN AND MAJOR STOCKHOLDER.

Served as Chief Executive Officer in charge of all aspects of the operation. Primary activities in sales management, direct field sales and customer relations. Responsible for financial adminstration, production operations and personnel administration. Assesssed future needs and created business planning for increasing market share, facilities capability and penetrating new market opportunity. Developed a new concept in contract services for blanket sales to large government and commercial prime contractors.

Exhibit 2   Excerpts from Jerry King's Dec. 9, 1987, Board Presentation

Introduction

The plan is a detailed road map for taking Applied CAD Knowledge, Incorporated (ACK) from the current sales volume to more than three million annual sales volume over the next three years. It identifies target markets, competitive environment, and sales tactics which will be used for achieving the sales projections during the plan period from January 1st 1988 through December 31st 1990. The projections show a monthly breakdown for 1988 and a yearly number for 1989 and 1990. The monthly projections were created on Lotus and provide for projected, forecasted and actual sales bookings for each month. As each month passes the actual numbers are entered and a goal status report is generated as part of the end of month reporting. At the end of each quarter a new quarter will be added so that there will always be four consecutive quarters of monthly projections.

The aggressive growth which is outlined will require significant expansion of facilities, personnel and equipment in order to maintain consistent QUALITY and ON TIME deliveries and insure REPEAT BUSINESS from established customers. It is required that the management

(continued)

Exhibit 2 *(continued)*

and the Board of Directors of ACK provide the necessary production controls and capital/operating budgets to support expansion commensurate with sales volume increases over the term of the plan.

The PCB design service market can be divided into three major segments. Each of these segments will include companies who design and manufacture electronic equipment for Commercial, Industrial, Aerospace and Military vertical market areas.

Major Accounts & Government Sub-Contractors (MA)

Major Accounts are Fortune 1000 companies. They present a significant opportunity for multiple board contracts and blanket purchase agreements. Any one company could fill ACK's capacity.

Primary Accounts (PA)

Primary accounts are companies who have been doing business for more that three years (not a start-up) and typically do between 5–500 million in annual sales. These companies represent the most consistent level of business. The type of contracts available from this market segment are usually on the level of one to four board designs per month. Typically, each board of project has to be sold separately at the project engineering level.

Venture Start-Up Accounts (VA)

Venture start-up companies usually are operating on stringent budgets. They typically have no internal CAD capability and therefore must rely on outside service. The business potential for this market segment is very significant. This market represents a high risk and therefore is avoided by the major competitors leaving more opportunity for the smaller operation. It is not unusual to obtain sole source product level contracts from companies in this market.

Bookings Projections

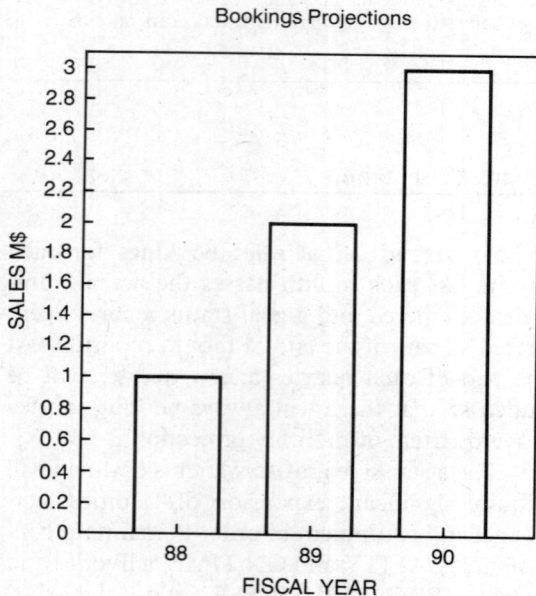

PCB Design Market

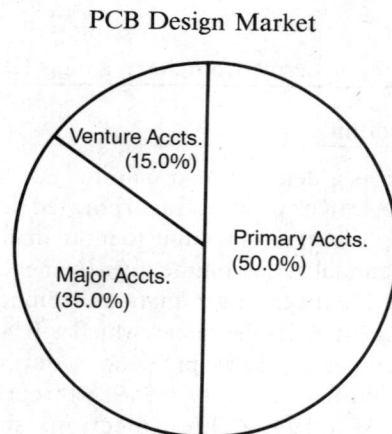

Source: Frost & Sullivan, Oct. 1985.

Exhibit 3 Sales Projections Presented to the Board, January 8, 1988

Forecast Q1 1988: Sales by Customer

Account Name	Jan. 50%	90%	Feb. 50%	90%	Mar. 50%	90%	Total 50%	Total 90%	Grand Total
Customer A	0.0	20.0	0.0	8.0	20.0	0.0	20.0	28.0	48.0
Prospect I	0.0	7.0	0.0	0.0	0.0	0.0	0.0	7.0	7.0
Prospect II	5.0	0.0	2.0	0.0	2.0	0.0	9.0	0.0	9.0
Customer B	0.0	0.0	12.0	0.0	0.0	0.0	12.0	0.0	12.0
Customer C	12.0	0.0	0.0	0.0	0.0	0.0	12.0	0.0	12.0
Customer D	0.0	0.0	12.0	0.0	0.0	0.0	12.0	0.0	12.0
Customer E	0.0	30.0	0.0	0.0	20.0	0.0	20.0	30.0	50.0
Prospect III	0.0	0.0	15.0	0.0	20.0	0.0	35.0	0.0	35.0
Prospect IV	0.0	0.0	15.0	0.0	20.0	0.0	35.0	0.0	35.0
Prospect V	0.0	6.5	0.0	0.8	0.0	3.8	0.0	11.1	11.1
Customer F	0.0	0.0	0.0	7.0	0.0	0.0	0.0	7.0	7.0
Total	17.0	63.5	56.0	15.8	82.0	3.8	155.0	83.1	238.1

Forecast FY 1988: Bookings by Product Type

	Service	Software	Total	Accum Total
January	33	15	48	48
February	48	5	53	101
March	53	15	68	169
Quarter 1	**124**	**35**	**169**	
April	60	5	65	234
May	68	15	83	317
June	75	5	80	397
Quarter 2	**203**	**25**	**228**	
July	80	15	95	492
August	85		85	577
September	88	15	103	680
Quarter 3	**253**	**30**	**283**	
October	90	8	98	778
November	95	15	110	888
December	98	15	113	1001
Quarter 4	**283**	**38**	**321**	

(continued)

Exhibit 3   *(continued)*

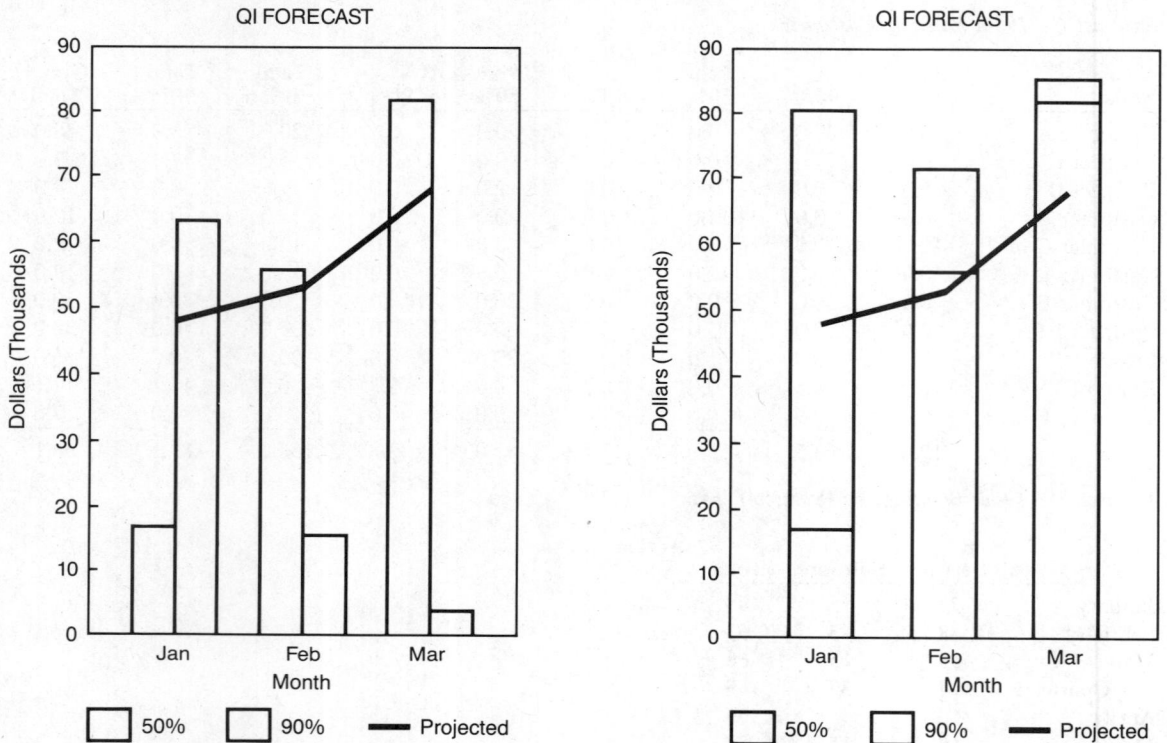

QI FORECAST

QI FORECAST

50%   90%   ▬ Projected

50%   90%   ▬ Projected

Exhibit 4   Monthly Sales and Month-End Receivables, Backlogs, Cash Levels (All in $000's)

	A/R	Sales	Backlog	Cash		A/R	Sales	Backlog	Cash
January 1986	18	20	20	$98	January 1987	13	3	—	7
February	—	10	—	N/A	February	40	21	—	8
March	18	10	12	62	March	35	28	22	6
April	18	10	20	28	April	32	22	37	11
May	24	20	26	26	May	25	22	50	5
June	—	10	—	N/A	June	50	50	90	10
July	14	25	—	18	July	90	58	30	10
August	70	50	30	15	August	—	25	—	10
September	90	40	—	8	September	34	25	50	21
October	50	30	—	26	October	62	48	9	8
November	19	5	10	17	November	50	24	—	—
December	24	10	18	14	December	14	34	9	33
					January 1988	8	6	—	19

Case 20

The Lincoln Electric Company, 1989

People are our most valuable asset. They must feel secure, important, challenged, in control of their destiny, confident in their leadership, be responsive to common goals, believe they are being treated fairly, have easy access to authority and open lines of communication in all possible directions. Perhaps the most important task Lincoln employees face today is that of establishing an example for others in the Lincoln organization in other parts of the world. We need to maximize the benefits of cooperation and teamwork, fusing high technology with human talent, so that we here in the USA and all of our subsidiary and joint venture operations will be in a position to realize our full potential.

George Willis, CEO, The Lincoln Electric Company

The Lincoln Electric Company is the world's largest manufacturer of arc welding products and a leading producer of industrial electric motors. The firm employs 2400 workers in two U.S. factories near Cleveland and an equal number in eleven factories located in other countries. This does not include the field sales force of more than 200. The company's U.S. market share (for arc-welding products) is estimated at more than 40 percent.

The Lincoln incentive management plan has been well known for many years. Many college management texts make reference to the Lincoln plan as a model for achieving higher worker productivity. Certainly, the firm has been successful according to the usual measures.

This case was prepared by Arthur Sharplin, McNeese State University, Lake Charles, LA 70601. Reprinted with permission.

James F. Lincoln died in 1965 and there was some concern, even among employees, that the management system would fall into disarray, that profits would decline, and that year-end bonuses might be discontinued. Quite the contrary, twenty-four years after Lincoln's death, the company appears as strong as ever. Each year, except the recession years 1982 and 1983, has seen high profits and bonuses. Employee morale and productivity remain very good. Employee turnover is almost nonexistent except for retirements. Lincoln's market share is stable. The historically high stock dividends continue.

A Historical Sketch

In 1895, after being "frozen out" of the depression-ravaged Elliott-Lincoln Company, a maker of Lincoln-designed electric motors, John C. Lincoln took out his second patent and began to manufacture his improved motor. He opened his new business, unincorporated, with $200 he had earned redesigning a motor for young Herbert Henry Dow, who later founded the Dow Chemical Company.

Started during an economic depression and cursed by a major fire after only one year in business, the company grew, but hardly prospered, through its first quarter century. In 1906, John C. Lincoln incorporated the business and moved from his one-room, fourth-floor factory to a new three-story building he erected in east Cleveland. He expanded his work force to 30 and sales grew to over $50,000 a year. John preferred being an engineer and inventor rather than a manager, though, and it was to be left to another Lincoln to manage the company through its years of success.

In 1907, after a bout with typhoid fever forced him from Ohio State University in his senior year, James F. Lincoln, John's younger brother, joined the fledgling company. In 1914 he became active head of the firm, with the titles of General Manager and Vice President. John remained president of the company for some years but became more involved in other business ventures and in his work as an inventor.

One of James Lincoln's early actions was to ask the employees to elect representatives to a committee which would advise him on company operations. This "Advisory Board" has met with the chief executive officer every two weeks since that time. This was only the first of a series of innovative personnel policies which have, over the years, distinguished Lincoln Electric from its contemporaries.

The first year the Advisory Board was in existence, working hours were reduced from 55 per week, then standard, to 50 hours a week. In 1915, the company gave each employee a paid-up life insurance policy. A welding school, which continues today, was begun in 1917. In 1918, an employee bonus plan was attempted. It was not continued, but the idea was to resurface later.

The Lincoln Electric Employees' Association was formed in 1919 to provide health benefits and social activities. This organization continues today and has assumed several additional functions over the years. In 1923, a piecework pay system was in effect, employees got two weeks paid vacation each year, and wages were adjusted for changes in the Consumer Price Index. Approximately thirty percent of the common stock was set aside for key employees in 1914. A stock purchase plan for all employees was begun in 1925.

The Board of Directors voted to start a suggestion system in 1929. The program is still in effect, but cash awards, a part of the early program, were discontinued several years ago. Now, suggestions are rewarded by additional "points," which affect year-end bonuses.

The legendary Lincoln bonus plan was proposed by the Advisory Board and accepted on a trial basis in 1934. The first annual bonus amounted to about 25 percent of wages. There has been a bonus every year since then. The bonus plan has been a cornerstone of the Lincoln management system and recent bonuses have approximated annual wages.

By 1944, Lincoln employees enjoyed a pension plan, a policy of promotion from within, and continuous employment. Base pay rates were determined by formal job evaluation and a merit rating system was in effect.

In the prologue of James F. Lincoln's last book, Charles G. Herbruck writes regarding the foregoing personnel innovations:

> They were not to buy good behavior. They were not efforts to increase profits. They were not antidotes to labor difficulties. They did not constitute a "dogooder" program. They were expression of mutual respect for each person's importance to the job to be done. All of them reflect the leadership of James Lincoln, under whom they were nurtured and propagated.

During World War II, Lincoln prospered as never before. By the start of the war, the company was the world's largest manufacturer of arc-welding products. Sales of about $4,000,000 in 1934 grew to $24,000,000 by 1941. Productivity per employee more than doubled during the same period. The Navy's Price Review Board challenged the high profits. And the Internal Revenue Service questioned the tax deductibility of employee bonuses, arguing they were not "ordinary and necessary" costs of doing business. But the forceful and articulate James Lincoln was able to overcome the objections.

Certainly since 1935 and probably for several years before that, Lincoln productivity has been well above the average for similar companies. The company claims levels of productivity more than twice those for other manufacturers from 1945 onward. Information available from outside sources tends to support these claims.

Company Philosophy

James F. Lincoln was the son of a Congregational minister, and Christian principles were at the center of his business philosophy. The confidence that he had in the efficacy of Christ's teachings is illustrated by the following remark taken from one of his books:

> The Christian ethic should control our acts. If it did control our acts, the savings in cost of distribution would be tremendous. Advertising would be a contact of the expert consultant with the customer, in order to give the customer the best product available when all of the customer's needs are considered. Competition then would be in improving the quality of products and increasing efficiency in producing and distributing them; not in deception, as is now too customary. Pricing would reflect efficiency of production; it would not be a selling dodge that the customer may well be sorry he accepted. It would be proper for all concerned and rewarding for the ability used in producing the product.

There is no indication that Lincoln attempted to evangelize his employees or customers—or the general public for that matter. Neither the chairman of the board and chief executive, George Willis, nor the president, Donald F. Hastings, mention the Christian gospel in their recent speeches and interviews. The company motto, "The actual is limited, the possible is immense," is prominently displayed, but there is no display of religious slogans, and there is no company chapel.

Attitude toward the Customer

James Lincoln saw the customer's needs as the *raison d'etre* for every company. "When any company has achieved success so that it is attractive as an investment," he wrote, "all money usually needed for expansion is supplied by the customer in retained earnings. It is obvious that the customer's interests, not the stockholder's, should come first." In 1947 he said, "Care should be taken . . . not to rivet attention on profit. Between 'How much do I get?' and 'How do I make this better, cheaper, more useful?' the difference is fundamental and decisive." Willis, too, ranks the customer as management's most important constituency. This is reflected in Lincoln's policy to "at all times price on the basis of cost and at all times keep pressure on our cost . . ." Lincoln's goal, often stated, is "to build a better and better product at a lower and lower price." "It is obvious," James Lincoln said, "that the customer's interests should be the first goal of industry."

Attitude toward Stockholders

Stockholders are given last priority at Lincoln. This is a continuation of James Lincoln's philosophy: "The last group to be considered is the stockholders who own stock because they think it will be more profitable than investing money in any other way." Concerning division of the largess produced by incentive management, he wrote, "The absentee stockholder also will get his share, even if undeserved, out of the greatly increased profit that the efficiency produces."

Attitude toward Unionism

There has never been a serious effort to organize Lincoln employees. While James Lincoln criticized the labor movement for "selfishly attempting to better its position at the expense of the people it must serve," he still had kind words for union members. He excused abuses of union power as "the natural reactions of human beings to the abuses to which management has subjected them." Lincoln's idea of the correct relationship between workers and managers is shown by this comment: "Labor and management are properly not warring camps; they are parts of one organization in which they must and should cooperate fully and happily."

Beliefs and Assumptions about Employees

If fulfilling customer needs is the desired goal of business, then employee performance and productivity are the means by which this goal can best be achieved. It is the Lincoln attitude toward employees, reflected in the following comments by James Lincoln, which is credited by many with creating the success the company has experienced:

> The greatest fear of the worker, which is the same as the greatest fear of the industrialist in operating a company, is the lack of income . . . The industrial manager is very conscious of his company's need of uninterrupted income. He is completely oblivious, evidently, of the fact that the worker has the same need.

> He is just as eager as any manager is to be part of a team that is properly organized and working for the advancement of our economy . . . He has no desire to make profits for those who do not hold up their end in production, as is true of absentee stockholders and inactive people in the company.

> If money is to be used as an incentive, the program must provide that what is paid to the worker is what he has earned. The earnings of each must be in accordance with accomplishment.

> Status is of great importance in all human relationships. The greatest incentive that money has, usually, is that it is a symbol of success . . . The resulting status is the real incentive . . . Money alone can be an incentive to the miser only.

> There must be complete honesty and understanding between the hourly worker and management if high efficiency is to be obtained.

Lincoln's Business

Arc-welding has been the standard joining method in shipbuilding for decades. It is the predominant way of connecting steel in the construction industry. Most industrial plants have their own welding shops for maintenance and construction. Manufacturers of tractors and all kinds of heavy equipment use arc-welding extensively in the manufacturing process. Many hobbyists have their own welding machines and use them for making metal items such as patio furniture and barbecue pits. The popularity of welded sculpture as an art form is growing.

While advances in welding technology have been frequent, arc-welding products, in the main, have hardly changed. Lincoln's Innershield process is a notable exception. This process, described later, lowers welding cost and improves quality and speed in many applications. The most widely-used Lincoln electrode, the Fleetweld 5P, has been virtually the same since the 1930's. The most popular engine-driven welder in the world, the Lincoln SA-200, has been a gray-colored assembly including a four-cylinder continental "Red Seal" engine and a 200 ampere direct-current generator with two current-control knobs for at least four decades. A 1989 model SA-200 even weighs almost the same as the 1950 model, and it certainly is little changed in appearance.

The company's share of the U.S. arc-welding products market appears to have been about forty percent for many years. The welding products market has grown somewhat faster than the level of industry in general. The market is highly price-competitive, with variations in prices of standard items normally amounting to only a percent or two. Lincoln's products are sold directly by its engineering-oriented sales force and indirectly though its distributor organization. Advertising expenditures amount to less than three-fourths of a percent of sales. Research and development expenditures typically range from $10 million to $12 million, considerably more than competitors.

The other major welding process, flame-welding, has not been competitive with arc-welding since the 1930s. However, plasma-arc-welding, a relatively new process which uses a conducting stream of super heated gas (plasma) to confine the welding current to a small area, has made some inroads, especially in metal tubing manufacturing, in recent years. Major advances in technology which will produce an alternative superior to arc-welding within the next decade or so appear unlikely. Also, it seems likely that changes in the machines and techniques used in arc-welding will be evolutionary rather than revolutionary.

Products

The company is primarily engaged in the manufacture and sale of arc-welding products—electric welding machines and metal electrodes. Lincoln also produces electric motors ranging from one-half horsepower to 200 horsepower. Motors constitute about eight to ten percent of total sales. Several million dollars has recently been invested in automated equipment that will double Lincoln's manufacturing capacity for 1/2 to 20 horsepower electric motors.

The electric welding machines, some consisting of a transformer or motor and generator arrangement powered by commercial electricity and others consisting of an internal combustion engine and generator, are designed to produce 30 to 1,500 amperes of electrical power. This electrical current is used to melt a consumable metal electrode with the molten metal being transferred in super hot spray to the metal joint being welded. Very high temperatures and hot sparks are produced, and operators usually must wear special eye and face protection and leather gloves, often along with leather aprons and sleeves.

Lincoln and its competitors now market a wide range of general purpose and specialty electrodes for welding mild steel, aluminum, cast iron, and stainless and special steels. Most of these electrodes are designed to meet the standards of the American Welding Society, a trade association. They are thus essentially the same as to size and composition from one manufacturer to another. Every electrode manufacturer has a limited number of unique products, but these typically constitute only a small percentage of total sales.

Welding electrodes are of two basic types: (1) Coated "stick" electrodes, usually fourteen inches long and smaller than a pencil in diameter, which are held in a special insulated holder by the operator, who must manipulate the electrode in order to maintain a proper arc-width and pattern of deposition of the metal being transferred. Stick electrodes are packaged in six- to fifty-pound boxes. (2) Coiled wired, ranging in diameter from .035″ to 0.219″, which is designed to be fed continuously to the welding arc through a "gun" held by the operator or positioned by automatic positioning equipment. The wire is packaged in coils, reels, and drums weighing from fourteen to 1,000 pounds and may be solid or flux-cored.

Manufacturing Processes

The main plant is in Euclid, Ohio, a suburb on Cleveland's east side. The layout of this plant is shown in Exhibit 1. There are no warehouses. Materials flow from the half-mile long dock on the north side of the plant through the production lines to a very limited storage and loading area on the south side. Materials used on each work station are stored as close as possible to the work station. The administrative offices, near the center of the factory, are entirely functional. A corridor below the main level provides access to the factory floor from the main entrance near the center of the plan. *Fortune* magazine recently declared the Euclid facility one of America's ten best-managed factories, and compared it with a General Electric plant also on the list:

> Stepping into GE's spanking new dishwasher plant, an awed supplier said, is like stepping "into the Hyatt Regency." By comparison, stepping into Lincoln Electric's 33-year-old, cavernous, dimly lit factory is like stumbling into a dingy big-city YMCA. It's only when one starts looking at how these factories do things that similarities become apparent. They have found ways to merge design with manufacturing, build in quality, make wise choices about automation, get close to customers, and handle their work forces.

Exhibit 1 Main Factory Layout

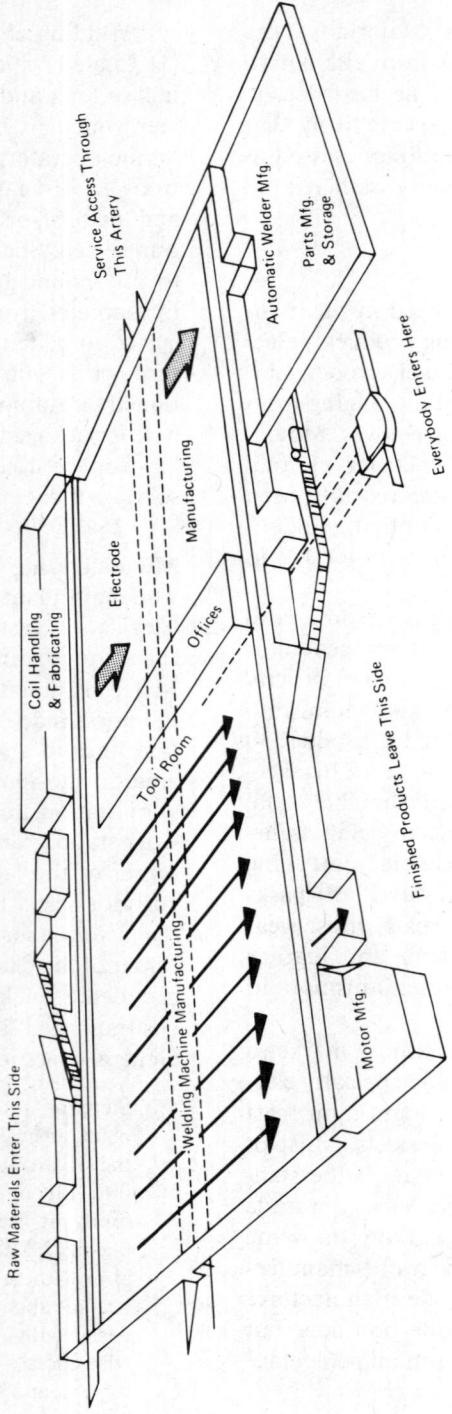

Raw Materials Enter This Side

Coil Handling & Fabricating

Electrode Manufacturing

Service Access Through This Artery

Automatic Welder Mfg.

Parts Mfg. & Storage

Tool Room

Offices

Everybody Enters Here

Welding Machine Manufacturing

Motor Mfg.

Finished Products Leave This Side

A new Lincoln plant, in Mentor, Ohio, houses some of the electrode production operations, which were moved from the main plant.

Electrode manufacturing is highly capital intensive. Metal rods purchased from steel producers are drawn down to smaller diameters, cut to length and coated with pressed-powder "flux" for stick electrodes or plated with copper (for conductivity) and put into coils or spools for wire. Lincoln's Innershield wire is hollow and filled with a material similar to that used to coat stick electrodes. As mentioned earlier, this represented a major innovation in welding technology when it was introduced. The company is highly secretive about its electrode production processes, and outsiders are not given access to the details of those processes.

Lincoln welding machines and electric motors are made on a series of assembly lines. Gasoline and diesel engines are purchased partially assembled but practically all other components are made from basic industrial products, e.g., steel bars and sheets and bar copper conductor wire.

Individual components, such as gasoline tanks for engine-driven welders and steel shafts for motors and generators, are made by numerous small "factories within a factory." The shaft for a certain generator, for example, is made from raw steel bar by one operator who uses five large machines, all running continuously. A saw cuts the bar to length, a digital lathe machines different sections to varying diameters, a special milling machine cuts a slot for the keyway, and so forth, until a finished shaft is produced. The operator moves the shafts from machine to machine and makes necessary adjustments.

Another operator punches, shapes and paints sheetmetal cowling parts. One assembles steel laminations onto a rotor shaft, then winds, insulates and tests the rotors. Finished components are moved by crane operators to the nearby assembly lines.

Worker Performance and Attitudes

Exceptional worker performance at Lincoln is a matter of record. The typical Lincoln employee earns about twice as much as other factory workers in the Cleveland area. Yet the company's labor cost per sales dollar in 1989, 26 cents, is well below industry averages. Worker turnover is practically nonexistent except for retirements and departures by new employees.

Sales per Lincoln factory employee currently exceed $150,000. An observer at the factory quickly sees why this figure is so high. Each worker is proceeding busily and thoughtfully about the task at hand. There is no idle chatter. Most workers take no coffee breaks. Many operate several machines and make a substantial component unaided. The supervisors are busy with planning and record keeping duties and hardly glance at the people they "supervise." The manufacturing procedures appear efficient—no unnecessary steps, no wasted motions, no wasted materials. Finished components move smoothly to subsequent work stations.

Appendix A includes summaries of interviews with employees.

Organization Structure

Lincoln has never allowed development of a formal organization chart. The objective of this policy is to insure maximum flexibility. An open door policy is practiced throughout the company, and personnel are encouraged to take problems to the persons most capable of resolving them. Once, Harvard Business School researchers prepared an organization chart reflecting the implied relationships at Lincoln. The chart became available within the company, and present management feels that had a disruptive effect. Therefore, no organizational chart appears in this report.

Perhaps because of the quality and enthusiasm of the Lincoln workforce, routine supervision is almost nonexistent. A typical production foreman, for example, supervises as many as 100 workers, a span-of-control which does not allow more than infrequent worker-supervisor interaction.

Position titles and traditional flows of authority do imply something of an organizational structure, however. For example, the Vice-President, Sales, and the Vice-President, Electrode Division, report to the President, as do various staff assistants such as the Personnel Director and the Director of Purchasing. Using such implied relationships, it has been determined that production workers have two or, at most, three levels of supervision between themselves and the President.

Personnel Policies

As mentioned earlier, it is Lincoln's remarkable personnel practices which are credited by many with the company's success.

Recruitment and Selection
Every job opening is advertised internally on company bulletin boards and any employee can apply for any job so advertised. External hiring is permitted only for entry level positions. Selection for these jobs is done on the basis of personal interviews—there is no aptitude or psychological testing. Not even a high school diploma is required—except for engineering and sales positions, which are filled by graduate engineers. A committee consisting of vice presidents and supervisors interviews candidates initially cleared by the Personnel Department. Final selection is made by the supervisor who has a job opening. Out of over 3,500 applicants interviewed by the Personnel Department during a recent period fewer than 300 were hired.

Job Security
In 1958 Lincoln formalized its guaranteed continuous employment policy, which had already been in effect for many years. There have been no layoffs since World War II. Since 1958, every worker with over two years' longevity has been

guaranteed at least 30 hours per week, 49 weeks per year.

The policy has never been so severely tested as during the 1981–83 recession. As a manufacturer of capital goods, Lincoln's business is highly cyclical. In previous recessions the company was able to avoid major sales declines. However, sales plummeted 32 percent in 1982 and another 16 percent the next year. Few companies could withstand such a revenue collapse and remain profitable. Yet, Lincoln not only earned profits, but no employee was laid off and year-end incentive bonuses continued. To weather the storm, management cut most of the nonsalaried workers back to 30 hours a week for varying periods of time. Many employees were reassigned and the total workforce was slightly reduced through normal attrition and restricted hiring. Many employees grumbled at their unexpected misfortune, probably to the surprise and dismay of some Lincoln managers. However, sales and profits—and employee bonuses—soon rebounded and all was well again.

Performance Evaluations
Each supervisor formally evaluates subordinates twice a year using the cards shown in Exhibit 2. The employee performance criteria, "quality," "dependability," "ideas and cooperation," and "output," are considered to be independent of each other. Marks on the cards are converted to numerical scores which are forced to average 100 for each evaluating supervisor. Individual merit rating scores normally range from 80 to 110. Any score over 110 requires a special letter to top management. These scores (over 110) are not considered in computing the required 100 point average for each evaluating supervisor. Suggestions for improvements often result in recommendations for exceptionally high performance scores. Supervisors discuss individual performance marks with the employees concerned. Each warranty claim is traced to the individual employee whose work caused the defect. The employee's performance score may be reduced, or the worker may be required to repay the cost of

Exhibit 2   Merit Rating Cards

QUALITY

Increasing Quality →

This card rates the QUALITY of the work you do.

It also reflects your success in eliminating errors and in reducing scrap and waste.

This rating has been done jointly by your department head and the Inspection Department in the shop and with other department heads in the office and engineering

DEPENDABILITY

Increasing Dependability →

This card rates how well your supervisors have been able to depend upon you to do things that have been expected of you without supervision.

It also rates your ability to supervise yourself including your work safety performance, your orderliness, care of equipment, and the effective use you make of your skills.

This rating has been done by your department head

IDEAS & COOPERATION

Increasing Ideas & Cooperation →

This card rates your Cooperation, Ideas and Initiative.

New ideas and new methods are important to your company in our continuing effect to reduce costs, increase output, improve quality, work safely and improve our relationship with our customers. This card credits you for your ideas and initiative used to help in this direction.

It also rates your cooperation – – – how you work with others as a team. Such factors as your attitude towards supervision, co workers, and the company; your efforts to share your expert knowledge with others, and your cooperation in installing new methods smoothly, are considered here.

This rating has been done jointly by your department head and the Time Study Department in the shop and with other department heads in the office and engineering

OUTPUT

Increasing Output →

This card rates HOW MUCH PRODUCTIVE WORK you actually turn out.

It also reflects your willingness not to hold back and recognizes your attendance record.

This rating has been done jointly by your department head and the Production Control Department in the shop and with other department heads in the office and engineering servicing the warranty claim by working without pay.

Compensation

Basic wage levels for jobs at Lincoln are determined by a wage survey of similar jobs in the Cleveland area. These rates are adjusted quarterly in accordance with changes in the Cleveland area wage index. Insofar as possible, base wage rates are translated into piece rates. Practically all production workers and many others—for example, some forklift operators—are paid by piece rate. Once established, piece rates are never changed unless a substantive change in the way a job is done results from a source other than the worker doing the job.

In December of each year, a portion of annual profits is distributed to employees as bonuses. Incentive bonuses since 1934 have averaged about ninety percent of annual wages and somewhat more than after-tax profits. The average bonus for 1988 was $21,258. Even for the recession years 1982 and 1983, bonuses had averaged $13,998 and $8,557, respectively. Individual bonuses are proportional to merit-rating scores. For example, assume the amount set aside for bonuses is 80 percent of total wages paid to eligible employees. A person whose performance score is 95 will receive a bonus of 76 percent (0.80×0.95) of annual wages.

Vacations

The company is shut down for two weeks in August and two weeks during the Christmas season. Vacations are taken during these periods. For employees with over 25 years of service, a fifth week of vacation may be taken at a time acceptable to superiors.

Work Assignment

Management has authority to transfer workers and to switch between overtime and short time as required. Supervisors have undisputed authority to assign specific parts to individual workmen, who may have their own preferences due to variations in piece rates. During the 1982–1983 recession, fifty factory workers volunteered to join sales teams and fanned out across the country to sell a new welder designed for automobile body shops and small machine shops. The result—$10 million in sales and a hot new product.

Employee Participation in Decision Making

Thinking of participative management usually evokes a vision of a relaxed, nonauthoritarian atmosphere. This is not the case at Lincoln. Formal authority is quite strong. "We're very authoritarian around here," says Willis. James F. Lincoln placed a good deal of stress on protecting management's authority. "Management in all successful departments of industry must have complete power," he said, "Management is the coach who must be obeyed. The men, however, are the players who alone can win the game." Despite this attitude, there are several ways in which employees participate in management at Lincoln.

Richard Sabo, Assistant to the Chief Executive Officer, relates job enlargement/enrichment to participation. He said, "The most important participative technique that we use is giving more responsibility to employees. We give a high school graduate more responsibility than other companies give their foremen." Management puts limits on the degree of participation which is allowed, however. In Sabo's words:

> When you use "participation," put quotes around it. Because we believe that each person should participate only in those decisions he is most knowledgeable about. I don't think production employees should control the decisions of the chairman. They don't know as much as he does about the decisions he is involved in.

The Advisory Board, elected by the workers, meets with the Chairman and the President every two weeks to discuss ways of improving operations. As noted earlier, this board has been in existence since 1914 and has contributed to many innovations. The incentive bonuses, for example, were first recommended by this committee. Every employee has access to Advisory Board members, and answers to all Advisory Board suggestions are promised by the following meeting. Both Willis and Hastings are quick to point out, though, that the Advisory Board only recommends actions. "They do not have direct authority," Willis says, "And when they bring up something that management thinks is not to the benefit of the company, it will be rejected."

Under the early suggestion program, employees were awarded one-half of the first year's savings attributable to their suggestions. Now, however, the value of suggestions is reflected in performance evaluation scores, which determine individual incentive bonus amounts.

Training and Education

Production workers are given a short period of on-the-job training and then placed on a piece-work pay system. Lincoln does not pay for off-site education, unless very specific company needs are identified. The idea behind this latter policy, according to Sabo, is that everyone cannot take advantage of such a program, and it is unfair to expend company funds for an advantage to which there is unequal access. Recruits for sales jobs, already college graduates, are given on-the-job training in the plant followed by a period of work and training at one of the regional sales offices.

Fringe Benefits and Executive Perquisites

A medical plan and a company-paid retirement program have been in effect for many years. A plant cafeteria, operated on a break-even basis, serves meals at about sixty percent of usual costs. The Employee Association, to which the company does not contribute, provides disability insurance and social and athletic activities. The employee stock ownership program has resulted in employee ownership of about fifty percent of the common stock. Under this program, each employee with more than two years of service may purchase stock in the corporation. The price of these shares is established at book value. Stock purchased through this plan may be held by em-

ployees only. Dividends and voting rights are the same as for stock which is owned outside the plan. Approximately 75 percent of the employees own Lincoln stock.

As to executive perquisites, there are none—crowded, austere offices, no executive washrooms or lunchrooms, and no reserved parking spaces. Even the top executives pay for their own meals and eat in the employee cafeteria. On one recent day, Willis arrived at work late due to a breakfast speaking engagement and had to park far away from the factory entrance.

Financial Policies

James F. Lincoln felt strongly that financing for company growth should come from within the company—through initial cash investment by the founders, through retention of earnings, and through stock purchases by those who work in the business. He saw the following advantages of this approach:

1. Ownership of stock by employees strengthens team spirit. "If they are mutually anxious to make it succeed, the future of the company is bright."

2. Ownership of stock provides individual incentive because employees feel that they will benefit from company profitability.

3. "Ownership is educational." Owners-employees "will know how profits are made and lost; how success is won and lost. . . . There are few socialists in the list of stockholders of the nation's industries."

4. "Capital available from within controls expansion." Unwarranted expansion would not occur, Lincoln believed, under his financing plan.

5. "The greatest advantage would be the development of the individual worker. Under the incentive of ownership, he would become a greater man."

6. "Stock ownership is one of the steps that can be taken that will make the worker feel that there is less of a gulf between him and the boss. . . .

Stock ownership will help the worker to recognize his responsibility in the game and the importance of victory."

Until 1980, Lincoln Electric borrowed no money. Even now, the company's liabilities consist mainly of accounts payable and short-term accruals.

The unusual pricing policy at Lincoln is succinctly stated by Willis: "At all times price on the basis of cost and at all times keep pressure on our cost." This policy resulted in the price for the most popular welding electrode then in use going from 16 cents a pound in 1929 to 4.7 cents in 1938. More recently, the SA-200 Welder, Lincoln's largest selling portable machine, decreased in price from 1958 through 1965. According to Dr. C. Jackson Grayson of the American Productivity Center in Houston, Texas, Lincoln's prices increased only one-fifth as fast as the Consumer Price Index from 1934 to about 1970. This resulted in a welding products market in which Lincoln became the undisputed price leader for the products it manufactures. Not even the major Japanese manufacturers, such as Nippon Steel for welding electrodes and Osaka Transformer for welding machines, were able to penetrate this market.

Substantial cash balances are accumulated each year preparatory to paying the year-end bonuses. The bonuses totaled $54 million for 1988. The money is invested in short-term U.S. government securities and certificates of deposit until needed. Financial statements are shown in Exhibit 3. Exhibit 4 shows how company revenue was distributed in the late 1980s.

How Well Does Lincoln Serve Its Stakeholders?

Lincoln Electric differs from most other companies in the importance it assigns to each of the groups it serves. Willis identifies these groups, in the order of priority ascribed to them, as (1) customers, (2) employees, and (3) stockholders.

Certainly the firm's customers have fared well over the years. Lincoln prices for welding machines and welding electrodes are acknowledged to be the lowest in the marketplace. Quality has consistently been high. The cost of field failures for Lincoln products was recently determined to be a remarkable 0.04 percent of revenues. The "Fleetweld" electrodes and SA-200 welders have been the standard in the pipeline and refinery construction industry, where price is hardly a criterion, for decades. A Lincoln distributor in Monroe, Louisiana, says that he has sold several hundred of the popular AC-225 welders, which are warranted for one year, but has never handled a warranty claim.

Perhaps best-served of all management constituencies have been the employees. Not the least of their benefits, of course, are the year-end bonuses, which effectively double an already average compensation level. The foregoing description of the personnel program and the comments in Appendix A further illustrate the desirability of a Lincoln job.

While stockholders were relegated to an inferior status by James F. Lincoln, they have done very well indeed. Recent dividends have exceeded $11 a share and earnings per share have approached $30. In January 1980, the price of restricted stock, committed to employees, was $117 a share. By 1989, the stated value, at which the company will repurchase the stock if tendered, was $201. A check with the New York office of Merrill Lynch, Pierce, Fenner and Smith at that time revealed an estimated price on Lincoln stock of $270 a share, with none being offered for sale. Technically, this price applies only to the unrestricted stock owned by the Lincoln family, a few other major holders, and employees who have purchased it on the open market. Risk associated with Lincoln stock, a major determinant of stock value, is minimal because of the small amount of debt in the capital structure, because of an extremely stable earnings record, and because of Lincoln's practice of purchasing the restricted stock whenever employees offer it for sale.

Exhibit 3 Condensed Comparative Financial Statements ($000,000)*

| | Balance Sheets | | | | | | | | |
	1979	1980	1981	1982	1983	1984	1985	1986	1987
Assets									
Cash	2	1	4	1	2	4	2	1	7
Bonds & CDs	38	47	63	72	78	57	55	45	41
N/R & A/R	42	42	42	26	31	34	38	36	43
Inventories	38	36	46	38	31	37	34	26	40
Prepayments	1	3	4	5	5	5	7	8	7
Total CA	121	129	157	143	146	138	135	116	137
Other assets**	24	24	26	30	30	29	29	33	40
Land	1	1	1	1	1	1	1	1	1
Net buildings	22	23	25	23	22	21	20	18	17
Net M&E	21	25	27	27	27	28	27	29	33
Total FA	44	49	53	51	50	50	48	48	50
Total assets	189	202	236	224	227	217	213	197	227
Claims									
A/P	17	16	15	12	16	15	13	11	20
Accrued wages	1	2	5	4	3	4	5	5	4
Accrued taxes	10	6	15	5	7	4	6	5	9
Accrued div.	6	6	7	7	7	6	7	6	7
Total CL	33	29	42	28	33	30	31	27	40
LT debt		4	5	6	8	10	11	8	8
Total debt	33	33	47	34	41	40	42	35	48
Common stock*	4	3	1	2	0	0	0	0	2
Ret. earnings	152	167	189	188	186	176	171	161	177
Total SH equity	156	170	190	190	186	176	171	161	179
Total claims	189	202	236	224	227	217	213	197	227

| | Income Statements | | | | | | | | |
	1979	1980	1981	1982	1983	1984	1985	1986	1987
Income	385	401	469	329	277	334	344	326	377
CGS	244	261	293	213	180	223	221	216	239
Selling, G&A***	41	46	51	45	45	47	48	49	51
Incentive bonus	44	43	56	37	22	33	38	33	39
IBT	56	51	69	35	30	31	36	27	48
Income taxes	26	23	31	16	13	14	16	12	21
Net income	30	28	37	19	17	17	20	15	27

*Columns totals may not check and amounts less than $500,000 (0.5) are shown as zero, due to rounding.
**Includes investment in foreign subsidiaries, $29 million in 1987.
***Includes pension expense and payroll taxes on incentive bonus.

Exhibit 4   Revenue Distribution

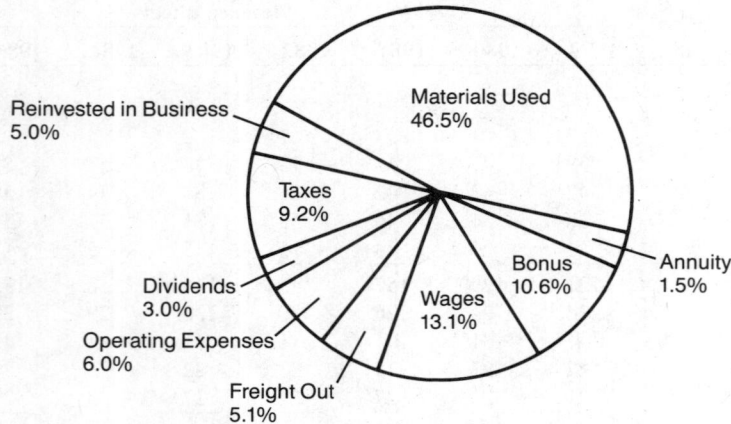

Reinvested in Business
5.0%

Materials Used
46.5%

Taxes
9.2%

Bonus
10.6%

Annuity
1.5%

Dividends
3.0%

Wages
13.1%

Operating Expenses
6.0%

Freight Out
5.1%

A Concluding Comment

It is easy to believe that the reason for Lincoln's success is the excellent attitude of the employees and their willingness to work harder, faster, and more intelligently than other industrial workers. However, Sabo suggests that appropriate credit be given to Lincoln executives, whom he credits with carrying out the following policies:

1. Management has limited research, development, and manufacturing to a standard product line designed to meet the major needs of the welding industry.

2. New products must be reviewed by manufacturing and all producing costs verified before being approved by management.

3. Purchasing is challenged to not only procure materials at the lowest cost, but also to work closely with engineering and manufacturing to assure that the latest innovations are implemented.

4. Manufacturing supervision and all personnel are held accountable for reduction of scrap, energy conservation, and maintenance of product quality.

5. Production control, material handling, and methods engineering are closely supervised by top management.

6. Management has made cost reduction a way of life at Lincoln, and definite programs are established in many areas, including traffic and shipping, where tremendous savings can result.

7. Management has established a sales department that is technically trained to reduce customer welding costs. This sales approach and other real customer services have eliminated nonessential frills and resulted in long-term benefits to all concerned.

8. Management has encouraged education, technical publishing, and long range programs that have resulted in industry growth, thereby assuring market potential for the Lincoln Electric Company.

Sabo writes, "It is in a very real sense a personal and group experience in faith—a belief that together we can achieve results which alone would not be possible. It is not a perfect system and it is not easy. It requires tremendous dedication and hard work. However, it does work and the results are worth the effort."

Employee Interviews

During the late summer of 1980, the author conducted numerous interviews with Lincoln employees. Typical questions and answers from those interviews are presented below. In order to maintain each employee's personal privacy, the names used for the interviewees are fictitious.

Interview with Betty Stewart, a 52-year-old high school graduate who had been with Lincoln 13 years and who was working as a cost-accounting clerk at the time of the interview.

Q. What jobs have you held here besides the one you have now?

A. I worked in payroll for a while, and then this job came open and I took it.

Q. How much money did you make last year, including your bonus?

A. I would say roughly around $20,000, but I was off for back surgery for a while.

Q. You weren't paid while you were off for back surgery?

A. No.

Q. Did the employee association help out?

A. Yes. The company doesn't furnish that, though. We pay $6 a month into the employee association. I think my check from them was $105.00 a week.

Q. How was your performance rating last year?

A. It was around 100 points, but I lost some points for attendance with my back problem.

Q. How did you get your job at Lincoln?

A. I was bored silly where I was working, and I had heard that Lincoln kept their people busy. So I applied and got the job the next day.

Q. Do you think you make more money than similar workers in Cleveland?

A. I know I do.

Q. What have you done with your money?

A. We have purchased a better home. Also, my son is going to the University of Chicago, which costs $10,000 a year. I buy the Lincoln stock which is offered each year, and I have a little bit of gold.

Q. Have you ever visited with any of the senior executives, like Mr. Willis or Mr. Irrgang?

A. I have known Mr. Willis for a long time.

Q. Does he call you by name?

A. Yes. In fact he was very instrumental in my going to the doctor that I am going to with my back. He knows the director of the clinic.

Q. Do you know Mr. Irrgang?

A. I know him to speak to him, and he always speaks, always. But I have known Mr. Willis for a good many years. When I did Plant Two accounting I did not understand how the plant operated. Of course you are not allowed in Plant Two, because that's the Electrode Division. I told my boss about the problem one day, and the next thing I knew Mr. Willis came by and said, "Come on, Betty, we're going to Plant Two." He spent an hour and a half showing me the plant.

Q. Do you think Lincoln employees produce more than those in other companies?

A. I think with the incentive program the way that it is, if you want to work and achieve, then you will do it. If you don't want to work and achieve, you will not do it no matter where you are. Just because you are merit rated and have a bonus, if you really don't want to work hard, then you're not going to. You will accept your 90 points or 92 or 85 because, even with that, you make more money than people on the outside.

Q. Do you think Lincoln employees will ever join a union?

A. I don't know why they would.

Q. What is the most important advantage of working for Lincoln Electric?

A. You have an incentive, and you can push and get something for pushing. That's not true in a lot of companies.

Q. So you say that money is a very major advantage?

A. Money is a major advantage, but it's not just the money. It's the fact that, having the incentive, you do wish to work a little harder. I'm sure that there are a lot of men here who, if they worked some other place, would not work as hard as they do here. Not that they are overworked—I don't mean that—but I'm sure they wouldn't push.

Q. Is there anything that you would like to add?

A. I do like working here. I am better off being pushed mentally. In another company if you pushed too hard you would feel a little bit of pressure, and someone might say, "Hey, slow down; don't try so hard." But here you are encouraged, not discouraged.

Interview with Ed Sanderson, 23-year-old high school graduate who had been with Lincoln four years and who was a machine operator in the Electrode Division at the time of the interview.

Q. How did you happen to get this job?

A. My wife was pregnant, and I was making three bucks an hour and one day I came here and applied. That was it. I kept calling to let them know I was still interested.

Q. Roughly what were your earnings last year including your bonus?

A. $37,000.

Q. What have you done with your money since you have been here?

A. Well, we've lived pretty well, and we bought a condominium.

Q. Have you paid for the condominium?

A. No, but I could.

Q. Have you bought your Lincoln stock this year?

A. No, I haven't bought any Lincoln stock yet.

Q. Do you get the feeling that the executives here are pretty well thought of?

A. I think they are. To get where they are today, they had to really work.

Q. Wouldn't that be true anywhere?

A. I think more so here because seniority really doesn't mean anything. If you work with a guy who has 20 years here, and you have two months and you're doing a better job, you will get advanced before he will.

Q. Are you paid on a piece rate basis?

A. My gang is. There are nine of us who make the bare electrode, and the whole group gets paid based on how much electrode we make.

Q. Do you think you work harder than workers in other factories in the Cleveland area?

A. Yes, I would say I probably work harder.

Q. Do you think it hurts anybody?

A. No, a little hard work never hurts anybody.

Q. If you could choose, do you think you would be as happy earning a little less money and being able to slow down a little?

A. No, it doesn't bother me. If it bothered me, I wouldn't do it.

Q. What would you say is the biggest disadvantage of working at Lincoln, as opposed to working somewhere else?

A. Probably having to work shift work.

Q. Why do you think Lincoln employees produce more than workers in other plants?

A. That's the way the company is set up. The more you put out, the more you're going to make.

Q. Do you think it's the piece rate and bonus together?

A. I don't think people would work here if they didn't know that they would be rewarded at the end of the year.

Q. Do you think Lincoln employees will ever join a union?

A. No.

Q. What are the major advantages of working for Lincoln?

A. Money.

Q. Are there any other advantages?

A. Yes, we don't have a union shop. I don't think I could work in a union shop.

Q. Do you think you are a career man with Lincoln at this time?

A. Yes.

Interview with Roger Lewis, 23-year-old Purdue graduate in mechanical engineering who had been in the Lincoln sales program for 15 months and who was working in the Cleveland sales office at the time of the interview.

Q. How did you get your job at Lincoln?

A. I saw that Lincoln was interviewing on campus at Purdue, and I went by. I later came to Cleveland for a plant tour and was offered a job.

Q. Do you know any of the senior executives? Would they know you by name?

A. Yes, I know all of them—Mr. Irrgang, Mr. Willis, Mr. Manross.

Q. Do you think Lincoln salesmen work harder than those in other companies?

A. Yes. I don't think there are many salesmen for other companies who are putting in 50- to 60-hour weeks. Everybody here works harder. You can go out in the plant, or you can go upstairs, and there's nobody sitting around.

Q. Do you see any real disadvantage of working at Lincoln?

A. I don't know if it's a disadvantage but Lincoln is a Spartan company, a very thrifty company. I like that. The sales offices are functional, not fancy.

Q. Why do you think Lincoln employees have such high productivity?

A. Piecework has a lot to do with it. Lincoln is smaller than many plants, too; you can stand in one place and see the materials come in one side and the product go out the other. You feel a part of the company. The chance to get ahead is important, too. They have a strict policy of promoting from within, so you know you have a chance. I think in a lot of other places you may not get as fair a shake as you do here. The sales offices are on a smaller scale, too. I like that. I tell someone that we have two people in the Baltimore office, and they say, "You've got to be kidding." It's smaller and more personal. Pay is the most important thing. I have heard that this is the highest-paying factory in the world.

Interview with Jimmy Roberts, a 47-year-old high school graduate, who had been with Lincoln 17 years and who was working as a multiple drill press operator at the time of the interview.

Q. What jobs have you had at Lincoln?

A. I started out cleaning the men's locker room in 1963. After about a year I got a job in the flux department, where we make the coating for welding rods. I worked there for seven or eight years and then got my present job.

Q. Do you make one particular part?

A. No, there are a variety of parts I make—at least 25.

Q. Each one has a different piece rate attached to it?

A. Yes.

Q. Are some piece rates better than others?

A. Yes.

Q. How do you determine which ones you are going to do?

A. You don't. Your supervisor assigns them.

Q. How much money did you make last year?

A. $47,000.

Q. Have you ever received any kind of award or citation?

A. No.

Q. Was your rating ever over 110?

A. Yes. For the past five years, probably, I made over 110 points.

Q. Is there any attempt to let others know?

A. The kind of points I get? No.

Q. Do you know what they are making?

A. No. There are some who might not be too happy with their points, and they might make it known. The majority, though, do not make it a point of telling other employees.

Q. Would you be just as happy earning a little less money and working a little slower?

A. I don't think I would—not at this point. I have done piecework all these years, and the fast pace doesn't really bother me.

Q. Why do you think Lincoln productivity is so high?

A. The incentive thing—the bonus distribution. I think that would be the main reason. The paycheck you get every two weeks is important too.

Q. Do you think Lincoln employees would ever join a union?

A. I don't think so. I have never heard anyone mention it.

Q. What is the most important advantage of working here?

A. The amount of money you make. I don't think I could make this type of money anywhere else, especially with only a high school education.

Q. As a black person, do you feel that Lincoln discriminates in any way against blacks?

A. No. I don't think any more so than any other job. Naturally, there is a certain amount of discrimination, regardless of where you are.

Interview with Joe Trahan, 58-year-old high school graduate who had been with Lincoln 39 years and who was employed as a working supervisor in the toolroom at the time of the interview.

Q. Roughly what was your pay last year?

A. Over $50,000—salary, bonus, stock dividends.

Q. How much was your bonus?

A. About $23,000.

Q. Have you ever gotten a special award of any kind?

A. Not really.

Q. What have you done with your money?

A. My house is paid for—and my two cars. I also have some bonds and the Lincoln stock.

Q. What do you think of the executives at Lincoln?

A. They're really top notch.

Q. What is the major disadvantage of working at Lincoln Electric?

A. I don't know of any disadvantage at all.

Q. Do you think you produce more than most people in similar jobs with other companies?

A. I do believe that.

Q. Why is that? Why do you believe that?

A. We are on the incentive system. Everything we do, we try to improve to make a better product with a minimum of outlay. We try to improve the bonus.

Q. Would you be just as happy making a little less money and not working quite so hard?

A. I don't think so.

Q. You know that Lincoln productivity is higher than that at most other plants. Why is that?

A. Money.

Q. Do you think Lincoln employees would ever join a union?

A. I don't think they would ever consider it.

Q. What is the most important advantage of working at Lincoln?

A. Compensation.

Q. Tell me something about Mr. James Lincoln, who died in 1965.

Q. You are talking about Jimmy, Sr. He always strolled through the shop in his shirtsleeves. Big fellow. Always looked distinguished. Gray hair. Friendly sort of guy. I was a member of the advisory board one year. He was there each time.

Q. Did he strike you as really caring?

A. I think he always cared for people.

Q. Did you get any sensation of a religious nature from him?

A. No, not really.

Q. And religion is not part of the program now?

A. No.

Q. Do you think Mr. Lincoln was a very intelligent man, or was he just a nice guy?

A. I would say he was pretty well educated. A great talker—always right off the top of his head. He knew what he was talking about all the time.

Q. When were bonuses for beneficial suggestions done away with?

A. About 15 years ago.

Q. Did that hurt very much?

A. I don't think so, because suggestions are still rewarded through the merit rating system.

Q. Is there anything you would like to add?

A. It's a good place to work. The union kind of ties other places down. At other places, electricians only do electrical work, carpenters only do carpenter work. At Lincoln Electric we all pitch in and do whatever needs to be done.

Q. So a major advantage is not having a union?

A. That's right.

Case 21

Wal-Mart Stores, Inc.

In January 1982, amid a distressed economy, Wal-Mart continues to pace the discount-chain industry, leaving K-Mart, Target, and Woolco behind. The chain emerged in 1962 with one store serving a small community in Arkansas and has grown to 491 stores serving 13 different states at the close of 1981. Jack Shewmaker, President of Wal-Mart, says the chain will continue to grow into markets where we can get the right profitability and return on investment.

History and Background

Wal-Mart Stores, Inc., headquartered in Bentonville, Arkansas, had its origin in the variety-store business. Sam Walton opened his first variety store, under the Ben Franklin franchise, in Newport, Arkansas, in 1945. One year later, he was joined by his brother, J. L. "Bud" Walton, now Senior Vice-President, who opened a similar store in Versailles, Missouri. The two brothers went on to assemble a group of 15 Ben Franklin stores, and subsequently developed the concept of larger discount department stores in communities of small size. This concept emerged in 1962 when the first Wal-Mart Discount City store in Rogers, Arkansas opened. Wal-Mart Stores, Inc., became a publicly held corporation in October 1970. After the company was listed on the over-the-counter market, stock began trading on the New York Stock Exchange in mid-

Source: This case was prepared by Monya Giggar, Gregg Gunchick, and David Miller, under the supervision of Professor Sexton Adams, University of North Texas, and Professor Adelaide Griffin, Texas Woman's University. Permission to use granted by Sexton Adams. This case is based on library research.

1972. The founder, Sam Walton, continues to serve as chairman of the board and chief executive officer.

In 1982, Wal-Mart has 491 discount department stores servicing the general merchandise needs of its customers. The discount stores range in size from 30,000 to 90,000 square feet, with the average store size being about 52,000 square feet. Wal-Mart stores are usually organized with 36 departments and carry merchandise such as wearing apparel for the entire family, household furnishings, appliances, and other hard-line merchandise. These stores are located in 13 states across the south and the southeast.

Unlike many other major discount chains, Wal-Mart has devoted itself almost exclusively to serving small towns and medium-sized cities. In their respective communities, Wal-Mart Discount Cities are the largest nonfood retailers. The largest cities in which the company operates, at this time, are: Little Rock, Arkansas; Shreveport, Louisiana; Springfield, Missouri; Huntsville, Alabama; Nashville, Tennessee.

Management

Wal-Mart has exercised a highly entrepreneurial, participatory, and goal-oriented style of management. Responsibility for Wal-Mart's style has been attributed to Sam Walton, chief executive officer and chairman of the board. Serving below him are some of the most respected top-level management personnel in the discount-store industry. Heading these top-level executives is Jack Shewmaker, President (see Exhibit 1).

One of the chain's historical strengths, though, has been that it has a single-minded phi-

Exhibit 1 Organization Chart

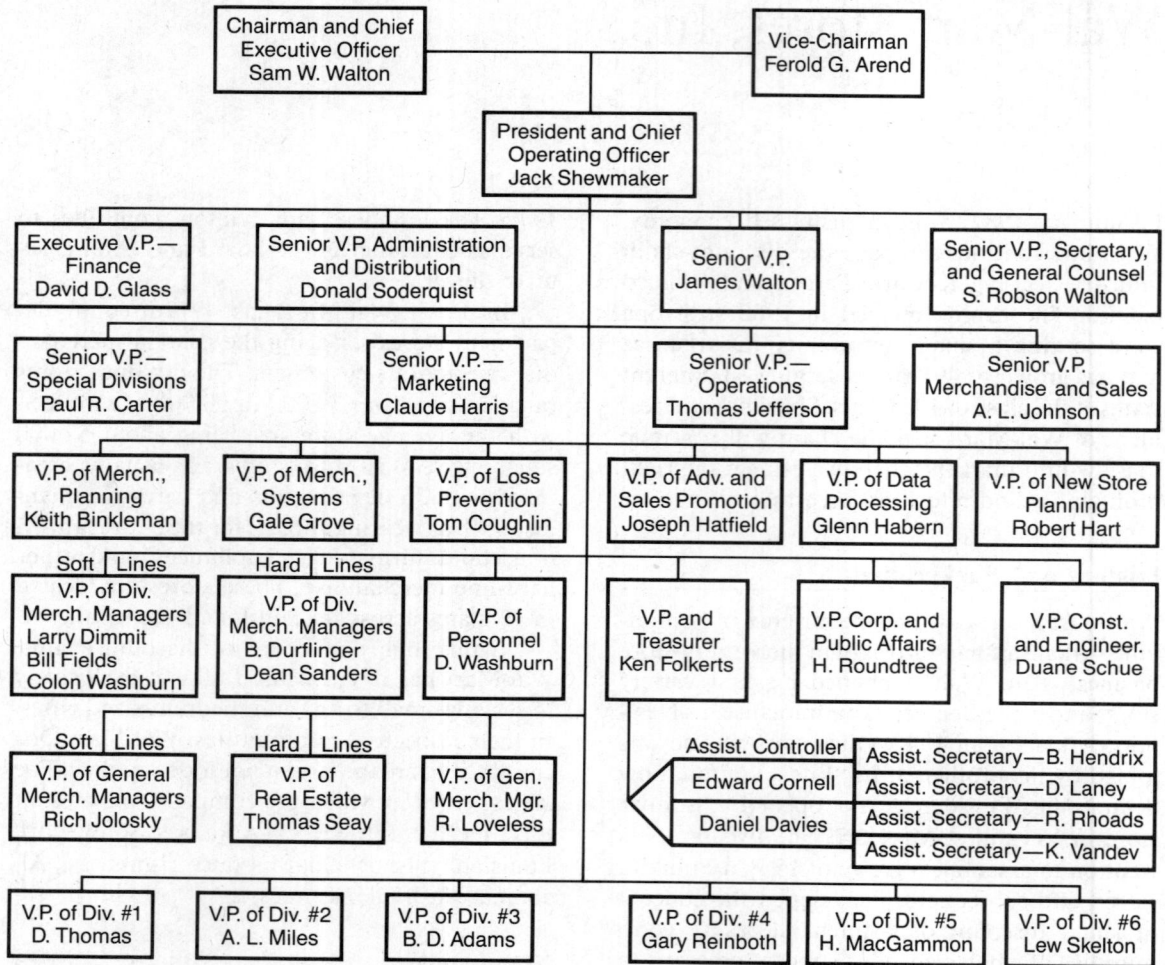

```
┌─────────────────────┐                              ┌──────────────────┐
│ Chairman and Chief  │                              │  Vice-Chairman   │
│ Executive Officer   │                              │ Ferold G. Arend  │
│  Sam W. Walton      │                              └──────────────────┘
└─────────────────────┘
           ┌───────────────────────┐
           │ President and Chief   │
           │  Operating Officer    │
           │   Jack Shewmaker      │
           └───────────────────────┘
```

Executive V.P.— Finance David D. Glass	Senior V.P. Administration and Distribution Donald Soderquist		Senior V.P. James Walton	Senior V.P., Secretary, and General Counsel S. Robson Walton

Senior V.P.— Special Divisions Paul R. Carter	Senior V.P.— Marketing Claude Harris		Senior V.P.— Operations Thomas Jefferson	Senior V.P. Merchandise and Sales A. L. Johnson

V.P. of Merch., Planning Keith Binkleman	V.P. of Merch., Systems Gale Grove	V.P. of Loss Prevention Tom Coughlin	V.P. of Adv. and Sales Promotion Joseph Hatfield	V.P. of Data Processing Glenn Habern	V.P. of New Store Planning Robert Hart

Soft | Lines	Hard | Lines				
V.P. of Div. Merch. Managers Larry Dimmit Bill Fields Colon Washburn	V.P. of Div. Merch. Managers B. Durflinger Dean Sanders	V.P. of Personnel D. Washburn	V.P. and Treasurer Ken Folkerts	V.P. Corp. and Public Affairs H. Roundtree	V.P. Const. and Engineer. Duane Schue

Soft | Lines	Hard | Lines			
V.P. of General Merch. Managers Rich Jolosky	V.P. of Real Estate Thomas Seay	V.P. of Gen. Merch. Mgr. R. Loveless	Assist. Controller Edward Cornell / Daniel Davies	Assist. Secretary—B. Hendrix / Assist. Secretary—D. Laney / Assist. Secretary—R. Rhoads / Assist. Secretary—K. Vandev

V.P. of Div. #1 D. Thomas	V.P. of Div. #2 A. L. Miles	V.P. of Div. #3 B. D. Adams	V.P. of Div. #4 Gary Reinboth	V.P. of Div. #5 H. MacGammon	V.P. of Div. #6 Lew Skelton

losophy that has kept it on the straight and narrow path established by Sam Walton 36 years ago. Sam's personal attitude has been reflected in the manner which he has established special relationships with many of the employees, whom he calls "associates." In the early years at Wal-Mart, Sam visited all the stores twice a year, exchanging open communication on ideas and problems. Theo Ashcraft, Vice-President of the Lease Department, said that Sam has always lis-

tened to people . . . learning (from them) everyday.

In 1982, the geographical expansion of Wal-Mart makes it impossible for Sam Walton to visit and communicate at a personal level with the employees of all 491 stores. Therefore, Jack Shewmaker has inherited many responsibilities, handed-down by the aging Sam Walton. Shewmaker, of the Sam Walton mold, is a strong believer in participatory management. He says,

"Wal-Mart's system is people supportive. This is a major factor in our operational strategy. We design programs so systems and procedures can be overridden by the manager, assistant manager, or the store manager who has first-hand contact with the problem." In addition to his support of Sam Walton's participatory management style, Shewmaker also maintains a personal relationship with Sam Walton, accompanying him on various hunting expeditions.

Grass-Roots Involvement

Wal-Mart practices management objectives called "grass-roots involvement." Jack Shewmaker refers to these objectives as "the involvement of our associates in every aspect of our business and the recognition of their ideas, suggestions, and problems is a key factor to our productivity gains." This policy was designed to provide continuous communication between top management and field operations. Starting at the store level, ideas and thoughts on improving the company's operations are written down by the associates and forwarded to headquarters. The overall corporate plan consolidates these individual goals and objectives to produce Wal-Mart's plan for action.

However, the corporate plans are composed in a centralized fashion at corporate headquarters. Every Saturday Sam Walton meets with the top-level executives and corporate planners to discuss future strategies. Sam continues to have the final word.

Another facet of Wal-Mart's strategy is an extension of the participatory management style to get employees involved. "We believe in sharing vital information on sales, expenses, and profits with every associate throughout the company," says Shewmaker. Among other vital information available, ". . . each month we prepare departmental reports showing percentage to total and comparative performance on sales, markdowns, inventory turnover, and gross margin. Each person is made to feel that he/she can affect the results."

Each of the store managers is evaluated on overall sales from his store, with consideration given to location and size of community. They are also evaluated on appearance, contributions in the form of ideas to corporate headquarters, and their ability to compete in their region.

Wal-Mart's most successful incentive program is its VPI or Volume Producing Item contest. This program allows individual store departments free rein to price and promote certain merchandise of their own choice. Walton claims that many faltering products have been revived as a result. "This is another way to keep people involved and thinking. Each month everyone knows where they rank in the chain and what percentage of a store's business they have," he explains.

The responses of Wal-Mart employees have been overwhelmingly in favor of the people-oriented programs. A clerk said that she "had worked for another chain for three years before coming to Wal-Mart, and I started off earning more here and there's no feeling of strain or pressure." A manager stated, "It's so much more open. You know where you stand all the time. You're not left in the dark."

Merchandising

Consumers' perceptions of Wal-Mart in Russellville, Arkansas, a typical Wal-Mart market, are just fantastic. In a Wal-Mart survey conducted in Russellville, many consumers responded positively to the chain with comments such as they have better quality merchandise, their prices are lower than K-Mart's, and they have a big selection. Wal-Mart's merchandising program has found the right combination of brand names, low prices, promotions and presentations, item merchandising, and fashion sense to attract and keep its customers.

Wal-Mart combines a strong brand-name merchandising philosophy with its domination of categories and subcategories. An example of its brand-name appeal is the Wrangler program. The complete size assortment of Wrangler jeans

are displayed in special dark-stained wooden cu-
bicles. Inside the display or adjacent to it in both
the men's and women's departments, are accessories (hats, belts, boots, and shirts) positioned
to encourage tie-in sales. Brand programs are
also extended to the hard lines. The Wal-Mart
strategy is that it carries all the usual hard-line
brands, but adds fringe items to bolster the price/
value perception of its shoppers. In health and
beauty aids, a line of old-favorite fragrances like
Wind Song, Jontue, and Emeraud is joined by a
selection of limited semirestricted lines, like
Charlie, Cie, Sophia, and Scoundrel. These limited additions are stocked heavily in multiple
facings on open shelves, unlike many other
chains that keep limited lines under lock-and-
key. The philosophy for having the lines accessible was that one cannot sell the lines where the
shoppers cannot get to them.

Another area where perception plays a key
role is in Wal-Mart's pricing policies. As one consumer states, Wal-Mart's prices are lower than
K-Mart's. The selection is better, too. Wal-Mart,
T.G. & Y., and K-Mart are often locked into
intense competition in the markets they all share
(small-towns and rural areas). In setting pricing
policies, each chain must devise an assortment
strategy. Of the two competitors, T.G. & Y. tends
to be overassorted—similar to the variety stores
of the past. K-Mart, on the other hand, tends to
narrow its assortments and fill-in the gaps with
private label brands, such as K-Mart toilet tissue
and facial tissue. Wal-Mart's strategy calls for
splitting the difference. First, it out-assorts K-
Mart, then it beats the prices offered by T.G. &
Y. Additionally, much of Wal-Mart's perceived
lower prices is revealed in a comparison of shelf-
prices of the three discount retailers that was conducted in Bartlesville, Oklahoma (1981). The results of the shelf-price study are shown in Exhibit
2. There were four random categories chosen and
several subcategories within these categories.
The total price differential for a 36-item market
basket amounted to less than 7½ percent between competitors. These results are indicative
of the closeness of the competition.

Much of Wal-Mart's success in developing
consumer perceptions is accredited to its promotional programs. The program emphasis provides the impact of name brands and good values
that make key departments dominant in the marketplace. "Power alley," a Wal-Mart promotional characteristic, is the high-powered promotional race track in all the stores. The alley
promotions are lined down each aisle in the
store's race track. In most stores, the power alley
will have 100 or more promotional tables or platforms. These tables/platforms contain merchandise with average tickets that are sometimes
100 percent lower than at most chains. This promotional effort is the key to the volume production that has enabled Wal-Mart to maintain
its growth. Included among the 100 or more tables and platforms that make up the total pro-
gram are assorted 2×2 ft. cubes, 3×3 ft. tables,
and 5 ft. square tables and platforms, occasion-
ally joined together. The 2×2 cubes are used
in health and beauty aids, with 18 to 24 items
set in a double row down the center of an interior
aisle. Requiring lower inventory investments,
the small cubes are also used to pull shoppers
into the automotive department located at the
right (or left) rear corner of the race track aisle.

Wal-Mart's strategy also entails the use of
item merchandising. It is a concept by which an
unusual "item" is positioned near or adjacent to
a department to build category dominance. To
create a bigger share of the bed-sheet market and
to build brand image, Cannon sheets at attractive
prices are promoted on a table adjacent to the
domestics department. The item sets the scene
for the particular department and serves as a way
to draw shoppers into the department. All Wal-
Mart chains practice this concept with their
"million-dollar" items. These are basic everyday
needs (sheets, socks, mattress covers) that help
build a category of major brand-name goods that
help build the brand-name image.

The profitable lure of apparel is also becoming increasingly evident in Wal-Mart stores.
Over the next five years, Wal-Mart intends to
build its stake in soft lines to 35 percent, ac-

Exhibit 2   Shelf-Price Comparison, Bartlesville, Oklahoma, Shelf Prices

Item	Wal-Mart	T.G. & Y.	K-Mart
H & BA			
Bayer 100's	$ 1.57	$ 1.60	$ 1.57
Excedrin X-Strength 100's	2.58	3.37	2.06[a]
Bufferin 100's	2.13	2.13	2.13
Bufferin A.S.	1.67[a]	2.09	2.43
Tylenol X-Strength 100's	3.54	3.27	3.29
Tylenol X-Strength 50's	2.33	2.53	2.33
Anacin 200's	3.68	3.97	3.68
Anacin 100's	1.42[a]	1.99	1.97
Flex 16oz. Shampoo	1.68	1.68	1.74
Suave Baby Shampoo 28oz.	1.06	1.14	1.48
Faberge Organic X-tra Body	1.18	1.18	1.18
No More Tears 16oz. Shampoo	2.62	3.12	1.97[a]
Wella Balsam 8oz. Shampoo	1.78	1.77	1.67
Head & Shoulders 15oz. tube	2.97	2.99	1.58[a]
Head & Shoulders 11oz. bottle	2.46	2.67	2.46
Prell tube 5oz.	1.92	1.72	1.92
Pert 15oz.	1.83[a]	2.44	2.13
Silkience 15oz.	2.56	2.78	2.16
Small Electrics			
Mr. Coffee 10 cup	22.88	22.99	24.97
GE automatic percolator	28.42	28.96	28.87
Regal Poly-Perk hot pot	9.96	9.99	10.62
Automotive			
Rain Dance 16oz.	5.54	5.99	5.07
Turtle Zip Wax 18oz.	1.84	2.17	2.07
Phillips TropArctic oil	0.97	0.95	0.97
Quaker State oil	0.97	0.95	0.97
Penzoil 10W-40	0.97	0.95	0.97
PL nondetergent	0.68	0.77	0.74
Hardware			
Powerlok II 20 ft.	11.57	12.99	12.48
Stanley 16oz.	8.44	5.67[a]	9.97
Steelmaster 16oz.	12.76	14.30	11.88
Black & Decker			
7104 Drill	16.88	17.87	15.77
7004 Drill	12.97	12.99	11.97
7504 Jig saw	12.97	11.77	13.48
7580 VSR drill	42.46	34.57	33.88
7308 Circular saw	29.96	35.97	27.88
7300 Circular saw 5½ in.	24.97	27.77	27.97
TOTAL	$284.19	$290.06	$268.31

Source: Discount Store News Research, December 14, 1981, p. 43.
[a]Sale item.

cording to the chain's executives. This is evident in the newer stores opened. In recent stores, the format is upgraded and total space-to-apparel and major soft-lines is as high as 43 percent. Wal-Mart has placed large, prominently placed departmental signs that tend to resemble J. C. Penney's signs. Brand emphasis is concentrated more and more on the apparel side of the store as is obvious with the Wrangler brand emphasis in boys', men's, and women's wear. Most store units also stock Garan knit sport shirts and display them on an eye-catching "brand displayer." Also, Wal-Mart is now trying to build identity in men's socks by displaying signs that read, "Alder from Burlington." Overall, Wal-Mart steers clear of no-names, especially in categories where image counts.

Advertising

The advertising policy, displayed in all Wal-Mart stores, is to take sale advertisements from any other store and match the price. Under this policy, historically, it has held advertising expenditures to 1.5 percent of sales or less. Recent expansion, however, will raise this level to about 1.7 percent of sales or nearly $2.4 billion a year. According to company sources, one third of that total will be spent on newspaper advertising, and television spots will be increased from $6 million to the $7 or $8-million dollar level. Expansion into urban areas has entered Wal-Mart into markets where television time, newspaper space, and radio time are substantially more costly.

In addition to its added level of expansion, Wal-Mart has begun running more expensive, up-scale advertising. In the small town of Fayetteville, Arkansas, where it was opening an 85,000 square foot store, Wal-Mart ran a 36-page, four-color, all-photo, magazine-size, "catalog" circular. This new style resembled a J. C. Penney's catalog. All 36 pages, 11 or so pages of apparel and the remainder of consumables, seasonal merchandise, and hardlines, were full four-color and the circular used models and/or product photography. In contrast to the bigger-store

advertisements, smaller units' circulars are usually 10-page broadsheets with false four-color on the front and back and black and white inside.

Wal-Mart is devising two separate merchandising and advertising strategies: the typical hard-line-oriented 40,000 to 50,000 square foot store and the 85,000 to 90,000 square foot stores that give greater emphasis to the fashion apparel side. This strategy is important to Wal-Mart's future in the ever-changing marketplace.

Distribution Centers

A basic practice of Wal-Mart has been to limit its store operations to about a 450-500-mile radius of distribution to centers, to achieve speed of restocking and savings in delivery costs. As Wal-Mart continues pushing its geographical limits, distribution that is cost-effective becomes more critical.

Located near headquarters in Bentonville, a 525,000 square foot distribution complex handled, in the past, 80 percent of all the goods sold by Wal-Mart. The expansion of the chain has resulted in additional distribution centers being constructed. In Searcy, Arkansas, an equal capacity center was opened to aid in Wal-Mart's expansion into southern Arkansas. Long-range plans called for the construction of a 512,000 square foot center in Palestine, Texas. This center fully came on-line, at the close of 1981. In 1982, a 900,000 square foot distribution center will be built in Cullman, Alabama.

The Palestine distribution center helped Wal-Mart penetrate the Texas border and Gulf Coast markets. Sam Walton is convinced that he can "double, even triple" the size of his company, just with locations in Texas and Louisiana. Shreveport, Louisiana, Houston, Corpus Christi, and Dallas—Fort Worth, Texas have been sited for the expansion of Wal-Mart. Management has already sited the Rio Grande valley and eight more sites in the area for prime expansion moves.

The new Alabama distribution center may be even more critical to the chain's expansion than the Palestine center. Coming on-stream in 1983, the center will provide overnight delivery into the states where the Big K acquisition brought the chain. It will extend into the Carolinas, Georgia, and Florida. These areas could be potential sites for Wal-Mart Country expansion.

Wal-Mart distribution centers (existing, as well as those to be built) are mechanized, utilizing conveyor systems to expedite the flow of merchandise and each serve an approximate proportion of the chain's stores. There are two additional distribution centers in Bentonville that are used for the inspecting and processing of fashion clothing; warehousing for jewelry and sporting goods; operations and accumulation of sale merchandise for shipment to stores as close to the sale as possible. The centers' radius span is to allow Wal-Mart's own trucking fleet to make deliveries in one day.

Wal-Mart trucks are expected to travel about 20-million miles in 1982 at a cost of about $18 million. The distribution centers' total expenses run approximately 2.5 percent of the goods shipped through them (now about 85 percent of the chain's total merchandise assortment). Wal-Mart's move toward establishing distribution centers and trucking fleets in Texas and Alabama is part of its long-range plan to expand its markets outward.

The Acquisition of Big K

Wal-Mart acquired the Kuhn's Big K chain, headquartered in Nashville, Tennessee, in August 1981. The total cost for 92 Big K stores, a large distribution center, headquarters, all of Big K's liabilities, and inventories within each store was about $100 million. Each store is estimated at costing $125,000 each to convert to the Wal-Mart label.

The conversion process (at the close of 1981) was first applied to the five least profitable Big K stores. This served as an acid test of the validity of the acquisition. According to Sam Walton, the average sales gains in these renovated stores have been in excess of 150 percent. In the

first quarter as part of the Wal-Mart chain, the renovated stores contributed $70 million in sales volume.

The purchase helped Wal-Mart's future plans become more attainable. With the Big K stores, Wal-Mart gained penetration of Tennessee, Kentucky, and large "clusters" in Alabama and Mississippi. It also brought Wal-Mart into the new areas of Georgia and South Carolina. Thus, by purchasing a bargain expansion and getting good locations that are profitable to the chain, Wal-Mart stands ready to face the future.

Financing

The company has financed its capital expenditures for expansion primarily through internally generated funds. Funds from operations, $74 million in fiscal 1981, are the primary source of liquidity for the company. For additional externally generated funds, Wal-Mart offered one million shares in 1981 that generated almost $33 million for the company. At fiscal year end, 1981, Wal-Mart had access to $176 million of unused short-term credit.

As far as controlling expenses, Wal-Mart has done so using several strategies: (1) negotiating harder with landlords for store sites (its current occupancy cost is 1.75 percent of sales), (2) store payrolls are tight—currently 7.5 percent (store managers work on smaller base salaries but with richer profit-sharing plans), (3) discouraging employee theft by sharing half the savings with employees, (4) tough bargaining stances on key line items from suppliers, and (5) advertising costs are kept at less than 1.2 percent of sales.

Wal-Mart's operating, selling, general, and administrative expenses (1981) rose 138 percent since 1977, and the cost of goods sold at the chain increased even more by 139.7 percent. Sales of the company rose 142.2 percent during that same period. Earnings for Wal-Mart also increased 193.8 percent since 1977.

The financial statements that follow detail Wal-Mart's impressive financial record. Exhibit 3 is the consolidated balance sheet, and Exhibit

Exhibit 3   Consolidated Balance Sheet

	January 31	
	1981	1980
	(Dollar Amounts in Thousands)	
Assets		
Current assets:		
Cash...............................	$ 6,927	$ 5,090
Short-term money market investments	11,528	—
Receivables	12,666	7,806
Recoverable costs from sale/leaseback......	31,325	15,557
Inventories...........................	280,021	235,315
Prepaid expenses	2,737	2,849
Total Current Assets	345,204	266,617
Property, plant, and equipment, at cost:		
Land................................	5,903	15,002
Buildings and improvements	51,200	42,287
Fixtures and equipment	80,411	56,072
Transportation equipment................	12,969	9,012
	150,483	122,373
Less accumulated depreciation	33,702	23,613
Net property, plant and equipment	116,781	98,760
Property under capital leases.............	152,882	109,608
Less accumulated amortization	23,721	17,806
Net property under capital leases	129,161	91,802
Other assets and deferred charges...........	1,199	700
Total Assets	$592,345	$457,879
Liabilities and Stockholders' Equity		
Current liabilities:		
Notes payable	$ 15,000	$ 25,080
Accounts payable	97,445	100,102
Accrued liabilities:		
Salaries.............................	11,229	12,889
Taxes, other than income	9,627	6,619
Other...............................	25,748	15,148
Accrued federal and state income taxes	11,907	5,365
Long-term debt due within one year	3,375	2,314
Obligations under capital leases due within		
one year	3,270	2,704
Total Current Liabilities	177,601	170,221
Long-term debt	30,184	24,862
Long-term obligations under capital leases	134,896	97,212
Deferred income taxes	1,355	740
Stockholders' equity:		
Preferred stock	—	—
Common stock.........................	3,234	1,512
Capital in excess of par value	67,481	35,064
Retained earnings......................	177,594	128,268
Total Stockholders' Equity..............	248,309	164,844
Total Liabilities and Stockholders' Equity...	$592,345	$457,879

Source: 1981 Annual Report.

4 is the consolidated statement of income. Exhibit 5 highlights the two-year comparison and the five-year financial review of Wal-Mart's performance. Exhibit 6 provides a review of 10 years of growth for Wal-Mart.

Wal-Mart vs. "The Other Guys"

Wal-Mart's five-year financial record through 1981 has paced the discount-store industry. Exhibit 7 shows five-year averages for Wal-Mart and two of its competitors. While running above the industry median, Wal-Mart has stiff competition to face. As Wal-Mart moves into larger metropolitan areas, its competition expands from Magic Mart, Gibson's, T.G. & Y., and K-Mart to include Dayton Hudson's Target, Woolworth, Murphy, and the Caldwell chain.

Although K-Mart is Wal-Mart's closest competitor, Target stores have been making moves to expand into Arkansas, Wal-Mart's home state. At the close of 1981, Target and Wal-Mart vie only in Nashville, Tennessee. However, the Dayton Hudson discount chain purchased three shuttered Woolco stores in Little Rock, an 80,000 square foot unit and two 10,000 square footers. The stores are to be remodeled in early 1982. Over the next two years, industry observ-

Exhibit 4 Consolidated Statement of Income

	Years Ended January 31		
	1981	1980 (Dollar Amount in 000)	1979
Number of stores in operation at the end of the year	330	276	229
Revenues:			
Net sales	$1,643,199	$1,248,176	$900,298
Rentals from licensed departments	5,331	4,804	6,344
Other income—net	6,732	5,288	3,271
	1,655,262	1,258,268	909,913
Costs and expenses:			
Cost of sales	1,207,802	919,305	661,062
Operating, selling and general and administrative expenses	331,524	251,616	182,365
Interest costs:	5,808	4,438	3,119
Debt	10,849	8,621	6,595
Capital leases	1,555,983	1,183,980	853,141
Income before income taxes ...	99,279	74,288	56,772
Provision for federal and state income taxes:			
Current	42,982	31,649	28,047
Deferred	615	1,488	(722)
	43,597	33,137	27,325
Net income	$ 55,682	$ 41,151	$ 29,447
Net income per share:			
Primary and fully diluted	$1.73	$1.34[a]	$.97[a]

Source: 1981 Annual Report.
[a]Adjusted to reflect the 100 percent stock dividend paid on December 16, 1980. See accompanying notes.

Exhibit 5   Wal-Mart's Financial Highlights

Two-Year Comparison
(Dollar amount in thousands)

	1981	1980
Current assets	$345,204	$266,617
Current liabilities. . .	177,601	170,221
Working capital	167,603	96,396
Current ratio	1.94	1.57
Stockholders' equity	$248,309	$164,844
Number of shares outstanding	32,342,445	30,242,522[a]

Five-Year Financial Review
(Dollar amounts in thousands except per share data)

	1981	1980	1979	1978	1977
Net sales	$1,643,199	$1,248,176	$900,298	$678,456	$478,807
Income before income taxes	99,279	74,288	56,772	40,847	30,857
Net income	55,682	41,151	29,447	21,191	16,039
Net income per share:					
Primary	$ 1.73	$ 1.34[a]	$ .97[a]	$ .74[a]	$ .58[a]
Fully diluted	1.73	1.34[a]	.97[a]	.71[a]	.54[a]
Number of stores in operation at the end of the period	330	276	229	195	153

Source: 1981 Annual Report.

[a]Adjusted to reflect the 100 percent stock dividend paid December 16, 1980 to holders of Wal-Mart common stock.

ers say that Texas appears a likely mark for expansion as Target currently covers the state with roughly half the number of stores as Wal-Mart.

The past performance of Wal-Mart in its smaller towns has been aided by its assimilation of technological advances. Exhibit 8 provides the data to support Wal-Mart's operational power among its competition. Thus, the expansive strength of Wal-Mart will be tested by all its competitors in the years to come.

Industry Trends

Within the discount-store industry, there is a definite trend toward upscaled merchandise presentation. K-Mart is adopting a new merchandising program that, for example, is dropping all syn-

thetic fibers in favor of natural blends. In addition, in view of Wal-Mart's success in rural markets, K-Mart is targeting expansion outside of metropolitan areas. Increasing emphasis on promotionally priced goods has caused reductions in many chains' profit margins. According to Kenneth Mache, president of Dayton Hudson (Target), this additional promotional activity will depress the bottom lines for the major chains by cutting into already reduced margins. To combat these problems, many discounters are turning to more updated apparel lines and cosmetics while at the same time reducing the number of items carried.

Macroeconomic factors have a direct impact on industry strategies. In the recessionary environment of early 1982, for example, discounters

Exhibit 6 Ten Years of Growth for Wal-Mart

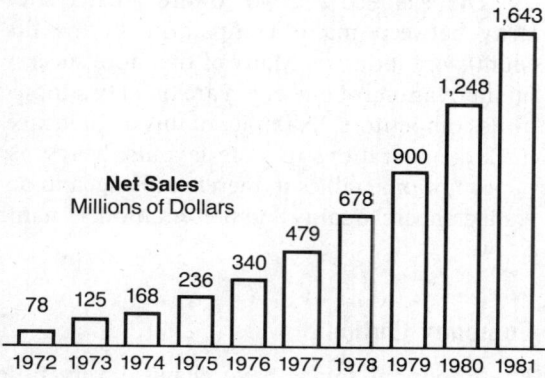

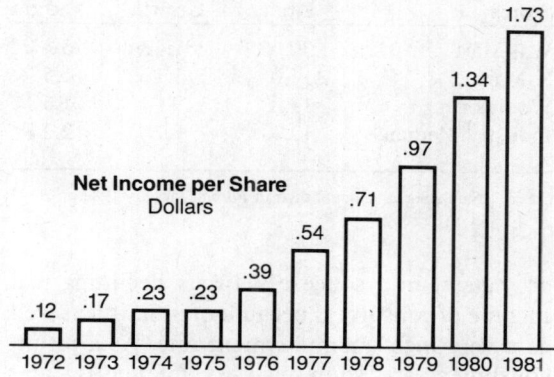

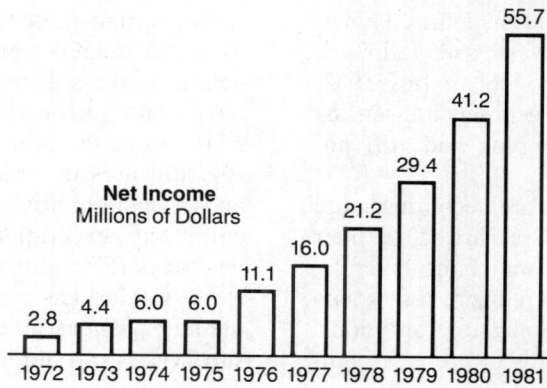

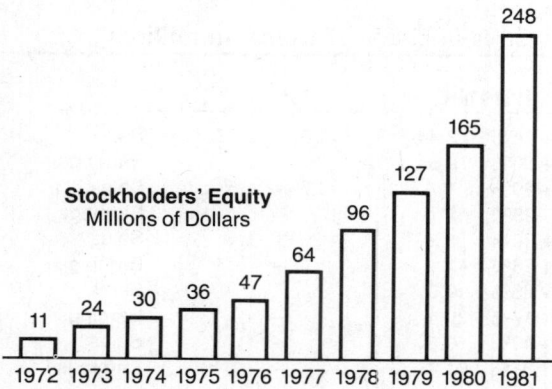

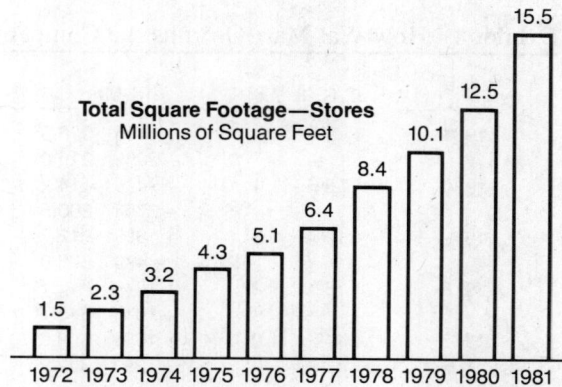

Ten Years of Growth for Wal-Mart

Net Sales
Millions of Dollars

1972	1973	1974	1975	1976	1977	1978	1979	1980	1981
78	125	168	236	340	479	678	900	1,248	1,643

Net Income per Share
Dollars

1972	1973	1974	1975	1976	1977	1978	1979	1980	1981
.12	.17	.23	.23	.39	.54	.71	.97	1.34	1.73

Net Income
Millions of Dollars

1972	1973	1974	1975	1976	1977	1978	1979	1980	1981
2.8	4.4	6.0	6.0	11.1	16.0	21.2	29.4	41.2	55.7

Stockholders' Equity
Millions of Dollars

1972	1973	1974	1975	1976	1977	1978	1979	1980	1981
11	24	30	36	47	64	96	127	165	248

Total Square Footage—Stores
Millions of Square Feet

1972	1973	1974	1975	1976	1977	1978	1979	1980	1981
1.5	2.3	3.2	4.3	5.1	6.4	8.4	10.1	12.5	15.5

Exhibit 7 Five-Year Averages

Stores	Return on Equity	Sales Growth	Profit Margin
Wal-Mart	30.6%	37.4%	3.3%
K-Mart	16.0	17.1	1.5
Woolworth	11.8	9.6	1.6
Industry Median	12.1	9.7	2.2

Source: "Sam's Song," as published in *Forbes,* January 1982.

are caught in a squeeze between declining real income of consumers because of inflation as well as a very high unemployment rate. As a result, consumers are shopping less frequently, and seeking out sale-priced items when they do shop. Of this, a Merrill Lynch analyst, Jeffrey Feiner, remarks, this pattern may reverse itself following the scheduled 10 percent tax cut in July 1982. But retailers believe that consumers are settling into the habit of sale shopping and will not change quickly.

Industry merchandisers are becoming more selective on the merchandise carried in their stores. Today's successful merchant carefully scrutinizes inventories, making sure that goods do not sit on shelves by stepping up promotions. The test for discounters in the future is to combine a low-cost structure with the most innovative merchandising techniques to move the goods.

There is also a trend toward greater similarity between major competitors in the discount-store industry. Many of the more successful innovations of one chain are quickly adopted by its competitors. Examples of this include race-track configurations in store layouts, heavy use of promotional tables in merchandising, and upgraded apparel quality and presentation, to name a few.

Company Outlook

The important things have changed very little for Wal-Mart over the years. The company still makes strong presentations of basic merchandise, still benefits from Sam Walton's entrepreneurial spirit, and still concentrates on the small towns and surrounding rural areas where the store can be the primary source for shoppers. It also still uses the best merchandise techniques and develops or attracts the best merchandise talent, always experimenting with new goods and new ways to present these goods.

Wal-Mart has evolved an intense, high-profile management style that brings together field supervisors and store managers into a chainwide

Exhibit 8 How Wal-Mart Outruns the Competition (Sales in billions/Earnings in millions)

	T.G. & Y.		K-Mart		Wal-Mart		Target		
1981	—		+14%	16.5	+28%	2.44	+26%	2.07	Sales
	—		−20%	210.0	+30%	79.5	—		Earnings
1980	+22%	1.4	+14%	14.2	+29%	1.7	+27%	1.5	Sales
	—		−27%	260.5	+26%	55.7	—		Earnings
1979	+19%	1.3	+13%	12.7	+38%	1.2	+20%	1.1	Sales
	—		+4%	358.0	+28%	41.1	—		Earnings
1978	+18%	1.2	+18%	11.7	+28%	0.9	—		Sales
	—		+18%	343.7	+17%	29.4	—		Earnings
1977	+14%	1.0	+18%	9.9	+42%	0.5	—		Sales
	—		+12%	302.9	+31%	21.4	—		Earnings

Source: Discount Store News Research, December 14, 1981, p. 13–14.

merchandising emphasis, providing new ideas for the company. The best ideas are put into the corporate framework and encouraged to be fulfilled. This is but one of several practices that have helped Wal-Mart gain its current status. Others include the perception of every day low prices by the consumers, and commitment to innovative, cost-control systems with the savings passed on to the consumer. The company utilizes technological advances in its operations for maximum efficiency and productivity. One example, is that the main computer in Bentonville talks directly to vendor computers, resulting in lower out-of-stocks.

Wal-Mart's 1981 annual report reflects its view of the future:

The retailing environment is constantly changing. Competition will continue to improve and become more intense. Life styles will change, and today's solutions will soon be obsolete. But, with a flow of new programs, with the continuing contribution of our dedicated associates and with our commitment to avoid any short-term strategy that does not enhance our long-range goals, we are convinced that improved productivity will be achieved. Our people have truly made the difference, and as they respond to the ever-changing environment, we will serve our customers with the "best value in town."

To Our Shareholders

What's Important Is You! You . . . our customers, associates, vendors and shareholders.

Record sales and earnings marked the year long celebration of our Company's Twenty-Fifth Anniversary. Sales increased 34% to $15.959 billion from $11.909 billion. Net income increased 39% to $627.643 million from $450.086 million. Fully diluted net income per share rose to $1.11, up 41% from $.79 in the prior year.

Sales increases in comparable stores were 11% which follows a 13% same store sales increase in the previous year. These levels of sales increases in our comparable stores indicate we continue to increase our market share. Strong sales advances in a period of very limited inflation and an otherwise slow-growth economic environment are a result of our dedicated associates performing better than ever before. During this past year, they concentrated on the operating philosophies that have sustained our growth in many different economic climates: improving customer service, offering our customers genuine value at the lowest possible everyday prices, effective inventory management, controlling and reducing expenses and listening to one another. We are proud of our associates and their accomplishments. Some of the highlights of these achievements are:

■ Sales productivity in comparable Wal-Mart stores reached $213 per gross square foot of store space, up from $194 last year and $145 just five years ago.

■ Our total retail space was expanded to 77.804 million square feet, a net increase of 14.531 million square feet, up 23% from last year. Store openings included 134 new Wal-Mart stores, 35

*Excerpts from Wal-Mart Stores, Inc. 1988 annual report, pp. 2–3, 12–15, 18–21.

Sam's Wholesale Clubs, six dot Discount Drug stores and two Hypermart★USA stores.

Total Store Square Footage (Millions of Square Feet)

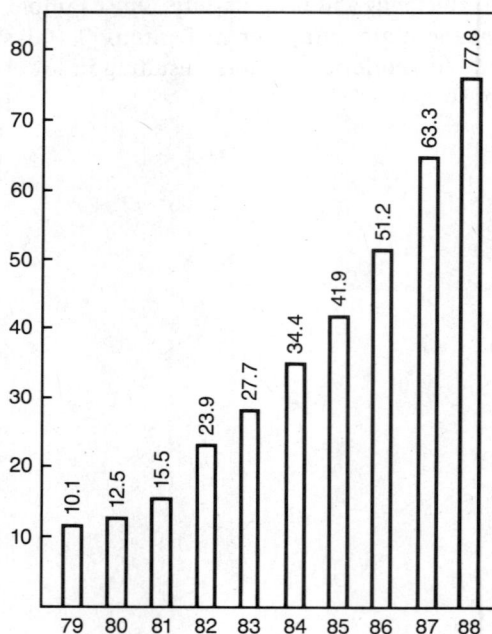

■ Our store renovation and update program included 20 relocations of existing stores into larger units, 25 expansions, 23 remodels, 77 stockroom additions and 106 facelifts and in-store refurbishings. These 251 projects on existing stores impacted 39% of Wal-Mart stores three years old or older.

■ Completion of the largest private satellite communication system in the United States which links all operating units of the Company and the general office with two-way voice, two-way data and one-way video communication. The inauguration of this system featured a live broadcast from Sam Walton to all Wal-Mart associates.

- The addition of 1.477 million square feet to our distribution center system capacity. We expanded three existing facilities and in January 1988, opened our 11th facility in Laurens, South Carolina, a 583 thousand square-foot facility.

- "Store-within-a-store", a new tool to involve and equip assistant managers with the necessary skills to develop their retailing careers, by giving them total management responsibilities for several departments within their assigned store, was successfully implemented in our Wal-Mart stores.

- Net profit as a percentage of sales increased to 3.9% this year compared with 3.8% last year. Planned reductions in initial markup, as well as the increased percentage of Sam's sales to the total and the pass-through of the lower federal income tax rates, were largely offset by a reduction in total expenses.

- Significant improvement in the Company's financial position as a result of strong profit production. Net income, net of dividends, raised shareholders' equity to $2.257 billion from $1.690 billion last year, a 34% increase which follows 32% and 30% increases in fiscal 1987 and 1986, respectively.

Percentage of Return on Common Shareholder's Equity (Millions of Dollars)

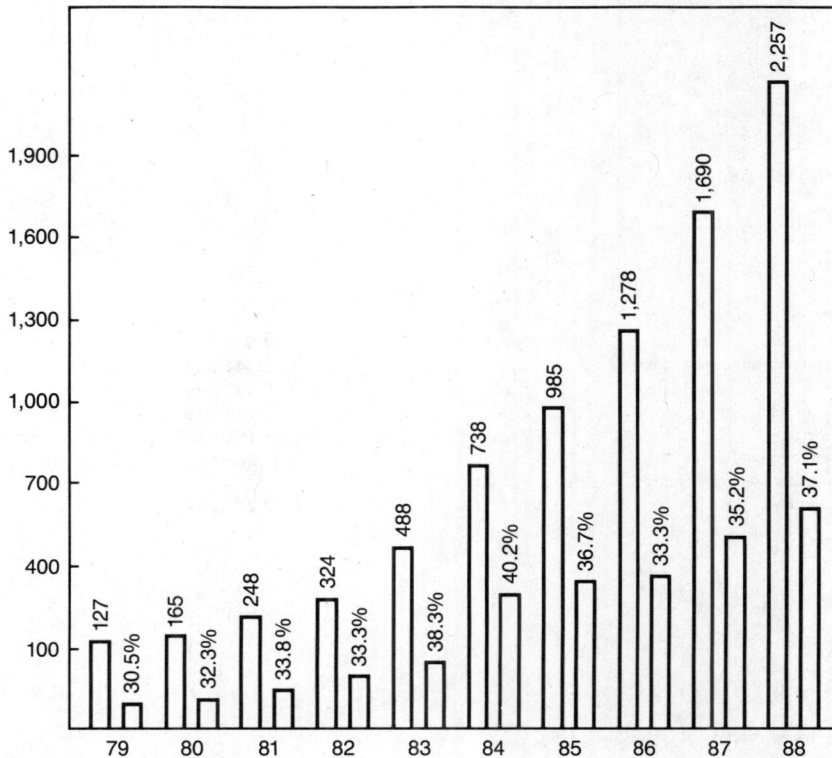

- Sam's Wholesale Clubs sales increased 62% to $2.711 billion from $1.678 billion a year ago, representing a 249% increase over sales of $776 million of just two years ago. Sam's opened 35 units this past year, 17 of which were acquired in the June, 1987 acquisition of Super Saver Warehouse Club, Inc. These 17 units are located throughout the Southeast, complementing existing Sam's units and accelerating Sam's market saturation.

- Hypermart★USA opened its doors in Garland, Texas, a suburb of Dallas, in December, 1987

Ten-Year Financial Summary

Wal-Mart Stores, Inc. and Subsidiaries

(Dollar amounts in thousands except per share data)	1988	1987	1986
EARNINGS			
Net sales	$15,959,255	$11,909,076	$8,451,489
Licensed department rentals and other income-net	104,783	84,623	55,127
Cost of sales	12,281,744	9,053,219	6,361,271
Operating, selling and general and administrative expenses	2,599,367	2,007,645	1,485,210
Interest costs:			
Debt	25,262	10,442	1,903
Capital leases	88,995	76,367	54,640
Taxes on income	441,027	395,940	276,119
Net income	627,643	450,086	327,473
Per share of common stock:			
Net income	1.11	.79*	.58*
Dividends	.12	.085*	.07*
Stores in operation at the end of the period			
Wal-Mart Stores	1,114	980	859
Sam's Wholesale Clubs	84	49	23
FINANCIAL POSITION			
Current assets	$2,905,145	$2,353,271	$1,784,275
Net property, plant, equipment and capital leases	2,144,852	1,676,282	1,303,450
Total assets	5,131,809	4,049,092	3,103,645
Current liabilities	1,743,763	1,340,291	992,683
Long-term debt	185,672	179,234	180,682
Long-term obligations under capital leases	866,972	764,128	595,205
Preferred stock with mandatory redemption provisions	–	—	4,902
Common shareholders' equity	2,257,267	1,690,493	1,277,659
FINANCIAL RATIOS			
Current ratio	1.7	1.8	1.8
Inventories/working capital	2.3	2.0	1.8
Return on assets**	15.5	14.5	14.8
Return on shareholders' equity**	37.1	35.2	33.3

*Adjusted to reflect 100% common stock dividend paid July 10, 1987.

**On beginning of year balances.

and Topeka, Kansas in January, 1988. Hypermart★USA may be described as a blend of the best of a Wal-Mart store, a combination supermarket/general merchandise store and a Sam's Wholesale Club. A true experiment, Hypermart★USA has received strong initial customer acceptance, but our ability to achieve satisfactory profit objectives is still unknown.

We are very pleased with fiscal 1988's profit and sales performance, but even more gratifying has been the opportunity to witness the further

1985	1984	1983	1982	1981	1980	1979
$6,400,861	$4,666,909	$3,376,252	$2,444,997	$1,643,199	$1,248,176	$900,298
52,167	36,031	22,435	17,650	12,063	10,092	9,615
4,722,440	3,418,025	2,458,235	1,787,496	1,207,802	919,305	661,062
1,181,455	892,887	677,029	495,010	331,524	251,616	182,365
5,207	4,935	20,297	16,053	5,808	4,438	3,119
42,506	29,946	18,570	15,351	10,849	8,621	6,595
230,653	160,903	100,416	65,943	43,597	33,137	27,325
270,767	196,244	124,140	82,794	55,682	41,151	29,447
.48*	.35*	.23*	.16*	.11*	.08*	.06*
.0525*	.035*	.0225*	.0163*	.0125*	.0095*	.007*
745	642	551	491	330	276	229
11	3					
$1,303,254	$1,005,567	$ 720,537	$ 589,161	$ 345,204	$ 266,617	$191,860
870,309	628,151	457,509	333,026	245,942	190,562	131,403
2,205,229	1,652,254	1,187,448	937,513	592,345	457,879	324,666
688,968	502,763	347,318	339,961	177,601	170,221	98,868
41,237	40,866	106,465	104,581	30,184	24,862	25,965
449,886	339,930	222,610	154,196	134,896	97,212	72,357
5,874	6,411	6,861	7,438	—	—	—
984,672	737,503	488,109	323,942	248,309	164,844	127,476
1.9	2.0	2.1	1.7	1.9	1.6	1.9
1.8	1.5	1.5	2.0	1.7	2.4	1.9
16.4	16.5	13.2	14.0	12.2	12.7	11.7
36.7	40.2	38.3	33.3	33.8	32.3	30.5

development of our associates. Once again, they have excelled, proving that together we can maintain profitable growth in diverse economic conditions and effectively compete against an ever changing and challenging retailing environment.

We approach this new year, fiscal 1989, confident in our people and the plans they have developed for continued success. We are cognizant of projected economic downturn and the continued sluggishness of the "oil patch", but we believe our strategies and plans will be executed, producing continued gains in market share, expense control and inventory management. We plan to expand our retail square footage to be-

yond 90 million. Construction will include 125 Wal-Mart stores, 18 Sam's Wholesale Clubs, two dot Discount Drug stores and two Hyper-mart★USA stores (one joint venture and one wholly owned). Expansions and relocations of 58 existing stores, including the relocation of three Wal-Mart stores into experimental combination supermarket/general merchandise stores to be operated as Wal-Mart SuperCenters, are also planned.

Exciting new concept development, experimentation, increased sales productivity, lower expenses, new store growth, advanced systems development and continued dedication to improved profitability is indeed challenging, but it's

Consolidated Statements Of Income

Wal-Mart Stores, Inc. and Subsidiaries

(Amounts in thousands except per share data)	Fiscal year ended January 31,		
	1988	1987	1986
Revenues:			
Net sales	**$15,959,255**	$11,909,076	$8,451,489
Rentals from licensed departments	**9,215**	10,779	13,011
Other income-net	**95,568**	73,844	42,116
	16,064,038	11,993,699	8,506,616
Costs and expenses:			
Cost of sales	**12,281,744**	9,053,219	6,361,271
Operating, selling and general and administrative expenses	**2,599,367**	2,007,645	1,485,210
Interest costs:			
Debt	**25,262**	10,442	1,903
Capital leases	**88,995**	76,367	54,640
	14,995,368	11,147,673	7,903,024
Income before income taxes	**1,068,670**	846,026	603,592
Provision for federal and state income taxes:			
Current	**432,133**	373,508	258,197
Deferred	**8,894**	22,432	17,922
	441,027	395,940	276,119
Net income	$ **627,643**	$ 450,086	$ 327,473
Net income per share	$ **1.11**	$ .79*	$ .58*

*Adjusted to reflect 100% common stock dividend paid on July 10, 1987.

See accompanying notes.

nothing new to Wal-Mart—it is Wal-Mart! Our confidence in our 200,000 dedicated Wal-Mart associates has never been stronger. Our 25 years of success and profitable growth are a direct product of their innovative ideas, commitment, suggestions, "entrepreneurial" spirit and hard work. These involved associates serve as the foundation of a mutually beneficial partnership with our customers, shareholders and suppliers.

This report is dedicated to this partnership and its 25 years of pride and success.

Sam M. Walton
Chairman

David D. Glass
President and
Chief Executive Officer

Net Income (Millions of Dollars)

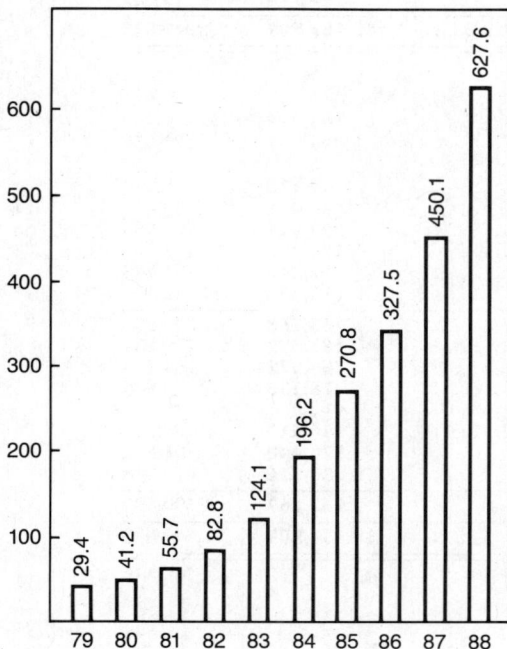

Year	Net Income
79	29.4
80	41.2
81	55.7
82	82.8
83	124.1
84	196.2
85	270.8
86	327.5
87	450.1
88	627.6

1,114 Wal-Mart Stores in 23 States
(Fiscal year ending January 31, 1988)

Wal-Mart Stores in Each State

State	Stores
Alabama	62
Arkansas	75
Colorado	17
Florida	75
Georgia	59
Illinois	57
Indiana	16
Iowa	18
Kansas	36
Kentucky	47
Louisiana	64
Minnesota	4
Mississippi	48
Missouri	101
Nebraska	10
New Mexico	15
North Carolina	12
Oklahoma	79
South Carolina	30
Tennessee	73
Texas	204
Virginia	2
Wisconsin	10

Source: Wal-Mart 1988 annual report

Consolidated Balance Sheets

Wal-Mart Stores, Inc. and Subsidiaries

(Amounts in thousands)	January 31,	
	1988	1987
ASSETS		
Current assets:		
Cash	$ **11,325**	$ 8,527
Short-term money market investments	**—**	157,018
Receivables	**95,928**	90,380
Recoverable costs from sale/leaseback	**126,917**	47,160
Inventories	**2,651,760**	2,030,972
Prepaid expenses	**19,215**	19,214
TOTAL CURRENT ASSETS	**2,905,145**	2,353,271
Property, plant and equipment, at cost:		
Land	**209,211**	134,351
Buildings and improvements	**621,023**	402,845
Fixtures and equipment	**855,926**	655,253
Transportation equipment	**46,301**	45,346
	1,732,461	1,237,795
Less accumulated depreciation	**374,193**	267,722
Net property, plant and equipment	**1,358,268**	970,073
Property under capital leases	**952,305**	832,337
Less accumulated amortization	**165,721**	126,128
Net property under capital leases	**786,584**	706,209
Goodwill	**47,034**	—
Other assets and deferred charges	**34,778**	19,539
Total assets	**$5,131,809**	$4,049,092
LIABILITIES AND SHAREHOLDERS' EQUITY		
Current liabilities:		
Notes payable	$ **104,382**	$ —
Accounts payable	**1,099,961**	924,654
Accrued liabilities:		
Salaries	**89,118**	62,774
Taxes, other than income	**81,064**	46,496
Other	**229,921**	159,985
Accrued federal and state income taxes	**120,773**	132,833
Long-term debt due within one year	**2,046**	1,448
Obligations under capital leases due within one year	**16,498**	12,101
TOTAL CURRENT LIABILITIES	**1,743,763**	1,340,291
Long-term debt	**185,672**	179,234
Long-term obligations under capital leases	**866,972**	764,128
Deferred income taxes	**78,135**	74,946
Common shareholders' equity:		
Common stock (shares outstanding, 565,112 in 1988 and 282,182 in 1987)	**56,511**	28,218
Capital in excess of par value	**170,440**	191,857
Retained earnings	**2,030,316**	1,470,418
TOTAL COMMON SHAREHOLDERS' EQUITY	**2,257,267**	1,690,493
Total liabilities and shareholders' equity	**$5,131,809**	$4,049,092

See accompanying notes.

Wal-Mart Stores, Inc.

Consolidated Statements Of Common Shareholders' Equity

Wal-Mart Stores, Inc. and Subsidiaries

(Amounts in thousands)	Number of shares	Common stock	Capital in excess of par value	Retained earnings	Total
Balance - January 31, 1985	140,223	$14,022	$189,907	$ 780,743	$ 984,672
Net income				327,473	327,473
Cash dividends:					
Common stock					
($.07* per share)				(39,302)	(39,302)
Preferred stock					
($2.00 per share)				(396)	(396)
Accretion of preferred stock					
redemption premium				(70)	(70)
Exercise of stock options	65	7	334		341
Conversion of preferred stock	86	9	977		986
100% common stock dividend	140,374	14,038	(14,038)		
Exercise of stock options	288	28	954		982
Tax benefit from stock options			3,352		3,352
Conversion of preferred stock	9	1	54		55
Other			(434)		(434)
Balance - January 31, 1986	281,045	28,105	181,106	1,068,448	1,277,659
Net income				450,086	450,086
Cash dividends:					
Common stock					
($.085* per share)				(47,850)	(47,850)
Preferred stock					
($1.50 per share)				(266)	(266)
Exercise of stock options	346	34	812		846
Tax benefit from stock options			5,122		5,122
Conversion of preferred stock	791	79	4,817		4,896
Balance - January 31, 1987	282,182	28,218	191,857	1,470,418	1,690,493
Net income				627,643	627,643
Cash dividends:					
Common stock					
($.12* per share)				(67,745)	(67,745)
Exercise of stock options	37	4	452		456
100% common stock dividend	282,219	28,222	(28,222)		
Exercise of stock options	821	82	1,739		1,821
Tax benefit from stock options			9,213		9,213
Other	(147)	(15)	(4,599)		(4,614)
Balance - January 31, 1988	565,112	$56,511	$170,440	$2,030,316	$2,257,267

*Cash dividends on common stock prior to July 10, 1987, have been adjusted to reflect the 100% common stock dividend paid on that date.

See accompanying notes.

Consolidated Statements Of Changes In Financial Position

Wal-Mart Stores, Inc. and Subsidiaries
(Amounts in thousands)

	1988	1987	1986
		Fiscal years ended January 31,	
Source of funds:			
Current operations:			
Net income	$627,643	$450,086	$327,473
Items not affecting working capital in current period:			
Depreciation and amortization	165,962	123,639	89,749
Deferred income taxes	3,189	22,432	17,922
Total from current operations	796,794	596,157	435,144
Net proceeds from exercise of options, and conversion of preferred stock	6,876	10,864	5,282
Additions to long-term debt	11,645	—	141,120
Additions to long-term obligations under capital leases	131,192	184,262	156,453
Reduction of other assets	1,522	1,300	18,609
Disposal of assets	37,341	90,920	9,913
	985,370	883,503	766,521
Application of funds:			
Acquisition of Super Saver Warehouse Club, Inc.			
Property, plant and equipment	10,422	—	—
Other assets	231	—	—
Goodwill	50,034	—	—
Long-term debt	(20,570)	—	—
	40,117	—	—
Additions to property, plant and equipment	527,960	403,660	350,667
Additions to property under capital leases	130,491	182,955	181,487
Reduction in long-term debt, including changes in current maturities	25,777	1,448	1,675
Reduction in long-term lease obligations, including changes in current obligations	28,348	15,339	11,134
Preferred stock conversions	—	4,902	971
Dividends paid	67,745	48,116	39,768
Additions to other assets and deferred charges	16,530	5,695	3,513
	836,968	662,115	589,215
Increase in working capital	$148,402	$221,388	$177,306
Changes in components of working capital:			
Increase (decrease) in current assets:			
Cash	$ 2,798	($ 723)	$ 7,398
Short-term money market investments	(157,018)	(8,150)	165,168
Receivables	5,548	32,718	12,084
Recoverable costs from sale/leaseback	79,757	(105,250)	10,021
Inventories	620,788	642,804	284,243
Prepaid expenses	1	7,597	2,107
	551,874	568,996	481,021
Increase (decrease) in current liabilities:			
Notes payable	104,382	—	—
Accounts payable and accrued liabilities	306,155	301,910	286,840
Accrued federal and state income taxes	(12,060)	43,434	16,040
Long-term debt due within one year	598	(157)	(1,377)
Obligations under capital leases due within one year	4,397	2,421	2,212
	403,472	347,608	303,715
Increase in working capital	$148,402	$221,388	$177,306

Case 22

The Home Depot, Inc.

Corporate Profile

At the close of fiscal 1989, The Home Depot was operating 118 retail warehouse stores selling a wide variety of building supplies and home improvement products to the rapidly growing do-it-yourself (D-I-Y) market and home remodeling professionals. Located in the Southeast, Southwest, West Coast, and Northeast regions of the United States, Home Depot warehouses range in size from 67,000 to 140,000 square feet of enclosed space; most stores have an additional 10,000 to 15,000 square feet of outdoor selling area for gardening and landscaping supplies. A typical warehouse store stocks approximately 30,000 items, including lumber, building materials, wall and floor coverings, paint, plumbing and electrical supplies, hardware, tools, and seasonal merchandise. Founded in 1978, The Home Depot is headquartered in Atlanta, Georgia, and is one of the select companies included in the Standard and Poor's 500 index.

The Home Depot, Inc., is a highly successful company within the home retailing industry. The company has been described by Montgomery Securities, Senior Retailing Analyst, Bo Cheadle as "one of the Premier Retailers in the United States. . . . This is going to be the Wal-Mart of the '90s" in terms of explosive sales growth

Source: Annual Report, The Home Depot, 1989.

Case prepared by Dorothy E. Brawley, Tommy Hackney, Carl Honaker, Jr., Mike Mahoney, and Denise West-Smith, Kennesaw State College. Copyright © 1990 by Dorothy E. Brawley. Reprinted with permission.

(Business Week, 3/19/90). The Company's goal is to become the first true national chain for building supplies in the D-I-Y market.

The success of the company can be attributed to a four prong strategy:

- Personnel training;
- A "customer cultivation" approach to service;
- Strong merchandising appeal; and
- New technology.

The success of the four prong strategy can be credited to the foresight of Mr. Bernie Marcus and Mr. Arthur Blank. Both spend significant time training the company's 118 plus store managers and 375 plus assistant managers. Mr. Marcus personally trains the managers on the company's "customer cultivation" philosophy. His charisma has instilled extreme loyalty from his employees. He inspires the dedication, motivation, and loyalty of his managers throughout the company. Mr. Blank maintains the immense day to day operations throughout the organization. He is strongly involved in selecting the individual store managers. The two men together have created a very successful team using their strengths collectively (AR, 89, p. 2).

Mr. Marcus and Mr. Blank are also dedicated to keeping an entrepreneurial spirit within The Home Depot, Inc. Both are committed to taking the necessary time to train employees and implement necessary procedures to instill the entrepreneurial spirit. They have been quoted as saying "We don't want to run Home Depot as a chain, we want to run it as (118) stores, and we do a great deal to support the stores on a store-by-store basis." The ". . . entrepreneurial environment is very precious to us. Without it, we wouldn't be Home Depot" (Retailers of the Year, *Fortune*, June 1988).

In 1989, the company's sales were $2.8 billion. *Fortune* ranked The Home Depot, Inc., as 38th in the top 50 retailers of the year based on sales. In March 1988 Standard and Poor's Corporation added the company to its 500 stock composite index. In the past 10 years, (1979–1989) The Home Depot, Inc., has been named Retailer of the Year in the home center industry twice and High Growth Retailer six times (89 *AR* p.1; *Fortune* 6/04/90, p. 324; *Wall Street Journal* 3/04/88, p. 18).

Historical Summary

The Home Depot, Inc., was organized by Mr. Bernard Marcus and Mr. Arthur Blank. It was conceived as a new kind of retail store that offered excellent service and low prices to attract higher sales volume. Mr. Marcus and Mr. Blank developed Home Depot into an operation of "Do-It-Yourself Warehouse" (D-I-Y) stores which sell a wide assortment of building materials and home improvement products. A company overview of Home Depot is presented in Exhibits 1, 2, 3, and 4.

In 1978 an investment banker, Mr. Ken Lagone, familiar with the record of Mr. Marcus, assembled a high-powered investor group to launch Mr. Marcus' Do-It-Yourself Warehouse concept. The investors included:

Name	Organization
Joseph Flom	Partner, Skadden, Arps, Slate, Meagher, and Flom
Robert Pirie	President, Rothchild, Inc.
Thomas Marcus	Executive, H. Ross Perot's Electronic Data Systems, Inc.
Thomas Walker	Executive, H. Ross Perot's Electronic Data Systems, Inc.
Frank Borman	Former Astronaut and Retired CEO of Eastern Airlines
Edward Cox	Private Investor

In total, $2 million was raised for the venture which assisted in opening the first two Home Depots in Atlanta, Georgia, on June 22, 1979. (*National Home Center News*, December 1986)

Exhibit 5, a time line, highlights the historical strategies—"patterns in the stream of actions"—of the Home Depot, Inc.

Although initial business was less than planned, an aggressive advertising program has vigorously increased annual growth in sales and earnings, within the past 10 years. Within the last three years (1986–1989) The Home Depot, Inc., has almost tripled its sales and quadrupled its net earnings.

Exhibit 6 presents a performance overview for the last 10 years, 1980–1989.

Mission and Goals

We have built, and will continue to build, our company on an honest and sincere belief in providing the best possible service to every one of our customers.

> Bernard Marcus
> Chairman and Chief Executive Officer
> (Annual Report, 1989, p. 2)

Growing the business by growing the market is a basic philosophy which has guided The Home Depot since day one. Take novice do-it-yourselfers, men and women who have never lifted a hammer, and educate them. Motivate them. Give them affordably priced supplies. Provide them with an array of quality name-brand merchandise. And make project shopping a convenient affair. The result? A growing number of satisfied, confident Home Depot customers who, time and time again, take on more and bigger building, repair, and home improvement projects which not only look good, and add value to

Exhibit 1   The Home Depot, Inc. Company
Overview, 1989*

General Information

Firm Name	: The Home Depot, Inc. 2727 Paces Ferry Road Atlanta, GA 30339 (404) 433-8211
Other Offices	: Fullerton, CA Piscataway, NJ
Trading Symbol	: HD
Trading Markets	: NYSE, PS, BO, MW, Ph
SIC #'s	: 5211–Lumber 5251–Hardware Stores
Industry	: Retail
Fortune 500 Number	: 38 (Retailers List)
Date Incorporated	: 1978
Date Public	: September 22, 1981
Distribution	: Regional • Northeast • West Coast • Southwest • Southeast

Strategy/Structure

Business Description	: Retailer of building supplies and home improvement products for do-it-yourself and home professional market
Identifiable Businesses	: Retail Distribution • Building Material Supplies, • Home Improvement Products
Strategy of Growth	: Single Business, Multi- Product Lines
Vertically Integrated	: No
Competitive Strategy	: Cost Leadership Broad Market Focus
Process of Growth	: Internal Growth—New Stores (Exhibit 2 and 3)
Structure	: Functional (Exhibit 4) Moving to Divisional— Geographic Holding Company Form

*All 1989 data refer to FY ending 1-28-90 unless otherwise specified.
Sources: 1989 Annual Report, p. 2, 4, 16, 32
1989 Form 10-K, p. 1, 2, 3, 4, 7
Fortune, 6/04/90, p. 324

their home, but make them feel good as well (89
AR, p. 5).

Specific objectives include:

▪ The Home Depot is committed to continuing
its *controlled expansion* at a new store rate of
approximately 25% each year. (AR, 1989, p. 2)
Management's goal is to open approximately 75
stores in the Northeast over the next five years
(1989, AR, p. 3). Their goal is to go national,
with $10 billion in sales from more than 350
locations by 1995. (*Business Week* 3-19-90, Will
Home Depot be the Wal-Mart of the '90s?)

▪ The Home Depot is committed to increasing
its *operating performance.* This includes becoming more efficient and profitable on a store by
store basis as measured by per store and per foot
sales growth, annualized inventory turnover; as
well as company wide growth in new stores, net
income, dividends, and stock price (1989, AR,
pp. 2–3).

▪ The Home Depot is committed to keeping its
entrepreneurial culture intact.

▪ The Home Depot continues its commitment
to being a *good corporate citizen* by being active
in and donating to charitable projects. The bulk
of the assistance is applied to two key issues:
affordable housing and "at-risk" youth (AR,
1989, p. 3).

Operations

Technology/Delivery

In order to distribute their product, Home Depot
pioneered the **discount warehouse** concept in the
retail building supply industry. Through the use
of large warehouse type retail distribution centers, Home Depot is able to bring a wide variety
of products to the market at competitive prices.
The latest in satellite and computer technology
is employed to manage the inventory and support distribution (1989, 10K, pp. 3-4).

Exhibit 2 Store Growth

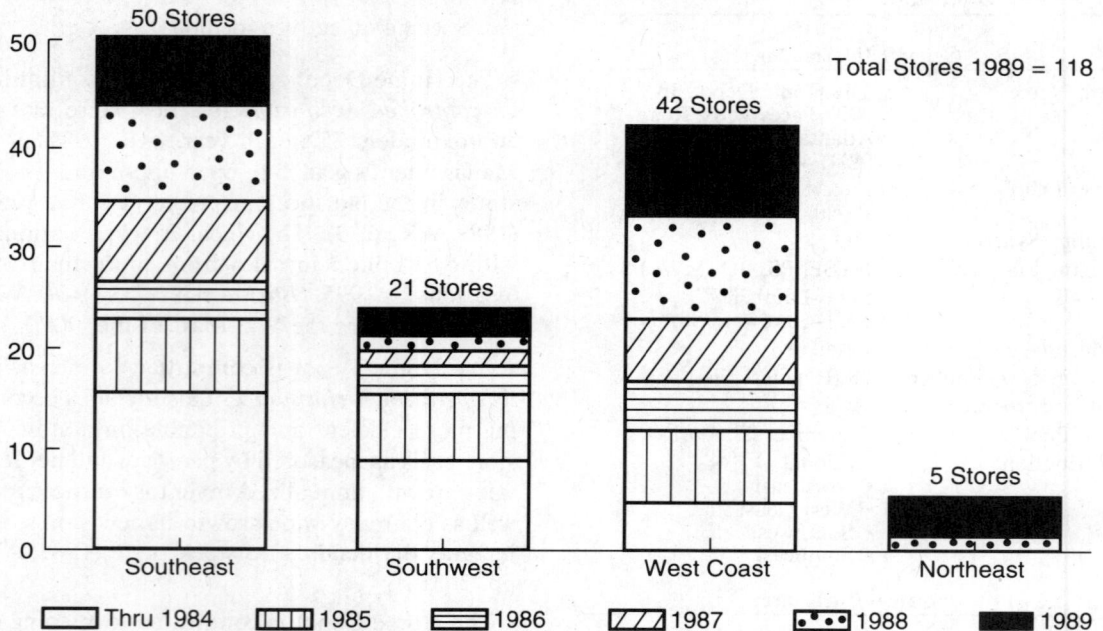

Inventory

The "Suggested Order Quantity" or SOQ system, is a computerized tool the chain provides each store for determining inventory reordering points. Since Home Depot's management asserts that the people in the store know the best required inventory levels, the SOQ approach is often modified by a store manager's own "gut feeling."

As much as 90% of reordering is performed by store managers based on information received from departmental personnel. With this amount of reordering performed in the store, it is imperative that company merchandisers stay abreast of inventory conditions (*National Home Center News*, June, 1988). This is accomplished through a $3.5 million store-wide satellite system which enables the company's computer systems to communicate with the headquarter's main-frame without the use of telephone lines (*Building Supply Home Centers*, June, 1988). Daily sales are also monitored utilizing this system.

Warehouse Concept

Mr. Bruce Berg (senior vice president of merchandising, Eastern Region) has stated, "we feel our only sales limitation is getting products to the floor fast enough." As a means of maximizing the warehouse format and therefore increasing profitability, Home Depot is now purchasing in pallet quantities. This concept allows products to be moved immediately to the sales floor (*Building Supply Home Centers*, June, 1988). The need for central warehousing is eliminated by utilizing each store as its own warehouse.

Store Openings/Location

As of April 6, 1990, the company has opened

Exhibit 3 Store Locations

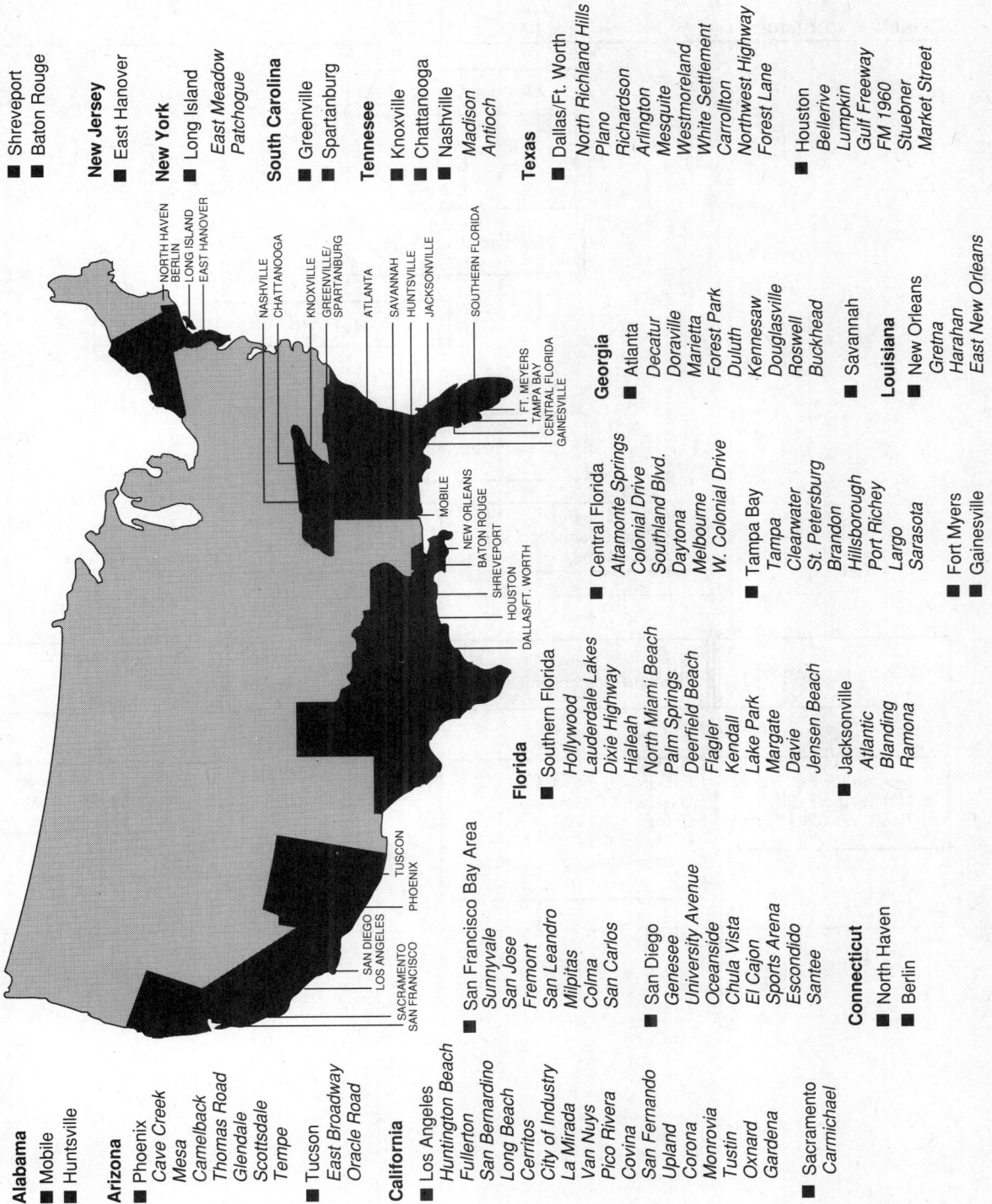

Alabama
- Mobile
- Huntsville

Arizona
- Phoenix
  - *Cave Creek*
  - *Mesa*
  - *Camelback*
  - *Thomas Road*
  - *Glendale*
  - *Scottsdale*
  - *Tempe*
- Tucson
  - *East Broadway*
  - *Oracle Road*

California
- Los Angeles
  - *Huntington Beach*
  - *Fullerton*
  - *San Bernardino*
  - *Long Beach*
  - *Cerritos*
  - *City of Industry*
  - *La Mirada*
  - *Van Nuys*
  - *Pico Rivera*
  - *Covina*
  - *San Fernando*
  - *Upland*
  - *Corona*
  - *Monrovia*
  - *Tustin*
  - *Oxnard*
  - *Gardena*
- Sacramento
  - *Carmichael*
- San Francisco Bay Area
  - *Sunnyvale*
  - *San Jose*
  - *Fremont*
  - *San Leandro*
  - *Milpitas*
  - *Colma*
  - *San Carlos*
- San Diego
  - *Genesee*
  - *University Avenue*
  - *Oceanside*
  - *Chula Vista*
  - *El Cajon*
  - *Sports Arena*
  - *Escondido*
  - *Santee*

Connecticut
- North Haven
- Berlin

Florida
- Southern Florida
  - *Hollywood*
  - *Lauderdale Lakes*
  - *Dixie Highway*
  - *Hialeah*
  - *North Miami Beach*
  - *Palm Springs*
  - *Deerfield Beach*
  - *Flagler*
  - *Kendall*
  - *Lake Park*
  - *Margate*
  - *Davie*
  - *Jensen Beach*
- Jacksonville
  - *Atlantic*
  - *Blanding*
  - *Ramona*
- Central Florida
  - *Altamonte Springs*
  - *Colonial Drive*
  - *Southland Blvd.*
  - *Daytona*
  - *Melbourne*
  - *W. Colonial Drive*
- Tampa Bay
  - *Tampa*
  - *Clearwater*
  - *St. Petersburg*
  - *Brandon*
  - *Hillsborough*
  - *Port Richey*
  - *Largo*
  - *Sarasota*
- Fort Myers
- Gainesville

Georgia
- Atlanta
  - *Decatur*
  - *Doraville*
  - *Marietta*
  - *Forest Park*
  - *Duluth*
  - *Kennesaw*
  - *Douglasville*
  - *Roswell*
  - *Buckhead*
- Savannah

Louisiana
- New Orleans
  - *Gretna*
  - *Harahan*
  - *East New Orleans*
- Shreveport
- Baton Rouge

New Jersey
- East Hanover

New York
- Long Island
  - *East Meadow*
  - *Patchogue*

South Carolina
- Greenville
- Spartanburg

Tennessee
- Knoxville
- Chattanooga
- Nashville
  - *Madison*
  - *Antioch*

Texas
- Dallas/Ft. Worth
  - *North Richland Hills*
  - *Plano*
  - *Richardson*
  - *Arlington*
  - *Mesquite*
  - *Westmoreland*
  - *White Settlement*
  - *Carrollton*
  - *Northwest Highway*
  - *Forest Lane*
- Houston
  - *Bellerive*
  - *Lumpkin*
  - *Gulf Freeway*
  - *FM 1960*
  - *Stuebner*
  - *Market Street*

Map labels:
NORTH HAVEN
BERLIN
LONG ISLAND
EAST HANOVER
NASHVILLE
CHATTANOOGA
KNOXVILLE
GREENVILLE/SPARTANBURG
ATLANTA
SAVANNAH
HUNTSVILLE
JACKSONVILLE
SOUTHERN FLORIDA
FT. MEYERS
TAMPA BAY
CENTRAL FLORIDA
GAINESVILLE
MOBILE
NEW ORLEANS
BATON ROUGE
SHREVEPORT
HOUSTON
DALLAS/FT. WORTH
SAN DIEGO
LOS ANGELES
SACRAMENTO
SAN FRANCISCO
TUSCON
PHOENIX

Exhibit 4 Structure

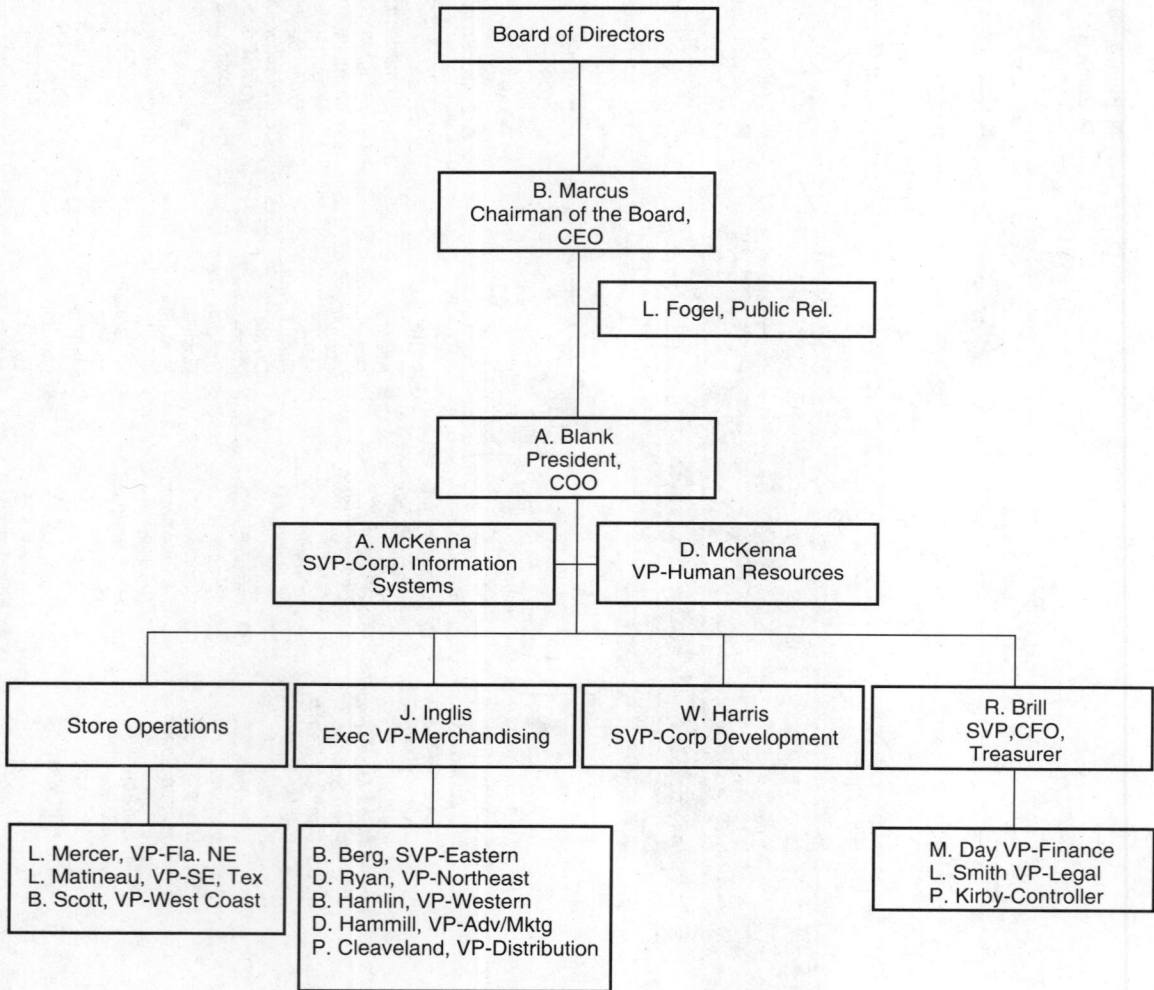

```
                        ┌─────────────────────┐
                        │  Board of Directors │
                        └─────────────────────┘
                                   │
                        ┌─────────────────────┐
                        │      B. Marcus      │
                        │  Chairman of the Board, │
                        │         CEO         │
                        └─────────────────────┘
                                   │
                                   │────────┌──────────────────────┐
                                   │        │ L. Fogel, Public Rel.│
                                   │        └──────────────────────┘
                                   │
                        ┌─────────────────────┐
                        │      A. Blank       │
                        │     President,      │
                        │        COO          │
                        └─────────────────────┘
```

A. McKenna SVP-Corp. Information Systems		D. McKenna VP-Human Resources

Store Operations	J. Inglis Exec VP-Merchandising	W. Harris SVP-Corp Development	R. Brill SVP,CFO, Treasurer

| L. Mercer, VP-Fla. NE
L. Matineau, VP-SE, Tex
B. Scott, VP-West Coast | B. Berg, SVP-Eastern
D. Ryan, VP-Northeast
B. Hamlin, VP-Western
D. Hammill, VP-Adv/Mktg
P. Cleaveland, VP-Distribution | | M. Day VP-Finance
L. Smith VP-Legal
P. Kirby-Controller |

Exhibit 5 Historical Time Line

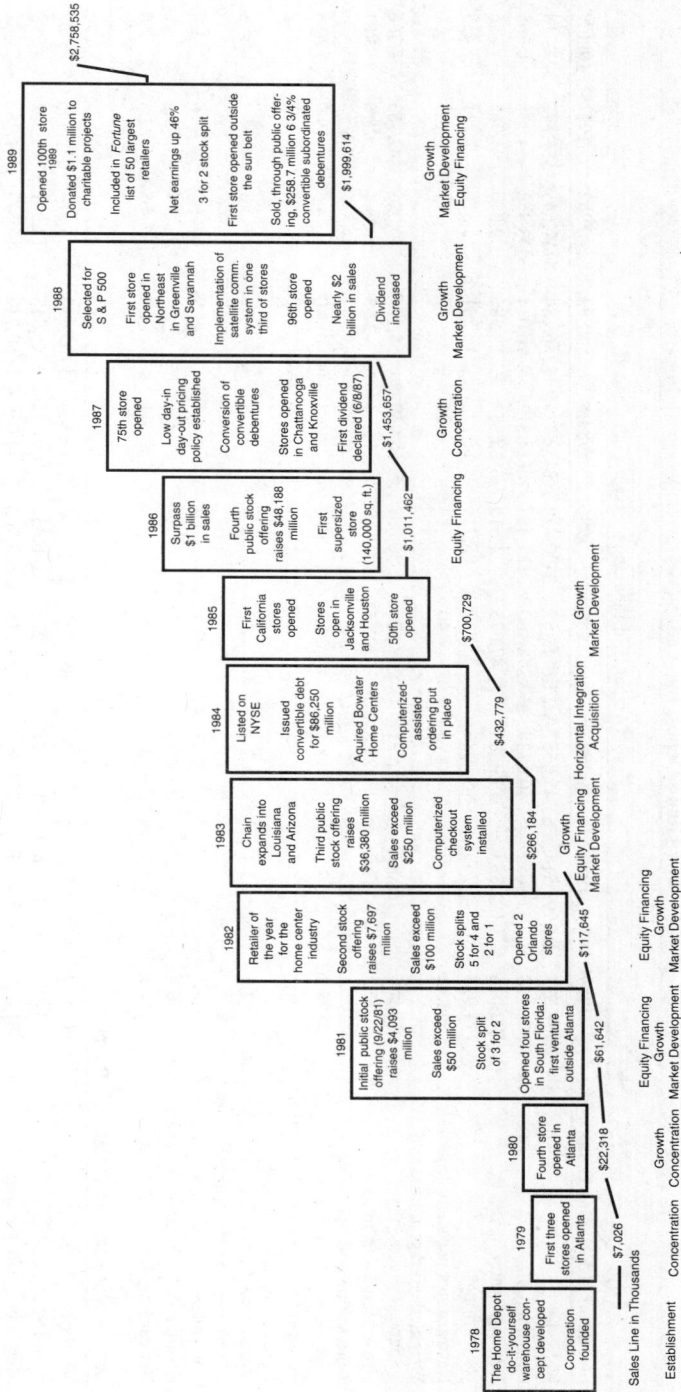

1978
The Home Depot do-it-yourself warehouse concept developed

Corporation founded

1979
First three stores opened in Atlanta

1980
Fourth store opened in Atlanta

1981
Initial public stock offering (9/22/81) raises $4,093 million

Sales exceed $50 million

Stock split of 3 for 2

Opened four stores in South Florida: first venture outside Atlanta

1982
Retailer of the year for the home center industry

Second stock offering raises $7,697 million

Sales exceed $100 million

Stock splits 5 for 4 and 2 for 1

Opened 2 Orlando stores

1983
Chain expands into Louisiana and Arizona

Third public stock offering raises $36,380 million

Sales exceed $250 million

Computerized checkout system installed

1984
Listed on NYSE

Issued convertible debt for $86,250 million

Aquired Bowater Home Centers

Computerized-assisted ordering put in place

1985
First California stores opened

Stores open in Jacksonville and Houston

50th store opened

1986
Surpass $1 billion in sales

Fourth public stock offering raises $48,188 million

First supersized store (140,000 sq. ft.)

1987
75th store opened

Low day-in day-out pricing policy established

Conversion of convertible debentures

Stores opened in Chattanooga and Knoxville

First dividend declared (6/8/87)

1988
Selected for S & P 500

First store opened in Northeast in Greenville and Savannah

Implementation of satellite comm. system in one third of stores

96th store opened

Nearly $2 billion in sales

Dividend increased

1989
Opened 100th store 1989

Donated $1.1 million to charitable projects

Included in *Fortune* list of 50 largest retailers

Net earnings up 46%

3 for 2 stock split

First store opened outside the sun belt

Sold, through public offering, $258.7 million 6 3/4% convertible subordinated debentures

$2,758,535

$1,999,614

$1,453,657

$1,011,462

$700,729

$432,779

$266,184

$117,645

$61,642

$22,318

$7,026

Sales Line in Thousands

Establishment   Concentration   Concentration   Growth   Concentration   Equity Financing   Growth   Market Development   Equity Financing   Growth   Market Development   Growth   Equity Financing   Market Development   Equity Financing   Horizontal Integration   Acquisition   Growth   Market Development   Equity Financing   Concentration   Growth   Market Development   Growth   Market Development   Equity Financing   Growth   Market Development   Equity Financing

Exhibit 6 Ten Year Selected Financial and Operating Highlights

The Home Depot, Inc. and Subsidiaries

(Amounts in thousands, except where noted)

	1989	1988	1987	1986	1985	1984(1)	1983	1982	1981	1980(1)
Statement of Earnings Data										
Net sales	$2,758,535	$1,999,514	$1,453,657	$1,011,462	$700,729	$432,779	$256,184	$117,645	$51,542	$22,318
Gross margin	766,758	539,652	403,739	278,160	181,457	114,319	70,014	33,358	14,735	6,855
Earnings before taxes	182,015	125,833	95,586	47,073	11,619	26,252	18,986	9,870	1,963	856
Net earnings	111,954	76,753	54,086	23,873	8,219	14,122	10,261	5,315	1,211	453
Net earnings per share (S)(2)	1.42	1.00	.75	.40	.14	.25	.18	.11	.03	.01
Weighted average number of shares(2)	78,980	76,883	71,991	59,805	56,807	56,930	55,877	50,025	47,363	48,366
Gross margin—% to sales	27.8	27.0	27.8	27.5	25.9	26.4	27.3	28.4	28.6	30.7
Store selling and operating expenses—% to sales	18.3	17.8	18.1	18.7	19.2	17.2	17.0	16.5	19.0	20.6
Pre-opening expenses—% to sales	.3	.4	.3	.3	1.1	.4	.9	.4	1.5	.2
General and administrative expenses—% to sales	2.5	2.4	2.6	2.7	2.9	3.0	2.9	3.3	3.7	4.3
Net interest expense (income)—% to sales	.1	.1	.2	1.1	1.2	(.3)	(.9)	(.2)	.6	1.8
Earnings before taxes—% to sales	6.6	6.3	6.6	4.7	1.7	6.1	7.4	8.4	3.8	3.8
Net earnings—% to sales	4.1	3.8	3.7	2.4	1.2	3.3	4.0	4.5	2.3	2.0
Balance Sheet Data and Financial Ratios										
Total assets	$1,117,534	$ 699,179	$ 528,270	$ 394,741	$380,193	$249,364	$105,230	$ 33,014	$16,906	$ 4,507
Working capital	273,851	142,806	110,621	91,076	106,451	100,110	49,318	12,901	5,502	1,399
Merchandise inventories	381,452	294,274	211,421	167,115	152,700	84,046	58,712	17,575	11,263	2,881
Net property and equipment	514,440	332,416	244,503	168,981	160,816	73,577	21,129	5,954	3,503	1,246
Long-term debt	302,901	107,508	52,298	116,907	199,943	117,942	4,384	236	3,738	1,013
Stockholder's equity	512,129	382,938	320,559	163,042	89,092	80,214	65,278	18,354	5,204	(285)
Book value per share (S)(2)	6.67	5.08	4.33	2.55	1.57	1.42	1.17	.72	.11	N/A
Long-term debt to equity—%	59.1	28.1	16.3	71.7	224.0	147.0	6.7	1.3	71.8	N/A

Current ratio	**1.94:1**	1.74:1	1.75:1	1.85:1	2.27:1	3.22:1	2.43:1	1.92:1	1.70:1	1.75:1
Inventory turnover	**5.9x**	5.8x	5.4x	4.6x	4.1x	4.2x	4.9x	5.8x	5.2x	6.2x
Return on average equity—%	**25.2**	21.6	21.1	20.3	9.7	19.3	24.5	45.1	58.7	N/A

Statement of Cash Flows Data

Depreciation and amortization	**$ 21,107**	14,673	10,646	$ 8,697	$ 5,193	$ 2,368	$ 903	$ 389	$ 176	$ 126
Capital expenditures	**204,972**	105,123	89,235	52,363	99,767	50,769	16,081	2,883	2,488	186
Cash dividends per share ($)(2)	**.11**	.07	.04	—	—	—	—	—	—	—

Customer and Store Data

Number of markets	**30**	24	19	17	15	11	7	3	2	1
Number of stores	**118**	96	75	60	50	31	19	10	8	4
Square footage at year-end	**10,424**	8,216	6,161	4,828	4,001	2,381	1,449	696	507	249
Change in square footage—%	**26.9**	33.4	27.6	20.6	68.0	64.3	108.2	37.3	103.6	36.1
Average square footage per store	**88**	86	82	80	80	77	76	70	63	62
Number of customer transactions	**84,494**	64,227	48,073	34,020	23,324	14,256	8,479	4,164	1,916	889
Average sale per transaction ($)	**32.65**	31.13	30.24	29.73	30.04	30.36	30.21	28.25	26.90	25.11
Number of employees	**17,500**	13,000	9,100	6,600	5,400	4,000	2,400	1,100	650	300

Other Data

Net sales increase—%	**38.0**	37.6	43.7	44.3	61.9	68.9	117.8	128.3	130.9	217.7
Average total company weekly sales	**$ 53,049**	$ 38,452	$ 27,955	$ 19,451	$ 13,476	$ 8,166	$ 4,927	$ 2,262	$ 991	$ 421
Weighted average weekly sales per operating store	**515**	464	418	355	343	366	360	281	187	107
Comparable store sales increase—%	**12.9**	13.4	18.0	7.0	2.3	14.0	31.0	46.8	57.5	55.4
Weighted average sales per square foot ($)	**303**	282	265	230	223	247	245	210	153	89
Advertising expense—% to sales	**1.1**	1.5	2.0	2.4	3.2	2.5	2.9	2.6	3.4	3.2

1 Fiscal years 1984 and 1980 consisted of 53 weeks, all other years reported consisted of 52 weeks.

N/A—Not applicable.

2 All periods have been adjusted for a three-for-two stock split-up declared in June 1989 and effected in the form of a dividend.

AR 1989, pg 1.

120 stores. Plans are to open 28 additional stores during the remainder of fiscal 1990. (1989 Form 10-K) New stores will generally be larger than existing stores; i.e., 140,000 square feet compared to 86,000 square feet—therefore selling space is expected to grow at a higher rate than the number of stores (1988 Annual Report).

Operations will oversee all new store openings, addition of new fixtures, plus remodeling of outdated locations.

The following illustrates the company's geographical locations.

Location	Number of Stores
Florida	30
California	33
Texas	16
Georgia	13
Arizona	9
Louisiana	5
Alabama	2
South Carolina	2
Tennessee	4
Connecticut	2
New Jersey	2
New York	2
	120

Home Depot's policy has been to expand by leasing second use space whenever possible. In order to secure strategic market locations, the company is finding it necessary to construct its own stores or to enter into lease commitments for stores to be built to company specifications (1989 Form 10-K, p. 6).

Home Depot's ultimate goal is to become the first true do-it-yourself *national chain*. Present strategy is aggressive expansion into markets where the company has already established a high profile and strong consumer acceptance; i.e., Southeast, Southwest, and the West Coast. Long-term strategy includes expansion nationally, with special emphasis over the next 5 years into the Northeast (1989, p. 3, Annual Report).

Merchandising

Product/Service

The products which Home Depot sells are building materials and home improvement items. They carry a wide offering of products including lumber, hardware, electrical and plumbing supplies, flooring, kitchen cabinets, home furnishings, and garden supplies. In addition to this product selection Home Depot offers its customers advice and knowledge on how to select and install these products. This service is provided through knowledgeable sales personnel, in-store demonstrations, and an assortment of pamphlets and how-to books (1989, 10K, pp. 2–3).

A typical Home Depot store will stock approximately 30,000 product items, including variations in color and size during the course of a year. Each store will carry a wide selection of quality and nationally advertised brand name merchandise. The following depicts Home Depot's product groupings ranked by each grouping's contribution to profitability for fiscal year 1989 (1989, p. 3 Form 10-K).

Product Group	% of Sales
Building Materials, Lumber, Floor and Wall Coverings	31.0%
Plumbing, Heating, and Electrical Supplies	29.5%
Seasonal and Specialty Items	14.5%
Paint & Furniture	12.9%
Hardware & Tools	12.1%
	100.0%

Through in-store demonstrations and professional clinics, Home Depot has developed a service frequently referred to as "customer cultivation." Customer cultivation is revealed through Home Depot employees who go beyond recommending appropriate products, tools, and materials. Sales personnel actually cultivate the customer by teaching/demonstrating methods and techniques of performing a job safely and efficiently. This unique aspect of the company's service will serve as a form of market research and keep employees alert to helping the next customer learn from the problems and successes of the last one (1989 Annual Report, pp. 6–8).

Customers/Markets
Home Depot's primary market is the retail distribution to the do-it-yourselfer and the small independent contractor. In the late 1970s Home Depot identified that there were an increasing number of homeowners with the inclination toward doing home improvement projects on their own. Their product and service offering was targeted towards this market. In addition to D-I-Yers, Home Depot also caters to the small independent contractors that like the advantages of purchasing their job supplies in one location at a price competitive with their traditional suppliers. Home Depot's regional market coverage is currently concentrated in the Southeast, Southwest, and West Coast. They are currently expanding into the Northeast in the continuing drive to be nationwide.

In 1989, The Home Depot has taken the idea of customer stimulation one step further and has identified programs which appeal to specific groups.

First, the company launched its Professional Business Customer (PBC) program for smaller contractors and commercial accounts such as property management firms and corporate maintenance departments. Qualified businesses receive the advantages of telephone ordering, merchandise delivery, and credit accounts (nonrecourse to the company), all of which motivate them to shop at The Home Depot.

A second, valued consumer group targeted by The Home Depot is the upscale, female shopper. Results of this program have been especially promising in the Northeast market, where a broader selection of high-end, decorating products are successfully being sold (1989 AR p. 8).

Purchasing
The company buys its merchandise from approximately 2,400 vendors. Since vendors are limited to handling no more than 10% of the company's purchases, the company is not dependent upon any single vendor (1989 Form 10-K, p. 3). The Home Depot only chooses vendors who possess the capability of keeping up with the company's sales and expansion.

Initial buying decisions are made at the corporate level by merchandise managers, who are also responsible for pricing, item selection, and presentation on the sales floor. The majority of reorders from vendors are made by store management personnel (1989, p. 3 Form 10-K).

Price
Home Depot stresses an "Everyday Low Pricing" strategy. This concept means across-the-board lower prices and fewer deep-cutting sales (*Building Supply Home Centers*, June, 1988). Professional shoppers are employed to regularly check prices at competitor's operations to ensure that everyday prices are competitive within each market (1989, p. 4, Form 10-K).

Utilizing a cost leadership strategy, the company's 1988 gross margin was 27.0%. When compared to the Home Center Composite gross margin of 26.87% (*Do-It-Yourself Retailing*, September, 1989), Home Depot's gross margin reveals operating efficiencies, good pricing policies, and strong ability to compete successfully with other companies in the do-it-yourself field.

Promotion
The company maintains an aggressive advertising program utilizing newspaper, television, radio and direct mail. All of the company's print advertising is prepared by its own staff which is responsible for context, layout, production, and media placement. Home Depot's advertising stresses competitive prices, broad assortments, and store services (1989 Form 10-K, p. 4).

Credit Card Program

In 1988 the company tested a new credit card program in Florida and Georgia. Home Depot has launched a new credit program for its Professional Business Customer (PBC) (1989 Annual Report, p. 8).

Human Resources

Employee Selection

Mr. Blank personally selects individuals for store manager positions. In an effort to obtain new ideas and skills applicable to the do-it-yourself industry, all executive level positions are recruited from outside the company.

The Home Depot selects people for its stores who relish the challenge of finding the right solution to the customer's needs. The Company seeks out individuals who want the opportunity to grow with the Company by building a career at The Home Depot (1989, Annual Report p. 6). An informal screening of sales floor applicants is performed prior to actual hiring.

Employee Training

The Company maintains an elaborate training program, in part conducted by top officers of the company. Eight times a year Home Depot conducts a six-day manager's course for assistant managers, store managers, and regional managers. The course covers such topics as:

- Management Information Systems;
- Effective Management;
- Profit Planning; and
- People Management.

Mr. Marcus himself conducts an all-day session on the Home Depot "religion," and an outside consultant teaches classes on effective delegation skills, time management, and personnel productivity (*National Home Center News*, December, 1986).

The company has instituted a formal employee orientation and training program under its Vice President—Human Resources. Currently, all sales floor personnel attend weekly training sessions conducted by manufacturers' representatives and the company's own staff. The Home Depot's policy is to hire and train personnel in the anticipation of future store expansion (1989 Form 10-K, p. 3).

Labor/Union Relations

The company has never experienced a strike or any work stoppage. Management believes that its employee relations are satisfactory. There are no collective bargaining agreements covering any of the company's employees.

Compensation

Home Depot has recently implemented a new bonus plan for store managers and executives at the regional manager level and above.

The plan was constructed around a primary performance indicator assigned to personnel categories subject to a bonus. Operations personnel were assigned return on assets (ROA) as their parameter, while merchandising personnel were assigned gross margin return on investment (GMROI) as their parameter.

Individuals assigned these performance incentives can earn up to 40% additional pay over their base salary for performance, plus 10% for superior sales performance (*National Home Center News*, December, 1988).

Sales floor employees receive above market wages for their services plus special recognition; i.e., service badges, for exceptional performance.

The company maintains an Employee Stock Ownership Plan (ESOP) for substantially all full-time employees (1989, p. 29, Annual Report). The plan allows participants to purchase company stock at a 15% discount from the stock's fair market value.

Information Systems

Home Depot's goal is to become the first true national D-I-Y chain. In order to obtain this goal, the company continues to stress low overhead and implement new technological systems in an effort to integrate separate stores. Such systems include (*Building Supply Home Centers*, June, 1988):

1. A *general ledger system* which helps executives analyze accounts-payable information by store. The system also tracks thousands of invoices dealt with each week.

2. A *broadcast video system*. The Home Depot Television Network, which allows management executives to conduct training courses and communicate via a two-way hookup.

3. *UPC coding* which eliminates the need for individual price stickers on products.

4. A *store-wide satellite data communications system* which enables the company's computer system to communicate with the headquarter's mainframe.

Finance

Capital Resources
The company has a revolving line of credit agreement for a maximum of $300 million. Management believes that availability of these funds, cash generated from operations, and/or its ability to obtain alternate forms of financing, (public stock offerings, convertible subordinated debentures, etc.) will enable the company to complete its store expansion program through fiscal 1991 (1989 Annual Report, p. 27).

Liquidity
Cash flow generated from store operations provides the company with a significant source of liquidity; e.g. working capital has shown recent improvement reaching $274 million in 1989. This is a good indication to short-term creditors that short-term debt will be paid when due. In addition, a portion of Home Depot's inventory is financed under vendor credit terms (1989 Annual Report, p. 1).

Dividend Policy
The Company did not declare dividends prior to fiscal 1987. During fiscal 1989, Home Depot paid a quarterly dividend of $.02 per share in March and $.03 per share in July, September, and December.

Future dividends will depend on the company's earnings, capital requirements, financial condition, and other influences considered relevant to the Board of Directors (1989 Form 10-K p. 8).

Financial Analysis
Exhibit 7 represents a Condensed Common-Size Comparative **Balance Sheet** for fiscal 1986, 1987, 1988, and 1989. This comparison illustrates:

- The relative importance of current assets (depicting a downward trend) versus noncurrent assets (depicting an upward trend). The upward movement in noncurrent assets is primarily due to the increase in property and equipment.

- A stable trend in current liabilities versus a downward trend in noncurrent liabilities. The reduction in noncurrent liabilities is due to utilization of liquid assets for reduction of long-term debt.

- Overall, continuous improvement in the financial position.

Exhibit 8 represents a Common-Size Comparative **Statement of Earnings** for fiscal 1986 through 1989. Here, all items on the Statement of Earnings are placed in common-size in terms of sales. This comparison illustrates:

- That approximately 72.5 cents out of every dollar of sales was required to cover the cost of goods sold over the past four years.

- That 2.86 cents out of every 1989 dollar of sales remained for profit as compared to only 2.4 cents profit in 1986.

- Even though operating expenses reveal a healthy dollar increase each year, on a relative basis, minimum change has occurred in expenses over the past three years.

Exhibits 9 and 10 highlight key ratios for The Home Depot, its key competitors, and the do-it-yourself industry. It should be noted that the comparison to Lowe's represents the most valid peer comparison.

Competition

The D-I-Y market is a dynamic and growing market. Currently estimated by the Home Improvement Research Institute to be in excess of $100 billion in sales (AR, HD, 1989, p. 4), the domestic industry is projected to grow to $138 billion by 1994 (*Do-It-Yourself Retailing*, September, 1989). The barriers to entry are limited as the technology is readily available, the capital requirement is not overwhelming and there are few trade or governmental restrictions on the industry. Because of this, there are a large number of competitors in the industry and the largest competitor has less than 3% market share. The following is a brief summary of the top 7 competitors of Home Depot.

Lowes—Headquartered in Wilkesboro, N.C., Lowes is the largest retailer of building materials and supplies in the country. Lowes has traditionally focused on the contractor/builder market but is redirecting its efforts toward the D-I-Y market. Ten years ago contractors accounted for 59% total revenue but in 1988 they only accounted for 41%. Management's current focus is to move towards 30% contractor business with the balance being in the D-I-Y segment. In 1989 Home Depot passed Lowes to become the largest home-repair chain in the country (*Business Week* 3-19-90).

Payless Cashways—To avert a takeover bid, senior management recently took the company private through a leveraged buy-out. This left the company with $1.1 billion in debt which will limit the capital available for financing growth. Plans for 1989 include opening 3 new stores in smaller markets not likely to attract large warehouse retailers and to put more emphasis on the contractor business.

Builders Square—After starting as Home Centers of America in Texas in 1983, Builders Square has been purchased by K-Mart and grown to 138 stores and $1.5 billion in sales in only 6 years. With K-Mart's financial backing, market share was taken at the expense of profits, as 1988 is reported to be the company's first profitable year. Builders Square's format is a direct copy of Home Depot although they only compete head to head in a few markets.

Grossman's—Since emerging from bankruptcy in 1986, Grossman's has only been able to manage 5 or 6% revenue growth per year. The weakening of the home construction industry in their primary market, the Northeast, will not help this trend. To counter this, they are shifting greater emphasis towards the D-I-Y market by remodeling existing stores. This strategy may come too late as the large warehouse retailers such as Home Depot and Hechinger's Home Quarters units start entering their markets.

Hechinger—Concentrated in the mid-Atlantic states, this long time building materials retailer has come on strong in the D-I-Y market during the last few years. Acquisition has been a significant element of their growth as they have recently acquired the Home Quarters Warehouse stores and the Triangle Building Supply retail division.

Wickes Company—After selling Wickes Lumber to a management group that took it private with a leveraged buy-out, Wickes Company remains a major player in the California D-I-Y market. Their Builder's Emporium and Orchard Supply Hardware are thriving although it remains to be seen if this diversified conglomerate will remain dedicated to the D-I-Y industry.

Home Club—This Zayre subsidiary experienced excellent growth in the West Coast and Southwest markets during 1988. With Zayre's financial backing they could be a significant player in the years to come if the trend continues. However, structural changes in the parent company could affect this segment.

Exhibit 7 The Home Depot, Inc.

Condensed Common-Size Comparative Balance Sheet

(Dollars in Thousands)

	FYE 2/1/87	Common Size %	FYE 1/38/88	Common Size %	FYE 1/29/89	Common Size %	FYE 1/28/90	Common Size %
Assets								
Cash and Equivalents	$ 17,124	4.34%	$ 25,595	4.85%	$ 15,853	2.27%	$ 69,525	6.20%
Short-term investments at cost	0	0%	0	0%	0	0%	65,856	5.89%
Amounts Receivable, Net	9,937	2.52%	15,228	2.88%	17,614	2.52%	38,933	3.48%
Merchandise Inventories	167,115	42.34%	211,421	40.02%	294,274	42.09%	381,452	34.13%
Prepaid Expenses	3,713	0.94%	5,043	0.95%	9,201	1.32%	10,474	.94%
Total Current Assets	197,889	50.13%	257,287	48.70%	336,942	48.19%	566,240	50.60%
Property and Equipment, Net	168,981	42.81%	244,503	46.28%	332,416	47.54%	514,440	46.03%
Other Assets	27,871	7.06%	26,480	5.01%	29,821	4.27%	36,854	3.30%
Total Assets	$394,741	100.00%	$528,270	100.00%	$699,179	100.00%	$1,117,534	100.00%
Liabilities								
Accounts Payable	$ 67,800	17.18%	$ 93,859	17.77%	$126,431	18.08%	$ 172,876	15.47%
Other Current Liabilities	39,013	9.88%	52,807	10.00%	67,705	9.68%	119,513	10.69
Total Current Liabilities	106,813	27.06%	146,666	27.76%	194,136	27.77%	292,389	26.16
Long-Term Debt	116,907	29.62%	52,298	9.90%	107,508	15.38%	302,901	27.10%
Deferred Income Taxes	6,988	1.77%	7,985	1.51%	13,960	2.00%	9,514	.85%
Other Long-Term Liabilities	991	0.25%	762	0.14%	637	0.09%	601	.05%
Total Liabilities	231,699	58.70%	207,711	39.32%	316,241	45.23%	313,016	28.00%
Stockholders' Equity	163,042	41.30%	320,559	60.68%	382,938	54.77%	512,129	45.83%
Total Liabilities and Stockholders' Equity	$394,741	100.00%	$528,270	100.00%	$699,179	100.00%	$1,117,534	100.00%

Sources: *1987 Moody's Industrial Manual.*
1989 Value Line.
1989 Annual Report, p. 22.
1988 Annual Report, pp. 22–23, 4–5.

Exhibit 8 The Home Depot, Inc.

Common-Size Comparative Statement of Earnings

(Dollars in Thousands)

	FYE 2/1/87	Common Size %	FYE 1/31/88	Common Size %	FYE 1/29/89	Common Size %	FYE 1/28/90	Common Size %
Sales	$1,011,462	100.00%	$1,453,657	100.00%	$1,999,514	100.00%	$2,758,535	100.00%
Cost of Merchandise Sold	733,302	72.50%	1,049,918	72.23%	1,459,862	73.01%	1,991,777	72.20%
Gross Profit	278,160	27.50%	403,739	27.77%	539,652	26.99%	766,758	27.80%
Operating Expenses:								
Selling and Store	189,290	18.71%	263,212	18.11%	356,831	17.85%	504,363	18.28%
Pre-opening	3,198	0.32%	4,608	0.32%	7,552	0.38%	9,845	.36%
General and Administrative	27,376	2.71%	37,678	2.59%	48,485	2.42%	67,901	2.46%
Total Operating Expenses	219,864	21.74%	305,498	21.02%	412,868	20.65%	582,109	21.10%
Operating Income	58,296	5.76%	98,241	6.76%	126,784	6.34%	184,649	6.69%
Other Income (Expenses)								
Interest Income	1,026	0.10%	761	0.05%	751	0.04%	13,320	.48%
Interest Expense	(12,249)	−1.21%	(3,416)	−0.23%	(1,702)	−0.09%	(15,954)	−0.58%
Total Other Income (Expenses)	(11,223)	−1.11%	(2,655)	−0.18%	(951)	−0.05%	(2,634)	−0.10%
Earnings before Interest and Taxes	47,073	4.65%	95,586	6.58%	125,833	6.29%	182,015	6.60%
Income Taxes	23,200	2.29%	41,500	2.85%	49,080	2.45%	70,061	2.54%
Net Earnings	$ 23,873	2.36%	$ 54,086	3.72%	$ 76,753	3.84%	111,954	4.06%

Sources: *1987 Moody's Industrial Manual.*
1988 Annual Report, pp. 4–5, 21.
1989 Value Line.
1989 Annual Report, p. 21.

Exhibit 9 The Home Depot, Inc.

Financial Ratio Analysis

	1986	1987	1988	1989	Trend	Industry*	Comparison to Ind.
Liquidity							
Current	1.85:1	1.75:1	1.74:1	1.94:1	Up	2.01:1	Low/Unf**
Quick	.29:1	.31:1	.22:1	.63:1	Up	.58:1	High/Fav
Working Capital ($000)	$91,076	$110,621	$142,806	$273,851	Up	$191,329	High/Fav
Leverage							
Debt/Assets	.57:1	.38:1	.43:1	.53:1	Up	.48:1	High/OK
Long-Term Debt/Equity	.72:1	.16:1	.28:1	.59:1	Up	.45:1	High/OK
Activity							
Asset Turnover	2.56 X	2.75 X	2.86 X	2.47 X	Down	2.28 X	High/Fav**
Fixed Asset Turnover	5.14 X	5.36 X	5.52 X	5.00 X	Down	5.35 X	Low/Unf
Inventory Turnover	6.05 X	6.88 X	6.79 X	7.23 X	Up	6.37 X	High/Fav
Accts. Rec. Turnover	101.79 X	95.46 X	113.52 X	70.85 X	Down	32.28 X	High/Fav
Avg. Collection Period	3.54 D	3.77 D	3.17 D	5.08 D	Up	11.15 D	Low/Fav
Profitability							
Return on Sales	2.36%	3.72%	3.84%	2.86%	Down	2.12%	High/Fav
Return on Investment	6.05%	10.24%	10.98%	7.07%	Down	4.81%	High/Fav
Return on Equity	14.64%	16.87%	20.04%	15.42%	Down	10.20%	High/Fav
Gross Profit Margin	27.50%	27.77%	26.99%	27.80%	Stable	26.78%	High/Fav

*Industry ratios equal average ratios of the following D-I-Y companies: 1) Home Depot 2) Grossman's 3) Lowe's 4) Hechinger's 5) Scotty's
**Unf = Unfavorable   Fav = Favorable
Sources: *1989 Annual Report*
Datext Information System
1990 Value Line

Exhibit 10 Retail, Do-It-Yourself Industry

1988 Financial Ratio Analysis

	Home Depot	Grossman's	Lowe's	Hechinger	Scotty's	Industry Average
Liquidity						
Current	1.94:1	1.82:1	1.94:1	2.48:1	1.89:1	2.01:1
Quick	.63:1	.37:1	.61:1	.94:1	.38:1	.58:1
Working Capital ($000)	$273,851	$95,000	$260,000	$250,000	$77,754	$191,329
Leverage						
Debt/Assets	.53:1	.64:1	.41:1	.40:1	.42:1	.48:1
Long-Term Debt/Equity	.59:1	.75:1	.26:1	.37:1	.27:1	.45:1
Activity						
Asset Turnover	2.47 X	3.25 X	2.31 X	1.63 X	1.76 X	2.28 X
Fixed Asset Turnover	5.00 X	9.78 X	4.81 X	3.52 X	3.66 X	5.35 X
Inventory Turnover	7.23 X	7.92 X	6.23 X	6.23 X	4.26 X	6.37 X
Accts. Rec. Turnover	70.85 X	29.62 X	21.74 X	16.07 X	23.10 X	32.28 X
Avg. Collection Period	5.08 D	12.15 D	16.56 D	22.40 D	15.59 D	11.15 D
Profitability						
Return on Sales	2.86%	1.50%	2.83%	2.78%	.61%	2.12%
Return on Investment	7.07%	4.87%	6.53%	4.53%	1.07%	4.81%
Return on Equity	15.42%	13.47%	11.60%	8.59%	1.94%	10.20%
Gross Profit Margin	27.80%	28.09%	24.39%	25.65%	27.97%	26.78%

Sources: 1989 Annual Report.
Datext Information System.
1990 Value Line.

Scotty's—Their historical dominance in Florida was erased by the entry of the D-I-Y warehousing giants, Home Depot and Builders Square. This has left management scrambling for a survival strategy while trying to deal with a takeover by the Belgium GIB Group.

As Home Depot pushes its way into the Northeast, its competitive situation will be altered considerably. Smaller local and regional competitors are being hit hard by the invasion. The past year Mr. Goodbuys Corp., a Philadelphia-based chain, has shuttered two Long Island stores and a third in New Jersey, citing the added competition from Home Depot. Channel Home Centers Inc. in Whipping, N.J., has scaled back on Long Island, while Hechinger Co. in Landover, Md., has decided against opening a Long Island store it already built. Supermarkets General Corp's Rickel Home Center chain is losing money and urging a format that may move it to home decorating. One rival vowing to fight back is Pergament Home Centers Inc. in Melville, N.Y. A number of Pergament stores are much

smaller than Home Depots' giants and emphasize hardware and paint. But the newest are just as large as Home Depot. President Michael Lurie insists his 35 store chain has enough clout to repel Home Depot. Some rival stores in the Northeast may be as well-stocked as a Home Depot, but analysts say the existing chains in the region will have to cut prices if they plan to compete head-on with Home Depot locations (*Business Week*, 3-19-90, Will Home Depot be the Wal-Mart of the '90's?).

From these summaries, it can be seen that the D-I-Y market is composed of competitors in various stages of business development. In order to graphically represent these diverse competitors, a Boston Consulting Group (BGC) competitive portfolio matrix has been employed. Exhibit 11 shows the top competitors in the D-I-Y industry. The size of the circles represents the relative sales volume of the company. The vertical axis represents the market growth rate of the company and the horizontal axis measures the market share of the company.

Exhibit 11 Competitor Portfolio

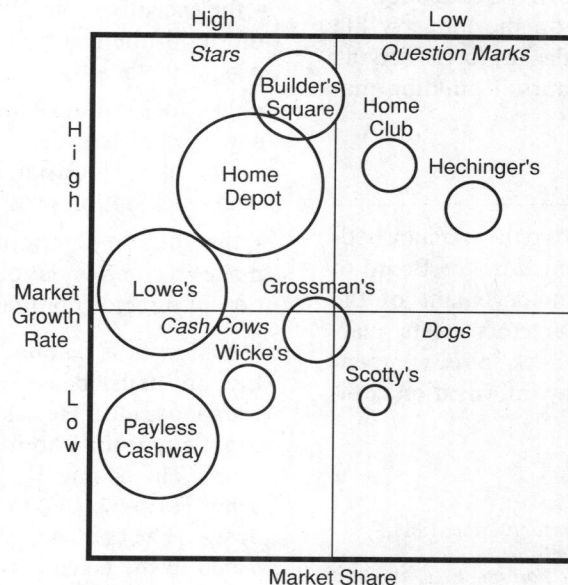

Within the Do-It-Yourself Industry, Hechingers and Home Club are in the growth stage as their primary focus at this time is to establish a significant market presence. Home Depot and Builder's Square are in competitive turbulence trying to develop customer loyalty by refining product price and service offering. Lowe's and Payless Cashways are the mature firms that are being pulled back into competitive turbulence by the onslaught of the D-I-Y warehouse retailers. To defend their markets they are directing focus towards the D-I-Y customer to replace lost business. Scotty's has also suffered in the face of D-I-Y retailer competition and is mired in the competitive turbulence. Within this industry segment, Wickes and Grossman's are in decline. Wickes has diversified into automotive and industrial supply and sold off its Wicke's Lumber unit. They may be moving away from the industry or they may be attempting to recycle themselves back into the D-I-Y segment through their Builders Emporium chain. Grossman's has had significant financial woes and unimpressive growth. They may divest portions of their operation and restructure in the near future. (Value Line Investment Surveys, 1989) See Exhibit 12 for each firm's placement on the industry life cycle. Exhibit 13 highlights the key forces driving competition in the do-it-yourself building materials industry.

Corporate Leadership

The Home Depot, Inc., relies on two major bodies for its leadership and direction, the Board of directors and the senior management of the Company. The Board of Directors meets quarterly to make decisions on stock splits, compensation of officers, and to stay informed on company matters. The board is a passive external coalition since Mr. Marcus and Mr. Blank make the majority of decisions for the company.

The senior management of The Home Depot, Inc., consists of 17 executive vice presidents, senior vice presidents, and vice presidents. Four executives are instrumental in setting the company's direction. They are Mr. Bernie Marcus, Mr. Arthur Blank, Mr. Jim Inglis, and Mr. Ron Brill. Marcus, Blank, and Chief Financial Officer Ron Brill get the credit for building Home Depot's strength. All three were fired from their top posts at the Handy Dan chain in 1978, after a long running feud about control with Sanford Sigoloff, then chairman of parent Daylin Inc. The trio decided to open a business and do things *their* way. Their overriding rule was to avoid bureaucracy (*Business Week*, March 19, 1990). A brief biography of the board of directors and senior management is listed below.

Mr. Bernard Marcus, *chairman of the board and chief executive officer.* Mr. Marcus is an inside member of the Board. He owns over 5 percent of the company's stock. He is a member on three of the board's committees:

- the executive committee that exercises the authority of the board of directors between meetings of the board;

- the stock option committee that determines and administers the employee incentive stock option plan, stock purchase plan, and non-qualified stock option plan; and

- the directors' nominating committee that makes recommendations to the board for selection of director nominees.

Mr. Marcus is cofounder of The Home Depot, Inc., and assisted in originating the do-it-yourself warehouse idea. He has been described as a charismatic type for whom retailing is a religion. He wants The Home Depot, Inc., to become the Sears Roebuck of the home improvement industry. The company's training program is dedicated to the belief that the company is not run by managers; it's run by missionaries whose

Sources: 1989 Form 10-K, pp. 3, 5–6.
1989 Annual Report, p. 32.
Proxy Statement, May, 1988.
"1988 Retailers of the Year," *Fortune*, June, 1988.
National Home Center News, 1986.
"The Fix Is in at Home Depot," *Fortune*, Feb., 1988.
Internal Interviews, October/November, 1989.

Exhibit 12   Industry Life Cycle

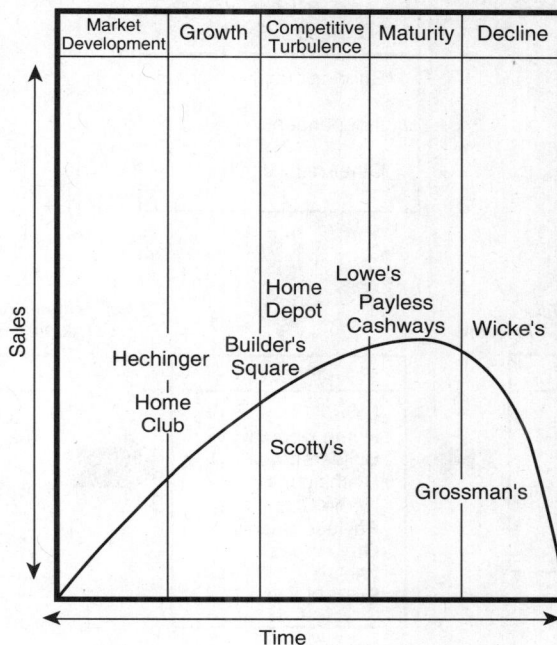

basic business beliefs are in the primacy of the customer and the store employee. Mr. Marcus dedicates up to 20% of his time training assistant managers, store managers, and regional managers on the company's mission and beliefs. Mr. Marcus is 61 years of age.

Mr. Arthur Blank, *president and chief operating officer.* Mr. Blank is an inside member of the board. He owns 1.9 percent of the company's stock and is a member of the executive committee and the stock option committee. Mr. Blank has been on the board since the company began in 1978. He cofounded the company along with Mr. Marcus and actively participates in The Home Depot, Inc.'s managerial training program, spending up to 50 percent of his time in this capacity. He has consistently supported and participated, along with other senior management, in the Outward Bound program. Mr. Blank encourages risk and was quoted as "getting irritated when they (the managers) sit pat and

follow what everybody else is doing." Mr. Blank is 47 years of age.

Mr. Ronald M. Brill, *senior vice president–chief financial officer* and *treasurer.* Mr. Brill is an internal member of the board. He owns .20 percent of the company's stock. He is not a member of the board's committees. He joined the company as a controller in 1978 and has advanced within the organization. He was elected treasurer in 1980, elected vice president of finance in May, 1981, and senior vice president and CFO in September, 1984. He also participates in the managerial training program explaining financial statements and terms in relationship to customer service. He was instrumental in the creation of the customer credit program. Mr. Brill is 46 years of age.

Mr. Kenneth G. Langone, *chairman of the board and president of Invemed Associates, Inc.,* is an external member of the board of directors. He owns 1.72 percent of The Home Depot, Inc.'s

Exhibit 13 Forces Driving Competition

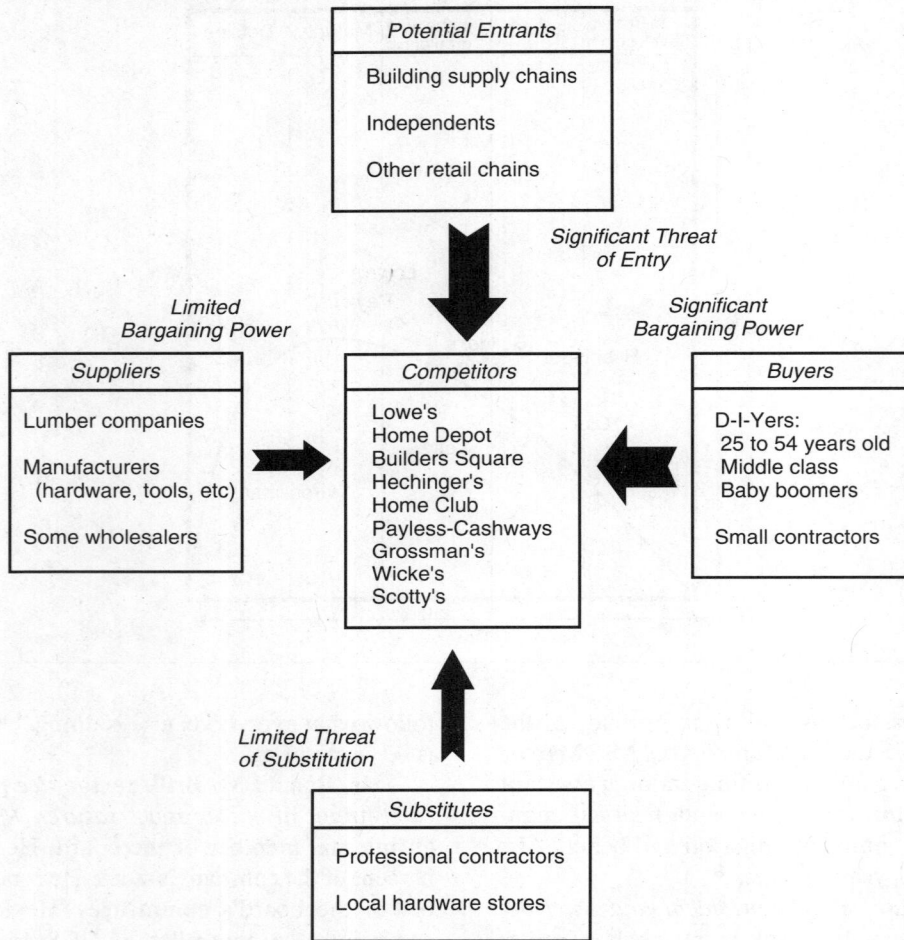

```
                    ┌─────────────────────────┐
                    │    Potential Entrants    │
                    ├─────────────────────────┤
                    │  Building supply chains  │
                    │  Independents            │
                    │  Other retail chains     │
                    └─────────────────────────┘
                              Significant Threat
                                  of Entry
```

Limited Bargaining Power

Significant Bargaining Power

Suppliers	Competitors	Buyers
Lumber companies	Lowe's	D-I-Yers:
	Home Depot	25 to 54 years old
Manufacturers	Builders Square	Middle class
(hardware, tools, etc)	Hechinger's	Baby boomers
	Home Club	
Some wholesalers	Payless-Cashways	Small contractors
	Grossman's	
	Wicke's	
	Scotty's	

Limited Threat of Substitution

Substitutes
Professional contractors
Local hardware stores

stock. Mr. Langone was instrumental in arranging the original investment capital to start The Home Depot, Inc. He had a previous profitable investment experience with Mr. Bernard Marcus and Daylin Corporation's subsidiary Handy Dan. He is a member of the board's executive committee, compensation committee, stock option committee, and directors' nominating committee. He and Mr. Marcus reside on the board of directors for The Ohio Mattress Company. He was contracted by The Home Depot, Inc., to con-

sult on investment banking matters for $100,000 during 1988. He has served on the board since the creation of the company in 1978. Mr. Langone is 54 years of age.

Mr. Milledge A. Hart, III, *chairman of the board of The Hart Group,* is an external member of the Board of Directors. He owns .54 percent of The Home Depot, Inc.'s stock. He is a member of the board's compensation committee, audit committee that selects the company's auditors, and the directors' nominating committee. He has served on the board since the creation of the company in 1978. Mr. Hart is 56 years of age.

Mr. Alan D. Schwartz, *managing director of corporate finance, Bear Stearns and Company,* is an external member of the board of directors. He owns .01 percent of The Home Depot, Inc.'s stock. He is a member of the audit committee. Mr. Schwartz is 40 years of age.

Mr. Frank Borman, *retired chairman of the board and chief executive officer of Eastern Airlines, Inc. and chairman of the board of Patlex Corporation,* is an external member of the board of directors. He owns .14 percent of The Home Depot, Inc.'s stock. He is a member of the audit committee. Mr. Borman was an original investor of the company and has served on the board for 8 years. Mr. Borman is 62 years of age.

Mr. Berry R. Cox, *director of Texas Commerce Bank and Texas Commerce Bancshares, Inc.,* is an external member of the Board of Directors. Mr. Cox owns .67 percent of The Home Depot, Inc.'s stock. He is a member of the audit committee and the compensation committee. He has served on the board for 13 years. Mr. Cox is 36 years of age.

Mr. Frederick DeMatteis, *chairman of the board for The Dematteis Organization,* a building and development organization, is an external member of the board of directors and owns .81 percent of The Home Depot, Inc.'s stock. He is a member of the audit committee and the compensation committee. He has served on the board for 13 years and is 67 years of age.

Mr. James Inglis, *executive vice president of merchandising,* joined the company in 1983. His original position was vice president of merchandising. He was promoted in 1988 to senior vice president of merchandising. He is the only executive-level officer in the company. He was previously employed with Dixieland. He is responsible for 160 plus people within his organization. His area purchases, advertises, and markets the 30,000 plus stock keeping units for the 120 stores.

Mr. W. Andrew McKenna, *senior vice president of corporate information systems,* recently joined the company in March, 1990. Prior to his position at Home Depot, Mr. McKenna served as partner-in-charge, management consulting, at Deloitte & Touche for ten years.

Mr. William E. Harris, *senior vice president of corporate development,* joined the company in 1986. He was previously employed with J.C. Penney. Mr. Harris assisted The Home Depot, Inc., with the original lease of J.C. Penney's Atlanta Treasury locations.

Mr. Bruce Berg, *senior vice president of merchandising,* joined the company in 1985 as vice president of merchandising. He was originally employed with Wickes Lumber.

Corporate Culture/Values

- Bernard Marcus is quoted as saying "our profits are due to our people." He spends one day a month training employees to instill his employee oriented values. Mr. Marcus views the organization (see Exhibit 14) as supporting the store manager.

- Two of the company's major strategies are personnel training and a customer cultivation approach to service.

- Decision making is pushed down to regional and store managers because they are close to the customer and know what the customer needs.

- Risk taking is encouraged by Mr. Marcus and Mr. Blank.

- Loyalty is a strong company value. One article referenced a statement that if you cut a Home Depot employee he would bleed "orange."

- The company is not run by managers but by missionaries whose basic beliefs are in the primacy of the customer.

- The officers of the company are perceived by the employees to really care about the employees who work for them.

- Reward systems such as service badges and incentive compensation are used to reinforce the importance of the employee and a focus on *anticipating* and *meeting customer needs.*

Exhibit 14 Culture Organization Chart

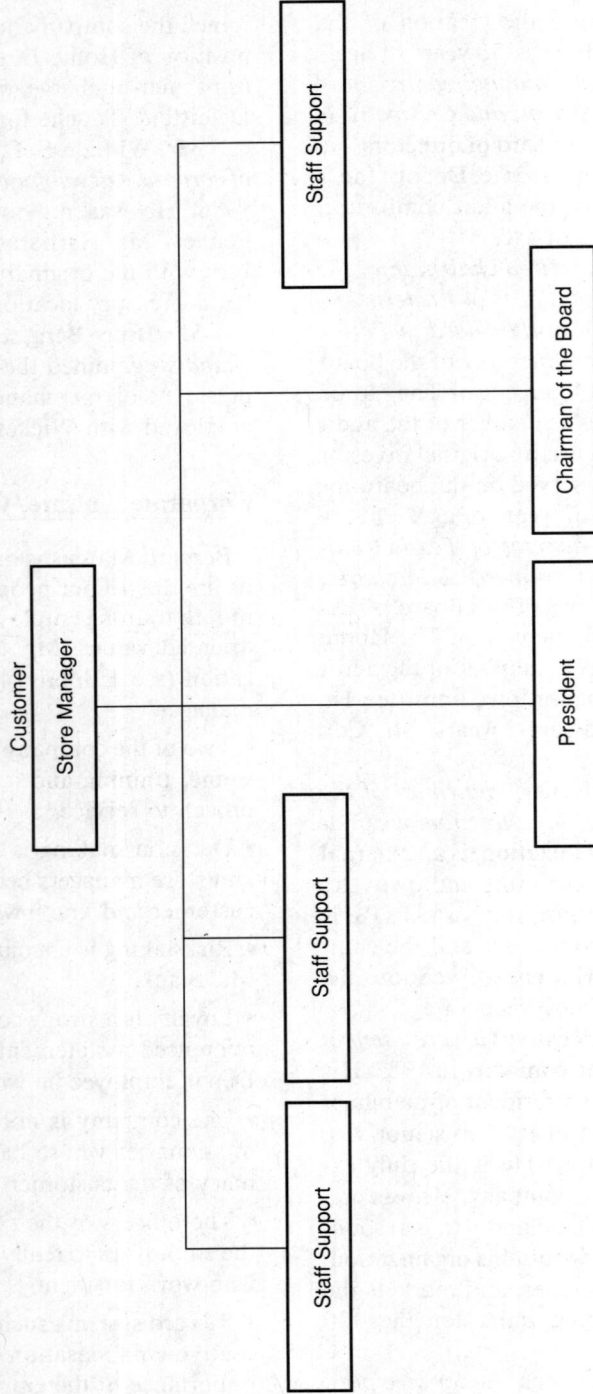

Customer

Store Manager

Staff Support

Staff Support

Staff Support

Chairman of the Board

President

Case 23

The Rise and Fall of Yugo America, Inc.

The five years that I invested in the Yugo project were rewarding and maturing for me, although I had a modest financial equity and a large amount of sweat equity invested in the company. In hindsight, there were areas where we failed, but I feel as though it all made a significant impact on the product and pricing aspect of the automobile industry.

William E. Prior
June, 1989

William E. Prior, co-founder, former chief executive and president of Yugo America, Inc., collected his thoughts and reflected on the past five years as he glanced across a crowded airport. It was June 1989, only five months after his company had declared bankruptcy. Looking back, he noted that the privately-held company had traveled a rocky road, yet made the most significant impact on the automobile industry in the decade.

It was 1983 when Prior and his two partners, Malcolm Bricklin and Ira Edelson, stumbled

This case was prepared by Carolyn Silliman and Jeffrey S. Harrison, Assistant Professor of Management, Clemson University, as the basis for class discussion rather than to illustrate either effective or ineffective handling of a managerial situation. The authors would like to acknowledge the helpful comments of David Grigsby on earlier versions of this case.

upon the idea of a company featuring a low-priced import. Bricklin, who was probably best known for the flashy sports car prototype that bears his name, was heading up the project as its main financial backer. Prior was the former president and general manager of Automobile Importers from Subaru, the nation's second largest Subaru distributor, a company Bricklin had founded after the collapse of his sports car project. Edelson was Bricklin's accountant and financial advisor. The three men had been researching the automobile industry, looking for a niche in the already crowded new car market. From their research, the men came to the conclusion that there was no "entry level car"; that is, there was not a new automobile inexpensive enough for the average first-time buyer. Bricklin, Prior, and Edelson concluded that they had discovered "a market in search of a product."[1]

Once the concept was conceived, the three entrepreneurs began their search for a low-priced, "no frills" mode of basic transportation. They determined that production costs would be too high in the United States, so they began evaluating the possibility of importing. In looking for a country which manufactured such a product, they wanted to meet three requirements:

1) The foreign company was not presently exporting to the United States, but desired to do so.

2) The overall quality of the car would be inferior to American and Japanese cars but could meet United States standards and consumer requirements.

501

3) The foreign company would be able to sell the cars at a low enough price for the new company to make marginal profits.[2]

Bricklin, Prior, and Edelson spent four months investigating and traveling to countries in pursuit of the "right" country and product that met the three requirements. They researched manufacturing plants in Brazil, Japan, Mexico, Poland, France, Romania, Czechoslovakia, England, and the Soviet Union before they discovered the Zastava car factory in Yugoslavia. Zavodi Crvena Zastava, Yugoslavia's leading automobile manufacturer, had been producing the Yugo GV model for five years and was quite receptive to Bricklin's proposal.[3] Bricklin, Prior, and Edelson toured the Yugoslavian plant in May 1984 and began discussing the terms of a contract that same month.[4]

Yugoslavian officials were eager to hear of the Yugo America venture. The country's economy was weak, and it owed (in 1985) approximately $19 billion to the Western world.[5] In order to purchase goods from the West, such as oil, steel, and electronics, Yugoslavia had to have "hard" currency (a universal currency of choice). The dinar, Yugoslavia's monetary unit, was not considered hard currency, so the country had to earn dollars by exporting. Yugoslavia's modest exports, including jewelry, tourism, furniture, leather, and sporting guns, did not contribute a significant sum in terms of national debt. Since cars are an expensive item, Yugoslavian officials saw the venture as a profitable method of increasing the supply of hard currency in their monetary economy.[6]

Bricklin and Zastava agreed that 500 Yugos should be shipped to a Baltimore port in early August, 1985, so that the cars would be in showrooms and ready to sell later that month. In addition, technicians would be trained at the Zastava plant prior to the launch in America, in order to guarantee customer satisfaction when the cars were sold and serviced. Bricklin and his partners returned to the United States in late May, 1984, and began setting up operations.[7]

Competitive Strategy

Competitive maneuvering among car manufacturers revolves around such factors as innovative options and styles, pricing, and brand name/reputation. Of these factors, Yugo's strategy focused on pricing. Innovative options and styles were not considered important, since the car was an older model and had no fancy options included in the base price. The company could not rely on reputation, since the company did not have an established name.[8]

Yugo America took advantage of a pricing scheme which set it apart from other automobile manufacturers. At $3995, it was the lowest priced car in America. Because price is important to most car buyers, Yugo felt that its low price strategy gave the company an advantage over other small cars. Major price competitors included the Toyota Tercel, Volkswagen Fox, Chevrolet Sprint and, later, the Hyundai Excel; however, the Yugo GV was priced below all of these competitors.[9] Instead of targeting families or status-conscious individuals, Yugo America made its car appealing to the first-time buyer looking for an economical subcompact.

Operations Begin

Four strategic decisions were made at the onset of operations:

1) The cars would be sold through "dual dealerships"; that is, Yugo would be a partner to an established retailer, such as Ford or Subaru. In this manner, Yugo America's executives hoped the public would associate its name with another successful manufacturer's name and reputation.

2) Prior, Bricklin, and Edelson decided that the company would import regionally rather than nationally. More specifically, Yugo America, with a home base in Upper Saddle River, New Jersey, would establish itself among Northeastern dealers. Approximately 23% of all import cars are sold in this region, and the Northeastern coast is the closest to Yugoslavia.

3) There would be a small number of dealers selling a large number of Yugos. The idea behind this decision was that the dealers would be making a substantial profit from the large number of cars, which would motivate them and encourage them to sell more.

4) The price of the car would be low, but the company would stress the fact that the car was of acceptable quality.[10]

The first task to accomplish before announcing the introduction of the Yugo GV in America was to set up a management hierarchy. As mentioned previously, Malcolm Bricklin was Yugo America's chief financial backer. As chairman, he owned 75% of the company. William Prior, who would act as president and head of operations, owned 1%. Ira Edelson owned 2% of the company and held the title of financial administrator. The remaining 22% was held by investors who were not involved in the management of the company.[11]

In February 1985, the company began recruiting automobile dealers. (The company's founders had been reviewing dealers for over four months, but the actual signing did not take place until February.) Tony Cappadona was hired as Dealer Development Manager and given the responsibility of locating established dealers who were interested in selling the Yugo. In addition, extensive surveys helped Mr. Cappadona determine the best area placement of Yugo franchises. By the end of July, the first 50 dealers were contracted in Pennsylvania, Massachusetts, New York, New Jersey, Connecticut, Rhode Island, Delaware, Maryland, and Washington, D.C.[12]

Some dealers were hesitant to sign because of the financial commitment involved. Pressure from Manufacturers Hanover Trust Company required that Yugo America produce 50 letters of credit by December, 1985. By the terms of agreement, dealers had to produce $400,000 stand-by letters of credit to cover at least two months of vehicle shipments. The dealer also had to pay $37,000 for a "start-up" kit and arrange financing for a "floor plan." A "floor plan" is an agreement between a financial institution and an auto dealership to finance the vehicles that are on the lot. The financial institution retains title to the automobiles until they are sold, which allows the financial institution to offer extremely attractive rates to the dealership, usually one to two percentage points above the prime lending rate. A typical "floor plan" would only require $600,000 of credit. However, the commitment of funds was excessive for such a risky operation. In response to these concerns, Yugo executives assured dealers that the Yugo GV would sell itself.[13]

Bricklin contacted Leonard Sirowitz, a New York advertiser, to write and launch a $10 million campaign prior to the debut of the Yugo GV. Sirowitz, who helped to create the Volkswagen Beetle advertisements during the 1960s, expected the Yugo advertisements to reach a potential one million buyers via newspapers, magazines, and television. He hoped to convince Americans that, despite their views of Communist Yugoslavia, the $3995 car was of sound quality.[14] Yugo's first slogan intended to catch the consumer's eye by asking, "The Road Back to Sanity: Why Pay Higher Prices?"[15]

In addition to trained technicians, Yugo's "support system" of quality parts and service was comprehensive. The company received 180 tons of spare parts to distribute among dealers during the summer of 1985. The company implemented the industry's first Universal Product Code inventory system, which enhanced the accuracy and efficiency of inventory processing. In addition, service schools were developed so that technicians would have no problems or questions when repairing the cars. For the "do-it-yourself" consumers, Yugo America published its own repair manuals and included a toll-free telephone number for assistance.[16]

The Yugo Arrives in America

The first shipment of 500 cars from the Zastava plant arrived in mid-August 1985 (the Yugo's features are listed in Exhibit 1). Ten cars were sent to each of the fifty dealers in the Northeast. Each dealer was instructed to reserve two cars as demonstration vehicles and to uphold this condition at all times. By the end of August, the cars were polished and ready for their national debut.[17]

Yugo's official entry into the automobile industry was announced on August 26, 1985. It was a long-awaited moment, and consumers were equally as excited about the car as the Yugo employees. The Yugo frenzy spread so quickly that 33 dealerships were added and 3000 orders were taken for cars by September 9. Customers paid deposits in order to reserve their cars, and by the end of 1985, a six-month waiting list was tallied. Indeed, Yugo's founders had discovered "a market in search of a product."[18]

During its first year of operations, which ended July 31, 1986, Yugo America, Inc., grossed $122 million from the sale of 27,000 automobiles and parts and accessories. The Yugo was hailed as the fastest selling import car in the history of the U.S.[19] The company employed 220 dealers throughout the Southeast and East Coast, and it was estimated that the consumer credit divisions of Chrysler, Ford, and General Motors financed one third of the Yugo retail sales.[20] At the end of July, Prior announced the expansion of the New Jersey home office to include a corporate planning department. He also informed reporters of Yugo's new slogan, "Everybody Needs a Yugo Sometime."[21]

Problems Begin

In February 1986, Consumer Reports published the first of two articles criticizing the Yugo GV. Reporters mocked Malcolm Bricklin for his other car ventures (the Subaru 360 and the Fiat Spider) which had recently failed. The writers pointed out that, after adding destination charges, dealer preparation fees, and a stereo, the price of the car exceeded $4600. The magazine's personal test evaluation was also published. It stated that the transmission was "sloppy," the steering was "heavy," the ride was "jerky," and the heating system was "weak and obtrusive."[22]

The writers continued by criticizing almost every aspect of the car, from seat coverings to the "not-so-spacious" trunk. The safety of the car was questioned, but could not be verified by government crash tests. It was noted, however, that the impact of a collision at 3 mph and 5 mph severely twisted and crushed the bumpers. It was estimated that repairing the damage to the front and rear bumpers was $620 and $461, respectively.[23] Twenty-one other defects were discovered, ranging from oil leaks to squealing brakes. A survey by J.D. Power and Associates (included in the article) concerning customer satisfaction revealed that over 80% of Yugo buyers had reported problems. In short, the writers did not recommend the Yugo GV at any price.[24]

The Yugo was facing increasing competition as well. In late 1985 Hyundai Motor America, a subsidiary of the giant South Korean industrial company, announced the American introduction of the Hyundai Excel for $4995. The Excel was a hatchback model that included standard features which were comparable to the Yugo GV. Therefore, the Excel posed a direct threat to the Yugo GV in the lower priced automobile market.

By mid-October, 1986, Yugo America responded to the Consumer Reports article and increasing consumer complaints by making 176 improvements to the car without raising its price.[25] Prior stated that Yugo spent between $2.5 and $3 million to improve its image through advertisements and national incentives. Independent dealers offered additional rebates, as well, in an effort to boost sagging sales.[26]

Looking ahead, Yugo America had hoped to introduce some new models, all within the lower price range. For 1987, the Yugo GV would be given a "face lift" to take on an aerodynamic look, and a convertible GV would be available later in the year. In order to meet the needs of couples and small families, Yugo anticipated the 1988 debut of a five-door hatchback, which would compete with the Honda Accord. A four-door sedan would be added to the line between 1989 and 1990, and a two-seater sports car named "TCX" would be the highlight of 1990.[27]

During 1986, there were rumors that Yugo America was considering a move to "go public" by issuing common stock, since the company was beginning to experience financial tension. The proposal was later canceled for two reasons. First, Bricklin did not want to surrender any of his equity (75%). Second, the company was starting to feel the effects of negative publicity, and financial consultants felt that the stock would not bring a fair price. For the time being, Yugo would remain a private company.[28]

More Trouble

In April 1987, *Consumer Reports* released its annual survey of domestic and foreign cars, and once again, Yugo's image was tainted. The writers criticized the Yugo GV from bumper to bumper, stating that "the manual transmission was very imprecise...the worst we've tried in years." As for comfort, "small, insufficiently contoured front seats" contributed to an "awkward driving position." In addition, the ride of the car was described as "noisy" and "harsh."[29]

Besides the negative description of the car's driving performance, the article publicized the results of an independent crash test. This test, which was not mandated by law, disclosed the results of a crash at 35 miles per hour among domestic and foreign automobiles. (The National Highway Traffic Safety Administration requires that all cars pass the national standard impact at 30 miles per hour.) The Yugo GV was among the 40% which did not pass the test.[30] In fact, it received the lowest possible ranking with respect to driver and passenger protection. The report indicated that the steering column "moved up and back into the path of the driver's head," and the seats "moved forward during the crash, increasing the load on occupants."[31]

Consumer Reports also reported that dam-age to the front and rear bumpers when hit at an impact of 3 and 5 mph was $1081, the highest in its class. This was particularly embarrassing to Yugo America, since many of its foreign competitors (including Toyota, Mazda, and Saab) escaped the collisions without a scratch.[32]

Before the second *Consumer Reports* articles, Yugo sold every car coming into its ports every month.[33] Sales in 1987 were the highest to date. From there, Yugo's problems started to catch up with the company. The negative image of the Yugo was apparent, and dealers were forced to offer $500–$750 rebates as an incentive to buy. In addition, several new programs and extended warranties were offered to entice customers. Monthly sales levels started to decline, and waiting lists became virtually obsolete.[34]

Through all of these problems, William Prior remained an exemplary figure for all of the Yugo/Global employees. As Tony Cappadona stated, "Bill added a lot of charisma and dedication to the company. He let the employees know that everyone was working to achieve a mission. They (the employees) didn't mind working 10 or 12 hours a day, because they saw Bill putting in twice as much."[35]

Changes in Ownership

The 1987 year was marked by the acquisition of Yugo America, Inc., by Global Motors, Inc., a company founded by Malcolm Bricklin. Bricklin established Global Motors as an umbrella corporation for importing cars worldwide. Gaining 91% of Yugo America, Global became its parent, distributor, and holding company, and it helped with the coordination and distribution of Yugos as they arrived at the Baltimore port.[36]

By 1988, Yugo America and Global Motors began contemplating the sale of a substantial portion of the company in an effort to avoid bankruptcy. In April, Mabon Nugent and Company, a New York investment firm, purchased Global Motors for $40 million.[37] Bricklin sold 70% of his equity for $20 million, and a debenture was purchased from Global for an additional $20 million. A management group headed by Prior and Edelson agreed to contribute $2.1 million to obtain 5.5% of the company. The management group would be awarded stock options periodically over the following three years, to bring the group's total ownership to 22%. Prior was named chief executive officer during the acquisition.[38]

The Final Year

By April 1988, the company's operating problems had also increased. Not only had the *Consumer Reports* articles thrashed the Yugo GV again, but dealers were beginning to undermine the company as well. William Prior stated that dealers would often persuade buyers to purchase one of their other brands instead of a Yugo. To make things worse, consumers could only receive 36-month financing with the purchase of a Yugo. Conversely, Ford Motor Credit and other financiers offered 60-month plans on their own cars, which resulted in lower payments. The thought of lower monthly payments was incentive enough for a prospective Yugo buyer to change his decision to purchase. If the former tactic did not persuade the buyer, the salesperson would criticize the Yugo directly and accentuate the features of the other line. Higher commissions on more costly brands increased the motivation of salespeople to move away from the Yugo.[39]

Even after deciding to buy a Yugo, many consumers ran into additional difficulties when they tried to obtain financing. Because the typical Yugo customer was a young, low-income, first-time buyer, lending institutions were hesitant to make high-risk loans to persons in this segment of the market. It was estimated that as many as 70% of all Yugo customers were declined for credit, since the majority had no previous credit history and a debt-income ratio of over 50%.[40] This common scenario was discouraging for both the customers and dealers. Enticing advertise-

ments lured customers in, and yet many could not obtain financing. The dealers became frustrated because of the amount of time and effort contributed to "put the deal together." Prior described the situation as "an inefficiency in the market."[41]

In an effort to hurdle these financing roadblocks, Yugo America announced in June 1988 that it would design its own program for financing.[42] The first-time buyer plan was administered through Imperial Savings Association, a $10-billion institution based in San Diego. Yugo and Imperial intended to protect themselves by charging a higher annual percentage rate—as much as four percentage points higher than those of other finance companies. In doing so, Yugo America could establish a "higher-than-average" reserve for loan defaults. Though the annual percentage rate was higher, buyers could finance the loan over 60 months so that monthly payments remained low.[43]

Approximately 50 dealers were enrolled in the program. Imperial was hesitant to allow all of the dealers to take advantage of Yugo Credit, since there were still some "bugs" in the system. Also, each state required separate licensing, and Yugo did not have the time to wait for acceptance in each state.[44]

The financing program was terminated after 90 days. One of the provisions of the plan required Yugo America to be "in good standing" financially. Bills were accumulating at Yugo and company debt was becoming unmanageable. Imperial Savings had to pull out.[45]

In November 1988, William Prior and 71 other employees were released from the company, leaving a "skeleton" crew of 71 remaining. Mabon Nugent's intentions were to cut costs in an effort to "relieve cash-flow pressures" and generate additional funds for product development. Marcel Kole, senior vice president and chief financial officer of Global Motors, temporarily replaced Prior as president and chief executive of Yugo America. Turnover within the company was high, and national advertising was brought to a halt.[46] Norauto LP of Ohio agreed to finance two shipments of Yugos backed by letters of credit. Norauto, a firm which aids bankrupt, terminated, or distressed companies, took possession of the cars until Yugo America could repay the $14.3 million letter of credit.[47]

Mabon Nugent and Company had written off $10.5 million as a loss in Global Motors by January 30, 1989. It was estimated that Global would need $10 million to "get back on its feet," but Mabon Nugent did not feel that contributing more money to a dying company was a worthy investment. The firm's partners considered selling the company to Zastava or private investors, but neither of the ideas were pursued.[48] Global officially filed for Chapter 11 bankruptcy on January 30, 1989.[49] Global's unaudited balance sheet reported in the petition for bankruptcy is contained in Exhibit 2.

A Hazy Future for Yugo, America

After declaring bankruptcy in January 1989, parent company Global Motors, Inc., discharged 250 (of 300) Yugo America employees. Zastava, honoring the warranty of the cars, began seeking financial backing so that the company could remain afloat. By February 1989, three lawsuits had been filed against Global Motors and Mabon Nugent and Company. William Prior sued the companies for breach of contract and Turner Broadcasting System in Atlanta filed suit demanding $182,000 for unpaid bills. A third lawsuit, by Imperial Savings, alleged that Mabon Nugent was "involved in the day-to-day operations of the company [Global]" before it (Mabon Nugent) actually took control of Yugo-Global in 1988. Mabon Nugent denied the charge.[50]

John A. Spiech became Yugo's new president and chief executive, succeeding Marcel Kole. Spiech, a veteran of the automobile industry, had full confidence in the company and its product, stating, "whatever happened wasn't the car's fault. It is still good, low-cost, reliable transportation."[51] He intended to take the company to the top, even though he was starting from the very bottom.

Notes

1. Personal interview with William Prior, former president, chief executive officer, and co-founder of Yugo America, June, 1989.

2. Ibid.

3. Ibid.

4. Ibid.

5. Ibid.

6. Ibid.

7. Personal interview with Tony Cappadona, former dealer development manager and market development manager of Yugo America, June 1989.

8. Prior, op. cit.

9. Ibid.

10. Ibid.

11. Ibid.

12. Cappadona, op. cit.

13. Ibid.

14. J. Fierman, "Can a Beetle Brain Stir a Yearning for Yugos?" *Fortune*, (May 13, 1985): 73.

15. Cappadona, op. cit.

16. Prior, op. cit.

17. Ibid.

18. "The Price is Right," *Time*, (September 9, 1985): 58.

19. J.L. Kovach, "We Don't Overpromise," *Industry Week*, (October 13, 1986): 73.

20. Ibid.

21. J.A. Russell, "Yugo Grosses $122 Million in First Year," *Automotive News*, (September 1, 1986): 42.

22. "How Much Car for $3990?" *Consumer Reports*, (February 1986): 84–86.

23. Ibid.

24. Prior, op. cit.

25. Kovach, op. cit.

26. Prior, op. cit.

27. J.A. Russell, "Zastava to Construct Plant For U.S. Yugos," *Automotive News*, (May 20, 1985): 2.

28. Prior, op. cit.

29. "The 1987 Cars," *Consumer Reports*, (April, 1987): 200–215.

30. Prior, op. cit.

31. "The 1987 Cars," op. cit., 200.

32. Ibid., 208.

33. Cappadona, op. cit.

34. Ibid.

35. Ibid.

36. Prior, op. cit.

37. J.A. Russell, "Bricklin's Import Firm Sold in $40 Million Deal," *Automotive News*, (April 18, 1988): 1, 56.

38. Ibid.

39. Prior, op. cit.

40. Ibid.

41. Ibid.

42. Ibid.

43. J. Henry, "Low Finance: Yugo Offers Loans to Spur Buyers," *Automotive News*, (August 1, 1988): 1, 51.

44. Prior, op. cit.

45. Ibid.

46. C. Thomas, "Prior Ousted: Shaky Global Trims Ranks," *Automotive News*, (November 14, 1988): 1, 58.

47. J. Henry, "Yugo, Liquidator in Accord," *Automotive News*, (March 27, 1989): 1.

48. J. Henry, "Global Struggles to Remain Afloat," *Automotive News*, (January 30, 1989): 1, 257.

49. Henry, (March 27, 1989), op. cit.

50. J. Henry, "More Yugo Grief—Maker Plans Termination," *Automotive News*, (February 20, 1989): 1, 51.

51. D. Cuff, "A Car Industry Veteran Will Try to Revive Yugo," *New York Times*, (March 17, 1989): D4.

Exhibit 1   Yugo GV Standard Features

Vehicle Type
Front-engine, front-wheel drive, four passenger, three-door hatchback.

Dimensions and Capacities
Wheelbase: 84.6 inches
Overall Length: 139.0 inches
Overall Height: 54.7 inches
Overall Width: 60.7 inches
Headroom: Front: 37.0 inches
             Rear: 36.0 inches
Legroom: Front: 39.0 inches
            Rear: 39.0 inches
Ground Clearance: 4.8 inches
Luggage Capacity: 18.5+9.0 cubic feet
Fuel Capacity: 8.4 gallons
Curb Weight: 1,832 pounds

Engine
Type: Single overhead cam, 1.1 liter 4-cylinder with aluminum cyl. head. Dual barrel carburetor
Bore & Stroke: 80 × 55.5 mm.
Displacement: 1116 cc.
Compression Ratio: 9.2:1
Horsepower: 54 hp at 5,000 rpm.
Torque: 52 lbs. at 4,000 rpm.

Drive Train
Transmission: 4-speed manual
Final Drive Ratio: 3.7
Gear Ratios: 1st-3.5, 2nd-2.2, 3rd-1.4, 4th-1.0, reverse-3.7

Suspension
Front: Independent, MacPherson struts, anti-sway bar.
Rear: Independent, transverse leaf spring with lower control arms

Brakes
Front: 8.0″ disc, power-assisted
Rear: 7.2″ drum, power-assisted
Rear brake proportioning valve

Wheels and Tires
Wheels: Steel
Tires: Tigar 145SR-13, steel-belted radials with all-weather tread design.

Electrical
Bosch electronic ignition
Alternator: 55 amp
Battery: 12 volt, 45 amp

Economy
City: 28 mpg
Highway: 31 mpg

Standard Equipment
1.1 liter 4-cylinder overhead cam engine
Front-wheel drive
4-wheel independent suspension
Power assisted brakes, disc front, drum rear
Front anti-sway bar
Rack and pinion steering
Color-coordinated fabric upholstery
Full carpeting, including carpeted luggage compartment
Reclining front seats
Folding rear seats—27.5 cu. ft. luggage space
3 grab handles
2 dome lights
Visor vanity mirror
Analog instrument gauges
Low fuel warning light
Steel-belted radial tires (145 × 13)
Lexan bumpers
Plastic inner front fender shields
Bosch electronic ignition
Rear brake proportioning valve
Full-size spare tire
Front spoiler
Hood scoop
Hub caps
PVC undercoating
Opening rear quarter windows
Rear window electric defroster
Quartz halogen headlights
Body side molding
Special owner's tool kit
Cigarette lighter
Locking gas cap
Dual storage pockets
Concealed radio antenna
Spare fuse and bulb kit
Night/day rear-view mirror
Electric cooling fan
Console

Source: Yugo America, Inc., promotional materials.

Exhibit 2 Global Motors Balance Sheet

**Global Motors, Inc., Balance Sheet
December 31, 1988 (Unaudited)
(In thousands of dollars)**

Cash	0
Due to/from subsidiaries	27,145
Due from manufacturer	15
Inventories	0
Prepaid and other current assets	48
	27,208
Property, plant, and equipment (at cost)	8
Less: Accumulated depreciation	(1)
	7
Investment in subsidiaries	223
Deferred charges	0
Total Assets	27,438
Acceptances payable	0
Accounts payable and accrued expenses	1,429
Notes payable	11,825
Due to/from subsidiaries	0
Estimated warranty (current)	0
	13,254
Estimated warranty (long-term)	0
Long-term debt	11,000
Minority interest	0
Shareholders' deficiency	3,184
Total liabilities and equity	27,438
	0

Source: Bankruptcy Docket Number 89 00680, filed January 30, 1989, United States Bankruptcy Court, District of New Jersey.

Case 24

Harley-Davidson: How Long Can the Eagle Stay Aloft?

The Harley-Davidson logo is the number one request in tattoo parlors across America (Spadoni, 1985). How could a manufacturer fail if its customers literally brand themselves with the company emblem? Few corporations, either in or outside of the motorcycle industry, have a product with such a strong brand loyalty, recognition, and reputation.

The Harley-Davidson name and eagle insignia inspire images of large and powerful motorcycles, James Dean, Marlon Brando, Hell's Angels—the "Wild Ones." The name stands for "real bikers" and a special type of individualistic freedom. However, image alone does not sell motorcycles, and does not ensure survival—even for Harley-Davidson. Efficient manufacturing, quality products, and effective marketing are all essential precursors for the development of a competitive advantage and profitability in the highly competitive and turbulent motorcycle industry. During most of the 1970s Harley-Davidson was weak in all of these areas and was reported to have been hours from declaring bankruptcy in 1985 (Reid, 1990).

In 1980 Harley-Davidson was the only American motorcycle manufacturer. It continued to survive while scores of other manufacturers died during the course of the century. Prior to the Great Depression, during the early stages of the motorcycle industry life cycle, there

This case was prepared by James A. Wolff and Douglas D. Baker of the Department of Management and Systems, Washington State University. Copyright © 1990. Reprinted with permission.

were many manufacturers in the United States. Increasing competition and the economic hardships of the 1930s killed most of these companies. At the beginning of World War II only two major American motorcycle manufacturers existed: Harley-Davidson and Indian.

There was a great deal of debate about which company made better machines, with many people preferring Indian because of their style and performance. At that time, Harley was known for the civility of its motorcycles, with one model being nick-named the "silent grey fellow" because of its quiet engine. During the war both companies supplied the armed services with thousands of bikes. However, after the war, Indian had production and marketing problems which, combined with increasing competition from British manufacturers, ultimately killed the company. The demise of Indian happened at a time when the motorcycle industry was set to experience tremendous market growth, as illustrated in Table 1.

During the 1950s, Harley's competition was from European companies such as Triumph, BSA, Ducati, Vincent, and even the German manufacturer BMW. Relative to Harley-Davidson, these companies made motorcycles that were small, light, and handled well. Harley's machines continued to have a strong following because of their traditional engine, reliable performance, and the fact that they were made in America. However, the increasing European competition was not strong enough to force Harley to make major changes in its motorcycles'

511

Table 1 U.S. Total Motorcycle Registrations, 1945–1988

Year	Total
1988	4,426,000
1985	5,216,000
1980	5,681,000
1975	4,964,000
1970	2,815,000
1965	1,382,000
1960	575,000
1955	450,000
1950	454,000
1945	198,000

Source: U.S. Department of Transportation, Federal Highway Administration for 1945–1975 motorcycle registrations. Motorcycle safety foundation, Irvine, California for 1980 and subsequent year motorcycle registrations.

designs or style. This relatively static position allowed other unlikely competitors to enter the industry.

One of these competitors was the Honda Corporation which, like BMW, went on to successfully manufacture automobiles. Mr. Honda began making three wheeled motorized carts toward the end of World War II to collect war scraps in Tokyo, such as unexploded American bombs. Soon his carts became more popular than his recycling. Seeing the strong demand, Mr. Honda began making small-engine motorcycles that proved to be a cheap and efficient form of transportation in war ravaged Japan.

Honda attempted to enter the American market with mid-sized motorcycles in 1959 but found few buyers. Later, an unforeseen opportunity presented itself when a Sears-Roebuck buyer observed Honda company couriers using small 50cc scooters in Los Angeles (Hill & Jones, 1989). The buyer proposed selling the small scooters through the Sears-Roebuck retail network. This chance opportunity provided Honda with a beachhead in the American market. Subsequent advertising campaigns depicting young men and women riding small and medium sized motorbikes appealed to a large market group not generally associated with motorcycles. The slogan "you meet the nicest people on a Honda" achieved a major image change for the American motorcycle industry. In the late 1960s and early 1970s the big four Japanese manufacturers (Honda, Kawasaki, Suzuki, and Yamaha) greatly increased sales by offering high quality products, in every conceivable market niche, at low prices. Twenty years later the Japanese companies continue to dominate the motorcycle market, as illustrated in Tables 2 and 3.

Meanwhile, Harley-Davidson continued to rely on its old designs and manufacturing processes. Their products were no longer the best and it was unclear as to whether the company had the ability or resources to meet the competition. In spite of these product limitations, Harley needed an infusion of cash to allow the company to expand to keep up with industrywide growth. In 1965, after 60 years of private ownership, Harley-Davidson held its initial public stock offering of 1.3 million shares (Reid, 1990). However, rather than solving problems, going public brought on the unanticipated specter of a hostile takeover.

In 1968, Harley executives discovered large blocks of stock were being purchased by Bangor Punta, a company with a reputation for feeding on profitable companies and then divesting the remains. Luckily, Harley found a white knight. With rapidly increasing sales in the motorcycle industry and a strategy to diversify into recreational consumer products, American Machine and Foundry (AMF) bought Harley. The plan was to update the manufacturing processes and designs and capitalize on Harley's long-standing reputation. AMF infused a great deal of capital into its new motorcycle division, and contracted with Porsche to design a new generation of engines. However, these engines were never produced and other attempts to revitalize Harley did not lead to financial success.

A number of factors contributed to AMF's failure to get Harley up to speed. One of the

Table 2 U.S. Motorcycle Imports by Engine Displacement, 1982–1988

	1982	1983	1984	1985	1986	1987	1988
Under 191 cc							
Units	312,891	175,212	191,856	355,670	241,250	156,485	133,828
$ Value	$152,019,038	$ 94,634,569	$ 97,761,709	$176,053,176	$152,153,709	$109,835,387	$107,923,087
191–490 cc							
Units	182,948	75,321	67,792	164,493	148,941	8,530	64,511
$ Value	$198,421,920	$ 82,609,575	$ 78,049,993	$183,019,603	$218,738,761	$105,170,653	$130,736,424
491–790 cc							
Units	298,182	215,975	141,716	177,605	129,932	0,841	67,101
$ Value	$532,150,656	$362,771,480	$256,491,632	$329,283,894	$291,693,936	$171,185,050	$189,330,629
Over 790 cc							
Units	119,625	65,093	34,828	31,274	28,702	20,694	18,394
$ Value	$226,188,672	$153,545,173	$ 88,441,983	$ 91,724,205	$ 99,838,528	$ 75,631,655	$ 82,913,454
Unspecified							
Units	3,557	8,612	5,228	4,296	844	1,324	073
$ Value	$ 1,387,633	$ 3,624,017	$ 2,641,863	$ 3,005,446	$ 338,616	$ 1,336,422	$ 881,279
Total							
Units	917,203	540,213	441,420	733,338	549,669	17,874	286,907
$ Value	$1,110,167,919	$697,184,814	$523,386,642	$783,086,324	$762,763,550	$463,159,167	$511,784,873

Scooters included; ATVs excluded.
Dollar Value = C.I.F. Value.
Source: U.S. Department of Commerce, Domestic and International Business Administration. *U.S. Motorcycle Imports*, Werner C. Single, Foreign Trade Services, New York,
New Jersey.

Table 3 New Motorcycle Registration Leading Brands by Market Share, 1983–1988

Make	1988 #	1988 Market Share	1987 #	1987 Market Share	1986 #	1986 Market Share	1985 #	1985 Market Share	1984 #	1984 Market Share	1983 #	1983 Market Share
Honda	1	39.0%	1	50.8%	1	55.0%	1	58.5%	1	57.7%	1	54.8%
Yamaha	2	23.0	2	19.8	2	17.8	2	15.7	2	18.6	2	19.0
Kawasaki	3	13.9	4	10.2	4	9.7	3	10.4	4	8.9	4	9.8
Suzuki	4	13.3	3	11.6	3	11.1	4	10.0	3	10.0	3	11.8
Harley-Davidson	5	9.4	5	6.3	5	5.0	5	4.1	5	3.7	5	3.3
BMW	6	0.8	6	0.7	6	0.9	6	0.8	6	0.6	6	0.6

Note: The market share for other brands was less than 0.5%.
R.L. Polk new registrations include the three most current model years. Some off-highway motorcycle and all-terrain vehicle new registrations are included.
California new off-highway motorcycle and ATV registrations have been added to 1983 new registrations, so that comparisons can be made with 1984 and subsequent years which include California off-highway registrations.
New York new registrations were not available from October 1983 through December 1984.
Oklahoma new registrations first became available in 1987.
Source: *New Motorcycle Registrations,* R.L. Polk and Co., Detroit, Michigan

major problems was the quality of the motorcycles. In 1980, fifty percent of the motorcycles moving off the assembly line were defective (Willis, 1986). Even those motorcycles of sufficient quality to move into the distribution channel could often be found leaking oil onto Harley-Davidson showroom floors. Surprisingly, one of the causes of the quality problem was the modernization of portions of their manufacturing facilities in 1977.

Along with the modernization came increased output pressures. However, increased output of quality products was hampered by the mismatch between the old craft-oriented design of the motorcycles and the new mass production facilities. Adding to these technological problems was the serious adversarial relationship between management and labor that developed in the latter half of the 1970s. Absenteeism was extremely high and employee complaints and grievances hampered the production process.

To further complicate matters Harley's manufacturing expansion came at an inopportune point in the industry life cycle. The aging of the baby boom generation in the 1960s led to a diminished number of young adults, as shown in

Table 4. The declining number of young adults, who had traditionally bought most motorcycles, was a factor leading to the peak in sales of new motorcycles for the industry in 1973 when 1,189,789 new units were registered. Since then, a steep downward trend in new motorcycle sales has taken place.

In 1981, faced with a declining motorcycle market, unrealized synergies, and a division with many internal problems, AMF sold the motorcycle company to a group of 13 Harley-Davidson managers at a large discount. Essentially, AMF felt that the hog (a nick name for Harley-Davidson motorcycles) had turned into a dog. The newly independent company faced a steep uphill battle for survival. In the 1960s, before Japanese competition, Harley enjoyed a 50% market share; in 1983 it was 3.8% (Daft, 1989). To compound these problems the U.S. economy entered a steep recession in the early 1980s. The strong competition, high operating costs, low quality, shrinking niche, and a cash poor position resulting from the leveraged buy out, left Harley-Davidson swimming in a pool of red ink for the fiscal years of 1981 and 1982. Many industry observers expected the company to crash.

Table 4 U.S. Population, Both Sexes (1000s)

Total Population	Census April 1 1960	Census April 1 1970	Census April 1 1980	Estimate 1986	Projections				
					1990	1995	2000	2005	2010
15–24 years old	24,020	35,441	42,487	39,027	35,863	34,804	36,468	38,343	38,048
25–34 years old	22,818	24,907	37,082	42,784	43,728	40,766	36,952	35,800	37,375
35–44 years old	24,081	23,087	25,634	33,069	37,827	42,266	43,841	40,881	37,131
45–54 years old	20,485	23,220	22,800	22,814	25,480	31,289	37,216	41,611	43,200
55–64 years old	15,572	18,590	21,703	22,230	21,363	21,324	24,158	29,762	35,430
Median Age	29.5	28.1	30.0	31.7	33.0	34.8	36.5	37.9	39.0

Source: U.S. Bureau of the Census.

The Turnaround at Harley-Davidson

The new management team of former AMF-Harley executives, led by CEO Vaughn Beals, had high aspirations for the reborn motorcycle manufacturer. To recover from the life threatening situation, Harley's management realized the need to better understand the competitive forces emanating from Japan. Chairman Beals and a handful of top executives visited Japanese motorcycle manufacturing facilities to obtain first-hand information. What they discovered was not a mystical secret of the Japanese culture or the technological wizardry of computerized robotic manufacturing facilities, but "the intelligent, efficient organization of the company's employees and production systems" (Willis, 1986).

Organizational Structure and Climate

To reduce costs and increase manufacturing efficiency, Harley-Davidson was reorganized. Shortly after the leveraged buy out (LBO) in 1981 the management structure was overhauled, eliminating layers of hierarchy. Chairman Beals reported "our biggest savings came from decreasing the number of salaried staff . . . this is where the greatest improvements in productivity have occurred" (Willis, 1986). In turn, production facilities were realigned into systems in which employees, from the production line up, had decision making responsibility for their particular areas.

A related step dealt with the introduction of quality circles. Quality circles were developed in Japan by a group of American management experts responding to Japanese requests for assistance in reconstruction after World War II (W. Edward Deming's statistical process control concepts and Joseph Juran's doctrine of Total Quality Control were combined in the early 1960s by the Japanese to form the first quality circles). Through adaptation and refinement, the concept developed slowly until 1970 when major industrial firms recognized its potential benefits. Quality circles taught workers to break a problem into small components, analyze key areas, and develop solutions to improve the product quality or the manufacturing process. The solutions or suggestions were then presented to management who had the responsibility for implementation.

Quality circles have played a key role in improving communication between production-line and supervisory staff at Harley. This improved communication has led to a number of operational innovations. For example, ideas were generated on how to do more in-house sourcing of components. By manufacturing more of its own components, Harley was able to provide increased job security, reduce costs, and improve the components' quality. Other programs initiated include: employee assistance programs, out-placement assistance, a job security committee, a voluntary peer review system, vocational college credit for quality circle training, a tuition refund program, a 401(k) savings program, an employee wellness program, several health and welfare programs, and cross training of most staff members (Willis, 1986). Through the use of such employee welfare programs, communications between labor and management have increased, costs have been reduced, and product quality improved. As a symbol of the new climate of cooperation, the union label is put on all bikes produced.

Production

In conjunction with Harley-Davidson's reorganization, a number of specific steps were taken to improve the manufacturing processes. With sales slowing to 31,000 units in 1982, quality at a low ebb, and the company losing money, manufacturing needed to become more efficient and effective. Similar to the elimination of unneeded levels of personnel, the implementation of just-in-time (JIT) inventory systems significantly reduced the large carrying costs of component and materials inventories. Harley-Davidson's JIT system, labeled MAN (materials as needed), successfully eliminated the need for stockrooms full of components and parts. With the MAN system, manufacturing and assembly components were delivered to the point of use at the time needed.

Coordination of the MAN system, with suppliers and vendors, provided management with significant challenges. Special vendor courses were instituted to demonstrate the benefits of JIT ordering and to aid in the coordination of changes in supplier manufacturing processes to accommodate the new system. In 1981, prior to full implementation of the MAN system, the annual inventory turnover rate was 4.5. By 1986 the turnover rate had dramatically increased to 23 times per year (Cayer, 1988).

Production efficiency and product quality were also attenuated by the difficulty of manu-

facturing the old V-twin motorcycle engine on the new automated production line, which AMF had developed. Similarly, there was a mismatch between some of the high tech manufacturing systems purchased by AMF and the older equipment still used to machine parts for the engines.

Traditionally, the company had relied upon quality inspectors and quality control personnel to maintain standards. With a scrap and rework rate approaching 50% in 1981, it was apparent that the traditional method had failed. To overcome the product quality problems inherent in Harley's existing manufacturing system, a method of statistical process control was implemented. The foundation of statistical process control is the detection and elimination of non-random causes of variability in product quality through engineering or manufacturing. The remaining common or chance causes of product quality variation are due to problems in the manufacturing process and can only be corrected by management action (Messina, 1987). Through the use of statistical techniques, product quality is monitored during the process (prevention) rather than at the end of the process (detection), when it is much more expensive to rework the product. The result of statistical process control was a reduction of scrap and rework costs by 60% to 70% with full implementation of the system and a percentage of "ready to ride" bikes off the assembly line rising from 50% in 1981 to 98% in 1986 (Reid, 1990).

Short Term Tactics

Just-in-time inventory and statistical process control provided more efficient manufacturing systems. The organizational restructuring, emphasis on improved work relations, and a more open management climate provided the motivation for implementation of the new production methods. With cost efficiencies and quality improvements under way, the problems of income and the competitive environment needed to be addressed.

Harley was facing declining sales, as was the entire industry. During this decline, sales dropped more rapidly than overhead costs could be reduced. Under such systemic conditions of decline, organizations frequently take drastic steps to reduce overhead expenses as rapidly as possible. For example, companies often liquidate assets. However, Harley's management decided that such a slash and burn tactic was not appropriate.

The assets would have been sold at a fraction of their value and would have left the company in a weak position for recovery. Rather, the company decided to use the excess plant capacity to generate additional income from sources outside of the motorcycle industry. Harley-Davidson ventured into defense contracting, manufacturing artillery-shell casings and rocket engines for target drones. These activities provided a contribution to overhead costs that the motorcycle division would have absorbed had the facilities been idle. Defense and other outside manufacturing contracts (e.g., computer peripherals and outboard marine engine components) became extremely important sources of income for Harley-Davidson through the recovery period. By 1986, non-motorcycle activities generated 25% of the income from operations.

Another tactic employed to increase income was the licensing of its name and logo. For Harley-Davidson, licensing allowed the company to regain control of the company image, provide a marketing medium to enhance general public perception of the end product (motorcycles), and produce a previously untapped source of profits. The Harley trademark has appeared on such diverse products as wine coolers, beer, denim apparel, Black Hills gold jewelry, men's cologne, motorcycle leathers, motorcycle accessories, children's three wheelers, and cigarettes. The popularity of the trademark license is due to the almost universal recognition and macho image of the company and its motorcycles (Spadoni, 1985). In general, these licensing agreements have been successful. However, the cigarette sponsorship has created some controversy as illustrated in the following editorial by David Sarasohn (1989).

Harley: The Smokes with Leather Filters

Sure, the surgeon general has determined that cigarette smoking is hazardous to your health.

Whatsamatter, you chicken?

After 25 years of arguing that, after all, nobody has ever produced color films of cigarette smoke actually turning into cancer inside a lung, the tobacco industry may be trying a different approach. The new plan is, don't fight the image of danger; use it.

Harley-Davidson cigarettes. They go with your leathers.

Suddenly, the familiar black-and-gold logo of a hundred motorcycle movies is decorating cigarette packs and billboards. The billboards never say anything about the cigarettes, such as, "Harleys will really strip your gears." They just show the logo and mention the cigarettes, or maybe a carefree couple on a motorcycle, and let the smoker figure it out for himself.

And, of course, the billboards include the required message from the surgeon general, maybe the one about cigarettes making your heart stop and your lungs fall out. But next to that big logo with the eagle on it, how can you worry about something like that?

After all, you expect to live forever.

According to several vendors around here, the cigarettes are selling.

The people who make Harley-Davidson motorcycles have not, of course, gone into the tobacco business, any more than they've gone into the T-shirt business or the New York Yankees go home and sew all those caps together. They've licensed the name, in this case to Lorillard Inc., which also makes Kents, Newports, and Old Golds.

Lorillard buys the Harley-Davidson rights, and Philip Morris buys the Bill of Rights. This is what America is all about.

Over the last decades, cigarette sales and the number of smokers have been declining, under a barrage of pressure from the surgeon general and various anti-smoking groups. Almost daily, scientists somewhere produce another study showing that cigarette smoking causes the average lung to resemble downtown Beirut. At the same time, lighting up in a public place exposes a smoker to a level of insult that until recently would have been grounds for a duel, or at least an enthusiastic fistfight.

Up to now, tobacco companies have responded by saying sure, cigarettes produce cancer in white mice, but who can trust white mice? They've also produced polite essays in support of personal freedom and civility, pointing out that your lungs are your personal property, to do with as you please.

And since much of society is willing to accept the same argument about an anti-tank gun, that even makes some sense.

Now, however, they're coming up with a new argument:

Varoom, varoom.

Obviously, if you're the kind of guy willing to spin your bike around a corner at 70—and you are, aren't you?—you're not going to worry about some medical research about what might happen 20 years from now.

The surgeon general probably doesn't even have a leather jacket.

Harley-Davidson cigarettes also help with another issue, the demographic repositioning of cigarette smoking. Cigarettes, like everything else in America, have usually been advertised as an elite product, vaguely English, with names like Kent, Newport, and Old Gold, and lots of sports cars in the ads.

The ultimate example of this trend, of course, was Benson & Hedges, featuring an actual English name and certifiably upscale people doing mystifying things in their magazine ads.

The cigarette market, however, has been changing. As cigarettes have become less socially acceptable in the middle class, smokers are increasingly younger and less educated. Even with filters and lights, the switch is from a sports car market to a motorcycle market.

Winston isn't sponsoring all those stock car races because the polo circuit was already booked.

So the surprise isn't that Harley-Davidson is now the name of a cigarette; it's that nobody thought of the idea before.

The next step, obviously, Smith & Wesson cigarettes, and maybe Doberman Pinscher Extra Longs.

Don't think of cigarette smoking as dangerous.

Think of it as daring.

Live fast, die young, and try not to cough too much around the curves.

Reprinted with Permission.

Marketing

In an effort to capitalize upon Harley's image among riders, the management became highly visible at industry events, sponsoring rallies and related activities. Company representatives always rode Harley-Davidson bikes at the events and mixed with Harley owners to continually stay in contact with their customers. The company-sponsored Harley Owners Group (HOG) is one example of the company's commitment to its customers. Another example is the Harley-sponsored group rides that began with the "Ride to Freedom" commemorating the rebirth of Harley-Davidson from AMF control, continuing with the "Liberty Ride" for the restoration of the Statue of Liberty, and most recently, the "85th Birthday Ride" celebrating Harley-Davidson's 85th year in business. In addition to these national events, Harley-Davidson also contributes support to many annual biker events such as the Blackhills Motorcycle Rally and the Muscular Dystrophy fund-raising rides.

An example of the Harley-Davidson marketing philosophy is demonstrated by their events organized for the 1989 Daytona Bike Week. The Harley agenda for the week included poker runs, seminars, women riders' workshops, shows, receptions, pool parties, and record hops, leaving very little spare time. An excerpt from an article in *Rider Magazine* (Bucher, 1989) typifies Harley-Davidson's after-market support: "The people at Harley-Davidson . . . understand that the price you sell a bike for, even the bike itself, is pretty much irrelevant. What you have to do is complete the loop and give people something to do with their machines: destinations, activities, a sense of belonging. To the Harley faithful, it really didn't matter what else was going on in Daytona that week. They had their own rally, they belonged." This type of support intensifies the loyalty of existing customers and contributes to the expansion of the company's customer base.

Another aspect of the Harley-Davidson marketing program, that met with tremendous success, was the test ride. Due to accident liability fears and the threat of theft, many dealers and manufacturers had refused customers test rides before the motorcycle sale was completed. Harley began to alter this policy by offering demonstration rides at rallies, later expanding the program nationally to dealers. The development of the demonstration ride as a marketing tool for dealers proved a boon to the sales of the big machines. By 1985, 6% of the participants in the test ride program purchased a Harley (Walsh, 1985).

Import Tariff

Perhaps the most controversial effort to turn around the company was a request for tariffs on imported motorcycles. Soon after completion of the buy out from AMF, Harley-Davidson executives began lobbying the International Trade Commission for a tariff on imported motorcycles. This request was specifically designed to protect Harley-Davidson's product niche from further Japanese encroachment. Early in 1983 the ITC ruled that imports posed a threat to the domestic motorcycle industry (Harley-Davidson) and in April of 1983 President Reagan imposed a tariff on imported motorcycles with engine displacements greater than 700 cc's. The tariff rate began at 49.4% in 1983 and declined each year thereafter to 14.4% in 1987 with an expiration of the tariff in 1988.

The stated purpose of the tariff was to stop the dumping of motorcycles by the Japanese and allow Harley-Davidson the opportunity to recover enough to be able to compete with the Japanese manufacturers (Pine, 1983). Ironically, the import tariff aided two Japanese companies, Honda and Kawasaki, against their Japanese rivals. Both companies had established manufacturing facilities for their larger bikes in the U.S. and thus avoided the tariff. Honda also took advantage of its flexibility in manufacturing to quickly produce bikes with engine sizes that were just below the 700 cc limit.

In the spring of 1987, amid much fanfare, Harley-Davidson requested an early end to the hard sought tariff imposed four years earlier. A Harley spokesperson stated that the request to rescind the tariff was largely a philosophical gesture designed to emphasize that existing legislation could be effective in facilitating a return to competitiveness by American industries (Bogart, 1987). Harley-Davidson was touted in many news and business articles as the epitome of an American company pulling itself up by the bootstraps to regain competitiveness in an industry dominated by foreign companies. President Reagan seized the opportunity to use Harley-Davidson as an example. He visited the York, Pennsylvania, assembly plant to laud the company's workers and management for their successful efforts. The president also cited the company's success with the tariff restrictions under existing trade laws, and voiced opposition to new and more restrictive trade legislation under consideration in congress. All Harley-Davidson needed was a little help; or did it?

In the final analysis the effects of the tariff were mixed. Due to the small quantity of European bikes imported and the high level of imports allowed before the tariff became effective, European motorcycle prices were not affected. Sales of Japanese motorcycles did decrease, but the major causes for the decline may not have been the tariff. During the initial stages of the tariff, the performance of the U.S. economy was weak. The economic downturn, combined with the shrinking demographics, led to a glut of motorcycles. In response, the big-four Japanese manufacturers initially reduced prices to shrink

Table 5 Motorcycle Owner Profile: Sex, Marital Status, Age, Education, Occupation, Income, Riding Experience, Motorcycle Ownership

	% of Total Owners			% of Total Owners	
	1985	**1980**		**1985**	**1980**
Occupation of Owner*			*Years Regularly Riding Motorcycles***		
Laborer/Semi-skilled	22.2%	20.7%	Under 3 years	13.9%	21.1%
Professional/Technical	18.3%	18.8%	3–5 years	22.3%	27.6%
Mechanic/Craftsman	14.7%	23.3%	6–10 years	28.3%	29.8%
Manager/Proprietor	9.1%	8.6%	Over 10 years	34.5%	18.6%
Clerical/Sales	8.1%	9.3%	Not Stated	1.0%	2.9%
Service Worker	6.4%	7.1%	**Median** (years)	8.0	6.0
Farmer/Farm Laborer	6.4%	4.6%			
Military	1.6%	1.9%	*Sex*		
Other	4.6%	0.0%	Male	91.3%	92.1%
Not Stated	8.6%	5.7%	Female	8.7%	7.9%
Age			*Highest Level of Education*		
Under 18	16.6%	24.6%	Grade School	8.6%	13.5%
18–24 years old	20.2%	24.3%	Some High School	16.0%	18.9%
25–29 years old	18.6%	14.2%	High School Graduate	36.5%	34.6%
30–34 years old	13.6%	10.2%	Some College	20.4%	17.6%
35–39 years old	8.7%	8.8%	College Graduate	12.0%	9.2%
40–49 years old	12.5%	9.4%	Post Graduate	4.8%	3.1%
50 and Over	7.9%	5.7%	Not Stated	1.7%	3.1%
Not Stated	1.9%	2.8%			
Median Age	27.7	24.0	*Total Motorcycles Ever Owned***		
Mean Age	29.7	26.9	1 motorcycle	22.4%	25.6%
			2 motorcycles	20.1%	21.4%
Household Income for Prior Year			3–4 motorcycles	26.8%	26.5%
Under $10,000	10.6%	9.1%	5–9 motorcycles	18.5%	16.0%
$10,000–$14,999	9.0%	13.0%	10 or more	11.0%	7.6%
$15,000–$19,999	11.2%	13.9%	Not stated	1.2%	2.9%
$20,000–$24,999	8.5%	12.9%	**Median** (cycles)	3.0	3.0
$25,000–$34,999	17.8%	12.5%			
$35,000–$49,999	13.9%	5.9%	*Marital Status*		
$50,000 and Over	6.8%	2.4%	Single	47.7%	51.7%
Unknown	22.2%	30.3%	Married	50.2%	44.3%
Median	$25,900	$17,500	Not stated	2.1%	4.0%

Note: The owner is defined as the primary rider, and the rider is the operator, not the passenger of the vehicle.
Source: *1980 Survey of Motorcycle Ownership and Usage,* conducted for the Motorcycle Industry Council by Burke Marketing Research, Inc., Cincinnati, Ohio, April 1981.
1985 Survey of Motorcycle Ownership and Usage, conducted for the Motorcycle Industry Council by Burke Marketing Research, Inc., Cincinnati, Ohio, February 1986.
*Based on owners employed.
**Scooters and ATVs not included.

inventories. Following the selldown of inventories, the imported large motorcycles' prices dramatically rose. As a result of this situation, many industry observers were critical of the import tariff and stated that it negatively affected the entire motorcycle industry by pushing prices up. For a profile of motorcycle owners, see Table 5.

Changes in the currency exchange rate between the U.S. and Japan also affected prices. In 1970 the exchange rate was 357.60 yen to the dollar, by 1980 the rate had fallen to 226.63 yen, and by 1986 the yen/dollar rate had dropped to 168.35 to 1. The result of this dramatic 16 year decline in currency exchange rates effectively raised the prices of Japanese products to American customers.

Finances

The Harley division management team reportedly purchased the company from AMF for 25 cents a share, clearly an indication of AMF's view of the future prospects for the motorcycle division (Anders, 1987). Even with this seemingly low price, Harley suffered under an extremely heavy debt load at a time when interest rates in the United States were at an all time high. The result of the combination of high interest, high debt, and poor sales was a $25 million loss in 1981 and $32 million in 1982. Bankruptcy was a real possibility.

The financing for the LBO was arranged by Citicorp Industrial Credit. During the early years of Harley's independence, the relationship with Citicorp was supportive. For example, Citicorp provided overadvance funding (a special arrangement to provide funds in excess of maximum amounts stipulated by original loan lending formulas) to cover the needs of Harley-Davidson.

As a result of Harley's improvements in production and marketing, the stronger U.S. economy, and the cooperation of Citicorp, the tide slowly began to turn resulting in a slim profit in 1983. A steady, conservative approach, concentrating on the strengths within the company and

a tight reign on costs led Harley-Davidson to an increased market share in 1984, a solid profit for the year, and a glimmer of light at the end of the tunnel. By 1985 Harley-Davidson was solidly in the black, posting a profit of $9.9 million (including $7.3 million in extraordinary credits from losses carried from prior years) on increasing sales and market share (Oneal, 1986). Although the company was revitalized and returning profits, it was laboring under a very large debt load from the leveraged buy out and the overadvances needed to continue operations in the lean years of 1981, 1982, and 1983.

The high level of debt, uncertainty about the future of the motorcycle industry, a less than favorable economic forecast from Citicorp economists, and a new account executive who was less than sympathetic to the plight of Harley-Davidson, precipitated a crisis that threatened the existence of the company. Citicorp senior executives were convinced that Harley could not survive an economic slowdown predicted for the last half of the 1980s. A decision was made by the bank in 1985 to "pull the plug" on Harley-Davidson. Harley executives were encouraged to arrange for another primary financing source, or face liquidation by the end of 1985. Citicorp reasoned there would be a greater chance of recouping the greatest portion of loans outstanding if the company was liquidated while it was profitable.

After many failed attempts to arrange refinancing and pay off Citicorp, a less than favorable deal was struck with Heller Financial Services on December 23, 1985, seven days from the bankruptcy/liquidation deadline. Although the deal was approved with time to spare, the actual funds transfer had to be completed prior to the close of business December 31. It was not until late afternoon on December 31, 1985, that all funds were transferred and verified, removing the specter of liquidation (Reid, 1990).

The result of this scramble for financing and the less than favorable terms of the new package, prompted Harley-Davidson executives to consider taking the company public. Reflecting on the company's dilemma, Vaughn Beals, Harley-Davidson's CEO stated "... private is better when you have the cash, but public is a lot better when you don't" (Deutsch, 1988).

Harley-Davidson completed its post LBO stock offering in July 1986, issuing 2 million shares of common stock at $11 per share, garnering net proceeds of $20 million. In addition to the stock offer, $70 million of 12.5% subordinated bonds, due in 1996, were issued. The proceeds of the offering allowed management to retire the high level of debt incurred from the LBO, and provided the means to acquire much needed machine tools to further modernize production processes.

The infusion of cash also resulted in a situation unique in Harley's recent history—an anticipated $50 million cash balance at the end of 1986 (Reid, 1990). After examining the trends in the motorcycle industry, the company's executives decided that they needed to spread their risks to other industries. With Harley's strong cash position, diversification by acquisition was chosen as the most logical means to accomplish the company's goals. Recent financial statements are reported in Tables 6, 7, and 8.

Holiday Rambler

Harley's executives felt that branded automotive aftermarket parts and recreational vehicles were the two most compatible industries for diversification (Reid, 1990). The management felt that these two industries would fit best with Harley's current skills and competencies in manufacturing and marketing. By coincidence, the Holiday Rambler recreational vehicle (RV) manufacturer came up for sale. Within three weeks of the initial contact, Harley-Davidson's board of directors authorized negotiations for the purchase of privately held Holiday Rambler Corporation. Two days later a formal agreement was reached to purchase the RV manufacturer for $155 million (Reid, 1990).

Holiday Rambler Corporation is a leader in the recreational vehicle and commercial truck/van body industry. The RV manufacturer consists of a diverse group of divisions and subsidiaries sharing a strength in manufacturing, a focus from which Harley hopes to realize operational synergies. The RV division manufactures and markets a broad range of recreational vehicles including Class A luxury motorhomes, competitively priced mini-motorhomes, travel trailers, fifth-wheel trailers, and Aviator van conversions. The Utilimaster subsidiary of Holiday Rambler manufactures truck transport vans and trailers and van bodies. They also introduced a front wheel drive walk-in mini van in August of 1988. Customers of the Utilimaster subsidiary include United Parcel Service, Ryder, and Federal Express. Other divisions of Holiday Rambler include Parkway Distributors, a large distributor of RV aftermarket parts and accessories; Nappanee Wood Products, a manufacturer of wood cabinetry and home furnishings; and Creative Dimensions office furniture.

Reflecting on the acquisition of Holiday Rambler, CEO Vaughn Beals stated "we're both really in the same business ... making big toys for big boys" (Reid, 1990: p. 129). This statement alluded to the possibility of marketing synergies that Harley-Davidson could develop. The RV manufacturer has market strengths in the premium segment of the RV market similar to Harley's strength in the motorcycle market. Additionally, both companies target a select group of customers whose recreational activities substantially influence their lifestyles.

Holiday Rambler may also prove to hold manufacturing and financial synergies for Harley-Davidson in an industry with substantial growth potential, however, the acquisition is not without its risks. At the time Harley entered negotiations for the company, Holiday Rambler executives were attempting to gain financing to acquire the firm. The RV manufacturer had been a family-held private corporation since its found-

Table 6 Consolidated Balance Sheets

December 31	1988	1987
	(in thousands, except per share amounts)	
Assets		
Current assets:		
Cash and cash equivalents	$ 52,360	$ 68,226
Accounts receivable, net of allowance for doubtful accounts	47,153	34,419
Inventories	97,661	83,748
Deferred income taxes	8,844	7,748
Prepaid expenses	5,273	3,763
Total current assets	$211,291	$197,904
Property, plant, and equipment, at cost, less accumulated depreciation and amortization	$110,788	$100,426
Goodwill	70,210	74,162
Deferred financing costs	4,495	7,194
Other assets	4,330	1,186
	$401,114	$380,872
Liabilities and Stockholders' Equity		
Current liabilities:		
Notes payable	$ 21,041	$ 19,958
Current maturities of long-term debt	12,188	8,377
Accounts payable	39,116	35,855
Accrued expenses and other liabilities	64,042	69,492
Total current liabilities	$136,387	$133,682
Long-term debt	135,176	178,762
Accrued employee benefits	3,309	642
Deferred income taxes	4,594	4,873
Commitments and contingencies (Notes 4, 5, 7, & 9)		
Stockholders' equity:		
Series A Junior Participating preferred stock, 1,000,000 shares authorized in 1988, none issued	—	—
Common stock, 9,155,000 shares issued in 1988 and 7,430,000 in 1987	92	74
Additional paid-in capital	76,902	41,741
Retained earnings	44,410	20,498
Cumulative foreign currency translation adjustment	374	730
	$121,778	$ 63,043
Less treasury stock (520,000 shares) at cost:	(130)	(130)
Total stockholders' equity	121,648	62,913
	$401,114	$380,827

Source: 1988 Harley Davidson Annual Report.

Table 7 Consolidated Statements of Income

Year Ended December 31	1988	1987	1986
	(in thousands, except per share amounts)		
Net Sales	$757,378	$685,358	$295,322
Operating costs and expenses:			
Cost of goods sold	572,162	518,670	219,167
Selling, administrative, and engineering	118,914	110,841	60,059
	$691,076	$629,511	$279,226
Income from operations	66,302	55,847	16,096
Interest income	4,249	2,658	1,138
Interest expense	(24,670)	(25,508)	(9,511)
Other–net	129	(2,143)	(388)
Income before provision for income taxes and extraordinary items	46,010	30,854	7,335
Provision for income taxes	$ 18,854	$ 13,181	$ 3,028
Income before extraordinary items	27,156	17,673	4,307
Loss of refinancing/debt repurchase, net of taxes	(1,468)	—	—
Additional cost of 1983 AMF settlement net of taxes	(1,776)	—	—
Benefit from utilization of loss, carry forward	—	3,542	1,411
Net income	$ 23,912	$ 21,215	$ 4,871
Per common share			
Income before extraordinary items	$ 3.41	$ 2.72	$ .82
Extraordinary items	(.41)	.55	.11
Net income	$ 3.00	$ 3.27	$ .93

Source: 1988 Harley-Davidson Annual Report.

ing, growing slowly from small travel trailer manufacturing to a position of prominence in the recreational vehicle manufacturing industry with a nationwide dealer network. Despite the indication that the acquisition would be a major subsidiary and operate as a separate entity, rumors of dissatisfaction and the possibility of wholesale defections by key Holiday Rambler executives were reported (Bohn, 1986). Also, there was uncertainty and apprehension from the Holiday Rambler dealer network over implications of the takeover. A statement regarding Holiday Rambler in the 1988 Harley Davidson annual report reflects the transition:

At Holiday Rambler Corporation, 1988 was a year of transition and opportunities. As the year

began, we knew the Company needed to set its sights on growth. To do that, we had to develop a strategy that would provide us with more competitive recreational products and a broader range of diversified products. We also had to streamline operations, institute improved business controls, and complete improvements to our manufacturing facilities. And that's exactly what we did.

During 1988, sales and market share in the RV division declined from 1987 levels. Two product lines within the RV division, Holiday House park model vacation homes and CAMP Industries low cost towables and Class C motorhomes, were phased out during the year. These actions were in response to a shift in the market toward the upper end of the industry's product offerings.

Table 8 Business Segments, Foreign Operations, and Major Customers

(a) Business Segments

The Company operates in three business segments: motorcycles and related products, transportation vehicles, and defense and other businesses.

Information by industry segment is set forth below. Operations of Holiday Rambler (transportation vehicles) are not included in 1986 since it was purchased effective December 31, 1986.

	1988	1987	1986
		(in thousands)	
Net sales			
Motorcycles and related products	$397,774	$324,614	$260,833
Transportation vehicles	351,987	342,979	—
Defense and other businesses	7,617	17,765	34,489
	$757,378	$685,358	$295,322

	1988	1987	1986
		(in thousands)	
Income from operations			
Motorcycles and related products	$ 50,112	$ 29,892	$ 16,686
Transportation vehicles	22,477	28,835	—
Defense and other businesses	321	722	4,633
General corporate expenses	(6,608)	(3,652)	(5,223)
	$ 66,302	$ 55,847	$ 16,096
Interest expense, net	(20,421)	(22,850)	(8,373)
Other	129	(2,143)	(388)
Income before income taxes and extraordinary items	$ 46,010	$ 30,854	$ 7,335

Source: 1988 Harley-Davidson Annual Report.

Hoped-for synergy from the acquisition may be years from reality if it ever materializes. Each industry has unique features that are not readily apparent to outsiders. Harley-Davidson knows the motorcycle industry very well. It is unclear whether the strengths Harley has developed in the motorcycle industry can be transferred to Holiday Rambler. If the acquisition can be assimilated successfully, Harley-Davidson will move away from major dependence upon the uncertain future of the motorcycle industry.

In 1987, the RV division provided more net sales contribution and almost the same net profit to Harley-Davidson as did the motorcycle division. Sales and profits of the motorcycle division in 1988 substantially exceeded the RV division, reflecting marketing and production adjustments necessary to adapt to market shifts in the RV industry. While these results do not indicate serious problems with the acquisition, the question remains whether Harley-Davidson can successfully transfer its manufacturing and marketing expertise to a new industry. Harley-Davidson also continues to vigorously pursue a diversification strategy in other areas: defense contracts, engine production for Briggs-Stratton, Acustar marine engine components, shower door production for Kohler Corporation, as well as computer peripherals (Harley-Davidson Annual Report, 1988).

The Recreational Vehicle Industry

There was steady growth in the RV industry, both in sales value and units sold, during the early 1980s. In 1988 shipments of recreational vehicles of all types were the highest of the decade. However, even at this peak, shipments were more than 100,000 units below 1978 levels, and less than half the level of 1973. According to industry reports shipments are expected to decline slightly through 1990, with a rebound expected during 1991 (RVIA Year-end Report, 1989). The trends evident from the above data reflect the industry's overwhelming dependence upon economic conditions.

The sharp decline in shipments experienced since 1973 was influenced by the rising gasoline prices of the mid 1970s and the sharp increase in interest rates from 1979 through 1981. Although the demographic trends (see Table 3) indicate a large portion of the population will be in their prime earning years during the 1990s, recreational vehicles are luxury items that are extremely sensitive to economic downturns, interest rates, and the price of fuel. If the industry is in a mature phase, pressures on pricing, and therefore profits, could be strong.

The decade ahead is filled with uncertainty for the RV industry. Recent trade reports indicate the U.S. economy is now more dependent upon foreign crude oil supplies than it was in the early 1970s. The U.S. economy has experienced its longest period of sustained expansion since World War II and may be ready for a downturn. These two factors characterize the pessimistic side of the outlook for the 1990s. However, everything is not gloom and doom. As indicated above, the baby boom generation will be in their prime earning years during the coming decade. Recent developments in the world political situation could mean economic opportunities for the export of goods and services from the U.S. or expansion of U.S. companies abroad. This situation could boost the domestic economy. Additionally, because of reduced tensions in the world, the "peace dividend" could become a

reality. A reduction in defense spending would reduce government expenditures and the budget deficit, possibly culminating in less pressure on domestic interest rates.

Any combination of these factors is possible, presenting the RV industry with a number of challenges. Positioning by manufacturers in the industry will be crucial to their economic success during the next decade. A number of opportunities exist, but threats are also present.

The Future

Harley-Davidson is clearly moving into a new phase of its history. After the long struggle from the edge of bankruptcy, the company must now position itself for challenges looming on the horizon. Crucial threats and opportunities exist on many fronts. An overarching issue will be how well the management can deal with the changing marketplace. Their efforts may be affected by the retirement of CEO Vaughn Beals in March, 1989. Although this transition may not cause the failure of the company, the new leadership can have a great impact on Harley-Davidson's future.

The new president is Harley's former chief financial officer Richard Teerlink. In a recent interview (Pacheco, 1989), he summarized Harley-Davidson future strategy: "Harley is going to remain dedicated to the motorcycle business. We're not going to go out on an acquisition binge and buy everybody out. We think it's important to have a balanced company so that when the motorcycle business may not be as good as it is today we are able to keep funding the motorcycle. We are committed to motorcycles. We are committed to both the customer and the touring market."

The evident long-run focus of this strategy is to use Holiday Rambler as a cash cow to fund the production of large motorcycles, the niche that Harley has traditionally occupied. In the short-run, the reverse may occur with the motorcycle division supporting Holiday Rambler. This strategy has a number of potential strengths and weaknesses. By continuing to focus on its traditional market, Harley will likely continue to build motorcycles having the familiar cruiser style and V-twin engine. While this has been an effective strategy in the recent past, there is no guarantee that this market will continue to be strong. In addition, it may ignore the potential for greatly increased growth and profits in the RV industry.

Even though the sale of Japanese bikes in Harley's niche have declined in recent years, the big four manufacturers may be poised to re-enter the market with improved machines. Many innovations are rumored to be coming from the Japanese manufacturers, including lightweight engines made from composite materials, oval pistons, electronically controlled engines and suspensions, swingarm front suspensions, anti-lock braking, and two-wheel drive.

Some innovations will be required to meet the increasingly stringent noise and air-pollution regulations. Surprisingly, two-stroke engines may be the answer to much of this environmental legislation. New computer controlled two-stroke engines are scheduled for introduction by the major automobile manufacturers in the mid 1990s and may be used by the motorcycle companies soon thereafter. These new engines are said to be cleaner, half the weight, and twice as powerful as current four-stroke engines, such as those used by Harley. If Harley is unable to meet these new technological requirements its profits may disappear.

Harley may also have sales problems due to the price of its motorcycles. In 1990, many of Harley's bikes retailed for over $10,000. Comparable Japanese motorcycles sold for 20% to 50% less. If the yen/dollar exchange rate shifts, the relative price of the Japanese bikes might be even less. Potentially, the Japanese can offer motorcycles with some of these new innovations, at a low price, and cut into Harley's sales.

Harley seems to be betting that major technological innovations will not affect their sales. This strategy seems to be based upon the long standing image and style of Harley-Davidson motorcycles. While the company does have a well established niche, it does not make Harley invulnerable to competition. A similar "steady as she goes" strategy almost killed the company following the initial entry of the Japanese manufacturers into the United States. Yet, if Harley does attempt to branch out of its current niche there are a number of obstacles.

Initially, the company needs to assess the market potentials for motorcycles and RVs. A number of important factors need to be considered, including: changing demographic patterns, demand by market niche, national economic conditions, disposable income for recreation machines, gasoline supplies and costs, and governmental safety regulations (e.g., laws requiring helmets and insurance).

If the company decides to expand in the motorcycle or RV markets, it must then decide upon the appropriate segments for growth. For example, Harley may have difficulty expanding out of the large motorcycle niche. In the 1970s the company attempted to build small motorcycles with two-stroke engines. These bikes directly competed with the Japanese manufacturers and had low sales. Harley also attempted to compete in the large sport motorcycle market with the introduction of its "cafe racer" in 1977. This bike was also a sales failure. There is, however, evidence to suggest that Harley might be able to successfully re-enter these markets, in spite of its cruiser-bike image. In the late 1980s the company developed a new off-road military motorcycle with an engine produced by the Austrian manufacturer Rotax. The goal was to manufacture these motorcycles for NATO troops. In the United States, Harley is selling engines to a small company, Buell, that produces an innovative on-road sport bike. In 1990, the Buell motorcycles successfully sold for nearly $15,000.

Sales in the traditional cruiser market segment might also be expanded overseas. With the economic unification of Europe in 1992, tariffs within Europe may be eliminated or reduced. However, imports into Europe may be limited.

Anticipating these economic and regulatory changes, a number of Japanese companies have been rumored to be attempting the purchase of Italian motorcycle manufacturers. There have also been rumors that General Motors will buy BMW and divest the motorcycle operations which have been loosing money in recent years. If Harley wants to increase sales in Europe, it may want to purchase manufacturing facilities such as those owned by BMW.

Within the United States, Harley must give serious consideration to expanding its production capabilities. Currently, the company sells all of the motorcycles that it can make. If demand does increase, due to factors such as changing demographics or the need for efficient transportation in congested urban areas, Harley's production capabilities will be even further stretched. Industry rumors in the early 1990s indicate that two of the Japanese companies are considering leaving the motorcycle industry. If they do, demand for Harley's bikes may further increase, and the company might consider purchasing one of the Japanese company's manufacturing facilities.

While considering these many growth possibilities, Harley must continue to be wary. With the passage of the crisis atmosphere and the increased production demands, the positive work climate in the factories may become strained. Workers may feel pushed to their limits and desire bigger rewards for the efforts leading to Harley's successes. However, by expanding production facilities, the company will increase its overhead and make it more vulnerable to economic downturns.

The company's profits and reputation may also attract the attention of corporate raiders. One such instance took place in October, 1989. Malcom I. Glazer, chairman of First Allied Investors Corporation, announced the intention to accumulate a controlling interest in Harley-Davidson (McMurray, 1989). This will probably not be the last attempt to take over Harley-Davidson. The current level of success enjoyed by

the company will continue to attract attention. The value of the company's parts may indeed be worth more than the combined entity. Holiday Rambler could be easily and profitably divested in a takeover. The Harley-Davidson trademark could be exploited as a valuable commodity. The company needs a strategic plan to deal with such acquisition attempts as well as to give an overall direction to the corporation.

Bibliography

Anders, G. (1987, January 2). Another round: Many firms go public within a few years of leveraged buy-out. *The Wall Street Journal*, pp. 1, 9.

Bogart, B. (1987). Harley-Davidson trades restrictions for profits. *Advertising Age*, August 10, p. S27.

Bohn, J. (1986, Dec. 8). Top RV firm sold to Harley-Davidson. *Automotive News*, p. 62.

Bucher, D. (1989, July). Letters from Daytona: A Bike-Week adventure in Florida worth writing home about. *Rider*, pp. 55–57.

Cayer, S. (1988, Oct. 13). Harley's new manager-owners put purchasing out front. *Purchasing*, pp. 50–54.

Daft, R. L. (1989). Case for analysis: Harley-Davidson. *Organization theory and design*, (3rd ed.), pp. 578–580.

Deutsch, C. H. (1988, April 17). Now Harley-Davidson is all over the road. *New York Times Magazine*, pp. 12–13.

Harley-Davidson Annual Report (1988). Milwaukee, WI.

Hill, C. W. L., & Jones, G. R. (1989). *Strategic management: An integrated approach*. Boston, MA: Houghton Mifflin.

Messina, W. S. (1987). *Statistical quality control for manufacturing managers*. New York: John Wiley.

McMurray, S. (1989, October 4). Harley-Davidson price run-up wasn't fueled by the smart money crowd, analysts say. *The Wall Street Journal*, p. C2.

O'Neal, M. (1986, July 21). Harley-Davidson: Ready to hit the road again. *Business Week*, p. 70.

Pacheco, B. A. (1989, November). Riding the crest: Richard Teerlink. *Rider*, pp. 35, 72.

Pine, A. (1983, April 4). Stiff motorcycle duties said to be aimed at spurring Japan to help US industry. *The Wall Street Journal*, p. 23.

Reid, P. C. (1990). *Well made in America: Lessons from Harley-Davidson on being the best.* New York: McGraw-Hill.

RVIA (1989). *Recreational vehicle industry association year end report 1988.*

Sarasohn, D. (1989). Harley: The smokes with leather filters. *The Oregonian*, November 22.

Spadoni, M. (1985). Harley-Davidson revs up to improve image. *Advertising Age*, August 5, p. 30.

Walsh, D. L. (1985, July). You meet the nicest people on a Harley. *American Demographics*, p. 18.

Willis, R. (1986, March). Harley-Davidson comes roaring back. *Management Review*, pp. 20–27.

Case 25

A Note on Starting an Entrepreneurial Business through Venture Capital

Throughout America more and more entrepreneurs are building successful businesses, which range from high technology to food franchising, from manufacturing products to providing services. Venture capital investments are spurring a good deal of the entrepreneurial momentum. In recent years investment bankers and venture capital firms have channeled funds into a variety of companies that demonstrated solid potential for profitable growth.[1]

Owning and managing a small firm is a risky undertaking, however. About 400,000 small businesses fail each year.[2] In fact, by their tenth year of existence, almost 90 percent of all small firms fail (Table 1a). Tables 1b and 1c present the overall new business failure rates and survival rates for one year and four years based on firm size.

The key to starting a successful firm is a good idea. Let us assume for this note that the idea is

a new one and that it is patentable. Let us further assume that the entrepreneur has completed the necessary market research and found the potential for this product, process, or service to be outstanding. What he or she lacks is funding.

Table 1b One-Year Survival Rates by Firm Size

Firm Size (employees)	Survival Percent
0–9	77.8%
10–19	85.5
20–99	95.3
100–249	95.2
250+	100.0

Source: Michael B. Teitz et al., "Small Business and Employment Growth in California," Working Paper No. 348 (Berkeley, Calif.: University of California, March 1981), 42.

Table 1a Overall New Business Failure Rates

By the End of:	Percentage that Fail
1st year	40%
2d year	60
10th year	90

Sources: Commerce Department; SBA; Dun & Bradstreet.

[1]*Raising Venture Capital: An Entrepreneur's Guidebook*, Deloitte, Haskins, and Sells, 1985, 72.

[2]Small Business Administration, *The State of Small Business, 1986*.

Copyright © 1989 Jeffrey S. Bracker

Table 1c Four-Year Survival Rates by Firm Size

Firm Size (employees)	D&B Study (1969–1976)	California Study (1976–1980)
0–19	37.4%	49.9%
20–49	53.6	66.9
50–99	55.7	66.9
100–499	67.7	70.0

Sources: David L. Birch, *MIT Studies, 1979–80*; and Michael B. Teitz et al., "Small Business and Employment Growth in California," Working Paper No. 348 (Berkeley, Calif.: University of California, March 1981), p. 22.

Table 2 Standard Deviations, *F*-Values: Projected Financial Ratios

	No. Samples Funded	No. Samples Unfunded	Std. Dev. Funded	Std. Dev. Unfunded	*F*-Values
Asset Management					
Sales/fixed assets	15	20	61.83	131.10	4.61**
Sales/current assets	16	21	0.92	1.36	2.18*
Working capital/total assets	17	22	0.51	0.63	1.53
Working capital/sales	16	20	0.32	0.61	3.52**
Profitability					
EBIT/sales	24	37	0.41	0.29	1.99
EBIT/total assets	17	22	0.61	0.54	1.40
EBIT/equity	13	20	0.68	0.56	1.47
Expense Management					
Fixed costs/sales	15	26	0.35	0.46	1.73
Gross margin	20	29	0.53	0.63	1.41
Capital Structure					
LT debt/equity	14	21	0.17	1.93	128.89**

*$p \cdot 0.05$; **$p \cdot 0.01$.
Note that due to lack of data in some plans it was impossible to calculate all ratios, so sample sizes vary.
Source: I.C. MacMillan and P.N. Subba Narasimha, "Characteristics Distinguishing Funded from Unfunded Business Plans Evaluated by Venture Capitalists," *Strategic Management Journal* 8 (issue 6, 1987): 583.

What Venture Capitalists Look For

Studies of successful and unsuccessful firms have indicated that firms with properly developed, implemented, and controlled plans are more likely to be successful in obtaining venture capital. A study that considered only the structure of the plan, not the content, distinguished funded from unfunded business plans evaluated by venture capitalists[3] (see Tables 2 and 3). The data revealed that plans that exhibit wide values from the norm go unfunded. It seems clear from the data that financial projections should conform to financial ratios for firms in similar competitive situations. Venture capitalists most often

[3]I.C. MacMillan and P.N. Subba Narasimha, "Characteristics Distinguishing Funded from Unfunded Business Plans Evaluated by Venture Capitalists," *Strategic Management Journal* 8 (issue 6, 1987), 582–583.

compare forecast figures and typical industry statistics in their early screening. Any differences from the industry should be explained in the plan. Failure to do this usually results in a rejection letter.

Many investment companies publish their investment criteria (Exhibit 1), yet it is still very difficult to obtain venture funding. In fact, only an estimated one in a hundred firms is funded through traditional venture capitalists. Exhibit 2 shows the sources of capital for entrepreneurs starting businesses that were previously nonexistent.

Most venture capitalists look for established industry niches to fund. Because they expect to see sound management practices, it is rare to see a venture funded that has limited management expertise. Mergers and acquisitions expert Robert Ouriel believes that venture capitalists look

Table 3   Standard Deviations, *F*-Values for Plan Structure

	No. Samples Funded	No. Samples Unfunded	Std. Dev. Funded	Std. Dev. Unfunded	*F*-Value
Marketing percentage of plan	27	55	0.12	0.31	6.67*
Financial percentage of plan	27	55	0.13	0.34	6.81*
Production percentage of plan	27	55	0.12	0.31	6.67*
Management percentage of plan	27	55	0.09	0.18	6.00*
Smallest expense item/largest expense item	16	34	0.12	0.30	6.25*

*$p < 0.01$.
Note that due to lack of data in some plans it was impossible to calculate all ratios, so sample sizes vary.
Source: I.C. MacMillan and P.N. Subba Narsimha, "Characteristics Distinguishing Funded from Unfunded Business Plans Evaluated by Venture Capitalists," *Strategic Management Journal* 8 (issue 6, 1987): 582.

at three things: management, management, and management.

A summary of characteristics of entrepreneurs, as proposed by various authors since the mid-1800s, is given in Table 4. Miner has developed a comprehensive theory of entrepreneurial achievement having at its root McClelland's[4] psychological theory of *n*Ach. Miner's theory specifies five role characteristics and their related motivational patterns.[5] These relationships are summarized as follows:

1. Achievement orientation: A desire to achieve through one's own efforts

2. Personal risk: A desire to take moderate risks

3. Feedback: A desire for some clear index of the level of performance

4. Personal innovation: A desire to introduce novel, creative, or innovative solutions

5. Planning: A desire to think about the future and anticipate future possibilities

A study of technologically innovative entrepreneurs found that these characteristics or motives were relatively strong among more suc-

cessful entrepreneurs.[6] Entrepreneurs who owned and managed small high-growth electronic firms were found to possess these characteristics as well as sophisticated business plans.[7]

These studies and others lead us to believe that many entrepreneurs are doomed because of a lack of drive and achievement. Barbato and Bracker (1988) studied dislocated (laid off) workers who desired to start their own businesses.[8] Even though they had been in sophisticated positions in large firms, they failed to produce sophisticated business plans for their potential companies after a 12-week training program. Further investigation also found them lacking in many of the motivational areas described by Miner. Therefore, there is a distinct difference between small business people and entrepreneurs. Entrepreneurship reflects a constellation of characteristics and behaviors, and these vary

[4]J.B. Miner, "Limited Domain Theories of Organization Energy," in C.C. Tinder and L.F. Moore, eds., *Middle Range Theory and Study of Organizations* (Boston: Martinus Nijhoff, 1980): 279–280.

[5]Miner, "Limited Domain Theories in Organization Energy," 334–336.

[6]N.R. Smith, J.S. Bracker, and J.B. Miner, "Correlates of Firm and Entrepreneur Success in Technologically Innovative Companies," *Frontiers of Entrepreneurship Research* 7, 337–353.

[7]J.S. Bracker, B. Keats, J.B. Miner, and J.N. Pearson, "Task Motivation, Planning Orientation, and Firm Performance," a paper presented at the National Academy of Management Meeting, Anaheim, California, 1988.

[8]R. Barbato and J.S. Bracker, "Dislocation and Potential Entrepreneurship," *Proceedings*, Santa Barbara Institute Directors Association National Meeting, San Francisco, California, 1988.

Exhibit 1 Investment Criteria of a Typical Investment Company

Industry
- Stable industries not subject to rapid technological change, or wide cyclical swings in volume and profit
- Presence of barriers to market entry

Size
- Revenues of at least $20 million
- Net income after tax of at least $1.5 million in the latest fiscal year or the average of the last three years

Profitability
- Proven record of profitability for a minimum of three years

Balance Sheet
- Relatively low debt/equity ratio

Price
- Purchase price that represents a realistic relationship to demonstrated profit performance

Location
- Anywhere in the United States

Equity Features
- Always required
- Percentage negotiable, never control

Preferred Size of Investment
- $1.0 million to $10.0 million

Purpose of Investments
- Leveraged buyouts
- Divestitures of subsidiaries and divisions
- Leveraged ESOP
- Growing companies

Types of Securities
- Private placements of
  - Subordinated debentures with common stock
  - Subordinated debentures with warrants
  - Preferred stock with common stock
  - Preferred stock with warrants

Types of Financing
- Sole investor/leader
- Lead with participants
- Participant, with another investor leading

Amortization/Redemption Schedules
- 5–10 years

Board of Directors Participation
- Attend board meeting as observer, and/or have the right to sit on the board

Businesses not Favored
- Start-ups
- Turnarounds
- Breaking even or unprofitable operations
- Real estate
- Commodity businesses with little or no control over pricing
- Highly capital intensive businesses that must reinvest most of their cash flow in plant and equipment or working capital in order to remain competitive

Source: Venture Capital Group, Bankers Trust Company, New York, NY.

among all individuals, including small business owners.

Smith identified two types of entrepreneur: opportunist and craftsman.[9] According to his ty-

[9]N.R. Smith, "The Entrepreneur and his Firm: The Relationship between Type of Man and Type of Company," Michigan State University, East Lansing, Michigan, 1967.

pology, the opportunist reflects an individual who reacts to a broad range of culture; exhibits breadth in education and training; and possesses a high level of social awareness, involvement, flexibility, confidence, and awareness of and orientation toward the future. The craftsman reflects the opposite on each dimension.

Exhibit 2   Sources of Capital for
Entrepreneurs Starting Businesses
Previously Nonexistent

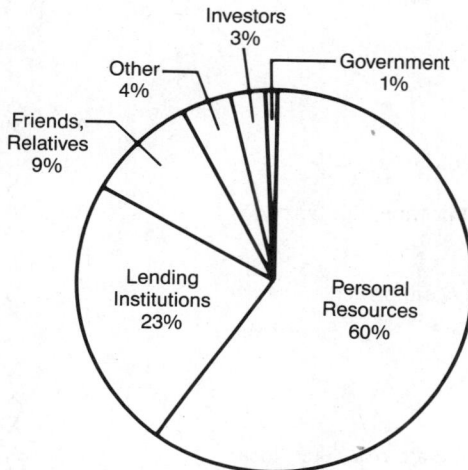

Source: National Federation of Independent Business

Smith's types are consistent with the literature.[10] In general, these typologies suggest that individuals who tend toward the craftsman orientation are motivated to do what they want to do, meet their personal and family needs, and avoid working for others. The opportunistic or managerial types are motivated by a desire to achieve economic gain and build an organization. This motivation is consistent with the goals of venture capital firms with regard to funding and represents the ability to build an organization that will return a significantly higher rate of return than a typical security investment.

[10]See J.W. Carland, Frank Hoy, W.R. Boulton, and J.C. Carland, "Differentiating Entrepreneurs from Small Business Owners: A Conceptualization," *Academy of Management Review* 9 (no. 2, 1984), 356; M.C. Casson, *The Entrepreneur* (Oxford, England: Martin Robertson, 1982); and A.C. Filley and R.J. Aldag, "Characteristics and Measurement of an Organizational Typology," *Academy of Management Journal* 21, 1978, 578–591.

Based on our knowledge of venture capital firm funding it seems clear that the business plan developed by the true entrepreneur plays a critical role not only in the success of the firm but in the acquisition of funds to start the firm. Numerous papers and books detail the structure of the plan. It should at a minimum contain: fundamental objectives, description of the company, the products, processes or services, the market, the competition, production and distribution, management, key business advisors, organizational chart, and projected financial information. Central to the plan is a section on how investors will see a return on their investment. The following is taken from a typical business plan:

> The company intends to go public in three to five years. If the company does not go public within that time, investors may realize a return on their investment from either a purchase of the company by a larger health care company, or the exchange of ownership through a pay-out schedule.[11]

The key to investment besides strong management is the construction and presentation of sound financial figures. The accounting firm of Deloitte, Haskins, and Sells has put together an outline of what the figures should look like. They are contained in three important sections: cash-flow forecast, income statement, and pro forma balance sheet (Exhibits 3, 4, and 5).

A Method for Approaching Venture Capitalists

Critical to making the venture capital deal is the method of approaching the venture capitalist. Many firms take a shotgun approach and send business plans to every venture capital firm mentioned in magazines such as *Inc.* or *Venture.* This approach usually brings multiple rejection letters, because the typical large firm might receive nearly a hundred plans a day to evaluate.

[11]Biosurge, Inc. business plan, 1987.

Table 4 Characteristcs of Entrepreneurs

Date	Author(s)	Characteristics	Normative	Empirical
1848	Mill	Risk bearing	X	
1917	Weber	Source of formal authority	X	
1934	Schumpeter	Innovation; initiative	X	
1954	Sutton	Desire for responsibility	X	
1959	Hartman	Source of formal authority	X	
1961	McClelland	Risk taking; need for achievement		X
1963	Davids	Ambition; desire for independence, responsibility; self-confidence		X
1964	Pickle	Drive/mental; human relations; communication ability; technical knowledge		X
1971	Palmer	Risk measurement		X
1971	Hornaday and Aboud	Need for achievement; autonomy; aggression; power; recognition; innovative/independent		X
1973	Winter	Need for power	X	
1974	Boiland	Internal locus of control		X
1974	Liles	Need for achievement		X
1977	Gasse	Personal value orientation		X
1978	Timmons	Drive/self-confidence; goal oriented; moderate risk taker; locus of control; creativity/innovation	X	X
1980	Sexton	Energetic/ambitious; positive setbacks		X
1981	Welsh and White	Need to control; responsibility seeker; self-confidence/drive; challenge taker; moderate risk taker		X
1982	Dunkelberg and Cooper	Growth oriented; independence oriented; craftsman oriented		X

Source: James W. Carland, Frank Hoy, William R. Boulton, and Jo Ann C. Carland, "Differentiating Entrepreneurs from Small Business Owners: A Conceptualization," *Academy of Management Review* 9 (No. 2, 1984): 356.

Venture capitalists like to have input into the firm by way of board seats. It would be quite difficult for partners of a California firm to sit on the board of a firm in Maine. Thus logistics of travel and time prompt the new firm to look for funding in its own region.

Most cities have venture capital clubs or associations. Often a contact through the entrepreneur's legal or accounting representation will result in a presentation to these groups. Many times press releases that result in newspaper articles alert venture capitalists to a firm's needs. An example is BioSurge Inc. in Rochester, New York. A short article about its product in *The Wall Street Journal* resulted in eight calls from local and regional venture capital firms.

The key, though, to contacting venture capitalists is personal contacts. Rarely do cold calls or unsolicited letters produce results.

Once the venture capitalist has become interested, the firm must prepare for initial meetings at both its own office and that of the venture firm. Usually the CEO or top financial officer meets initially with the venture capitalist. This meeting is usually a check on figures, a discussion of possible forms of financial participation, and an expressed desire to examine additional information. Often this information is referred to as due diligence. Exhibit 6 is taken from BioSurge's due diligence package. This presents further knowledge of the company and allows the venture capitalist's staff to examine specific technical

Exhibit 3   Cash Flow Forecast

The following format can be used to prepare the cash flow forecast:

BEGINNING CASH BALANCE
CASH RECEIPTS:
      Collection of Receivables
      Interest Income
         Total
CASH DISBURSEMENTS:
      Accounts Payable
      Payments of Other Expenses
      Income Tax Payments
         Total
NET CASH FROM (USED FOR) OPERATIONS
SALE OF STOCK
PURCHASE OF EQUIPMENT
DECREASE (INCREASE) IN FUNDS INVESTED
SHORT-TERM BORROWINGS (REPAYMENTS)
LONG-TERM BORROWINGS (REPAYMENTS)
ENDING CASH BALANCE

This format shows cash receipts and disbursements from operations separate from financing activities and capital acquisitions. It clearly shows the monthly changes in cash flow from operations and will indicate when operations will begin to generate a positive cash flow.

    The financing activities are segregated. In using this format, estimate a minimum cash balance to be maintained at the end of every month and project enough borrowings to give you that minimum cash balance. Any excess cash generated during a month is used to repay debt or is invested in money market funds; any shortage of cash is made up by drawdowns of funds previously invested or by additional borrowings.

Source: *Raising Venture Capital: An Entrepreneur's Guidebook*, Deloitte, Haskins, and Sells, 1985.

Exhibit 4   Income Statement

The following format can be used in preparing the income statement:

SALES
COST OF SALES:
      Material
      Labor
      Overhead
         Total
GROSS MARGIN
OPERATING EXPENSES:
      Marketing
      Research and Development
      General and Administrative
         Total
INCOME (LOSS) FROM OPERATIONS
INTEREST INCOME (EXPENSE)
INCOME (LOSS) BEFORE TAXES
TAXES ON INCOME
NET INCOME (LOSS)

To assist the potential investor in evaluating your company, include some operating statistics on the income statement. Calculate your gross margin and each major expense category as a percentage of sales. If any of these statistics are significantly different from industry averages, you should explain why.

Source: *Raising Venture Capital: An Entrepreneur's Guidebook*, Deloitte, Haskins, and Sells, 1985.

details. In the example of BioSurge, these would be its FDA documentation and the strength of its patent applications.

    Up to this point the entrepreneur has not revealed any significant technical or marketing information that would have been considered confidential. The presentation of filed patents and, in the case of BioSurge, FDA documentation are crucial business secrets that must be closely controlled. The entrepreneur must make sure that the venture capitalist does not represent a competitor or potential competitor. A signed confidentiality agreement is crucial at this stage. Exhibit 7 provides an example of such an agreement.

    What remains now are the negotiations with the venture capital firm. If this is the entrepreneur's first deal, it is important to be accompanied by legal counsel at all times. Most venture capitalists do not like to negotiate initially with attorneys, but having them present is in the best interest of the entrepreneur. However, a con-

Exhibit 5 Pro Forma Balance Sheet

The following format can be used for a pro forma balance sheet:

ASSETS:
Current assets:
      Cash
      Investments
      Accounts Receivable
      Inventory
           Total
Property, Plant, and Equipment—net
    TOTAL ASSETS
LIABILITIES AND STOCKHOLDERS' EQUITY:
Current liabilities:
      Short-Term Debt
      Accounts Payable
      Income Taxes Payable
      Accrued Liabilities
           Total
Long-Term Debt
Stockholders' equity:
      Preferred Stock
      Common Stock
      Retained Earnings (Deficit)
           Total
    TOTAL LIABILITIES AND
    STOCKHOLDERS' EQUITY

The pro forma balance sheets will help investors to evaluate your understanding of asset management.
    Investors use a variety of financial statistics to assist them in evaluating companies. You should calculate these statistics and include them in your forecast. This will make the investors' evaluations easier and show them that you considered these ratios in formulating your plan.

Source: *Raising Venture Capital: An Entrepreneur's Guidebook*, Deloitte, Haskins, and Sells, 1985.

Exhibit 6 Contents Page from a Due Diligence Package

TABLE OF CONTENTS
Introduction to Officers/Directors
Listing of Business Advisors
Organizational Structure
Corporate Resolutions/Agreements
FDA Documentation
Patent Applications

sulting firm can easily assist in lieu of an attorney in the early stages. One such firm is Alimansky Venture Group in New York. Exhibit 8 lists many of the items about which the entrepreneur needs to be knowledgeable when negotiating the deal.

    The final decision for the entrepreneur is the percentage of the company to give up. This is a function of economic position, experience, stage of business development, risk involved, and many additional factors. Two of the most common methods today are the sale of preferred stock or private placements. Exhibits 9 and 10 present some of the advantages and disadvantages of each method.

    Ultimately the entrepreneur will determine whether the firm is successful. No amount of advisors or money can make a poor idea work. Careful attention to detail and a willingness to work long hard hours and plow revenues back into the firm are musts.

Exhibit 7　Sample Confidentiality Agreement to Business Secrets

CONFIDENTIALITY AGREEMENT

This Agreement is made this _____ day of _____, 1988, by and between BioSurge, Inc., a Delaware corporation with a place of business of 919 Westfall Road, Rochester, New York, 14618 (hereinafter referred to as "BioSurge") and _____, a _____ organized and existing under the laws of _____ and having a place of business at _____ (hereinafter referred to as "Company").

WHEREAS, the parties hereto desire to discuss areas of mutual interest and benefit, including but not limited to Company investing in BioSurge; and

WHEREAS, in the course of such discussions Company desires to review and evaluate certain Confidential Information (as hereinafter defined) of BioSurge; and

WHEREAS, BioSurge is willing to disclose the Confidential Information to Company only pursuant to the terms of this Agreement;

NOW THEREFORE, in consideration of these premises and mutual covenants herein contained, the parties mutually agree as follows:

1. CONFIDENTIAL INFORMATION. The term "Confidential Information" shall include all information disclosed by BioSurge to Company, or known to Company as a consequence of the relationship between BioSurge and Company, whether in oral, written, graphic or machine-readable form including but not limited to products, plans, procedures, prototypes, clients, trade secrets, patents, copyrights, business information, financial information, ideas and data, including information relating to research, development, manufacturing, purchasing, pricing, selling and marketing. Confidential Information shall not include any information that was known to Company and documented in its files or was in the public domain, publicly known or readily available to the trade or public prior to the date of disclosure by BioSurge, and which is made known by Company to BioSurge with ten (10) days of such disclosure.

2. NON-DISCLOSURE COVENANT. Company agrees that the Confidential Information shall at all times remain property of BioSurge, and that it shall not use the Confidential Information for its own benefit or the benefit of any third party or disclose the Confidential Information to any third party without prior written consent by BioSurge.

3. PROTECTION OF CONFIDENTIAL INFORMATION. Company agrees to use all reasonable means, not less than those employed by Company to preserve and safeguard its own confidential information to maintain the Confidential Information secret and confidential. The Confidential Information shall not be disclosed or revealed to anyone except employees of Company who have a need to know the information and who have entered into a secrecy agreement with Company under which such employees are required to keep confidential the proprietary information of Company, and such employees shall be advised by Company of the confidential nature of the information and that the information shall be treated accordingly. Company shall be responsible for any use or disclosure of the Confidential Information by any of its employees or agents.

4. RETURN OF CONFIDENTIAL INFORMATION. Upon termination of discussions between the parties, or upon request of BioSurge, Company shall immediately return to BioSurge (or at BioSurge's request, destroy) all Confidential Information, including any copies thereof.

5. REPRESENTATION. Company warrants and represents that it is not currently an affiliate of or a substantial investor (with 5% or more equity or voting interest) in an entity whose products are substantially similar to or competitive with BioSurge's proposed products and will immediately inform BioSurge of any such affiliation or interest.

6. EQUITABLE RELIEF. The parties hereto agree that monetary damages shall be insufficient to fully compensate BioSurge for its losses in the event Company violates the provisions of this Agreement. In addition to seeking monetary damages, BioSurge therefore shall be entitled to enjoin Company from violating or continuing to violate the provisions of this Agreement, and Company shall not raise as a defense to any action or proceeding for any injunction the claim that BioSurge would be adequately compensated by monetary damages.

7. TERM. This agreement shall remain in full force and effect both during discussions between the parties and thereafter, whether or not Company actually invests in BioSurge.

8. MISCELLANEOUS.
   8.1 *Severability*. If any part, term or provision of this Agreement shall be held unenforceable, the validity of the remaining portions or provisions shall not be affected thereby.
   8.2 *Modification*. This Agreement shall not be modified or terminated except in writing signed by both parties.
   8.3 *Governing Law*. This Agreement shall be governed by and construed in accordance with the laws of the State of New York.

IN WITNESS WHEREOF, the parties hereto have executed this Agreement as of the day and year first above written.

BIOSURGE, INC.
By: _____
Name: _____
Title: _____
COMPANY
By: _____
Name: _____
Title: _____

Source: BioSurge Inc., Rochester, N.Y.

Exhibit 8 Venture Capital Negotiation Checklist

1. Amount of financing
2. Type of security (e.g., convertible preferred)
3. Price (possibly including performance-based securities)
4. Prefinancing valuation
5. Purchasers
6. Exchange of debt securities
7. Dividend provisions (e.g., preference)
8. Liquidation preference
9. Rights upon merger or consolidation
10. Conversion rights (if applicable)
11. Rights upon a public offering (e.g., automatic conversion, payment of accrued dividends)
12. Antidilution provisions (e.g., stock splits, stock dividends, new stock issued at a purchase price less than the conversion price for this round)
13. Option to require the company to repurchase all or part of the securities issued
14. Voting rights (e.g., on preferred stock)
15. Protective provisions (e.g., consent of 50 percent of holders of new securities required for change in rights)
16. Information rights (e.g., monthly financial statements, annual operating plan, board seat, etc.)
17. Registration rights (e.g., demand registration, "piggyback" registration, S-3 rights, registration expenses, transfer of rights, standoff provisions within 90 days, etc.)
18. Right of first refusal to purchase pro rata any new shares
19. Key man insurance
20. Market standoff agreement (e.g., for 90 days)
21. Employee matters:
    a) Vesting of stock granted to new employees
    b) Proprietary information
    c) Reserved employee shares
    d) Employment contracts
22. Amendments to rights of existing stockholders
23. Conditions to financing (e.g., legal documentation, due diligence, etc.)
24. Investment banking agreement with [our company]
25. Legal fees and expenses to investor's attorney
26. Approval of accounting firm
27. Shareholders agreement
28. Representations and warranties

Source: Alimansky Venture Group Inc., New York, NY, 1988.

Exhibit 9   Obtaining Capital through the Sale of Preferred Stock

Advantages

1. Failure to meet offering terms will not result in bankruptcy.
2. The cost of raising capital is about 30 percent less when preferred is issued instead of secondary common stock.
3. Borrowing reserve and financial insurance are preserved.
4. Preferred carries no maturity unless investors require a sinking fund to guarantee the annual buy-back of a certain number of outstanding shares.
5. If the financial condition of the company is strong, the quality of the common shares is undiminished, nor are debt ratios altered by a preferred offering.

Disadvantages

1. In order to guarantee buy-back of a certain number of shares outstanding every year, the company may have to either establish a sinking fund from available cash, or reissue new shares of preferred to finance the buy-back.
2. If the offering terms are too restrictive in order to satisfy investors, the offering may limit future unsecured borrowing or other long-term debt financing.
3. The quality of common shares may diminish during bad economic times if too much preferred is issued.
4. Management must pay ongoing costs to keep the preferred offering in registration.

Source: Jennifer Lindsay, *The Entrepreneur's Guide to Capital: The Techniques for Capitalizing and Refinancing New and Growing Businesses* (Chicago: Probus Publishing, 1986), 45.

Exhibit 10   Obtaining Capital from Private Investors

Advantages

1. Management can avoid some or all of the time-consuming SEC registration/disclosure requirements of public ownership.
2. Management can raise capital in less time and at slightly less cost by not going public.
3. Friends, employees and associates can acquire private company stock at a more beneficial price with a private offering.
4. More control is retained by company founders/owners/management by remaining private with an exempt offering.

Disadvantages:

1. Regulation D limits the number and qualification of private investors, as well as the amount raised, in some offerings.
2. Resale of private shares is restricted and lack of a public market creates other obvious resale constraints.
3. Private companies do not receive as much media and analyst attention as public entities do.
4. Share price may be lower because of limitations on the number of purchasers and on resale of shares.
5. Private companies cannot apply for NASDAQ or stock exchange listing.

Source: Jennifer Lindsay, *The Entrepreneur's Guide to Capital: The Techniques for Capitalizing and Refinancing New and Growing Businesses* (Chicago: Probus Publishing, 1986), 54–55.

Case 26

Walsh Petroleum

John Walsh sighed as he looked again at the financial statements his accountant had delivered that morning. When John's father died two years ago, his accountant had advised against selling the business. "It's a good business, John," he said, "and I think you could do a lot to improve it."

While Walsh Petroleum, Inc. had increased profits in 1985, John still considered them unacceptably low. Company sales had declined for the third straight year, and, while John realized that other oil distributors faced the same problems, he had to wonder what type of future he could expect if he stayed with the family business. Now 31 years old and just married, maybe he should consider selling the business and starting another career before he got too old.

Company History

Walsh Petroleum was founded in 1957 by John's mother and father as commission agents in the oil business. By 1976, the senior Walsh converted the company to a conventional oil distributorship. Both the family and the company

This case was prepared by George A. Overstreet, Jr., Stewart C. Malone, and Bernard A. Morin. The authors gratefully acknowledge the financial support of the General Electric Foundation and the McIntire School of Commerce at the University of Virginia in the preparation of this case. As well, the cooperation and assistance of the two closely held corporations represented herein is deeply appreciated.

were well respected in the local community, and the company grew steadily. The 1970's and early 1980's were a period of relative prosperity for Walsh Petroleum. Dollar sales in 1982 were four times higher than sales in 1977 (although most of this increase was a result of increased unit sales prices). Nonetheless, profits were at their highest level in 1982. A year later, sales gallonage started a decline that had continued unabated. In 1984, John's father died, leaving John's mother and John to manage the firm.

Company Operations

Walsh Petroleum distributed oil products throughout a seven-county area of the southeastern United States. Their marketing area was semi-rural, but contained two county seats with populations of 15,000 and 25,000. The area's proximity to a growing, major metropolitan city was expected to result in higher-than-average population growth over the next ten years, but in no way was the area likely to become a suburb of the city. The firm represented a major branded oil company and carried a full line of petroleum products. There were three basic classes of customers for Walsh:

Reseller Accounts

Walsh served as a distributor of oil products to ten reseller locations, most of which were local gas stations. Gaining new reseller customers depended more on financial considerations than marketing techniques, since gasoline and oil products were generally considered commodities, and most distributors offered similar types of services. When a new gas station was about to be constructed (an event that had been occurring with decreasing frequency over the past twenty years), the operator would contact several distributors such as Walsh. The distributor would formulate a proposal based on expected sales gallonage. In return for an exclusive, long-term contract to supply the location with gasoline and oil products, the distributor provided the station with fuel storage tanks, pumps, remote consoles and a canopy. Walsh's profit margin per gallon declined as the reseller's volume climbed based on a sliding scale. If up to 50,000 gallons a month were delivered he received 4.5¢ over delivered cost (including freight). If 50,000 to 65,000 gallons a month were delivered he received 4.0¢ per gallon. For 65–75,000 gallons he received 3.65¢, and for over 75,000 gallons he received 3.5¢ per gallon. Over the course of the contract the station operator could switch suppliers if he/she was willing to make a settlement on the equipment provided by the original distributor.

John had recently audited the profitability of his reseller accounts and found that many of the accounts yielded over a 20% after-tax IRR.[1] New reseller contracts also tended to be very lucrative, but there were relatively few high-gallonage locations left in Walsh's trading area, and only two or three new reseller accounts were out for bid each year. The capital requirements for such investments had grown over the years and ranged from $60,000 to $100,000.

In addition to the ten contract locations, Walsh operated a reseller location itself, on which it had constructed a convenience store (C-store). This diversification move was initiated by Mr. Walsh, Sr. in 1983. The C-store facility was located on 3.0 acres with 300 feet of road frontage on a 4-lane U.S. highway. The property had been appraised at $356,000 and included not only the convenience store but also the bulk storage fa-

cilities (144,000 gallons). Mrs. Walsh personally owned the site and leased it to Walsh Petroleum at $4,000 per month ($2,500 for the bulk storage plant and $1,500 for the C-store). The property had a $100,000 note payable over five years at 9%.

Home Heating Oil
Active accounts numbered 624, of which 325 were classified as automatic (with refills scheduled by the distributor). While the home heating oil business was relatively profitable, it was also highly seasonal, and, thus, efficient utilization of equipment and personnel was viewed as a problem. Some other distributors had taken on equipment sales and service, as well as related businesses such as air conditioning, in order to balance the seasonality of fuel oil sales. John had concluded that heating oil sales would have to double in order to justify the equipment investment and personnel training for an in-house sales/service department.

Commercial/Agricultural Accounts
Approximately 120 businesses and/or farms maintained their own tanks and pumps for which Walsh supplied oil products. While these accounts had generally shown some degree of loyalty to their petroleum supplier, there was no contractual relationship that would prevent them from changing suppliers.

Within Walsh Petroleum's trading area, there were currently three other gasoline and oil distributors. Competitive pressures were moderate for existing gasoline reseller and home heating oil accounts, but John had recently noticed an increased level of competition for the one or two new reseller locations that were constructed each year. None of the four distributors possessed a large competitive advantage over the others. Each competitor had about the same level of sales, and all possessed a similar amount of financial resources. Since gasoline and oil products have a significant freight cost to value ratio, distributors of these products generally had a

---

[1]See Appendix B for a discounted cash flow analysis of a recent reseller investment.

trading radius of approximately 75 miles around their terminal or distribution point. While the local competitors did not really worry John, some of the distributors that served the nearby metropolitan area were significantly larger than Walsh, and a move by one of these larger competitors into Walsh's trading area could well upset the competitive equilibrium that had evolved over the years.

Family and Management

Mrs. Walsh assumed the chairmanship of the company following the death of her husband, and she held 52% of the voting stock of the corporation (the remaining 48% being held equally by John and his 2 younger brothers). Having worked with her husband for several years, she was very knowledgeable about the firm's operations. While she held the title of chairman, Mrs. Walsh's duties consisted of supervising the convenience store adjacent to the distributorship and maintaining relationships with the fuel oil customers. A prominent citizen of the local community, Mrs. Walsh also served on the town council.

John Walsh had been employed as a geologist with an energy consulting firm in Denver prior to 1982. When he was visiting home one weekend, he mentioned to his father that he was concerned that his career would be hurt by the recent recession in the oil drilling business. Later that weekend, while having coffee together in the local donut shop, John, Sr. said, "John, our business here is changing rapidly, too. If you have any interest in joining the family business, you better make up your mind soon, because I may just sell the business rather than put up with all the changes that are occurring."

John returned to Denver, but after several months he decided that the opportunity at Walsh Petroleum might offer a better future than his current job. John returned home in late 1982 and began to learn the business from his father. Not only did John assume many of the administra-

tive duties, but he also managed the marketing relationships with the major accounts.

John's two younger brothers were not active in the management of the business at the time, although each held 16% of the corporate stock. Richard was 26 years old and was employed in another city. Daniel was a sophomore in college.

Aside from John and his mother, Walsh Petroleum employed three clerks and four driver/maintenance workers. The three clerks handled much of the administrative paperwork for both the oil distributorship and convenience store. Convenience stores have a multitude of vendors, all of whom expect payment within ten days. Managing the payables took a great deal of time, and Walsh's bookkeeping clerk had complained on more than one occasion that she couldn't keep up with the workload. All of the accounting was done manually, and John planned to install a computer system in the near future.

In addition, there were two full-time and three part-time workers at the convenience store. Salaries and benefits for these workers corresponded to industry averages, and all employees were non-unionized. During the first quarter of 1986, John purchased a new tractor/trailer for $60,000 (9,000 gallon capacity). In addition, Walsh had three older "bobtail" trucks for short deliveries (2,000 gallon capacity), and two used service delivery vans.

The Oil Distribution Industry

Few industries have experienced the volatility and changes connected with the oil business in the past 15 years. In 1973, the Arab oil embargo resulted in a 119% increase in the price of crude oil during a twelve-month period. While demand fell slightly from 1973 to 1981, prices were expected to continue climbing. Spurred by higher prices, oil exploration and refinery construction continued to increase. In 1981, President Reagan decontrolled gasoline and crude oil prices. The acquisition price of crude oil began to drop, and demand also fell as the world economy entered a recession.

Exhibit 1   Average Miles per Gallon 1974–85

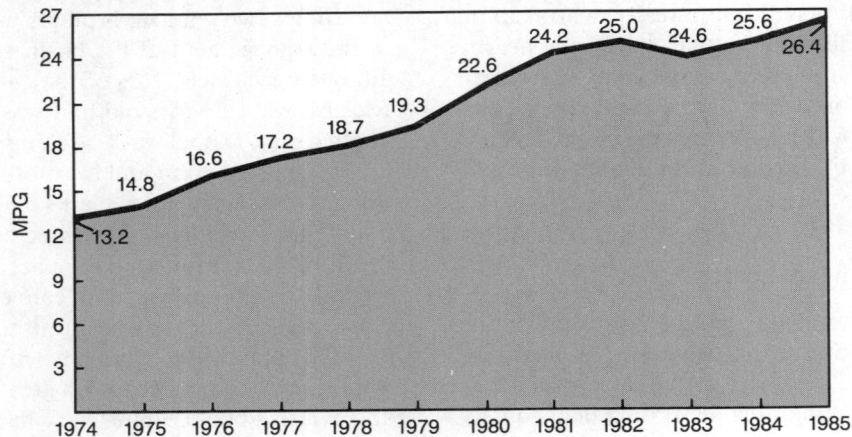

Source: *Forbes,* Citing National Highway Traffic. Safety Administration Data, October 8, 1986, p. 198.

The changes that occurred upstream in the oil production industry had a large impact on the independent petroleum market in the following way:

1. Between 1974 and 1985, American auto manufacturers doubled the miles per gallon of new cars, from 13.2 MPG to 26.4 MPG (see Exhibit 1).

2. During the same period, gasoline consumption of passenger cars declined from approximately 75 billion gallons to 65 billion gallons (see Exhibit 2).

3. The number of service stations (defined as outlets with 50% or more dollar volume from the sale of petroleum products) fell from 226,459 in 1972 to 121,000 in 1985 (see Exhibit 3).

In addition to these changes, oil distributors also faced declining margins, increased real estate costs, and a proliferation of environmental regulations.

News for distributors had not been all bad. The past two years had seen firmer gross profit margins and increased gallonage pumped. Al-

though the market had not recovered to the volume levels of the late 1970's and early 1980's, gasoline gallonage used by motorists increased 1.5% in 1983, 1.5% in 1984, and 3.4% in 1985.[2] A significant portion of the increased demand had to be attributed to the oversupply of world crude and, hence, to lower prices during each of the last three years (−3.3% for 1983, −1.6% for 1984, and −1.6% for 1985).

Independent petroleum marketers are entrepreneurs involved in the sale and distribution of refined petroleum and ancillary products. While the exact number of the companies was unknown, one trade association report estimated their number between 11,000 and 12,000 in 1985.[3] In terms of size, the trade association membership is broken down in Table 1.

Independent petroleum marketers have responded to the pressures in their industry in one

_____

[2] *1986 State of the Convenience Store Industry,* National Association of Convenience Stores, Inc., Alexandria, VA, p. 7.

[3] *1985 Petroleum Marketing Databook,* Petroleum Marketing Education Foundation, Alexandria, VA (1985), p. 12.

Exhibit 2   Gasoline Consumption, 1947–1990 (Passenger Cars)

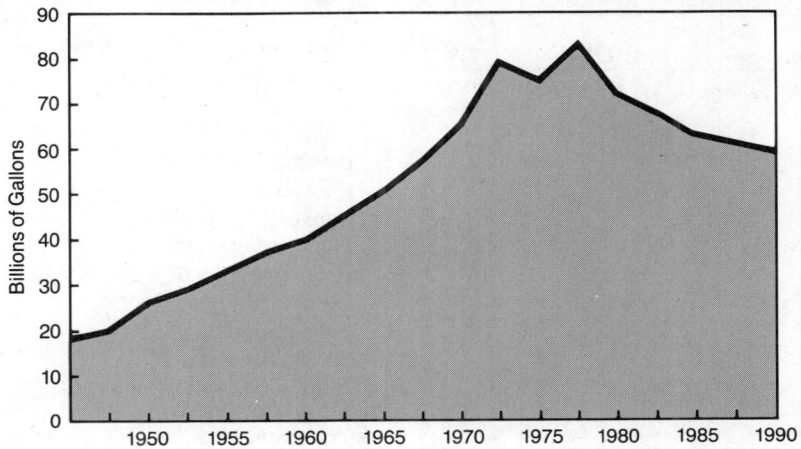

Source: American Petroleum Institute, *Basic Petroleum Data Book,* January 1983, for 1947–1981 figures; 1985 and 1990 projections based on Data Resources, Inc. (DRI), Petroleum Investor's Relations Association (PIRA), and PACE Company Consultants and Engineers (PACE) average projections.

Total U.S. gasoline demand in 1982 was 6.5 million barrels per day. DRI, PIRA, and PACE estimates for 1985 gasoline demand are 6.0, 5.9, and 5.7 million barrels per day, respectively, averaging to 5.87. Their respective 1990 estimates of 5.4, 5.2, and 5.3 million barrels per day average to 5.3. We have applied the 1978–1981 average ratio or total gasoline demand to gasoline consumption for passenger cars to these 1985 and 1990 DRI, PIRA, and PACE averages.

Exhibit 3   The U.S. Gasoline Station Population (1972–1982)

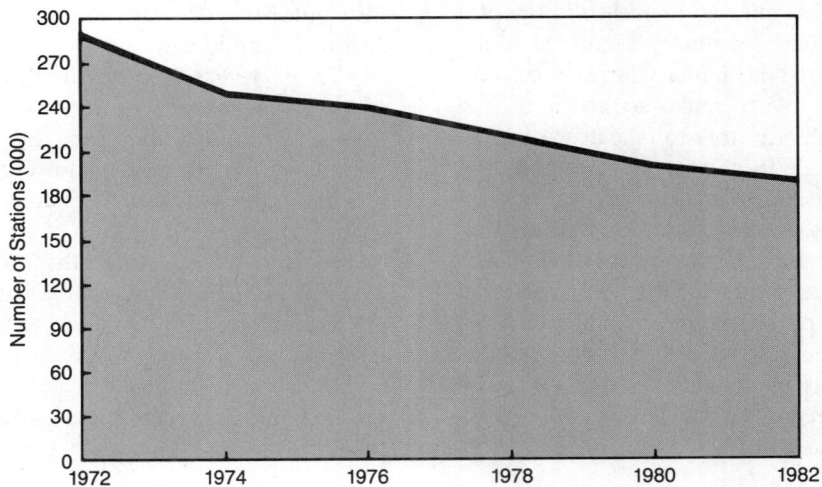

Source: *Lundberg Letter,* October 8, 1982.
Note: Unlike DOE, Lundberg includes gasoline retailers who derive less than 50% of their revenues from the sale of gasoline.

Table 1 Percentage of Marketers by Size Distribution

Millions of Gallons Sold	1984	1982
Less than 1.0 MM gallons	13.8	18.0
1.0 – 2.49	23.8	26.3
2.5 – 4.99	21.9	20.8
5.0 – 7.49	12.2	9.7
7.5 – 9.99	6.6	6.7
10.0 – 14.99	9.3	7.1
15.0 – 19.99	3.8	2.8
20.0 – 24.99	2.2	1.8
25.0 – 29.99	1.7	1.4
30.0 – 39.99	1.8	1.5
40.0 – 49.99	1.1	1.2
50.0 and above	1.8	2.7
Average Volume	7.80	7.12
Median Volume	3.91	3.18

Source: *1985 Petroleum Marketing Databook* Petroleum Marketing Education Foundation, Alexandria, VA (1985), p. 12

Table 2 1984 Diversified Operations

Operations	Number of Operations
Auto Repair/Maintenance Center	7,081
Auto/Truck/Trailer Rentals	638
Beverage only stores	228
Car washes	2,961
Convenience stores	14,235
Fast food operations	1,002
Heating/Air conditioning service	3,189
Kerosene heater sales	1,275
Lube centers	1,549
Plumbing service	501
Tires/Tires, Battery and Accessory stores	3,507
Truck stops	1,734
Towing service	911
Coal sales	164
Other	1,000

Source: *1985 Petroleum Marketing Databook*, Petroleum Marketing Education Foundation, Alexandria, VA (1985), p. 15.

of two ways: diversification or consolidation (mergers and acquisition). Table 2 shows the number of diversified operations for companies belonging to the major trade association.

Aside from diversifying into other areas, the number of acquisitions had increased in the past few years, spurred by industry decontrol. Independent marketers, particularly larger ones with the capital available to make acquisitions, had acquired other distributors to take advantage of economies of scale in storage, distribution, and other areas such as billing and general administrative services. A 1984 study found that 56 of 135 marketers had purchased one or more marketing companies within the last five years, and 24 of the 56 had purchased more than one.[4] Most of the acquisition activity occurred among marketers with assets greater than $1MM. Of the 90 firms in this category in the sample, 46 had acquired one or more businesses during the period.

As a result of increasing profit pressure, a number of operating changes had occurred on the distribution level.[5] First, the total number of distributor-owned transportation vehicles had declined dramatically from 106,868 in 1982 to 96,972 in 1984. Second, distributors had decreased the amount of their storage facilities from a 2.3 billion-gallon capacity in 1982 to 1.7 billion in 1984. Finally, credit terms to distributors had tightened. In 1982, net 30 day payment terms were reported by 21% of trade association members, while in 1984 this percentage had dropped to 8.2%. These changes and others had led gasoline and oil distributors to redefine the term "good customer." Whereas in the 1960's and 1970's, distributors were willing to inventory product and deliver relatively small amounts of gasoline on small "bobtail" trucks, the new mar-

[4] *1984 Petroleum Marketing Databook,* Petroleum Marketing Education Foundation, Alexandria, VA (1984), p. 19.

[5] *1985 Petroleum Marketing Databook,* Petroleum Marketing Education Foundation, Alexandria, VA (1985), pp. 15–16.

ket realities made these practices less attractive. Instead of inventorying product, successful distributors would now send a large transport truck (9,000-gallon capacity) to the terminal, or distribution point, and transport the gasoline directly to one service station. Since it was inefficient to have the large truck tied up making multiple deliveries, the customer emphasis was on the volume gas station with tank capacity large enough to handle one large delivery. The "mom-and-pop" gasoline retailer was now considered undesirable. John Walsh stated, "In 1980 we considered a good account one that pumped 20,000–25,000 gallons per month, while in 1986 we consider a good account to be in the range of 40,000–50,000 gallons per month."

In addition to the deregulation of gasoline and crude oil prices in 1981, another regulatory development that affected oil distributors was the issuance of EPA regulations regarding leakage of gasoline from underground steel storage tanks. According to one authority, as many as 30% of steel tanks currently in the ground might be leaking.[6] Since both past and present owners of property with underground tanks could be held legally liable for leakage pollution, many companies were completely removing older tanks (more than 10–15 years old) at a cost of approximately $1,000 for a 1,000–3,000 gallon tank. The cost of removing and then reinstalling a similar size tank cost approximately $6,000. If there was a minor leak, clean-up costs would be approximately $5,000 extra. Liability insurance for tank leakage had become exceedingly expensive and difficult to obtain, especially for older, single-wall steel tanks.

The Current Situation

From his study of trade journals and attendance at industry conferences, John Walsh had concluded that basic industry trends portended a bleak future for Walsh Petroleum unless some

---

[6]Plenn, Steffen W., *Underground Tankage: The Liability of Leaks,* Petroleum Marketing Education Foundation, Alexandria, VA (1986), pp. 9–12.

substantial changes were made in the company's strategy. It seemed apparent to John that his company had to do something different or get out of the business. Being relatively young, John was confident that he could start a career elsewhere, but he enjoyed living in his hometown of Lancaster and liked the idea of being his own boss. Furthermore, his mother was currently receiving an annual salary of $50,000 in addition to rent she received on the C-store. If they sold the company, would the proceeds generate sufficient income to replace his mother's current income?

If they decided not to sell the business, John wondered how the business could be changed? He had received an offer to purchase a competitor, Valley Oil, only weeks before.

The Valley Oil Alternative

In many respects, it seemed as though Valley Oil faced the same problems as Walsh. The two companies sold basically the same product lines, although Valley's percentage of heating fuel sales was higher than Walsh's. This aspect of Valley was attractive to John, since heating fuel commanded higher margins than gasoline (25¢ per gallon versus 8 to 10¢ per gallon), and customers were a little less sensitive to price than gasoline resellers. Overall, though, Valley's unit sales were declining and unit profit margins were being squeezed. Many of Valley's contract resellers were low volume accounts and had experienced declining sales volumes. Furthermore, their underground tanks were old.

The owner of Valley had died recently, and Valley's current 55-year old CEO wanted to get out of the business. Valley's CEO had sent along a copy of the company's recent financial statements which John had given to a consultant to value Valley Oil for him (see Appendix C). Valley's CEO said that, while the company wasn't for sale on the open market yet, he felt that an $800,000 offer would buy the company. John's consultant didn't think Valley was worth that much, but John was skeptical of the consultant's conclusions because the consultant did not have experience in the petroleum business.

John thought that acquiring Valley Oil could offer some unique advantages—advantages that many other potential acquirers could not realize. First, many of the selling and administrative expenses that Valley incurred could be performed by Walsh's personnel. A potential buyer from outside the industry would probably have substantially higher operating costs than John would have.

Rather than beginning his analysis with what employees he would be able to eliminate from Valley's payroll, John decided to examine how many people he would have to add to Walsh Petroleum to serve Valley's customers. He figured that initially he would need at least two additional clerks to handle the scheduling and the billing for Valley accounts. Two additional full-time drivers would be needed for deliveries and two seasonal drivers for fuel oil. Salaries for clerks and drivers were estimated at $9,000 and $18,000 a year, respectively, and fringe benefits would probably add about 35%. John thought he could get someone to manage the new business at $30,000 (benefits included). John also felt that if he could get his computerized accounting system up and running within a year for approximately $40,000 he might be able eventually to eliminate one of the clerks. John was also pleased with the thought that the acquisition of Valley would allow him to spread the significant upfront investment in hardware and software over a greater number of accounts, and by adding a delivery scheduling module to the computer system he should be able to schedule his deliveries more efficiently. In addition, John's accountant recommended that he use a conservative tax rate of 30% in his analysis of Valley.

Even with the operating savings John might be able to utilize, Valley would probably be an attractive acquisition to some of the large distributors in the nearby city. Compared to the fierce competition in that city, John's trading area would probably look very attractive to them. While John's knowledge of the local market gave him an advantage, the larger, city-based distributors could achieve many of the operating cost savings that John was contemplating. By purchasing Valley, John felt his gross profit margin would improve due to a reduced level of competition.

The more John thought about the possibility of combining Walsh and Valley, the more likely it seemed that he wouldn't need most of Valley's physical assets to service the accounts he would be acquiring. John had scheduled a lunch with Valley's CEO to discuss the possibility of the acquisition. John's hopes of only acquiring Valley's customers were quickly dashed. Valley's CEO stated that if he was getting out of the business, he was going to sell the whole business as a unit, not hold a "rummage sale". Moreover, he seemed firm about the price of $800,000. The rise in Valley's gross profit margin in 1985 had continued through the first half of 1986 because of the unprecedented drop in oil prices and "sticky" retail prices. However, John knew that Valley's CEO would want to sell the business this year before long-term capital gains rates expired.

A big issue in John's mind was how to finance the acquisition. Neither he nor his mother had enough liquid funds outside the business to acquire Valley. Valley's owners indicated that they might be willing to hold a note, but they would require certain covenants regarding Walsh Petroleum's financial condition in order to protect their position. Also, personal guarantees from John, his mother, and his brother would be required. John decided to try to get Valley's owners to finance 75% of the acquisition price over 10 years. While he would have to pay a premium over the prime rate, in his opinion it might still be a good investment.

The C-Store Alternative

One of the relative bright spots in Walsh Petroleum's operation had been the C-store. C-stores originated as a convenient alternative to the traditional grocery store, and the premise that consumers would pay higher than grocery store prices in exchange for convenience proved correct. Since customers typically bought only a few items, checkout lines were very short. C-stores carried a relatively limited product line of items generally regarded as necessities. Milk, bread, and beer and wine made up a substantial percentage of C-store sales. Although a majority of the products sold in C-stores carried a very similar product mix, opportunities did exist for C-Store operators to differentiate themselves. A number of operators offered video rentals, hot food service (hot dogs, pizza, etc.), and other amenities. Geographic location was also a critical success factor. Customers selected a C-store based on its proximity to their home or their daily route of travel.

Many motor fuel operators had taken the traditional gas station, closed the maintenance bays, and remodeled them into small convenience stores (800–1200 sq. ft.) with gasoline pumps out front. Likewise, convenience store operators, such as Southland (7-Eleven), added self-service gas pumps. According to the National Association of Convenience Stores, gasoline margins averaged 7.3%, while non-gasoline margins averaged 32.2%.[7]

In early 1982, the Walshes had commissioned a marketing consulting group to conduct a feasibility study of a C-store location adjacent to the fuel oil distributorship. The location had approximately 300 feet of frontage on a major highway, and the traffic count looked as though it would make the operation feasible. Mr. Walsh, Sr. had remodeled an existing 2-bay station, and within two years the unit was meeting and then exceeding the marketing consultants' projections.

Walsh Petroleum currently owned an unoccupied two-bay service station on a corner lot with good access from all directions and a stable

traffic flow in a growing, nearby community. In the past the Walshes had leased the property to a number of service station operators. None of them had been able to make a success of the operation, and it was John's opinion that the day of the "traditional" two bay station was past its prime. Customers wanted either the pricing and convenience of a self-service station or a super-premium station that provided clearly superior maintenance and service. The turnover of operators was consuming much of Walsh's time, and the station would often sit empty.

John had felt that it might be possible to demolish the station and erect a C-store with self-serve gasoline pumps on the site. To investigate this possibility, John commissioned the same market research firm that had provided the feasibility study for the original C-store to analyze the new location. This firm had developed a forecasting model that would generate fairly accurate sales estimates for both gasoline and in-store sales for a C-store. Among the many variables included in the model was highway traffic flow, store size and layout, distance to the nearest existing C-store, as well as a variety of demographic data on the area. John's corner lot had a traffic count of 14,000 vehicles per day on the main road and 4,000 vehicles a day on the side street. The resulting sales forecast for gasoline was 915,000 gallons with a 24 month maturity and 410,000 gallons in year 1. Kerosene sales were forecast at 7,500 gallons in year 1 and 10,000 gallons per annum thereafter. Inside sales items totalled $213,000 (year 1), $428,000 (year 2), maturing at $530,000 in year 3. Expected margins were 50¢ a gallon for kerosene, 8¢ a gallon for gasoline, and 32% for inside sales.

At the same time, an architectural firm had been retained as a design consultant. Table 3 shows the costs that had been estimated under John's close supervision. Another option John had was to build a C-Store using his major oil supplier's generic C-store design plan. The generic design included a smaller C-store (40 × 50 feet) under a 90 × 40 feet canopy with pumps

[7]"Why the C-store Image Race Could Lead to a Shakeout," *National Petroleum News,* Sept. 1987, p. 40.

Table 3 C-store Estimated Costs

Appraised value of lot	$100,000
Building ($\approx$ $60 for 2400 sq. feet of C-store)	144,400
Market Research	1,000
Equipment Costs:	
Gas equipment	150,000
Food equipment	60,000
Canopy	17,500
Capitalized Site Plan (consultant)	20,000
Inventory:	
Food	40,000
Fuel	14,500
Net Operating Capital	20,000
TOTAL	$567,400
Salvage Value:	
Gas equipment	$13,500
Food equipment	6,000
Canopy	1,750
Capitalized site plan	0
Asset lives:	
Gas equipment	5 years
Food equipment	7 "
Canopy	10 "
Site plan & building	31.5 "
Depreciation Method:	
Gas, Food & Canopy Equip.—Dou. Decl. Bal.	
Site plan & building—Straight Line	

on either side of the store (35 feet from pump to entrance). The advantage to this design was that the major oil company would refund Walsh 2¢ per gallon on all gallons sold (up to 150,000 gallons per month) for 36 months and provide a detailed site plan without charge. John felt he would lose some inside sales with their fatter margins and he wouldn't get to build his own C-store identity and goodwill. The overall cost would be approximately the same for the two options, and John was uncertain which choice was best from a marketing point of view.

Based on those of his other store, John estimated the operating expenses per annum for the new store as follows: salaries and benefits for a 126-hour week at $80,000, utilities at $14,000, property taxes at $2,000 and other miscellaneous expenses at $20,000.

While the research pertaining to the original C-store had been highly accurate, John wondered how reliable the model could be in forecasting future sales for the proposed C-store. Since even the major highways were relatively undeveloped in his rural market, there were certainly some desirable road frontage locations near his site. As a matter of fact, there was a one-acre site directly across the street that could be used for a C-store location. While he had considered buying the property as a defensive move, he felt he really couldn't afford to buy it at $150,000.

John felt that the threat of new C-store competitors was very real. Even though a half-million dollar investment for a C-store was a substantial investment to John, this sum might look like a real bargain to the major C-store chains that had been paying up to a million dollars for prime suburban locations. Surely, John reasoned, a competing C-store within a mile or two of his location would adversely affect the validity of his financial projections. The design consultant had added a drive-in window at a cost of approximately $25,000 to differentiate the store and build customer loyalty. John felt a drive-in window would add 15% annually to projected inside sales.

At a recent petroleum distributors conference, John discussed his C-store plans with several fellow distributors. Most felt that the generic C-store designs offered by the major oil companies were too small to provide the maximum level of in-store sales, particularly in a rural market. They questioned the wisdom of the drive-in window, suggesting a car-wash operation instead.

While John felt the C-store alternative had potential, he also was aware that the move had its risks. Nationally, the number of C-stores had increased rapidly. At the end of 1981, there were 38,000 C-stores, and only 16,416 of these sold gasoline. Just four years later, the C-store population had reached 61,000, with 33,500 selling gasoline.[8]

There was general agreement in the industry that the danger of C-store saturation was greatest in suburban areas, but that substantial opportunities remained in both urban and rural markets. One rural operator, who competed successfully in towns with as few as 1,000 residents, said, "For the rest of the industry, the mark-up on gas is six to eight cents a gallon, while we get eight to ten cents. Often we are the only gas station in town."[9] While gas margins would be higher in rural areas, C-stores often increased margins on other products as well. Fast foods and video rentals were extremely profitable in the absence of strong competitors. Pizza, for example, carried a 70% profit margin. One C-store/pizza vendor said that the pizza concept probably wouldn't work in cities where people could go to a Pizza Hut, "but out in the rural areas, there's no place else to get a good pizza."[10]

Until recently, most of the competitors in the C-store industry were convenience store chains, such as Southland, and locations operated by independent oil distributors. There were increasing indications that the big oil refiners were entering the industry in force. Eight refiner/supplier oil companies, such as Texaco, Mobil, and Exxon, were ranked in the top 50 C-store operators. Many industry observers expected that the entry of the big-oil-owned C-stores would touch off a price war in the industry, particularly in the in-store segment. The rationale behind this expectation was that oil companies would lower in-store merchandise mark-ups in order to increase pump gallonage. However, the major oil companies had tended to concentrate on the urban areas, leaving the rural markets to the distributors.

[8]*Id.*, p. 41.
[9]"Rural vs. Urban: A Site Selection Dilemma," *Convenience Store News,* BAT Publications, New York, NY, July 13-August 2, 1987, p. 54.
[10]*Id.*, p. 54.

The Future of Walsh Oil

During one of the recent executive education programs John had attended, a few sessions had been devoted to evaluating investment opportunities. He knew that he should try to determine an appropriate hurdle rate to use. There were some discussions at these sessions about calculating a cost of capital, but that seemed too academic and complicated. Instead, he went to the library and looked up various interest rates and decided to add a couple of percentage points to them. He figured that a small company like his would have to pay somewhere between 2 and 5 percent over the going rate. The interest rates as of August 1986 are listed in Table 4.

As he reviewed his notes from the training sessions, John found that real estate investments were evaluated differently than other types of investments. Rather than using the total acquisition price as a measure of cash outflow, real estate investments were analyzed on the basis of equity cash outflow to determine the payback. One of John's friends in the real estate business told him that, rather than using the purchase price of the acquisition as a measure of its cost, he should use the down payment, or the immediate cash outflow, as the cost measure and calculate a levered rate of return on investment.

John scheduled an initial meeting with his banker to see what type of financing he might be able to obtain. While the banker expressed interest in the C-store, he didn't feel that the bank would be willing to lend funds for the acquisition of Valley Oil. "John, it's just too risky for us," he said. "Valley's assets just aren't liquid enough

Table 4 Selected Interest Rates–
August 1986

Prime rate charged by banks	7.75%
U.S. Treasury bonds–ten years	7.17%
Corporate bonds–Aaa seasoned	8.72%
Home mortgages–FHLBB	10.26%

to qualify as high quality collateral. With those old tanks and trucks, we would never get our money out. Now the C-store is something I could sell to the loan committee. It's my guess that we could finance 80% of the land and building at 11.5% for 15 years.[11] In addition, we could finance 80% of the equipment including the site plan over 7 years at a 9.75% fixed rate."

The banker paused, as if unsure how to proceed. "You know, John, what I'm about to bring up is somewhat sensitive," he said, "so just tell me to stop if I'm out of line. I've watched you work like a dog over the past year to turn your business around, but at some point you have to start thinking about yourself. You can work like hell for thirty years and still only be a minority stockholder. If your mother and two brothers wanted to sell out at some point in the future, all your efforts, not to mention your career, are down the drain."

"Here's an alternative you might just think about," said the banker. "Walsh Petroleum owns the C-store site you are talking about developing. Why don't you buy the land personally and construct the C-store on it? We here at the bank would lend you the money, although we would probably have to have Walsh Petroleum guarantee the loan. You could then lease the C-store back to Walsh Petroleum, and start building up some personal equity for yourself through the real estate investment."

As John Walsh pondered his alternatives, one thing seemed certain to him—he would have to take action very soon. Many of his friends he met at the trade association meetings seemed to be complacent about the pressures on their industry at this time, but as John glanced at the financial statements again, he knew that a few more years like these past two would threaten not only his family's financial security, but his own as well. After all, he was really the only member of the family whose income was directly

related to the future of Walsh Petroleum. He remembered the discussion of these issues at a recent dinner with his mother and brothers.

"John, I agree with the idea of expanding the business, and I think it would have pleased your dad," said Mrs. Walsh, "but you have to remember that Walsh Petroleum is really all I have. If we take on too much debt, and get into trouble, I don't know what I'll do in my old age."

"I see your point, Mom," said John, "but the fact is that I'm the only one in the family who is devoting the rest of my life to running the business. You already own C-store #1, and Richard and Daniel either don't want to be in the business or aren't sure yet. I don't want to sound selfish, but my interest in the business is only 16%. I don't want to wake up when I'm fifty and find that I've spent my whole life running this business for the rest of the family and have relatively little to show for it."

Richard puffed on his pipe and said, "John, I'm not sure the C-store alternative is a good idea for the family business. Sure, it's a good deal for you personally, but the rest of us have to guarantee your loan at the bank. I think Walsh Petroleum should give serious consideration to the Valley Oil deal."

"And why do you think that Valley is better than the C-store?" asked John.

"The main reason," Richard replied, "is that Walsh Petroleum is primarily a gasoline distributor. The original C-store was a great idea of Dad's, but the oil business is this family's cash cow. This is an opportunity to take out a competitor. We all agree there aren't a whole lot of new people going into this business, but if a big gasoline distributor in the region buys Valley, then Walsh Petroleum has got some major problems on its hands. The increased competition could certainly lower our gross margin one-to-two cents a gallon, and we all know that there are two large distributors that are interested in Valley."

"But, Richard, can't you see that we're in a declining industry?" said John. "If you looked

---

[11]It should be noted that the bank is refinancing land that Walsh currently owns.

at those financials I sent you, it should be obvious that our gallonage has been declining for several years."

"What do you think, Daniel?" asked Mrs. Walsh. "After all, it's as much your business as it is John's or Richard's."

"I think that John and Richard both have good points," said Daniel." "While John is the only one of us three in the business now, I may want to join the company when I finish school, and I really don't care to be a clerk in a convenience store. And while John certainly has a right to try to accumulate some wealth, I don't know that using the family business's credit rating to guarantee his personal investments is really fair to the rest of us. After all, John is at least getting a decent salary, and Richard and I don't even receive any dividends."

"Wait a second, Dan," said John, somewhat resentfully. "I'm not riding a gravy train here. My thirty thousand dollar salary at Walsh is no higher than what my market worth is, and especially the way things are going, my upside po-

tential is much lower than I could get working for someone else. Even more importantly, the family couldn't find anyone else to do this job for any less than what I'm getting."

The family discussion had ended without resolving anything, but John was certain the business would be worth substantially less if he was unable to turn the operation around. Aside from the purely financial considerations, John knew that the major oil companies were now evaluating their distributors on sales levels and sales growth. A distributor in an attractive market who wasn't showing the appropriate level of sales or sales growth might soon find itself without a supply contract.

Further, while John was anxious to stop the decline in the company's financial performance, he also felt strongly that the business's plan he developed now should lay the foundation for the business growth for the next five-to-ten years. The questions in his mind were, "How do we do it, and is it worth the trouble?"

Appendix A

Walsh Petroleum Statement of Income for the Years Ended 1981–1985

	Year 1981	Year 1982	Year 1983	Year 1984	Year 1985	
Gallons:						
Premium	386,144	687,087	584,076	617,420	593,777	
Unleaded	1,193,536	1,236,757	830,002	898,065	841,184	
Regular	1,930,719	2,656,736	1,660,004	1,290,969	1,039,110	
Lube	24,847	17,793	18,184	16,660	15,725	
Heating Oil	491,583	409,267	327,845	373,609	335,054	
Diesel	375,478	373,704	338,249	348,420	327,098	
Kerosene	79,769	96,215	99,733	138,555	125,182	
Other Products	1,810	414	713	5,301	10,682	
Total	4,483,886	5,477,973	3,858,806	3,688,999	3,287,812	
Sales:						
Premium	322,225	533,091	551,540	517,510	533,998	
Unleaded	1,195,855	1,493,304	1,020,024	1,019,856	881,903	
Regular	2,385,763	2,967,718	1,633,912	1,187,458	854,324	
Lube	84,438	64,681	66,005	60,491	58,988	
Heating Oil	533,368	478,842	368,498	411,344	364,539	
Diesel	397,663	410,090	332,637	345,317	310,858	
Kerosene (Gasahol in '80)	92,252	119,845	117,952	162,359	147,066	
Other Products	53,960	10,757	48,261	140,259	177,768	
Net Sales	5,065,524	6,078,328	4,138,829	3,844,594	3,329,444	
Cost of Sales:						
Beginning Inventory	77,420	84,927	84,804	136,862	131,592	
Purchases Net of Discounts	4,725,693	5,691,682	3,885,577	3,528,264	2,942,582	
Ending Inventory	4,803,113	5,776,609	3,970,381	3,665,126	3,074,174	
	84,927	84,804	136,862	131,592	149,007	
Cost of Sales	4,718,186	5,691,805	3,833,519	3,533,534	2,925,167	
Gross Profit	347,338	386,523	305,310	311,060	404,277	
Selling, General and Admin. Expenses						
Licenses and Non-Income Taxes	22,447	22,462	18,472	22,604	8,917	
Vehicle Expense	23,362	41,510	36,837	43,950	32,583	
Officers' Salaries	68,248	63,370	53,970	52,952	50,780	
Other Salaries and Wages	78,763	92,138	121,160	135,692	140,623	
Other Expense	132,880	135,589	136,903	127,892	150,957	
Depreciation	46,524	68,676	72,842	73,404	69,441	
Interest on Borrowing Needs	6,457	7,410	11,232	11,999	9,299	
Operating Income (Loss)	(31,343)	(44,632)	(146,106)	(157,433)	(58,323)	
Earnings on Marketable Securities	4,456	2,853	3,009	2,943	3,739	
Other Income (Expense)	83,587	112,425	103,109	144,878	85,038	← Hauling income
Earnings before Taxes	56,700	70,646	(39,988)	(9,612)	30,454	
Provision for Federal Income Taxes	6,590	11,870	(15,294)	(2,229)	2,485	
Net Income	50,110	58,776	(24,694)	(7,383)	27,969	

Note: Inventory is recorded on a lifo basis.

Walsh Petroleum Balance Sheet for the Years Ended 1981–1985

	Year 1981	Year 1982	Year 1983	Year 1984	Year 1985	
Assets						
Current Assets						
Cash	36,305	7,704	38,510	55,652	14,003	
Marketable Securities	0	0	0	0	0	
Accounts Rec.	262,047	254,809	190,673	143,802	155,839	
Inventories	84,927	84,804	136,862	131,592	149,007	
Refundable Taxes	3,964	0	27,194	2,665	200	
Prepaid Exp.	5,756	7,121	13,698	8,625	9,609	
Notes Receivable	0	0	0	0	9,368	
Other Current Assets	0	0	0	0	116,607	← Key man life insurance pay off (cash)
Total Current Assets	392,999	354,438	406,937	342,336	454,633	
Property Plant and Equipment						
Land	25,201	28,134	25,489	34,893	30,544	← Market value $100,000
Buildings	0	0	0	0	0	
Equipment	154,029	140,493	163,011	130,797	144,965	← Market value $100,000
Vehicles	51,930	60,678	42,367	37,032	24,604	← Market value $18,000
Furniture and Fixtures	5,544	3,730	3,449	4,102	3,425	
Total	236,704	233,035	234,316	206,824	203,538	
Less Accumulated Depreciation	0	0	0	0	0	
Net Property Plant and Equipment	236,704	233,035	234,316	206,824	203,538	
Other Assets						
Long-Term Investments	677	1,202	1,202	1,202	1,202	
Deposits and Licenses	0	0	0	0	0	
Cash Surrender Value—Officers Life	30,970	35,117	690	3,116	0	
Loan Fees—Net	370	277	195	0	0	
Advances to Affiliated Companies	0	0	0	0	0	
Total Other Assets	32,017	36,596	2,087	4,318	1,202	
Total Assets	661,720	624,069	643,340	553,478	659,373	
Liabilities						
Current Liabilities						
Accounts Payable	264,812	155,012	157,254	80,624	98,505	
Notes Payable	0	0	50,000	30,000	0	
Current Portion of Long-Term Debt	18,163	18,315	18,204	17,900	50,675	
Construction Loan Payable	0	0	0	0	0	
Income Taxes Payable	334	4,506	0	235	2,485	
Advances from Officers	0	0	0	0	0	
Accrued Expenses	42,834	45,944	55,125	44,424	40,724	
Other Current Liabilities	0	0	522	846	0	
Total Current Liability	326,143	223,777	281,105	174,029	192,389	
Long-Term Debt	19,849	10,305	0	0	0	
Other Long-Term	14,572	30,054	26,992	51,592	0	← Equipment demand note payable net of current maturities at Prime +1
Total Liabilities	360,564	264,136	308,097	225,621	192,389	
Owners Equity	301,157	359,933	335,240	327,856	466,984	
Total Liabilities and Owners Equity	661,721	624,069	643,337	553,477	659,373	

Note: Walsh has limited underground tank liability due to placing tanks in resellers name, and having installed double-walled tanks @ the bulk plant over the past 5 years.

Walsh Petroleum Ratio Analysis for the Years Ended 1981–1985

Ratio Analysis	Year 1981	Year 1982	Year 1983	Year 1984	Year 1985
Dupont Analysis:					
Return on Sales	0.99%	0.97%	−0.60%	−0.19%	0.84%
· Asset Turnover	7.66	9.74	6.43	6.95	5.05
= Return on Assets	7.57%	9.42%	−3.84%	−1.33%	4.24%
· Financial Leverage	2.20	1.73	1.92	1.69	1.41
= Return on Equity	16.64%	16.33%	−7.37%	−2.25%	5.99%
Gallonage DuPont:					
Return on Sales	1.12	1.07	−0.64	−0.20	0.85
· Asset Turnover	6.78	8.78	6.00	6.67	4.99
= Return on Assets	7.57%	9.42%	−3.84%	−1.33%	4.24%
· Financial Leverage	2.20	1.73	1.92	1.69	1.41
= Return on Equity	16.64%	16.33%	−7.37%	−2.25%	5.99%
Activity:					
Fixed Asset Turnover	21.40	26.08	17.66	18.59	16.36
Sales Growth (Dollars)	13.48%	19.99%	−31.91%	−7.11%	−13.40%
Sales Growth (Gallons)		22.17%	−29.56%	−4.40%	−10.88%
Profitability:					
Gross Margin	6.86%	6.36%	7.38%	8.09%	12.14%
Salaries Ratio (Offic. Salar. ÷ Sales)	1.35%	1.04%	1.30%	1.38%	1.53%
S,G, & A Ratio (S,G & A ÷ Sales)	6.43%	5.84%	8.88%	9.96%	11.53%
Working Capital Usage:					
Days Payable	19.08	9.31	13.87	7.65	10.80
Collection Period (Days)	18.88	15.30	16.82	13.65	17.08
Days Inventory	6.12	5.09	12.07	12.49	16.34
Cash Cycle ((Collect. + Inv.) − Days Pay)	5.92	11.09	15.02	18.49	22.62
Leverage:					
Total Debt/Assets	54.49%	42.32%	47.89%	40.76%	29.18%
Long-Term Debt/Assets	0.03	0.02	0.00	0.00	0.00
Liquidity:					
Current Ratio	1.20	1.58	1.45	1.97	2.36
Acid Test Ratio	0.94	1.20	0.96	1.21	1.59

Walsh Petroleum Common Size Statement of Income for the Years Ended 1981–1985

	Year 1981	Year 1982	Year 1983	Year 1984	Year 1985
Sales:					
Premium	6.36%	8.77%	13.33%	13.46%	16.04%
Unleaded	23.61%	24.57%	24.65%	26.53%	26.49%
Regular	47.10%	48.82%	39.48%	30.89%	25.66%
Lube	1.67%	1.06%	1.59%	1.57%	1.77%
Heating Oil	10.53%	7.88%	8.90%	10.70%	10.95%
Diesel	7.85%	6.75%	8.04%	8.98%	9.34%
Kerosene	1.82%	1.97%	2.85%	4.22%	4.42%
Other Products	1.07%	0.18%	1.17%	3.65%	5.34%
Net Sales	100.00%	100.00%	100.00%	100.00%	100.00%
Cost of Sales:					
Beginning Inventory	0.00%	0.00%	0.00%	0.00%	0.00%
Purchases Net of Discounts	1.53%	1.40%	2.05%	3.56%	3.95%
	93.29%	93.64%	93.88%	91.77%	88.38%
Ending Inventory	94.82%	95.04%	95.93%	95.33%	92.33%
	1.68%	1.40%	3.31%	3.42%	4.48%
Cost of Sales	93.14%	93.64%	92.62%	91.91%	87.86%
Gross Profit	6.86%	6.36%	7.38%	8.09%	12.14%
Selling, General and Admin. Expenses					
Licenses and Non-Income Taxes	0.44%	0.37%	0.45%	0.59%	0.27%
Vehicle Expense	0.46%	0.68%	0.89%	1.14%	0.98%
Officers' Salaries	1.35%	1.04%	1.30%	1.38%	1.53%
Other Salaries and Wages	1.55%	1.52%	2.93%	3.53%	4.22%
Other Expense	2.62%	2.23%	3.31%	3.33%	4.53%
Depreciation	0.92%	1.13%	1.76%	1.91%	2.09%
Interest on Borrowing Needs	0.13%	0.12%	0.27%	0.31%	0.28%
Operating Income (Loss)	−0.62%	−0.73%	−3.53%	−4.09%	−1.75%
Earnings on Marketable Securities	0.09%	0.05%	0.07%	0.08%	0.11%
Other Income (Expense)	1.65%	1.85%	2.49%	3.77%	2.55%
Earnings before Taxes	1.12%	1.16%	−0.97%	−0.25%	0.91%
Provision for Federal Income Taxes	0.13%	0.20%	−0.37%	−0.06%	0.07%
Net Income	0.99%	0.97%	−0.60%	−0.19%	0.84%

Walsh Petroleum Common Size (% of Assets) Balance Sheet for the Years Ended 1981–1985

	Year 1981	Year 1982	Year 1983	Year 1984	Year 1985
Assets					
Current Assets					
Cash	5.49%	1.23%	5.99%	10.05%	2.12%
Marketable Securities	0.00%	0.00%	0.00%	0.00%	0.00%
Accounts Rec.	39.60%	40.83%	29.64%	25.98%	23.63%
Inventories	12.83%	13.59%	21.27%	23.78%	22.60%
Refundable Taxes	0.60%	0.00%	4.23%	0.48%	0.03%
Prepaid Exp.	0.87%	1.14%	2.13%	1.56%	1.46%
Notes Receivable	0.00%	0.00%	0.00%	0.00%	1.42%
Other Current Assets	0.00%	0.00%	0.00%	0.00%	17.68%
Total Current Assets	59.39%	56.79%	63.25%	61.85%	68.95%
Property Plant and Equipment					
Land	3.81%	4.51%	3.96%	6.30%	4.63%
Buildings	0.00%	0.00%	0.00%	0.00%	0.00%
Equipment	23.28%	22.51%	25.34%	23.63%	21.99%
Vehicles	7.85%	9.72%	6.59%	6.69%	3.73%
Furniture and Fixtures	0.84%	0.60%	0.54%	0.74%	0.52%
Total	35.77%	37.34%	36.42%	37.37%	30.87%
Less Accumulated Depreciation	0.00%	0.00%	0.00%	0.00%	0.00%
Net Property Plant and Equipment	35.77%	37.34%	36.42%	37.37%	30.87%
Other Assets					
Long-Term Investments	0.10%	0.19%	0.19%	0.22%	0.18%
Deposits and Licenses	0.00%	0.00%	0.00%	0.00%	0.00%
Cash Surrender Value—Officers Life	4.68%	5.63%	0.11%	0.56%	0.00%
Loan Fees—Net	0.06%	0.04%	0.03%	0.00%	0.00%
Advances to Affiliated Companies	0.00%	0.00%	0.00%	0.00%	0.00%
Total Other Assets	4.84%	5.86%	0.32%	0.78%	0.18%
Total Assets	100.00%	100.00%	100.00%	100.00%	100.00%
Liabilities					
Current Liabilities					
Accounts Payable	40.02%	24.84%	24.44%	14.57%	14.94%
Notes Receivable	0.00%	0.00%	7.77%	5.42%	0.00%
Current Portion of Long-Term Debt	2.74%	2.93%	2.83%	3.23%	7.69%
Construction Loan Payable	0.00%	0.00%	0.00%	0.00%	0.00%
Income Taxes Payable	0.05%	0.72%	0.00%	0.04%	0.38%
Advances from Officers	0.00%	0.00%	0.00%	0.00%	0.00%
Accrued Expenses	6.47%	7.36%	8.57%	8.03%	6.18%
Other Current Liabilities	0.00%	0.00%	0.08%	0.15%	0.00%
Other Financing Needed	0.00%	0.00%	0.00%	0.00%	0.00%
Total Current Liability	49.29%	35.86%	43.69%	31.44%	29.18%
Long-Term Debt	3.00%	1.65%	0.00%	0.00%	0.00%
Deferred Taxes	2.20%	4.82%	4.20%	9.32%	0.00%
Total Liabilities	54.49%	42.32%	47.89%	40.76%	29.18%
Owners' Equity	45.51%	57.68%	52.11%	59.24%	70.82%
Total Liabilities and Owners' Equity	100.00%	100.00%	100.00%	100.00%	100.00%

Walsh Petroleum Common Size (% of Sales) Balance Sheet for the Years Ended 1981–1985

	Year 1981	Year 1982	Year 1983	Year 1984	Year 1985
Assets					
Current Assets					
Cash	0.72%	0.13%	0.93%	1.45%	0.42%
Marketable Securities	0.00%	0.00%	0.00%	0.00%	0.00%
Accounts Rec.	5.17%	4.19%	4.61%	3.74%	4.68%
Inventories	1.68%	1.40%	3.31%	3.42%	4.48%
Refundable Taxes	0.08%	0.00%	0.66%	0.07%	0.01%
Prepaid Exp.	0.11%	0.12%	0.33%	0.22%	0.29%
Notes Receivable	0.00%	0.00%	0.00%	0.00%	0.28%
Other Current Assets	0.00%	0.00%	0.00%	0.00%	3.50%
Total Current Assets	7.76%	5.83%	9.83%	8.90%	13.65%
Property Plant and Equipment					
Land	0.50%	0.46%	0.62%	0.91%	0.92%
Buildings	0.00%	0.00%	0.00%	0.00%	0.00%
Equipment	3.04%	2.31%	3.94%	3.40%	4.35%
Vehicles	1.03%	1.00%	1.02%	0.96%	0.74%
Furniture and Fixtures	0.11%	0.06%	0.08%	0.11%	0.10%
Total	4.67%	3.83%	5.66%	5.38%	6.11%
Less Accumulated Depreciation	0.00%	0.00%	0.00%	0.00%	0.00%
Net Property Plant and Equipment	4.67%	3.83%	5.66%	5.38%	6.11%
Other Assets					
Long-Term Investments	0.01%	0.02%	0.03%	0.03%	0.04%
Deposits and Licenses	0.00%	0.00%	0.00%	0.00%	0.00%
Cash Surrender Value—Officers Life	0.61%	0.58%	0.02%	0.08%	0.00%
Loan Fees—Net	0.01%	0.00%	0.00%	0.00%	0.00%
Advances to Affiliated Companies	0.00%	0.00%	0.00%	0.00%	0.00%
Total Other Assets	0.63%	0.60%	0.05%	0.11%	0.04%
Total Assets	13.06%	10.27%	15.54%	14.40%	19.80%
Liabilities					
Current Liabilities					
Accounts Payable	5.23%	2.55%	3.80%	2.10%	2.96%
Notes Payable	0.00%	0.00%	1.21%	0.78%	0.00%
Current Portion of Long-Term Debt	0.36%	0.30%	0.44%	0.47%	1.52%
Construction Loan Payable	0.00%	0.00%	0.00%	0.00%	0.00%
Income Taxes Payable	0.01%	0.07%	0.00%	0.01%	0.07%
Advances from Officers	0.00%	0.00%	0.00%	0.00%	0.00%
Accrued Expenses	0.85%	0.76%	1.33%	1.16%	1.22%
Other Current Liabilities	0.00%	0.00%	0.01%	0.02%	0.00%
Other Financing Needed	0.00%	0.00%	0.00%	0.00%	0.00%
Total Current Liability	6.44%	3.68%	6.79%	4.53%	5.78%
Long-Term Debt	0.39%	0.17%	0.00%	0.00%	0.00%
Deferred Taxes	0.29%	0.49%	0.65%	1.34%	0.00%
Total Liabilities	7.12%	4.35%	7.44%	5.87%	5.78%
Owners' Equity	5.95%	5.92%	8.10%	8.53%	14.03%
Total Liabilities and Owners' Equity	13.06%	10.27%	15.54%	14.40%	19.80%

Walsh Petroleum Statement of Income as a % of Assets for the Years Ended 1981–1985

	Year 1981	Year 1982	Year 1983	Year 1984	Year 1985
Sales:					
Premium	0.4870	0.8542	0.8573	0.9350	0.8099
Unleaded	1.8072	2.3929	1.5855	1.8426	1.3375
Regular	3.6054	4.7554	2.5397	2.1454	1.2957
Lube	0.1276	0.1036	0.1026	0.1093	0.0895
Heating Oil	0.8060	0.7673	0.5728	0.7432	0.5529
Diesel	0.6010	0.6571	0.5170	0.6239	0.4714
Kerosene	0.1394	0.1920	0.1833	0.2933	0.2230
Other Products	0.0815	0.0172	0.0750	0.2534	0.2696
Net Sales	7.6551	9.7398	6.4333	6.9462	5.0494
Cost of Sales:					
Beginning Inventory	0.1170	0.1361	0.1318	0.2473	0.1996
Purchases Net of Discounts	7.1415	9.1203	6.0397	6.3747	4.4627
	7.2585	9.2564	6.1715	6.6220	4.6623
Ending Inventory	0.1283	0.1359	0.2127	0.2378	0.2260
Cost of Sales	7.1302	9.1205	5.9588	6.3842	4.4363
Gross Profit	0.5249	0.6194	0.4746	0.5620	0.6131
Selling, General and Admin. Expenses					
Licenses and Non-Income Taxes	0.0339	0.0360	0.0287	0.0408	0.0135
Vehicle Expense	0.0353	0.0665	0.0573	0.0794	0.0494
Officers' Salaries	0.1031	0.1015	0.0839	0.0957	0.0770
Other Salaries and Wages	0.1190	0.1476	0.1883	0.2452	0.2133
Other Expense	0.2008	0.2173	0.2128	0.2311	0.2289
Depreciation	0.0703	0.1100	0.1132	0.1326	0.1053
Interest on Borrowing Needs	0.0098	0.0119	0.0175	0.0217	0.0141
Operating Income (Loss)	−0.0474	−0.0715	−0.2271	−0.2844	−0.0885
Earnings on Marketable Securities	0.0067	0.0046	0.0047	0.0053	0.0057
Other Income	0.1263	0.1801	0.1603	0.2618	0.1290
Earnings before Taxes	0.0857	0.1132	−0.0622	−0.0174	0.0462
Provision for Federal Income Taxes	0.0100	0.0190	−0.0238	−0.0040	0.0038
Net Income	0.0757	0.0942	−0.0384	−0.0133	0.0424

Walsh Unit Sales Trends (1984–1987)

		Avg. Gal./Month (000's)		
Unit	Type	1984	1985	1986 (EST)
1	4,000 Sq ft rural grocery, owner change in 1984	6.0	10.5	10.8
2	Village 2-bay, financial problems, cash only, pool hall	11.7	16.8	14.3
3	5,000 sq ft rural grocery in low growth area	—	—	8.2
4	C-store in growing rural area	—	6.7	18.1
5	2-bay station with marina service, new C-store competition	20.3	17.9	20.7
6	Rehab 2-bay on front of bulk plant property, owned by mother and leased to corporation, good location on four-lane with crossover access, growth area	28.4	35.3	37.5
7	3-bay station in low-growth rural area, father and son	9.9	9.9	10.1
8	1,500 sq ft rural grocery with new owner, business recovery	14.0	9.1	11.6
9	3,000 sq ft rural C-store with interceptor location, sell on consignment with Walsh controlling price, considering canopy to be leased by Walsh from owner	17.6	18.8	20.0
10	3,000 sq ft rural C-store with interceptor location	21.9	22.4	22.7

Appendix B

Reseller Investment Analysis

Investment

Underground Costs:	
Storage Tanks & UG Lines	0
Electr. Tank Mon. & Probes	0
Submersible Pumps	0
Installation	0
Fuel Inventory	0
Total	0

Aboveground Costs:	
Dispensors	25,000
Remote Console	3,500
Canopy	8,000
Signage	1,500
Installation	32,000
Total	70,000

Asset Lives:	
Canopy	10 yrs.
All Other	5 yrs.

Financing to Retailer:	
% Equity	100.00%
Principle	25,000
Interest Rate	9.00%
Term	60 Mo.

	1	2	3	4	5	6	7	8	9	10
Operating Costs:										
Property Taxes	500	500	500	500	500	500	500	500	500	500
Maintenance	0	2,000	2,000	2,000	2,000	2,000	2,000	2,000	2,000	2,000
Revenues/Gallon:										
Gasoline	$0.045	$0.045	$0.045	$0.045	$0.045	$0.045	$0.045	$0.045	$0.045	$0.045
Diesel	$0.045	$0.045	$0.045	$0.045	$0.045	$0.045	$0.045	$0.045	$0.045	$0.045
Kerosine	$0.300	$0.300	$0.300	$0.300	$0.300	$0.300	$0.300	$0.300	$0.300	$0.300
Sales Mix:										
Gasoline	90.00%	90.00%	90.00%	90.00%	90.00%	90.00%	90.00%	90.00%	90.00%	90.00%
Diesel	5.00%	5.00%	5.00%	5.00%	5.00%	5.00%	5.00%	5.00%	5.00%	5.00%
Kerosine	5.00%	5.00%	5.00%	5.00%	5.00%	5.00%	5.00%	5.00%	5.00%	5.00%
Total Gallons	450,000	450,000	450,000	450,000	450,000	450,000	450,000	450,000	450,000	450,000
Tax Rate	30.00%	30.00%	30.00%	30.00%	30.00%	30.00%	30.00%	30.00%	30.00%	30.00%
Discount Rate	12.00%									

NOTE: Arrangement here centers around placing the underground tanks in the reseller's name. Walsh loans $25,000 to the reseller for this purpose, as noted above. Terms of the loan and the necessity for such are subject to negotiation.

Financing Schedule

	Month: 1	2	3	4	5	6	7	8	9	10	11	12
Balance	25,000	24,669	24,335	23,998	23,659	23,318	22,974	22,627	22,278	21,926	21,571	21,214
Payment	519	519	519	519	519	519	519	519	519	519	519	519
Principle	331	334	336	339	342	344	347	349	352	355	357	360
Interest	188	185	183	180	177	175	172	170	167	164	162	159

Depreciation Schedule

	Year: 1	2	3	4	5	6	7	8	9	10
Canopy	1,600	1,280	1,024	819	655	524	419	336	268	215
Other	24,800	14,880	8,928	5,357	3,214					

Cash Flow Analysis

	Year: 0	1	2	3	4	5	6	7	8	9	10
Revenues:											
Gas		18,225	18,225	18,225	18,225	18,225	18,225	18,225	18,225	18,225	18,225
Diesel		1,013	1,013	1,013	1,013	1,013	1,013	1,013	1,013	1,013	1,013
Kerosine		6,750	6,750	6,750	6,750	6,750	6,750	6,750	6,750	6,750	6,750
Total		25,988	25,988	25,988	25,988	25,988	25,988	25,988	25,988	25,988	25,988
Operating Costs:											
Taxes		500	500	500	500	500	500	500	500	500	500
Maintenance		0	2,000	2,000	2,000	2,000	2,000	2,000	2,000	2,000	2,000
Depreciation		26,400	16,160	9,952	6,176	3,869	524	419	336	268	215
Total		26,900	18,660	12,452	8,676	6,369	3,024	2,919	2,836	2,768	2,715
Interest Earned		2,082	1,693	1,267	802	293					
Pretax Income		1,169	9,020	14,803	18,114	19,911	22,963	23,068	23,152	23,219	23,273
Less: Taxes		351	2,706	4,441	5,434	5,973	6,889	6,920	6,946	6,966	6,982
Net Income		818	6,314	10,362	12,680	13,938	16,074	16,148	16,206	16,253	16,291
Plus:											
Depreciation		26,400	16,160	9,952	6,176	3,869	524	419	336	268	215
Principle Repayments		4,146	4,535	4,960	5,425	5,934					
Less:											
Initial Principle	(25,000)										
Below Ground Cost	0										
Above Ground Cost	(70,000)										
Cashflow	(95,000)	31,364	27,009	25,274	24,281	23,742	16,599	16,567	16,542	16,522	16,506
Present Value of Annual Cashflows	(95,000)	28,004	21,531	17,990	15,431	13,472	8,409	7,494	6,681	5,958	5,314
Cumulative Present Value Position	(95,000)	(66,996)	(45,465)	(27,475)	(12,044)	1,427	9,837	17,331	24,012	29,970	35,284
IRR	22.02%										
MPV	35,284										

Appendix C

Valuation of Valley Oil Co.

Purpose and Methodology

Fair market value is defined as "the price at which the property would change hands between a willing buyer and a willing seller when the former is not under any compulsion to buy and the latter is not under any compulsion to sell, both parties having reasonable knowledge of relevant facts" (Rev. Rul. 59–60).

Revenue Ruling 59-60 also outlines many techniques appropriate in the determination of fair market value. Among these are the following:

- the economic outlook in general and the condition and outlook of the specific industry in particular;
- the nature of the business and the history of the enterprise from its inception;
- the book value of the stock and the financial condition of the business;
- the earning capacity of the company; and
- whether or not the enterprise has goodwill or other intangible value.[1]

Bearing these points in mind, the analysis will consider the following:

I. Condition of Industry

II. Condition of Company
    A. Position within market and life cycle
    B. Financial trends and earnings capacity
    C. Income-based value
    D. Goodwill potential

III. Adjusted asset value

IV. Conclusion

---

[1]Burke, Frank M. *Valuation and Valuation Planning for Closely Held Businesses* (Prentice-Hall: Englewood Cliffs, N.J., 1981), pp. 27–7.

I. Condition of Industry

At present, the picture in the petroleum marketing industry is glum; according to a National Petroleum News study, industry observers see a fallout rate of over 17% for the 1985–87 period. Through 1990, the rate is even higher; observers expect little more than two-thirds of the jobbers will still be in business by 1990.[2] Over the past decade, jobber returns have been falling drastically. According to data collected by the Petroleum Marketing Education Foundation, after tax return on equity has fallen from almost 20% in 1979–80 to only 6.9% in 1984–85 (see Table 5). This falling return comes from two main sources. First, as demand remains weak and the age of assets increases, total asset turnover, an asset productivity measure, falls significantly. Second, because of the pressure put on prices by deregulation and by the elimination of benefits from refiners,[3] profit margins have dropped drastically. Although margins improved in 1985, and so far in 1986, these are the result of a market phenomenon, sticky retail prices during periods of unprecedented price decline. In other words, the improvement is a temporary result of the reluctance of marketers to pass price declines on to the consumer. Upon return to normal equilibrium, one finds that the marketer is squeezed from both sides, volume and margin.

Given these factors, it seems logical to place the petroleum marketing industry late in the life cycle. The industry has shown several classic examples of mature (stage three) behavior:

---

[2]Reid, Marvin. "To Stay In or Sell Out," *National Petroleum News,* August 1985, p. 45.

[3]*Id.* p. 46.

Table 5 Industry DuPont Analysis

Year	Profit Margin ·	Total Asset Turns ·	Financial Leverage Multiplier =	ROE
1976–1977	1.03	4.85	2.33	11.6
1977–1978	0.87	5.40	2.55	12.0
1978–1979	0.92	5.20	2.49	11.9
1979–1980	1.24	6.25	2.57	19.9
1980–1981	0.97	7.21	2.66	18.6
1981–1982	0.58	7.44	2.47	10.7
1982–1983	0.55	7.80	2.51	10.8
1983–1984	0.59	6.87	2.39	9.7
1984–1985	0.47	6.12	2.37	6.9

■ Sales, as a percent of assets, have trended down dramatically, showing both old, deteriorating assets and market overcrowding.

■ Fallout has reached an all-time high, with a definite buyer's market developing.[4]

■ Prices have declined to unprecedented lows.

■ The market is composed of fewer, but larger, firms.

This placement in the mature stage of the cycle suggests that, barring revolutionary changes in the industry, nothing but decline can be foreseen.

II. Condition of Company

A. Life Cycle and Market
Valley Oil finds itself in the middle of this declining industry. Its position in the life cycle does not seem to be much better; in fact, Valley appears to have advanced into the early decline stage. Several factors contribute to this assessment:

■ Sales/total assets have declined from over 5.8 in 1983 to only 5.31 in 1985. On a gallonage basis, where price fluctuations have less impact, there has still been a close to fifty percent decline since 1979.

[4]*Id.* p. 47.

■ Assets are at an unprecedented old age. An attached chart illustrates the old age of Valley's storage tanks.

■ Sales, on both an absolute dollar and a gallonage basis, are declining steadily. Although the actual percentage varies from year to year, the overall trend is distinct.

What does this imply for Valley? First, the firm must cope with trying to maintain market share and profitability in an environment where the potential for both is shrinking. Second, the firm must attempt this in spite of its own inherent limitations; it is burdened with older, shrinking-volume resellers, as well as aged vehicles and tanks.

B. Financial Trends and Earning Capacity
The firm's financial statements do not yield a picture any more bright. First, the downward trend in sales is disturbing. Second, excluding the first half of 1985, the same trend has applied to margin. The combination of these two factors places a vise grip on profitability. In fact, if it were not for the margin windfall in the first half of this year, Valley would have taken a major blow.

C. Income-based Value
In any discounted, income-based valuation, two factors must be determined: the discount rate and the earnings base. Theoretically, the discount rate can be assumed to be the rate of return which an investor could earn on a portfolio of similar risk assets. As a starting point, one can consider that for the week of August 1, the Standard and Poor's 10-bond utility average yielded 9.03%. This range of 9% is consistent with performance over recent months and actually low for the past decade. Working from this starting point, one can logically assume that there would have to be some risk premium; therefore, a minimum capitalization rate would be 10%. As an earnings base, one can use a weighted average of

the last five years. This both eliminates any unusual blip in the last year and takes into account the overall trend (See Table 6).

When this average earnings figure is capitalized at 10%, an income-based valuation of $367,280 is determined. Using a more reasonable discount rate of 12% yields a value of $306,067.

D. Goodwill Potential

A study by David Nelson, a consultant to the Petroleum Marketing Education Foundation, shows that, of 37 sales studied in 1983, 19 received "goodwill". This ratio was down from 13 out of 18 in 1981.[5] In addition to the quantitative evidence suggesting that large blue sky premiums are a thing of the past, there are several logical arguments to support this point:

▪ More and more firms are entering the market on the selling side, suggesting a definite oversupply.[6]

▪ The firm is completely unleveraged, yet it can barely support its current operating costs. Margins are insufficient to cover fixed costs, leaving hauling fees and finance charges as the only means of profit.

Given that the industry trend is toward little or no blue sky, that Valley would be one of many firms entering the market, and that its margins do not even indicate profitable gallonage, it seems unreasonable to attach any goodwill to the earnings base or to an asset valuation.

III. Adjusted Asset Value

Another step that must be taken in any valuation is an assessment of the asset value of the company. If this market-related asset value is higher that the income-based value, then the business has negative operating value and is worth more liquidated.

[5]*Id.* p. 47.

[6]*Id.* p. 47.

Table 6

Year	Wt. Factor	Income	W · I
1981	1	(1,536)	(1,536)
1982	2	38,032	76,064
1983	3	40,920	122,760
1984	4	42,219	168,876
1985	5	36,951	184,755
	15		550,919

Weighted Average Earnings = $36,728

When this step is taken with Valley, the analysis is fairly simple (see attached chart for complete analysis). All of the current assets can be liquidated at their book value except for accounts receivables. These must be carried across to market less a 10% bad debt adjustment. This brings the value of total current assets to $620,557.

Adjustments for the fixed assets are a bit more complex. First, the land/buildings account must be adjusted to $100,000 market value. Equipment, with the exception of tanks, is valued at about $20,000 (79 pumps @ $250). The vehicles have an appraised market value of $156,500. The market value for furniture and fixtures is $7,050, giving a total market value to long-term assets of $283,550. The next step to be followed is to deduct any liabilities. These are deducted at book value of $203,569.

The final step in the adjusted asset valuation is to consider any hidden assets or liabilities. These can take several forms:

▪ Undervalued real estate which could actually bring much more than its book value;

▪ Exclusive distribution contracts or other market-related, hidden assets; and

▪ Contingent liabilities such as pending lawsuits or potential lawsuits from sources such as leaking underground tanks.

The first of these is ruled out by the fact that Valley owns only one piece of real estate, which was recently appraised and is included in the valuation at its appraised value of $100,000. Neither does the second factor enter into the value—Valley has no unique market-related advantages.

The question of contingent liabilities is important; the possibility that one or more of the approximately 90 tanks could develop or already possess a leak is far from remote. According to Steffen Plenn, author of *Underground Tankage: The Liability of Leaks,* as many as thirty percent of the steel tanks currently in the ground may be leaking. What's worse, that number is expected to rise. The volatile nature of this problem is most clearly seen in its propensity to wind up in court. Plenn explains that these leaks, when discovered, are disasters of a magnitude that will not avoid court.[7] The most serious implication, however, is that the liability has historically extended to all owners of the tanks, both past and present, vis-a-vis the concept of joint and several liability. Thus, in the process of any rationally executed liquidation, the seller would have to remove each of the older tanks. In the case of Valley, this cost would amount to approximately $90,000.[8] Deducting this contingent tank liability (cost of removal) from the previously computed values yields a liquidation value of $610,538.

IV. Conclusion

This now presents us with two different values for consideration:

(1) The income-based value of $367,280 and

(2) The adjusted asset liquidation basis of $610,538.

Realizing that

■ the liquidation value exceeds the income-based value;

■ there is a trend toward decreasing blue sky premiums;

■ goodwill is usually paid for growing or unusually profitable gallons, of which Valley has none;

■ there is a significant contingent liability attached to the tanks, all of which cannot be eliminated by tank removal (due to potential for previous leaks); and, finally,

■ Valley is a declining firm in a mature industry, we recommend use of the adjusted asset liquidation value of $610,538 as our best estimate of market value.

Adjusted Asset Valuation Valley Oil Co.

	Book	Market
Assets:		
Cash	26,558	26,558
A/R	421,308	421,308
Inventory	153,135	137,821
Refundable Taxes	3,888	3,888
Prepaids	25,883	25,883
Notes Receivable	5,099	5,099
Land/Building	79,942	100,000
Equipment	247,258	20,000
Vehicles*	310,000	156,500
Furn. & Fixt.	37,896	7,050
Less: Acc. Depr.	(475,238)	—
Total Asset Value	835,729	904,107
Liabilities		
A/P	(196,670)	(196,670)
Income Taxes Payable	(6,899)	(6,899)
Total Liabilities Value	(203,569)	(203,569)
Less: Contingent Tank Liability	—	(90,000)
Total Value	632,160	610,538

*One two year old tractor/trailer (9,000-gallon capacity), two older "bobtail" trucks (2,000-gallon capacity) and one older service van.

---

[7]Plenn, Steffen W., *Underground Tankage: The Liabilities of Leaks,* (Petroleum Marketing Education Foundation: Alexandria, Virginia, 1986), pp. 9–12.

[8]Ascertained in conversation with a local contractor. Confirmed by recent removals of similar tanks.

Valley Oil Co. Income Statement
Information for the Years
Ended 1984 and 1985

	1984	1985
Other Expenses:		
Advertising	6,254	6,921
Office expense	7,066	10,566
Utilities	5,033	4,806
Insurance	15,360	37,855
Telephone	3,327	4,310
Rent*	27,163	27,940
Professional fees	7,483	10,503
Repairs	34,445	32,026
Directors fees	4,800	4,800
Travel	5,982	10,178
Dues and subscriptions	4,786	4,442
Contributions	1,520	4,403
Sales promotion	5,705	5,736
Miscellaneous	—	673
Pension plan expense	1,072	—
Employee benefits	28,834	33,448
Bad debts	28,091	25,552
Total	186,921	224,159

*Rent on bulk plant and corporate office.

Valley Oil Co. Statement of Income for the Years Ended 1981–1985

	Year 1981	Year 1982	Year 1983	Year 1984	Year 1985
Gallons:					
Premium	NA	NA	NA	NA	382,869
Unleaded	NA	NA	NA	NA	1,152,730
Regular	3,956,353	3,316,151	4,004,842	3,101,595	1,418,560
Lube	NA	NA	NA	NA	NA
Heating Oil	978,113	1,004,000	1,057,131	1,137,072	1,267,011
Diesel	NA	NA	NA	NA	NA
Kerosene	286,870	286,430	262,802	310,066	315,739
Other Products	NA	NA	NA	NA	NA
Total	5,221,336	4,606,581	5,324,775	4,548,733	4,536,909
Sales:					
Premium	NA	NA	NA	NA	358,038
Unleaded	NA	NA	NA	NA	1,038,871
Regular	NA	NA	NA	3,061,113	1,222,758
Lube	NA	NA	NA	95,781	100,922
Heating Oil	NA	NA	NA	1,172,390	871,031
Diesel	NA	NA	NA	NA	355,966
Kerosene	NA	NA	NA	364,573	359,583
Other Products	NA	NA	NA	NA	92,493
Net Sales	4,734,881	4,332,049	4,657,833	4,234,277	4,279,681
Cost of Sales:					
Beginning Inventory	211,832	210,000	192,449	153,639	160,344
Purchases Net of Discounts	4,292,934	3,873,798	4,138,784	3,752,969	3,714,003
	4,504,766	4,083,798	4,331,233	3,906,608	3,874,347
Ending Inventory	210,000	192,449	153,639	160,344	153,135
Cost of Sales	4,294,766	3,891,349	4,177,594	3,746,264	3,721,212
Gross Profit	440,115	440,700	480,239	488,013	558,469
Selling, General and Admin. Expenses					
Licenses and Non-Income Taxes	23,584	24,450	25,943	25,810	22,252
Vehicle Expense	100,471	61,397	85,365	74,066	81,748
Officers' Salaries	45,500	49,414	48,700	51,000	53,100
Other Salaries and Wages	155,843	142,087	154,104	148,434	162,161
Other Expense	145,081	168,015	168,076	186,921	224,159
Depreciation	44,428	38,032	36,920	54,639	61,015
Interest on Borrowing Needs	10,025	3,496	5,272	7,144	11,203
Operating Income (Loss)	(84,817)	(46,191)	(44,141)	(60,001)	(57,169)
Earnings on Marketable Securities	8,746	14,493	5,134	6,426	8,103
Other Income (Expense)	72,552	74,672	90,703	96,501	95,066 ←Hauling income
Earnings before Taxes	(3,519)	42,974	51,696	42,926	46,000
Provision for Federal Income Taxes	(1,983)	4,942	10,776	707	9,049
Net Income	(1,536)	38,032	40,920	42,219	36,951

(From 1981 to 1984, gallonage data is available only as aggregate gasoline sales—these are entered as regular. Likewise, during the entire five year period, heating oil and diesel are combined under heating oil. During the same time period, dollar values are often unavailable.)

Valley Oil Co. Balance Sheet for the Years Ended 1981–1985

	Year 1981	Year 1982	Year 1983	Year 1984	Year 1985
Assets					
Current Assets					
Cash	64,468	31,922	24,076	10,000	26,558
Marketable Securities	0	0	0	0	0
Accounts Rec.	656,187	579,313	471,803	470,120	421,308
Inventories	210,000	192,449	153,639	160,344	153,135
Refundable Taxes	33,054	0	0	9,920	3,888
Prepaid Exp.	2,636	1,535	1,526	1,766	25,883
Notes Receivable	1,804	40,277	14,481	59,342	5,099
Other Current Assets	0	0	0	0	0
Total Current Assets	968,149	845,496	665,525	711,492	635,871
Property Plant and Equipment					
Land	79,942	79,942	79,942	79,942	79,942
Buildings	0	0	0	0	0
Equipment	207,463	216,139	208,116	207,873	227,444
Vehicles	247,339	274,634	253,153	279,634	255,355
Furniture and Fixtures	5,032	21,588	22,393	24,388	30,464
Total	539,776	592,303	563,604	591,837	593,205
Less Accumulated Depreciation	392,800	430,332	427,310	392,465	422,781
Net Property Plant and Equip.	146,976	161,971	136,294	199,372	170,424
Other Assets					
Long-Term Investments	0	0	0	0	0
Deposits and Licenses	0	0	0	0	0
Cash Surrender Value—Officers' Life Insurance	0	0	0	0	0
Loan Fees—Net	0	0	0	0	0
Advances to Affiliated Companies	0	0	0	0	0
Total Other Assets	0	0	0	0	0
Total Assets	1,115,125	1,007,467	801,819	910,864	806,295
Liabilities					
Current Liabilities					
Accounts Payable	670,524	474,892	272,434	295,092	196,670
Notes Payable	0	45,000	0	50,000	0
Current Portion of Long-Term Debt	0	0	0	0	0
Construction Loan Payable	0	0	0	0	0
Income Taxes Payable	0	4,942	5,832	0	6,899
Advances from Officers	0	0	0	0	0
Accrued Expenses	0	0	0	0	0
Other Current Liabilities	0	0	0	0	0
Other Financing Needed	0	0	0	0	0
Total Current Liabilities	670,524	524,834	278,266	345,092	203,569
Long-Term Debt	0	0	0	0	0
Other Long-Term	0	0	0	0	0
Total Liabilities	670,524	524,834	278,266	345,092	203,569
Owners Equity	444,601	482,633	523,553	565,772	602,726
Total Liabilities and Owners' Equity	1,115,125	1,007,467	801,819	910,864	806,295

Valley Oil Co. Selected Ratios

Ratio Analysis	Year 1981	Year 1982	Year 1983	Year 1984	Year 1985
DuPont Analysis:					
Return on Sales	−0.03%	0.88%	0.88%	1.00%	0.86%
· Asset Turnover	4.25	4.30	5.81	4.65	5.31
= Return on Assets	−0.14%	3.78%	5.10%	4.64%	4.58%
· Financial Leverage	2.51	2.09	1.53	1.61	1.34
= Return on Equity	−0.35%	7.88%	7.82%	7.46%	6.13%
Activity:					
Fixed Asset Turnover	32.22	26.75	34.17	21.24	25.11
Sales Growth (Dollars)	−16.28%	−8.51%	7.52%	−9.09%	1.07%
Sales Growth (Gallons)	−30.65%	−11.77%	15.59%	−14.57%	−0.26%
Profitability:					
Gross Margin	9.30%	10.17%	10.31%	11.53%	13.05%
Salaries Ratio (Officers Salaries + Sales)	0.96%	1.14%	1.05%	1.20%	1.24%
S,G,& A Ratio (S,G, & A + Sales)	9.94%	10.28%	10.35%	11.48%	12.70%
Working Capital Usage:					
Days Payable	51.69	40.01	21.35	25.44	16.77
Collection Period (Days)	50.58	48.81	36.97	40.52	35.93
Days Inventory	16.19	16.21	12.04	13.82	13.06
Cash Cycle ((Collect.Pd. + Inven.) − Days Pay.)	15.08	25.01	27.66	28.91	32.22
Leverage:					
Total Debt/Assets	60.13%	52.09%	34.70%	37.89%	25.25%
Long-Term Debt/Assets	0.00	0.00	0.00	0.00	0.00
Times Interest EBIT	−7.46	−12.21	−7.37	−7.40	−4.10
Liquidity:					
Current Ratio	1.44	1.61	2.39	2.06	3.12
Acid Test Ratio	1.13	1.24	1.84	1.60	2.37

Valley Oil Co. Common Size Statement of Income for the Years Ended 1981–1985

	Year 1981	Year 1982	Year 1983	Year 1984	Year 1985
Sales:					
Premium	NA	NA	NA	NA	8.37%
Unleaded	NA	NA	NA	NA	24.27%
Regular	NA	NA	NA	72.29%	28.57%
Lube	NA	NA	NA	2.26%	2.36%
Heating Oil	NA	NA	NA	27.69%	20.35%
Diesel	NA	NA	NA	NA	8.32%
Kerosene	NA	NA	NA	8.61%	8.40%
Other Products	NA	NA	NA	NA	2.16%
Net Sales	100.00%	100.00%	100.00%	100.00%	100.00%
Cost of Sales:					
Beginning Inventory	4.47%	4.85%	4.13%	3.63%	3.75%
Purchases Net of Discounts	90.67%	89.42%	88.86%	88.63%	86.78%
Ending Inventory	95.14%	94.27%	92.99%	92.26%	90.53%
	4.44%	4.44%	3.30%	3.79%	3.58%
Cost of Sales	90.70%	89.83%	89.69%	88.47%	86.95%
Gross Profit	9.30%	10.17%	10.31%	11.53%	13.05%
Selling, General and Admin. Expenses	0.00%	0.00%	0.00%	0.00%	0.00%
Licenses and Non-Income Taxes	0.50%	0.56%	0.56%	0.61%	0.52%
Vehicle Expense	2.12%	1.42%	1.83%	1.75%	1.91%
Officers' Salaries	0.96%	1.14%	1.05%	1.20%	1.24%
Other Salaries and Wages	3.29%	3.28%	3.31%	3.51%	3.79%
Other Expense	3.06%	3.88%	3.61%	4.41%	5.24%
Depreciation	0.94%	0.88%	0.79%	1.29%	1.43%
Interest on Borrowing Needs	0.21%	0.08%	0.11%	0.17%	0.26%
Operating Income (Loss)	−1.79%	−1.07%	−0.95%	−1.42%	−1.34%
Earnings on Marketable Securities	0.18%	0.33%	0.11%	0.15%	0.19%
Other Income (Expense)	1.53%	1.72%	1.95%	2.28%	2.22%
Earnings before Taxes	−0.07%	0.99%	1.11%	1.01%	1.07%
Provision for Federal Income Taxes	−0.04%	0.11%	0.23%	0.02%	0.21%
Net Income	−0.03%	0.88%	0.88%	1.00%	0.86%

Valley Oil Co. Common Size (% of Assets) Balance Sheet for the Years Ended 1981–1985

	Year 1981	Year 1982	Year 1983	Year 1984	Year 1985
Assets					
Current Assets					
Cash	5.78%	3.17%	3.00%	1.10%	3.29%
Marketable Securities	0.00%	0.00%	0.00%	0.00%	0.00%
Accounts Rec.	58.84%	57.50%	58.84%	51.61%	52.25%
Inventories	18.83%	19.10%	19.16%	17.60%	18.99%
Refundable Taxes	2.96%	0.00%	0.00%	1.09%	0.48%
Prepaid Exp.	0.24%	0.15%	0.19%	0.19%	3.21%
Notes Receivable	0.16%	4.00%	1.81%	6.51%	0.63%
Other Current Assets	0.00%	0.00%	0.00%	0.00%	0.00%
Total Current Assets	86.82%	83.92%	83.00%	78.11%	78.86%
Property Plant and Equipment					
Land	7.17%	7.93%	9.97%	8.78%	9.91%
Buildings	0.00%	0.00%	0.00%	0.00%	0.00%
Equipment	18.60%	21.45%	25.96%	22.82%	28.21%
Vehicles	22.18%	27.26%	31.57%	30.70%	31.67%
Furniture and Fixtures	0.45%	2.14%	2.79%	2.68%	3.78%
Total	48.40%	58.79%	70.29%	64.98%	73.57%
Less Accumulated Depreciation	35.22%	42.71%	53.29%	43.09%	52.44%
Net Property Plant and Equip.	13.18%	16.08%	17.00%	21.89%	21.14%
Other Assets					
Long-Term Investments	0.00%	0.00%	0.00%	0.00%	0.00%
Deposits and Licenses	0.00%	0.00%	0.00%	0.00%	0.00%
Cash Surrender Value—Officers' Life Insurance	0.00%	0.00%	0.00%	0.00%	0.00%
Loan Fees—Net	0.00%	0.00%	0.00%	0.00%	0.00%
Advances to Affiliated Companies	0.00%	0.00%	0.00%	0.00%	0.00%
Total Other Assets	0.00%	0.00%	0.00%	0.00%	0.00%
Total Assets	100.00%	100.00%	100.00%	100.00%	100.00%
Liabilities					
Current Liabilities					
Accounts Payable	60.13%	47.14%	33.98%	32.40%	24.39%
Notes Receivable	0.00%	4.47%	0.00%	5.49%	0.00%
Current Portion of Long-Term Debt	0.00%	0.00%	0.00%	0.00%	0.00%
Construction Loan Payable	0.00%	0.00%	0.00%	0.00%	0.00%
Income Taxes Payable	0.00%	0.49%	0.73%	0.00%	0.86%
Advances from Officers	0.00%	0.00%	0.00%	0.00%	0.00%
Accrued Expenses	0.00%	0.00%	0.00%	0.00%	0.00%
Other Current Liabilities	0.00%	0.00%	0.00%	0.00%	0.00%
Other Financing Needed	0.00%	0.00%	0.00%	0.00%	0.00%
Total Current Liabilities	60.13%	52.09%	34.70%	37.89%	25.25%
Long-Term Debt	0.00%	0.00%	0.00%	0.00%	0.00%
Deferred Taxes	0.00%	0.00%	0.00%	0.00%	0.00%
Total Liabilities	60.13%	52.09%	34.70%	37.89%	25.25%
Owners' Equity	39.87%	47.91%	65.30%	62.11%	74.75%
Total Liabilities and Owner's Equity	100.00%	100.00%	100.00%	100.00%	100.00%

Valley Oil Co. Common Size (% of Sales) Balance Sheet for the Years Ended 1981–1985

	Year 1981	Year 1982	Year 1983	Year 1984	Year 1985
Assets					
Current Assets					
Cash	1.36%	0.74%	0.52%	0.24%	0.62%
Marketable Securities	0.00%	0.00%	0.00%	0.00%	0.00%
Accounts Rec.	13.86%	13.37%	10.13%	11.10%	9.84%
Inventories	4.44%	4.44%	3.30%	3.79%	3.58%
Refundable Taxes	0.70%	0.00%	0.00%	0.23%	0.09%
Prepaid Exp.	0.06%	0.04%	0.03%	0.04%	0.60%
Notes Receivable	0.04%	0.93%	0.31%	1.40%	0.12%
Other Current Assets	0.00%	0.00%	0.00%	0.00%	0.00%
Total Current Assets	20.45%	19.52%	14.29%	16.80%	14.86%
Property Plant and Equipment					
Land	1.69%	1.85%	1.72%	1.89%	1.87%
Buildings	0.00%	0.00%	0.00%	0.00%	0.00%
Equipment	4.38%	4.99%	4.47%	4.91%	5.31%
Vehicles	5.22%	6.34%	5.43%	6.60%	5.97%
Furniture and Fixtures	0.11%	0.50%	0.48%	0.58%	0.71%
Total	11.40%	13.67%	12.10%	13.98%	13.86%
Less Accumulated Depreciation	8.30%	9.93%	9.17%	9.27%	9.88%
Net Property Plant and Equip.	3.10%	3.74%	2.93%	4.71%	3.98%
Other Assets					
Long-Term Investment	0.00%	0.00%	0.00%	0.00%	0.00%
Deposits and Licenses	0.00%	0.00%	0.00%	0.00%	0.00%
Cash Surrender Value—Officers' Life Insurance	0.00%	0.00%	0.00%	0.00%	0.00%
Loan Fees—Net	0.00%	0.00%	0.00%	0.00%	0.00%
Advances to Affiliated Companies	0.00%	0.00%	0.00%	0.00%	0.00%
Total Other Assets	0.00%	0.00%	0.00%	0.00%	0.00%
Total Assets	23.55%	23.26%	17.21%	21.51%	18.84%
Liabilities					
Current Liabilities					
Accounts Payable	14.16%	10.96%	5.85%	6.97%	4.60%
Notes Payable	0.00%	1.04%	0.00%	1.18%	0.00%
Current Portion of Long-Term Debt	0.00%	0.00%	0.00%	0.00%	0.00%
Construction Loan Payable	0.00%	0.00%	0.00%	0.00%	0.00%
Income Taxes Payable	0.00%	0.11%	0.13%	0.00%	0.16%
Advances from Officers	0.00%	0.00%	0.00%	0.00%	0.00%
Accrued Expenses	0.00%	0.00%	0.00%	0.00%	0.00%
Other Current Liabilities	0.00%	0.00%	0.00%	0.00%	0.00%
Other Financing Needed	0.00%	0.00%	0.00%	0.00%	0.00%
Total Current Liabilities	14.16%	12.12%	5.97%	8.15%	4.76%
Long-Term Debt	0.00%	0.00%	0.00%	0.00%	0.00%
Deferred Taxes	0.00%	0.00%	0.00%	0.00%	0.00%
Total Liabilities	14.16%	12.12%	5.97%	8.15%	4.76%
Owners' Equity	9.39%	11.14%	11.24%	13.36%	14.08%
Total Liabilities and Owners' Equity	23.55%	23.26%	17.21%	21.51%	18.84%

Valley Oil Co. Statement of Income as a % of Assets for the Years Ended 1981–1985

	Year 1981	Year 1982	Year 1983	Year 1984	Year 1985
Sales:					
Premium	NA	NA	NA	NA	0.4441
Unleaded	NA	NA	NA	NA	1.2885
Regular	NA	NA	NA	3.3607	1.5165
Lube	NA	NA	NA	0.1052	0.1252
Heating Oil	NA	NA	NA	1.2871	1.0803
Diesel	NA	NA	NA	NA	0.4415
Kerosene	NA	NA	NA	0.4002	0.4460
Other Products	NA	NA	NA	NA	0.1147
Net Sales	4.2461	4.2999	5.8091	4.6486	5.3078
Cost of Sales:					
Beginning Inventory	0.1900	0.2084	0.2400	0.1687	0.1989
Purchases Net of Discounts	3.8497	3.8451	5.1617	4.1202	4.6063
Ending Inventory	4.0397	4.0535	5.4018	4.2889	4.8051
	0.1883	0.1910	0.1916	0.1760	0.1899
Cost of Sales	3.8514	3.8625	5.2101	4.1129	4.6152
Gross Profit	0.3947	0.4374	0.5989	0.5358	0.6926
Selling, General and Admin. Expenses	0.0000	0.0000	0.0000	0.0000	0.0000
Licenses and Non-Income Taxes	0.0211	0.0243	0.0324	0.0283	0.0276
Vehicle Expense	0.0901	0.0609	0.1065	0.0813	0.1014
Officers' Salaries	0.0408	0.0490	0.0607	0.0560	0.0659
Other Salaries and Wages	0.1398	0.1410	0.1922	0.1630	0.2011
Other Expense	0.1301	0.1668	0.2096	0.2052	0.2780
Depreciation	0.0398	0.0378	0.0460	0.0600	0.0757
Interest on Borrowing Needs	0.0090	0.0035	0.0066	0.0078	0.0139
Operating Income (Loss)	−0.0761	−0.0458	−0.0551	−0.0659	−0.0709
Earnings on Marketable Securities	0.0078	0.0144	0.0064	0.0071	0.0100
Other Income	0.0651	0.0741	0.1131	0.1059	0.1179
Earnings before Taxes	−0.0032	0.0427	0.0645	0.0471	0.0571
Provision for Federal Income Taxes	−0.0018	0.0049	0.0134	0.0008	0.0112
Net Income	−0.0014	0.0378	0.0510	0.0464	0.0458

Valley Oil Co. Gallonage Based Total Asset Turnover

Year	Tot. Asset Tur.
1979	9.95
1980	7.51
1981	4.52
1982	4.34
1983	5.89
1984	5.31
1985	5.28

Valley Oil Co. Annual Station Gallons (1985)

Stations:*	
1.	346,279
2.	160,316
3.	128,620
4.	111,702
5.	105,036
6.	116,286
7.	37,894
8.	19,746
9.	121,440
10.**	244,802
11.	304,772
12.	189,422
13.	196,152
14.	148,226
15.	47,118
16.	130,472
17.	100,106
18.	220,440
TOTAL	2,728,829

*Reseller locations with contracts ranging from 2–5 years.
**Wholly owned by Valley Oil with appraised value of $100,000 (good potential, 4-lane interceptor, C-store location).

Valley Oil Co. Capacity and Age of Tanks

Sites*	Capacity	Age	Type	Product	Sites*	Capacity	Age	Type	Product
1.	4000	12	steel	gas	14.	2000	14	"	"
	4000	12	"	"		1000	14	"	"
	3000	25	"	"	15.	1000	12	"	"
	4000	25	"	"		1000	12	"	Diesel
	3000	25	"	"		2000	12	"	F.O.
2.	2000	7	"	"	16.	10000	10	"	Gas
	2000	7	"	"		2000	10	"	"
	1000	2	"	"	17.	2000	10	"	"
3.	1000	8	"	"	18.	1000	5	"	"
	1000	8	"	"		1000	5	"	"
4.	1000	10	"	"	19.	1000	9	"	"
	1000	10	"	"		1000	9	"	"
	1000	10	"	"		1000	9	"	"
5.	2000	20	"	"	20.	10000	35	"	Diesel
	1000	20	"	"	21.	20000	15	"	F.O.
	1000	20	"	"		20000	15	"	"
6.	1000	12	"	"		20000	15	"	"
	1000	10	"	Diesel		20000	15	"	"
	1000	10	"	"		20000	15	"	Gas
7.	1000	15	"	Gas		20000	15	"	"
	1000	15	"	"		20000	15	"	"
	2000	10	"	"		20000	15	"	"
	1000	1	"	"		10000	15	"	"
	1000	1 month	"	"		6266	35	"	Kerosene
8.	1000	25	"	"		6266	35	"	"
	2000	3	"	"		5631	35	"	"
	2000	3	"	"		6266	35	"	"
	2000	3	"	"		6266	35	"	"
9.	2000	10	"	"		6769	35	"	"
	4000	11	"	"	22.	4000	10	"	Gas
	3000	11	"	"		4000	10	"	"
	3000	11	"	"		3000	10	"	"
	1000	11	"	"		3000	25	"	"
10.	1000	12	"	"		3000	25	"	"
	1000	5	"	"	23.	1000	20	"	"
11.	1000	15	"	Diesel		1000	20	"	"
	1000	15	"	Gas	24.	2000	7	"	"
12.	10000	15	"	"		1000	7	"	"
	4000	15	"	"		1000	7	"	"
	4000	15	"	"		1000	7	"	Kerosene
	1000	15	"	Kerosene	25.	2000	11	"	Gas
13.	1000	12	"	Gas		2000	11	"	"
	1000	12	"	"					
	1000	12	"	"					

*Sites include reseller locations, large individual users, and bulk plant (No. 21).

Appendix D

Motor Fuel Marketers—Indust. Avg. Firms W/Assets $500M–$1MM
  Statement of Income for the Year ($000's)

	Year 1980	Year 1981	Year 1982	Year 1983	Year 1984	Year 1985
Gallons:						
Premium	3,936.0	2,920.0	3,189.0	3,532.0	542.4	380.8
Unleaded	0.0	0.0	0.0	0.0	1,286.3	1,193.4
Regular	0.0	0.0	0.0	0.0	1,385.2	2,241.8
Lube	0.0	0.0	0.0	0.0	0.0	0.0
Heating Oil	746.0	245.0	295.0	342.0	287.0	366.3
Diesel	777.0	853.0	920.0	982.0	1,558.4	1,241.1
Kerosene	0.0	0.0	0.0	0.0	59.2	71.3
Other Products	47.0	40.0	65.0	30.0	104.2	62.0
Total	5,506.0	4,058.0	4,469.0	4,886.0	5,222.7	5,556.7
Sales:						
Premium	0	0	0	0	0	0
Unleaded	0	0	0	0	0	0
Regular	0	0	0	0	0	0
Lube	0	0	0	0	0	0
Heating Oil	0	0	0	0	0	0
Diesel	0	0	0	0	0	0
Kerosene (Gasahol in '80)	0	0	0	0	0	0
Other Products	0	0	0	0	0	0
Net Sales	5,775.9	4,930.7	5,427.6	5,241.6	5,646.4	5,086.5
Cost of Sales:						
Beginning Inventory	0.0	158.5	135.4	140.4	143.5	97.7
Purchases Net of Discounts	5,402.0	4,510.2	5,000.1	4,816.5	5,117.3	4,595.7
	5,402.0	4,668.7	5,135.5	4,956.9	5,260.8	4,693.4
Ending Inventory	158.5	135.4	140.4	143.5	97.7	76.4
Cost of Sales	5,243.2	4,533.3	4,995.1	4,813.4	5,163.1	4,617.0
Gross Profit	532.7	397.4	432.5	428.2	483.3	469.5
Selling, General and Admin. Expenses						
Licenses and Non-Income Taxes	25.9	32.4	28.0	19.8	20.4	22.5
Vehicle Expense	69.9	65.2	61.7	58.4	58.5	63.6
Officers' Salaries	49.1	40.6	42.9	40.8	55.4	50.4
Other Salaries and Wages	152.0	104.5	115.2	118.6	96.5	126.2
Other Expense	140.4	81.8	109.7	115.2	144.2	125.9
Depreciation	39.3	37.4	37.9	44.3	53.1	50.6
Interest on Borrowing Needs	19.2	22.4	22.0	16.0	18.5	26.2
Operating Income (Loss)	36.9	13.1	15.1	15.1	36.7	4.1
Earnings on Marketable Securities	0.0	0.0	0.0	0.0	0.0	0.0
Other Income (Expense)	38.0	30.4	26.0	35.3	20.3	32.1
Earnings before Taxes	74.9	43.5	41.1	50.4	57.0	36.2
Provision for Federal Income Taxes	19.4	11.0	8.8	11.8	12.9	11.6
Net Income	55.5	32.5	32.3	38.6	44.1	24.6

Motor Fuel Marketers—Indust. Avg. Firms W/Assets $500M–$1MM
Balance Sheet as of 12/31

	($000's) Year 1980	Year 1981	Year 1982	Year 1983	Year 1984	Year 1985
Assets						
Current Assets						
Cash	79.7	54.2	67.5	87.2	64.7	34.2
Marketable Securities	19.4	14.5	12.8	17.6	6.4	14.8
Accounts Rec.	247.5	224.0	235.2	263.0	264.0	194.4
Inventories	158.5	135.4	140.4	143.5	97.7	76.4
Refundable Taxes	0.0	0.0	0.0	0.0	0.0	0.0
Prepaid Exp.	0.0	0.0	0.0	0.0	0.0	0.0
Notes Receivable	0.0	0.0	0.0	0.0	18.0	23.7
Other Current Assets	20.0	30.1	21.1	16.6	26.6	47.9
Total Current Assets	525.1	458.2	477.0	527.9	477.4	391.4
Property Plant and Equipment						
Land	0	0	0	0	0	0
Buildings	0	0	0	0	0	0
Equipment	0	0	0	0	0	0
Vehicles	0	0	0	0	0	0
Furniture and Fixtures	0	0	0	0	0	0
Total	0	0	0	0	0	0
Less Accumulated Depreciation	0	0	0	0	0	0
Net Property Plant and Equipment	287.1	225.4	215.5	248.8	244.9	218.7
Other Assets						
Long-Term Investments	0.0	0.0	0.0	0.0	10.7	28.9
Deposits and Licenses	0	0	0	0	0	0
Cash Surrender Value—Officers' Life Insurance	0	0	0	0	0	0
Loan Fees—Net	0	0	0	0	0	0
Advances to Affiliated Companies	0	0	0	0	0	0
Total Other Assets	25.4	20.6	25.5	29.1	23.2	43.9
Total Assets	837.6	704.2	718.0	805.8	745.5	654.0
Liabilities						
Current Liabilities						
Accounts Payable	237.7	200.1	190.3	203.2	166.9	121.0
Notes Payable	27.5	29.6	46.1	35.7	68.7	109.8
Current Portion of Long-Term Debt	30.9	15.9	15.4	12.7	0.0	0.0
Construction Loan Payable	0.0	0.0	0.0	0.0	0.0	0.0
Income Taxes Payable	0.0	0.0	0.0	0.0	6.9	1.5
Advances from Officers	0.0	0.0	0.0	0.0	0.0	0.0
Accrued Expenses	0.0	0.0	0.0	0.0	0.0	0.0
Other Current Liabilities	67.3	38.4	39.5	43.3	63.4	66.5
Other Financing Needed	0.0	0.0	0.0	0.0	0.0	0.0
Total Current Liabilities	363.0	284.0	291.3	294.9	305.9	298.8
Long-Term Debt	157.4	130.7	105.1	122.3	98.7	85.9
Other Long-Term	2.7	2.9	8.7	4.3	0.0	0.0
Total Liabilities	523.1	417.6	405.1	421.5	404.6	384.7
Owners' Equity	314.5	286.6	313.0	384.3	340.9	269.4
Total Liabilities and Owners' Equity	837.6	704.2	718.1	805.8	745.5	654.1

Motor Fuel Marketers—Indust. Avg. Firms W/Assets $500M-$1MM Ratio Analysis

Ratio Analysis	Year 1980	Year 1981	Year 1982	Year 1983	Year 1984	Year 1985
DuPont Analysis:						
Return on Sales	0.96%	0.66%	0.60%	0.74%	0.78%	0.48%
· Asset Turnover	6.90	7.00	7.56	6.50	7.57	7.78
= Return on Assets	6.63%	4.62%	4.50%	4.79%	5.92%	3.76%
· Financial Leverage	2.66	2.46	2.29	2.10	2.19	2.43
= Return on Equity	17.65%	11.34%	10.32%	10.04%	12.94%	9.13%
Gallonage DuPont:						
Return on Sales	1.01	0.80	0.72	0.79	0.84	0.44
· Asset Turnover	6.57	5.76	6.22	6.06	7.01	8.50
= Return on Assets	6.63%	4.62%	4.50%	4.79%	5.92%	3.76%
· Financial Leverage	2.66	2.46	2.29	2.10	2.19	2.43
= Return on Equity	17.65%	11.34%	10.32%	10.04%	12.94%	9.13%
Activity:						
Fixed Asset Turnover	20.12	21.88	25.19	21.07	23.06	23.26
Sales Growth (Dollars)	−14.63%	10.08%	−3.43%	7.72%	−9.92%	
Sales Growth (Gallons)	−26.30%	10.13%	9.33%	6.89%	6.40%	
Profitability:						
Gross Margin	9.22%	8.06%	7.97%	8.17%	8.56%	9.23%
Salaries Ratio	0.85%	0.82%	0.79%	0.78%	0.98%	0.99%
S,G, & A Ratio	7.57%	6.58%	6.59%	6.73%	6.64%	7.64%
Working Capital Usage:						
Days Payable	15.00	14.81	12.80	14.15	10.79	8.68
Collection Period (Days)	15.64	16.58	15.82	18.31	17.07	13.95
Days Inventory	10.02	10.02	9.44	9.99	6.32	5.48
Cash Cycle	10.66	11.79	12.46	14.16	12.59	10.75
Leverage:						
Total Debt/Assets	62.45%	59.30%	56.41%	52.31%	54.27%	58.81%
Long Term Debt/Assets	0.19	0.19	0.15	0.15	0.13	0.13
Times Interest EBIT	2.92	1.58	1.69	1.94	2.98	1.16
Liquidity:						
Current Ratio	1.45	1.61	1.64	1.79	1.56	1.31
Acid Test Ratio	1.01	1.14	1.16	1.30	1.24	1.05

Case 27

Brooktrout Technology, Inc.

It's violent out there, and people in violent industries sometimes get killed. It's violent because it's changing rapidly. There are bodies all over the place in the voice mail segment. Computerm, for example, has $14 million invested and sold out for a pittance.

There are some very big companies, like AT&T, that are our potential customers—but they can also produce their own electronic messaging products. When you go to these big companies it's like walking underneath elephants: you just hope the elephant doesn't step on you. But they don't move real fast, so you can watch out for them.

It was June of 1989, and Eric Giler, president of Brooktrout Technology, Inc., knew his company was at a crossroads.[1] What strategy would best bring the high growth he wanted, while minimizing risk? Giler faced tough choices in mar-

[1]This case has accompanying videotapes of Eric Giler in a question and answer session in front of an Executive MBA class that can be purchased from Northeastern University, College of Business Administration, Boston, MA 02115.

This case was prepared by Raymond M. Kinnunen and Wendy Vittori, of Northeastern University, and by John A. Seeger, of Bentley College, as a basis for class discussion. Financial statements have been disguised. Distributed by the North American Case Research Association. All rights reserved to the authors and the North American Case Research Association. Permission to use the case should be obtained from the authors and the North American Case Research Association. Copyright (c) 1990 Raymond M. Kinnunen and John A. Seeger. Reprinted with permission.

keting and finance as he wondered how to capitalize on his firm's technical skills.

Brooktrout designed and built electronic messaging systems—the equipment which automatically answers a business telephone and accepts a message for a specific individual. Some products were full systems in their own cabinets; others were separate electronic cards to be plugged into computers. Brooktrout sold mainly to original equipment manufacturers (OEMs) in the telecommunications industry. Its customers included some of the world's largest builders of telephone equipment.

Brooktrout Technology was founded in 1984 by Eric Giler, David Duehren, and Patrick Hynes; all had worked together previously at Teradyne, Inc. The new company lost money in each of its first five years, but Eric expected 1989 to be profitable, with sales approaching $5 million (Exhibit 1 shows financial data on the company). Eric commented,

> It's high risk, but also high reward. We can build a $100 million company in this business; after all, it's a multi-billion dollar industry. The expertise we have is our technology. We understand what makes it possible to do electronic messaging and our goal in life is to sell it on an OEM basis to companies that need it. We will make a product that is cheaper, or faster.

Telecommunications Industry: History

On January 8, 1982, American Telephone and Telegraph Company agreed to end its 48-year history as a regulated monopoly. In its total life-span of 106 years, the company had created the telecommunications system which served as a world model. AT&T provided local phone service through its wholly-owned geographic subsidiaries (e.g. New England Telephone and Telegraph) to 80% of American homes. Through its Western Electric manufacturing arm, it made virtually all of the nation's telephone equipment. Through its Bell Laboratories—renowned as the leading electronics R&D center of the world—it developed new technologies (including, for example, the first transistors.) Unfettered by competition, AT&T devoted itself to providing superb quality and service. By regulation, it was assured a profit based on its investment. AT&T's assets base thus grew phenomenally; by 1984, when the company was divided, its total of $150 billion in assets dwarfed the size of most nations' economies. In assets and profits, AT&T was the largest company in the world.

For most of its history, to preserve the quality of its lines, AT&T absolutely prohibited any other company's equipment from being attached to its network. The historic Carterfone decision in 1968 made it legal for non-Bell equipment to be attached to public lines; the first privately-owned telephone answering machine, barred by AT&T for years, now had to be admitted to the network and the market for terminal equipment was opened.

As a monopoly, AT&T had been restrained from competing in the open marketplace; at the same time it was often criticized for commercial practices which made market penetration difficult for makers of specialized terminal equipment. In the industry, it was widely thought that AT&T saw itself as the major potential competitor to IBM in the computer industry. In the 1982 agreement, settling an anti-trust suit by the government, the company officially acceded to being dismantled. Its local telephone operating companies, still working as regulated monopolies, were spun off into seven regional holding companies. The breakup—the largest financial transaction in world history—was completed in late 1983. AT&T was now free to compete. (See Exhibits 2 and 3 for comparative sizes of the units, before and after the breakup.)

Telecommunications Industry: Structure

The telecommunications industry consisted of three major segments—local telephone companies, long distance carriers, and telephone equipment manufacturers—and one relatively small segment, information products and services, where Brooktrout Technology competed. (Exhibit 4 gives examples of leading entrants in all four segments.)

The information products and services segment resulted from the combination of computer and telecommunications technologies during the 1980s. These combined technologies made it possible for data to be processed as well as transmitted by the communications networks, thus creating "intelligent communications" (new products combining hardware innovations, computer technology, and software). By 1989, this segment of the telecommunications industry was a hotbed of competitive marketing activity, with contenders ranging from heavyweights like AT&T's own Bell Laboratories, to entrepreneurial newcomers such as Brooktrout Technology, Inc.

Local Exchange Operators

Before deregulation, local telephone companies were the only source for all telephone equipment and services. After deregulation, many vendors began to supply the market. Businesses began to purchase and install their own private branch exchanges (PBXs), which performed all the telephone functions that were internal to a given business. PBXs were sold based on lower costs, more features, and greater control for a business over its phone usage than the telephone company's standard service could offer.

With competition increasing, local telephone companies enhanced the level of service they provided beyond simple transmission. Since pricing on local phone calls was regulated, their principal competitive weapons were additional services. The telephone companies turned to the private sector for equipment they could sell in competition with the industry newcomers. Thus the new manufacturers of telecommunications equipment had two markets—one to businesses, and another to the telephone companies who in turn sold to businesses.

New opportunities for products and services continued to grow. In 1988, a court decision permitted local telephone companies to transmit information services. Options such as call-forwarding and call-waiting could now be offered to even single-line subscribers. In the future lay provision of services such as stock quotations and transactions, and merchandise selection and purchase, all through the telephone company. A recent advance allowed multiple phone numbers to be channeled to a single line, a cost-effective solution for home businesses with only one phone line. Publishing and computer/telecommunications integration were major new business thrusts.

Long-Distance Carriers

Long distance transmission continued to be dominated by AT&T following deregulation, with 87% of the long distance customers handled by AT&T in 1988. The only major competitors to AT&T were MCI and US Sprint, each with 5–6% of the customer base. Both of these new firms were pursuing high-growth strategies in 1989 based on the lower cost and higher quality of fiber optic, microwave and satellite transmission technologies.

Low costs were vital in selling telecommunications services to business. Dedicated long distance services, where a corporation owned its own satellite network, were also attracting a share of the total long distance transmissions in the United States. Long-distance carriers were beginning to install these end-to-end transmission services for large customers. This connected long-distance service directly to a PBX, eliminating the need to connect via the local exchange.

Telephone Equipment Manufacturers

After deregulation, the decision on what equipment to buy and where to install it was made by the customer, who could lease or purchase as much or as little equipment as desired, from a vendor of its choice. Private branch exchange (PBX) equipment sales grew tremendously, breaking $3 billion per year in 1988.

Twenty years after the Carterfone decision, the market for "customer premise" equipment had grown to $8 billion per year, but the growth rate was expected to slow from 8.7% in 1988 to 4.8% by 1992. Several larger firms (AT&T, Northern Telecom, Siemens) together controlled more than 50% of the market. However, smaller manufacturers, like TIE Communications, had made inroads by offering lower prices, enhanced features (least-cost routing, voice messaging, and other advanced exchange and information services), quality of service, testing, and maintenance. Under this kind of competitive pressure, prices of electronic components fell by half every two to three years.

Small entrepreneurial manufacturers and software houses (like Brooktrout Technology) provided many of the innovations behind new services. These small firms might sell to the larger equipment firms, to the regional Bell operating companies, and/or to the end users themselves. Acquisition and merger activity was high (see Exhibit 5), as larger firms brought these high-technology skills in-house.

Information Products and Services

The compound annual growth rate for the information products and services segment was forecast to be approximately 25% from 1988 to

1992.[2] Some of the major subsegments (examples are given in Exhibit 4) were Data Access and Retrieval, Transaction Processing, and Electronic Messaging (the segment where Brooktrout Technology competed).

Electronic Messaging products allowed users to send and receive messages from other users, by voice, data, or image transmission. The messaging product either replaced or augmented a person-to-person phone conversation. Specific examples included electronic mail, facsimile, and voice messaging.

Principal "Voice Store and Forward" (VSF) products were telephone attendant systems, voice messaging, and voice response systems. Telephone attendant systems replaced a switchboard operator with an automated system—a "silicon Sally" computerized voice which prompted the caller to enter codes in order to route a call to the proper extension. Voice messaging provided for recording, storing, and playing back messages, as with a simple telephone answering machine but using a much more flexible computer storage and retrieval technology. Voice response systems could carry on a dialogue with the caller in order to perform functions such as order-taking and account inquiry.

Although VSF was a small subsegment within the overall telecommunications industry, in 1989 it was growing very rapidly (see Exhibit 6). From revenues of $200 million in 1986 and $426 million in 1988, the VSF segment was expected to reach $1 billion in 1990.[3]

Voice Store and Forward
Brooktrout Technology in 1989 competed in the Voice Store and Forward segment, with products in both voice messaging and facsimile messaging. A VSF system was based on a technology known as "digital signal processing," used to capture voice signals and convert them into a string of

digital "bits" which could be computer processed. Only a few VSF manufacturers, such as Brooktrout, had developed in-house expertise in this basic technology.

Traditionally, voice-processing applications had required the processing power of a host minicomputer, and products based on these large systems still represented the vast majority of the market in 1989 (see Exhibit 7). However, the new generation of more powerful personal computers was creating an increasingly strong alternative for low-end VSF host computers. In fact, the market researcher, Dataquest, had predicted:

> The low-end segment [of VSF] brings to the voice messaging market what PCs brought to the computer industry—cost-effective, flexible, powerful applications processors for small to medium-size businesses or organizations.

Others had forecast that PC-based systems were not likely to achieve significant market share, because telephone answering machines and service bureaus could provide the services needed by a small user at a lower cost (almost no cost with a telephone answering machine). Service bureaus used large-scale VSF systems based on mini or mainframe computer hosts, and rented voice messaging services to companies without their own on-site VSF systems. This could be a cost-effective alternative to PC-based systems for small users who needed the sophisticated capabilities of VSF. Even larger firms were contracting service bureaus for voice services. Probe Research, Inc., forecast VSF service bureau revenues to be $271 million by 1990.

Local telephone companies were also looking at the opportunities that voice messaging might offer. Ameritech, one of the regional Bell companies, had acquired Tigon Corp., the nation's largest voice messaging service bureau (with corporate clients like Ford Motor Co.), in late 1988. Bell Atlantic had recently contracted with Boston Technology, a small voice messaging company founded in 1986, for its newly introduced central-office-based voice processing

---

[2] *Telephony*, May 16, 1988.

[3] "Voice Mail Matures: Sales Boom as Applications Explode." *Teleconnect*, September, 1988.

system. Although Boston Technology had first developed small, stand-alone systems, "from the beginning, we believed that there was a need for a huge voice processing system," said Greg Carr, the firm's president. "Their proposal got our attention immediately," commented Kathy Maier, Bell Atlantic's product manager for enhanced voice services. "Its size—1536 ports, 7000 hours of voice storage capacity, support of 104,000 voice mailboxes—is a major factor."[4]

Facsimile machines were the most recent addition to the electronic messaging segment. These machines, which were priced as low as $600 in 1989, used digital signal processing technology similar to that used in VSF to transmit images via telephone lines. Sales of facsimile machines in 1988 of $2.2 billion were projected to reach $6.6 billion by 1992.[5]

Electronic mail involved computer-to-computer communication of data (rather than voice) messages. Although more expensive and not so easy to use as VSF or facsimile (because it required specialized training for each user), electronic mail had the great advantage of transmitting both messages and data in a format that could be understood and further manipulated by computer programs.

Distribution

The distribution system for Information Products and Services was complex. For example, all of the following were being used to distribute Voice Store and Forward systems.

Local Exchange Operators. Telephone companies purchased VSF equipment on an OEM basis, to build into the equipment they sold for their own telephone services, such as Centrex. GTE, for example, offered many services including Telemessager (voice mail) and Telemail (electronic mail).

---

[4] *Telephony*, November 14, 1988.
[5] *Communications Week*, February 20, 1989.

Telephone Equipment Manufacturers (OEMs). These firms purchased and incorporated VSF products into their own devices, such as PBXs. In some cases, they would simply license the VSF technology and manufacture the actual products themselves. Many of these manufacturers would customize their VSF systems in order to differentiate their end products in the mind of the end-user, even though the components might have a common origin. The identity of the VSF manufacturer was generally not revealed in the end product. Prominent among these original equipment manufacturers were AT&T, Rolm, TIE, and Iwatsu. The largest suppliers of VSF products to OEMs were Brooktrout, Genesis, and AT&E.

Telephone System Dealers. Dealers were either independent or affiliated with an equipment manufacturer. Independent dealers generally carried multiple brands of business telephone systems, PBXs, and other telecommunications equipment. There had been an increasing trend for equipment manufacturers to integrate forward by purchasing independent dealers. As a result, some of the dealers sold only one brand of equipment (e.g. Rolm or GTE), while others still represented multiple brands. Dealers generally provided complete installation and maintenance service.

Service Bureaus. Purchased large VSF systems to be time-shared by both small and large businesses.

Computer Stores. Low-end VSF systems could be sold as add-on circuit boards for personal computers, through computer stores.

Direct Sales. Some firms, most notably Natural Microsystems, had promoted and sold their products directly to end-users, using methods such as direct mail or advertising directed to the personal computer owner.

Historically, PC-based VSF systems had been sold principally on an OEM basis to the telephone equipment manufacturers. Some two-thirds of VSF manufacturers' revenues were derived from OEMs. The remaining third was split between direct sales and computer and telephone system dealers.

Industry Trends

Several key trends were apparent to the telecommunications equipment industry at the end of the 1980s. Competition seemed likely to intensify. World-wide markets were likely to appear as multinational firms spread their use of electronic messaging and overseas telephone companies upgraded their services. Prices were expected to decline as Asian manufacturers and new entrants brought lower costs into mainstream products. Continued reduction of the regulations on the Bell Operating Companies could translate to faster market expansion and larger shares for their OEM purchases. Rapid acceptance of new technologies, as exemplified by the history of the facsimile machine, could make any new product an overnight phenomenon. The appearance of new applications for electronic messaging products was likely, but what they would be was unknown.

In technology, customers and suppliers alike were pushing for adoption of industry-wide communications standards, rather than vendor-specific codes. This trend influenced the entire computer/software industry; it would eliminate the many difficulties that existed in 1989 in transferring information across networks containing hardware from many different makers. Information service providers stood to benefit directly from standardization, as their products could be used on a wider array of equipment.

In 1989, the information products and services industry was dynamic, complex, and highly unpredictable. A key phrase for the future of the telecommunications industry appeared to be system integration. One industry analyst stated:

Computers can switch phone calls, and PBXs can do computing. [We can] predict a day, perhaps five or ten years away, when system integration for the business customer will include not only telephone service but word processing, commercial data processing, and facsimile data transmission.[6]

Brooktrout Technology, Inc.: History

In 1984, Eric Giler, Dave Duehren, and Pat Hynes—a technical marketer and two design engineers—founded Brooktrout Technology to take advantage of the technical ideas they had begun to think about at their previous jobs. With their expertise in digital signal processing, they felt they could integrate voice messaging with text, graphics, image processing, and data communications—putting all the functions into a single piece of hardware.

Armed with a business plan projecting $3 million in sales the first year, they began to seek financing. Eric Giler reflected on the early efforts:

We thought at first that raising capital would be easy. But when we tried, we found doors closing on use for two reasons. One, we were young. Second, the venture capitalists couldn't believe that people would talk to machines, even if the systems worked perfectly. So for the first six months we operated the company out of an apartment.

Eric and his partners decided to seek money privately, and in several private placements in the first two years raised $1.5 million from approximately 50 investors. In 1987, a major telephone equipment manufacturer injected $1 million in cash for a minority equity position. By 1989 Brooktrout had raised a total of $2.5 million to finance its growth, and was anticipating its first profitable year (Exhibit 1 shows financial data and projections). The founders, equal own-

---

[6] Gerald R. Faulhaber, *Telecommunications in Turmoil: Technology and Public Policy.* Cambridge, MA, Ballinger, 1987, pp. 129–130.

ers from the beginning, still retained a 30% ownership stake in Brooktrout.

Eric Giler, Brooktrout's president had received an undergraduate degree in management science from Carnegie-Mellon and an MBA from Harvard (in 1982). Pat Hynes (V.P. of Engineering) and Dave Duehren (V.P. of R&D), were electrical engineers. Both had bachelors degrees from M.I.T.; Duehren's M.S. was also from M.I.T., while Hynes's was from Columbia. Hynes, an avid trout fisherman, chose the name for the new company.

In 1987 Eric hired Stephan Ide, a twenty-year veteran in telecommunications and a former consultant to Brooktrout, as Vice President of Sales and Marketing. Ide had founded and served as president of Computer Telephone Corp., a publicly-held company with $14 million in sales. In 1988, Bob Leahy, former Controller and Treasurer of Cambridge Robotic Systems, was hired as Treasurer. Leahy, holder of a B.S. in Accounting from Bentley College, brought a diverse background in high-technology finance. Eric was comfortable with the progress they had made building the top management team as well as the technical organization; by mid-1989, six additional engineers—hired directly out of local colleges—supplemented the efforts of Hynes and Duehren. Another five worked in production and seven in marketing. "We have the team in place; now we have to figure out how to grow it," said Eric.

Brooktrout Products

The first products to be made by Brooktrout were for voice messaging. At the time, Eric Giler said, this seemed the most logical segment to enter: the technology was just beginning to take off, while the facsimile machine as an image communication device was not that far along. They then moved into the imaging segment with a circuit board facsimile messaging system ("Fax-Mail"), which enabled computer data to be translated electronically into facsimile images. With Fax-Mail, a PC user could send a computer file straight to the facsimile transmitter, without printing out the image first. (See Exhibit 8 for a description of Brooktrout's voice and fax products in mid-1989).

In mid-1989, Fax-Mail was sold at retail to end users for installation in their own personal computers, at a price of $499. The voice messaging products ranged in price from $5,000 to $20,000 retail. Most were sold to OEMs, at discounts up to 50 percent.

Brooktrout also did some design work under contract to specific customers. (Even AT&T had made inquiries about Brooktrout's capabilities.) A current contract with a major manufacturer was developing data transfer between modems and facsimile machines. A major advantage of designing under contract was avoiding the need to raise additional capital for the research effort. However, in the end Brooktrout might not have full rights to the products they developed.

Brooktrout Strategy

Traditionally, individual companies specialized in either voice, data, or image communication. Brooktrout believed these three modes of communication would become integrated in the near future, as the technology of digital signal processing became cheaper and better. Eric commented:

> Nobody does all three. Our goal over the long term is to provide solutions in all three areas, for all the major telecommunications and computer manufacturers. We want to do something different from what other people are doing, based on our expertise in technology and our understanding of what makes electronic messaging possible.

Brooktrout estimated it had 5 to 10% of the voice segment market, selling against 30 to 40 competitors. Several of those were achieving success by selling further down the distribution channel, directly to dealers. Brooktrout, on the other hand, still sold its voice mail products mainly to OEMs. An advantage to selling to the OEMs, Eric said, was the ready access gained to certain segments of the industry. For instance, TIE Communications had developed a product suing Brooktrout's technology that they sold to the Bell Operating Companies. TIE had access to the people in Nynex, Ameritech, etc., where Brooktrout did not.

Occasionally Brooktrout was called upon by their OEMs to assist in developing end-user applications for their products. Although this required additional effort, successful applications translated directly into more demand for Brooktrout's products.

Brooktrout had major OEM agreements for its voice and fax products with TIE, the second largest Customer Premise Equipment (CPE) supplier of small business phone systems behind AT&T, and with the American division of Iwatsu, a major Japanese equipment manufacturer. Both TIE and Iwatsu built Brooktrout products into their own offerings; both also labeled the Brooktrout equipment with their own name and sold it separately. TIE's dealers sold only TIE products, where Iwatsu dealers also sold products made by other manufacturers.

Although Eric felt that selling to OEMs was the best bet for the future, his sales department saw things differently. They believed the company could grow more rapidly by promoting and selling through dealers. Eric reported

> What the salespeople are saying is, "Here we have stuff we can sell now. We can make money. We can sell lots of them." The problem I have is that our organization is not set up to deal directly with dealers.

All the sales department employees had either worked for dealers or owned their own dealerships. Eric felt, however, that the Brooktrout organization was not prepared to meet the needs of dealers or the dealers' customers. For example, operating manuals and instruction books would be required, along with 24 hour telephone and technical support. He said,

> We can sell to dealers to the extent it furthers our OEM goals. To the extent it isn't supporting those goals, I'm not sure it's worth it. Recently a potential investor complained about our selling to OEMs. He said, "Oh, that's the wrong way to do it. What you do is sell to users, then the users like it and they tell the dealers; the dealers like it and they tell the manufacturers, and the manufacturers have to have it."
>
> I never thought of it that way. The reason I never thought of it is simple: that's what you do when you have money!

Although distribution was an important consideration, many industry experts felt that market timing was also a critical success factor. The major task was to build a competitive product. Once the product was sold to an OEM and incorporated in its products, it became very difficult for competitors to dislodge it. Eric commented,

> The biggest competitive advantage I've seen in this business is what I call the first mover advantage. The guy who's first to do something kicks ass. It doesn't matter what anyone else does. Over the long haul, that's our best bet. And it probably doesn't matter where in the channel you sell as long as you're the first mover.
>
> Anyone can do anything—that's my premise. I have never seen anything in technology that is totally proprietary. You have to be careful though. There are also the pioneers with arrows in their backs; I've seen a bit of that also.

Sometimes being first was not that easy. The facsimile circuit board for personal computers was first introduced by a small California firm, Gamma Fax, while Brooktrout's similar product—fully designed and ready for production—sat on the shelf. Eric had felt the market wasn't ready: "naw, fax for personal computers? Who understands that stuff?" Now Brooktrout had to make up for the first-to-market advantage that Gamma Fax had captured.

The Future
Eric and his partners aimed to be the first company to fully integrate voice, data, and image

messaging—"tying all these things together; that's the long-term vision." Brooktrout would soon have the key technology they needed for that integrated product, as a result of one of their current development contracts. To exploit the new opportunity, however, would take more capital and other resources than Brooktrout had available in mid-1989.

> I have the product idea: a voice machine that will let a company handle requests for literature with no human intervention at all. The customers call in and the machine asks what they want. When it defines what literature they want, the machine faxes the stuff to them instantly. The customer should love it: he doesn't even have to wait for the mail, much less for some clerk to fill the request. There isn't any other product like that, anywhere.
>
> If I had the money I would pursue it right now. I know it's going to hit. But I have to consider the effects of more stock dilution. I'd really prefer not to sell any stock.
>
> But people don't operate strategically on a day-to-day basis. If a venture capitalist called me right now and made the right kind of deal I would take the dilution.

Eric was at a crossroads. He knew that the capital structure of Brooktrout, with fifty shareholders, was not very attractive to venture capitalists. It had actually scared some away. And he had other products, too, which had not been brought to market because of capital needs.

He wanted to bet on the new product where literature could be requested over the phone. That concept was very different. It would allow Brooktrout to diversify its customer base and, if successful, could possibly get them to the point of going public or being acquired by a larger company. But, he asked, what market channel would best reach all the potential users of such a product?

Eric also knew that there was some merit in selling directly to dealers as the salespeople wanted, and that being first was the "best possible thing to do."

> Say we go out and raise more money and get diluted. Does the stock's value get pumped up? Some of the investors want out now. We have fifty investors and there's not a day that goes by that I don't talk to one of them.
>
> If I had the capital resources right now I would just be the best voice and fax company around. There is nobody there yet. We know it's going to be a big market; it doesn't take a rocket scientist to figure that out. It does take some thinking about how you want to position yourself, because it's a very fragmented set of business opportunities. Do you want a turnkey setup? Do you want to sell to OEMs? Do you want to build a system or do you want to just sell components?
>
> This is a very complex industry. There are people who spend their lives trying to figure this stuff out; they get paid a lot of money for being wrong. I've never seen so many consultants in all my life.

When asked where he thought Brooktrout would be in five years, Eric replied:

> Five years is too long to project in a violent industry. I would probably like to see the harvest point before that. If your business is really hot, it's very hard to maintain your independence, because the thing grows and you get assimilated into something whether you want to or not. Ultimately, you go public or you get acquired. We just want to keep playing the game—growing the beast as big as we can.
>
> From a personal perspective, it will be fun at $10 million [in sales]. That's when it starts to get fun. You're not playing around as much, and you have enough mass to expect the bottom line to hit about 15%. That's what I'd like to see.

Exhibit 1 Brooktrout Technology, Inc.

Statement of Operations ($000)

	1985	1986	1987	1988	Projected 1989	Projected 1990
Revenues						
Voice					$3,490	$6,396
Facsimile					1,231	3,444
Total Revenues	$271	$ 510	$1,378	$2,418	$4,721	$9,840
Cost of Sales						
Voice					1,920	3,518
Facsimile					391	1,722
Total Cost of Sales	114	191	566	1,076	2,311	5,240
Gross Profit	157	319	812	1,342	2,410	4,600
Operating Expenses						
Sales and Marketing	79	134	425	682	685	1,118
Research and Development	214	553	354	568	726	1,332
General and Administrative	289	622	474	422	568	925
Total Expenses	582	1,309	1,253	1,672	1,979	3,375
Net Interest Expense	(5)	(175)	(391)	(120)	(110)	(198)
Net Income/(Loss)	($430)	($1,165)	($ 832)	($ 450)	$ 321	$1,027

Financial Statements Balance Sheet ($000)

	1985	1986	1987	1988
Assets				
Current Assets				
Cash	$ 96	$ 82	$ 274	$ 122
Accounts Receivable	115	74	318	402
Inventory	62	44	124	236
Other Current Assets	0	26	5	24
Total Currents Assets	273	226	721	784
Property and Equipment (net of accumulated depreciation)	86	81	101	119
Other Assets	26	16	13	8
Total Assets	$385	$ 323	$ 834	$ 912
Liabilities and Shareholders' Equity				
Current Liabilities				
Accounts Payable	110	126	254	440
Notes Payable	72	160	102	90
Current Portion of Long-Term Debt	12	28	85	84
Other Liabilities	70	71	86	140
Total Current Liabilities	264	385	527	754
Notes Payable to Stockholders	88	416	578	548
Other Long-term Debt	6	340	300	331
Total Liabilities	358	1,141	1,405	1,633
Net Stockholders' Equity	28	(818)	(571)	(722)
Total Liabilities and Stockholders' Equity	$385	$ 323	$ 834	$ 912

Exhibit 2 Brooktrout Technology, Inc. Values and Operating Results of Leading Telephone Companies (All figures in millions of dollars)

	Assets	Sales	Market Value	Net Profit
AT&T (1983)	149,530	69,403	59,392	5,747
AT&T (1988)	35,152	35,210	30,868	−1,669
Bell Operating Companies, 1988				
Ameritech	19,163	9,903	12,888	1,237
Bell Atlantic	24,729	10,880	14,013	1,317
BellSouth	28,472	13,597	18,504	1,666
Nynex	25,378	12,661	12,997	1,315
Pacific Telesis	21,191	9,483	12,934	1,188
Southwestern Bell	20,985	8,453	12,129	1,060
U.S. West	22,416	9,221	10,548	1,132
Other firms, 1988				
GTE	31,104	16,460	14,520	1,225
MCI Communications	5,843	5,137	5,498	356

Source: "The Forbes 500s," *Forbes*, April 30, 1984 and May 1, 1989.

Exhibit 3 Brooktrout Technology, Inc.

Rankings of Leading Telephone Companies

(figures give rank among the top 500 American businesses, including banks and financial services firms)

	Assets	Sales	Market Value	Net Profit
AT&T (1983)	1	3	2	1
AT&T (1988)	36	9	4	n/m
Bell Operating Companies, 1988				
Ameritech	85	66	28	19
Bell Atlantic	63	51	22	16
BellSouth	52	38	12	13
Nynex	60	41	26	17
Pacific Telesis	75	72	27	24
Southwestern Bell	79	83	32	30
U.S. West	69	73	38	27
Other Firms, 1988				
GTE	41	32	20	20
MCI Communications	271	154	81	142

n/m = not meaningful.
Source: "The Forbes 500s," *Forbes*, April 30, 1984 and May 1, 1989.

Exhibit 4

Segments of the Industry (and Examples of Active Competitors)

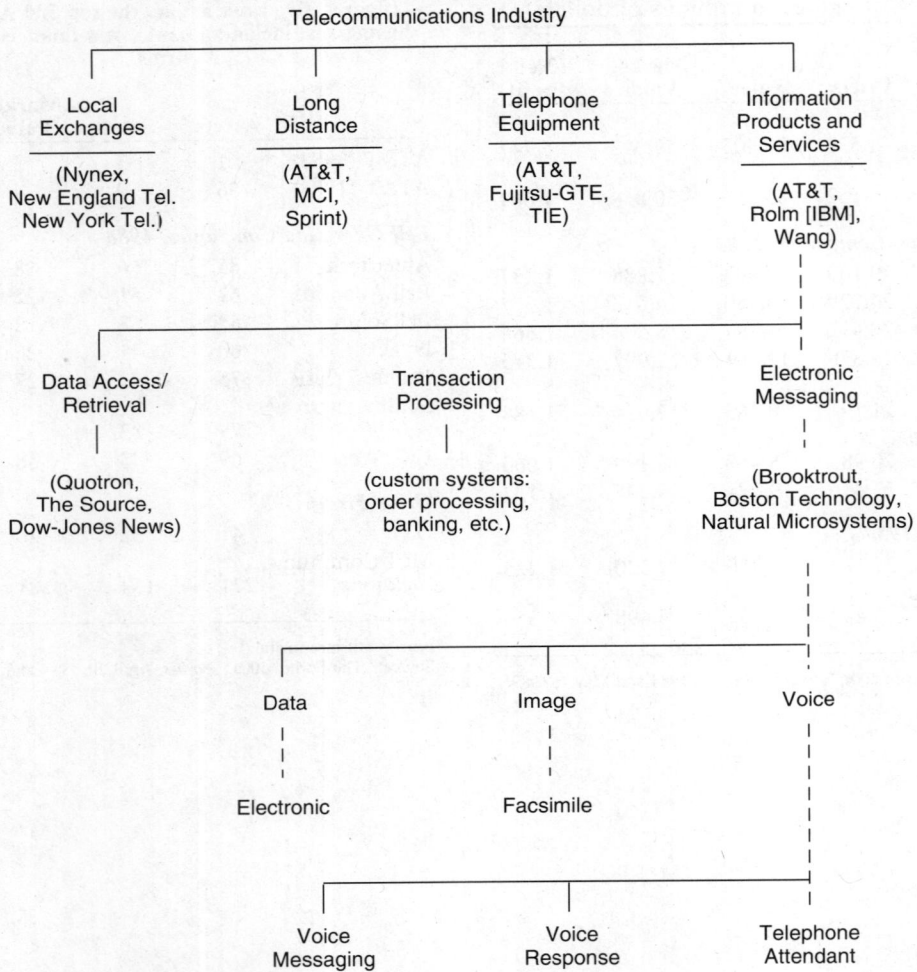

Telecommunications Industry

Local Exchanges	Long Distance	Telephone Equipment	Information Products and Services
(Nynex, New England Tel. New York Tel.)	(AT&T, MCI, Sprint)	(AT&T, Fujitsu-GTE, TIE)	(AT&T, Rolm [IBM], Wang)

Data Access/ Retrieval	Transaction Processing	Electronic Messaging
(Quotron, The Source, Dow-Jones News)	(custom systems: order processing, banking, etc.)	(Brooktrout, Boston Technology, Natural Microsystems)

Data	Image	Voice
Electronic	Facsimile	

Voice Messaging	Voice Response	Telephone Attendant

Exhibit 5   Brooktrout Technology, Inc.

Merger and Acquisition Activity in Consumer Premises Equipment Firms
(Representative Activity, 1987–1988)

| | C.P.E. Sales ($ millions) | | | |
	1986	1987	1988[a]	Acquired by
CPE Manufacturer				
Contel/Executone	$268	$305	$335*	Isotek/Vodavi
Tel Plus Comm., Inc.	255	283*	320	Siemens
RCA Telephone Systems	120	130	140*	Mitel
Universal Comm. Systems	87	106*	n/a	BellSouth
Jarvis Corp.	36	38*	40	Isotec
All American Businessphones	25	28	30*	TIE[b]
Gray Communications	25	22	25*	AIM Tel
Henkel & McCoy/Telecom	19	21*	25	Star Datacom
Interconnect Comm. Corp.	7	22*	38	Inter-Tel
	$842	$955		

*Year of acquisition.
[a]Estimated sales following acquisition.
[b]Acquisition proposed.
Source: *Telephony*, April 11, 1988.

Exhibit 6 Brooktrout Technology, Inc.

The Market for Telecommunications, 1988
(in $ millions)

	1988 Revenues	Projected Compound Annual Growth Rate*
Public Network Services		
Local Services	$ 87,558	
Long Distance Services	52,400	
Cellular/Public Data Nets	2,842	
Total Network Services	$142,800	
Business Communications Equipment Market: Voice		
Private Branch Exchanges (PBXs)	$ 3,182	2.6%
Key Systems	2,316	0.9
Facsimile	1,041	17.8
Voice Messaging	426	23.6
Automated Call Distribution	284	7.1
Call Accounting	281	4.4
Video Teleconferencing	264	26.5
Phones	125	6.9
Integrated Voice-Data Terminals	73	2.9
Total Voice Equipment Market	$ 7,992	
Business Communications Equipment Market: Data		
Local Area Networks	$ 2,400	22.4%
Modems	1,200	−6.2
Front-end Processors	625	6.7
Network Management Systems	457	13.8
Private Packet Switching	432	17.0
T-1 Multiplexors	403	12.9
Statistical Multiplexors	299	−5.5
Circuit/Data Switching Units	122	12.7
Data PBXs	85	−4.7
Total Data Equipment Market	$ 6,023	

*Estimated annual growth rates for the period 1988–1992
Source: Dataquest, Inc., *Forecast '88*

Exhibit 7   Brooktrout Technology, Inc.

VSF Equipment Market (1987)

System Size	Number of Ports*	System Size as % of Total Market	% Market Share for Segment Size	
Large Systems (main-frame)	32–1500	52%	Rolm	45
			AT&T	13
Medium Systems (mini-computer)	8–32	47	Centigram	17
			Opcom	17
			Rolm	14
			Wang	13
			Digital Sound	11
			Genesis	11
			AT&T	3
Small Systems (personal computer)	1–8	1	Natural Microsystems	30
			Brooktrout	20
			AT&T	15

*Ports are the number of telephone lines a system is capable of accommodating simultaneously. System capacities here are estimates by Eric Giler.
Source: Frost and Sullivan, Report Number A1867, 1988 (quoted with permission)

Exhibit 8   Brooktrout Technology, Inc.

Brooktrout Products, as of Mid-1989

Voice Messaging:

Operator Plus
- Advanced call processing systems for small and medium sized companies.
- Automated attendant, voice messaging, and voice response capabilities.
- Digital Signal Processing technology to record, store, and play back digitized human voice.
- Up to six ports capacity.
- Up to 24 hours of stored messages.

V-Mail 210/DID
- Allows outside callers to leave messages for individuals without dialing extensions, mailbox numbers, etc.
- Each user assigned an individual Direct Inward Dial number.
- Ideal for answering services, voice mail service bureaus, and cellular telephone sites.

Phoneware 470
- Development system.
- Speeds creation of telephone-based speech processing applications software.
- Ideal for voice-prompted order entry, voice bulletin boards, and information dissemination.

Fax Messaging:

Fax-Mail Systems
- Complete hardware/software systems.
- Allows personal computers and fax machines to communicate worldwide over standard telephone lines.
- Plugs into any IBM PC/XT/AT or compatible computer.
- Permits PCs to receive transmissions from fax machines, store files on disk, display them on PC monitors, or print them out.
- Compatible with CCITT Group III fax (machines transmitting a letter-sized page in less than one minute).

Case 28

Environcare

The Lawn Care Industry

In 1984, about 14,000 companies will provide about $2.75 billion worth of lawn care services for over four million residences. In 1982 lawn service revenues totaled $1.85 billion. Total revenues have increased by almost 50 percent in just two years.

Thirty-nine chemical lawn care companies had revenues in excess of $1 million in 1983, a 75 percent increase over 1978, when 22 firms had sales above $1 million.

It is estimated that only 16 percent of the potential market—50 million single-family residences—has been penetrated. The market has grown at a rate of 30 percent to 35 percent per year from 1975 to 1983, and it is forecast to continue at the same rate of growth for the next eight years.

Most lawn care firms are privately owned and have annual revenues of less than $200,000. However, the giant of the industry, Chem-Lawn, whose headquarters is in Columbus, Ohio, had $200 million in 1983 sales. It has 167 branches throughout the United States and served 1.3 million homes in 1983. The larger lawn care companies, such as Chem-Lawn, Lawn Doctor, Ever-Green Lawns, Orkin Lawn Care, and Nitro-Green Corporation, either own their own branch operations or have franchise units throughout the United States.

This case was prepared by James W. Clinton, Professor of Management, University of Northern Colorado, Greeley, Colorado, as a basis for class discussion rather than to illustrate either effective or ineffective organizational practices. Presented at Midwest Case Writers Association Workshop, 1984. Reprinted with permission.

Chemicals are used not only to nurture lawns but also to control pests, both inside and outside of residences and commercial establishments. Firms that provide residential pest control include the Orkin Exterminating Company, the largest in the world, Airex, and numerous other local and regional companies. The control of pests in lawns, trees, and bushes (termed ornamentals) is generally handled by firms other than those that provide interior structural applications. The lawn care firms usually do not compete against exterior pest control firms since the latter spray trees and ornamentals, utilizing spray equipment of a different technology and applying chemicals that are primarily preventive and not restorative—as is the case in lawn care.

Landscaping firms, another segment of outside home care, are concerned with the design of a lawn or garden, the selection of appropriate grasses, trees, flowers, and ornamentals. They utilize their creative talents to create a unique lawn and garden that is tailored to each customer's preferences. They are not at all like the lawn care and pest control specialists that apply similar chemicals to most of the residences that they treat.

Also concerned with residential exterior care are those individuals or companies that trim, cut down, and remove trees. They utilize high-technology tree, limb, and leaf shredders and "cherry-picker" extension vehicles to trim or remove tall tree branches. Trees are removed either to improve the aesthetic appearance of the residence or to eliminate a blighted or diseased condition.

Growth and Development of the Industry

The growth and prosperity of professional lawn care companies and those firms that provide related services are due to a combination of the factors discussed below.

Health Concerns

The public is concerned about the possible harmful health effects associated with handling chemicals. The chemical, DDT, was an acceptable pesticide for use around the home and garden for some time after World War II. Rachel Carson's 1962 book, *Silent Spring,* alerted the public that our environment was being adversely affected by the indiscriminate use of chemicals. The public began to carefully scrutinize the use of chemicals in pest control and lawn care after it was learned that "Agent Orange," which was used as a defoliant—destroyer of all growing plants—in the Vietnam War, may also have caused major injury to those who conducted the aerial applications of this herbicide or who were present in the areas contaminated by it.

Today there is increased public concern and awareness of the dangers and toxicity of certain chemicals. Consumers are more wary of manufacturer's claims and also are apprehensive about the potential hazards associated with the use of chemicals on their own lawns, trees, plants, and shrubs. Because of this awareness, and their sensitivity to the dangers of being exposed to or ingesting hazardous chemicals, homeowners are more willing to allow chemical lawn care firms to look after their property.

Leisure Time

Homeowners, until 5 or 10 years ago, tended to spend a great deal of time around their homes on weekends, performing miscellaneous chores and making minor home repairs. Today's homeowners place a greater value on their leisure time and prefer to engage in activities other than yard work. The lawn professionals are willing to perform these services, which many homeowners now disdain and consider to be drudgery, for a fee.

Economics

Families today have larger incomes because there are now more families with two wage earners and they can afford the lawn care fees. In addition, because it buys its chemicals in bulk in wholesale quantities, it is frequently possible for the lawn care service to treat a lawn more cheaply than if the homeowner were to purchase the materials at a retail store and administer the treatment.

Home Appearance

The professional lawn care companies use specialized mechanical sprayers that ensure uniform application of the necessary chemicals. This uniformity produces a consistently even and visually pleasing effect on the lawns. Too many homeowners have experienced the erratic operation of a home lawn spreader that produced a striped effect on their lawns—visual proof to all the neighbors that the homeowner was either too cheap to buy a workable lawn spreader or was incompetent and unable to operate the spreader correctly. In other words, a homeowner can hide the wood-working mistakes around the house, but a botched lawn job is there for all the neighbors to see.

An Investment

The price of the average home in many parts of the United States is over $100,000. The value of a home is not separated from its lawn and garden growth. Consequently, the expenditure of perhaps $150 or more a year is seen as a sound investment in enhancing the property value of a residence. Some lawn care firms go after the upscale homeowner. Clark-Morrell Inc., of Georgia, directs its efforts at the one out of ten homeowners who is interested in "quality care and maintenance," and leaves the other potential customers who are price-conscious to the competition. The company has been very successful.

Rocky Mountain Pest Control Company

The Rocky Mountain Pest Control Company (RMPCC) was established in 1976 in Longmont, Colorado, to provide interior pest control services for residences within 25 miles of Longmont. Included in this radius were the cities of Loveland and Boulder, Colorado.

The founder of RMPCC was David Tokarz, its president. Mildred Tokarz, his wife, is secretary-treasurer. In 1978 David Moon joined the company as its vice president in charge of sales and operations. Its 1978 sales were $39,000. Since 1978 RMPCC has been successful in obtaining several major commercial accounts. Its 1983 revenues were $260,000.

In the early 1980s RMPCC received an increasing number of requests from its customers for pest control services for their trees and ornamentals. Tokarz and Moon, however, did not have the expertise or the manpower to provide such services and typically referred their customers to a lawn care firm or tree spray firm with which they were acquainted.

In the fall of 1982 RMPCC decided that the addition of tree and ornamental spraying to their existing line of business would be a valuable complementary service. They also decided that they would expand their geographic base as quickly as possible because they believed that the tree and ornamental spray business was about to experience significant growth. Through contacts in the industry, they learned that Welco Spray Inc., of Greeley, was available for sale if the price and terms offered were acceptable to the owner. RMPCC's offer of $140,000 for Welco was refused by its owner.

Until the fall of 1983 Tokarz and Moon made no further effort to expand their services or geographic coverage. At that time they again offered to buy Welco Spray Inc. They increased their offer by $40,000 to $180,000. The assets to be purchased consisted of the firm's five trucks, its spray equipment, and its customers' accounts list. They also planned to retain the firm's employees and utilize their expertise. RMPCC proposed terms of no money down and $1,500 a month for ten years, plus interest.

The owner of Welco rejected RMPCC's offer. He made no counter proposal, and gave no reason for his rejection of the offer. RMPCC executives concluded that Welco's owner believed that RMPCC would be unable to service the debt obligation to Welco.

Formation of Environcare

The officers of RMPCC, during their visits to Greeley to bargain with the owner of Welco Spray, became acquainted with Don Smith, Welco's general manager. They were impressed with his technical knowledge of the pest spray business and also believed that he had the ability to manage an operation of similar scale on his own. He had the experience and expertise that they lacked and he was also familiar with the geographic area into which RMPCC wished to expand. Accordingly, after being rebuffed by the owner of Welco, they asked Don Smith if he was interested in being the general manager of a company that would be separate from RMPCC. Smith agreed and Environcare was incorporated in the state of Colorado in February 1984.

Organization

David Tokarz is president of Environcare. David Moon is secretary, and Don Smith was appointed vice president in charge of operations. The firm was incorporated as a separate company because RMPCC's officers believed that state licensing requirements for pest control were too complicated. They believed that it would be very easy for them to violate state licensing requirements unknowingly and either be fined or have their operation suspended for a period of time. The Division of Licenses requires that a firm that is licensed to spray trees and ornamentals have a separate license for applying structural (interior) treatments. Consequently, Environcare is licensed only to spray trees, ornamentals, livestock, and weeds. The employees of Environcare, therefore, are not required to take the additional five licensing tests for structural pest control that are administered by the state of Colorado.

David Moon will handle the marketing and perform limited spraying duties. Part-time help will be hired initially to assist Don Smith spray trees and ornamentals.

Finance

Environcare was capitalized with an initial investment of $25,000, which was borrowed from the Bank of Boulder. The loan consisted of a long-term note for $25,000, due in March 1987, at an interest rate of 1 percent over the prime rate, to be adjusted monthly. The firm authorized the issue of 50,000 shares of common stock, which have not yet been issued.

The company purchased a Ford F-350 pickup truck for $8,000, an FMC high-pressure sprayer for $9,000, and liquid spray and wettable powder supplies for $3,000. It maintained $5,000 for other current expenses, such as advertising, promotion, and salaries.

Environcare plans to sell its services on credit. Bills will be due within 30 days of receipt. The firm will also provide for installment payments over a three-month period. They will offer commercial accounts the option of paying on a quarterly basis or after each spray application. Year-round maintenance accounts, requiring a monthly payment throughout the year, will be offered to both residential and commercial accounts.

Richard Foster, publisher of *Pest Control Technology,* has drawn the following profile of the typical lawn care small business:

High net profit before taxes	30%
Average net profit before taxes	20%
Minimum cash investment	$15,000
Average cash investment	$20,000
Stability of the business	Moderate
Risk factor of the business	Moderate
Growth potential	High

In conjunction with this profile, Foster has also developed the following first-year pro forma income statement as a guide for the small-business lawn care entrepreneur:

Table 1 Pro Forma Income Statement, First Year, Lawn Care Service Business

Expense Item	Millions of Dollars	Percent of Total
Marketing and administration	$ 29.6	23%
Labor	25.8	20
Chemicals/fertilizer	34.8	27
Vehicles/equipment	10.3	8
Advertising/promotion	7.7	6
Rent	3.9	3
Gas/repairs/insurance	12.9	10
Telephone/office expense	3.9	3
	$129.0	100%

Foster estimates that the typical lawn service entrepreneur will break even during his first year and service a total of about 700 customer accounts.

Marketing

Environcare's officers believe that radio advertising is the quickest way for a new firm to reach the public and obtain customer recognition. Also, they chose to emphasize radio because they believe that most potential clients are over 35 years of age and, as homeowners, listen to the radio for community programs and announcements. They plan to use radio spots on two Greeley stations—the times and dates to be arranged but prior to the beginning of the spraying season. The messages will be humorous and will be handled by an advertising agency in Longmont.

Environcare will advertise in the "Work Force" classified ad section in three newspapers so that it can reach potential customers in Boulder, Loveland, Fort Collins, and Boulder (see Figure 1). Its employees will make personal contacts to solicit business. David Moon will also

Figure 1 Northern Front Range, Colorado (Mileages between Greeley and Adjacent Cities)

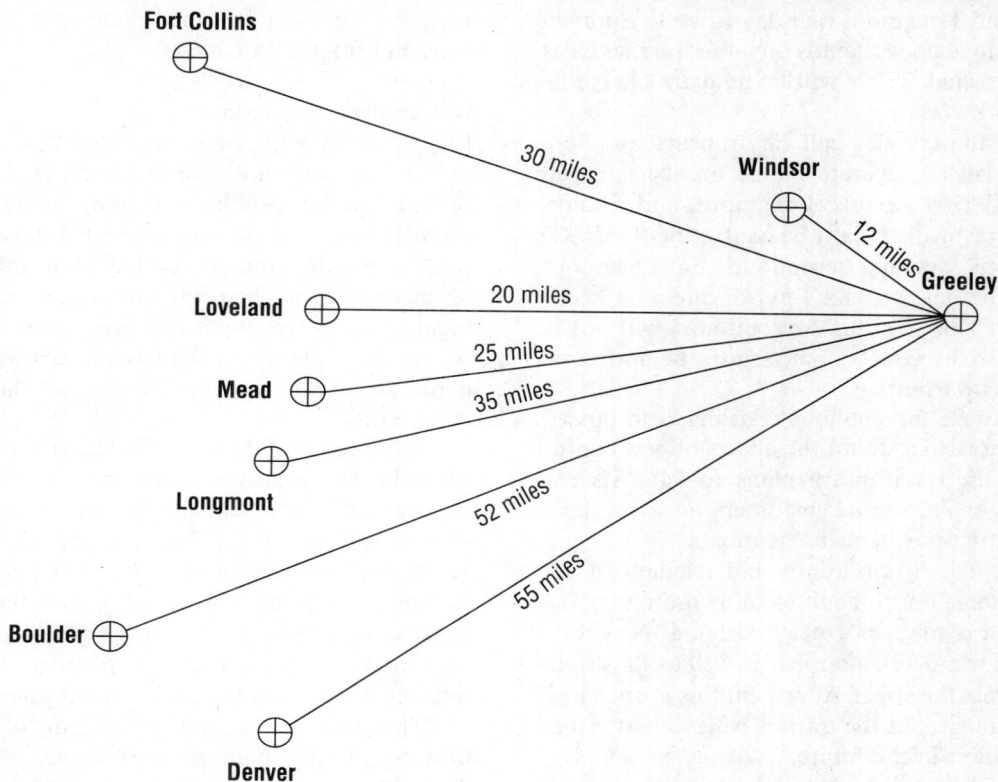

canvass customers, both commercial and residential, by phone. The firm will have an exhibit booth at local home and garden shows held annually in the spring in Greeley, Boulder, and Fort Collins.

Environcare plans to send out three mailings to present customers of RMPCC to solicit business for Environcare. The first mailing will notify customers that they can now receive tree and ornamental spray services from an RMPCC company. The second and third mailings will inform and educate customers about the value of spraying in the high plains and Rocky Mountain foothills (Boulder). Mailers will also be sent to Greeley residents selected by Don Smith, a life-

time Greeley resident, and to commercial firms in the Greeley-Boulder area identified by Don Smith, and Dave Moon. Each mailing of 2,600 pieces will consist of a letter and an enclosed flyer describing Environcare, the services that it provides, its connection with RMPCC, and information about tree and ornamental spraying.

Operations

Environcare will handle both residential and commercial accounts for exterior pest control. Requests for structural pest control treatments will be referred to RMPCC, which, in turn, will provide Environcare with tree and ornamental spray referrals.

Environcare plans to conduct tree spraying in Greeley four days a week and in Boulder/Loveland/Longmont one day a week. Spraying is also done on weekends on an individual basis, as contracted. There will be no extra charge for weekend work.

Customers who call Environcare by phone (there will be separate phone numbers for the Greeley, Fort Collins, Longmont, and Boulder exchanges) will actually be contacting RMPCC's telephone operator/receptionist in Longmont. She will then contact Environcare in Greeley through Don Smith. A receptionist will not be hired for the Greeley office until the additional business warrants it.

Because the public is considered to possess little knowledge about the effects of pest control chemicals, Environcare plans to have its employees explain to its customers the advantages and limitations of such chemicals.

Because of environmental regulations and restrictions, it is difficult to spray more than one home at a time in a neighborhood. Neighbors next door must be notified, as well as those who live across the street. At present this is not a legal requirement, but the owners believe that it may be required in the future.

Neighborhood contact is made in order to avoid lawsuits, harassment by neighbors, or possible adverse publicity. Personal contact with the neighbors is necessary. If possible, the homeowner is asked to assist in notifying his neighbors. Neighbors are inconvenienced because they must close their doors and windows and keep their pets inside their homes while the spray is being applied and for several hours thereafter. A few neighbors are uncooperative and make it difficult for some residences to be sprayed.

The fee for the spray application is determined individually. It depends on the location of the customer, the type of insect, the density of the ornamentals and trees, the area to be covered, and, because of the hazard to fish, the proximity of the plantings to be sprayed to lakes and streams. If such a hazard exists, the trees must be injected with a systemic chemical that converts the tree to a poisoned plant and kills the bugs and insects on contact.

Government Regulations

In accordance with the laws of the state of Colorado, pest control employees must be both licensed and bonded because they apply toxic chemicals in and around inhabited areas. Licensing is not required for the application of fertilizer, also a chemical but not toxic. The bonding requirement ensures that the applicator is capable of absorbing the costs of accidents or harm to people or property due to chemical treatments.

If the chemical to be applied carries a "Danger" label, it is highly toxic and requires that the applicator be certified by the Environmental Protection Agency (EPA). There are approximately 15 categories of chemicals used in tree and ornamental spray that are classified as dangerous. Because of widespread concerns about chemicals, their labeling is much more stringent and restrictive than was the case 5 to 10 years ago.

The state of Colorado's Division of Plant Industry, Department of Agriculture, licenses those who are engaged in pest control and the spraying of trees and ornamentals. There are 15 different categories for licensing, including ornamental pest control for insects and plant diseases; agricultural, industrial, and right-of-way weed control; aquatic pest control, turf pest control, and forest and rangeland pest control.

A licensed individual is expected to know which chemical is appropriate for application in various topographies, the problems encountered in high winds, and how liquids and wettable powders are combined to produce both a curative and a preventive treatment.

Technology

The equipment used for lawn and tree spray has had evolutionary changes during the past three decades. Improvements have increased the efficiency of the pumps used in spraying. The pumps, because they are now smaller, are more mobile and permit easier access to customer lawns. Application times are therefore shorter than before. (In fact, applications are accomplished so quickly that some customers think that they are not getting their money's worth.) Spray nozzles have also been improved so that the application velocity is increased. This allows the sprayers to reach the highest of trees. The City of Denver uses a spraying device that looks like an old civil war cannon but that in reality is a high-powered machine capable of spraying a large number of trees in a very short period of time. Some tree sprayers utilize a device called a roto-mist. It too is capable of rapid coverage of a large area. It is ideal for commercial applications.

There is the possibility that biological insect control will achieve wider acceptance than is the case today. Parasitic wasps are used to eat fly larvae, predatory snails can control slugs, ladybugs can control aphids, and so on. The potential of this type of control is uncertain, and there are few companies that have the expertise to conduct such operations. The Greeley area has many feed lots, and flies are a constant problem. Biological insect control would appear to be an efficient and economical method of controlling such pests. Lace wings, predatory bugs, are used in greenhouses to eat the white flies that attack greenhouse plants. The greenhouses now receive the lace wings direct from an insectary, also called a "bug farm." The best-known insectary in the United States is the Rincon-Vitova, which has three plants in California.

Climate and Insects

Greeley is located on the high desert plains. The humidity is very low and the sun's rays, because of the city's high altitude, are direct and intense. The arid environment, coupled with the heat, makes it more difficult for plants and lawns to

survive and thrive. Deeper root systems are needed and proper watering is critical.

Greeley's climate is conducive to the proliferation of a wide variety of insects because the temperatures normally are not cold enough to kill off either the insect's larvae, pupae, or eggs, or even the insects themselves, during the winter months. Different insects thrive in the area's dry climate; others thrive in the dampness that exists around riverbanks, streams, and ponds. This results in a large infestation of insects of one type or another.

There is a wide variety of insects that attack Colorado trees, lawns, and shrubs. The sod webworm feeds on the root systems of grass plants. Grasshoppers are attracted to the leaves of bushes. Elm leaf beetles, elm bark beetles, leaf roller worms, and tent caterpillars, if untreated, will quickly infest trees.

Chemical Applications

The liquid sprays used are primarily systemic. That is, they are absorbed into the plant or tree and spread internally throughout the tree. The pests are destroyed when they touch the tree or plant. This poison is especially effective for use with tall trees when the applicator/technician is not sure that the spray treatment has reached the uppermost branches.

Frequently used liquid chemicals are meta-systox-R and Dursban. They are dangerous because they are toxic contact chemicals, i.e., they can cause severe irritation upon contact with the skin. They are safely applied only by licensed technicians, and then only under carefully controlled conditions.

The wettable powders do not dissolve in water. The water serves as an agent to deliver the powder to the tree. The wettable powders have a residual life equal to that of soluble powders. They simply adhere to the tree after the water spray evaporates. The choice of wettable powder or liquid spray depends on the type of insect to be eliminated.

Contact poison chemicals are used against leaf-chewing insects that either absorb the poison on contact with the tree or ornamental or ingest the poison when they chew the poisoned leaves.

Spraying and lawn service contractors must know the watering habits of their customers to ensure that their lawn treatments are effective. Too much or too little water can cause plant and turf problems. Therefore the care and feeding of lawns and gardens is a cooperative venture between the homeowner and the applicator.

The Greeley Market
In 1980, according to U.S. Bureau of the Census figures, there were 20,700 housing units in Greeley. There were estimated to be 21,300 housing units in Greeley in 1984. Slightly more than half of these units are privately owned single-family homes. Somewhat less than half are rental units, either single or multifamily units. The median value of a Greeley single-family home, as of January 1984, was $61,500. Approximately 37 percent of Greeley is zoned either business (10.5 percent) or industrial (26.3 percent). Greeley's physical area covered 21.1 square miles in 1982. This is about one-third larger than its size in 1980, and 148 percent larger than its 1970 area of 8.5 square miles.

Greeley's 1983 population was estimated to be 56,000. Residents under 18 years of age accounted for 28 percent, those between 19 and 64 represented 62 percent, and those over 65, 10 percent. The median family income in Greeley in 1980 was approximately $19,200. Families above the median family income, according to Don Smith, are estimated to use spray treatments twice as frequently as lower-income families. Greeley's water supply and reserves are conservatively expected to be adequate for the city's projected growth for the next 20 years.

Don Smith believes that about one-third of Greeley's residents, i.e., 7,000 homes, have their lawns chemically treated by commercial firms. For about an annual $125 fee, a homeowner receives lawn treatments to fertilize the lawn, kill weeds, and destroy insects harmful to lawns. He also estimates that only about 2,000 residents utilize spray services for trees and ornamentals. On the average, each residence that uses a spray service obtains two treatments per year at $35 per application. (Note: Of the $35 spray application fee, labor is estimated by Don Smith to represent $2.00 of the cost, materials $.80, and truck and spray pump fuel, $.70, for a total of $3.50.)

Greeley schools and city and local governments typically have their own lawn and maintenance employees care for their lawns. Tree spraying, however, is usually let out for bids. Don Smith estimates that this business amounts to $20,000 annually. Shopping centers and local business properties are estimated to represent a present market of $10,000 for tree spraying and $5,000 for lawn care. Property management companies, which administer rentals, apartment complexes, condominiums, and townhouses, represent an estimated present market of $20,000, equally divided between lawn care and tree spraying.

Don Smith estimates that 25 percent of his expected annual revenues will be derived from spraying lawns and that the remainder will come from spraying trees and ornamentals.

Estimated Regional Market Potential
The area in which the Rocky Mountain Pest Control Company and Environcare operate is located along Colorado's Northern Front Range—an area approximately 20 miles wide, running east (from Greeley) to west (Boulder), and about 75 miles long, from north (Fort Collins) to south (Denver). Don Smith estimates that the Fort Collins market potential is about the same as Greeley, that Loveland and Longmont combined represent about one-half of Greeley's potential, and that the Boulder metropolitan market is larger than Greeley's potential by a factor of five. These estimates apply to both lawn care and tree and ornamental spraying.

The Competition
Two companies, Welco Spray Inc. and Greeley

Spray Service, are estimated to have divided the Greeley market pretty much between themselves for the last ten years, with respect to both the spraying of trees and ornamentals and chemical lawn applications. Within the past year, two franchise operations have entered the Greeley market—Ever-Green Lawns and Nitro-Green. These two firms provide only chemical lawn treatments.

There are about 15 firms in Greeley that provide spray service or lawn care, or both. (A discussion of the major competitors will follow.) There are also individuals from outside Greeley who provide lawn care. Some may be conducting their business in violation of a local ordinance, since they may not have a Greeley license to operate. Don Smith anticipates no major change in the nature of the competition. However, he believes it possible that a Denver company or a new franchise operation may enter the Greeley area.

Welco Spray Inc. Welco Spray Inc. was founded in 1966 by J. L. Williams. At first, he sprayed only trees and ornamentals. Pest control services were added in 1975 because a major customer requested this service and assured Williams of a significant return on his investment.

In the fall of 1983 Welco had approximately 3,000 customers. It also had additional inactive accounts—due to customers moving from the area, deaths, switching to another spray company, or just stopping the use of spray services entirely.

Before Environcare was incorporated, Welco had three full-time and four part-time employees. Welco owned five trucks (including five portable spray tanks), a roto-mist machine, two weed sprayers, and a combination tractor-sprayer.

Welco had a good reputation for quality service and, since it was a local firm, a high degree of visibility and acceptance. Welco is only one of three firms that provide both lawn care and tree and ornamental pest control in the Greeley area. It is estimated that lawn care represents 10 percent of its business and trees and ornamentals 90 percent.

Its customer file, which was extensive and comprehensive, was one of Welco's major assets. On the other hand, the firm appeared to lack expertise in money management. It frequently was late in paying its bills. It also had more equipment than appeared to be warranted by its sales volume. One truck generally sat idle in the parking lot.

Welco's sales rose from $15,000 in 1966 to a peak of $175,000 in 1977, and gradually declined to $160,000 in 1983. The firm's expenses were such that during this period it made a profit for only one year (detailed data were not available).

Nitro-Green Nitro-Green has its headquarters in Bismarck, North Dakota. Its 1983 gross revenues, for the treatment of 17,000 lawns, were $1.5 million. It had 20 franchises at the beginning of 1984. One of its strengths is that it is a franchise operation and potential customers have confidence in the name. Its equipment is good, and its trucks, painted in "industry colors" of white and green, are mobile advertisements for their product. Nitro-Green advertises primarily through flyers and inserts that appear in the local newspaper. They also use four-column-wide ads in *The Greeley Tribune,* the city's only daily newspaper.

A local professional sprayer thinks that Nitro-Green employees may not be as knowledgeable about chemicals as they should be in relation to specific pests. That is, they may not use the most effective chemical to treat a particular type of insect. Nitro-Green employs 5 or 6 employees, has three spray trucks and tanks, and has a spray rig set up on a pickup truck. Nitro-Green provides both lawn care (90 percent of its business) and tree spraying (10 percent). One weakness that Don Smith sees is that the firm may not have enough equipment to satisfy customer interest generated from their advertising, which appears to be very effective.

Ever-Green Lawns Ever-Green of Golden bought out Nutra-Lawn of Greeley, a privately owned company, in 1983. It opened a warehouse/office in Windsor, Colorado, 12 miles from Greeley. This is the Golden company's fifth branch. The company reported that its decision to enter the Greeley-Windsor-Fort Collins area was made after it had conducted a market research study of residents in the area.

The Ever-Green Lawns Corporation has gross sales of over $10 million in 1983 for all of its franchise operations. The company was recently purchased by the Hawley Group of London, England, which has additional interests in industrial cleaning and pest control.

The company advertises extensively in the Denver metropolitan area on local television stations, whose signals are received in Greeley with ordinary housetop antennae. It also uses four-color brochures that are inserted in *The Greeley Tribune* and the two major Denver metropolitan dailies that are delivered to Greeley residents. The company also advertises on radio. It continuously solicits business by phone and sends direct mailers to homes, using the mailing lists obtained from the company that it bought out—Nutra-Lawn. There are at least three employees in the Windsor office phoning for new business in the local area.

The company's facility in Windsor is more modern and more complete than any of its competitors. Its clean white and green vehicles are very visible advertisements on wheels. It appears to have very strong financial resources. When they are first hired, all of its specialized applicators/technicians are required to attend a one-week school run by the parent company in Boulder. They also attend a refresher course every year. A possible weakness is that the firm is not Greeley-based. Each truck is required to do 30 lawns a day, and that may be a high standard for all of its employees to meet. Ever-Green deals exclusively with lawn fertilization. Their employees are not licensed to apply the pest control chemicals associated with tree and ornamental spraying.

Greeley Spray Service The Greeley Spray Service is a subsidiary of Kincaid Tree Service of Fort Collins, Colorado. Its manager is well known and respected by his Greeley customers. However, he comes to Greeley only once or twice a week to perform spray applications. The firm's trucks do not have the distinctive and appealing appearance associated with Nitro-Green and Ever-Green Lawns. Because they come to Greeley infrequently, they do not provide service with the responsiveness and regularity that some Greeley residents prefer.

General Spray and Lawn Service and Colorado Lawn Care Service These two companies lack modern and efficient spray applicator equipment. According to Don Smith, their employees are neither as experienced nor as well trained as those associated with the firms previously discussed. Colorado Lawn Care Service provides both lawn care and pest control spray services.

Competitive Market Share Data Don Smith, vice president of Environcare, estimated that at the approach of the 1984 season the market for the spraying of trees and ornamentals and lawn care was distributed as follows:

Table 2 Estimated Market Shares of the Greeley Area Lawn Care and Trees/Ornamental Spray Business, December 1983

Firm	Trees/ Ornamentals	Lawn Care
Welco Spray	80%	10%
Ever-Green Lawns	0	30
Nitro-Green	2	30
Greeley Spray Service	16	0
General Spray and Lawn Service	1	1
Colorado Lawn Care Service	1	1
Other firms (from Denver, Mead, Loveland, and Fort Collins)	—	28
	100%	100%

Plans for The Future

Don Smith, the general manager of Environcare, hopes some day to own his own business, and that business may be Environcare. He has a target of $500,000 gross sales annually. He also would like to explore the possibilities of biological applications for pest control. At the present time, however, he is devoting all of his time to the start-up of Environcare's tree and ornamental spray business. He comments: "I am not interested in getting into the landscaping business. I think the quality of service I now provide would decline if our services became too broad. I prefer to be friends with the landscapers rather than their competitor. I can provide service to ten landscaping firms. If I am their competitor, I will only get my own referrals for spray service—and none of theirs. Before we can even consider expanding our line of services, we have to learn how to walk before we can run."